***Black Separatism and Social Reality: Rhetoric and Reason***

Other Books of Related Interest

Halpern, F. – *Survival: Black/White*

Katz, P. – *Towards the Elimination of Racism*

# *Black Separatism and Social Reality: Rhetoric and Reason*

Editor
Raymond L. Hall
Dartmouth College

PERGAMON PRESS INC.
New York / Toronto / Oxford / Sydney / Frankfurt / Paris

*Pergamon Press Offices:*

| | |
|---|---|
| U.S.A. | Pergamon Press Inc., Maxwell House, Fairview Park, Elmsford, New York 10523, U.S.A. |
| U.K. | Pergamon Press Ltd., Headington Hill Hall, Oxford OX3, OBW, England |
| CANADA | Pergamon of Canada, Ltd., 207 Queen's Quay West, Toronto 1, Canada |
| AUSTRALIA | Pergamon Press (Aust) Pty. Ltd., 19a Boundary Street, Rushcutters Bay,sN.S.W. 2011, Australia |
| FRANCE | Pergamon Press SARL, 24 rue des Ecoles, 75240 Paris, Cedex 05, France |
| WEST GERMANY | Pergamon Press GmbH, 6242 Kronberg/Taunus, Frankfurt-am-Main, West Germany |



**Library of Congress Cataloging in Publication Data**

Main entry under title:

Black separatism and social reality.

Includes index.
1. Black nationalism–United States–Addresses, essays, lectures. 2. Pan-Africanism–Addresses, essays, lectures. I. Hall, Raymond L.
E185.6.B63 1976 320.5'4 75-34419
ISBN 0-08-019510-5
ISBN 0-08-019509-1 pbk.



Printed in the United States of America

To my mother, Anna May Gregory, who first taught me to find and explain cause before foolishly and blindly accepting effect.

# *Contents*

# *Contributors*

**Ladun Anise** – A Nigerian from Yorubaland, he teaches political science at the University of Pittsburgh. He is interested in American politics generally and black politics in particular.

**Imamu Ameer Baraka** – Author, playwright, activist and social thinker, he has recently embraced Marxism as the most viable liberation strategy for black people.

**Robert S. Browne** – Formerly an economics professor at Fairleigh-Dickinson University, his ideas are regarded by some as the ideological model for the Republic of New Africa (RNA). He now heads the Black Economic Research Center in New York City.

**Stokely Carmichael** – Catapulted into national headlines on the theme of Black power in the mid-1960s as chairman of the now defunct Student Non-Violent Coordinating Committee (SNCC), he now heads the African Peoples Party headquartered in Conaky, Guinea, and the Black United Front in Washington, D.C.

**Locksley G.E. Edmondson** – A native of Jamaica, he is now Senior Lecturer in the Department of Government at the University of the West Indies, Mona, Jamaica. He formerly taught political science at Cornell University.

**Dennis Forsythe** – Born in the West Indies, he has taught at McGill University in Montreal and now teaches sociology at Howard University.

**James A. Geschwender** – A keen observer of the black community, he has written extensively on some aspects of black life. He is Chairperson of Sociology at the State University of New York at Binghamton.

**Raymond L. Hall** – A student of social movements, he wrote his dissertation–which subsequently became a book–on black separatist social movements. He earned his Ph.D. degree at Syracuse University and teaches sociology at Dartmouth College.

**William B. Helmreich** – Author of *The Black Crusaders,* he has long been interested in Afro-American and African relations in particular and intergroup relations in general. He teaches sociology at the City University of New York.

**Milton R. Henry** – Born in Philadelphia, he is a 1950 graduate of the Yale Law School, a close friend of the late Malcolm X, and a founder of the Republic of New Africa. He now practices law in Detroit.

**Lewis M. Killian** – Co-author of *Racial Crisis in America* (1964) and author of *The Impossible Revolution: Black Power and the American Dream,* among others, he is Professor of Sociology at the University of Massachusetts, Amherst.

**Willie B. Lamousé-Smith** – Born in Cape Coast, Ghana, he has taught at the Free University of Berlin, Makere University in Uganda, and Syracuse University. He is now Director/Dean of African and Afro-American Studies at the University of Maryland, Baltimore.

**Richard A. Long** – Professor of English at Atlanta University, he organized the Conference on Afro-American Studies (CAAS) beginning in 1968. This conference was among the forerunners in pointing the way for developing Black Studies Programs.

**Arline Sakuma McCord** – Co-author with Charles V. Willie of *Black Students on White College Campuses*, she has authored numerous works in the area of urban education, stratification, and sex roles. She is Associate Professor of Sociology at Hunter College.

**William M. McCord** – Author of *Lifestyles in the Black Ghetto, Mississippi Summer, Springtime of Freedom,* the *Origins of Alcoholism*, etc., he has taught at Harvard, Stanford, and Rice Universities. He is presently Chairperson of Sociology at the City University of New York.

**Clarence J. Munford** – Associate professor of History, University of Guelph, Guelph, Ontario, he received his doctorate in History from the University of Leipzig.

**Thomas Pettigrew** – Long a keen observer of intergroup relations, he authored *A Profile of Negro Americans* and *Racially Separate or Together*, among numerous other works on the subject. He is Professor of Social Relations at Harvard.

**Bayard Rustin** – A co-founder of the Congress of Racial Equality (CORE), and a long-time activist and eloquent spokesman for black-white solidarity in the labor movement, he is presently Director of the A. Philip Randolph Institute in New York City.

**Bernard E. Segal** – A participant in the civil rights movement in the 1960s and author of *Racial and Ethnic Relations*, he pays close attention to theoretical issues in intergroup relations. He is Professor of Sociology at Dartmouth College.

**Socialist Workers Party** – Headquartered in New York City, the Socialist Workers Party (SWP) is a Trotskyite Socialist organization which attempts to accommodate both socialism and black nationalism.

**Howard F. Taylor** – A social psychologist specializing in small groups, he authored the important book *Balance Theory in Small Groups* and has recently completed a book on the Gene-I.Q. controversy. He is Associate Professor of Sociology at Princeton University.

**S. Jay Walker** – A prolific writer on black American literature, having written a book on the subject, he received his training at the University of Nottingham. He is Professor of English and Director of the Black Studies Program at Dartmouth College.

**Ronald Walters** – A prolific author on, and an activist in, black politics, he received his training in International Relations. He is Associate Professor of Political Science at Howard University.

**Charles V. Willie** – Author of several works on the black family, among others, and an activist-scholar in the civil rights and women's movements, he has been chairperson of Sociology and Vice President for Student Affairs at Syracuse University. He is now a professor in the School of Education, Harvard University.

**Brunetta Reid Wolfman** – A specialist in Urban Studies, she has long been involved with the black and women's movements. She is a Special Assistant, President's Office, University of Massachusetts, Boston.

# *Foreword I*

WILLIAM McCORD

The contemporary debate over black separatism has a long history, almost as long as the black presence in America. Both blacks and whites have argued for and against racial separation as a mechanism for achieving black liberation. As an example, some 130 years ago Frederick Douglass, a black man, passionately contended that blacks and whites could live together in mutual harmony if they so desired. At the same time, John Brown, a white man, vehemently argued for the establishment of a separate black nation. Brown believed that his ill-fated attack upon the federal armory at Harper's Ferry would not only lead to a revolt but to the abolition of slavery and the creation of a black country comprised of Virginia and other parts of the South. He contended that violence would give birth to an economically and politically autonomous realm governed by freed black men. Ironically, Frederick Douglass – an ex-slave and another great emancipator – dismissed the idea as utopian and totally impractical. In their correspondence, Douglass chided John Brown for ignoring economic reality.

As this splendid book demonstrates, the argument did not end with John Brown's defeat nor with the North's eventual victory. In the early 20th century, Booker T. Washington, W.E.B. DuBois, and Marcus Garvey continued the debate in bitter, often vituperative terms. Washington opted for economic advance while accepting social and political segregation; as Jay Walker's article brilliantly demonstrates, Washington – "a separatist in golden chains" – won superficial approval from the white community of his times. He had to repay dinners with Theodore Roosevelt and Queen Victoria, however, with exclusion from Pullman cars and the refusal of immigrant maids to clean his room in a Southern hotel. DuBois, a black Harvard aristocrat, went through many mutations: advocacy of an elitist integration for educated blacks, a flirtation with Marxism, and eventual espousal of Pan-Africanism from his self-imposed exile in Ghana. Garvey (that strange mixture of charlatan, idealist, and visionary) stirred the hopes of millions of blacks with the dream of returning in glory to Africa. After his ill-starred ships sank one after the other and lawsuits punctured his empire, Garvey and "Garveyism" faded into dismal oblivion.

In the 1930s, the Communist Party revived the ideal of separatism in its proposal for an independent black republic (strangely reminiscent of Milton Henry's writings in this volume); this proposition, too, met its death at the hands of the Depression.

In the modern era, as Raymond Hall incisively demonstrates in his dissection of contemporary ideological perspectives, the ideal of black separatism flourished in ghettoes and prisons, on political podiums and Muslim pulpits, from college dormitories to Broadway stages. While emotionally moving and morally valid, many of the ideological statements reproduced in this book still would appear to ignore reality. C.J. Munford, for example, argues from a Marxist perspective that "racial discrimination is an essential mode of imperialist exploitation." This may sound reasonably like Marxism but not when put in the context of Marxist logic. Munford states that automation is a capitalist tool leading to the elimination of black unskilled workers. According to Marx, in contrast, automation meant the death of capitalism since, by discharging workers, capitalists automatically eliminated their source of surplus value. Thus, from a strictly Marxist point of view, capitalists would *welcome* the unskilled black worker as their last remaining source of profit.

Imamu Ameer Baraka (who recently denounced black nationalism in favor of Marxism-Leninism) earlier argued for a set of "black" values and lists a magical seven of them. There is nothing wrong with the values, but they are neither parochially black nor are they backed by any other proof than Baraka's assumption that they are "good."

Milton Henry and the Black Muslims advocate a separate black state, but its realization seems dependent upon God's whims. This is an unfortunately slim reed to lean on. Paraphrasing Stalin, one might ask how many divisions can God mobilize?

The list could go on and on, but the fact remains that most separatist ideologies – whether they drape themselves in the "hard-headed" realism of Marx or a faith in God – lack any sense at all as to how they might fulfill their dreams in the cold world of political, military, and economic reality.

In the third part, Thomas Pettigrew does a yeoman's job in exposing the similarities of white racist assumptions and black separatism. And Bayard Rustin, an elder statesman of the black movement but one often accused of being an "Uncle Tom," realistically assesses the prospects of black separatism.

This book serves an eminently useful purpose in bringing together for the first time many of the diverse ideologies of a

Carmichael and the Pan-Africanists, of Marxists and the Black Panther Party and others. Devoid of pragmatism, however, these ideologies parade without the Emperor's clothes.

In the last part of the book, William Helmreich presents a comprehensive review of the history of separatist thought and an excellent bibliography concerning the relation of Afro-Americans with Africa. Lewis Killian dissects white attitudes and points to the very real danger of a violent eruption between whites and blacks. With his usual incisive brilliance, Howard Taylor demolishes the arguments of those who contend that intelligence decisively separates blacks from whites.

Taylor also presents another side to the question discussed by Ronald Walters at the end of the volume: Is there a need for a distinct, "black" social science? Apparently Walters believes that the unique experience of blacks in America necessitates a separate discipline. Taylor, on the other hand, cogently argues "that while certain uses and applications of the scientific method are racist, the scientific method itself is relatively free from institutional racism." His articles demonstrate beyond question that the canons of good research are indispensable in evaluating the pronouncements of contemporary racists. Indeed, the entire last part of the book illuminates the ways in which unbiased social science can help to resolve ideological issues.

Thus, in a vital and literate way, the book raises fundamental issues that have recurred throughout the last century and continue unabated today:

> Should black Americans seek their political destiny apart from white Americans?
>
> Should white liberals be eschewed as allies, as merely "covert racists"?
>
> Can economic growth within the black community eventually lead to true "black power"?
>
> Is the destiny of black Americans linked intrinsically with that of Africa, or, as was the view of Tom Mboya, Gamal Abdul Nasser, and Julius Nyerere, must Africans pursue their own fate separately from their "American cousins"?
>
> Should a cultural revolution" among blacks precede any other form of liberation?

As the very disparity of the articles produced in this fine book demonstrate, no one can answer these questions with assurance. In the middle 1970s, the data are too confusing and contradictory to lead to a definitive policy. Those who look to economic advance as the key to black progress, for example, might take heart from the 1974 report of the President's Council of Economic Advisors. It indicated that black families earned 76 percent of the income of white families (as opposed to 57 percent in 1959). Young black families almost achieved parity with whites (blacks under 35 earned 93 percent of the income of white families of the same age). In fact, by any standard, black female college graduates earned more money than white women. These facts would hearten Booker T. Washington but they do not lighten the burden of continuing discrimination.

Political separatists could gain confidence from the fact that 374 blacks won office in the South during the by-elections of 1974 – although the South remained under resolute white control.

Intellectuals who view education, particularly in black studies, as a road to advance could happily cite the fact that more black students than ever before were enrolled in college in 1974. They would have to face the disheartening fact, however, that the proportion of black students in American colleges has significantly declined since 1965.

Whether blacks should take an economic, political, or education road to achieving true freedom – whether expressed in a separatist culture or not – still remains an open issue. That is exactly why this book offers a unique opportunity for both blacks and whites to explore the role of separatism in our society. We owe a great debt to Raymond Hall for crystallizing the issue in this fine work.

The whole ideal of black separatism is today a vibrant issue in American society. John Brown's body may be rotting in his grave, but his dream keeps marching on. I personally hope that Frederick Douglass' wisdom will prevail over John Brown's ghost.

# *Foreword II*

S. JAY WALKER

In any discussion of black separatism in its traditional sense – that is, the hope for the establishment of an Afro-American state somewhere on the continent of Africa or the lopping off of a few of the United States for a separate black republic somewhere on this continent – only one fact need be remembered:

The fact is that it is not going to happen.

The periodic resurfacing of this idea in one form or another – from the establishment of Liberia in the early 19th century, to the Nigerian explorations of Martin Delany just before the Civil War, to the Pap Singleton vision of a black Kansas in the years following the war, to the Marcus Garvey movement of the 1920s, to the Elijah Muhammad movement of the '60s and the plethora of imitators which exist today – says something, certainly, about the degree of black discontent with our "assigned" place within the structure of American society.

Yet with the persistence of the vision of a black Israel has persisted also a willful refusal to look at the historical, political, economic, and psychological conditions which make all such visions no more than fantasies diverting much of our energies and thoughts away from the actions that can and must be taken within the framework of American citizenship.

The contemporary separatist fantasies tend to be based, one and all, on the most shockingly careless parallels with modern world history: the establishment of the State of Israel and the massive reparations paid to that state by the Federal Republic of Germany in the aftermath of the Nazi holocaust, the Mau Mau revolution which freed Kenya, and the Algerian Revolution against the French. All indicate the ability of a determined nationalist group to carve out a state for itself, against overwhelming population or overwhelming military odds; the German support for Israel indicates that a nation may be brought to recognize the wrongdoing of its forebears and to make amends for that wrongdoing in cold cash. None of these situations, however, has the remotest applicability to the visions of black separatism.

The founding of the State of Israel is regarded as the pattern for the establishment of an Afro-American state on the continent of Africa, but the realistic parallels are ominous rather than encouraging. The separatists would seem to be hypnotized by the sheer bulk of the African continent into ignoring the fact that Africa is not "empty" but, on the contrary, in terms of lands habitable in the light of present technology, is overcrowded. There is no African nation – and probably not all of them together – that could absorb 22 million foreigners (and foreigners is precisely what black Americans are in Africa) without disaster to its own socio-economic structure. Liberia, for instance, is only slightly larger than the state of Tennessee, and has a population of less than two million.

Any Afro-American state organized in Africa would thus have to be taken by force from its present inhabitants, precisely as Israel had to take Palestine from its indigenous peoples; in so doing, it would establish precisely the same legacy of hatred and bitterness which keeps the Middle East the most dangerous area of the globe. No black separatist could possibly announce an intention to reduce the people of, say Sierra Leone, to the status of Arabs in the Jewish State; the doctrines of Pan-Africanism preclude such an announcement. Yet none, either, has been willing to say where or how such a state might be established without doing just that.

Even given that willingness, there is another factor that makes the Israeli parallel, in Watergate terms, inoperative. When the State of Israel was founded in 1948, the full horror of the Nazi death camps was fresh in everyone's mind, and Palestine was under the "protection" of Great Britain and the United Nations, dominated at the time by the Atlantic Alliance. It was a relatively easy thing for the West to assuage its own conscience by partitioning someone else's homeland. (It should not be forgotten that at about the same time Britain very generously offered to "give" Uganda as a homeland for Israel.) The idea that the United Nations today, no matter how touched by the plight of blacks in America, would, or could, repeat that action flies in the face of all the realignments of power that have taken place in that organization in the past 25 years.

An African solution, then, is out. African nations may welcome a few black Americans who can bring to them highly developed skills: educators, medical personnel, technicians – exactly, in fact, those blacks who are most economically viable in the United States. They can do nothing at all to benefit the black masses.

The partitioning of the United States, perhaps most imaginatively stated in what Fletcher Knebel called the GAMAL plan – Georgia, Alabama, Mississippi, and Louisiana – is, if anything, even more farfetched. Basic outlines for establishing a black nation in that territory are two. The first is that white America, in some sudden conversion to righteousness, will recognize its past misdeeds and its inability to correct them and will, as an act of justice, cede the crescent states as the basis for a black republic, with an orderly exchange of populations – all whites in those states moving north or west and all blacks in the rest of the nation moving in to take their places. This plan also suggests that the United States will "support" the new nation for the next half century, or "until it can get on its feet."

The second scenario involves no such light on the road to Damascus but rather protracted guerrilla warfare taking place throughout the United States – the Mau-Mau and the film, *The Battle of Algiers,* are the putative models here – until America, despairing of achieving domestic tranquillity in any other way, cedes the states and arranges the transfer of populations. In other words, the Civil War is to be refought, this time as a series of inner-city shoot-outs, and this time with success to the secessionists.

What is most remarkable about these schemata is that they rest on basic assumptions that are totally contradictory. Those putting them forth claim: (a) that the United States as a whole is beyond redemption in its commitment to racism and so no possibility of justice may be looked forward to in this country; at the same time, that the United States will, at enormous cost to itself and out of pure altruism, divest itself of part of its territory; or (b) that the United States is beyond civilized restraint in its treatment of black people and will eventually commit genocide on all of us; at the same time, that the United States would hesitate to use the full arsenal of its power to destroy or intimidate every black in the country before it would cede a single square mile of land. To accept either the peaceful or warlike argument for partition requires having it both ways at once.

The Mau-Mau and Algerian revolts as patterns for military success are simple romanticism. In both Kenya and Algeria the revolutionists, though outgunned, had an enormous edge in population, and could absorb ten to one and one hundred to one losses and still succeed. What might work for such a majority is useless for a minority. Further, in both African situations, the insurgents had the benefit of friendly neighbors, of borders over which arms and supplies could be smuggled and hard-pressed insurgents could retreat. Neither Mexico nor Canada would seem to fill that condition for black America, even were there any center of black population, with the exception of Detroit, within easy striking distance of either country. The People's Republic of North Korea may occasionally send fraternal greetings to the Black Panther newspaper, but the People's Republic of North Korea would be able to send little other than sympathy in a fight.

And, finally, neither Britain nor France was as emotionally involved in Kenya or Algeria as the United States would be in GAMAL. For all the loud talk of Algeria being "part of Metropolitan France" and the slogans of "Algeria c'est Francais," the average Frenchman never seems to have believed for a moment that the North African state was anything other than a colony – or at least not to the point of willingness to die to keep it. The United States, for its part, has expressed a willingness – at times, one feels, an eagerness – to grant independence to Puerto Rico any time that a plurality of Puerto Ricans requests it, and it is Puerto Rico – not the GAMAL states – which stands in relationship to the United States as Algeria stood to France. The same factor that sent the Union into the bloodiest of our wars in 1861, the prospect of dismemberment of the essential body of the United States, would send it to war again, and any politician or political party that refused to commit maximum armed strength to prevent that dismemberment would be destroyed in the next election by the approximately nine million southern whites forcibly expatriated from their homes.

For these very practical reasons, then, separatism in its classic sense is not going to occur. But perhaps the greatest obstacle to the establishment of a black state lies beyond the physical, in the psychological realm that has historically prevented the success of separatist movements. That is the fact that the vast majority of black Americans have no interest whatsoever in a separate state.

This determination to stay in the United States, come what may, has been a continuous source of irritation to separatist leaders as well as the subject for some of their best lines. Malcolm X, before his own abandonment of separatism, used to say, "These Negroes don't want no nation; they're trying to crawl back on the plantation!" It was a good quip; except for the loaded terms "crawl back" and "plantation," it was totally accurate. For the black American, by and large, has been given no model to suggest that his welfare would be bettered in a separate state.

For those who see themselves as leaders of the state, certainly, the rewards are many; even the poorest of states can be manipulated to produce a cornucopia of honors, power, wealth; one need look no further than the Caribbean for examples. But independent states have certainly not always served to improve the welfare of their ordinary citizens, and black Americans, made hard-headed and pragmatic by long experience, have asked questions of the separatists that have not been answered; questions which one feels, at times, the separatists have not yet asked themselves.

Precisely how, for instance, does one aid the massive unemployment problem of blacks by moving all of them into states that are already among the most depressed in the nation? Precisely how does one improve the health services of blacks by removing them from the reach of those white medical facilities to which they presently have access? Would the independent state be, in fact, self-sufficient in the production of food and in basic industries, or would it, in order to survive, become the client of one of the great powers? Does black America presently wield the technical know-how, does it possess the capital for independence, or would it find itself obligated to some kind of technical peace corps and to the investments of other nations to keep its economy running? In the 1950s and '60s, the United States attempted to strangle Cuba, not through military might but through the simple and quite legal expedient of refusing to trade with it. The Castro regime was saved through massive infusions of Soviet aid, roughly one million dollars a day. What does an increasing climate of detente have to say about the ability of small states today to play one great nation off against the other?

But of course man does not live by bread alone. It is quite possible that black Americans would accept a lessened standard of living if they saw no other way to gain that increase of personal freedom and dignity toward which all men aspire. This is, in fact, the only thing that the black separatists might reasonably offer in competition to life in the United States.

The unfortunate thing is that they seem to offer nothing of the sort. Quite the contrary. As the United States moves, however grudgingly, in the direction of greater personal liberty, black separatist movements seem to tend toward greater authoritarianism and repression. In the name of purification of the people, the Fruit of Islam has the right to invade the homes of members of the Black Muslims, checking and enforcing the codes of diet, dress, work, and morality; it is a violation of personal privacy that makes the recent unlamented "no-knock" bill look like the model of permissiveness. Eldridge Cleaver, in Algiers, placed that most harmless and free-spirited of all rebels, Timothy Leary, under "house arrest" to teach him "revolutionary discipline." As most of us begin to recognize the self-defeating nature of punitive law codes, a Harlem separatist leader announces that in "the new nation" crime will be eliminated by the simple expedient of publicly severing the right hand of every convicted felon, while members of rival separatist groups assault, assassinate, execute, and massacre each other in numbers that make the Kent State unpleasantness appear by comparison a friendly neighborhood dispute.

As even the most red-necked press stops going into orgies of recrimination over whom Frederick Douglass or Jack Johnson married, the separatists begin similar orgies to indicate that the marriage choices of Diana Ross or Sly Stone are something other than their own personal business. In fact, it is possible to run through virtually the entire list of controversial issues on individual liberty in the nation today – the equality of women, censorship of the press and films, gay liberation, population control – and to find that on each of them black separatists take a conservative if not a reactionary stance; one that, not to put too fine a face on it, would seem to differ little from the puritanism of Maddox Country or Hitler's Germany.

The questions are, then, how is black separatism to come about and what are blacks to gain from it if it does? The answers, respectively, would seem to be "no way" and "nothing." As a result, black separatist programs across the country, which peaked in 1968-1969 today are moribund. The Muslims grow vaguer and vaguer about both the date and place of coming forth from among the white devils, and seem to be concentrating their efforts on the acquisition of land and real estate: a hospital here, a farm there, an ornate mosque in this state, a modern meat-packing plant in that – scarcely the most portable property for people planning an exodus. The Panthers, having lost each replay of the Battle of Algiers, have laid down their guns and taken to participatory politics; while Imamu Ameer Baraka has recently (December 1974) apostatized from the separatist faith in such a stunning volte-face that we may soon be calling him LeRoi Jones again. What remains of the genuine movement are a few obscure keepers of the dimming flame, without policy or program or organization, repeating almost as incantations the old slogans and awaiting another period of despair to bring them again to the fore.

For despair and the peak of black separatist sentiment go hand in hand. It is always at those hours which look bleakest for black America – the killings of King and Robert Kennedy and the election of Nixon, the aftermath of the "Red Summers" following World War I, the betrayal of Reconstruction, the apparent failure of the Abolitionist movement just before the Civil War – when the unexamined "anyplace but here" becomes most attractive. It is upon examination of the idea that it loses force.

Yet it never completely dies, nor is it completely valueless. For if black separatism reminds black Americans that we are exactly that, Americans, and that we have no home in Africa, and if it reminds us that some of the systems and ideologies prepared for us by other blacks are not precisely what we want, it also reminds us of what we do want and reminds us that as blacks we have a common cause and a common identity that can be turned into a tool for achieving it.

That tool is the recognition of our roots here, the recognition of the strength, the dignity, and the discipline with which our grandparents and parents struggled to put us within striking reach of equality. It is the realization of the oneness of the desire of human beings to be respected for what they are and the responsibility of human beings to respect others for what they are. Few black Americans, I suspect, are given to Fourth of July panegyrics, and still fewer to wearing American flag lapel pins a la Nixon. But very, very few have given up, or have any intention of giving up on this country, for the simple reason that it is ours. We are here, we are going to stay here, and thus our task is to make this place closer to what it should be – more free, more just, more humane.

We are not "trying to crawl back on the plantation," if plantation it is. We have never left it. We are simply determined now to make part of it truly our own.

# *Preface*

This book, with its diversity of contributors, represents a range of perspectives, ideas, orientations, and ideologies that all directly or indirectly address the question of black separatism – pro and con – from the vantage point of their own realities. The majority of contributors are black, some are white, and some are women; some are black separatists and others are not. Some are not black Americans, but black nevertheless, sharing the commonality of membership in the black Diaspora and presenting their views on black separatism in America. Their diversity should at least contribute to our knowledge of black separatism and, whatever our ideas or sentiments regarding separatism, after reading this book we should all hopefully gain an insight into how others rationalize positions and ideas we might dismiss as irrational, radical, deviant, or dangerous. It is, after all, *their* reality from the same social system in which we live.

Putting together such a wide range of papers was both frustrating and challenging. It was sometimes frustrating for me to have to "listen" to others instead of "talking" when I differed very much with them on certain points; but it was nevertheless challenging for me to be able to arrange and present the discussion as I so desired. And I did some "talking" too! In a way, editing the book was similar to creating a mosaic: after asking certain individuals to contribute specific articles, it was left to me to arrange the articles in a scheme that I felt was both satisfying and appealing. The different parts should be self-explanatory, but in each one I generally posited my rationale for the arrangement of the articles.

I am indebted to a number of people for their suggestions, encouragement, and contributions toward the completion of this work. First, I want to thank the contributors, most of whose articles appear in this book for the first time and the rest who allowed me to reprint their works. I particularly want to thank my mentors, friends, and colleagues – William M. McCord, Charles V. Willie, and Willie B. Lamousé-Smith – for their involvement other than their contributions of original articles. My friends and colleagues at Dartmouth College, S. Jay Walker and Bernard E. Segal, deserve special mention for the many hours they spent both writing articles and a foreword for the book and nudging and sometimes pushing me to complete it. I am also grateful to Gene Lyons for taking time out of his busy schedule to critically read this manuscript. Special thanks also to Marshall H. Segall, a longtime special friend, who critically read the entire manuscript and made valuable suggestions for its improvement.

Finally, I am most grateful to the Social Science Research Council for providing me office space, copying privileges, and solitude for the final stage of completion. While I was there David L. Sills, Alice L. Morton, Judy Poehler, and Madora G. Blake were especially helpful. At Dartmouth, Judy Jones, Ann Fellows, and Donna Musgrove provided clerical help. I thank them very much. Even in the process of becoming a crotchety, irritable, uptight author, I remained aware of Terry Tarun Hall's contributions in many ways. As usual, I alone am responsible for the book's shortcomings.

Raymond L. Hall

# Part I
# Introduction

RAYMOND L. HALL

## DEFINITIONS

This book explores the phenomenon of black separatism, an ideological perspective on how to achieve freedom that is almost as old as the black presence in America. When discussed by whites, it is often done so disparagingly, if at all, implying that black separatism is an illogical and misguided reaction to white oppression. On the other hand, when viewed by blacks, it is seen either as a utopian, once-and-for-all solution to the complexity of race relations in the United States or as a juvenile, simplistic, and impractical means of coping with oppression in a complex, urbanized, technological society. In either case, however, black and white Americans – separately or together – seldom calmly or rationally discuss black separatism from an informed, enlightened position. Most people have made up their minds about what black separatism is, concluding that it is simply what "radical" blacks call "black nationalism." They then know who its proponents are likely to be and what its total ideological configuration is. Most often, they are all wrong on all counts.

Black nationalism as an ideological construct is complex and diverse, incorporating political, cultural, territorial, and economic factors. For example, black separatism is a sub-category of black nationalism, but there are many more branches to the tree of black nationalism: a cultural nationalist may believe it to be superior to Western culture. But a black nationalist may also believe that black and white territorial separation is unnecessary, accepting that cultural nationalism is only a part of American pluralism. An "economic" nationalist may believe that blacks should strive to control their economic destiny; "political" nationalist may believe that blacks should elect their own (black) officials and politically control areas where blacks are in the majority; other nationalists believe in "community control," ranging from control of black communities in urban settings to all-black towns and cities. All of these forms of "nationalism" reflect the size and diversity of views that may be enunciated under the umbrella of black nationalism, and all stem from the idea of racial solidarity. All of these "nationalisms" could constitute separatism if stretched to their logical extremes but not necessarily so if insistence on total black and white separation is omitted.

Black separatism is a sub-category of black nationalism which posits that blacks and whites ideally should form two separate nations. However, until the ideal of black and white national separation is a reality, separatism often manifests itself in one or more of the above forms of black nationalism. It is worth repeating that a separatist is *always* a nationalist, but a nationalist is *not always* a separatist.

Separatist dimensions may also be characterized as beginning with local or community black separatism, later including the black nation or "nation within a nation" idea, and finally embracing Pan-Africanism as the ultimate manifestation of black nationalism/separatism. Pan-Africanism, based on the same concept as Zionism, holds that all black peoples – wherever they are – are of African descent and are all members of the black or African Diaspora. Following the logic of Pan-Africanism, eventually all black peoples would "return" to Africa from all points of the Diaspora. The return of members of the African Diaspora is only one dimension of Pan-Africanism; the other is chiefly concerned with African unity on a continental basis. In this connection, it is primarily concerned with unity first as a protective measure against white minority dominance and ultimately with political, social, and economic unity to compete and negotiate in a world of political and economic blocs. The latter manifestation of Pan-Africanism transcends race as the binding solidarity element and theoretically includes white racist regimes if they abandon the oppression of black African peoples.

But, more to the point, some black separatists ultimately envision the revival of Mother Africa's power through the return of her skilled, trained, and technologically efficient Diaspora children. Others are content to regard Africa proudly as their ancestral homeland with no intention of returning to live, but still replenishing their "soul" supply with visits. These "recharges" may, however, serve to keep the fires of separatism burning in the United States; the "Black Nation," once established, may base its sociocultural organization on an "African" model: Tanzania's Ujamaa, or some ancient or current tribal system of the Ibo, Efik, Ijaw, Yoruba, Ibibio or usually some other (West) African group. The Black Nation would be geographically located in the United States (or somewhere in North America) but would receive its sociocultural sustenance from an African source.

The scope of black separatism is indeed wide and its

contemporary expression is as diverse and multifaceted as are its historical roots. Contemporary separatist manifestations may be found in organizations whose ideologies were originally oriented toward integration, such as the Congress of Racial Equality (CORE) and the now-defunct Student Non-Violent (later National) Coordinating Committee (SNCC). The Black Panther Party, allegedly a Marxist-Leninist organization advocating worker (black and white) solidarity, also based part of its appeal on black nationalism/separatism. US (as opposed to "them"), headed by Mulana Ron Karenga, is a cultural nationalist organization basing its separatist ideology on the distinct differences between African and European culture, positing the superiority of African culture over European culture. Although these cultural, social, and political aspects of separatism do not always call for geographical and territorial separation between blacks and whites, there are some aspects that do.

The Nation of Islam and the Republic of New Africa, for example, straightforwardly reject the idea of blacks and whites living in the same society. The Nation of Islam, or the Black Muslims as they are popularly called, claim whites are "devils" and the "natural enemy" of black people. Blacks should separate themselves from the "devil" by establishing a black nation in Africa; short of that, the white devils should compensate blacks for kidnapping and slavery by giving them land somewhere in the United States and enough reserves to sustain the black nation until it can "go for itself."

The Republic of New Africa (RNA) also bases its ideology on complete black and white territorial separation. Rejecting the idea of returning to Africa, it proposes to establish the Black Nation in the five states of South Carolina, Georgia, Alabama, Mississippi, and Louisiana. According to the RNA, since a significant number of blacks already live in these states, and blacks and whites in northern urban areas are engaging in increasingly conflictive relationships, blacks ought to return to these states, become a political majority, and "be a black nation."

Separatist tendencies are also seen in the establishment of black caucuses within predominantly white organizations: some examples include the Caucus of Black Sociologists, which grew out of disenchantment with the American Sociological Association, and the African Heritage Studies Association, which emerged from disenchantment with the African Studies Association. In general, black organizational separation occurred in most predominantly white organizations, and this form of "separation" is the classical form of "splintering" from "parent" organizations. The splintering results from blacks concluding that separation is the most expedient way of controlling their own destinies.

## HISTORICAL BLACK SEPARATISM

Though contemporary black separatism has quickened and revitalized aspects of black culture and highlighted another dimension of the black experience in America, it should be emphasized that separatism has deep historical roots. To promote an understanding of contemporary separatism, it is valuable to construct a synoptic history of separatist-nationalist thought up to the present time. Such a synopsis will provide a "map" of these historical manifestations with a view toward laying a foundation for the exploration of separatism's contemporary social reality.

Our synopsis of historical black nationalism suggests that – based on the idea of racial solidarity – it has taken many forms, including territorial separatism, emigrationism, and a specific variant, Back-to-Africanism. *Emigrationism* meant that blacks felt it best to leave the United States entirely, moving to Canada, Mexico, and the West Indies to establish their own societies and to escape white oppression. *Back-to-Africa* meant literally to return to Africa, to the ancestral homeland as opposed to the non-southern United States or some other part of the world.[1] Between these three general headings fall other separatist nuances which some classify as separatist expressions: "slave rebellions" or liberation efforts, church or "religious" separatism, convention movements, black political parties, migration, and other efforts to bring about self-determination.

Though black separatism has deeper roots, historians usually point to its initial expression as "religious" or church separatism. Specifically, the first separate black Baptist Church was founded at Silver Bluff, South Carolina, in the 1770s. The first black Episcopal Church, founded by Absalom Jones in the 1880s, emerged from the refusal of white parishioners to allow blacks to "integrate" their worship service as did the founding, in 1815, of the African Methodist Episcopal (AME) Church in Philadelphia by Richard Allen. Blacks had always been allowed to worship in the same church building with whites – as long as they stayed in their "place" in the lofts and balcony areas. Reverends Allen and Jones, among others, were not satisfied with this arrangement – thinking that the Almighty might also disapprove – and they descended from their lofty positions to worship with their white brethren, only to face coercive physical removal. Brothers Allen and Jones vowed never again to "bother" their white brethren. Later, in 1816, they formed a separate AME Convention in Philadelphia.[2]

It is very easy to chronicle expressions of black people playing important "integration" roles in the nation's emergence. Crispus Attucks was credited with being the first to die for the American cause of freedom in the Revolutionary War; Salem Poore and Peter Salem, among many, fought side by side with their white compatriots against British oppression (one of these gentlemen of color was responsible for dispatching Major Pitcairn to his Maker).[3] Yet, these instances of black sacrifice and contributions notwithstanding, white Americans, even in the midst of British oppression, continued to hold blacks as slaves; on the other hand, the many blacks who joined the British were promised their freedom if they fought against their colonist oppressors. Even though Britain lost the war, those blacks who fought in the British ranks won their freedom: the British allowed many to return to Africa and others settled in Canada and even in England itself; they even established Sierra Leone in West Africa specifically to accommodate manumitted slaves and other free blacks who wanted to return.[4]

There is ample evidence to suggest that Africans brought to America as slaves always wanted to return to Africa. That is a major reason why slaveholders concocted elaborate measures to keep them from escaping. Nevertheless, many managed to escape from slaveholding areas and were somehow able to return to Africa.[5] Most, of course, were not.

In 1791, the "black revolt," led by Toussaint L'Ouverture

in Santo Domingo, resulted in the first independent black republic in Central America and sent shock waves through the slaveholding areas in the United States.[6] More precautions were immediately instituted to guard against slave revolts. In 1800 Gabriel Prosser was apprehended for planning a slave revolt in Virginia; in 1821, Denmark Vesey was also apprehended for planning a slave revolt. In 1831, "Nat" Turner got beyond the planning stage, killing 55 whites before he and his coconspirators were finally caught. Herbert Aptheker and others have documented the occurrence of many slave revolts and speculated about the possibility of others.[7]

Some have suggested that these slave revolts are examples of black separatist expression. I am somewhat dubious, largely because they raise as many questions as they emphatically answer one: blacks hated slavery with a passion, and revolting against it was one possible – though desperate and dangerous – way of escaping. However, struggling for freedom still leaves the question of whether they sought to separate from whites *qua* whites, or whether they simply wanted to go "north to freedom." If the latter was the case, as it most often was, then one would have to stretch the concept of separatism too far for it to retain any meaning. My position is that slave revolts can only be classified as separatist expressions on a case-by-case basis.

Separatism, expressed through emigration, can be seen in the activities of Paul Cuffee, a wealthy black New Bedford, Massachusetts ship merchant who used his own resources to transport blacks to the West Coast of Africa. In 1816, Cuffee was instrumental in the founding of the American Colonization Society (ACS), whose purpose was to aid in the transportation of blacks to Africa.[8] The ACS played a role in black emigration schemes for well over a hundred years, and therefore will intermittently appear in this synopsis.[9]

In 1822, at the behest of the ACS, the United States government established Liberia – as the British had earlier done with Sierra Leone – as an African "homeland" for manumitted slaves and "free blacks" who wanted to emigrate there. The role of the ACS in promoting African emigration was seen by slaveholders as a way of "interfering" with their capital and meddling in their profit-making ventures. It was criticized almost as often by blacks as a conspiracy to rid the United States of black people. Nevertheless, it did receive black emigrants and white support in promoting black emigration.

The abolitionist movement opposed the ACS, arguing that more effort should be spent fighting the abolition of slavery than promoting black emigration. Thus, the late 1820s and '30s found the abolitionist movement in full swing. The appearance of the first black newspaper, *Freedom's Journal,* in 1827, also urged abolitionism. Both the ACS and the abolitionists were, in essence, pressure groups using moral suasion as their chief weapon in the black freedom struggle. David Walker, a black, used-clothing dealer in Boston, made this point clear in 1827 when he issued an "appeal" to the slaveholders to free their slaves and, at the same time, urged blacks – if necessary – to take up arms to win their freedom.[10] He was not in favor of African emigration and, along with Richard Allen, denounced it as a conspiracy by whites to rid the country of blacks. Walker's militant appeal was characterized by the ACS and abolitionists as counterproductive; they argued that it would harden the slaveholders' position and weaken northern sentiment by conjuring up a picture of bloodshed and chaos.

In general, during the period from the 1770s to the 1830s, emigration for the most part was concerned with returning or taking southern slaves to Africa. While there was some black emigration sentiment on the part of "free blacks" in the North, they generally rejected it, preferring to remain in the United States. Thus, emigration flourished under dire (slavery) circumstances, and waned (in the North) when oppression was not unusually harsh. By the 1830s, however, northern blacks began to step up their pace in agitating for freedom for southern slaves as well as for themselves.

Elements of separatism in these stepped-up activities can be seen in the Convention movement, when some blacks in the organization began to speak of black nationalism – the "nation within a nation" idea. In fact, the Convention movement itself may be seen as blacks organizing to promote their own ends (it is indeed comparable to the black caucus activity of today).[11] Other groups sprang from the Convention movement, thinking it too nationalistic. Thus, ACS, abolitionist, and Convention movement activity continued into the 1840s, when black "militant" activity escalated. In 1843, for example, Henry Highland Garnett, a black minister of a white congregation in Troy, New York, called for black slaves to revolt against their oppression. At the Convention meeting that year, he tried to get the National Convention to publish his speech urging slaves to revolt, but the meeting was not that militant and the resolution failed to pass. Later, in 1848, he wrote a treatise on the subject and published it privately along with "Walker's Appeal."[12] (Walker had been mysteriously murdered on June 28, 1830, in his Boston used-clothing shop.)

The 1850s found northern blacks continuing to escalate their integration as well as their separatist activities. But, ironically, as blacks sought justice and equality in the American mainstream, they were constantly rebuffed, winning only a few concessions here and there. These rebuffs served as a catalyst for them to seek redress of their grievances by means of self-determination. As a result of the major political parties excluding or paying little attention to black voters, in 1855 a group of blacks in New York City called for an independent black political party.[13]

The Compromise of 1850, the Dred Scott Decision in 1857, and other oppressive and repressive measures led many blacks to conclude that it was best to leave the United States. Frederick Douglass, for example, an avowed integrationist, decided in late 1859 that he would move to Haiti. Martin Robinson Delany agitated for migration and emigration, living for a while in Canada and later exploring the possibility of black emigration to West Africa. Alexander Crummell, a longtime civil rights activist, finally moved to Liberia under the auspices of the ACS. In general, the times did not bode well for those who advocated that blacks should stay in the United States and pursue an integrationist course. At this point, those taking up an integrationist stance were pejoratively called "stay-at-homes."[14]

Even Abraham Lincoln, who later issued the Emancipation Proclamation, felt that because of inherent racial differences, blacks and whites should live in separate societies. John Brown, a Connecticut Yankee, had even deeper feelings about black separation. He "went to the barricades" at Harpers Ferry to secure arms for blacks so that they could defend their "black nation."[15] Though his plan failed and the black nation did not materialize, migration and emigration – aided and abetted by black pessimism, black nationalism, and the ACS – continued as dominant themes.

The 1850s, then, was a decade characterized by an intensive national policy debate between the pro-slavery South and the generally anti-slavery North. The main issue centered around maintaining equilibrium between the admission of slave and free states to the Union. The North felt that slavery was a moral question, that no human should be legally classified as a slave because this *ipso facto* denied the pursuit of happiness, among other things. The South, on the other hand, felt that slavery was an economic question and that national policy should not deny a class (read: the South) the right to pursue its economic opportunities in its customary manner. These conflicting perspectives became the center of the nation's political debate. Blacks, taking their cues from the northern and southern protagonists, either advocated emigration, conceding southern victory, or migration, believing northern arguments regarding the "rights of man." Toward the end of the '50s the increased nationalism, emigration tendencies, the Dred Scott decision, and the desperate John Brown Harpers Ferry incident indicated that the South had not won the debate, but was not losing it, either. Many blacks, like Douglass and Delany, felt that the stalemate was really a loss for black equality. As they prepared to leave the United States, a predictably "minor incident" at Bull Run turned out to be not so predictable and not so minor. It was, in fact, among the first major battles of the Civil War. Blacks and whites, North and South, felt that the "final solution" to the question of slavery and race would be attained through the war. Douglass and Delany stayed, with Delany serving as a Captain (he had received training in medicine at Harvard). Emigration ceased, and migration (of blacks from South to North) increased with thousands of blacks serving in the Union army.

### Black Separatism from 1865 to 1900

The end of the Civil War found blacks legally free (thanks to Lincoln's Emancipation Proclamation and the 13th Amendment), but still victims of poverty, prejudice, and discrimination, confronted by the problems of an increasingly industrializing, urbanizing, and expanding nation. Though reconstruction was designed to aid the newly freed slaves, it did not do enough, long enough, to change radically the traditional power relations. By the end of the '60s, the Republican Party was ready to compromise its commitment to black equality in favor of promoting commercial and industrial national progress. The Democratic Party, the party of white redemption, again openly advocated "Jim Crowism" and black subordination. By the election of 1876, the North, the Republican party, and Rutherford B. Hayes – its standard bearer and the winner of the Presidential election – withdrew Union troops from Louisiana in return for southern Democratic cooperation in commercial-industrial matters. Thus, the Compromise of 1877 again ushered in completely white "redemption" (read: black oppression) and again, as always, blacks reacted with "nationalistic" responses.

In 1879, for example, "Pap" Singleton, the "Moses of the Negro people," led an exodus of blacks from the Deep South to Kansas. There, he argued, blacks could be free of white oppression by establishing all-black communities.[16] He later also embraced African emigration after whites engaged in a "Kansas exodus" (there is no mention that they were led by a "Moses," however).

The ACS, as usual in times of increased white hostility, continued its emigration efforts. This time it was aided by Bishop Henry McNeil Turner, an ardent separatist-emigrationist, who felt that the place of blacks was in Africa, not in the United States.[17] In addition, African emigration was given a shot in the arm by Professor Edward Wilmont Blyden, a West Indian transplanted to Liberia. He, too, believed that all blacks should return to their ancestral homeland and he came to the United States advocating this position in a whirlwind tour around the country. Despite the fact that there were not many takers, this event pointed up the fact that emigration was no longer a one-way street – some Africans, too, were interested in the "return" of their American cousins.[18] Blyden came at the invitation of the ACS and Bishop Turner, but he was also welcomed by proponents of an emigration bill before Congress in 1892 – the Butler Bill – which would have provided passage for blacks who wanted to return to Africa. Blyden advocated its passage, but it failed to pass Congress, because, among other things, its implementation would have been prohibitively expensive.

Despite the failure of the Butler Bill, the 1890s witnessed a multiplicity of plans and schemes for black emigration. Many were ill-conceived and dishonest, others were honest but ill-conceived, and still others were well-conceived but dishonest; there were a smattering of honest schemes and some were mildly successful – that is, successful in the sense that a small number of blacks were transported to Liberia, though not many of those who went remained; of those that remained, not many survived. But the point that African emigration received tremendous attention in the 1880s is crucial to understanding the next phase of black separatism: Pan-Africanism.

It should be clear at this point that black separatism manifested itself in the form of migration (moving away from the South) and emigration (initially slaves returning to Africa, but after emancipation, free-blacks, responding to their circumstances outside the South, also embracing emigrationism and promoting it). Particularly after the "1877 Compromise" emigrationism again became popular because of increased subordination in the North and South. From that time, black "civil rights" steadily deteriorated and by the 1890s even the Populists were in the process of abandoning blacks, a position they had initially championed.[19] However, with Populists like Tom Watson and "Pitchfork Ben" Tillman, what could one expect of the Populist Party? By the mid-1890s, the deep economic recession (Panic of 1894) did not exactly contribute to friendly race relations.

The southern mechanization of agriculture, in essence, worsened the already bad relations between the black and white sharecroppers and "crop-lieners." Receiving the short end of a very long stick, blacks were "pushed" out of the moribund southern agricultural scene and "pulled" to the industrial North. The 1890s witnessed the infant stage of this demographic shift which would dramatically increase in the 20th century. But even in its infancy, it was enough to help usher in an increased emphasis on African emigration or Pan-Africanism.

The beginning stages of the huge impending black demographic change, an increase in the number of African emigration schemes, and the death in 1895 of Frederick Douglass, were all to have profound ramifications for black separatism in the 20th century. Douglass, the eloquent spokesman for integration, would be replaced by another extraordinarily adept and cunning race conciliator, Booker T. Washington. In his speech at the Cotton States Exposition in Atlanta in 1895, he told his immediate Southern audience that the races could be as "separate as the fingers on the hand," but could work together for "mutual progress." Moreover, he opted to forego political and social equality in favor of economic pursuits. W.E.B. DuBois, who graduated from Harvard with a Ph.D. in 1895, later denounced Washington's position and labeled his speech the "Atlanta Compromise." DuBois, though no separatist, played a significant role in the Pan-African movement from 1900 to his death in Ghana in 1963.

We should again make the point that black separatism, through whatever medium, was a reaction by a relatively few against oppression; the majority continued to espouse stay-at-home sentiments. The Afro-American League, organized in the early 1890s and headed by T. Thomas Fortune, for example, was a militant civil rights organization demanding equality in the United States. Though ths decade was one least conducive to civil rights progress (considering the 1894 panic, among other things, the *Plessy vs. Ferguson* Supreme Court decision, and the impending virtual re-triumph of Jim Crow), most blacks who engaged in political activity did so in an attempt to make things better where they were – North or South. It is crucial that this be clearly understood because it underscores the following two points: (1) separatism, whether through migration or emigration, was not the modal tendency of black people – it was a last-ditch effort to minimize oppression; (2) making things better where they were was to become one component of the next major black leader's ideological appeal: Booker T. Washington admonished southern blacks to "let their buckets down where they were" and eventually he was successful in influencing northern blacks to do the same. Therefore, civil rights activity, emigration, increasing white oppression, and the shifting black population would set the stage for the escalation of black nationalism in the 20th century.

**Twentieth Century Black Separatism**

The turn of the century ushered in stirrings among blacks that eventually culminated into one of the most significant black nationalist/separatist mass movements ever produced by black people in the United States. Around this time, black migration from the South to the northern urban areas – later escalated by the advent of World War I – transformed rural ex-slaves into proletarians. Shortly after the First World War, the black presence in urban America prompted hostility and resistance by whites in response to demands for black equality in housing, employment, and even recreation. Out of these denials came the East St. Louis and Chicago riots, among others, in 1917 and 1919, respectively. In the early '20s emerged the Harlem or "Negro" Renaissance, the cultural wing of the newly awakened "New Negro," and Marcus Garvey – black nationalist leader par excellence. After the wane and eclipse of Garvey and Garveyism, black separatism did not disappear. Indeed, it lingered and festered – subdued and dormant to be sure – from Garvey's demise until the late 1950s and '60s when it again burst forth with ferocious intensity, culminating in separatist expressions which had a generally invigorative liberating effect on blacks and often elicited fearful bewilderment among whites.

At the turn of the century, Booker T. Washington was the acknowledged leader – by blacks as well as whites – of the nine to ten million blacks in America.[20] His "non-militant" leadership earned him the title of "Uncle Tom" (see Chapter 8 in this volume) among most of his contemporary militant black compatriots and, of course, among today's militant blacks. On the other hand, there are also those who view his leadership, in retrospect, as viable separatism, and it is still often inadvertently utilized by many contemporary separatists. Was Washington a covert separatist? I answer in the affirmative and my reasons are included in Part II of this volume (see Chapter 7).

Other black leaders than Washington offered programs aimed at black liberation. Among them was W.E.B. DuBois, one of the organizers of the first Pan-African Congress held in London in 1900. In this connection, DuBois is linked with the initial developments of Pan-Africanism, which later took on a "militant" separatist character. However, domestically, DuBois was the antithesis of a separatist, opposing Washington's separatism by organizing the "Niagara Movement" in 1906, which opposed Washington's acquiescence to political and social equality in favor of economic separatism. Moreover, DuBois was instrumental in the founding of the National Association for the Advancement of Colored People (NAACP) in 1909. Others, such as William Monroe Trotter (who received a master's degree from Harvard around the same time that DuBois received his Ph.D.) also opposed Washington's program.[21] On the whole, most of Washington's critics opposed him for abandoning political and civil rights for blacks.

This raises the question, then, of what Washington's separatist expressions were if most blacks favored integration and utilized civil rights activities to achieve it. In short, Washington chose to accept the reality that white southerners had "redeemed" the South by taking away the vote, had segregated public transportation and education, and had generally reduced not-far-from-slavery blacks to "free-slave" status. He argued that to ignore this reality by agitating for equality through civil rights activity was folly and that the best alternative for blacks would be to work for economic advantage – and eventual self-sufficiency and self-determination – through groundings in "commerce, the trades, and vocational pursuits."[22] Achieving proficiency in these areas was far superior to liberal arts training where one would "spend a dollar on opera" rather than investing it for profit. To this end, he geared Tuskegee Institute to the vocational trades, and urged black businessmen in the North to focus on the acquisition of property, newspapers, and other capital and profit-producing enterprises. These economic undertakings, he argued, were more fruitful than agitating for political and social rights. Not that he particularly opposed these rights for blacks, but he felt they would come automatically with economic determination. This economic separatism, then, was the foundation of Washington's program for black liberation. His over-emphasis on economic self-determination was the basis for opposition to his program. His opposition was integration- and civil-rights-oriented and thus beyond the purview of our emphasis on black separatism. But since separatism is more often the flip side of the integration coin, there are times when integration efforts "explain" or highlight the meaning of separatism. Pan-Africanism is a case in point.

Since my essay will explore specific details of Washington's "separatism" (see Chapter 7 in this volume), I can proceed here to examine how Washington's separatist expression shaded into the next phase of Pan-Africanism and its militant advocate, Marcus Garvey.

Pan-Africanism espoused by DuBois and the other leaders of the civil rights movement in its early stages merely argued that the colonial powers should grant freedom to their African colonial territories. Once free, these African nations could then pursue a policy of African unity for their mutual development: if blacks of the Diaspora wanted to return to Africa, they should and would have the opportunity to do so.

DuBois himself, however, generally opposed African emigration, exerting most of his Pan-African energy on African colonial freedom. Despite his opposition, however, the first decade of the 20th century found emigration sentiments still high. For example, "Chief" Alfred Sam launched an emigration scheme in 1913 that was partly successful.[23] Washington, a shrewd and perceptive observer, realized that Pan-Africanism and African emigration sentiments were real. Though he opposed emigration in favor of economic separatism at home, he did sponsor programs and opportunities for blacks to return to Africa. His program was oriented around economics and he eventually founded the African Union Company in 1913 that was designed to promote commercial relations between black Americans and Africans. His untimely death in 1915, however, prevented his Pan-African plans from unfolding.

In 1915, when the ardent Pan-Africanist-separatist Henry McNeil Turner died, the impetus for Pan-Africanism was temporarily lost. The outbreak of the First World War also contributed to Pan-Africanism's decline, embroiling the colonial powers in a fratricidal struggle and the rest of the world in watchful waiting.

The renewal of interest in Pan-Africanism did not wait long. At the invitation of Booker T. Washington, Marcus Garvey was preparing to come to the United States to look at Tuskegee Institute as a model for what could be done for his Jamaican compatriots.[24] Washington died in 1915 before Garvey's scheduled visit, but in 1916 Garvey arrived anyway and began organizing for his program in Harlem, the "capital" of black America. After many setbacks and disappointments, Garvey established the Universal Negro Improvement Association (UNIA) in Harlem, and around 1919, his program caught on and he became the talk of the town – and eventually of the world (see Chapter 21 in this volume).

Garvey preached that Africa was the black homeland and that in order to free Africa from colonial domination, all blacks from the Diaspora should "march back to Africa 400 million strong" and free her from colonial oppression. In order to do so, he organized the Black Star Line as both a commercial venture and ostensibly a scheme to transport blacks back to Africa. Thus, African emigration took on a back-to-Africa character, militantly demanding that Diaspora blacks be allowed to return to Africa.

In the meantime, in addition to planning for the eventual separation of blacks and whites on a national basis, Garvey organized the Negro Factories Corporation so that blacks could pursue their own separate economic goals through such means as cleaning establishments, grocery and clothing stores, bookstores, beauty parlors, barbershops, and a host of other small business enterprises. Garvey was able to combine Washington's economic program with a militant form of African emigration.

He was able to do so for a variety of reasons. Among them were the huge migration of rural southern blacks to northern industrial urban centers as a result of industries "pulling" cheap black labor and of the mechanization of southern agriculture. Washington's program was initially geared to aid southern blacks, but as his fame spread and black migration swelled northern urban ghettoes, he also tried to speak to the needs of urban blacks. He again urged northern blacks to concentrate on economic enterprises and the development of skill levels, but his counsel to soft-pedal civil rights did not sound the same to northern blacks because, among other things, they were more educated than his southern peasants; they were as a class more sophisticated and had not generally faced the same kinds of oppression southern blacks had. Only recent black migrants understood him and his position, and they were content to listen if not to internalize his admonishments.

After Washington's death, Garvey galvanized the latent hostility, forged a vision of Africa, organized a program of redemption, and freed blacks from the fear of white reprisal. In short, he was able to take Washington's separatist economic program and add militant African emigration or Back-to-Africa ingredients, which resulted in the largest black mass movement up to that time. Garvey, unlike Washington, was not a covert separatist, but rather an open advocate of black national separation with Africa as the black nation.

Though Garvey and the UNIA captured the imagination of blacks and elicited fear from whites, his vision of the black nation in Africa and viable economic separatism in the United States fell victim to UNIA-organizational squabbles, mismanagement, and outright thievery and external American and colonial control mechanisms. The Black Star Line and the Negro Factories Corporation were at the outset underfinanced and ill-managed, while his Back-to-Africa proposal involving Liberia crumbled due to international monopoly capital and colonial designs. In 1924, he was convicted of "defrauding through the mails" and sentenced to the federal penitentiary in Atlanta. Pardoned and exiled in 1927, Garvey returned to Jamaica and eventually to London, where he died in 1940. His dream – like most dreams – was not realized during his lifetime, but he did set an example of how blacks could pursue their separate destiny, and that pursuit continued after the eclipse of Garvey and Garveyism and continues today.[25]

Though his was the loudest voice, Garvey was not the only proponent of separatism. The African Blood Brotherhood – led at one point by Cyril Briggs, one of Garvey's fellow West Indians – was also a militant anti-white separatist group. Claude McKay (see Chapter 21 in this volume), Langston Hughes, and other black artists and intellectuals wrote and spoke about Mother Africa. These were not necessarily expressions of separatism, but they were indications that Africa no longer had the same kind of pejorative meanings for blacks as it did for whites. There are those, too, who suggest that the Harlem Renaissance had a nationalistic wing. It is clear that Garvey led the militant nationalists, and his decline did not spell the end of nationalism-separatism.

However, Pan-Africanism did suffer a severe defeat with Garvey's decline; even the DuBois-led, nonmilitant brand had less appeal. Other concerns were drawing the attention of black Americans. Garvey's successful appeal to the black masses was not lost, however, on the Communist Party (CP). In 1928, the Party, at the behest of the Communist International (Comintern), fashioned a separatist program in the United States based on Garvey's success. The CP called it "Self-Determination in the Black Belt," suggesting that blacks constituted a "nation within a nation." Moreover, it was argued that the racial question in the United States had become a national question because blacks in the Black Belt had evolved a separate culture from whites, therefore qualifying, according to the Comintern's definition, for nationhood.

The Self-Determination policy was not received with enthusiasm by the American CP, which had to administer the inane, ill-conceived idea, or by blacks, who were to be the beneficiaries of the "nation" (see Chapter 14 in this volume). By 1933, the Black Belt policy had given way in all but name to a "United Front" strategy.[26]

The CP was not the only organization addressing itself to the question of black separation, though it was at that time the only predominantly white one to do so. In the early 1930s, the Moorish American Science Temple, organized in 1913 by Timothy Drew, was an example of blacks rejecting their "Negroness" in favor of Asiatic identity. The Nation of Islam, founded in Detroit in 1932, also emphasized black people's "Asiatic" heritage, and it is still one of today's most viable separatist organizations.[27] The Ethiopian Peace Movement was representative of black identification with Ethiopia and the Forty-Ninth State Movement, founded in 1934, centered its appeal around the idea of establishing a 49th state for black people (at that time the United States consisted only of the 48 continental states).

In general, the 1930s were characterized by the proliferation of small, sect-like separatist groups with none approximating the size and intensity of the Garvey movement. Many of Garvey's followers had joined other separatist organizations – the Nation of Islam, for example. Daddy Grace and Father Divine both received ex-Garveyites, and although these were not separatist movements per se, they had so few white members that, for all practical purposes, Garveyites and other black separatists could escape from the white world.[28] One of the reasons for subdued separatism was the advent of the Great Depression and the subsequent "deliverance" of the New Deal. In other words, the militant separatist organizations seldom had viable economic programs to sustain their membership and, consequently, the New Deal programs became much more attractive. People usually opt for "meat to eat" over "pie in the sky," and thus, the dire economic situation took the steam out of their prior militant orientations. Consequently, from around the mid-1930s, separatism gave way to increasing emphasis on "getting a piece of the pie" (here and now) rather than on separation. The Don't-Buy-Where-You-Can't-Work campaigns may be seen as a form of economic separation in that blacks in many large cities demanded that white-owned stores hire black workers. Some insisted that blacks take over some of these white-owned stores in black communities.

The late 1930s to the mid-1940s witnessed the Second World War and black activity centered around legal battles by the NAACP and agitation for equal or fair employment. In the latter connection, the A. Philip Randolph-led March on the Washington Movement (MOWM) temporarily took a separatist/nationalist turn when Randolph threatened to appeal to the black masses in an effort to pressure President Roosevelt to deal with black unemployment during the war. The March never took place, but the threat of one was enough to influence the President to issue an executive order banning discrimination in industries with federal contracts. The effectiveness of the order is another story and a sorry one at that.[29]

From the 1940s to the late '50s, separatism remained limited to locally oriented small-scale group efforts in large metropolitan areas. The only organization during this period to promote a national separatist campaign was the Nation of Islam. By the end of the 1950s, Malcom X, who was converted to the Nation of Islam while in a Massachusetts prison in 1947, had gained national prominence as the quick-witted, ascerbic, and charismatic Minister of the Nation of Islam.

By 1960, the impact of Rosa Park's refusal in 1955 to stand on a bus in Montgomery, Alabama so that a white man could have her seat led to the rise of Martin Luther King, Jr.'s leadership of the civil rights movement and the resultant intense integration focus. The intensity of the integration movement did not, however, eliminate separatism as an alternative. Rather, it led many blacks to contemplate Malcolm X's rhetorical question, "Integrate into what?" The March on Washington in August of 1963 was the beginning of the end of blacks and whites struggling together for integration. The passage of the 1964 civil-rights bill was followed by a general resurgence of black separatism and militant black civil rights activity. Around 1964, riots began to occur throughout the country, culminating in Detroit in 1967.

Black militancy and separatism in the 1960s have been characterized by some as the "Black Revolution," a label to which I take exception. It constituted a black rebellion, Harold Cruse reminds us, but does not fit any rigorous definition of revolution. Revolution connotes a drastic, complete change in power relations, and that has never occurred between blacks and whites in the United States.

The question that perplexes many people is, why was there a proliferation of separatism among blacks when things were ostensibly getting better? Why did the Congress of Racial Equality (CORE), founded as an interracial, nonviolent organization, and the Student Non-Violent Coordinating Committee (SNCC) opt for separation around the mid-1960s? Why did the Black Panther Party, allegedly a Marxist-Leninist organization, take the un-Marxian position of not allowing whites to become members? How did the Republic of New Africa come to adopt the separatist position of five southern states for the Black Nation? These and other questions are the subject matter of this book, and a number of people will answer them in a variety of ways.

Black separatism, then, is not a recent phenomenon, but goes far back into American history. Hopefully, this brief synopsis has provided continuity regarding its salient characteristics in the context of that history. It points up a history that many Americans do not know, and one that many would prefer to forget; for still others, it is a history reflective of the long denial of basic humanity to black people. Black separatism is an attempt by black people to take their destiny into their own hands, and to forge their own future unhindered by the power of white separatists who, under the circumstances, hold veto power over black survival.

## THE SOCIAL REALITY OF BLACK SEPARATISM

Academic scholars usually treat black nationalism as a "social problem" or as "deviant behavior" on the part of those blacks who embrace it. This treatment stems in part from the past acceptance of consensus rather than conflict models and theories of social behavior. Black separatism usually receives little or no attention. Laypeople generally greet black nationalism with misunderstanding, fear, and hostility. Black separatism is always met with fear, hostility, and social control mechanisms designed to eradicate it as quickly as possible and to insure its perpetual moribundity. What these academic and lay reactions are suggesting, perhaps, is that the idea of American pluralism, if it is to retain any meaning for black Americans, can and must accept certain aspects of black nationalism – such as its emphasis on black cultural distinctiveness – that does not require a reordering and reshuffling of the economic, political, and social status quo. Most people know little or nothing about black separatism and consequently deny its existence. But black separatism does exist and, as the historical synopsis has shown, it has evolved over time. It is a social reality in American society.

This work then explores several aspects of the reality of black separatism from several perspectives, making it clear that people in the same society, existing and operating in the same social milieu, react differently, for different reasons, to the same societal conditions: the suggestion that the reaction of those blacks who embrace separatism as a liberation tactic or strategy in struggling against real or imagined white oppression is a pathological one on their part is at best arbitrary considering that social reality is multifaceted and multidimensional. What, then, is social reality and what is the best way to approach and analyze it?

From the beginning of scientific observation of human interaction and behavior, social scientists and other keen observers have pondered and wondered, theorized and philosophized over the question of reality. And the question of the social construction of reality remains an elusive phenomenon for social scientists. One could argue that the social construction of reality is the central concern and, therefore, the raison d'etre of social science. One thing is for sure: the complexity of the social construction of reality demands multifaceted and multidimensional approaches and strategies. These strategies and approaches notwithstanding, social reality continues to elicit controversy mainly because it continues to defy and elude a widely accepted definition. Nevertheless, for the purpose of this work, and hopefully to minimize ambiguity, an operational conception – as opposed to a definition – of social reality is necessary: social reality may be conceptualized as the sum total of human interaction in a given society and the consequent individual and group-patterned reactions in relationship to components of the physical environment which together represent relative constructs from the absolute empirical social world.

It follows that there is a high degree of predictability resulting from patterned social relations, and yet the range of possible reactions to social stimuli remains beyond consistent accurate prediction. Our conceptualization of social reality is merely an attempt to straddle the Plato-Aristotle debate: there is an ultimate empirical social world, but individuals, groups and societies can only experience part of ultimate reality. Moreover, *social and physical phenomena together* comprise *ultimate* reality, but humans, individually or collectively, can only construct *social* reality. Even the human physical environment is merely the objectivization of social conceptions, and, in the end, still remains the social construction of reality. Thus, objective and subjective reality are, in the final analysis, equal though potentially opposite aspects of a unitary phenomenon. This conception of reality follows the argument of Gehlen, and Berger and Luckman; they, of course, may disagree with how I articulate it.

The above conception and subsequent discussion of social reality still leaves unasked a most significant question: Since there are at least three types of dimensions to the "social construction of reality," what are they and how can we tell which one(s) we are dealing with at a particular time? The first construction is the subjective reality of the actor(s) – i.e., those studied by the social scientist; the second, actually a second-order construction, the social scientist takes for granted an already constructed reality based on his own ideas, concepts, position – i.e., his own perception of social realization; third is the social scientist's theories (construction) of how the actors'/subjects' realities are constructed. Here is where the social scientists must be very careful about the validity, reliability, and replicability of his construction because it is too often the case that there is little or no relationship between the social reality that is manifest in the minds of the actual social actors and the social reality that is manifest in the mind of the investigating social scientist. This is not to suggest that there should not be different perceptions of the actor's situation. This depends largely on "where one is coming from," i.e., whether the perception is that of the actor or that of the social scientist. It is also not to suggest that the actor can always "realistically" understand and describe his or her situation. Here is where the social scientists can play a most significant role if they do not (often like the actors themselves) dogmatically insist that their view is the most accurate construction in town – in the face of evidence to the contrary. But social scientists, unlike the actors they investigate, have tools, disciplines, and other social scientists to keep check on the validity and reliability of their constructions. Hence, the social scientist must always pay close attention to the question of "which reality"? At what time? But he must above all else understand (here I would rather use the German word *Verstehen*) the actor's construction. And only certain social science tools can be used for that! We shall discuss this latter matter in more detail below. At this point, let us discuss some other problems associated with the social construction of reality.

### The Need for Interdisciplinary Approaches

One of the reasons why it is difficult for social scientists to "accurately" explore social reality stems from social science fragmentation. It is a given that no specialist in any one of the social sciences today can understand all aspects of social life, nor will many make the claim to do so. Specialists need the support of other specialists in other social science disciplines in order to attempt to construct a complete – or nearly complete – configuration of social reality.

But specialization has not always been the *modus operandi* of the social sciences. Comte and Marx specifically and 19th-century founders of social science in general did not favor this division. Comte, for example, maintained that "social phenomena are fundamentally connected with one another and that study of a particular category of phenomenon is sterile." Marx felt that no social phenomena could be validly analyzed in isolation; economic, political, historical and sociological phenomena are all ultimately linked in a dialectical manner and reality cannot exist outside these interrelationships. To promote the unitary character of the social sciences, Comte favored "specialists in generalities" and Marx called for a cosmogony for social science. Neither view stemmed the tide of disciplinary proliferation.

However, many contemporary social scientists recognize the fundamental value of early arguments against divisions within social science; at the same time, they also recognize the reasons for disciplinary divisions in the search for social reality. That is, the complexity of social life in a complex, dynamic society such as the United States demands that social life be approached from a variety of perspectives, recognizing that no one social scientist can adequately come to grips with the problems and complexities. Hence, the structure of higher education and the complexity of social life mandate disciplinary specialization. For example, there are courses called the *politics* of poverty, the *economics* of poverty, the *history* of poverty, the *sociology* of poverty, the *psychology* of poverty, etc., as though there were no interrelationship among the different approaches. This is not to place a value on the offerings themselves, but to ask how one is to gain a complete picture of poverty without crossing disciplinary lines and, at the same time, to point up how the search for social reality in social science has been fragmented – to the chagrin of Comte and Marx, to be sure.

*My position is that social reality can best be explored by approaching it from a general social science or interdisciplinary/multidisciplinary perspective rather than from a single disciplinary perspective.* If one focuses on the social construction of reality as the key concept, an emphasis in this direction, in fact, mitigates the serious and persistent controversy over which of the social sciences "best" depicts and promotes the understanding of social reality and social life. The straddling of disciplines then becomes normal as a result of this approach. Let me reiterate my point that social reality is a slippery and elusive character and its multidimensionality is the reason for social science fragmentation in the first place.

### Methods and Approaches

Social scientists have at their disposal a wide range of theories and methods to foster understanding, description, and explanation of social phenomena and social life. Their task, therefore, is to choose from among them the most accurate and "realistic" ones for understanding and communicating their findings to others. Both quantitative and qualitative approaches and methods allow the researcher to pay close attention to the scientific elements of reliability, validity, and replicability.

It is my opinion that the social reality of black separatism can best be initially explored by using qualitative methods and approaches. Put another way, qualitative approaches, methods, and techniques such as symbolic interactionism, phenomenology, participant observation, in-depth interviewing, etc. – in short, ethnomethodology – are best suited for getting at the "inner reality" of the separatist phenomenon.

Qualitative methods allow the researcher to examine and interpret the empirical social world from the perspective of the subjects being investigated. Frequently, inflexible use of the natural science model dictates that the investigator's theory, paradigm, concept, and technique conform to the dictum of the natural scientific method; thus, it may egregiously distort the subjective and intersubjective reality of aspects of social life the social scientist is constructing. Human interaction and behavior, individually or in groups, is a complex process and its comprehension requires that the social scientist have maximum qualitative as well as quantitative information regarding the attitudes, situations, and environments comprising the social world of those under investigation. To accomplish this "inner perspective," it is often necessary that the social scientist have close and sometimes intimate contact with the social phenomenon under investigation: he or she must interact with and touch it, should feel its anxiety and ordeal as well as its enchantment and pleasure, and, above all, should feel some compulsion to explain the social continuum of winners and losers. Too often social scientists explain the winner's rationale and perspective without explaining that, in our social milieu, winning is causally linked with losing. Without this existential knowledge, the social scientist's data must be regarded as inadequate, lacking in credibility, and advertently or inadvertently misleading. For with or without these crucial existential perspectives from the empirical social world, the modern social scientist implicitly or explicitly answers Howard Becker's question, "Whose Side Are We On?" The controllers or the controlled? The oppressor or the oppressed?

For example, phenomenology, which many perceive as exploring the "obvious," allows multidimensional explorations of reality by affording the opportunity of momentarily escaping our own subjectivity and entering the intersubjective (putting ourselves on the role of another) world of separatist (for the purpose of this work) reality. Through phenomenological reductionism, we can question our own taken-for-granted assumptions about the empirical social world by probing our because-of (our own views of our actions) reality by adopting in-order-to (others' reactions to our acts which shape our ends) postures. We may then be able to transcend our own subjectivity as well as put into some perspective idealized and formalized social science reification (treating social things as physical objects). The gene-I.Q. controversy, which is treated in Part VI of this book, is an example.

It follows that it is imperative to "know" others to be able to gain this phenomenological perspective. This knowledge can often be best gained through "intimate" qualitative methods of data gathering. In other words, the interpretation of quantitative data about black separatism, for example, cannot be valid unless and until separatist perspectives are included, unless, of course, the purpose is control rather than understanding. Put another way, quantification yields very little regarding separatist emotions, perspectives, desires, anxieties, dreams, and fears. But it will yield much of what controllers fear and desire and what they will tolerate and what they will crush.

Questions of whether or not social science or the social scientist is value-free, or, what are the "best" methods, etc., are still, after many years of debate, very important ones for the social scientist. And they are volatile and controversial. But taking positions on these questions should not blind one to the wide range of social science methods and approaches. Let's look at three general approaches. In the first instance, there is the humanistic approach, characterized by European intellectualism and social criticism. This orientation has led to challenges of some American values and the social importance of fundamental issues and a theoretical perspective of humanism. Humanism then contributed to the action-oriented position characterized by the model of the "social engineer," aimed at the solution of social problems and interested in the social importance of segmental problems; pragmatic liberalism is its theoretical perspective. The third course emphasizes the scientific orientation identified with the scientific method of the natural sciences. This orientation emphasizes ethical neutrality, logic and mathematics, and rigorous statistical analysis; its theoretical approach may be classified as European positivism or contemporary American neo-positivism. All these approaches, separately or together, are concerned with the business of making some systematic sense out of human interaction and behavior.

In summary, it is incumbent on the social sciences to become involved in – not detached from – the needs of the real world and there is also need to utilize theoretical, methodological, and conceptual schemes that promote a closer tie with the empirical social world. In order to promote a closer tie with social reality, we must utilize the best theories and methods – quantitative or qualitative – *based on a strict social* view of the inner and outer perspectives of social questions. Social Scientists should not forget that social reality exists only in the empirical social and not in the methods used to measure it.

In the following essay I attempt to explore the appeal of separatism from the separatist perspective, keeping in mind that separatism is not the same to all who embrace it as a philosophy or strategy. Rather, it has several dimensions, and I attempt to explore several of them by employing the "ideal type" approach, suggesting that separatism's appeal emanates from several loci in American society. The data were derived from interviews, questionnaires, participant observation, memoranda, letters, pamphlets, organizational newspapers, etc. From these sources, I derived my second-order "ideal type" constructs of the separatist appeal and its social reality.

## NOTES

[1] See John H. Bracey, August Meier, and Elliott Rudick (Ed.), *Black Nationalism in America* (New York: Bobbs-Merrill, 1970), pp. XXVI - XXIX.

[2] See Richard Allen, *The Life, Experience and Gospel Labors of the Rt. Rev. Richard Allen* (Philadelphia: Lee & Yocum, 1888).

[3] See John Hope Franklin, *From Slavery to Freedom,* 3rd Edition (New York: Random House, 1969), p. 128.

[4] See Benjamin Quarles, *The Negro in the Making of America* (New York: Collier Books, 1964), Chapter 2.

[5] See Philip D. Curtin (Ed.), *Africa Remembered: Narratives by West Africans From the Era of the Slave Trade* (Madison: University of Wisconsin Press, 1968); also Thomas R. Frazier (Ed.), *Afro-American History: Primary Sources* (New York: Harcourt, Brace & World, 1970), Part One.

[6] See C.L.R. James, *The Black Jacobins: Toussaint L'Ouverture and the Santo Domingo Revolution* (New York: Vintage Books, 1963, first published in 1938).

[7] See Herbert Aptheker, *American Negro Slave Revolts* (New York: Columbia University Press, 1943); also his *Nat Turner's Slave Rebellion* (New York: Humanities Press, 1966); John Lofton, *Insurrection in South Carolina: The Turbulent World of Denmark Vesey* (Yellow Springs, Ohio: Antioch College Press, 1964); John Henrik Clarke (Ed.), *William Styron's Nat Turner: Ten Black Writers Respond* (Boston: Beacon Press, 1968); also Arna Bontemps, *Black Thunder* (New York: MacMillan, 1936).

[8] See Paul Cuffee, *A Brief Account of the Settlement and Present Situation of the Colony of Sierre Leone in Africa* (New York: Samuel Woods, 1812); Sheldon H. Harris, *Paul Cuffee – Black America and the Africa Return,* (New York: Simon and Schuster, 1972).

[9] See Edwin S. Redkey, *Black Exodus: Black Nationalist and Back-To-Africa Movements, 1890-1910* (New Haven: Yale University Press, 1969); Philip J. Staudenraus, *The African Colonization Movement, 1816-1865* (New York: Columbia University Press, 1961); Henry N. Sherwood, "Paul Cuffee and His Contribution to the American Colonization Society," Proceedings of the Mississippi Valley Historical Association for the year 1912-1913, 6(1913), pp. 307-402.

[10] Charles M. Wiltse (Ed.), *David Walker's Appeal in Four Articles* (New York: Hill and Wang, 1965, originally published in 1829).

[11] See Howard H. Bell (Ed.), *Minutes of the Proceedings of the National Negro Conventions, 1830-1864* (New York: Arno Press, 1969); Lerone Bennett, Jr., "First National Convention," *Ebony*, Vol. XXX, No. 4 (February 1975), pp. 128-132.

[12] Henry Highland Garnett, "An Appeal to the Slaves of the United States," in Bracey, *et al., Black Nationalism in America.*

[13] Bracey, *et al., Black Nationalism in America.*

[14] See Philip S. Foner, *The Life and Writings of Frederick Douglass*, Vol. II (New York: International Publishers, 1950); Martin R. Delany, *The Condition, Elevation, Emigration and Destiny of the Colored People in the United States Politically Considered* (Privately published by the author in 1852) in Frazier, *Afro-American History;* also Martin R. Delany and Robert Campbell, *Search for a Place: Black Separatism and Africa, 1860* (Ann Arbor: University of Michigan Press, 1969); J.T. Holly and J. Dennis Harris, *Black Separatism and the Carribbean, 1860,* edited by Howard H. Bell (Ann Arbor: University of Michigan Press, 1969).

[15] See W.E.B. DuBois, *John Brown* (New York: New International Publishers, 1962, originally published in 1909).

[16] See Roy Garvin, "Benjamin or 'Pap' Singleton and His Followers," *Journal of Negro History,* Vol. xxxiii, No. 1 (1948), pp. 7-23; Walter L. Fleming, " 'Pap' Singleton, the Moses of the Colored Exodus," *American Journal of Sociology,*

Vol. XV (July 1909), pp. 61-82; John G. Van Deusen, "The Exodus of 1879," *Journal of Negro History,* Vol. XXI, No. 2 (1936), pp. 111-129.

[17]See Edwin S. Redkey, *Respect Black: The Writings and Speeches of Henry McNeil Turner* (New York: Arno Press, 1971); also his discussion or Turner in *Black Exodus;* see also Redkey's "Bishop Turner's African Dream," *Journal of American History*, Vol. 54, No. 2 (September 1967).

[18]See Hollis R. Lynch, *Edward Wilmot Blyden – Pan Negro Patriot 1832-1912* (London: Oxford University Press, 1970); also Lynch's *Black Spokesman – Selected Published Writings of Edward Wilmot Blyden* (New York: Humanities Press, 1971).

[19]See Raymond W. Logan, *The Betrayal of the Negro: From Rutherford B. Hayes to Woodrow Wilson* (New York: Collier Books, 1968).

[20]See W.E.B. DuBois, *The Souls of Black Folk* (Chicago: A.C. McClurg & Co., 1903; August Meier, *Negro Thought in America, 1880-1915: Radical Ideology in the Age of Booker T. Washington* (Ann Arbor: University of Michigan Press, 1963).

[21]See Stephen R. Fox, *The Guardian of Boston: William Monroe Trotter* (New York: Atheneum, 1970).

[22]See Booker T. Washington, *Future of the American Negro* (New York: Small, Maynard, 1899); Samuel R. Spencer *Booker T. Washington and the Negro's Place in American Life* (Boston: Little, Brown, 1955); see other references in Chapter 7 of this volume.

[23]See William E. Bittle and Gilbert Geis, *The Longest Way Home: Chief Alfred C. Sam's Back-To-Africa Movement* (Detroit: Wayne State University Press, 1964).

[24]Amy Jacques Garvey, *Garvey and Garveyism*, (London: Collier-MacMillan, 1963).

[25]See Edmund David Cronon, *Black Moses: The Story of Marcus Garvey and the Universal Negro Improvement Association* (Madison: University of Wisconsin Press, 1955); see also Cronon's second edition; Robert Brisbane, *The Black Vanguard: Origins of the Negro Social Revolution 1900-1960* (Valley Forge, Pa.: Judson Press, 1970), Chapter 4; Robert G. Weisbord, *Ebony Kinship: Africa, Africans and the Afro-American* (Westport, Conn.: Greenwood Press, (1973), Chapter 2; *Marcus Garvey, Philosophy and Opinions on Africa for the Africans,* edited by Amy Jacques Garvey (London: Frank Cass, 1967, first published in 1923); see especially Theodore G. Vincent, *Black Power and the Garvey Movement* (Berkeley: Ramparts Press, 1971).

[26] See Wilson Record, *The Negro and the Communist Party* (New York: Atheneum, 1971, originally published in 1951); Benjamin Davis, Jr., *The Negro People and the Communist Party* (New York: International Publishers, 1943); also Davis' *The Path of Negro Liberation* (New York: New Century Publishers, 1947).

[27]See E.U. Essien-Udom, *Black Nationalism: A Search for Identity in America* (New York: Dell Publishing Co., 1962), Chapter 2; C. Eric Lincoln, *The Black Muslims in America* (Boston: Beacon Press, 1961), especially Chapter 3.

[28]See Vincent, *Black Power and the Garvey Movement,* pp. 251-256.

[29]See Herbert Garfinkel, *When Negroes March: The March on Washington Movement in the Organizational Politics for FEPC* (New York: The Free Press, 1959).

# 1
# *Explorations in the Analysis of Black Separatism* *

RAYMOND L. HALL

This section of the introduction is concerned with how and why black separatist movements emerge and why separatism appeals to some individuals and not to others. The question of why one movement rather than another appeals to certain individuals is a complex matter that continues to baffle and intrigue, plague and enlighten students of social movements. Part of the complexity stems from the fact that quite often the individual cannot identify the motivational factors that led him or her to join a social movement. In some cases, however, individuals intentionally obfuscate or hide their ulterior motives for joining movements. But if the individual is unclear about his or her motivations to join, this is where the social scientist unwraps his vast array of investigative and analytical tools to probe various motivational possibilities. The particular tools chosen by the social scientist to more closely approximate the social reality of individual motivation – and to ascertain why certain movements appeal to particular individuals – must consider the general nature and character of the individual's social context, individual personality, and the ideology resulting from the two preceding variables. Approaching these questions from the social movement's perspective affords one the opportunity of simultaneously exploring aspects of group dynamics and individual roles, relationships, and interaction in that process.[1]

Social movements are derived from and constructed around societal conditions where individuals feel that they should band together to promote or resist change. Ideology may be regarded as the component that draws and (along with morale) holds together disparate movement elements such as age, religion, class, geographic differences, etc. Movement ideology – as we have seen in the historical introduction – does not crop up overnight, and individuals do not suddenly or spontaneously join a movement based solely on its ideology. Individuals, to be sure, join movements because they offer answers to certain dissatisfactions prompted by societal conditions in relation to their unique experiences.

The appeal of black separatism must first be understood in the context of American society and how societal conditions prompt certain individuals to come to accept separatist ideology. Since black separatism has never enjoyed overt mass commitment, it raises the question of whether only certain personality types embrace separatism. It also raises other important questions: Does black separatism appeal only to young blacks? Does it appeal only to blacks on the lower end of the socioeconomic scale, or does it cut across class lines? Why are there multiple organizations with separatism as part of their ideology? Why is there not just one black separatist organization with all black separatists adhering to its ideology? This chapter will consider these and other questions in exploring the appeal of black separatism. The exploration begins with how whites generally perceive blacks in the United States, which may suggest that white perceptions and behavioral patterns toward blacks heighten the appeal of black separatism.

Many whites believe that black people came into existence in 1619 because, in the past, textbooks acknowledged the arrival in Jamestown of 20 blacks in that year. Moreover, most Americans know little or nothing about the history of Black Africa, except pejorative references to it as the "Dark Continent." Perhaps, they have been entertained by stories of African safaris or, if affluent, would like to personally undertake one. In the past – if not now – most Americans cheered Tarzan as he outfoxed hundreds of black "natives" to save Jane or Boy and then escape to their tree house by swinging through thick lion- and snake-infested jungles (regardless of the fact that lions inhabit savannas, *not* jungles, and that jungles are too thick for Tarzan-like swinging!).

These two prevalent misconceptions – that black people, and hence black history, began in 1619, and that the Hollywood/television myth of white superiority applied even in Africa – contribute to the popularly accepted myth that black Americans have no culture.[2] How could they, one argument goes, when they had none in Africa; if they developed one in the United States, it has to be sun-burned white culture. There are those who are more sophisticated and know that all people(s) have cultures and even acknowledge that culture cannot be evaluated as good or bad, fair

*A revised version of this paper appears in Raymond L. Hall, *Black Separatism: Emergence Development and Consequences* (Hanover, N.H.: University Press of New England, 1976). Data for this paper were gathered from the Nation of Islam, Republic of New Africa (RNA), Congress of Racial Equality (CORE), Student National Coordinating Committee (SNCC), and the Black Panther Party through participant observation, interviews, newspapers, organizational memoranda, personal correspondence, primary source books, etc. See the above citation for a fuller explanation of how the "ideal types" were derived.

or poor. Even among those few, however, the prevalent view is that, yes, black Americans have a culture because they have all the necessary qualifying characteristics. But, since white culture is so dominant and white oppression so pervasive, blacks can only have a "culture of poverty" or a "deviant" subculture, or a "culture of oppression."

Any one of the three stereotypes of black culture can be used as justification for continued denial of black freedom, justice, and equality of opportunity. That is, in the past blacks were excluded from the mainstream of American society by slavery, then peonage, later combined peonage and proletarianization, and, finally, almost impossible mobility because white society denied them the educational basis necessary to participate in technological development and its present state of advanced and complex cybernation; in all these stages they were denied the basic tools for equal participation – politically, economically, educationally, and socially. The denial of these pursuits individually or collectively, by whatever means, could be otherwise described as oppression; no further qualifications were needed. And it continues today. More basically, the past denial of equal opportunity through slavery, peonage, etc., is often the basis for the present-day denial of opportunity, i.e., "inferior genes" – low I.Q., "uneducable," "culturally disadvantaged," etc. It is the same kind of oppression by exclusion with another name, only the justification had changed. It is still upon the black that the rationale of white separatism is built. But black separatists – unlike white separatists – prefer not to be coy and elusive with words; they see it as white racism and they call it that. Consequently, they call for blacks to cease attempting to "integrate" into a social system that has in the past and continues to circumvent their integrative efforts. Instead, they urge blacks to construct parallel (separate) societies where they can finally be free of white oppression and where they can live their own existential, political, economic, and social reality.

In this connection black separatism and black separatist movements might be characterized as consciously or unconsciously acting as a catalytic change agent by proposing and attempting to implement a set of political and sociocultural arrangements for black people that might differ from and, in some essential ways, oppose those of the larger society. The larger society's opposition means that more than attitudes are at issue; existing power relations become a (sometimes the only) central aspect of a movement's program. The separatist group has to maintain its separate identity in order to act as a catalyst, but identity is not an end in itself. On the contrary, contemporary black separatist movements are also concerned with influencing the larger society, forcing concessions that correspond with the movement's goals for itself and for those it claims to represent.

Whether or not a separatist movement organization seeks to alter customary power relations depends on a variety of factors. If whites readily respond to what it is separatists demand, the existing power relations are maintained in a type of responsive reform. If not, the separatist movement organization seeks to force change, thus risking the charge of being branded utopian at best, revolutionary at worst. Transforming power relations seems to be the most common reason cited for separatism in the first place, since approved methods of redress do not seem to be available or effective. Thus, separatists are not necessarily opposed to the ideology and values of the larger society at first; they are dissatisfied with their pragmatic application by whites in the larger society. Distrust develops out of dissatisfaction; out of distrust, the withdrawal of the attribution of legitimacy or appropriateness to the larger society's lifestyle and values. Hence, the bitterness of total failure or limited success in seeking change for the black masses in the power arrangements eventually drives certain former reformists to conclude that the only way to attain their goals is to take it upon themselves to carry the separatist movement's banner to the barricades. When the breakaway group (separatists) prepares for more drastic measures to uphold the "true" separatist ideals and goals, its core of "true believers" severely strains possible relations with the still more moderate members of the reform-oriented group. The end product of the process is separatism; the human end products are called separatists.

In summary, the point needs repeating that black separatism is not only geared to eliminate black oppression, but also to enhance black culture and black lifestyles. In fact, each black separatist movement organization studied made special efforts to emphasize black culture and history. Put another way, identification with Africa and emphasis on black awareness, highlighting black cultural roots and in general "doing one's own black thing," are efforts to overtly reject white sterotypes of black inferiority as well as to exhibit pride in blackness. In general, contemporary black separatist movements quickened and revitalized black culture, contributing to the development of positive black images and models. While it may be a distortion of reality to attribute the resurgence of black awareness and pride solely to the black separatist movements, one could safely suggest that they played a significant role in its development.

All black separatist proposals are aimed at combating white oppression and seeking to free blacks from the shackles of cultural imperialism. The following are among some of the black separatist proposals described in this chapter: proposals to bring about separatism within the already constituted society by taking over southern states to establish a "nation within a nation" (RNA), establishing black-controlled communities (CORE), replacing the racist capitalist government with revolutionary black nationalists (Black Panther Party), taking political control where blacks are in the majority (SNCC), and establishing black separation from whites "by any means necessary" (The Nation of Islam). All these proposals somehow speak to the need for a Pan-African or Third World perspective.

What must always be remembered is that all these proposals are attempting to describe the black condition in American society and, at the same time, are seeking a way out of black subordination. But they come to different conclusions based on their organizational analysis of the problem. Though each organization has different proposals, they all agree on some form of separatism. Here the question of what kind of person is likely to join one of these movements in particular and the black separatist movement in general can be addressed.

## INDIVIDUAL TYPES IN THE SEPARATIST MOVEMENT

It is here that anti-separatists should for the moment lay aside their stereotypes and try to understand why black separatism has had a long tenure in the United States. Try to understand that black separatism is no more than the black struggle for justice, equality, and humanity against racism (both individual and institutional), injustice, and the historical and contemporary American denial of a fair chance for dignified black survival.

The modal behavior of black Americans regarding liberation suggests that most blacks – past as well as present – want only a fair chance to compete and get along in what is an obviously far from perfect society. Why should it be so difficult to get so little? Why should there be so much physical and emotional pain and hardship to take hold of a promise long made but never more than partially and grudgingly met? Is the covenant that white America made with black America no more than the sign of God's covenant with Abraham – a pretty rainbow, a mere vision of life on vapor that cannot be grasped or that disappears when viewed from a different angle? Is there a white American who could say for certain and in good conscience that his own achievements would have been the same if *his* great-grandparents had been slaves and his grandparents landless serfs, sharecroppers, or proletarians at the very bottom of the totem pole weighted down with disdain, inhumanity, hate, or oppressive indifference? Is there a black American – no matter how affluent, respected, and "accepted" – who has not felt torment and despair, frustration and anger, guilt and confusion, knowing that this once most "open" of all societies (for whites) would never open for most black people? Many whites cannot understand why so many blacks seem confused and angry; the seeming confusion more often than not stems from white perceptions, not black confusion. A few individual blacks have always been able to successfully play around in the system; nevertheless, most blacks have been and continue to be American political, social, and economic scapegoats. Hence, logic be damned – things are not getting better and the logical way to "make it" takes too long; even if a black person treads the long road to "success," he is more often than not denied the benefits of his long-suffering pursuit. Even if he is successful, he knows that when millions of other blacks try to duplicate his efforts, their attempts will result in complete or partial denial of the fruits of their labor.

In the final analysis, a black separatist social movement is more than an ideology: it is comprised of people – individuals and groups that design, implement, manipulate, and transform movement ideologies, tactics, goals, and every facet of a social movement. Though much of this chapter is "academic," it is ultimately about people, individuals, and groups seeking justice in American society. It is about people who have been denied the fruits of their labor; it is also about people who are materially secure, but insecure about the denial of security to their brethren who have earned it but do not possess it. It is about people who at first unconsciously accepted the American Dream in all its utopian splendor, but later realized that it was a nightmare dressed in sheep's clothing; it is also about people who hold onto the dream while struggling to unmask the nightmare, hoping that it is a sheep in wolf's clothing. It is about people who seem to have given up struggling for dignified black existence in America; it is also about people who seem to have given up but would contend for the opportunity to awaken from the nightmare and seize the time to strive for a peaceful, idyllic slumber that comes after the struggle. It is also about people who have given up on America and its promise. They all ask the same question: how, without separatism, can black people – individually and collectively – feel that they are controlling their own destiny or affecting anything of consequence?

These movement people – these separatists – might be people you know or people like them whom you have known. At different places and in different times, perhaps, we have all been these people. Can you grasp that, despite white stereotypes, the people in separatist movements are, after all, people? They are not all the same, though they share similar longings. They are not all bad, though some might have done apparently stupid or perhaps evil things. They are not all good, though some have been steadfastly noble and self-sacrificing. They are not all certain – though some had developed a dogged purpose and conviction that they were right; others use iron will and purpose and courage to block out and cover their fears and longings and ordinary human desires. Some want simply to be left alone.

Now begins the task of referring to several member types, again with the customary caveat that reality is more complex, so that actual people quite often represent different combinations of these types. Before beginning, another small but important set of distinctions should be made in order to clarify the following presentation. At one extreme, there is the larger society; at the other, the separatist movement. Between these two lies the original group – the parent body from which separatist movement organizations have sprung. For ease of translation, here is a scorecard with some concrete players: (1) "general society" = the United States or American society; (2) "original group" = SCLC, NAACP, or the integration-oriented civil rights movement in general; and (3) "separatist movement" = any black separatist movement organization or the ones indicated above. It is assumed that each member "type" has, in fact, joined a separatist movement organization.

### The "Value-Suspended Ideologist"

The value-suspended ideologist overtly rejects the values of the general society in favor of those promoted by a separatist movement; however, he *subconsciously* operates under the general society's value constraints. Thus, he is in limbo between partially rejecting the original group's reformist values and ideology and accepting those of the separatist movement. He usually overcomes his dilemma by promoting the separatist movement's *ideology,* but not necessarily its *values.* For example, a separatist movement's ideology might have as one of its tenets the rejection of things material; the value-suspended ideologist may rhetorically support the movement's anti-material stance. However, subconsciously, because of his original socialization into the general society's materialistic mode (by being deprived of valued material things and admonished to strive to get them or by having had them as a matter of course), he may not subscribe to the movement's nonmaterialistic values, but may promote its ideology. Evidently, this member type is marginal; the strength of his separatist affiliation is unpredictable. He may become a staunch movement supporter or he may defect. How can he be explained?

People do operate consciously or unconsciously on the basis of their prior socialization. However, rare as the real accomplishment may be, many do believe that they can totally reject their background and prior value orientations. The value-suspended ideologist, thinking that he has rejected the values held by the general society and the original group, is ostensibly committed to the separatist movement's values and ideology. Here we need to explore the relationship between the values and ideology of the general society, the original group, and separatist movement.

In many instances, the values of the three groups are basically the same, but the way the original group seeks to promote change in power relations with the general society is unsatisfactory to certain other members in the original group; these members may often opt for an alternative which results in separation or splintering, as it were. That is, the original group does not function – to the dismay of certain members – in the "right" way to promote change quickly enough. The real problem, then, is not necessarily basic value differences, but dissatisfaction with the original group's change-promoting tactics; this dissatisfaction produces factions and finally separation (schismogenesis). Consequently, separatism arises in this instance because some members in the original group can effect sufficient pivotal input to change the original group's operating tactics. The disaffected members then form their own group to apply pressure to the general society in order to change power relations – the first case of separatism. The separation may become ideological to the point of promoting separatism from the general society as a tactic in order to have a dramatic impact on prompting changes in power relations – the second case of separatism.

Both cases of separatism may stem from means of attaining ends, not from basic value differences; both groups, the original group as well as the separatist group, are seeking ways to change the power relations between the general society and the black masses. That is, both groups are attempting to influence the general society to live up to the ideals and values that all three groups may share. But the separatist group seeks to influence change by promoting ideological alternatives to those of the original group. For example, the general society claims that everyone should have "equal opportunity" in every phase of American life – a value held by most Americans. When translated to action, white Americans generally deny blacks equal opportunity; in the past as well as at present, organizations such as the NAACP, the Urban League, Southern Christian Leadership Conference, *et al.* – and in many instances the separatist movements themselves – originated to seek equal opportunity for black Americans.

Hence, in order to promote equal opportunity for black people, the separatist group may propose alternative ideological routes for achieving values shared by all concerned. Taking the example further, the general society demands that the "American Dream" be pursued through the democratic process of majority rule. However, majority rule would continue to militate against black equal opportunity because numerical factors suggest that blacks cannot effect sufficient political input to produce systemic change based on that concept. Because original groups linger under the illusion of influencing linear change through the system, separatist movements propose changing the power relations thorugh "revolutionary black nationalism" (Panthers), making the five southern states into an "independent black nation" (RNA), "community control" of the black ghettoes (CORE), "black political control" where blacks are the majority (SNCC), or complete "racial separation" of blacks and whites on a nonlinear basis "by any means necessary" (Muslims).

The outcome of these interrelationships can be that the value-suspended ideologist may promote the separatist group's ideology, but his values may not significantly differ from those held by the original group or the general society. On the other hand, the separatist group may develop fundamental value differences from those held by the general society and the original group. Consequently, the value-suspended ideologist may also completely abandon his socialized values for those held by the separatist group; he could also abandon the separatist group and return to the original group. Hence, in either case, his values are no longer suspended by ideological ambivalence if he ultimately chooses one or the other.

### The Transient Exchanger

A member who comes to consistently reject the values *and* ideology of the general society and original group and accepts those of a separatist group might be called a "transient exchanger." The total rejection of the general society's socialization, as well as that of the original group(s) for that of the separatist movement points to the likelihood that he might – if a more attractive situation were to occur – exchange his present separatist ideological values for another set. This type of member is easily swayed by nonsubstantive arguments, glittering generalities, and charismatic personalities. The real basis of his motivations is least known by himself, but is easily detected by those who can make use of him for their own purposes. He can easily be convinced to become a "true believer" or even a fanatic. In general, a case could be made that he is prone to exchange ideological and value sets because he neglects to examine them in relationship to real basic needs in order to foster change. Perhaps he sees only rapid or even radical change as important factors in altering power relations.

### The Progress-Fixated Member

A third type of separatist member may view separatism only as a step forward in attaining the "true" ideals of the group. The most important factor concerning this member is that he sees only "progress" in separatism without ever examining the direction in which the separatist group is going; he never entertains the possibility that the movement might be retrogressive. His obsession with progress leads him to accept the particular separatist movement's goals, values, and ideology as progressive to such an extent that he becomes what might be called "progress fixated." The utility and logic of the separatist movement's ideology and values are of little significance to the progress-fixated member because the idea of separatism per se is the dominant, all-encompassing factor. In short, separatism is *the* ideology, *the* value, and *the* goal he seeks most.

### The Vacillating Utopia-Seeker

A fourth type of member is one who is personally well-off in terms of money, education, status, and prestige. Usually his well-being comes as a result of hard work over a long period of time. He is familiar with the total range of positions on the socioeconomic scale in terms of lifestyles, values, and potential ideology that each relative group on the scale would embrace. He usually has become impatient with institutionalized approaches to solving problems. Therefore, knowing the importance of mass movements in terms of protests and demonstrations, he proposes to short circuit the institutional approach by embracing a separatist organization in order to effect change in the general society.

His continued membership in the separatist movement usually depends on his position in the organization. His past experience and knowledge of the way changes are made in the general society set him aside from being a mere rank-and-file member; he is impatient with the often irrelevant and petty preoccupations that concern the rank-and-file. He assumes that the other members of the organization are as aware of the necessary steps to a solution as he is.

He usually emerges as a leader of the separatist organization – its ideologue, the major charismatic figure, the intellectual, the central organizing force, or some other post of major importance to the maintenance of the organization. Moreover, in times of financial stress and strain, he may use his own resources to sustain the organization. No separatist movement can do without such members.

Still, he is called a vacillating utopian because prior to his separatist affiliation he espoused the virtues and values of the general society and achieved success by societal standards. He became successful because he possessed the character, personality, and ability to negotiate with power networks in the larger society. It was only after having achieved success through established standards that he became restless and generally dissatisfied with the status of his oppressed brethren and the manipulation of power to keep them that way. For example, if the law indicates that a good education can only be obtained through desegregation "with all deliberate speed" while those who control the change mechanism manipulate the law to nullify the legal end product, then the vacillating utopian-seeker becomes dissatisfied with the application.

His best chance to redress the balance, as he perceives it, is to join organizations oriented toward reform of the existing power relations in the general society; he then joins a reform-oriented movement – his second utopia. But in reality reform measures do not appeal to him because he already knows the route that reform-oriented movements take – i.e., the established, "legal," and "acceptable" channels. For him, the route is long and slow; the end product – assuming it survives the "legitimate" channels – is so compromised that it is, for all practical purposes, ineffective in bringing about the changes he desires.

The only choice left for him is to seek other means of making changes. A separatist route seems appropriate and appealing. In it he sees an opportunity to bring about his third utopia. In short, he moves from one "utopian" extreme to another. He is necessary to the movement, but he is also risky. Once his staying power is used up, he can well become cynical and bitter, feeling ineffectual or unappreciated. Then, making the best of a bad bargain, he may well return to conventional success, unsatisfied but safe.

### The Latent Revolutionary

A fifth kind of separatist can be called a "latent revolutionary." He is apathetic about his relation to society in general and has only lukewarm enthusiasm for the separatist movement. He does not seem to become overly excited about anything. He wanders from organization to organization before settling on one more or less to his liking. Even his colleagues may dislike or distrust him.

He is, however, the one individual – whether the movement knows it or not – who can be counted on to act out its extreme rhetoric. In most movements designed to rearrange power relations, there are two levels of goals: (1) the real or expected goals, which are not articulated, and (2) goals articulated in extreme terms. In the second instance, leaders of the movements are aware that these goals are articulated to begin the negotiating process with the constituted authority. The intention (the first instance) is to reach a *rapproachement* somewhere in the middle – i.e., a compromise between the separatist movement's extreme rhetorical demands as a goal and what the constituted authority is prepared to offer.

The latent revolutionary is prepared to act on the extreme rhetoric articulated by the movement as a justification for its intended goals. That is, if a movement publicly posited that "revolution came through the barrel of a gun," but in reality meant "if you don't make some concessions, there will be trouble," the latent revolutionary would act on the "gun-barrel" rhetoric. Another example might be in order. In the Women's Liberation movement, in its early stages of development, some women used extreme rhetoric to the effect that women who were married were merely "domestic prostitutes" and should begin to deal with that circumstance. Apparently, the real meaning or the anticipated compromise was that men and women should share the chores of marriage on an equal basis – i.e., dishwashing, baby care, housecleaning, etc. However, the latent revolutionaries acted on the "domestic prostitute" rhetoric and demanded "payment per diem" or else – and burned their bras in the process.

In the end, the latent revolutionary may be responsible for delegitimizing the separatist movement in terms of membership recruitment; more than likely his actions force – or justify – the constituted authority's use of coercive power to curb the movement's activities. If the movement is aware of the latent revolutionary before he joins, it may take extra precautions to dissuade him from joining. Consequently, the latent revolutionary may not find a movement organization that will meet his requirements. He may then have to act out his repressed revolutionary impulses – "his thing," as it were – in acts of random aggression or suicidal forays directed against the constituted authority or its symbols. His actions are done in the name of "the brothers," "the sisters," "the struggle," the "revolution," "my people," etc. It may be that his actions influence others to "take care of business," "off the pig," or "attack male chauvinism," etc. The other possibility is that an extremist organization may be functional (as a safety valve) in preventing the random aggression of the latent revolutionary. If his grievances, disaffected hostility, and indignation cannot be directed by an organization, it is likely that he will act out his belligerence at random in any place and at any given moment in time.

## SOCIETY AND PERSONALITY IN THE SEPARATIST MOVEMENT ANALYSIS

The above descriptions of "ideal type" individuals must be seen in light of specific societal conditions. They should be viewed as persons seeking to cope with problems that drive them to the separatist movement. The focus, then, shifts from these individuals to the society that produces them.

When the values and ideology held by one segment of a population are in direct opposition to those held by another, the conflict is usually dealt with by overtly or covertly suppressing the less powerful segment. The suppression may result in value transformation, value conflict, value suspension, or any combination. Individuals with a less powerful value system have to contend with the two-value systems – the operational system of the general society and the subordinate value system. Hence, the "value-suspended ideologist" tends to embrace movements with ideologies that seem to offer solutions to his problems, but he does not necessarily embrace the movement's values even though he has deep reservations about his own socialized values. Consequently, value suspension results from the feeling of insecurity in the general values (normative) that oppose his subcultural values and from the partial abandonment of his subordinate values because they do not meet his needs.

The more complex the society, the more complex the values and value structure tend to be. Differential values are sure to exist in an urbanized, technological, heterogeneous, pluralistic society. Because of the proliferation of "value change-inducers" – i.e., urbanism, technology, pluralism, heterogeneity, etc. – values tend to become flexible and more susceptible to reevaluation and change. The temporary nature of the values and ideology held by the "transient exchanger" emanate from the multifaceted stimuli influencing him first one way and then another. He eventually opts for the separatist route because it is a stimulus from another direction. He has already been exposed to the "programs" of the general original societies, but the appeal of these programs has lost its impact. Thus, the new separatist appeal becomes attractive. As the "transient exchanger" is highly susceptible to further changes in his value and ideology structure, the separatist organization may be only a temporary stopping point for him.

The transient nature of the values of the "transient exchanger" usually does not come as a result of psychological problems or as maladjustment to the structural complexity of society or as a form of deviancy. Rather, the flexible position comes as a result of the society's institutionalized obstacles against his cause – that is, the general society does not hold his value as important and he responds by not having hard and fast value definitions. He develops "situational values" and his definition of the value situation is flexible and, in some cases, spontaneous.

Some separatists do not necessarily embrace separatism out of total pessimism and despair. Rather, they are optimistic that the separatist route will result in progress. They are convinced that change only means progression toward the realization of their conceptions of society's true values and ideals. The separatist movement to them represents only positive change. The fact that a separatist movement can promote resistance and hostility in the general society never disturbs them. Thus, the "progress-fixated" member can also be called an optimist who joins the movement because he is convinced that no change is possible in the existing situation; to him, the separatist route represents a positive means of attempting to redress the balance.

However, the "progress-fixated" member can be understood in light of the historical and traditional optimism possessed by black people in the United States. One could say that blacks have survived the degradation of the American system because they have remained optimistic that things will get better – often because they can get no worse. From the interior of Africa, through triangular trade, to the auction blocks, to the plantation, to the cotton fields – a few in the plantation house – and all of the horrors of slavery, inhumanity, prejudice, discrimination, and inequality, many blacks maintain their optimism. This optimism stems from the conviction that tribal customs, Christianity, and promised freedom will see them through and that in the end all will be well. This is not to suggest that a few individuals and some groups do not lose faith or commit suicide or attempt to overthrow the oppression that has engulfed them. In a sense, that is what this book is about. But the bulk of the black population retains unfaltering optimism, which has brought them through untenable circumstances.

This same dogged optimism and ability to hope where there was no hope, to see light where there was none, to make a way where there was no way seem to characterize some members of separatist groups or organizations. It could thus be said that the "progress-fixated" member is an extension of traditional and historical strains in the black experience. He is oriented toward progress (sometimes blindly) because, without this optimism for betterment and progress, he will cut the historical and traditional ties – in essence, he will lose his black soul.

Utopia may be defined as any romantic or metaphysical state of an imaginary and perhaps unrealizable state of society free from human imperfections. Utopia may be thought of as the construction of ways and means for the fulfillment or attainment of the dreams for that perfect society. Hence, conscious societal improvement by ideas, actions, and definitive agencies of social modification may indeed be said to provide a "resting place" for society's utopia-seeking members.

The synonyms for "resting places" are portrayed in the popular concepts of success, prosperity, advancement, esteem, etc., and indicate that one is reaping the highest status and benefits of one's society – the ultimate fulfillment of one's dreams. Once this pinnacle has been reached, the aurora and magnificence one can call utopia may not seem as fascinating as it was while in the process of attainment.

Consequently, the "utopia-seeker" is likely to become dissatisfied with utopia as defined by the general society because he is limited by it. That is, despite his competence, intelligence, and drive, he still faces obstacles that result from his origin and/or his activities and the stigma society has placed on these. This is a constant source of frustration. Thus he becomes more sensitive to the plight of people in the society who cannot find means of coping with their situations through constituted channels. Eventually his sympathy changes to actual support. His utopia in the general society now becomes an unconscionable reality and the values and ideology of the reform alternative conquers his fancy.

After awhile, the once dreamed of alternative "utopia" becomes commonplace and the desire to find the "real" utopia becomes overwhelming. Thus, the "vacillating utopia-seeker" finds himself again dissatisfied and restless. The urge to seek another utopia forces him to disregard the previous move to the reform – original group – movement. He seeks the next utopia in a separatist movement because, after he has traveled the "straight and narrow" reform path, he finds that he still lacks fulfillment.

The separatist movement may fulfill his expectations of utopia for a time; it may even serve as his permanent utopia – or it can only serve as a temporary resting place. He may then seek another utopia in direct opposition to the separatist movement, to its left or right. Thus, he may provide the impetus to bring about a splinter movement within the separatist movement. His incessant search for utopia may even lead him back to the original point of departure – i.e., the values, ideology, and structure of the general society.

To understand the actions of the "utopia seeker," one must understand American society and how it thwarts and frustrates some of its members who aspire to make it to the top in their chosen endeavor. On the one hand, theoretically, the society encourages all Americans to achieve to their maximum potential and, on the other, it defines, delimits, and carefully admits certain minority people to positions of power and authority. Because the society shuts off the mobility mechanisms for most, there is never any assurance that those few it does admit will forever "conform." It is from these few that the utopia-seeker is likely to emerge.

The emergence of the utopia-seeker seems to center around his concern and sympathy with the plight of the underclass of his particular group. The politicization of the underclass – prompted by recent emphasis on the black masses – has produced a vacuum in terms of viable underclass leadership. It is seldom, if ever, in Western society that viable national leadership emerges from the underclass; national leadership usually comes from high-ranking classes on the socioeconomic scale. If viable leadership does come from the underclass, as it recently has in black communities, it is usually confined to the local community or it takes on the trappings of leadership patterns other than those of underclass people.

After becoming a member of the separatist group, the utopia-seeker still has to cope with success as defined by the general society. He has to decide on ends or means. Is the utopia of the general society repugnant to him because he found the values inadequate or does he find the values repugnant because the general society refuses to live up to its ideology of freedom and justice for all? The relationship between the values and ideology of the separatist group and the general society becomes significant in answering this question. Here the determination can be made of whether or not the separatist group will be catalytic in influencing the parent body or the general society to bring about congruence between stated goals and reality. This determination will illuminate the utopia-seeker's relative direction.

At present, the evidence points to the conclusion that most of those blacks who "make it" do not become utopia-seekers in the sense that they opt for separatism.[3] However, there is evidence that many – or more – blacks who have "made it" are tending in the direction of becoming concerned about the relative intransigence of meaningful change to blacks in the general society.[4] This tendency could develop into a very significant factor in the future.

The desire to maintain contact with one's social and cultural heritage may be universal. In order to form a holistic concept of the diversity and complexity of human societies, it is necessary to have some form of contact with them. Whether this contact can be transformed into permanent, comfortable acceptance is problematic; it will depend upon whether the acceptance is voluntary or involuntary. If it is voluntary – in the case of members of one culture voluntarily living in another culture, as whites living in Black Africa – then there is the opportunity to reconstruct one's own culture in an "alien" setting. If, on the other hand, one lives involuntarily as a minority within a dominant culture, constantly experiencing alien cultural dominance – through symbols and authority, implicitly inferring one's own inferiority – one might become exclusively engrossed in reconstructing one's own culture. This cultural reconstruction might take on separatist characteristics and might result in desultory and nonchalant recognition of the dominant cultural reality. The consequence of this dominance may produce, among other things, the latent revolutionary.

Finally, apathy toward the "host or alien culture may result in overt attempts to live in original sociocultural styles. Finding it impossible to do so, the latent revolutionary then seeks out individuals and movements that are closely aligned to his own thinking – and lifestyle. He literally takes the movement's ideology and is prepared to act on it.

One movement(s) may prove too "tame" in implementing its ideology; he moves on. If, after seeking peer companionship in the movement(s), he fails to find an acceptable outlet, he may then decide that he must make the society conducive to *his* sociocultural reality. He may attempt to bring his reality into fruition by acting alone, or he may seek out other "latent revolutionaries" and together they will begin to take steps to implement their sociocultural reality.

In summary, "ideal type" individuals found in black separatist movements join for many reasons. The easiest general conclusion that can be made relative to their membership is that they join because white oppression drives them to movements seeking solutions to their individual and collective problems. However, it is also true that there are movement members who are at peace with or have made it in the dominant society. Thus, the easy conclusion flies in the face of evidence to the contrary. What else, then, can be said about reasons for membership in black separatist movements?

In the first place, the five "ideal type" individual members above are not meant to exhaust individual types found in black separatist movements; they are only meant to give the reader a "feel" for some general member characteristics. No doubt there are members who in no way resemble any one or combination of the above five ideal types; they may join for a myriad of reasons ranging from companion preference, fascination with movement symbols or ceremonial behavior, to a desire to learn black history – both African and black American – or to keep up with "what's goin' on" locally and nationally, etc. These reasons are not necessarily related to white oppression in linear proportion. That is, when black people are together they do not spend all of their time discussing or thinking about white racism or white oppression; by the same token, they are not preoccupied with it when they are at organizational or movement meetings – even though the organization may have originated and met specifically for that purpose. To react incessantly to white racism would render individuals as well as organizations incapable of supplying black people with other human needs such as understanding, camaraderie, love, and culture-sustaining activities enjoyed as a matter of course by ethnic Americans; rather, blacks may be belligerent, hateful, paranoid, and schizophrenic. To the contrary, despite individual, institutional, and systemic white racism and oppression, blacks have remarkably stable mental health.[5] There are whites who suggest – using questionable scientific methods – that all black people bear the "mark of oppression."[6] (If this were true the results would produce not just a few blacks who were tagged as "militants" or "revolutionaries," but, rather, millions of blacks seeking to displace their aggression!) In short, many blacks join movements not in reaction to white oppression but simply to enhance their own sociocultural and psychological individuality.

Secondly, since separatist movements do, in fact, propose to effect black liberation, many join movements simply to do what they can for the black cause and for black people. Doing what they can for black people may or may not be the same as reacting against white oppression.

Diagram 1 suggests the path of the "ideal types" from the general society to the original group and finally to the separatist movement organization. The diagram should be read as follows: Everyone is initially born into a social system (#1), in this case the American system; consequently, generalized norms, taboos, sanctions, mores, folkways, etc. are more or less consciously and unconsciously internalized by each individual. Of course, the initial socializing agency or institution is the family, which may possess an infinite variety of ethnic, racial, and nationality combinations. Further, religious, educational, economic, and political institutions, among others, also play important roles in individual socialization. No matter how these institutions or socializing agencies differ internally, all the variations are somehow consistent with the general ideological and value system. If not, they are in constant conflict with societal control agencies. For example, communism and the Communist Party in the United States are anti-capitalist and propose a different system of governing. Both ideas are generally opposed by the American free enterprise system as well as the American democratic process. Hence, an American Communist is in constant ideological (and, logically, value) conflict with the general American system. But, most important, though a Communist may oppose the ideology and values, his behavior must reflect the "American way" or he will be removed (incarcerated) to a facility especially for those "improperly socialized."

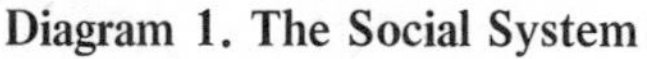

**Diagram 1. The Social System**

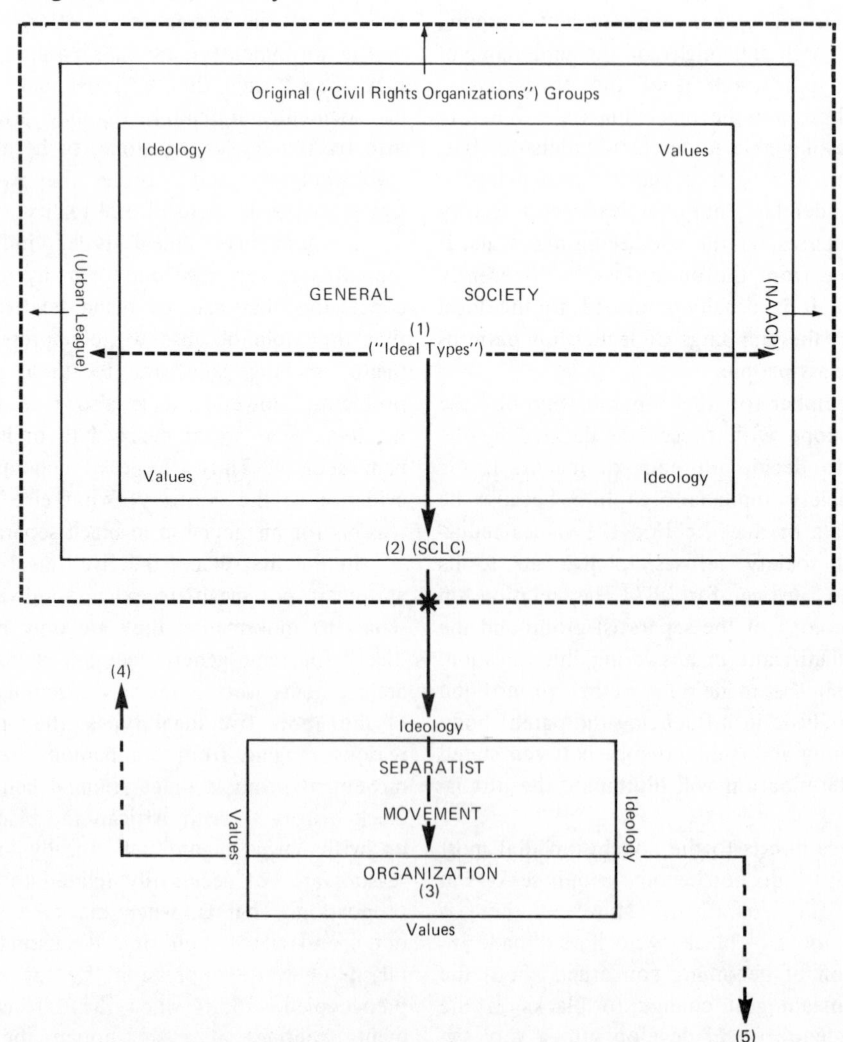

Incarcerated individuals aside (for whatever reason), most individuals in a social system abide by its rules. There are, however, alternatives for those who do not agree with the rules: (a) they can oppose them by acting in direct opposition and face incarceration for being a "threat to society," or (b) they can attempt to reform the existing reality. The second alternative takes us to the *specific society* (#2 in the diagram). Found here are most social movements aimed at reforming the existing system, and these movements may be left wing or right wing, radical or conservative, moderate or liberal. In short, these individuals cannot effect or resist change to their satisfaction in the general society by working directly in the system. As a result, a group of like-minded individuals form to work at effecting change outside the "normal" change mechanism(s).

The original group also has an ideology and values; however, they usually reflect those of the general society. They may be exactly the same as those in the general society, but the concern of the group is with how they are implemented, whether they are denied to a specific group(s), or if they need to be modified for specific needs.

The original group is usually the first stopping place for our ideal types. They all usually exhibit their dissatisfaction with the general society by attempting to reform it. Note they are still within the social system. If unsuccessful or if change does not occur to their satisfaction, they then move to the separatist movement organization (#3). As the diagram suggests, the separatist movement organization is seen as having complete independence from the general and specific societies: it has its own set of values, its own ideology, and its own organizational structure. (We have suggested that the separatist movement's values and ideology may also reflect those of the general society and the original group, but it is dissatisfied with how the change mechanism is affected.)

What happens to the ideal types once they join the separatist movement? Many different things. Implicit in this chapter in treating the separatist movement is the assumption that they act as catalytic agents in fostering change in the general society. This assumption is predicated on the notion that it is most difficult – if not impossible – for individuals to completely abandon their prior socialization. Turner and Killian make the point as follows:

> The values held by members of most separatist movements are extensively identified with those of the parent body [original group] . . . Because of the underlying value identity and because of the sacrifices demanded by sustained separatism, separatist values are usually short-lived.[7]

The implication is clear: on the one hand, because of the value identification with the original group and, consequently, the general society, members tend in the direction of reidentification with the original group and/or the general society or both (represented by #4). Put otherwise, according to Turner and Killian, ". . . the values of separatism may gradually be displaced by a return to conventionality within the movement itself."[8]

On the other hand, movement members as well as the movement itself might develop even more contempt for the original group and the general society; in this instance the movement and/or certain members in it might opt for a more extreme position (and tend in the direction of #5).

In short, the individual types may find the separatist movement an adequate means of working for and expressing their disaffection with the general society and original groups. They may remain loyal members, content with the movement's values and ideology. Then again, they may come to grips with their disaffection and return to their original socialized values. Finally, members may find the separatist movement an inadequate vehicle for expressing and acting out their disaffection and they may move to a more extremist position.

The question of age is an important aspect of membership in contemporary separatist movements. Cameron observed that "age alone is not a precise index of abilities, but it has been accepted as one for so long that it influences most people's attitudes as strongly as if it were an absolute quality in itself."[9] It is commonly suggested that black separatist movements tend to attract young blacks. In that the black population is younger than the white (21.5 percent and 28.5 percent, respectively), there is some truth in the suggestion. Moreover, in general, today's black youths seem to be more open-minded about other liberation strategies, including black separatism, as alternatives to integration. But when separatist movement organizations are analyzed for membership age, there does not seem to be much difference between the "old" and the "young."

**Diagram 2. Movement Organization Age Profile***

| Movement | Leadership | Age of Susceptibility* | Membership | Most likely place of recruitment |
|---|---|---|---|---|
| Nation of Islam | The Late Elijah Muhammad<br>Wallace Du–Muhammad–Mid-40s | all ages | all ages | urban ghettoes |
| CORE | Roy Innis<br>middle-aged (over 40) | all ages | all ages | lower middle to middle-class urban |
| SNCC** | Carmichael Brown 20s | <twenties> | college age youth | college campuses |
| Panthers | Newton Seale Cleaver<br>late 20s early 30s | <twenties> | teens to 30s | urban ghettoes |
| RNA | Omari Obadele<br>mid-40s | <all ages> | youth to middle age | urban ghettoes |

*These represent average organizational ages computed from membership data.
**Refers to SNCC in its heyday.

The Republic of New Africa is a militant separatist movement organization, but its officials are men in their 40s: Brother Omari Obadele is in his mid-40s and Robert Williams, the organization's former honorary president, and Milton Henry are men approaching their 50s. The separatist Nation of Islam was headed by the Elijah Muhammad who was over 70 (see Diagram 2), while his successor son, Wallace, is in his mid-40s. Henry Highland Garnett, Bishop Henry M. Turner, Booker T. Washington, W.E.B. DuBois, and Marcus Garvey were all past 35 (Garvey was 28 when he came to the United States). Floyd McKissick, Roy Innis, James Farmer, Albert Cleage, and other "militant" leaders are also middle-aged men.

However, SNCC had and the the Black Panther Party has relatively young leadership and membership, basically because the former originated around and recruited from college campuses, while the latter recruited mainly from unemployed blacks from the streets. When CORE and SNCC began to embrace separatism, "the two organizations recruited people, *mostly youth*, who were drawn by the militant image. . . ."[10] Naturally their initial membership would be comprised of young blacks. However, the membership of both organizations shifted over time. The Nation of Islam's age distribution also tended to tilt in favor of younger membership. However, from observation, there is fair representation in all age categories.

Youth was a factor in the appeal of separatist movement organizations in the more "militant" movements – i.e., the Black Panther Party and SNCC. The significance is in the number of *active* members who are young (under 30) and whether or not they persist in their militancy. Because of the movement's ideological appeal in light of societal conditions, all blacks are susceptible to membership in any of them. In the final analysis, it may be more accurate to indicate that appeal is more related to individual ideological orientations because the contemporary separatist movements are comprised of *all* age categories.

Although the question of appeal was partially dealt with in the "ideal type" age analysis, it is also intimately related to organizational structure and ideology. But that is another matter.

In conclusion, the appeal of black separatism is seen as a complex interplay between society and the individual. The question of whether separatism only appealed to the black masses on the lower end of the socioeconomic scale has a double-edged answer: yes, separatist movements tended to be comprised of lower status individuals because most blacks in American society are in the lower socioeconomic status categories; however, from our "ideal types" it can be seen that separatism's appeal is not limited to status. The answer to the question as to why there is not just one separatist organization instead of several organizations with separatist programs is simply that people perceive inequality and oppression differently and each constructs his own social reality and decides how to deal with it.

## NOTES

[1] Barry McLaughlin (Ed.), *Studies in Social Movements: A Social-Psychological Perspective* (New York: The Free Press, 1969), pp. 69-71.

[2] For an excellent discussion of this point see Melville J. Herskovits, *The Myth of the Negro Past* (Boston: Beacon Press, 1958, originally published in 1941).

[3] See Charles V. Hamilton, "The Silent Black Majority," *The New York Times Magazine* 1970, pp. 25, 26, 42, 44, 46, 47, 49.

[4] In addition to "Black Caucuses," which means that blacks operate as a separate group *in larger (white) organizations,* black professionals are forming, in proliferating frequency, separate black organizations. The impact of this development is making a real and lasting change which at this time cannot be determined.

[5] See Charles V. Willie (Ed.), *Racism and Mental Health* (Pittsburgh: The University of Pittsburgh Press, 1973).

[6] For example, Drs. Abraham Kardiner and Lionel Oversey in their book, *The Mark of Oppression: Explorations in the Personality of the American Negro,* despite their "advice to the reader" not to draw pejorative conclusions about black people, write: ". . . the Negro occupies a unique position in American culture, being separated from the majority white group by a caste barrier. The Negro still bears the psychological scars created by caste and its effects. It is these scars that we have chosen to call 'the mark of oppression.' " The inference here is clear: without contact with whites, blacks cannot have "normal personalities." Logically, the obverse is also true. What is "unscientific" is the use of a sample of 25 blacks, including a "criminal and a drug addict." Moreover, as the independent variable, they write: "Our constant control is the American white man. We require no other control." Black people will no longer tolerate white culture and social organization being used as "the standard"; rather, black culture alone is their standard.

[7] Ralph Turner and Lewis Killian, *Collective Behavior* (Englewood Cliffs, N.J.: Prentice-Hall, 1972), p. 333.

[8] *Ibid.*

[9] William B. Cameron, *Modern Social Movements* (New York: Random House, 1966), p. 38.

[10] August Meier and Elliott Rudwick, *CORE* (New York: Oxford University Press, 1973), p. 1.

# Part II
# The Case for Separatism

Following our argument that social reality is multifaceted and multidimensional, this section explores several perspectives and approaches that advocate black nationalism/separatism. These are, of course, only examples of separatist arguments, since other important perspectives, for a variety of reasons, are not included here. The Nation of Islam and the Congress of Racial Equality (CORE) have already been mentioned. I reiterate that the articles in this section are only small samples from a universe of national and local separatist groups and ideologies.

Part II begins with Browne arguing that cultural differences between blacks and whites (among other things) are sufficient to merit black and white separation in the United States. Baraka augments Browne's position, suggesting that black people should adhere to a "black or African value system" as opposed to a European centered one. Note that Baraka wrote this article prior to his "conversion" to a Marxist perspective. Henry, then a spokesman for the RNA, elaborates on reasons why blacks should concentrate on establishing a separate black nation in the five southern states of South Carolina, Georgia, Alabama, Mississippi, and Louisiana. Long, writing in the climate of 1969, amid the clamor for the establishment of Black Studies programs, contends that the challenge of Black Studies is to "combat academic imperialism, white paternalism, black intellectual nihilism, and deemphasize materialism" and to establish viable programs or let those who oppose them "hie to the hills." Stokely Carmichael, who led SNCC's separatist wing in 1966, suggests that blacks should concentrate on Pan-Africanism because blacks are an African people and their homeland is in Africa, not the United States. This position, of course, is in direct opposition to that of Henry and the Republic of New Africa. In the final chapter in this section, it is argued that Booker T. Washington was really a separatist, believing that economic self-determination would lay the foundation for dignified black survival and self-determination.

# 2
# *A Case for Separatism**

ROBERT S. BROWNE

There is a growing ambivalence in the Negro community which is creating a great deal of confusion both within the black community itself, and within those segments of the white community that are attempting to relate to the blacks. It arises from the question of whether the American Negro is a cultural group, significantly distinct from the majority culture in ways that are ethnically rather than socioeconomically based.

If one believes the answer to this is yes, then one is likely to favor emphasizing the cultural distinctiveness and to be vigorously opposed to any efforts to minimize or to submerge the differences. If, on the other hand, one believes that there are no cultural differences between the blacks and the whites or that the differences are minimal and transitory, then one is likely to resist the placing of great emphasis on the differences and to favor accentuating the similarities.

These two currents in the black community are symbolized, and perhaps over simplified, by the factional labels of separatists and integrationists.

The separatist would argue that the Negro's foremost grievance is not solvable by giving him access to more gadgets, although this is certainly a part of the solution, but that his greatest thirst is in the realm of the spirit – that he must be provided an opportunity to reclaim his own group individuality and to have that individuality recognized as having equal validity with the other major cultural groups of the world.

The integrationist would argue that what the Negro wants, principally, is exactly what the whites want – that is, that the Negro wants "in" American society, and that operationally this means providing the Negro with employment, income, housing, and education comparable to that of the whites. This having been achieved, the other aspects of the Negro's problem of inferiority will disappear.

The origins of this ideological dichotomy are easily identified. The physical characteristics that distinguish blacks from whites are obvious enough; and the long history of slavery, supplemented by the post-emancipation pattern of exclusion of the blacks from so many facets of American society, are equally undeniable. Whether observable behavioral differences between the mass of the blacks and the white majority are more properly attributable to this special history of the black man in America or are better viewed as expressions of racial differences in lifestyle is an arguable proposition.

What is not arguable, however, is the fact that at the time of the slave trade the blacks arrived in America with a cultural background and a lifestyle that was quite distinct from that of the whites. Although there was perhaps as much diversity amongst those Africans from widely scattered portions of the continent as there was amongst the European settlers, the differences between the two racial groups were unquestionably far greater, as attested by the different roles which they were to play in the society.

## INTEGRATIONIST AND SEPARATIST VIEWPOINTS

Over this history there seems to be little disagreement. The dispute arises from how one views what happened during the subsequent 350 years.

The integrationist would focus on the transformation of the blacks into imitators of the European civilization. European clothing was imposed on the slaves; eventually their languages were forgotten; the African homeland receded ever further into the background. Certainly after 1808, when the slave trade was officially terminated, thus cutting off the supply of fresh injections of African culture, the Europeanization of the blacks proceeded apace. With emancipation, the national constitution recognized the legal manhood of the blacks, United States citizenship was unilaterally conferred upon the ex-slave, and the Negro began his arduous struggle for social, economic, and political acceptance into the American mainstream.

The separatist, however, takes the position that the cultural transformation of the black man was not complete. Whereas the integrationist is more or less content to accept the destruction of the original culture of the African slaves as a *fait accompli*, irrespective of whether he feels it to have been morally reprehensible or not, the separatist is likely to harbor a vague sense of resentment toward the whites for having perpetrated his cultural genocide, and he is concerned to nurture whatever

*Robert S. Browne, "A Case for Separation," in Robert S. Browne and Bayard Rustin, *Separatism or Integration: Which Way for America? – A Dialogue* (New York: A. Philip Randolph Educational Fund, 1960), pp. 7-15. Reprinted by permission of the author.

vestiges may have survived the North American experience and to encourage a renaissance of these lost characteristics. In effect, he is sensitive to an identity crisis which presumably does not exist in the mind of the integrationist.

To many observers, the separatist appears to be romantic and even reactionary. On the other hand, his viewpoint strikes an harmonious chord with mankind's most fundamental instinct – the instinct for survival. With so powerful a stimulus and with the oppressive tendencies congenitally present in the larger white society, one almost could have predicted the emergence of the burgeoning movement toward black separatism. Millions of black parents have been confronted with the poignant agony of raising black, kinky-haired children in a society where the standard of beauty is a milk-white skin and long, straight hair. To convince a black child that she is beautiful when every channel of value formation in the society is telling her the opposite is a heart-rending and well-nigh impossible task. It is a challenge that confronts all Negroes, irrespective of their social and economic class, but the difficulty of dealing with it is likely to vary directly with the degree to which the family leads an integrated existence. A black child in a predominantly black school may realize that she doesn't look like the pictures in the books, magazines, and TV advertisements, but at least she looks like her schoolmates and neighbors. The black child in a predominantly white school and neighborhood lacks even this basis for identification.

## THE PROBLEM OF IDENTITY

This identity problem is not peculiar to the Negro, of course, nor is it limited to questions of physical appearance. Minorities of all sorts encounter it in one form or another – the immigrant who speaks with an accent; the Jewish child who doesn't celebrate Christmas; the vegetarian who shuns meat. But for the Negro the problem has a special dimension, for in the American ethos a black man is not only "different," he is classed as ugly and inferior.

This is not an easy situation to deal with, and the manner in which a Negro chooses to handle it will be both determined by and a determinant of his larger political outlook. He can deal with it as an integrationist, accepting his child as being ugly by prevailing standards and urging him to excel in other ways to prove his worth, or he can deal with it as a black nationalist, telling the child that he is not a freak but rather part of a larger international community of black-skinned, kinky-haired people who have a beauty of their own, a glorious history, and a great future. In short, he can replace shame with pride, inferiority with dignity, by imbuing the child with what is coming to be known as black nationalism. The growing popularity of this latter viewpoint is evidenced by the appearance of "natural" hair styles among Negro youth and by the surge of interest in African and Negro culture and history.

## BLACK POWER, BLACK CONSCIOUSNESS, AND AMERICAN SOCIETY

Black Power may not be the ideal slogan to describe this new self-image that the black American is developing, for to guilt-ridden whites the slogan conjures up violence, anarchy, and revenge. To frustrated blacks, however, it symbolizes unity and a newly found pride in the blackness with which the Creator endowed us and which we realize must always be our mark of identification. Heretofore this blackness has been a stigma, a curse with which we were born. Black Power means that henceforth this curse will be a badge of pride rather than of scorn. It marks the end of an era in which black men devoted themselves to pathetic attempts to be white men and inaugurates an era in which black people will set their own standards of beauty, conduct, and accomplishment.

Is this new black consciousness in irreconcilable conflict with the larger American society?

In a sense, the heart of the American cultural problem always has been the need to harmonize the inherent contradiction between racial (or national) identity and integration into the melting pot which is America. In the century since the Civil War, the society has made little effort to find a measure to afford the black minority a sense of racial pride and independence while at the same time accepting it as a full participant in the larger society.

Now that the implications of that failure are becoming apparent, the black community seems to be saying "Forget it! We'll solve our own problems." Integration, which never had a high priority among the black masses, now is being written off by them as not only unattainable but as actually harmful – driving a wedge between those black masses and the so-called Negro elite.

To these developments has been added the momentous realization by many of the "integrated" Negroes that, in the United States, full integration can only mean full assimilation – a loss of racial identity. This sobering prospect has caused many a black integrationist to pause and reflect, even as have his similarly challenged Jewish counterparts.

## INTEGRATION – A PAINLESS GENOCIDE?

Thus, within the black community there are two separate challenges to the traditional integration policy which long has constituted the major objective of established Negro leadership. There is the general skepticism that the Negro, even after having transformed himself into a white black-man, will enjoy full acceptance into American society; and there is the longer range doubt that even should complete integration somehow be achieved, it would prove to be really desirable, for its price may be the total absorption and disappearance of the race – a sort of painless genocide.

Understandably, it is the black masses who have most vociferously articulated these dangers of assimilation, for they have watched with alarm as the more fortunate among their ranks have gradually risen to the top only to be promptly "integrated" off into the white community – absorbed into another culture, often with undisguised contempt for all that had previously constituted their racial and cultural heritage. Also, it was the black masses who first perceived that integration actually increases the white community's control over the black one by destroying black institutions, and by absorbing black leadership and coinciding its interests with those of the white community.

The international "brain drain" has its counterpart in the black community, which is constantly being denuded of its best trained people and many of its natural leaders. Black institutions of all sorts – colleges, newspapers, banks, even community organizations – are experiencing the loss of their better people to the newly available openings in white establishments, thereby lowering the quality of the Negro organizations and in some cases causing their demise or increasing their dependence on whites for survival. Such injurious, if unintended, side effects of integration have been felt in almost every layer of the black community.

## NEGRO DISTRUST OF WHITE AMERICA

If the foregoing analysis of the integrationist *vs.* separatist conflict exhausted the case, we might conclude that all the problems have been dealt with before, by other immigrant groups in America. (It would be an erroneous conclusion, for while other groups may have encountered similar problems, their solutions do not work for us, alas.) But there remains yet another factor which is cooling the Negro's enthusiasm for the integrationist path: he is becoming distrustful of his fellow Americans.

The American culture is one of the youngest in the world. Furthermore, as has been pointed out repeatedly in recent years, it is essentially a culture that approves of violence, indeed enjoys it. Military expenditures absorb roughly half the national budget. Violence predominates on the TV screen and the toys of violence are best-selling items during the annual rites for the much praised but little imitated Prince of Peace. In Vietnam, the zeal with which America has pursued its effort to destroy a poor and illiterate peasantry has astonished civilized people around the globe.

In such an atmosphere the Negro is understandably restive about the fate his white compatriots may have in store for him. The veiled threat by President Johnson at the time of the 1966 riots, suggesting that riots might beget programs and pointing out that Negroes are only ten percent of the population was not lost on most blacks. It enraged them, but it was a sobering thought. The manner in which Germany herded the Jews into concentration camps and ultimately into ovens was a solemn warning to minority peoples everywhere. The casualness with which America exterminated the Indians and later interned the Japanese suggests that there is no cause for the Negro to feel complacent about his security in the United States. He finds little consolation in the assurance that if it does become necessary to place him in concentration camps it will only be as a means of protecting him from uncontrollable whites. "Protective incarceration" to use governmental jargonese.

The very fact that such alternatives are becoming serious topics of discussion has exposed the Negro's already raw and sensitive psyche to yet another heretofore unfelt vulnerability – the insecurity he suffers as a result of having no homeland which he can honestly feel is his own. Among the major ethnocultural groups in the world he is unique in this respect.

## NEED FOR NATIONHOOD

As the Jewish drama during and following World War II painfully demonstrated, a national homeland is a primordial and urgent need for a people, even though its benefits do not always lend themselves to ready measurement. For some, the homeland constitutes a vital place of refuge from the strains of a life led too long within a foreign environment. For others, the need to reside in the homeland is considerably less intense than the need merely for knowing that such a homeland exists. The benefit to the expatriate is psychological, a sense of security in knowing that he belongs to a culturally and politically identifiable community. No doubt this phenomenon largely accounts for the fact that both the West Indian Negro and the Puerto Rican exhibit considerably more self-assurance than does the American Negro, for both the former groups have ties to an identifiable homeland which honors and preserves their cultural heritage.

It has been marvelled that we American Negroes, almost alone among the cultural groups of the world, exhibit no sense of nationhood. Perhaps it is true that we do lack this sense, but there seems to be little doubt that the absence of a homeland exacts a severe if unconscious pride from our psyche. Theoretically, our homeland is the U.S.A. We pledge allegience to the stars and stripes and sing the national anthem. But from the age when we first begin to sense that we are somehow "different," that we are victimized, these rituals begin to mean less to us than to our white compatriots. For many of us they become form without substance; for others they become a cruel and bitter mockery of our dignity and good sense; for relatively few of us do they retain a significance in any way comparable to their hold on our white brethren.

The recent coming into independence of many African states stimulated some interest among Negroes that independent Africa might become the homeland which they so desperately needed. A few made the journey and experienced a newly found sense of community and racial dignity. For many who went, however, the gratifying racial fraternity which they experienced was insufficient to compensate for the cultural estrangement that accompanied it. They had been away from Africa for too long and the differences in language, food, and custom barred them from experiencing that "at home" sensation they were eagerly seeking. Symbolically, independent Africa could serve them as a homeland: practically, it could not. Their search continues – a search for a place where they can experience the security that comes from being a part of the majority culture, free at last from the inhibiting effects of cultural repression and induced cultural timidity and shame.

## "THIS LAND IS OUR RIGHTFUL HOME"

If we have been separated from Africa for so long that we are no longer quite at ease there, then we are left with only one place to make our home, and that is in this land to which we were brought in chains. Justice would indicate such a solution in any case, for it is North America, not Africa, into which our toil and effort have been poured. This land is our rightful home, and we are well within our rights in demanding an opportunity to enjoy it on the same terms as the other immigrants who have helped to develop it.

Since few whites will deny the justice of this claim, it is paradoxical that we are offered the option of exercising this birthright only on the condition that we abandon our culture, deny our race, and integrate ourselves into the white community. The "accepted" Negro, the "integrated" Negro, are mere euphemisms, hiding a cruel and relentless cultural destruction which is sometimes agonizing to the middle class. A Negro who refuses to yield his identity and to ape the white model finds he can survive in dignity only by rejecting the entire white society, which ultimately must mean challenging the law and the law enforcement mechanisms. On the other hand, if he abandons his cultural heritage and succumbs to the lure of integration, he risks certain rejection and humiliation along the way, with absolutely no guarantee of ever achieving complete acceptance.

That such unsatisfactory options are leading to almost continuous disruption and dislocation of our society should hardly be cause for surprise.

## PARTITION AS A SOLUTION

A formal partitioning of the United States into two totally separate and independent nations, one white and one black offers one way out of this tragic situation. Many will condemn it as a defeatist solution, but what they see as defeatism may better be described as a frank facing up to the realities of American society. A society is stable only to the extent that there exists a basic core of value judgments that are unthinkingly accepted by the great bulk of its members. Increasingly, Negroes are demonstrating that they do not accept the common core of values that underlies America – whether because they had little to do with drafting it or because they feel it is weighted against their interests.

The alleged disproportionately large number of Negro law violators, of unwed mothers, of illegitimate children, of non-working adults *may* be indicators that there is no community of values such as has been supposed, although I am not unaware of racial socioeconomic reasons for these statistics also. But whatever the reasons for observed behavioral differences, there clearly is no reason *why* the Negro should not have his own ideas about what the societal organization should be. The Anglo-Saxon system of organizing human relationships certainly has not proved itself to be superior to all other systems, and the Negro is likely to be more acutely aware of this fact than are most Americans.

This unprecedented challenging of the "conventional wisdom" on the racial question is causing considerable consternation within the white community, especially the white liberal community, which has long felt itself to be the sponsor and guardian of the blacks. The situation is further confused because the challenges to the orthodox integrationist views are being projected by persons whose roots are authentically within the black community – whereas the integrationist spokesmen of the past often have been persons whose credentials were partly white-bestowed. This situation is further aggravated by the classical intergenerational problem – with black youth seizing the lead and speaking out for nationalism and separatism whereas their elders look on askance, a development which has at least a partial parallel within the contemporary white community, where youth is increasingly strident in its demands for a thoroughgoing revision of our social institutions.

## THE BLACK NATIONALISTS

If one were to inquire as to who the principal spokesmen for the new black nationalism or for separatism are, one would discover that the movement is essentially locally based rather than nationally organized. In the San Francisco Bay area, the Black Panther party is well known as a leader of the tactics of winning recognition for the black community. Their tactic is *via* a separate political party for black people, a format which I suspect we will hear a great deal more of in the future. The work of the Black Muslims is well known, and perhaps more national in scope than that of any other black nationalist group. Out of Detroit there is the Malcolm X Society, led by attorney Milton Henry, whose members reject their United States citizenship and are claiming five southern states for the creation of a new Black Republic. Another major leader in Detroit is the Rev. Albert Cleage, who is developing a considerable following for his preachings of black dignity and who has also experimented with a black political party, thus far without success.

The black students at white colleges are one highly articulate group seeking some natonal organizational form. A growing number of black educators are also groping toward some sort of nationally coordinated body to lend strength to their local efforts for developing educational systems better tailored to the needs of the black child. Under the name of Association of Afro-American Educators, they recently held a national conference in Chicago which was attended by several hundred public school teachers and college and community workers.

This is not to say that every black teacher or parent-teacher group that favors community control of schools is necessarily sympathetic to black separatism. Nevertheless, the general thrust of the move toward decentralized control over public schools, at least in the larger urban areas, derives from an abandoning of the idea of integration in the schools and a decision to bring to the ghetto the best and most suitable education that can be obtained.

## GHETTO IMPROVEMENT EFFORTS

Similarly, a growing number of community-based organizations are being formed for the purpose of facilitating the economic development of the ghetto, for replacement of absentee business proprietors and landlords by black entrepreneurs and resident owners. Again, these efforts are not totally separatist in that they operate within the framework of the present national society, but they build on the separatism that already exists in the society rather than attempting to eliminate it. To a black who sees salvation for the black man only in a complete divorce of the two races, these efforts at ghetto improvement appear futile – perhaps even harmful. To others, convinced that co-existence with white America is possible within the national framework if only the whites will permit the Negro to develop as he wishes and by his own hand rather than in accordance with a white-conceived and white-administered pattern, such physically and economically upgraded black enclaves will be viewed as desirable steps forward.

Finally, those blacks who still feel that integration is in some sense both acceptable and possible will continue to strive for the color-blind society. When, if ever, these three strands of thought will converge toward a common outlook I cannot predict. In the meanwhile, however, concerned whites wishing to work with the black community should be prepared to encounter many rebuffs. They should keep ever in mind that the black community does not have a homogeneous vision of its own predicament at this crucial juncture.

# 3
# *A Black Value System**

IMAMU AMEER BARAKA (LE ROI JONES)

*Umoja* (Unity) – To strive for and maintain unity in the family, community, nation, and race.

*Kujichagulia* (Self-Determination) – To define ourselves, name ourselves, and speak for ourselves, instead of being defined and spoken for by others.

*Ujima* (Collective Work and Responsibility) – To build and maintain our community together and to make our brothers' and sisters' problems our problems and to solve them together.

*Ujamaa* (Cooperative Economics) – To build and maintain our own stores, shops, and other businesses and to profit together from them.

*Nia* (Purpose) – To make as our collective vocation the building and developing of our community in order to restore our people to their traditional greatness.

*Kuumba* (Creativity) – To do always as much as we can, in the way we can in order to leave our community more beautiful and beneficial than when we inherited it.

*Imani* (Faith) – To believe with all our heart in our parents, our teachers, our leaders, our people, and the righteousness and victory of our struggle.

The 7 principles are 7 because the number is a meaning-symbol for this world. As a throw of dice it speaks of spiritual concepts and scientific principles. It is because of this that the seventh day was the culmination, as a period of devotion and meditation, for the six days of divine work. Sun-Day. So Maulana speaks of spiritual concepts and scientific principles embodied as a morality system – complete in itself, as a contemporary black philosophy old as the sun.

The 7 principles are the spine and total philosophy of the US organization. They are simple in what they say, but total in that they evoke all the levels of meaning associated with philosophical systems.

The 7 principles are "10 commandments" yet more profound to us – US because they are pre and post 10 commandments at the same time. If there is *Umoja*, for instance, thou cannot kill, steal, bear false witness, commit adultery, or any of the things the western world thrives on. The commandments are fulfilled by the initial need of blackness for unity – oneness.

But unity is political too. The meaning vibrates as a totality. Spiritual unity is the needed completion of physical and mental unity. (The doctrine is made up of the three sides of the ancient pyramid – physical, mental, and spiritual – in each of its statements. The three pyramids of the US symbol meaning "our traditional greatness," and by this, our traditional understanding') The 7 principles are solutions to the political dilemma of Black people. I would say solutions to the political dilemma of all men, but I recognize that we are different by virtue of our concerns and the context of our lives.

We, the different peoples, are as different rays of light, each bent to particular articulation of the initial life force, and at different stages of evolution (self-consciousness). All men would benefit by the 7 principles. But the black man has created them out of his *specific* need. The balancer of East and West, completer of this cycle.

*Umoja* (definition: To strive for and maintain unity in the family, community, nation, and race). We are a *body* of people, the large Being of Blackness. The many of us are parts of the body. The whole cannot function *as it will* (Kujichagulia – Self-Determination) if it is scattered, the head one place, the heart another. Physical unity. Mental unity. We must think one way of total movement to liberate ourselves. Each has a function but as complementary parts of a whole. All organizations, *organs* really, they must function as of the whole body.

*Ujima* – Collective Work and Responsibility. All of the organs must function by the same will. We must have a head with control over all the organs. The I's must be our many eyes and be a basis for seeing in all the places.

One being in harmony with itself, this is the first need to be satisfied before we can deal with an outside world. But it is internal unity that makes a single will, which is self-determination. What we will be, what we will do, are questions only we ourselves have the proper answers to.

The concept of *oneness* is old and black and spiritual. The One God. And the 7 principles are a religious creed, in its most practical application, a code of common morality.

We need a value system to be predictable in our behavior, Maulana has said. Predictable, meaning stable, pointed toward a

*From *The Black Scholar,* November 1969, by permission.

single goal. The liberation of our soul, mind, and body. A value system is the spine of all cultures. What is good or bad aside from specific interpretation in specific context? Through unity, we arrive at self-determination and can then proceed to collective work and responsibility (in the organs, or as each one teach one, or painting a wall), *Ujima.* The value system selects the goal, we apply ourselves to it, live by it, the rest follows. Why Moses gave the commandments for the same result, as a best way to live. And they will *raise* us.

So that Maulana Karenga's doctrine is first a value system. It sets forth a value system, to be followed, called Kawaida, literally ("that which is customary, or traditionally adhered to, by black people"). A nation is only as great as that set of values it *actually* practices . . . no matter what it says, e.g., witness America (white and negro). The value system is how you live, to what end. And Kawaida is, as the doctrine teaches, "a weapon, a shield, and a pillow of peace."

One cannot have a slave's mentality and hope to be free, or one *can hope*, but that will not make anything really happen. The freeing of the mind, before anything else can happen. The people *must actually want* to be free. Want it bad enough to be it.

A value system that is itself the way of life of a free man of high morality, is what the Kawaida teaches. A morality (more) is *the meaning* of what people do. Culture is how they live, morality is what it means. What it means as cause and effect, past what you or anyone else might *think*. What happens as a result of . . . is what morality directs. And there is a finality to this path-making that is part of the heaviest truth. To live better, you must live better. It is simple and complex.

Kawaida, or the doctrine of Maulana Karenga, is the measure of that "better" life. It is African, because we are African, no matter that we have been trapped in the West these few hundred years. But by the quality of what our lives *meant* we have transformed the white man. The value system especially as the Nguzo Saba begins to focus it, can give us the identity, purpose, and direction to move to that better life. At each level it is a contrast to Euro-American *morality*, because first it is based on teachings that are superior to the practiced morality of Euro-American civilization. It is also a value system beneficial to black people. And there is no reason for the practiced value system of Euro-America to be beneficial to black people, quite the contrary, it has always been absolutely detrimental to black people. For instance the fourth principle of the Nguzo Saba is Ujamaa, collective or cooperative economics.

But Ujamaa is not, as it has been called, "African Socialism," it is Ujamaa. If anything you could say European Ujamaa, but never the reverse. The reason? Ujamaa is the traditional way of distributing wealth for the black man. It is an economic attitude older than Europe, and certainly older than the term Socialism. Which finally is another thing, coming from the European definition, since the European definition is a state that will exist "after the decay of capitalism." Ujamaa has always been the African *attitude* towards the distribution of wealth (until the decay that made our kingdoms fall). It has never been a European attitude, but rather a *theory*. Can you dig it? (See Julius Nyerere's paper *Ujamaa in Uhuru na Umaja.*)

The "decay of capitalism" theory is also another aspect of the European attitude of "world revolution," and do not mistake my meaning, I am talking about the lifestyle of violence. Vita (violence or war) in Swahili equals *life* in Latin. When we say "revolution" we mean the restoration of our national sovereignty as a people, a people, at this point, equipped to set new paths for the development of man. We mean the freeing of ourselves from the bondage of another, alien, people. We are not warring upon our own society among ourselves. These pigs are no kin to us. We are trying to destroy a *foreign oppressor.* It is not "revolution" but *National Liberation.*

When you speak of capitalism you speak of the European mind. We do not want to be Europeans. No, not of any persuasion. Just as the, as he calls them, "economic radicals" of the '20s tried to stop J.A. Rogers, whom they called "a black capitalist," from doing his research and rewriting our destroyed archives saying Rogers was "chauvinistic" and suffered an "inferiority complex"; they said he should be studying people like "Marx, Engels, and Lafargue and be preparing for the worker's utopia which was just around the corner . . ." (See Introduction to Rogers' "World's Great Men of Color, Vol. 1"). *But are not Marx, Engels and Lafargue just another list of "great" men . . . but great white men,* or at least white men thought great by one particular group of white men? Another group of white men might give you another list . . . like say Washington, Jefferson, Lincoln, Kennedy, etc. But it is, either way, still a commitment to Euro-American values, to whiteness.

In order to free ourselves, and this may come as a shock to many "hip negroes," we are going to have to do it ourselves! For ourselves. Yes, the world will benefit, but they are not going to do it, any more than you helped free the Chinese! If you cannot have faith in blackness, in the black mind and the black man to find a way out of this slavery, you are full of despair, or else emotionally committed to white people. Which is the terrible truth for many of us, even our so-called "revolutionaries." They are so committed to whiteness that they must find a way to make white relevant some way. The Right will not save us so the Left will. This group of white people will not do it, but this other group of white people will. (Do not misunderstand, we will take aid from a scorpion, but we must not confuse our identity. Or try to crawl under rocks, with scorpions.)

Another fallacy of many "revolutionaries" is the "right around the cornerism" that Rogers cites and Maulana Karenga always emphasizes as dangerous. There is no such thing. The work of National Liberation is hard and its resolution is to be sought but not fantasized as the result of unprepared spontaneous outbursts of emotionalism. It is work. It will only be achieved by disciplined, dedicated people, with a value system that allows them to persevere and remain healthy and rational and committed for as long as it takes no matter what happens to anybody or everybody else.

Too often so called revolutionaries without a black value system, like Kawaida, do exactly the same things as the oppressor-people and, as I said, they are always emotionally committed to the oppressor people. They speak the same language, think the same things valuable, have the same "taste." In fact they are so much the same they can make alliances that are unnatural as far as the natural lifestyles of the new peoples are concerned. The bush-smoking, wine drinking, homo-superhetero sexual bellbottomed life of the hippy (a truly interracial though white committed phenomenon) is just a phase of death rattle for a culture and a people. The magnetism of the final death will compel to death all those with the jingling matching magnets around their brains.

An epoch passes because it is played out. To imitate the played out is to simulate, and then not to be able to stop, death.

So *Nia* purpose. What is your purpose, for anything? For being alive? If you are black your purpose should be the building of Black. The Nguzo Saba says our purpose must be the rebuilding of our people to their traditional greatness. One reason for the stress on history, if you do not even know of your traditional greatness, then you will not aspire to anything but dry rock white "radicalism" (like some 1930s vampire rerisen again from the grave to suck black people's blood) as some kind of alternative to the maggoty pork that exists. But neither is our shot, brother. Initially our purpose is *Nation building.* To raise black people to "our traditional greatness." National Liberation, as Malcolm called it.

Karenga stresses cultural nation for the same reasons that Mao continues his cultural revolution on a continuous basis in China even after his political revolution has been realized. It is a constant process. The minds of the people are the most important factor of any movement, without them you can have nothing else. And we do not have to settle for maggoty pork or renewed draculaism (a white "radical"). We can have and be ourselves.

But you must have the cultural revolution – i.e., you must get the mind before you move another fuhtha. There is no violent revolution except as a result of the black mind expanding, trying to take control of its own space. Our armies are not yet formed, as armies. We cannot fight a war, an actual physical war with the forces of evil just because we are angry. We can begin to build. We must build black institutions. In all the different aspects of culture. Political, Religious, Social, Economic, Ethical, Creative, Historical – institutions all based on a value system that is beneficial to black people.

All these institutions will be alternatives to the Euro-American or Negro institutions that exist, but will exist in their own right as expressions of the black sensibility, and not merely as reactions to an alien sensibility. If Mao does not control the minds of the Chinese, his political victories are lost, his military is hostile, Maoism is another name for what was. Ghana should have had a continuous cultural revolution. To maintain the consciousness of the people. So that they could not be taken off by the criminal sickness of the white-led Negro mentality that reinvaded Ghana. If the chief of state of Biafra names as his country's national anthem "Finlandia," then we know where his politics are right off. The internationalization of a white value system will always militate for white decisions about the way things should be. Whether it is a national anthem or an economic system.

Black creativity, *Kuumba*, is the sixth principle. Which tells us how we must devise a way out of our predicament. How we must build, with what methodology. In what emotionalism, the fire of blackness. So that even Ujamaa is Kuumba in regards to the distribution of wealth among men. For the European, Ujamaa, like jazz, is a saying, a pretending illusion, rather than a being. And we are not racists when we say this, we are merely recognizing the traits of different peoples.

When we call white people evil it is based on empiricism, not theory. Do you remember how you Africans got here to the Western Hemisphere in the first place? (I mean as slaves, not as Egyptians and Moorish explorers and settlers.) The recital of the horrors black people have suffered at the hands of the white makes us racists? Only to the white, or the *white committed.* Herodotus came up with the Teutonic Origins theory of why white was best and how the rest were not, on a descending xenophobic scale all the way down to us. A theory, not a fact. The lynching and oppression and enslavement of black people by European, and the capacity for such cruelty by the European mind is fact, not theory. It is empirical, we have witnessed, and lived through it, are still living through it. And just because some dude wants to sleep with a white woman, let him not call those of us who do not racists. There are facts, to which any honest man had better bear witness.

When we said, Black Art, we meant Kuumba. The spiritual characteristic of revelation through the creative. The artist is respected in Bantu philosophy because he could capture some of the divinity. Because it flowed through his fingers or out of his mouth, and because he would lend this divinity to the whole people to raise them in its image, building great nations reared in the image of righteousness. What is soul (like the one sun the sole solar force, in this system) our connection, our relation with the infinite. And it is feeling, like inner revelation, that is the connection, the force of the uncreated, which we constantly make reference to, bringing into creation. Yehh! we scream, bearing witness to the power of Kuumba.

But black creativity is what will save us – not just "artists" but all of us – after all is said and done – nothing else. An antidote to birth or mind control! The Ngnzo Saba itself is one of the strongest examples of Kuumba. And each idea or act that animates our lives must be measured against the Nguzo Saba in each of its components. You must ask of each new idea or dissociation that comes to mind, what does this have to do with bringing about unity for black people, what does it contribute to black people's self-determination – does it have anything to do with Ujima, collective work and responsibility, and so on. So, for instance, a "black TV program" with a straight haired sister dancing a Martha Graham – Merce Cunningham – esque tribute to the ghetto (?) is not Kuumba – neither the dance nor the program.

A nation coming into being is a new creation. It must be willed into existence by itself. It is new – it is literally something other than what exists.

*Imani* is faith – Faith in your leaders, teachers, parents – but first faith in *blackness* – that it will win. Faith in Nationalism, that *we* can build *ourselves* into a conscious nation once again – that we can free ourselves, from the chain of white commitment – this is all that binds us to slavery – *the fact that we are emotionally committed to it* – to being slaves.

Imani is the supra rational aspect of Nationalism, but the aspect that we cannot survive without. We must believe past 2 + 2 or 180 *vs.* 40 that the number we want is the one we can achieve.

Simple faith, like church people say and that's what we want – hardrock emotional faith in what we're doing. The same way your grandmamma used to weep and wring her hands believing in Jeez-us, that deep deep connection with the purest energy, this is what the Nationalist must have. Can you understand this? That we must believe past any bullshit "rationale" that we may or may not achieve based on 7 million subjective-objective variables. We must believe in Nationalism. We must believe in the justness of our struggle and the certainty of our victory. *No matter how long this might take*. There is no time. Only change.

Nationalism must be the basis for our entire lives. It must be the content and initiator of anything we do. Always, as the formulator of any act must be the need to see that act contribute to the building of a Nation. That is our purpose, Nationalism our direction. Black is our identity. The totality of these as a life focus is simple faith, even before it exists as spirituality. But that is what faith is, if it is directed toward grace – spirituality.

We say spirituality because the spiritual is the blessing of life. It is what all life points toward. Complete consciousness and Nationalism, at this point, is the definer and director of our people toward the goal of absolute, yes, absolute consciousness.

So the 7th principle, Faith, is actually one with the 1st – to create the whole, the one (it's what Umoja means).

There is nothing anyone can do about the fact of the Nguzo Saba. It does – they do – exist. Now it is only for the studying or aspiring Nationalist to accept these principles as the clearest statment of the badly needed new value system.

It is spiritual without being religious. That is, it moves to the higher levels of human aspiration but describes no ritual dogma. The Nguzo Saba would organize the morality of the would-be Nationalist, give him a new and more relevant morality, to begin to build Blackness anew.

As long as we are commited to old ways and ideas, to paraphrase Toure, we will never move from where we are. A value system is a describer of your life on the planet, how you lived, in what manner and for what reasons, i.e., to what purpose. If you do not consciously create a new value system, one that is quite different from the rest of crazy America's – you will be exactly what crazy America is and die the way she dies.

But we want to survive. We want life. We want to build and create. We do not want a modified version and what exists, we want the totally new –newly claimed but as the eastern, the tradition, the African, the black –i.e., we want a whole different version of men's life on earth. We do not want what Marx wanted or what Abbie Hoffman wants. We want our new black selves as absolute masters of our own space. Can you dig it *space*, and I repeat it for all these simple "black" crypto-hippies who believe in Malcolm solely *because he is dead* – *Space* is what we are fighting for. And it manifests itself as anything or everything. Institutional space, living, i.e. human space, thinking space, or the actual planetroom una fahamu? Like they say, land. It is all space. CAN YOU UNDERSTAND??

But the point man is Malcolm never had a *doctrine* – we learned from him because he was straight and true but he made no doctrines, no real *organization*, and we must face this. This is *our* work now, today, to organize better than Malcolm did. Can you understand? Malcolm's teachings must now be analyzed, formalized, and a structure and program issued out of them.

Elijah had a formal teaching, something close to a doctrine and Malcolm sprang from it, but made some other decisions. But he, Malcolm, made no doctrine. But now a doctrine has been made, formalized around a black value system, and this is what we need. How you live is how you project and how you will project. Your progeny, your creations are products of life, manifestations of your way, scenes from your path. The Nguzo Saba is the key to the new Nationalism. It is the key to the new learning. And that learning is the complete doctrine of Maulana Karenga.

The Nguzo Saba is the first, the basic, primary teaching. The rest of the doctrine, covering the completeness of modern experience is a black ideology in toto. A path itself in blackness and Nationhood.

The doctrine now is in the head and hands mostly of organization people and a few key organizers and student leaders around the country. (*The Quotable Karenga* is a light sampling of some of the doctrine's content.) But soon it will be published and available to most of us. It is the central ingredient of the new nationalist organization. It will transform black people and by doing this, transform, yes, America.

You better get ready for it.

# 4
# *An Independent Black Republic in North America**

MILTON R. HENRY

About this idea of "separation," it is imperative that first we arrive, if we can, at some fundamental truths.

The real problem with the institution of chattel slavery in America was that it tended to rob, and did rob, the enslaved African of his understanding of what was really essential for the full enjoyment of life. It tended to erase any understanding of those values which made life meaningful and worthwhile, and to render the enslaved African a perceptionless and cultureless babe, hopelessly caught up in a whirling vortex of incomprehensible and foreign situations from which any hope of escape was simply not able to be entertained.

Today, as descendants of the enslaved African, we try importantly to regain our spiritual and psychological balance because we live in the time of the resurrection – i.e., the time when a people awake from their deaf, dumb, and blinded state, emerge from their spiritual tombs, and come forth to the fulness of life.

In the Hebrew book of Genesis we are told that, at the creation, man was instructed by his creator to "be fruitful; to multiply; to replenish the earth; to subdue it; and to exercise dominion over all living things which move upon the face of the earth."

The critical words in the passage are: "Male and female created he them, and blessed them, and said to them, be fruitful, multiply, replenish *the earth*, and subdue it." We think that in these words God gave man two precise preconditions for a healthy existence. Number one, the use of the sexes for procreation of the species; and, number two, the subduing and domination of the earth, or the land. The *sina qua non* for health – man tied to man and, equally important, man tied to the living earth.

The ancient Indian sages believed that the feet of man should always touch and come in contact with the earth; otherwise man would lose contact with the great spirit of the universe. As a consequence, the Indian brave wore fine moccasins of the thinnest of skins, in order that he remain strong in battle and not insulated from the pulsating and living earth processes.

The Indian saw the earth, the land, as a sustainer and reviver of the internal spirit of man; thus, the Indian would see in today's concrete buildings and paving the glaring evidence of a people who, having no life spirit whatever or love of nature, were doing everything possible to block out and insulate themselves from life and life's dynamic spiritual processes.

Whatever truth there is contained in these various ideas, Robert Ardrey, of recent days, now writes about the "Territorial Imperative" and presents the argument that all animals on the face of this planet are driven by a fundamental unconscious inner urge to stake our territories over which they must exercise complete dominion; and that, whether bird or lion or man is subjected to scrutiny, there is to be observed the same unmistakable urge and need for "territory" – a need to have a piece of land and to be able to control it against all intruders. Ardrey claims that the need for territory seems to be even stronger than the need for sex, and finds that only those species that are on the verge of extinction, such as the great gorilla, exhibit any declining or waning interest in territory.

The urge therefore for territory seems to be an innate, deeply rooted part of the nature of all living species of animal except those about to become extinct. Living animals everywhere seem to know that land is in fact the basis for freedom, justice, independence, and equality – and most living animals know that sovereignty and power over land are essential for any kind of life. Sovereignty, of course, being simply the right to exercise dominion over a piece of land, coupled with the power to preserve that right against all outside intrusion and assault.

On analysis, the greatest observable evil inherent in the system of American chattel slavery, and what seems to me to be the most degrading thing about it, is that it destroyed the essential inclination of the persons enslaved to unashamedly seek out, seize, and exercise dominion over some land.

I say this because it seems to me that in the final analysis no man can exist anywhere in this world and be considered normal who does not have some inner desire to control the land or the house in which he must live.

Admittedly, the black experience in North America was a terrible and painful one. That our ancestors were conditioned – mind, soul, and body – in a socially indefensible experiment there can be no doubt. That the end of the experiment was to

*Speech given by Milton R. Henry at the Conference on "Problems of Black Liberation Movement" at Guelph, Ontario, Canada, Saturday, March 4, 1970. Reprinted by permission.

modify the character of a whole race of people was, in truth, criminal and unforgivable; that it succeeded so well is, even today, difficult to fathom.

Most men catapulted into the mechanism of a system such as that put into operation against our African ancestors would quickly suffer from neurosis and derangement. In a space of less than four years, the Jews at Treblinka, Dachau, and Buchenwald lost 2000 years of scrupulous religious preconditioning, and begged for the privilege of serving on Judenrats and of becoming security guards and crematoria operators and, in thousands of individual instances, curried the favor of SS guards while others openly set upon the total destruction of their race.

How much more was it to be anticipated that the African should suffer difficulties in reasoning and perception after hundreds of years of cruel manipulation and conditioning?

When we understand how deeply the African had in the past related himself to his tribe, and its history, and to his ancestors whose existence he saw as being tied to his own through one thread, connecting himself and the present with those dead and those yet to be born — when we reflect upon the true philosophical meaning of such an attitude, then we can begin to understand somewhat the dimension of the tragic disorientation which must have taken place in the being of the African transplanted to the new world.

His past life had rested upon "community" and "Ujaama" — upon the need for collective concern among, and responsibility for, the tribe. His transplantation to the Americas abruptly tore him from everything his life had come to rest upon — his history, his institutions, and his philosophies.

There is nothing that can be said of the North American slave experience that would adequately condemn it. But at the very least all observers would have to admit that there can be found no comparable historic parallel to the horror and inhumanity of it.

Its horror lay largely in the fact that it was not simply designed to overpower and subdue the will of the enslaved; it was designed to modify, distort, and remake the instinctive drives of an entire race of men and women so that they would not be able to reason or distinguish fact from fancy, or to desire those things that other men desired. It was hoped to make of a man an articulate, obedient beast of burden which would have a special desire to serve loyally and love its master more than itself, notwithstanding any degree of cruelty imposed upon it.

Hitler sought to destroy a people; for that, he was condemned. The slave master sought objectively, by his program, to make a utilitarian, unfeeling, unthinking, undesiring humanoid — a unique impersonal living tool and thing which would self-generate and keep bringing into being for his own use offspring so modified from the normal that they would in turn willingly serve the system of horror.

The enslaver intended that these captured men and women should slowly come to see themselves and their institutions as nothing — to forget the things of the past — to forget and despise their languages and tribal identities and any meaningful connection they might have had with any land. The enslaver intended that these men and women should be drawn to and attracted by his white skin, stringy hair, and passionate devotion to the unbridled use of power. And black men were.

The black man who resisted conditioning and indoctrination was disposed of as the useless by-product of the social experiment. He was simply killed and removed from the system.

The "useful" end-product of the system was this denatured black man — made a "Negro." He was a special breed of life — sport in the human species — like a peculiar strain of dog that would neither bark, bite, nor eat meat, and that had no ability to follow a scent, or inclination to chase a cat or a fox — i.e., a "freak" among the dog family.

And this manufactured "Negro" was every bit as much a freak or sport among the human family as that dog described above. Here we saw a humanoid, devoid of the normal instincts which most members of the human family possess — lacking any desire whatever to take control of land and to go for himself — loving his master much more than himself or his mate or his own offspring, and happily reveling in his state of subjugation — evidencing no inclination whatever to make any of the vital decisions affecting his own life.

The South African experimenters who produced that species of dog that will only attack black men have not yet reported to us whether the descendants of these peculiar and freakish dogs regain their natural inclination to attack white and black alike; and we do not really know whether, so far as this American "Negro" is concerned, he will ever be able to overcome the effects of the past and regain his full humanity and all of his natural instincts, including his will to control his own life, to have some land, and to exercise sovereignty over that land for the benefit of himself and his posterity.

That is the question and the great fear that remains foremost in my mind today. Any fair evaluation of the majority thinking among blacks living in this country will suffice to strengthen that doubt.

Our most renowned pre- and post-Civil War political spokesman, Frederick Douglass, who so eloquently castigated the slave masters on their celebration of Independence Day while holding a quarter million blacks in chains, spoke from his figurative knees to white men, and not black men, begging and imploring them to let black men loose from their bonds — so that they might the better participate with the white man in running whatever kind of system white men had going for them. Check him out if you don't believe it. He considered John Brown's plan for a separate state for liberated slaves to be extreme and unrealistic. He considered the American Colonization Society, which hoped to transport black men back to their homelands in Africa, to be "that old offender against the best interests, and slanderers of the colored people."

His considered end, eloquently fought for, was freedom for blacks to join their enslaver — the kidnapper, raper, and murderer of his family, and the open despoiler of everything black, brown, or yellow. He wanted to see black men join this monster in his nefarious empire building, cannibalistic activities — as a junior partner in the enterprise — as a sharer in the arch-criminal's ill-gotten gains.

So pervasive has the spiritual malignancy affecting black men in North America been, whether of intellect or not, that even Harvard-trained, Berlin-educated W.E.B. DuBois, failing to comprehend the true outreach of Garvey's call for a Black Man's Government, argued with sincere conviction against the questions posed by Garvey in his program for complete liberation.

Even as late as the middle decade of the 20th century, long after DuBois had perceived that the problem of the 20th century was the problem of the color line, Martin Luther King spoke with conviction and assurance to millions of black men who, sharing the dream of Frederick Douglass, wanted inclusion into the system run by Satan himself.

And, Martin Luther King was, and is, glorified and made a Messiah, a modern-day Moses, by thinkers such as Bayard Rustin, A. Philip Randolph, Roy Wilkins, Whitney Young, and a host of lesser "leaders" who devote themselves to selling the lie that separation is the last resort of "desperate men," violent men, who are such because the system has failed to let them share its goodies.

These prophets of integration and partnership have always, throughout our North American experience, been given great notoriety and currency and accolades from the slave master and his children. And the merits of separation, land, and power have always been pooh-poohed by white men and talked and thought of almost exclusively by black men with a superior love for their people and for true liberation.

Henry Highland Garnett, who stated so well that it would better if we all died right now than pass our wretchedness on to successive generations, tried his very best to get Frederick Douglass to understand what the American Colonization Society was really talking about. He tried, over one hundred years ago, to make Douglass understand the difference between running your own house and being a house nigger who helped to run someone else's.

John Brown, a white man, tried to convince Douglass that once black men had been freed they should establish their own separate land in what would now be the foothills of Virginia, West Virginia, and Kentucky. He tried mightily to convince Douglass that this was the only way the freed slave, who had purchased his liberation through struggle, could protect his existence. Douglass, for some inexplicable reason, refused to countenance any political separation of territory from the then constituted United States.

Marcus Garvey came along a little later. He asked the simple question: Where is the black man's government – his Army, his Navy, his men of great affairs? He answered his own question for millions of black men and women by saying simply, "I cannot find them." And, with a spark divinely given, he said, "I shall help to make them." And he put his vision to work. He made black men proud of being black. He made black men turn to their roots – to Africa – to building for self, and to commerce with other black persons around the world. He made black men see themselves as a majority African people. And he argued that black men should return to Africa and strengthen it, leaving this white man to his just destiny. In the years of Garvey's heyday, DuBois contended with his separatist thinking, though it must be said, to his great credit, that he came to understand in later years and to be a great force, along with Kwame Nkrumah, for Pan-Africanism and African Nationalism in the broadest and highest sense of those terms.

After Garvey, the Hon. Elijah Muhammad talked of Black Nationhood and Black Statehood – as did Oscar Brown Sr., talking of a separate state for blacks; but no one really heard what these more recent black thinkers were saying to a whole race of people. It was not heard until Malcolm X came to repeat what Messenger Muhammad had taught him and to enlarge upon those ideas – namely, that we are an African people, in the wilderness of North America; a nation of people, enslaved and held captive, with a community of suffering and a common experience and lifestyle and humor that has welded us in every sense into a separate nation in the midst of another white nation. Malcolm made it clear that our oppression had been common to us all simply because we were black – and for no other reason.

No one really wanted to believe Malcolm when Martin Luther King was telling us so eloquently and sweetly that one day the oppression would end, that justice would flow down like a river, and righteousness like a mighty stream. No one really wanted to believe Malcolm when Martin was making clear the meaning of a dream in which he saw little black boys and little white boys playing ring-around-the-rosy on the red clay hills of Georgia. No one really wanted to believe Malcolm when Martin was pleading so eloquently for integration into the white man's nation – and suggesting to the slave masters' children, as Douglass had done a century before, that integration ought to be effected because the system was losing the benefit of black talents which it ought to coopt for the sake of the smooth operation of the system.

No – Malcolm, like the prophets of separation and liberation before him, was not to be given any currency or accorded any respectability in the white media; and, of course, if he couldn't be regarded in the white media, he certainly couldn't be respected in black quarters.

The one redeeming thing about our history in North America has been, as we look back on it, that there have been those few men whose spirits have tingled with the very thought of self-determination and land – whose souls and minds and hearts have been truly free – men whose thoughts have broken through the barrier of all the intellectual nonsense forced on black men over the years. And, because of those few men, we know today that some fires in human hearts are truly unquenchable – that the love of family, tribe, and nation will not be extinguished by hundreds of years of torture, mistreatment, rape, robbery, murder, and cruelty.

Isaiah promised that God would not suffer the smoking flax to be extinguished, nor the bruised reed to break; though the attempt to suppress our weakly burning and smoking fires for nationhood and to break us as a people has been made for over 400 years, we can announce this afternoon that we are not broken as a people, and our fires for liberation and nationhood and land are not out. In spite of all the past, the wormwood and the gall, we can today announce with Jeremiah that "We have not been consumed" and we have not died out.

In spite of it all, the fever and the boils, the loss of sons and daughters, possessions and wealth, and esteem, we announce today, along with Job, that our "latter will be more blessed than our beginning"; when we consolidate our nation, "we shall have restored to us more than we had before of beautiful sons and daughters, wealth, and self-esteem."

In spite of it all, the assaults of the incarnate offspring of Satan, we declare today that God has given his angels charge over our nation, to keep it in all its ways against the terror that comes by night and the pestilence that flies by day.

In spite of it all, we declare this afternoon, along with Joel and Isaiah, that old black men are dreaming dreams of nationhood and land – that they are mounting up with wings like eagles, they are running their course without getting tired, and are walking on two feet without feeling faint.

To Bayard Rustin and all of his persuasion, we declare this morning that the thrust for separation is not some ploy designed to get white folks to help us share in the tainted goods this nation has so unjustly wrenched off the backs of the exploited black, brown, and yellow people of this earth.

We declare to you that our thrust for self-determination is not a gimmick – or a publicity stunt. It is not a power play aimed at getting a better position in the white man's system; and it actually has nothing whatever to do with helping white men survive. *It simply has to do with the matter of freeing black men from the grip of white men.* Can you dig that, Bayard?

We are a nation of field niggers, as Malcolm said. We want to run our own house – the way we want to run it, not according to the old masters' plan. And, in a deeply spiritual sense, we ask with Paul, "What commerce hath righteousness with unrighteousness?" We want to build a new and better society in a new and better world. Can you dig that, Bayard Rustin? We want to be able to deal with other nations of the world, diplomatically, representing the interests of our black nation. We are sick and tired of never being able to hear our desires and wishes articulated in and among the nations of the world. We are tired of not being able to help our brothers diplomatically in South Africa, Rhodesia, Mozambique, and wherever else oppression and aggressive cannibalistic white power operates to the detriment of black people. Can you dig that, Bayard Rustin? Is there something freakish about that desire?

More than diplomatically, we want to deal with other nations of the world through our own men of great affairs – commercially, aesthetically, and culturally. We want our sons and daughters to have open commerce with all the peace-loving peoples of the world. Not on the basis of economic cannibalism, but on a fair and equitable basis, with mutual respect and regard. Can you dig that?

More than on a foreign level, we want to end the crime, the social dislocation, the unemployment, the spiritual degradation among our own people at home. Government can plan an overall economy. Government can get rid of unemployment. Government can operate relevant schools and eliminate illiteracy and ignorance. Government can, in fact, eliminate poverty. Can you dig that, Bayard Rustin?

We want spiritual and social excellence. The end to the use of narcotics and other artificial stimulants and props made so much a part of this white man's thing. And we want our own theater, dance, and art – free and uncontaminated by white folks. Can't you dig that?

We are a nation of great resources. When men possessed of skills combine, and these skills are applied to land, you have a true measure of national size and greatness. Based on this formula, we, as a nation of 40 million of the most trained blacks on earth, when put in touch with a land mass that has agricultural potential, timber and minerals, and that has access to the sea lanes, can become potentially the greatest nation on earth.

Japan, with 90 million people pressed into a land mass one-tenth the size of the United States – lacking iron, bauxite, copper, gold, silver, zinc, tin, lead, cotton, or wood pulp – has, by application of its people's intellectual and technical skills to their available and importable resources, made itself into the third greatest industrial power on earth.

Black men, with 40 million trained people, dedicated to the making of a new life for themselves, operating on a land mass one-sixth the size of the United States, could become the greatest industrial nation on earth. Only our lack of faith in what we are and what we possess could prevent us from reaching that goal.

If the Japanese, by dividing their skilled persons into Zaibatsus, or families such as Mitsui (devoted to banking and trading and mining) or Mitsubishi (devoted to heavy industries, chemicals, and electronics) or Sumitomo, or Yasuda (devoted to their various economic pursuits) could make their nation viable, how much more so could this black man in America do the same.

Young black men, on graduating from universities, would enter the service of their nation, giving it full loyalty and helping their nation to develop its overall potential.

What is to prevent us from running our own seaports and traversing our own shipping lanes, from undertaking our own economic course, and from assisting those of our brothers who are beleaguered militarily? Nothing at all – but our own slavish devotion to master.

Demographic and geographic conditions rationally dictated that the RNA settle upon the land mass represented by the present states of Mississippi, Louisiana, Alabama, Georgia, and South Carolina as the only possible location for the new African nation. Whenever we mention acquiring this land mass for the nation, some "Negro" of little vision or faith asks how we intend to get that land – if we expect the Congress to give it to us. Actually, we expect to acquire the land through both diplomatic and political means, but we also are keeping full in mind the case of the Cherokee Nation and the State of Georgia.

Those who know anything at all about the Cherokee Indians know that prior to the coming of the white man they extended their influence over the entire lower eastern coastal area of the United States. And, at the time of the coming of the white adventurers from Europe, their sovereignty was supreme in the territories where they resided. With typical honky arrogance, Europeans sailed down the Atlantic coastline, looked toward the shores being traversed, and said, "Everything within our sight is ours and subject to our power."

Most of us sitting here cannot even visualize this type of mentality. Certainly, we could not look upon a strange land and bring ourselves to utter, "Everything in there is ours." But this was the mentality of that European monster who came to the New World in search of plunder. When he came ashore, he came with his smile and a willingness to smoke the Indian's peace pipe. Indians with some acquaintance with these strangers and their devious ways would have been suspicious of their ingratiating manner, but they could not have had any basis for suspicion since in all their experience they had never met any men like those in basic dishonesty.

Almost contemporaneous with the smiling and the smoking of the peace pipes, came elaborate, wordy documents for the Indians to sign, drafted by the whites to define the conditions under which the two peoples would occupy the Cherokee land. That such documents were sought by the whites and made necessary for the joint occupation of the land by the whites should have alerted the Indians to the inherent dishonesty and craft of the newcomers. But, it was only after the signing of 18 such documents, more properly "treaties," that the Cherokee began to understand the nature of the trouble they were in for. Up to that point, the Cherokee were an acknowledged and recognized sovereign nation of people. They had their own laws, their own customs, their own ways of marrying, punishing criminals, and adjusting relations and disputes between individual members of the tribe. They had their own religion and their own scheme and system of justice.

As the whites signed treaty after treaty with the Cherokee, they successively expanded their land holdings and pushed the Cherokee back from the Atlantic coastal areas into a small land mass in the center of the State of Georgia. Finally, after they had flooded the land with as many cracker scum as they could cull out of the dark recesses of Europe, they demanded that the Cherokee submit to their legal authority and repair to their courts, which they (in breach of their own skillfully prepared treaties) had erected in Georgia upon land admittedly within the sovereign control of the Cherokee. In protest against this violation, the Cherokee took his cause to the United States Supreme Court and, in 5 Peters (U.S. Reports), we read what happened. Justices Marshall and Jackson wrote illuminating opinions for the court, but it is Justice Jackson whose words hold the most meaning for us today.

Justice Jackson, speaking fully for the cracker mentality, said crudely out of his blatant white power bag that this matter *was not one for the decision of any court;* that the matter was a matter *to be reserved to the sword;* that where one nation asserts its sovereignty over another nation, it is the duty of the nation imposed upon to assert its own power against the intruder or forfeit any claims or pretensions of sovereignty. If the intruder cannot be successfully resisted, then the one imposed upon must forget all talk of sovereignty. In other words, for him and the U.S., "sovereignty" is solely a matter of who has the sharpest and most powerful sword; all other questions, either moral or legal, are subordinate to that question.

Thus, the law is that when someone wants to interpose his authority over your life, your institutions, your entire way of thinking, and make you over into what he says you ought to be, it is not a question to be debated at law at all. It is a question in which the final arbiter is, in *white folks' minds*, the sword. That is the Supreme Court speaking – not me.

But we are not foolish enough to believe that blacks can assert "sovereignty" over five states of the United States at this moment and not experience the "cut of the sword." We are wise enough to believe that the same God who has preserved us from destruction over 400 years of white oppression can, and will, show us the means by which the potential sword can be broken into ploughshares and the spear into pruning hooks, and the U.S. can be made to study the art of war no more.

Without discussing military tactics, we know perfectly well that you cannot preserve or own anything that you can't protect. You can't have a wife, a child, or anything at all that you can't protect. The states we choose can be protected against outside aggression by the acquisition of internal political power within the area and the diplomatic courting of friendly nations outside the area.

When we look at the Port of New Orleans, we note that it faces on the Gulf of Mexico, that the Gulf also faces Cuba, Haiti, and the Islands, borders on Mexico and touches Guyana and other parts of South America.

When we look at South Carolina, we find it to be important to the maintenance of our sovereignty. Once, in the past, its ports were used against us as a means of helping the slaver get his ill-begotten cargo to these shores. We think that perhaps this process could be reversed out of those same ports, and there are important reasons why this must be so.

This morning I heard the brothers speaking of the problems and needs of our brothers engaged in the South African struggle for freedom and liberation. I have the feeling, before it is all over, that South Carolina will furnish an important link with black people on the African continent and that the existence of independent South Carolina ports makes possible the realistic furnishing of military, medical, and other assistance to our beleaguered African brothers, and vice versa.

Our acquisition of land and free access to the seas is essential to true black liberation. To hope that beleaguered blacks in Africa can be aided by blacks on this side of the ocean, as we in the RNA envisage such aid must be given, is sheer folly, since blacks, *because of U.S. sovereign law*, are kept from engaging in any commerce from U.S. ports, except in accord with laws oriented to protect and preserve worldwide white power interests.

Only a free and independent government can open the now tightly shut avenues to commerce and cooperation which must exist between these two branches of the same human family, now artifically separated from one another by a mere 6000 miles of ocean and pervasive white law and power.

Like a genie in a bottle, whose awesome power can never be realized until he escapes from its confines, the power and might of blacks in the new world to aid the liberation of blacks in the old is restricted by our own lack of independence and the overall extention of U.S. sovereignty over black lives. The cork to our bottle is U.S. sovereignty. The cork is removed only by political independence.

Apart from these considerations, I like the land mass we have chosen. I also like North Carolina, and I frankly do not see how we could neglect to include North Carolina with its beautiful weather and fragrant pines, mountains, and coastal beaches. But, I equally like South Carolina and Mississippi, the bay and the gulf areas – Biloxi and Gulfport – all the area . . . just beautiful. In my mind's eye I can see them converted into black resorts for black people. Do you understand what I am talking about?

Then run down into Georgia and farther on into Florida and contemplate the land. Yet, when I look at the land, I do not see its natural beauties alone. I see electrical wires already strung. One of the things I observed in Ghana were young men stringing electrical wires on posts in Accra, a major city of the country. When I look around the most remote rural areas of Mississippi, Louisiana, Alabama, Georgia, and South Carolina, I see electrical and telephone wires and radio and television towers. I anticipate that after we take over, nobody is going down there and pull up a single one of those lines – not a single one. We intend to take everything as it is – the infrastructure intact. We want every last high tension tower down there, every last power line. We want every last television tower, every last radio tower. It is our infrastructure, and we are going to need it to run our own nation. So we don't want anybody blowing up anything down there in those five states. We intend to have, and will have, law and order in this regard.

Then look at the Gulf Coast in Louisiana. Here you've got the great Mississippi River. And you also have shrimp boats and offshore oil rigs. And, I am sure the crackers operating these things now don't know what I see in my mind's eye. How did they get it? They ought not ask me how I am going to get it. How the hell did they have nerve enough to walk into Africa and take my ancestors? And now the kidnapper dares to question me as to the means by which I intend to get a piece of land. I would say frankly that I intend to take it by the same right that you took my ancestors from their homeland. That's how I intend to get it: by the same right that justified you taking and using me. That's how I am going to get it. In any event, the issue is not one for white people to decide. The issue in the first analysis is one for black men to decide.

I tell you, as a matter of fact, that if white people were moral they wouldn't object to our plans, because the moral man would understand that when he has taken from a whole people he ought to try to make right what he did wrong. Jesus said that if you do wrong against somebody, there is only one way to make it right. Go to the one wronged. Tell him you acknowledge your wrong to him. Give him back what you took from him. Ask for his forgiveness. And then you can have reconciliation. Don't you know that that's the only way this world can be straightened out? There's no way in hell that six percent of the world's people can continue to gobble up 75 percent of the world's goods without there being trouble. Jesus said again how wrong it was to have this world's goods and, seeing what your brother needs, withhold it from him and say the love of God dwells in you. I agree. It simply is not possible.

But, further, under Anglo-Saxon legal principles, if I kidnapped anybody in this room and took him to my home and started working him, and he had the chance to escape from my clutches, he could take me into court anywhere in this country and get relief against me. Number one, the penalty for kidnapping – for me to go around and kidnap anybody and carry him even 15 feet against his will – is death. That's what Robert Williams is fighting about right now. The penalty for kidnapping all over this country is death.

Bruno Richard Hauptman was said to have kidnapped one little honky child from a guy named Lindbergh. He was said to have stolen and killed just one little brat. People in the United States got so up in arms that they called the Congress in session. Congress didn't come up for air until it had drafted a law that provided that anybody that put his hand on another human being and moved him one inch against his will with the intent to use him for his benefit would have to die. The penalty for kidnapping was announced by the Congres to be death. Congress so ordained. I didn't. Now, if the penalty for kidnapping one little honky brat is death, what the hell ought the penalty be for kidnapping 100 million Africans from their native land and transporting them 6000 miles from their homes to serve the kidnapper?

If we can sit here this afternoon and consider the value Congress put on the head of one honky child, we ought to wonder how a whole race of black people can be so indifferent to the value of the millions of black lives, personality, and minds destroyed by the monster kidnapper. If we can eat our meals without being disturbed, under the circumstances, then we are indeed freaks – something is unquestionably wrong with us.

We are simply saying, evaluating what has been done to us by his own standards, that a capital crime was committed in bringing us here to these shores. And, if I stole you, in a historical sense, and took you to my house and worked you, and you got away from me, if I didn't suffer the death penalty the next thing you could do to me is take me into court anywhere in this land for a civil judgment. I don't know of one state in this land where you couldn't take me into court. And you know what the court would do to me? Number one, if I stole you and took your labor, I would have to give an account. How much labor did you do for me? I would have to sit down and listen where you told the court that you shined my silver or my shoes, or that you cut my grass. And the court would say that cutting grass is worth $1.59 per hour. Then the court would add it all up and render an account for the value of your service to me, saying, everywhere in this land, that I didn't have a right to steal the product of your labor without paying you. Judgment would be entered against me and in your favor for the amount of the account. Whatever the account was, then that's what the judgment would be. That's the judgment due for my stealing a man and taking his labor.

Yet, when James Forman says there ought to be reparations given them, black people sit around this country and they criticize that. Whites yell likewise, "We ain't going to give you no reparations." "We never stole nobody." They have the temerity to say to you, "I never had no slaves." "I don't owe you nothing."

Well, I want to go back and give you another example. The law in every state of this union is that if I go down to a bank and steal the bank's money and put it in my basement, and the bank comes down after I die and my wife is sitting over there in the house with all that gold, my wife can't tell the bank that it is not their money. The law says that a thief never acquires title to stolen property. The fact that you kept the property for a time doesn't convey any title to the property. Neither the thief, nor his heirs, can ever acquire title to stolen property; therefore, the gold that I stole out of the bank must be restored to the bank, and neither my wife nor my children, nor anyone else, can use that gold and come back and tell the bank, "I'm sorry, we're not going to give it back to you." There is no theory of law that justifies this. Further, the bank would be entitled to recover all of the wealth that you obtained as a result of your use of the money stolen from it, on the theory that a thief cannot be "unjustly enriched" at the expense of his victim.

Eric Williams, in his book *Capitalism and Slavery,* says that basically the United States doesn't have a damn thing in this system of theirs that wasn't traceable to, and paid for by the system of black chattel slavery. If he said the whole goddamn system was built on the backs of black men, then I am actually entitled to the whole damn system.

If stolen labor is responsible for whatever financial preeminence this nation has, then I say to this nation that it owes the descendants of the stolen laborers all that has so unjustly resulted therefrom. That's the law – and fair is fair.

But more than that, I say that there is another principle of law operating here, and that principle of law relates to punitive damages. If I stole you and took you and used you, not only ought I to pay you back the value of your stolen labor, but I ought to have to pay you enough money to make everybody understand that I realized the gravity of the wrong I had perpetrated upon you. So, I would have to pay you exemplary, or punitive, damages. Damages large enough to make it hurt me. You would be entitled to enough money to make me feel something of the weight of the wrong I had done you.

White people in this country think it is all right to just pass over their injustices. They feel they don't have to do anything at all for black folks, that they actually haven't done anything wrong to them, notwithstanding that they are all the unworthy beneficiaries of the wealth produced from criminally coerced labor. And, they have no compunctions against using the ill-gotten wealth to enslave, cripple, and exploit weaker nations in this world.

But nowadays we say that you've got to pay. Now you can sit down with us as we have attempted to compel the United States Government to do by delivery of our diplomatic note to the State Department which set forth the basis of reparation.

We didn't ask for very much. We wanted only $400 billion in cash. That's really chump change – not very much at all. We want, in addition to the monetary settlement, the transfer of five states to our sovereignty – then we can be friends. That's the basis for healing the wounds of the past – for making reconciliation.

We don't want the U.S. to pay it to us individually. Don't give me any $15 or $20 or $10 down. We don't want it individually. Make the reparations payable to the nation. And then the nation will go on from there. Once we have the nation consolidated, all of these white folks can do whatever they want to do to the north of our borders. They can do their thing in their own way, subject of course to the fact that we are not going to be allied to them in doing whatever they want to do; subject, of course, also to the fact that we are going to be interested in black liberation throughout the world – black liberation. Subject also to the fact that we are not going to be controlled by them, or be their little black puppet, notwithstanding anything anyone might think to the contrary.

And so, what we are saying simply is that this would be a fair basis for a peaceable resolution of the race problem in the United States. The Good Book says that the sins of the fathers will be transferred down to the children of the third and fourth generations. And God knows the Scripture is accurate as to the United States. The United States is about to tear apart, and it is being torn apart at the seams by conditions spawned by former generations of slaves.

The United States defies the immutable laws of the universe and the Creator when it expects that it can take all of the benefits that have derived from its institution of slavery for hundreds of years and now does not attempt to do justice toward those so cruelly wronged.

There is actually but one proper way to handle the problem, and we offer that way in the RNA.

Moved by divine urgings and as latter-day prophets, we predict dire consequences for the United States unless it acts, as God requires, to heal the wounds of the broken-hearted, to grant deliverance to the captives, and to set at liberty those who are bruised. We, as black men, conscious of the meaning and nature of the past four hundred years of oppression, hope that we can pass on to our posterity an opportunity for life markedly different from that either we or our ancestors have known in this land. That is what the Republic of New Africa is all about.

We are not talking about getting a little piece of land under the control and domination of the United States Government. We are talking about getting free of the United States – of separating from all that has oppressed in the past – of exercising our own sovereignty. To that end, we have a flag. The flag, of course, is simply a symbolic representation of what we are all about.

The red in our flag is in the middle, and red means what red means in anybody's flag. Everywhere I have seen red and asked anybody about it, it meant "blood." We have black on the bottom and green on the top, over the blood. The green on the top means life – the opportunity for life, the eternal cycle, the refresher. Green on the top and black on the bottom. The black man, the black nation, on the bottom, because we have not yet gotten to the land represented by the green on the top.

It is the reverse of Kenya's flag. Kenya has its colors the other way arond, obviously because the black man is on top, theoretically – in Kenya he has the land. There are two spears in the middle, over the blood, so there is no mistaking what they are saying when you look at the Kenyan flag. It took "bloodshed" to get the land. In the RNA flag we, the black, are on the bottom. To get to the land we will, of course, have to shed (and we have shed) blood. History confirms the reality of this assessment. The Bible likewise confirms that except there be a shedding of blood there can be no remission of sin.

And then we, each of us, say something which reminds us of our commitment and obligation, and it goes like this:

> Freely and of my own will, I am joined with my brothers and sisters in a just and sacred cause; namely, to defend the community against armed attack, and to build a new and better society in a new and better world.

Not just locally, the whole world to be reformed – a new and better society in a new and better world. Further, we say:

> I swear that I will not betray this trust – not from cowardice, not from laxiness – not through treachery – nor any other means – to our black brothers and sisters, born and yet unborn, on our lives, this we swear.

Thank you very much.

# 5
# *Pan-Africanism—Land and Power**

STOKELY CARMICHAEL

Whether we want it or not, there are divisions among black Africans living in the United States, the Caribbean, and on the African continent, divisions which have been imposed on us by Europeans. There are geographical divisions, countries such as Senegal and Mauritania, Mozambique and Guinea, created by Europeans as they struggled for the wealth of Africa. Then there are political divisions and economic divisions, again imposed on us by Europeans.

Now they are planning to impose on us grave cultural divisions and, most of all, to divide us by naming us different things. If you are in San Francisco, for example, and you see a Japanese or a Chinese walking down the street, you do not say that there goes an American Japanese or a Japanese-American. You say simply that there goes a Japanese – period. Yet, probably, that Japanese cannot speak Japanese at all; he may be third or fourth generation in America. But no one calls him a Japanese-American. The first thing you call him is a Japanese; because a person is defined, really, at first by his physical presence, or in terms of his ancestral stock. Whether they are Chinese, Japanese, or African. The same is true of the Indians. Even in America, when you see a red Indian, you do not say he is an American; you say he is an Indian. The same is true for East Indians; the same for Phillipines. Wherever you see them, in any part of the world, you call them Chinese or what not.

The same is not true for Africans.

Let's ask ourselves why.

If you see an African in Europe, you do not say that he is an African. If you see him in America you do not call him an African. He may be Negro; he may be West Indian; he may be everything else but African. That is because Europe took its time to divide us carefully, quite carefully. And they gave us different names so that we would never, always never, refer to ourselves by the same name, which helped to insure that there would always be differences. If you say you are West Indian, it is fairly obvious that you are something different to be set apart from an African. An American Negro and an African also obviously are not the same thing.

One of the most important things we must now begin to do is to call ourselves "African." No matter where we may be from, we are first of all and finally Africans. Africans. Africans. The same also happens to be true of North Africa. When they say "Algerians" or "Egyptians," they are talking about Africans because Africa happens to be one solid continent. Among Africans there are and must be no divisions. They are just Africans – period.

You must also understand that there are two types of oppression, basically. One is exploitation. Another is colonization. With exploitation, one is economically raped; for example, in the 1930s the labor movement was a response to economic exploitation. Rich white people, in that instance, were exploiting poor white people. But there is another type of oppression – colonization. Colonization is not just the economic raping of someone, not merely taking a lot of money away. Colonization deals with destroying the person's culture, his language, his history, his identification, his total humanity. When one is colonized, one is totally dehumanized. So that when the victims of colonization fight, they are fighting for a process of humanization.

This is entirely different from the fight of people who are only exploited. The people who are exploited fight just for economic security. The colonized fight beyond economic security, far beyond. And so, it seems to me that as we begin the search for allies and coalitions we can only form alliances and coalitions based on whether those people are fighting for the same thing, fighting the same fight that we who have been colonized are fighting. In other words, people who are fighting for their humanity. This means, for example, that all non-white people who have been colonized can join hands, understanding of course that our fights remain entirely different.

The people who have been colonized by white folk, let us say, in Asia, are fighting the same fight but a different fight because of culture, humanity. Their way of life is and will be entirely different from ours. But they are fighting nonetheless and fighting for a humanity of their own, albeit the same thing in a sense that we are fighting for, to affirm our humanity. We are fighting to affirm our humanity. We are fighting to affirm our humanity. With those non-white people we can begin to move so long as they understand precisely what the fight is all about and that we may differ in some respects.

In America, folk seem to think that the revolution there –

*From *The Black Scholar*, November 1969, by permission.

if there is such a thing, or even if there will be such a thing – will all be over in five years, when actually we are talking about a generation of struggle. That is why they always have deep questions in their minds to trouble them. They fail to understand that the struggle we are talking about inside America is only symptomatic of a world-wide struggle against Europe and its satellites. America, in fact, is nothing but Europe. The white people in America are not Americans but, in fact, are Europeans. When we call them Americans, we allow them to escape; we define them incorrectly. We should call them Europeans and understand that they never belonged to America, that they took that continent from somebody else. When you call them Americans you forget that they were Europeans because you give them the theory of native origin, that they came out of America. Where did Americans come from? They come from America – that is, somebody you call American. But if you say that they are Europeans (which is what they are), then the question arises as to where they came from – Europe. What are Europeans doing in what is now called America?

We must understand that because it shows how deep our struggle really, really, really is. These are things we do not even think about, because, if you see what I have been saying up to now, you also will see that, in the final analysis, the struggle is going to be waged with Europeans against non-Europeans. And that means that America is European. That means that our struggle is not five or ten years but is, in fact, a generation. Once we understand that our struggle is at least a generation, then we do not even have to worry about so many little things. We will know, then, that we are not going to see any really concrete or substantive victories in our fight for at least five or ten years. I mean to say anything really concrete enough for us to look at and say that that is what we have been able to do.

At this point, it becomes important that you have people of African descent – scattered over the Western hemisphere by Europeans, scattered across the West Indies and used so long as slaves – bound together in a unified struggle for their liberation. This is not impossible inasmuch as we have people today all over the world moving forward in the quest for liberation against their oppressors.

Because I understand so clearly the foregoing factors, the ancestral roots of the problem, I have concluded that the solution has to be Pan-Africanism. Everybody – DuBois, Padmore, or whoever – always comes back at last to Pan-Africanism. Pan-Africanism is not just some nonsensical black nationalism. Even white philosophers understand this fact. For example, Plato in *The Republic* talks about the theory of Antaeus.* The parable of Antaeus, says Plato, shows that the philosopher king has come up out of the earth, that the people grew out of the earth. They were asking "Where are we from?" Plato says that you must always answer that question: "Where are we from?" In his book he says that the people come out of the earth, have grown up there, so that they always fight for that earth; and for the ideas that come out of that earth. And they always will. So black people (us) come out of that earth, and we always will; and so black people (us) must stop running around in circles. We have to have our theory of Antaeus – where we are from. If black people in the States say "where are we from?" they must wind up at Africa. One must know one's beginning, who one is, before one knows where one is going.

People who regard Pan-Africanism negatively, who think that it is a racist theory, ought to read George Padmore's book, *Communism or Pan Africanism.* Padmore is clear on this. Writing around the 1930s, and one of the advisers to Dr. Nkrumah, Padmore was crystal clear on the point that we must talk about Pan-Africanism. I believe that people who talk about "Marxism-Leninism" so hard, in such a hard line, are people who are groping for an answer. They seize on "Marxism-Leninism" as if it were some sort of a religion. Marx becomes, in essence, Jesus Christ. Now anything you cannot answer you take over and bow to Marx. That, in my view, is absolutely absurd. At least for me.

I cannot claim to understand all of Marxism-Leninism. I have read very little of them and understand little of what I have read. So, for me to jump up and say that I am a Marxist-Leninist is for me to be intellectually dishonest and, in fact as well, a damn liar. Yet, though I do not fully understand all that you folk are talking about, I do have certain universal concepts which happen to agree with the things that Marx was talking about. But, just because I have these concepts does not mean that Marx was the man who taught them to me. I knew them before I read Marx. So, even if I agree with them, why now should I call myself a Marxist? Tunisian Ibn-Khaldun spoke of Marx's concept of surplus value, for example, as early as the 15th century. Why should I give Marx the credit for plagiarizing Khaldun? Marx only wrote down universal truths about oppression. He did not invent all of them.

Everybody can arrive at these truths himself. I don't need necessarily to read Marx, though Marx wrote it down more fully. I give Marx the credit for writing it down, of course, for being a good writer. But Marx wrote down the universal truths of those who came way back before Marx. Right here in Algeria there was Ibn-Khaldun. For me, to always look to Marx is once again to give the credit for everything good to Europe. Once again I continue to stress my own inferiority as an African. Ready to unify my country, I continue to look to a European, Marx, to unify me. I say "Marx, Marx, Marx," and once again I am looking to Europe. People with this approach do not believe that they themselves can originate something worthy, which becomes very damaging.

People in that frame of mind are going in circles and they of course are going to be aided by our oppressors. They are going to be aided whenever they travel in circles. When a man's lost and you know that he is going in circles trying to get to you, you do not tell him "Look, man, you are going in circles." Even if you did you would be unable to show him the proper path. If you said "Look, man, you are going in circles," he would get mad at you and keep on moving. He would lay back and then he would say, "O.K. man, let's go." Don't get in a man's way when he's going in circles.

And yet, I view the struggle in the States as part and parcel of the entire world struggle, particularly the black world struggle. That is to say, I cannot see the struggle in the States as any different from the struggle anywhere else where men are fighting against a common oppressor. Our fight is clearly a fight against both capitalism and racism. One does not get rid of capitalism without fighting against racism.

I cannot agree with the ideology that says that capitalism

*Antaeus was a giant wrestler who was invincible as long as he was touching his mother, the earth.

and racism are two different entities unto themselves. I would have you struggle against both. To get rid of capitalism – I repeat – is not necessarily to get rid of racism. As a matter of fact, I think that black people ought to know this better than anyone else. I think that, in terms of reality and history and my own ideology, all of the movements that we have been building up in terms of black nationalism, from the sit-ins for coffee to "black power," run straight to Pan-Africanism. We always come back to that.

We need a base that can be used for black liberation, a land that we can say belongs to us. We do not need to talk too much about it. That will harm the struggle. When one needs a base one needs also to prepare for armed struggle. To seize any of the countries in Africa today that are dominated by white people who have physically oppressed us is to confront an armed struggle, a prolonged struggle.

But once we have seized a base we will be on our way. We will then have to demonstrate our willingness to fight for our people wherever they are oppressed. I believe that people basically defend their own kind, as America did during the Spanish Civil War. In the Middle East they did it even in 1967 with Israel. People who didn't have any rights in that country were flying in from all over the world to fight. There's nothing wrong with our doing the selfsame thing. It can be done and, most important, we are trying to secure a political ideology as we seek a state. We are beginning to understand our movements and to see how we can move politically, so that we begin to talk clearly and critically now about Pan-Africanism. It is a discussion that must begin.

There are many people who live in Europe and America who support lands which do not belong to them. Concretely. They wage so large a propaganda campaign that one cannot say anything about their country without being automatically labeled "anti . . ." to the point where one is even afraid to move for fear of falling into that label. If we obtain a bigger base than they have we can do a better job than they do because we have more rights to be in Africa than they have to be where they are.

Malcolm X said that one fights for revolution but that in the final analysis revolution is based on land. He was absolutely correct. You have to have land in order to produce, in order to feed, shelter, and clothe your people. People fight the revolution not solely for ideas; they fight also for a better way of life, and they incorporate new ideas introduced to them that promise a better way of life. People do not just fight for ideas, unless they are sure that they can see a better way of life coming out of those ideas.

Thus, unless one can feed and clothe and shelter people who want to fight for these better ideas, there is nothing for them to fight for. In order to have a revolution one must have a clear and viable alternative for the masses, one they can understand and follow, one that can move them to struggle. I do not think that in the States there can be a clear and viable alternative for black people. I am almost convinced that there cannot be. That is not to say that the struggle cannot and will not continue.

But we cannot begin to understand clear and viable alternatives until we first obtain a land base. We have to have a land base. I think that the best place for that is Africa and in Africa the best place is Ghana. Black people in the United States meanwhile must begin to understand that there now needs to be a clear sharpening of our ideologies. Our ideology must be Pan-Africanism, nothing else. I am almost convinced of that. Once we get a land base we can begin to experiment with it and develop it and go about the concrete tasks of nation building.

One of the problems of black people is that we are always afraid to put up leaders. I don't know why. We have some fear of putting up leaders and following a leader. What we always look for instead is merely someone who has an idea. We all will agree with the idea but fail nonetheless to give concrete support to that man. We keep saying that the man is not important, that the idea alone is important, but that is not necessarily true. You have to have someone who is capable of implementing the idea. Our enemies have recognized this and, whenever they find someone able to implement a viable idea, they move to destroy him. All the time. They kill him physically, or isolate him politically, or ruin his name among us.

We allow that to happen and only after he has been destroyed does he become a hero for us. By that time it is too late. Now everybody is wearing Malcolm X T-shirts and Malcolm X, blah, blah, blah. But Malcolm today would be more important to us alive than dead, although in death he has become more famous. We need him now, and we need to know what he would do in the present case, because at least he had some ideas about where he was going before the rest of us did. He was ahead of us. We have caught up with him today in a sense but he would still be ahead of us, hopefully growing at the same rate that we are growing. But we never protect our leadership while our leaders are alive. We are afraid to do that.

We never understand history because history is always moved forward by a single person. China would not be China were it not for Mao Tse-tung. That is not to say that somebody else would not have led China, but it would not be what China is today. Vietnam would not be Vietnam without Ho Chi-minh. France would not be France without De Gaulle. England would not be England without Winston Churchill. We have to understand that. Now I have traveled all around the world. I have looked and I have seen. I have been waiting for and seeking a black man outside of our generation who knows what is going on. I have found one – Dr. Nkrumah. He knows precisely what the struggle is. We should bring Dr. Kwame Nkrumah back to Ghana. I would not deny that he made some mistakes. But he was the first person to talk about Pan-Africanism as a concrete term. And he demonstrated his willingness to fight. He sent his troops to the Congo and mobilized his troops to move to Zambia when problems developed there. He trained many guerrillas. He was the first to give Lamumba assistance. He gave his country as an open base for every African freedom fighter or liberation movement. He trained his youth in the concept of Pan-Africanism. It was he who started the whole drive for African nationalism. Dr. Nkrumah was one of the first people to wake me up. It was he who began to wake up everyone. He is the person who can bring our fight together and give us some direction to fight. We need such a person, and Dr. Nkrumah happens to be that person as far as I am concerned.

But the fact that we start in Ghana does not mean that we stop in Ghana. We must fight for the unification of Africa. That's what Pan-Africanism is all about. The unification of the mother continent at this time must take priority. The unification of the African continent is entirely different from African unity. They are two different things. They are two different terms and they are two different things. African unity means you have different states who come together and talk, talk, talk, talk. Unification of Africa means you have one state – Africa. Everybody speaks the same language, one government, one army.

So that you start in Ghana for the unification of Africa, and you recognize, if you are intelligent, that South Africa is not going to be removed by talk. It is not going to be removed by talk. It is not going to be removed by Britain, by the UN, or by anybody. Nor is it going to be removed by a handful of guerrillas. It is only going to be removed by the entire black world standing up against it, because when in fact the final confrontation over South Africa, for example, takes place, the black man will see that he is not just fighting whites in South Africa. He is fighting all of Europe, because all of Europe is going to actively defend South Africa.

We must begin to move. The whole black world must begin to move, though we will not even be able to see anything concrete for at least five to ten years. Then we begin to understand precisely our direction. We are coming closer; we are more sharply defined now. We have always been moving. Let's go back to the 1960s: we start a move for integration – a cup of coffee. Even before we got the cup of coffee, we recognized where else we were going. We were moving for the vote. By the time they were getting ready to give us the vote, we recognized that that was not it either. So now we recognize that it is Pan-Africanism.

It becomes more and more sharply defined now. It has taken since the 1960s, almost ten years, to understand precisely where we are going. Ten years to take us to Pan-Africanism, and it will probably take us another ten to sharply define what that is all about. We mistakenly believe that we can solve the problems of the United States in five years. Then, when the five years have come and gone and the problem remains unsolved, our people grow tired and say: "Well, you've been jiving me. You said five years." We should prepare ourselves for 25 years. We should always say 25, at least 25. One generation will have to fight, because there are people who are always attuned to fighting if you have indoctrinated one generation thoroughly, prepared them to fight. Then all subsequent generations are prepared to fight. Vietnam is clearly a case of that readiness.

I believe that as you study you struggle and struggle. It's like a math problem. If you are given a math problem, you may sit up all night working with it before, finally, things click and the problem is solved within five minutes. But that does not mean that you could come here and solve it in five minutes whenever you please. Before you solve it in five minutes, you have to sit down and go through that whole process of trying everything you know. If you have tried and you have eliminated all the possibilities, you now come to the one correct one. The same is true for us; that's what we have been doing in our struggle.

Pan-Africanism wants to save as many black people as possible. We will lose some. Some will even die in the struggle. We know that, but there's no need for us to emphasize those deaths. We want to emphasize what is alive. Revolution is not about dying; it is about living. People do not understand that. You kill to live; you die to live. It is not just about dying. We no longer have to prove that we are bad by dying. We want to live. Fratricide, for instance, is something that we must not in any way encourage. It is okay to back down from a fight with one's people. The impression of Pan-Africanism especially is that one must be aggressive and intolerant against the enemy; but, with one's people one must always be humble. If one says one is really serving the people, one must be humble. You are always humble to him whom you serve.

We must always be political. I think that culture, for example, is always very political. It always has been and always will be. It means that at this point Africa is ready to launch its real liberation. In order to launch its liberation, it must have a culture because a culture represents the values, the values for which one fights. If one is fighting for a revolution, one is talking about more than just changing governments and power, and that is changing the value system. What carries that value system is one's culture. What we have here is the beginning of people who are trying to grope for a real fight with the culture.

Culture is a cohesive force. It is what keeps people together. Culture is very important in the fight because a lot of people have fought against their oppressors yet maintained the culture of their oppressors; and culturally they are the same as their oppressors. They haven't fought for anything actually. All they have done is change powers, but that is not a revolution. You have to understand that changing powers is not a revolution.

Black people in America, Africans who live in America, especially must understand that and begin to alienate our people completely from the culture and values of Western society. That is going to be particularly difficult because all of us live within those values and it is going to be hard for us to root them out. I mean that it is like people who say that they want to be black. But being black is an awfully hard job in the United States.

It is very, very difficult, and we have to constantly try to understand the rejection of Western values and the picking up of new values. It is very, very difficult. But our first task is all the more to alienate our people at every chance we get from the Western culture and values, because once they are alienated there will be no influence over them. That is what we are seeking. We are seeking to stop all influence of Western culture on our people – completely. We must stop it; so we move to alienate. That is number one. Then number two: we move to give a concrete ideology that the people in the United States will adopt. They have a lot of technical skills and a lot of information which they could begin to put to the aid of the unification of Africa – spiritually, morally, and politically.

At the same time, there will be struggles inside the United States, always moving on different levels as black people keep trying to get a better way of life. These struggles will continue. I cannot say that I know exactly which way to go, but I think that some trends are very important. For example, the trends in black studies are very, very important, and they must continue because what is at stake is not the subjects but the attitude, the attitude of black people having the right to have the education that will benefit black people.

Those are the skirmishes. They are the beginnings because the rulers are not going to let us have a truly black studies or a truly black university. In the final analysis one can not have a black university in any other society than a black society because the job of the university is to propagate the values and institutions of that society. In the United States, a black university, a truly black university, is going to be totally anti-American, not just possibly anti-American, but anti-American to the point where it urges people to destroy, dismantle, disrupt, tear down, level completely in America. So you cannot have that, but that is precisely the job of the black educator, to train his people how to dismantle America, how to destroy it.

What those black study groups should now do is not just talk about Africans living in Africa, but Africans living all over the world, so that the subjects will become concrete subjects related to Africans in Africa, Africans in the Caribbean, Africans in the United States, Africans in Canada. We have to understand also that Egypt is in Africa; Algeria is in Africa. They are African and even the Arabs are going to find that the African world must come first because that is where they are continentally. They are African. That's the roots, and that's where we all have to come from.

# 6
# *Black Studies: Year One**

RICHARD A. LONG

Over 70 years ago, at Atlanta University, DuBois sought to begin a series of scientific studies of the Negro problem in America. His venture was rewarded with only a modicum of success. There was adequate encouragement at Atlanta University, poor then as now. But he rapidly discovered that philanthropic organizations and agencies, supposedly wholly dedicated to spreading the blessings of science everywhere, were a little less than enthusiastic about scientific studies of the Black man. His tale is told with affecting dispassion in *Dusk of Dawn* and again in Chapter 13 of his second autobiography, written when he was in his 90s.

In 1919, DuBois engaged in the first steps in his lifelong unattained dream, the *Encyclopedia Africana*. He was doomed to disappointment, though he pursued the idea during his long years as editor of the *Crisis* and again on his return to Atlanta University in the 1930s.

Nevertheless, the interest in the world and the background of Afro-Americans so carefully nurtured by DuBois, by Carter Woodson, by Benjamin Brawley, by Kelly Miller, and by many other eminent Black scholars of the first half of the 20th century, took a feeble hold in the hearts and minds of earnest Black seekers after truth. An important chapter in this quest for self-enlightenment was the formation of ladies' literary societies throughout the nation, at least one named for DuBois himself, and that back in 1906.

The strands and strains of the history of the study of Black folk by Afro-Americans is itself a story worth exploring and telling. Indeed, it requires exploration and telling if only because so much confusion, so much obfuscation, so much deliberate manipulation of the truth – some in ignorance, some in malice – is now the order of the day.

No people have believed more passionately in the American dream than Black Americans, though none had more reasons to disbelieve. This very faith has had disastrous consequences both for their hearts and their minds, for their souls and their science. For, consciously, Black people – Black scholars, Black thinkers – have acquiesced in a reading of their history and their experience that has been biased, inaccurate, and unscientific in the extreme. The reading in which they have acquiesced is one which, defining all history in Euro-American terms, has sought to make of Black Americans a mirror people, reflecting (usually badly) what they have been taught by the cultural arbiters of planet earth. The Black folk intelligence long ago grasped the point and expressed it in a pithy dramatic epigram:

> Black girl: Mirror, mirror, on the wall who is the fairest one of all?
>
> Mirror: Snow White! And don't *you* forget it.

The examination of this phenomena, this acquiescence in Euro-American values, is itself a proper inquiry for Black studies, for it will serve as a warning against the newer excesses that are already in full swing, as well as some of the older ones that have merely assumed Black masks. All such excesses bring truth to the service of tyranny, science to the service of cynics, and man to the service of myth.

In recent years, we have had, as part of a general reevaluation of the Euro-American ethos, the discovery that all has not been well in the study of the Black man, in what is taught (or not taught) about him, in what is written (or not written) about him, in what is examined (or not examined) about him. The discovery of such an obvious truth is not in itself remarkable, and that discovery is indeed only incidental to a larger truth – one that has always been perfectly obvious to all – that the Black man has fared ill in the world that Europeans have made. It is the reformulation of that truth, of that reality, that has engendered in its wake the demand that the study of the Black man be reformulated as well. The disproportion in the study of the Black man functions structurally in the injustice he experiences. This disproportion is a consequence of that injustice. In turn, it nurtures that injustice, provoking both a positive and a negative rationale for it.

The negative rationale is clear enough. Examine the curriculum of 90 percent of American colleges of a short year ago and you will find that nowhere can the most diligent eye find any evidence from course offerings that Black men have lived and breathed, struggled and fought, labored and created. This fact must be placed in historical perspective. Colleges of 100

*The author reminds the reader that this paper was written in the climate of 1969.

years ago carried in their course offerings little that had affected any division of the human race outside of the Hebrew Bible and the Greco-Roman world. But those colleges frankly disclaimed any competence to deal with the modern world. The American university of last year presumed to speak on all subjects to all men, and its spokesmen insisted quite vehemently that this was what they were doing. These omniscient curricula said in effect: "of the Black man there is nothing to say."

A small number of American colleges, among which the Black colleges had an important place – a fact, pointedly forgotten and ignored in the higher and rarer air where some Black studies decisions are now being made –counted the Black man in. But there, more often than not, a positive rationale for injustice was provided, for the Black man was a problem, a social disaster, a misfit.

For several years, we have had growing by leaps and bounds, a series of interrelated activities grouping around the concepts of disadvantage, cultural deprivation, social fragmentation, and psychological shipwreck. The rewards in this enterprise have been great for certain schools (none Black), for certain individuals (none Black), and for certain foundations and agencies (none Black). It is equally obvious that nowhere, anywhere, have substantive numbers of Black people, the object of so much energy and so much solicitude and so much expenditure, profited or gained or been advanced. Operation Culturally Deprived has become a mammoth industry, a classic boondoggle in the good old American tradition. Pilot study has succeeded pilot study. Model after model has been devised. The single, unvarying characteristic in all of this monumental activity exploitive of the situation of Black people is that Black people are almost never included in any of its planning and that all previous findings, knowledge, and insights (especially when they have issued from the work of Black scholars) are studiously ignored. The industry has been subjected to a scathing analysis in a recent *Freedomways* article by Dean Edward Weaver of Atlanta University.

Now, and as it were, suddenly, we have Black Studies. Not the non-study of Black people. Not the study of the culturally deprived. But study, positively oriented, based on the search for truth, for meaning, and for significance. Now we have Black Studies. But do we? Here in this first year of the Black Academic Revolution we have a literal explosion in course offerings and programs in colleges from Puget Sound to the Florida keys. But do we have Black Studies? Or are we being set up for another giant academic boondoggle that will evade rather than focus upon its ostensible object?

Certain trends and tendencies need to be noted at the moment, for the Black Studies picture is already extremely complex and threatens to become even more so. One tendency to be noted and deplored is the imperialistic approach. In the November issue of *Negro Digest*, editor Hoyt Fuller takes Mary Washington College and one Mr. Singh to task for establishing a *Black Studies Journal* in Fredericksburg, Virginia – that jewel of the Confederacy. This is clearly an act of imperialism motivated by opportunism. If Mary Washington College has had any significance at all, it is as a symbol of inaccessibility to Black people. There are surely few there now. It is, therefore, an act of presumption for it to attempt to preempt this field. If Mary Washington College has suddenly become a center for Black Studies, a journal emanating from that institution would still be hard to take, but there is not even faint justification for it. There is such a thing as academic good manners. Such an act as the establishment of a Black Studies Journal at Mary Washington College is a classic violation of this code. What do you think would be the reaction if an American college that had recently refused Jewish students were to announce itself as the home of a Jewish Studies journal? Can you imagine the consequences? In the name of decency, I invite Mary Washington College and the scholars who have rushed to the editorial board of that journal to reconsider what is clearly an act of imperialism, and I urge those interested in Black Studies everywhere to be wary of such enterprises since their very mode of conception precludes their undertaking the tasks that they announce in any constructive manner.

A second tendency is paternalism. This is kindlier in manner but equally arrogant and is, I regret to say, found everywhere money is dispersed in the name of Black Studies. Certain foundations, guided by arrogant program administrators, have already decided where the Black Studies Movement should go and propose spending their money so as to make it go in those directions. The pattern of spending of the Ford Foundation is very revealing in this regard. It has siphoned large grants to parts where Black people were unknown, with the aim of darkening the student population and the curriculum. So far as I know, these grants are never accompanied by any conditions that assure anything more than a certain amount of activity. When approached last year about supporting the first Conference on African and African-American studies at Atlanta University, the Ford Foundation blew hot and cold and finally decided it could not do anything. It was as if it had suddenly became clear that something constructive might be done about Black Studies in a Black institution, and there is, to my knowledge, no desire in those circles to see this happen.

Another tendency to be noted with some concern is a nihilistic one, which approves the existence of Black Studies but which disclaims any attempt to set up a verifiable content for such programs. In many instances such an attitude results from misunderstanding the demands of Black students for Black teachers on the faculties of their institutions. Few Black students are so naive as to believe that it is pigment cells rather than brain cells that learn and teach. But they are dealing with people who unconsciously believe this, and it is necessary to shock them out of their mythology. Establishing a Black Studies program on a completely individual and particular basis (whether this is called autonomy or not) is academic nihilism and the alacrity with which certain respectable institutions accepted such alternatives is an indictment of them for triviality. I want to make it clear, however, that in many other institutions the abolition of archaic administrative practices in connection with Black Studies programs cannot but be salutary for the whole institution.

A fourth tendency to be deplored is materialism. In a year's time, Black Studies has become a major software industry, responsive to the needs of the marketplace – a marketplace dominated by prejudice and its ally, ignorance. When we consider that this marketplace consists largely of schools and colleges, it must give us pause. Every few days a new software operation surfaces, sometimes out of conventional publishing, sometimes out of nowhere. And the profit motive is written all over the operation. One of the high priorities for those few of us who have some authority in this field is to develop at least a warning system so that time and money are not squandered on the products of what is rapidly becoming little short of criminal activity.

Having looked at four dangerous external tendencies, all of which constitute challenges to Black Studies – namely imperialism, paternalism, nihilism, and materialism – I now turn to a fundamental internal tendency, that of Black/White Studies.

The only process involved in setting up Black Studies programs in most institutions up to the moment has been the assembling of materials in the manner in which this is done for other courses, sticking the label "Black" on it, and opening the door to the classroom. What is not fully appreciated is that the materials available, for the most part, are worthless. They grow out of an ethnocentric bias so complete as to be laughable if it were not the tragedy of the age. The ultimate contribution of Black Studies can be to bring about an academic and intellectual revolution in which the whole story is told. But the whole story lies beneath the tissue of facts and non-facts; it is imbedded in premises and assumptions never once examined. Hence we note a proliferation of Black Studies courses that are merely analogous to other courses taught in the institution, with no indication that their premises are to be new, fresh, tentative. The music of Black people requires something quite different from Euro-American musical theory as Alan Lomax has so brilliantly demonstrated. The behavior of Black people will of course be aberrant if the norms do not take them into account. I see little awareness of this in the construction of Black Studies courses, but this awareness is priority number one.

In Black/white Studies, we find the conventional schools staking our territory. There is Black Freudianism, Black existentialism. These are all European constructions, not wholly applicable to American life or even to all of Europe, and yet they are generalized into world-explaining theories, and the facts of life play second fiddle to them in analyses of Black reality. They generate only Black/white Studies, aided and abetted by statistics that exclude Black people from the norms.

Black Studies is also challenged by the Cultural Deprivation Establishment. Entrenched in the nation's schools and benevolent agencies is a large career army that has earned its spurs and its bread by posing as authorities on the culturally deprived. They have conducted projects and studies, for the most part of massive irrelevancy and frequently really dangerous in their import and scope. They have been financed by government and foundation. And they are loathe to be replaced by any new orientation on their captive subject. Being pragmatists all, they are committed to the I would rather switch than fight philosophy. Accordingly we are seeking before our eyes a fabulous example of shape-shifting – the Cultural Deprivation Establishment becoming the Black Studies Establishment. I say to this, enough! Let them clean up the debris they have created. I would confine the specialists on the culturally deprived to their specialty and, as it falls to pieces before their eyes and those of their donors, let them all hie to the hills.

# 7
# *Booker T. Washington: Separatist in Disguise?**

RAYMOND L. HALL

The contemporary mood of black America, and the black separatist movements in particular, would, for a number of reasons, take any attempt at portraying Booker T. Washington as the leader of a black separatist movement as a bad joke or outright heresy. According to those who do not appreciate Washington's separatist image, he was not a "revolutionary" in the Malcolm X or Stokeley Carmichael sense, and his "Tuskegee Machine" as an organization did not operate like that of the Black Panther Party. He was not even a "militant" in his own time. Indeed, Washington even has an "Uncle Tom" image among many black Americans who claim no association with "militant" movements; he is almost universally considered by blacks to have "sold out" black interests and black dignity to the white power structure. In short, many black Americans who have any occasion to think about Washington view him and his program as accommodationism, which is regarded as an unfortunate part of black history long past. Some even conclude that Washington's leadership was an abnormal, atypical coincidence in the black separatists struggle for self-determination in America.

Black reservations about Washington's leadership are heightened in that during his time and even today most whites knowing anything about him judge him and his program as one of the most "respectable" and "responsible" ever produced by the "Negro" race – a veritable "final solution," as it were.

What was it about his program that has elicited such visceral reactions among blacks and between blacks and whites? Why is he in fact almost universally praised by whites as having a virtual "final solution" to the race question, when today, as well as in his time, many blacks regard him as misrepresenting the black cause for dignified survival? Why is it that today he has such a negative image among the predominantly young, predominantly militant, all-black separatist movements?

The obvious answer is that contemporary black separatists as well as other black Americans view Washington in a particular historical perspective. Because Washington did not overtly call for "a nation within a nation" or Black Power or posit a "revolutionary" program for black self-determination or embrace African emigration (Back-to-Africa) does not mean that he opposed any or all these alternatives, even though he may have on occasion said so. The truth more often than not can be found between examining what people say and what they do. By taking Washington's statements literally, in the short run his critics may have missed the point of his actions; in the long run his actions may still prove prophetic and beneficial to contemporary black self-determination.

Generally, taking the long view, one of the most salient facts in the black struggle in America is that there is a historical continuity in the fight for equality and self-determination. Many groups and individuals have sprung up to combat the same social reality – injustice, inequality, and the lack of choice meted out to black people by the general society. This chapter takes the position that Booker T. Washington was one of those individuals and that his movement was an attempt to alter the social reality of black oppression and powerlessness in America. The contemporary separatist movements should find it useful to study past social movements because the history of these movements may offer the opportunity to assess the contemporary prospects of "success" and "failure."

Most of the contemporary separatist movements only utilize past "militant" black social movements – and even some militant white examples, such as John Brown's raid – as models. The selection of particular past movements for ideological reasons may, in the long run, inhibit the ability of contemporary separatist movements to make use of functional elements from "non-militant" movements. The Washington movement may be an example. Despite the critics who maintain that Washington was an accommodationist, the position this work takes is that his movement's activities fit solidly in the tradition of separatist movements. What follows is an attempt to explain why.

## THE AGE OF BOOKER T. WASHINGTON: ACCOMMODATION OR SEPARATISM?

Booker T. Washington was born a slave in Franklin County, Virginia.[1] He was not sure of the place or date, but suspected that he was born in 1858 or 1859. He vividly remembered the slave quarters and the particular cabin where he lived with his mother, sister, and brother until the end of the Civil War when the slaves were declared free.

He received no schooling while he was a slave, though on several occasions he carried his slave owner's daughter's books

*Written especially for this book.

to the schoolhouse door. He wrote, "The picture of several dozen boys and girls in a schoolroom engaged in study made a deep impression upon [him], and [he] had the feeling that to get into a schoolhouse and study in this way would be about the same as getting into Paradise."

After the slaves were legally freed in 1863, his family moved to West Virginia where Washington worked in the salt furnaces. It was here that his mother somehow got him a book: a Webster's "blue-book" speller. He had to teach himself to read; he was further motivated because there came to Malden, West Virginia, a black boy from Ohio who could read. Eventually a school was opened and an ex-soldier from Ohio was made the teacher.

At first, Washington was not able to attend school full time because his stepfather did not share his enthusiasm for learning. However, Washington's mother arranged for the teacher to give him lessons at night. Later Washington was able to attend the day school. He went to work in the morning until nine, then to school, and then to work again in the afternoon for a couple of hours.

Washington tired of working in the coal mines (by this time he had also terminated his "day schooling") and took a job working for a white woman who was very hard to get along with. He made out fine with his new job, however, and the woman even urged him to read and learn. With the encouragement of his mother, he decided to go to Hampton Institute in Virginia. He arrived at Hampton with 50 cents in his pocket.

He was admitted to Hampton and worked as a janitor to pay his way. After his second year, he returned home. While he was there, his mother died. Without means and unable to get employment, he had no way of continuing his schooling. Fortunately, he was asked to return to Hampton two weeks early in order to help clean up before school opened, enabling him to earn enough money to continue his studies.

He finished Hampton in 1875 as an honor student. According to him, his greatest benefits from Hampton were his contact with the principal, General S.C. Armstrong, and learning that education meant "independence and self-reliance" and "the ability to do something which the world wants done." He returned home to teach in Malden after graduation.

He returned to Hampton as a teacher in 1879 primarily to work with a group of native Americans that General Armstrong had brought from the western United States. In addition to directing the study of native American students, Washington was asked by General Armstrong to head a night school for students who could not pay for day school. He did, and the night school became "one of the permanent and most important features of the institution." Even while in charge of the native American students and the night school, Washington pursued further studies. There were other things in store for Booker T. Washington.

"In May 1881, near the close of my first year in teaching the night school, in a way that I had not dared expect, the opportunity opened for me to begin my life work." When the white citizens of Alabama, charged with the responsibility of selecting a person to head a school for blacks, approached the principal of Hampton Institute, he had no white person to recommend. But the reputation that Booker T. had made immediately put him in the position for the recommendation from General Armstrong. "Several days passed before anything more was heard about the matter. Some time afterward, one Sunday evening during the chapel exercises, a messenger came in and handed the General a telegram. At the end of the exercises he read the telegram to the school. In substance, these were his words: *Booker T. Washington will suit us. Send him at once.*"

At first there was white opposition to having a black principal, but Washington eliminated most of it by assuring the whites that the education he was offering would not influence blacks from the rural areas to become "uppity" or make them disdainful of service in the white community. He therefore gained the support of the whites of Alabama, and he was also able to benefit from northern philanthropy. Tuskegee Institute, founded in 1881, grew rapidly. Several thousand acres of land were procured, many buildings were constructed, and many students from all over the United States and several foreign countries came to the institution.

By the mid 1880s, Washington's reputation and influence were known far beyond the Institute's immediate surroundings. Many people all over the United States believed that Washington's program of education and self-help for blacks and his policy of cooperation with whites in "all things essential to mutual progress" would lead to a solution of the race problem.

Because of his prominence in the black community – and his acceptable leadership by the white power structure – Washington was invited to give a speech at the Cotton States Exposition held in Atlanta, Georgia, in 1895. The speech he gave solidified his leadership position until his death in 1915. The speech placated whites, North and South, and Washington was firmly entrenched as the "Compromiser" between the North, South, and black people. John Hope Franklin observes that,

> (I)n his celebrated address at the Cotton States Exposition in Atlanta in 1895, he placated white supremacists by renouncing social equality with the whites and to pursue careers in "agriculture, mechanics, in commerce, in domestic service, and in the professions." . . . He called for the intelligent management of farms, ownership of land, habits of thrift, patience, and perseverance, and the cultivation of high morals and good manners.[2]

In general, after his Atlanta Exposition speech, Washington became even more influential as a black spokesman. Many whites felt that he represented the "final solution" to the race problem. He received large contributions from industrialists to carry on the work at Tuskegee, and thus became *the* spokesman for black people. He wielded more power within the black community than anyone else had ever done. Some of his authority over black people was derived from his political influence and from his popularity with the philanthropists. No black schools received contributions from Carnegie, Rockefeller, and others without Washington's support. He cultivated influential black leadership in the black communities, and it was virtually impossible to achieve a major position in the black churches if Washington or his position was attacked. He kept the black press in line by judicious advertisements and contributions. There were a few exceptions, but for the most part, the black press was not critical of his leadership.[3]

From the mid-1890s to his death, the majority of articulate southern blacks supported Washington. This was true even of many of the northern intellectuals. Those few who deemed it feasible to contest Washington's leadership found it to be an impossible task, and they often became apathetic. Not all of his backers accepted his total program, however. Many who were for his program at first later changed their minds, and some of his early critics, including W.E.B. DuBois, became his supporters. But the fact is that for many reasons he enjoyed enormous support in the black community. DuBois, who was not a Washington supporter in Washington's lifetime, except very early, pointed out that "Easily the most striking thing in the history of the American Negro since 1876 is the emergence of Mr. Booker T. Washington . . . with the largest personal following . . . Today he stands as the one recognized spokesman of his ten million fellows, and one of the most notable figures in a nation of seventy million."[4]

Some of the reasons for Washington's support in the black community – as well as in the white community – have been indicated above. In summary, inclusive reasons for his support include the following:

1. The times were hard for blacks; protest agitation, and political action had not worked. Therefore, many felt – or hoped – that his method would work. Rayford Logan puts it this way:

> . . . Washington unmistakably accepted a subordinate position for Southern Negroes . . . he renounced social equality . . . he asked for a chance to gain a decent livelihood. Washington was convinced, and rightly so, that it would have been folly to ask in 1895 for equal rights for Negroes.[5]

2. Many may have seen in his emphasis on economic development and black support of black business an opportunity to become independent of white business.

3. A third factor in Washington's support in the black community was his power over political appointments.

4. Along with his influence over philanthropic contributions and the black press, his political clout helped to make his ideas and philosophy more palatable to blacks than they otherwise would have been.

5. Finally, the very prominence of Washington himself drew support for his program. His fame made his ideas and philosophy more attractive, and his image of success made him a model to millions.

## WASHINGTON'S LEADERSHIP OBJECTIVES

What exactly were Washington's ideas on black self-determination, and why did they create hope and support on the one hand and, on the other, apathy and opposition? What was his program, and how was it to be implemented? Was his ultimate aim accomodation, or was it a mechanism in achieving functional and viable separation for black people? Emma Thornbrough quotes a white Washington contemporary speculating that ". . . the Tuskegeean was silently preparing the way for assimilation and amalgamation of the races . . . or something equally dangerous – the building of a separate Negro nation within a nation."[6] These and other questions will be explored in the following analysis.

Separation to Washington was not something that had to be brought about – it already existed, designed and enforced by white people. As a matter of fact, it was institutionalized. Therefore, in his Atlanta "Compromise" speech he stated that "(I)n all things that are purely social we can be as *separate* as the fingers, yet one as the hand in all things essential to mutual progress." In the same speech he observes "the wisest among my race understands that the agitation of questions of social and political equality is the extremist of folly. . . ." What he may have been saying is that the most important thing for black people to do is to let whites rest with the fact that blacks do not want to socialize with them or to agitate for political equality. But blacks will work with and for them until economic self-sufficiency is achieved; separation is a reality – reconstruction is over, and whites are afraid that blacks want to become political forces again. Since whites have institutionalized "Jim Crow" and taken the ballot, blacks should adhere to the gospel of wealth (money), and then later participate as equals.

The objectives of Washington's leadership included making ex-slaves and not-far-from-slavery-ex-slaves viable men and women in American society in general and in their communities in particular. The basis of Washington's prescription for the development of rural black self-determination centered around vocational, industrial, and domestic training. Tuskegee Institute became the vehicle through which he manifested his objectives. He believed that blacks should make themselves useful where they lived; thus, in time, they could become self-sufficient citizens. In the meantime he thought

> . . . the whole future of my race hinges on the question as to whether or not it can make itself of such indispensable value that the people in town and the state where they reside will feel that our presence is necessary to the happiness and well-being of the community. No man who continues to add something to the material, intellectual, and moral well-being of the place in which he lives is long left without proper reward. This is a great human law which cannot be permanently nullified.[7]

The self-sufficiency aspect would follow, according to Washington, because they would have had the proper grounding through agriculture, mechanics, commerce, ownership of land, patience, thrift, and perseverance. Thus, educational pursuits should initially follow these directions and prescriptions. Washington apparently took the position that before meaningful self-determination can be achieved, it must be preceded by self-sufficiency. Genovese speculated that

> He [Washington] knew that slavery had ill-prepared his people for political leadership; he therefore retracted from political demands. He knew that slavery had rendered manual labor degrading; he therefore

> preached the gospel of hard work. . . . He knew that slavery had undermined the family and elementary moral standards; he therefore preached self-reliance and self-help.[8]

Clearly, Washington spoke to the immediate means of separating illiterate ex-slaves from dependence upon the ex-slavemaster by advocating industrial and vocational training. Since he became *the* spokesman for all blacks, he had to broaden his platform to include northern blacks as well as the black bourgeoise everywhere. What was his plan for bringing about or maintaining black bourgeoisie self-sufficiency and then self-determination? It must be answered that if Washington was clandestinely a separatist, he had a program for the ex-slaves on the lowest end of the socioeconomic scale – which was self-sufficiency or self-help – *and* a separatist program for the bourgeoisie and intellectuals.

If Washington's prescription for lower class blacks to gain self-determination was industrial and vocational training and then self-sufficiency, his prescription for the black bourgeoisie was economic independence. He believed that, "Brains, property, and character for the Negro will settle the question of civil rights . . . Good school teachers and plenty of money to pay them will be more potent in settling the race question than many civil rights bills and investigation committees."[9] Moreover, Washington exposed his plan to a fuller extent when he indicated that

> But asked, would you confine the negro to agriculture, mechanics, and domestic arts, etc.? Not at all, but along the lines that I have mentioned is where the stress should be laid *just now* and for many years to come. We will need and must have many teachers and ministers, some doctors and lawyers and statesmen; but these professional men will have a constituency or a foundation from which to draw support just in proportion as the race prospers along economic lines. . . . If this generation will lay the material foundation, it will be the quickest and surest way *for the succeeding generation* to succeed in the cultivation of the fine arts, and to surround itself even with some of the luxuries of life, if desired.[10]

Here one may posit that Washington saw the need to have a firm foundation upon which to base his black bourgeoisie separatism. But he was opposed by DuBois, who wrote: "The question then comes: Is it possible, and probable, that nine millions of men, can make effective progress in economic lines if they are deprived of political rights. . .?"[11] His answer was no. DuBois took this position in 1903 – i.e., that business was not the way to black viability without political equality. But it is confusing to note that DuBois was largely responsible for the position that Washington took. DuBois proposed at an Atlanta University Conference in 1899, "The organization in every town and hamlet where colored people dwell, of Negro Business Men's Leagues, and the gradual federation from these of state and national organizations."[12] One year later Washington established the National Negro Business League!* But apparently DuBois changed his mind about Washington's methods and philosophy emphasizing economic self-sufficiency. DuBois later felt that the philosophy of the NAACP was the right path – i.e., that political and social agitation would enhance economic equality. In the 1930s he again changed his mind about the NAACP approach and indicated that "There are manifest difficulties about such a program . . . first of all it is not a program that envisages any direct action of Negroes themselves for the uplift of their socially depressed masses."[13] DuBois then indicated that blacks must concentrate on economic self-sufficiency, looking to "fit himself into the new economic organization which the world faces."[14] Washington had already stated in 1895 in his "Atlanta Compromise" speech that, ". . . No race that has anything to contribute to the markets of the world is long in any degree ostracized. . . . The opportunity to earn a dollar . . . is worth infinitely more than the opportunity to spend a dollar. . . ."[15] Moreover, Washington had already stated that ". . . Good school teachers and plenty of money to pay them will be more potent . . . than . . . bills . . . and committees." Forty years later DuBois belatedly came to the same basic conclusion that Washington did: black people must develop separate economic self-sufficiency.

In retrospect, at the height of the controversy between Washington and DuBois, DuBois could not accept the idea of a separate economy for blacks because it was incompatible with the idea of integration into the dominant white economy. From the outset, Washington's attitude was bourgeois – practical and pragmatic based on the reality of long-standing black exclusion from meaningful participation in the general economy. In order for him to lay his separatist – independent, as it were – foundation he had to have racial peace. Washington's role in the development of an economic program to counteract the social position of black people was of utmost importance in contributing to black bourgeois separatism. That is, Washington may have been attempting to "raise" a separate class of black capitalists as a separate counterpart to white "Robber Barons." What is certain is that he attempted to bring about a separate black economy in the age, as DuBois describes it, "of unusual economic development."

DuBois also objected to Washington's stress on vocational and industrial training. It is true that Washington emphasized these areas, but it is also true that he did not object to purely academic education. Washington argued that he thought it somewhat strange and the height of absurdity for a child to spend valuable time learning French grammar "amid the weeds and dirt of a neglected home." But Washington also said he favored any kind of training, whether in the languages or mathematics, that gives strength and culture to the mind.

*"It was this group that was especially instrumental in the burgeoning of the philosophy of racial solidarity, self-help, and the group economy, the rationalization of the economic advantages to be found in segregation and discrimination – to use a phrase commonly employed in *Those Days.* Washington's National Negro Business League was the platform on which this group expressed its point of view." August Meier, "Negro Class Structure and Ideology in the Age of Booker T. Washington," *Phylon* (Fall, 1962), p. 258. (Emphasis in the original.)

Yet education had different meanings to Washington and DuBois. To Washington, education meant that

> . . . while the Negro should not be deprived by unfair means of franchise, political agitation alone would not save him, and that back of the ballot he must have property, industry, skill, economy, intelligence, and, character, and that no race without these elements could permanently succeed.[16]

DuBois, on the other hand, called for the education of the "talented tenth" of the black population, arguing that every race possessed a number of talented individuals and that this "tenth" should be recognized and embraced to "uphold the race." Both objectives seem to have merit, and the two philosophies, despite their differences, are complementary. Washington felt that *before* there could develop political involvement there must exist an educational and skill base, while DuBois felt that blacks must have the franchise *irrespective* of their educational background.

The upshot of the controversy was the temporary polarization of the two philosophies. Booker T. Washington institutionalized his position through the Negro Business League, his string of newspapers, Tuskegee Institute, and his many disciples who became established, educated individuals in the various communities. DuBois' position was institutionalized through the "Niagara Movement" and its outcome, the National Association of Colored People (NAACP). The controversy continues today in various guises. In retrospect, it seems that during Washington's and DuBois' time it would have been the height of folly to expect blacks – only a generation away from legal slavery – to be sophisticated enough, as a mass, to compete politically with the white majority in North and South. It was a *fact* that blacks were disenfranchised, and to argue against this reality was idealistically valid but realistically unsound. To assert that blacks should have the ballot and that they should participate in political life was right, but it was also right that Washington should advocate a route by which the masses of black people could find other ways to seek viability in American society. Not all blacks were of the "talented tenth," and not all wanted to become agricultural workers, blacksmiths, domestic servants, mechanics, or skilled laborers. The approaches of both Washington and DuBois were needed at the time for they reflected the diversity of black people hoping for an answer in a situation they did not control. However, again finally accepting Washington's original position, DuBois came to the conclusion in 1940 that the education of blacks could not best be served in white schools because "they would not in most cases receive decent treatment nor real education . . . it is not theory but fact that faces the Negro in education. He has education in large proportion and he must organize and plan these segregated schools so that they become efficient, well-housed, well-equipped, with the best teachers . . . properly paid teachers for educating their children."[17] Washington had already stated "brains, property, good schools and well-paid teachers will do more. . .!"

Washington was influential among those economically destitute blacks living in the intimidating atmosphere of the Klan-controlled, post-Reconstruction South. His advocacy of vocational training – which to the black separatist and most nationalists is a means of retaining the educated black in a servile position – often represented a way of achieving a livelihood where no alternative means of advancement was possible. It is of utmost importance to note that Washington's program was acceptable to his followers by virtue of the fact that it suited their past experiences. He addressed himself to ex-slaves, not to northern, "militant," highly trained intellectuals. He urged ex-slaves to escape from the bottom – extreme bottom – of a socioeconomic hierarchy, a position to which many of them were bitterly reconciled since they had no hope of ever extricating themselves. What is obvious to some – and what others deliberately ignore – is that once Washington's prescriptions were followed, the doors did open vistas that were never dreamed of before. The foundation that he laid was done in the face of apprehensive ex-slavemasters who were unable to foresee the consequences of vocational training for the masses and, of course, liberal arts training for the "talented tenth."

In this connection it must be observed that those who controlled the power in the South *did accept* Washington's movement but did not or could not totally *manipulate* it. That is, the ex-slavemasters in the South did not want their ex-slaves to have *any* education.[18] But Washington gained their confidence and did educate many black people in their presence. The fact is that those who worked their way through the shops and classrooms of Tuskegee did so to improve their conditions. "If they had gained the tacit approval of persons interested in not having them progress too far, this fact does not convert them into dupes, nor does it qualify the reality of their ambitions."[19]

From some of the words and deeds indicated above, a fairly sound case can be made that Washington favored servile separation – blacks on the bottom and whites at the top. One scholar has described Washington as a "separatist in golden chains."[20] However, a closer look at Washington may give a clearer indication of his intentions. Was he ultimately an accommodationist or was he laying the foundation for viable black separation? Was he a covert black nationalist?

Washington's public image was that of an accommodator, but as a private man he contradicted his public stance. He ostensibly denounced higher education for the masses because he knew that as a group they were hardly literate. His own children, however, received training in the trades through a grounding in the liberal arts. Overtly he urged blacks to accept for a time the separate-but-equal doctrine, but he entered social circles both at home and abroad that few southern whites could.

Booker T. Washington was a very complex man. Outwardly he was a simple, good-natured man who, some have said, was naive about many things – certainly about the "goodness" of southern whites. But was he really? In public, Washington spoke of the friendly relations between blacks and whites in the South, but "clandestinely spent thousands of dollars financing the fruitless test cases taken to the Supreme Court against the southern disfranchisement amendments [and even] on one occasion he hired a lobbyist to defeat legislation that, if passed, would have encouraged segregation on interstate trains in the North."[21] None other than DuBois himself was quoted as saying, "Actually Washington had no more faith in the white man than I do."[22] Washington was certainly not politically naive either. Rather, he was a consummate politician, cunning and calculating. One example of his political acuity was that if he were laying the foundation for viable black separatism, he was placating Southern whites in the process ("viable black separatism" meaning the ability of black people to determine *their own* destiny wherever they lived, North or South).

Typically, the cunning Washington denied any interest in politics

> ... and urged Negroes to soft-pedal the desire for the franchise; behind the scenes, he was the most influential politician in the history of American Negroes, and surreptitiously fought the disfranchisement laws. He served as political adviser on Negro affairs to Presidents Roosevelt and Taft.[23]

As a matter of fact, all blacks who were appointed to office by Theodore Roosevelt and most of William Howard Taft were recommended by Washington. Some of them were Robert H. Terrell, who served as judge of the municipal court in Washington, 1901-1921: Charles W. Anderson, collector of internal revenue in New York, 1905-1915; and William H. Lewis, assistant attorney general, 1911-1913. These were the highest black executive and judicial appointments made up to that time. Another example of Washington's cunning in achieving his ends in the midst of oppression was his "use" of *The New York Age* and its editor.

T. Thomas Fortune, the militant editor of *The New York Age,* founded the Afro-American League in 1890. At its initial convention Fortune set forth the tone:

> ... It has been charged upon us that we are not made of the stern stuff which makes the Anglo-Saxon race the most consummate masters of hypocrisy, of roguery, of insolence, of arrogance, and of cowardice, in the history of races.... Attucks, the black patriot – he was no coward! Toussaint L'Overture – he was no coward! Nat Turner – he was no coward! And the two hundred thousand black soldiers of the last war [Civil War] – they were no cowards! If we have work to do, let us do it. And if there comes violence, let those who oppose our just cause "throw the first stone." We have wealth, we have intelligence, we have courage; and we have a great deal of work to do.[24]

The relevance of Fortune to Washington is that *The New York Age* was a "radical" platform where black Americans were able to voice their opinions. By 1895, the Afro-American League – founded in 1892 – had become defunct and was revived in 1898 as the Afro-American Council. The Council in many ways was a continuation of the earlier convention movement. It was captured in the early 1900s by Washington and its resolutions became far less militant than before, although it continued to ask for full constitutional rights for black people. Overtly, it seemed as if Washington was "silencing a militant," but a closer examination shows that he used the Council to secretly attack the disfranchisement constitutions of the southern states in 1903-1904. Moreover, the Council exemplified and explicitly articulated the view that only through united collective efforts, through race unity and self-help, could black men achieve their citizenship rights.[25]

Many of Washington's critics charged him with subsidizing publications – like *The New York Age* – in order to silence critics by buying them off, as it were. But Washington sold the *Age* and denied interest in it; meanwhile he continued to subsidize it. Why? "The argument centers around whether Washington maintained anonymous participation so as not to offend wealthy and white non-militant beneficiaries or in order to manage the volley from his black critics."[26] It is unlikely that he needed the *Age* to manage volleys in that he had several other news organs through which he could do the same.

A separatist/nationalist, if anything, is ultimately proud of his race and its achievements. What did Washington have to say about race pride and the race's achievement past, present and future? Those who charge Washington with "Uncle Tomism" and telling "darky" stories to his white benefactors – which is the antithesis of race pride – must also account for the black version of his "darky" stories. His black version preached that

> We have reached a period where educated Negroes should give more attention to the history of their race: should devote more time to finding out the true history of the race, and in collecting in some museum the relics that mark its progress.... We should have so much pride that we would spend more time in looking into the history of the race, more effort and money in perpetuating in some durable form its achievements, so that from year to year, instead of looking back with regret, we can point to our children the rough path through which we grew strong and great.[27]

If he truly believed in black assimilation and that blacks should really be subservient to whites, why would he speak of race pride and the importance of preserving black heritage for posterity? It seems hardly coincidental that in 1915, the same year of Washington's death, Carter G. Woodson, the renowned black historian, established the Association for the Study of Negro Life and History; in 1916 the publication of the *Journal of Negro History* began. In 1913 Washington had instituted "Negro Health Week" and, after the establishment of Woodson's Association, "Negro History Week" became, up to this day, an annual event. (However, the Association's name has been changed to fit the times – at one time it was "Afro-American" Life in place of "Negro" Life, and "Negro" History Week is now Black History Week.)

To Washington, Jews served as the best model of solidarity. He writes:

> We have a very bright and striking example in the history of the Jews in this and other countries. There is perhaps no race that has suffered so much, not so much in America as in some of the countries of Europe. But these people have clung together. They have had a certain amount of unity, pride and love of race; and, as the years go on, they will be more and more influential in this country – a country where they were once despised, and looked upon with scorn and derision. It is largely because the Jewish race has had faith in itself. Unless the Negro learns more and more to imitate the Jew in these matters, to have faith in himself, he cannot expect to have any high degree of success.[28]

Washington possibly could not have imagined Hitler's atrocity against the Jewish people, but he did foresee their inclusive role in the American mainstream. Perhaps Washington could never envision black assimilation in white American society; hence, this may have been the significant factor in the Tuskegee-sponsored establishment of the all-black town of Mound Bayou, Mississippi, which exists to this day. Some have speculated that the establishment of this all-black town was Washinton's way of institutionalizing "ideologies of self-help, economic development, and racial solidarity."[29] The present-day all-black towns, as well as the "black central city," are not unrelated to this early attempt by Washington to create black separate viability; only the setting has changed.

In the final analysis, Washington's ulterior motives will never be known. The above attempts to portray Washington as the leader of a separatist/nationalist movement is done with full knowledge of Washington's leadership shortcomings. As John Hope Franklin observes, "during his lifetime, lynchings decreased only slightly, the Negro was effectively disfranchised, and the black workers were systematically excluded from the major labor organizations; but Washington's influence, sometimes for better and sometimes for worse, was so great that there is considerable justification in calling the period 'The Age of Booker T. Washington.' "[30]

## NOTES

[1] Booker T. Washington, "Up From Slavery," in *Three Negro Classics* (New York: Avon, 1965), pp. 29-205, *passim.*

[2] John Hope Franklin, "Introduction," *Three Negro Classics.*

[3] Samuel R. Spencer, Jr., *Booker T. Washington and the Negro's Place in American Life* (Boston: Little, Brown & Co., 1955), p. 163.

[4] W.E.B. DuBois, *The Souls of Black Folk* (Greenwich, Conn.: Fawcett, 1961), p. 42.

[5] Rayford W. Logan, *The Betrayal of the Negro*, 2nd edition (New York: Collier, 1965), pp. 280-281.

[6] Emma L. Thornbrough, "Booker T. Washington as Seen by His White Contemporaries," *Journal of Negro History* (April 1968), p. 162.

[7] Washington, "Up From Slavery," p. 182.

[8] Eugene D. Genovese, "The Legacy of Slavery and the Roots of Black Nationalism," *Studies on the Left* (November-December 1966), pp. 14-26, in Thomas Wagstaff (Ed.), *Black Power: The Radical Response to White America* (Beverly Hills, Calif.: Glencoe Press, 1969), p. 139.

[9] Washington, "Up From Slavery," p. 141.

[10] Booker T. Washington, *Future of the American Negro* (Boston, Mass.: Small, Maynard, 1899), pp. 227-228. (Italics added.)

[11] DuBois, *The Souls of Black Folk*, p. 49.

[12] "Resolutions of the Atlanta University Conference on the Negro in Business," in W.E.B. DuBois (Ed.), *The Negro in Business* (Atlanta, Ga.: Atlanta University Publications, No. 4, 1899), p. 50. Seen in John H. Bracey, August Meier, and Elliott Rudwick (Eds.), *Black Nationalism in America*, (New York: Bobbs-Merrill, 1970), pp. 262-263.

[13] W.E.B. DuBois, *The Dusk of Dawn: An Essay Toward an Autobiography of a Race Concept* (New York: Schocken Books, 1968, first published by Harcourt, Brace & World, 1940), p. 193.

[14] *Ibid.*, p. 199.

[15] Washington, "Up From Slavery," p. 149.

[16] *Ibid.*, p. 141.

[17] DuBois, *Dusk of Dawn*, p. 201.

[18] See Ray Stannard Baker, *Following the Color Line: American Negro Citizenship in the Progressive Era* (New York: Harper Torch Books, 1964, originally published by Doubleday, Page, 1908). His insight into the southern mind relative to education is significant. He observes "... the majority view in the South was more or less hostile to the education of the Negro, or, at least, to his education beyond the bare rudiments" (p. 282).

[19] Hans Toch, *The Social Psychology of Social Movements* (New York: Bobbs-Merrill, 1965), p. 238.

[20] S. Jay Walker, "Booker T. Washington: Separatist in Golden Chains." See Chapter 8 in this volume.

[21] August Meier and Elliott M. Rudwick, *From Plantation to Ghetto* (New York: Hill and Wang, 1966), p. 181.

[22] Donald J. Calista, "Booker T. Washington: Another Look," *Journal of Negro History* (October 1964), p. 251.

[23] Meier and Rudwick, *From Plantation to Ghetto,* p. 181.

[24] T. Thomas Fortune, from an address in "Official Compilation of Proceedings of the Afro-American League National Convention, 1890," in Bracey, Meier, and Rudwick, *Black Nationalism in America*, pp. 212-222.

[25] *Ibid.*, pp. 211-212.

[26] John P. Flynn, "Booker T. Washington: Uncle Tom or Wooden Horse," *Journal of Negro History,* July 1969, **54**: 262-274.

[27] Booker T. Washington, *Future of the American Negro,* p. 182.

[28] *Ibid.*, pp. 182-183.

[29] August Meier, "Booker T. Washington and the Town of Mound Bayou," *Phylon* (Winter 1954), p. 400.

[30] John Hope Franklin, *From Slavery to Freedom,* 3rd edition (New York: Random House, 1969), p. 397.

# Part III
# The Case Against Separatism

There is general agreement that blacks in the United States are victims of white oppression, both institutional and systemic. Black separatists contend that blacks can only escape this oppression by separating from whites through "community control" of black communities, establishing a geographically separate nation in the United States, or leaving (emigrating from) this country and "returning" to Africa. In short, separating from whites "by any means necessary." While many blacks accept much of what the separatists say about the nature of the black condition, they still oppose separation as a solution to the dilemma. Those who oppose separation regard separatism as a romantic and utopian dream; that in reality whites are not about to allow the establishment of a "black nation" in the United States. The most efficacious way of promoting black liberation, they argue, is to launch a broadside attack against institutional and systemic oppressive forces.

The first article by Walker rejects the idea that Booker T. Washington was a separatist. If he was, his "golden chains" prevented him from effectively promoting black liberation. Pettigrew makes the point that though the call for racial separation is appealing to many – black and white alike – its practical consequences negate the possibility of fruition. We shall, therefore, remain – uncomfortable to be sure – racially together. The McCords suggest that changes in class and other status categories will eventually dull separatism's appeal. Moreover, in a highly urbanized and technological society such as the United States, separatism becomes subject to other forces militating against its development. Walker, the director of one of the most successful black studies programs in the country, and writing about contemporary black studies, contends that separate black studies programs do not demand intellectual rigor. Moreover, white administrators – assuming that the program is located on a white college or university campus – use them as a way of "keeping blacks quiet" by "giving them what they want." Rustin, that venerable figure in the civil rights struggle, takes the separatists to task for giving up what black gains have already been made. Moreover, he contends, the black separatists have not come up with a viable program – if they have a program at all.

# 8
# *Booker T. Washington: "Separatist" in Golden Chains**

S. JAY WALKER

*In all things purely social we can be as separate as the fingers, yet one as the hand in all things essential to mutual progress.*

With those words, spoken at the Atlanta Exposition of 1895, Booker T. Washington vaulted into national prominence. Almost overnight he became *the* black leader, the Wizard of Tuskegee, the man to be consulted by educator, philanthropist, and President alike on any and all questions having to do with "the Negro problem."

In our day there has been a reawakening of interest in Washington, particularly on the part of many for whom hope or expectation of any meaningful integration has died and who seek to create an economic independence of white America. Booker Washington's foundation programs – to establish freedmen on a firm financial basis as homeowners, independent farmers, and artisans and his early advocacy of black-run schools and black businessman's leagues – are said to make him the progenitor of groups that seem as removed from Tuskegee, in style and spirit, as Elijah Muhammad's Lost-Found Nation of Islam and James Farmer's Soul City, U.S.A. They are said, in fact, to establish his claim as the father of black separatism.

This is a title which we would do well to scrutinize carefully. Washington's achievements were many (we may someday recognize as the greatest of these his persuasion of northern philanthropists to build black public schools for an indifferent state of Alabama). But Washington's apparent bland acceptance of the "fact" of segregation did not make him a separatist. Separatism requires power: not only the will to stand alone, but also the ability. And power, the power to bring about his larger dreams, escaped Washington to the very end of his life. He enjoyed the simulacrum of power: he could reward and punish those more helpless than himself, and he enjoyed public notice, public deference, admission to circles closed to other blacks. But essentially his position was that of Zenobia, Queen of Palmyra, who rode before Caesar garlanded, crowned – and in chains of pure gold.

What is obscured by Washington's success in making Tuskegee the wealthiest and most famous black college in the nation is the failure of his larger design, precisely that design on which rests his claim as the founder of separatism. The contented, prosperous black masses in the south never emerged, nor did the voluntary granting by whites of political power. Black businesses, with a few notable exceptions, remained marginal, most successful in those areas in which they had a captive clientele – i.e., supplying services that whites refused to blacks. Nor did achievement necessarily bring respect in its wake. Washington himself was the very model of the self-made man, and not at all reticent about admitting it; yet Washington suffered astonishing vituperation, attack, and mistreatment – most of which he preferred not to put on record.

It may be worthwhile, therefore, to look at Washington's work and ideas, most cogently set down in *Up From Slavery* in 1901, and to look as well at the aftermath of Washington's life, at what he did not say and what he did not accomplish.

More than half a century after his death, the meaning of Booker T. Washington's career, the career itself and its aftermath, remain a mystery – an enigma only compounded by successive studies.

Was he the tower of wisdom that he seemed, or a weak and vascillating time-server? Was he, with his insistence on black property and black business, the father of black nationalism, or was he, with his insistence on "the folly of agitation," the father of an indifferent black bourgeoise? We now know that he secretly used funds to support civil rights cases in the courts. Did he also secretly use funds to sabotage civil rights organizations that might have offered his leadership competition? We still do not know. We circle around the figure, dazzled by its complexity, by what Arthur Link called its protean strengths and weaknesses. But at the heart, where there should be understanding, there remains a great void.

Certainly, Washington is the most honored black American who ever lived. No black has received from this nation as much official praise, as many official honors, as this man, born in slavery, received both in his lifetime and afterwards.

Within a decade following World War II, Washington was given six signal notices. In 1946 the Commonwealth of Virginia purchased the land on which he was born to establish the Booker T. Washington Birthplace Memorial. In the same year, Congress authorized the minting of Booker T. Washington Memorial Half Dollars. In 1948, Virginia erected a replica of the cabin in which he was born on the Birthplace Memorial. In 1948 and again in 1956, Congress authorized the issuance of Booker T. Washington postage stamps, and, in 1956, President

*Written especially for this book.

Eisenhower signed a bill which made the Birthplace a National Monument. It is an astouding array of honors; indeed, so unlike those paid to any other black man that they alone should give us pause, should suggest that we ought to look closely to see who this man was and why he was so honored.

Certainly Washington's place in black history is secure. He was a spokesman, in his day *the* spokesman, for the black viewpoint. He was a highly influential educator, a prolific writer, and an orator in constant demand upon the public platform.

Yet, perhaps John Hope Franklin was exaggerating when he called Booker T. Washington one of the most powerful men in the South. Washington was powerful as long as he said what his white backers wanted to hear. He had the power to destroy or cripple black opponents and the power to advance the careers of blacks – and even some whites – whom he favored. He was powerless to halt or even slow the tide of segregation, disenfranchisement, and terror sweeping across the South, even to protect himself from insult on his own campus. He was personally honored; his school flourished and prospered. The chains he wore were golden, but they were nevertheless chains.

Washington's *Up From Slavery* falls into a pattern beloved of the late 19th century – the Horatio Alger epics of young men going, through a combination of courage, hard work, and good morals, from rags to riches, of boys being born paupers and becoming presidents, if not of the nation at least of corporations and, one supposes, of colleges. Benjamin Franklin's *Autobiography* is the 18th-century prototype of those books, and certainly Washington's picture of his early struggles and his later description of his tremendous personal success must be the culmination of the type.

There are clear reflections of Benjamin Franklin in Washington's book. Every schoolchild sooner or later hears the story of Franklin as a poor boy entering Philadelphia, spending his last pennies on loaves of bread, and walking down the main street of the city munching one of them and being laughed at by the proper Philadelphians – among them his future wife. The point of that story, of course, is our knowledge that Philadelphia was the city over which Franklin was later virtually to reign. *Up From Slavery* gives us an almost identical anecdote. As he traveled to Hampton to attend school, Washington ran out of money and so, in Richmond, slept several nights under a raised wooden sidewalk. Many years later he was tendered a reception by "the colored citizens of Richmond" and his mind, he tells us, was far more on that nearby sidewalk under which he had slept than on the honors being paid him.

In addition to the parallel anecdotes there is a philosophical connection between the Washington and the Franklin autobiographies that is far more important. Both are classic statements of the Protestant ethic, that familiar concept that work is good, that work builds character, that work will necessarily be rewarded. Today we regard the ethic in purely secular terms. What we tend to forget is that the present concept had a religious origin, that it was the *Mayflower* group, that third wave of immigrants to America and the first in search of religious freedom, who imported the ethic as part of their religious faith.

The Calvinistic concept of election – the idea that a limited number of people were predestined for salvation – carried the implication that those people could be known by their demeanor, by the plainness of their dress, and the plainness of their lives, could be known by their hard work, their honesty, and their trustworthiness. And because they possessed all these virtues, they would also be known by the fact that they were rewarded with wealth during their lifetimes. People who worked hard, were honest, saved their money, had the respect of their neighbors and protection of the law, were more than likely to be materially successful.

Gradually, what happened was that these characteristics – "the way of wealth" Benjamin Franklin called them – were taken as virtues in themselves, not because they indicated that a man was elected by God for salvation, but because they brought about success in a success-oriented society.

What were those virtues? Ambition, first of all. Hard work, thrift, trustworthiness, cleanliness, earnestness, sobriety, chastity, tranquility, moderation, orderliness, silence, and finally, humility, although as Franklin slyly suggested, if one had the first 12, it was rather difficult to be humble as well.

It is almost impossible to exaggerate the degree to which these virtues are imprinted on the American spirit, built into the American ideal. The nation as a whole feels that it is "immoral" for someone not to work, and part of its distrust for artists and intellectuals – except for the very "successful" ones – is that there is no tangible sign that they *do* work.

From the concept that work is good of itself, we tend to make various nonproductive adjectives (unambitious, lazy, prodigal, dilettantish) pejoratives; we treat them as sins even when they injure no one. And I suspect that even most of us who consider ourselves "liberated" from the ethic feel essentially the same way.

If for instance, tomorrow I were to win one million dollars in the New York State lottery, and announce that I intended to spend the money on a year-long beer blast, I would be the subject of denunciation from pulpits, editorial columns, and probably the Congress for months. On the other hand, if I were to state that I was putting the money into Xerox stocks and municipal (tax-free) bonds, the same sources would say that I was being very prudent, very wise, a "good and faithful servant."

But it would, in fact, make very little difference what I did with that windfall. My income as a teacher is sufficient to my needs, if not to my aspirations; my profession is, I suppose, as secure as a profession ought to be; and we are obviously all in serious trouble if the only thing that stands between us and the welfare rolls is a ten million-to-one shot at a lottery. Yet, I know that my own background would simply not allow me to "throw away" – and that's the way I would think of it – that million dollars in enjoying myself. Like it or not, I, like most of my Depression-reared generation, am tied to the Protestant ethic.

And I believe this to be our national characteristic. In a very real sense, Middle America's objection to the counterculture is an objection founded on the Protestant ethic. It is that "hippies" are not ambitious, they are not hard-working, they don't make a fetish of cleanliness, they don't make a fetish of sobriety or chastity and certainly not of silence or humility.

Faced with this, hard-hat patriotism translates into a concept of material success: America is a good country because it is a country where you can make it, where you can work, and through work become wealthier than your father had been. This suggests that the Protestant ethic has shifted position. From being the mere visible sign of salvation, the symbol of faith, it has become the faith itself. It is that, I feel, which is the only possible explanation of the really obscene hatred which the hard-hat displays toward the hippie, exemplified by the spate of "they should have killed more" statements that followed the Kent State massacre.

It is not as simple as beer versus grass or marriage versus free love or even to bomb or not to bomb Indochina or Saudi Arabia. Rather, it is that the counterculture is a calculated assault on the nation's most cherished ideals and virtues – its real faith. It not only holds that faith up to scorn and execration – and what, after all, is the burning of the flag other than the 20th-century equivalent of smashing images during the Thirty Years' War or spitting on the cross during the Crusades? – but more dangerously, it seems to tempt the children of Middle America itself into heresy, thus threatening, in a very real manner, Middle America's immortality. In the turn of the decade clash between hippies and hard-hats, we glimpsed not the possibility of a civil but of a religious war.

We seem to be, here, at some remove from the Wizard of Tuskegee, but in fact we are not. The Protestant ethic burns brightly in the majority of black separatist organizations – again, the Black Muslims are the best example – and the primary lighter of that torch was Booker T. Washington. Benjamin Franklin set down the ethic as the way to wealth and Washington picked it up and proclaimed it as *the* means, *the* method of elevation for the newly freed slaves.

Where did Washington get these ideas? We can see them being shaped in the early pages of *Up From Slavery*. As a boy, Washington was ambitious; he wanted to go to school, to make something of himself. He didn't quite know how or in what, but he wanted to succeed. And the success symbols that he saw around him were largely symbols that were dominated by New England Protestantism. The South – the old, rather careless and inefficient South – had lost the war. The plantations lay deserted or destitute. The masses of freed blacks, also lackadaisical, scraped out a bare living in misery. But there were some people around who were neither lackadaisical nor destitute, and one of these, a Mrs. Viola Ruffner, had a tremendous influence on him.

When Washington went to work for Mrs. Ruffner at the age of 12, he took on a job that a number of small black boys had already quit. Viola Ruffner was a hard mistress, one who insisted that the yard be kept clean of every twig and every piece of paper; who insisted that the windows be not only spotless, but polished and shining. She wanted every picket in place on every fence, and every fence whitewashed. She insisted, in a word, on thoroughness, on the painstaking carrying out of any job undertaken. And Mrs. Ruffner was not a Southerner; she was a Vermont Yankee. Washington had come into contact with an example of the people who had demonstrated their superiority in the only way that was ever to mean anything to him: by success, winning. (Years later, his first major address was to be entitled "The Force that Wins.") From them, he learned the secret, a pattern for success from which he was never, publicly, to diverge for the rest of his life.

The formula was almost immediately put to the test. When Booker T. Washington arrived to enroll at Hampton Institute, having run out of money and slept under sidewalks enroute, he must have looked very much like an 1872 caricature of a black hippie: unwashed, uncombed, and ragged; and Mrs. Mary Mackie, the Lady Principal of Hampton, understandably disconcerted at the apparition before her, was not at all certain that this was the kind of student she wanted in her school. But she let him hang around for awhile and finally asked him to sweep a classroom next door. It was like throwing Brer Rabbit into the briar patch: Washington went about the cleaning with the thoroughness he had been taught by Mrs. Ruffner. He swept the floor three times, he found a cloth and dusted the furniture four times, he cleaned and polished the windows, he went into every closet and every corner. Thus, when Miss Mackie came to inspect his job, rubbing her handkerchief over woodwork and furniture, she found the place to be scrupulously clean, and she remarked quietly, "I guess you will do to enter this institution."

It was more than an entrance examination to Hampton; in his first personal test, Washington had applied the Protestant ethic and had succeeded brilliantly. Then, the Principal of Hampton, General Armstrong (again, like Miss Mackie and Mrs. Ruffner, a New Englander – part of that crusade of the Yankee schoolteachers who had come into the South to educate the newly freed blacks) quickly recognized Washington as an exemplar of all that he wanted of his new charges and encouraged him, loaned him money, and found jobs for him. Armstrong made it possible for him to be a success at Hampton, and finally it was Armstrong who sent Washington to Tuskegee to begin his life's work there.

Thus Washington's own background had been a demonstration that the ethic *would* work. It is obvious, of course, that there was a tremendous need for the Protestant ethic among the newly freed blacks. As Frederick Douglass had pointed out, the system of slavery was one that worked against ambition (because there was no point in a slave being ambitious), against hard work (because a slave's work benefitted only his master), and against thrift (because a slave could not legally own anything). These habits, which had been wrenched out of blacks by the peculiar institution, were precisely those in which they would most need to be retrained for their success as free men.

The need for elements of the Protestant ethic in any society from Puritan New England to Communist China is, of course, clear. But Washington failed to see the limitations of that ethic. He seemed to feel that only the accomplishments of physical labor were really valuable. He had very little concept of the arts, of the higher professions, as being beneficial. He saw no need for black sculptors or philosophers and very little possibility of black doctors or lawyers or engineers. These services, he felt, could and would be provided by whites. He elevated cleanliness to a subreligion in itself: "The gospel of the tooth-brush," but at the same time his whole educational program gradually inculcated a contempt for the intellect as intellect – "mere book learning," Washington called it.

The effect on black education was largely disastrous. The Tuskegee example was so pervasive, and economically so successful, that it became a characteristic of the South that black schools were industrial schools. Viewing the old "separate but equal" state education system in the South establishes a pattern: the University of Tennessee was white and Tennessee Agricultural and Mechanical College was black, the University of Florida was white and Florida A & M was black, the University of Mississippi was white and Alcorn A & M was black. Again and again this pattern was imposed on black education, public and private, and, as a result, the liberal arts and professional institutions of the blacks were weakened as money was diverted from them toward the industrial schools.

In the 20th century, anti-intellectualism was still visible at Tuskegee Institute itself. The distinguished visiting black scholar, E. Franklin Frazier, was once reprimanded by the Dean of Tuskegee for carrying books across the campus. The Dean's fear: white people might "get the impression that Tuskegee was training the Negro's intellect rather than his heart and hands." By the later 1950s, when I taught there, resentment of this attitude was beginning to subvert the faculty itself. The famous statue of Washington as he "lifted the veil of ignorance from his people" stood at one of the central crossroads of the campus. It was inevitably referred to, courtesy of Ralph Ellison, as "the statue of Booker T. Washington pushing the veil of ignorance down over the head of the Negro."

But was this concept of total "working with the hands" actually Washington's? There is reason to doubt that it was. Obviously, he borrowed some of it from Hampton; just as obviously Frederick Douglass had urged the importance of industrial training before Washington's birth. But there was a third, and a more ominous source of inspiration. In Chapter Twelve of *Up From Slavery*, Washington tells of two people who had given him a good deal of help in devising his program. One of these, J.L.M. Curry, was a former Confederate officer; the other Morris K. Jessup, was a northern industrialist. Frankly, when I read of a Confederate general and a northern industrialist getting together to decide the "proper method of elevating the Negro," I get worried.

What, in fact, the South wanted was peaceable blacks, blacks who would not compete with whites and would continue to act in service roles. The North wanted peace, of course – an end to the agitation of "the color question," as they called it – and it wanted, at the same time, a pool of black labor sufficiently skilled to be able to man factories. Most of the factories were still in the North; the flight to the union-free fields of Dixie had not yet begun. But labor unions were becoming more and more powerful in the North and the industrialists wanted a pool of semi-skilled black labor that they could use as a counterweight to the unions, that could be used to tell the unions that if they didn't shape up, their jobs could easily be filled by blacks.

And this is exactly what happened. In the late 19th and early 20th centuries, blacks were used as strike breakers, a situation that fueled the antagonism between blacks and labor unions that exists to this day. Washington, then, gave the white South and the industrial North what they wanted. In return, he asked for peace, for protection, and for the ability of blacks to prosper. The white South and North, by and large, got what they wanted; whether Washington got what he wanted remains questionable. But what is clear, I think, is that Washington neglected even to ask on behalf of blacks for the rights and dignities that belong to them as free men, and without which neither peace, protection, nor prosperity could be anything but a vain and idle fancy.

When Washington walked onto the stage for his Atlanta Exposition Speech on the 18th of September in 1895, he was reaching consciously for the mantle of black leadership that had been Frederick Doulgass. Douglass had been dead for seven months and, in fact, there was no one to take his place. Monroe Trotter and W.E.B. DuBois were both too young and insufficiently well known. There was a leadership vacuum, and Washington projected himself into that vacuum. He simply assumed leadership; he convinced whites that he was the black leader, and in that way he very largely convinced blacks of the same thing.

One wonders what kind of leadership Washington was prepared to give. One wonders always whether he would have dared make the Atlanta Exposition speech had Douglass still been alive. I suspect he would not have for fear that Douglass' bellowed outrage would have driven him straight back to Alabama to bury himself in the Tuskegee swamps for the next ten years. But Douglass was dead; there was no one prestigious enough to deliver that blast, and so Washington became, through lack of competition, the recognized spokesman for Black America.

Since he did replace Frederick Douglass, it is perhaps cruel, but nevertheless perfectly justifiable, to look at a contrast between Washington and the man he replaced. A black contemporary, Kelly Miller, who knew both well, assessed the two men:

> Douglass was like a lion, bold and fearless. Washington was lamb-like, meek and submissive. Douglass escaped from personal bondage, which his soul abhorred. But for Lincoln's Emancipation Proclamation, Washington would have risen to esteem and favor in the eyes of his master as a good and faithful servant. Douglass insisted upon his rights; Washington insisted upon duty. Douglass held up to public scorn the sins of the white man. Washington portrayed the faults of his own race. Douglass spoke what he thought the world should hear. Washington spoke only what he thought it was disposed to listen to. Douglass' conduct was actuated by principle; Washington's by prudence.

The contrast is almost vicious in its terms, but if we take almost any of Douglass' speeches and set it side by side with Washington's Atlanta speech, the assessment stands up. Washington's speech at the Atlanta Exposition was essentially a message of "cool it! don't rock the boat! don't make waves!" He said to American blacks that they must simply abandon, at least for the time being – an indefinite entity – their struggle for real American citizenship, abandon their struggle to move into the mainstream of American life as equals. In exchange, he claimed the whites would immediately aid blacks toward prosperity and eventually give them those political "privileges" with which Washington felt the white South would be generous once blacks had learned respectability.

Obviously, there is a great deal to be said for the principles of being both respectable and amenable. Soft speech is not totally without value. But complete acquiescence to the "realities" of life was a very dangerous thing to propose at a point in which the rights of blacks were systematically being stripped away. This was the period in which the Ku Klux Klan and other terrorist organizations were ending black voting in the South. It was the period in which the Supreme Court had struck down the Civil Rights Act of 1875. It was the period in which segregation was being imposed in greater and greater degree on public transporation, on accommodations, on public facilities, on shelter, and it was precisely at this moment that Washington chose to state to a national audience that these things were really not very important.

Rather, he gave in the Atlanta speech the beloved old image of the black as the good darky, of blacks as good and faithful servants, compounded of loyalty, generosity, trustworthiness, and fidelity to their masters. He told tender stories of old black servants who had ministered to the parents of his white listeners in their illnesses and followed their bodies with tear-brimmed eyes to the graves. He told stories of slaves who had been allowed to go North before the Civil War to work for their freedom and, even after the Civil War had given them that freedom, insisted on paying to their masters all that they had contracted for.

It was an image that was deliberately designed as soothing, an image that said to the South, "you have nothing to fear from black people," and because it said that there was nothing to fear, it also said, in effect, "you can treat them any way that you have a mind to." That image was not only derogatory in its suggestion of blacks spinelessly accepting whatever kind of treatment was offered them, but was compounded by Washington's catalogue of the little peccadilloes of black folk, a catalogue that happened to fit nearly his audience's concept of racist stereotypes. In Atlanta, Washington smilingly praised the progress of Negroes who had started freedom with only "a few quilts and pumpkins and chickens (*gathered from miscellaneous sources*)," thus "acknowledging" that blacks were incurable chicken and watermelon thieves.

Frederick Douglass had once rebuked a fellow Abolitionist's crowd-warming "darky-stories" with the line, "Very funny. I felt as though someone were trampling on my mother's grave!" But both Washington's autobiography and his nationwide speeches featured such stories, suggesting that light-skinned blacks could be identified by the size of their feet and that blacks became ministers because the cotton field was so large and the sun so hot that they believed they had been called upon to preach.

He stressed again and again the image of the over-educated black as a clownish charlatan determined to live by his wits; and, central to all of it, he indicated that the "wisest" of his race understood that it was folly to agitate for political privileges, that it was folly to agitate for social rights, but rather that it was all-important that blacks be allowed to work, to serve.

It was more than simply coincidental, I think, that the year after Washington delivered the Atlanta Exposition speech, the Supreme Court handed down the Plessy-Ferguson Decision of 1896 making separate but equal accommodations an acceptable interpretation of the Fourteenth Amendment. It would be foolish to suggest, of course, that the Supreme Court had waited for Booker T. Washington's speech before it acted. Very obviously, the components of the Court and the direction of American social and economic philosophies had determined that that decision would have been handed down regardless of what Washington said. But effectually, Washington's acceptance of segregation *before* the ruling undercut the grounds of those who opposed that decision. Justice Harlan, who wrote a dissenting opinion insisting that the Constitution was colorblind and that the Court had no right to impose segregation on a portion of the citizenry, was immediately attacked in the press for demanding more for blacks than blacks wanted for themselves. Booker T. Washington had *told* the nation what blacks wanted.

The effect of the Atlanta Exposition speech, then, was to undermine, in its own time and for decades to come, any concerted resistance to segregation. It was to provide segregationists with the argument that wise men, like Washington, were satisfied with the status quo, that it was only radicals, only revolutionaries, only bad niggers, who wanted change.

But Washington himself very quickly began to find out that he had bitten off a bit more than he could chew, that the faith that he had deposited in the white South was returning an almost nonexistent rate of interest.

He tells us in *Up From Slavery*, for instance, that he favored a restricted ballot fairly and equally applied, that he did not favor illiterate blacks, or illiterate whites for that matter, being able to vote, but felt that the ballot ought to be based on education, or on income or property taxes. But the white South almost immediately began to pass legislation that did not even make a pretense of equal restriction.

In 1900 a Virginia convention met to rewrite the State Constitution. The previous Constitution had been written as part of Reconstruction, in order for the State to regain admission to the Union, and the Commonwealth had now decided to rewrite it yet again. Carter Glass, the chief spokesman for "respectable" Virginia, announced, "We are here to discriminate with a view to the elimination of every Negro voter who can be gotten rid of, legally, without materially endangering the numerical strength of the white electorate." The Constitution was duly written so that blacks could not vote and whites could. And this is precisely what happened all over the South. During my tenure at Tuskegee Institute, there was not to my knowledge a faculty member who voted, since none could get past the "literacy examinations" which every surrounding sharecropper passed with ease.

What had happened here? I don't think we can reasonably say that Booker T. Washington was simply treasonous, that in exchange for personal pomp and circumstance he decided to sell out blacks. Nor can it be demonstrated, as some of Washington's supporters have suggested, that he was "yessing the man to death," smiling in his face to gather contributions and then pouring huge portions of them back into the covert financing of civil rights suits. There was something more human – and sadder – than either of those Machiavellian interpretations. Washington could have profited from the "book-learning" that he scorned. Instinctively wise in personal relations, he suffered from a desperate narrowness of experience, of vision, that led him to expect more than he had any right to of the white South. He had forgotten that success under the Protestant ethic required not only work, thrift, and honesty, but also protection of the law. For legal protection, he attempted to substitute the patronage and good will of the ruling whites, and the results were disastrous.

The people by whom Washington had been shaped, Mrs. Ruffner, Miss Mackie, General Armstrong, were both fair and (by their own lights) benevolent. The people with whom he first came into contact when he moved into Tuskegee, the old aristocracy, were also fair-minded. They may have had their own conceptions of the "proper" place of blacks; but they placed little tangible obstacle in the way of a black fulfilling any potential that he had – possibly because it never occurred to them that that potential might constitute a challenge. Washington seems to have believed that the South was still ruled by its aristocracy, by the descendants of the old plantation class, who were supposed to have had some sense of *noblesse oblige* to "their people," the kind of benevolent paternalism that Washington had found in his "perfect man," General Armstrong.

In fact, what was happening at the very moment that Washington was delivering his Atlanta speech was that the degenerated populist movement of the 1890s was putting the southern political reins in the hands of the lower middle class and the white sharecroppers – the "redneck" vote. In Faulknerian terms, power was slipping from the Sartorises into the hands of the Snopeses, and the Snopeses had no sense whatsoever of *noblesse oblige*. They were the people who had always been in most direct competition with the slaves and who had blamed the slaves, not the slaveowners, for their pitiable condition. It was this class, and not Washington's white aristocracy, that almost immediately began to produce a series of demagogues, men like Tillman and Vardamann and Talmadge, who ruled the South for decades, and whose philosophical descendants, Eastland, Maddox, and Wallace, largely rule it today.

The implications for Washington's materialistic program were no less disastrous. Without political power, he was dependent on the good will of the white South to aid and protect the black in gaining an economic foothold. In the Atlanta speech he had said that "whatever other sins the South may be called to bear, when it comes to business, pure and simple, it is in the South that the Negro is given a man's chance in the commercial world." Giving "a man's chance" to someone who was not considered a man, meant, in fact, providing him with guardians, with a community that believed at large that it would be "a shame to cheat poor, ignorant Nigras."

In the New South, cheating poor ignorant Nigras ceased to be a shame and became a regional pastime. Black sharecroppers paid inflated prices for their "furnishing" at the credit store, and paid them over and over again as the boss kept the records. Let a black man prosper on his farm or paint his house, and the assessor, in whose election he played no role, skyrocketed his taxes. Let a white man lay claim to his property and the black's day in court, if he were lucky enough to get that far, was played out before a white judge, a white jury, and with white attorneys, any of whom would be ruined, socially, financially, and politically, if he took a black man's word against a white's. And the behavior of southern police and sheriffs need not even be discussed.

In some rural areas, blacks did prosper, often when they had the friendship and support of some "Mister Andy" or "Captain Johnson," influential enough to call off the heat. But it was insufficient; Washington's dream of an independent, prosperous, and advancing black yeomanry was stillborn.

The real tragedy of Booker T. Washington's life is that he must eventually have realized that his gamble on the benevolence of the white world had in fact failed. During the early 1900s, when Washington was at the height of his fame, Senator J.K. Vardamann of Mississippi made a speech widely reported throughout the country, one which Washington could scarcely have missed. Vardamann had this to say:

> I am just as opposed to Booker T. Washington as a voter with all his Anglo-Saxon reinforcements as I am to the coconut-headed, chocolate-colored typical little coon, Andy Dotson, who blacks my shoes every morning. Neither is fit to perform the supreme function of citizenship.

It was painfully typical of the experiences that Washington was to undergo. At the beginning of the century, Theodore Roosevelt invited him to dinner in the White House, and a storm of denunciation immediately broke over the heads of both men. The Rough Rider did not repeat the invitation. In Indiana, an immigrant chambermaid indignantly refused to clean Washington's hotel room, for which heroism the citizens of New Orleans awarded her one thousand dollars and those of Houston five hundred. In New York a white man clubbed him to the ground for being in the vestibule of a "white" apartment house. The assailant was acquitted, one of the judges remarking that Washington "had no business in the house," while Senator Vardamann weighed in with the comment that the attacker "proved himself not a man by not killing Washington on the spot."

Even on his own campus he was not totally safe; on one occasion Governor Oates of Alabama, invited to deliver the Commencement address, suspected a note of militancy in the preceding speaker and took umbrage. Thrusting aside his prepared speech, he stormed,

> I want to give you niggers a few words of plain talk and advice. . . . You might as well understand that this is a white man's country, as far as the South is concerned, and we are going to make you keep your place. Understand that. I have nothing more to say to you.

That was, in essence, the South's answer. Washington had offered an olive branch at Atlanta and the white South had thrown it back in his face.

The black reaction to Washington's olive branch wasn't really a great deal better. *Up From Slavery* spends a good deal of time telling the reader that there was some adverse black reaction at first, but that this quickly died away. In fact, the reaction never died; it slackened for awhile and then began to grow ominously. The autobiography also includes an interesting anecdote about the initial black reaction: with his usual humility (the 13th virtue), rather than praising the effect of his own speech, Washington reprints a newspaper report that praised it. The article, in the New York *World*, tells us that there was "a ragged, ebony giant" squatting in the aisle and listening intently to Washington, and that when the ovation rose to its height, the giant burst into tears, "perhaps without knowing just why." I have, personally, always suspected that he knew exactly why he was crying; it was because he had that old "here we go down the river again" feeling.

But whether or not that is true, Washington was clearly aware during this period of his life that there was a sense among blacks that he *had* sold out, that this speech was what DuBois called "The Atlanta Compromise," and that the name of Uncle Tom, whose virtues Washington admired, was being tailored, with no admiration whatsoever, to fit him.

And thus the end of *Up From Slavery* becomes a tally of personal triumphs intermingled with evasions. He tells us of having tea with Queen Victoria and Susan B. Anthony, of receiving an autographed picture of the Dutchess of Westminister, of being honored by presidential visits and having receptions given him. He nowhere mentions being insulted or humiliated. He dwells on the exhibition of a work by a black painter, Henry Tanner, in the Luxembourg Gallery as proof that true worth never goes unmerited, yet ignores the fact that Tanner had, in fact, fled to Paris because it was impossible for a black artist to exhibit in the United States. He praises his own brand of Industrial Education as sweeping the nation, but sent his own daughter to Wellesley and his son to Fisk.

He tells us that the Ku Klux Klan no longer exists, that the fact that it ever had existed is almost forgotten, and that no one could expect it to rise again. The statement is in direct and astounding contradiction to the statistics of Tuskegee Institute itself, which recorded that in 1901, the year that Washington was writing, 130 blacks were lynched – that is, better than one every three days. Not a word about lynching sullies the optimistic pages.

He tells us of the contrast between his treatment on trains and oceanliners and that received by Frederick Douglass in a manner to suggest that segregation was atrophying. And yet he gives himself away by speaking of enjoying train travel "when I am permitted to ride where I may be comfortable," an indication that he was not always so permitted.

In fact, so desperate is this whistling in the dark, this attempt to pretend that everything is all right, that one almost feels sorry for Washington. Here is a man who set out to do good, who learned his lessons well and applied them assiduously, only to discover that the world was not as easily captivated as was Miss Mackie. Senator Vardamann, Governor Oates, the judge in New York, the immigrant chambermaid, the townspeople of Houston and New Orleans, the nameless train conductors and assorted ruffians, all told him clearly that, no matter how often he brushed his teeth and bathed, no matter how honest, ambitious, intelligent, and Uriah Heep-humble he was, to them he remained just another nigger, to be kept in his place with the rest. One almost feels sorry for him; almost, but not quite.

For whenever one begins to feel sorry for Booker T. Washington, some typical characteristic recurs to ease the sorrow. If only he had been able to admit the possibility that he might be wrong! Not admit that his life had been a failure, that is perhaps too much to expect from any mortal, but only to admit that there might possibly be another way, that other blacks might be as sincere as he, as intelligent as he, and yet wish to follow an independent program. This was the one thing that Washington could not, would not, do. Rather he devoted the energy of his last years to the relentless pursuit of his "enemies" within the black race: From driving W.E.B. DuBois out of Atlanta University, to sabotaging the Niagara Movement, to having Monroe Trotter arrested for "disturbing" a meeting he held, to threatening Judge Terrell with the loss of his position if his wife continued her activities in the N.A.A.C.P. In Louis Harlan's phrase, he was "king of a captive people," and he would brook no brother near the throne.

Yet the future was not to belong to Booker T. Washington; black history in the first half of the 20th century was largely a history of fighting against his legacy, and the honors heaped on Washington by the Virginia and Federal governments in the 1940s and '50s can now be seen as an attempt to restore his icon as a bulwark against the oncoming civil rights agitation.

The icon was never to be rebuilt; even before his death, the struggle was on to undo the effects of his career. And the chief undoer of that career was a man called William Edward Burghardt DuBois.

Curiously enough, it might all have been different had DuBois preceded Washington rather than followed him. We can see today that there is in fact the potential for large-scale black economic independence: the size of the black middle class, a majority (bare, but nevertheless a majority) for the first time in history; the increase of education with the concomitant increased pool of technicians and professionals; and, above all, the effects of the civil rights decisions and legislation of the 1950s and '60s, all of them the direct results of DuBois' life work, have given black America an effective option – the power to choose whether they wish separation or integration.

That power simply did not exist in Washington's day, and powerless, Washington's nascent black nationalism was doomed. One may quibble with the second clause of Kwane Nkrumah's dictum, "Seek ye first the political kingdom and all else shall be added unto you," but without at least a share in the political kingdom, nationalism and separatism alike are sounding brass and tinkling cymbals.

# 9

# *Black Studies: Equal or Separate**

S. JAY WALKER

Two startling innovations have marked higher education in the United States in the course of the last decade.

The first has been a sharply increased enrollment of black students, fueled in part by the crisis of conscience brought on by the Civil Rights Movement, in part by the availability of government and foundation funds for the education of minority students, and in part by federal pressure. As a result, the overall number of black undergraduates has more than doubled, and in some institutions increased ten- and 20-fold. My own college, Dartmouth, as an example, now has more black students enrolled, approximately 300, than it graduated in the first 200 years of its existence.

With the enrollment of minority students there has come another change, perhaps in the long run as significant. The pattern of American education itself is undergoing an adjustment, sometimes abrupt, sometimes gradual. Those subjects that were taught unquestioned for generations have been challenged as misrepresentation. "American History" and "American Literature," it has been pointed out, have not been that at all, but rather essentially "White American History" and "White American Literature."

It is easy to see now, if we look at the syllabi and textbooks of the 1940s and the 1950s, that black Americans were the invisible men of American studies. In history, there was some mention of blacks having to do with causes of the Civil War but there was rarely any study of the anti-slavery activity carried out by black men and women for decades before the War: Sojourner Truth and Harriet Tubman and Frederick Douglass might as well never have existed. And the Civil War itself was treated as having solved the issue for all time. From these texts one could assume that once Lincoln signed the Emancipation Proclamation, the black, except for some highly indecorous shenanigans called Reconstruction (promptly and effectively put down by all right-thinking people), simply vanished. He was likely to turn up now and again as an athlete bringing glory to the flag – Jesse Owens at the 1936 Olympics in Berlin; Joe Louis defeating Max Schmeling for the heavyweight championship – and one might also get some passing mention of Booker T. Washington founding a famous school or George Washington Carver turning the peanut into an industry in itself. But for the most part the black man simply was not included in American history.

If he was not a part of American history, he was even less visible in American literature. Anthologists might now and again include something from Phillis Wheatley – preferably the lines " 'Twas mercy brought me from my pagan land" – and perhaps one of Paul Lawrence Dunbar's dialect poems. But any black writing which seemed to suggest that all was not for the best in this best of all possible worlds was rigorously excluded from the textbooks. It is interesting, for instance, to note that the 1941 edition of the *Oxford Companion to American Literature* (edited in the United States) devotes seven and one-half column inches to Margaret Mitchell and *Gone With the Wind*, three inches to Richard Wright, and two inches to Langston Hughes. Nor, for that matter, was the situation much better when Americans looked beyond the natural boundaries. Courses and books devoted to world literature generally dealt with European literature – occasionally straying as far afield as the Hebrew scriptures – and world history seemed generally to have occurred on the European continent – in which Egypt somehow held honorary membership.

It was not simply the increased presence of black students that brought about attention to this discrepancy in the education system. In colleges where black students had previously enrolled in large numbers (indeed, in black colleges throughout the country), the situation was much the same. It was rather a combination of that black enrollment and the *Zeitgeist*. Something new had begun to happen in the Afro-American mind since a black woman named Rosa Parks had refused to stand up on a Montgomery bus in 1955, a black man named Kwame Nkrumah had raised the colors of an independent Ghana in 1957, and a Black Muslim named Malcolm X had begun to dominate network television in the early 1960s. Black Studies was thus the outgrowth of the way in which black people had begun to look at themselves by the end of that decade and the way in which they demanded that the white world look at them as well.

It was in many ways a startling demand; startling both in its source, from which had been expected gratitude rather than criticism, and its Emperor's-new-clothes statement that the "authorities" did not always know best. It is of considerable credit to the flexibility of most American educational institutions that, faced with the arguments put forth by black students, they looked at themselves, admitted the justice of

*Written especially for this book.

many of them, and set about realigning academic priorities. That realignment can be seen clearly in the difference between the history and literature textbooks of the late '50s and the late '60s. In the text of the '50s, the black is still invisible; in the '60s, he is all but ubiquitous.

But more than new texts were needed. Scholars themselves came to admit that in fact they knew little or nothing of black Americans, that there was a pressing need for organized study of what was actually the experience, the culture, and the aspirations of blacks. With the admission there was, of course, also resistance. Teachers were as much given to inertia as anyone else, and indeed the nature of their profession made scholars particularly prone to the worship of tradition. The very fact that the study had not been done before seemed to a number of faculty members an admirable reason for not doing it now.

Nevertheless, the innovation was adopted with relatively little acrimony. Some members of the academic establishment were hostile, some were indifferent, some seemed resigned to the regretable fact that 1966 was not 1926, and others were quite sincerely concerned about the advisability of hastily instituting an entirely new dicipline. But a larger number recognized the fact that the academic community had not carried out its responsibilities to all members of the community. Still buoyed by the domestic idealism of the Kennedy-Johnson era, they were attracted by the belief that an increase of knowledge could bring increased social justice and by the idea that a new era of scholarship might liberate them from the stale mythologies of their own disciplines.

And so Black Studies came to be. There were immediate and serious problems: no one knew exactly what a Black Studies Program should be; no one knew whether it should concentrate on blacks in the United States, whether it should attempt to cover the entire Pan-African area, or even at what point one could draw a line of demarcation and establish one work as Black Culture and the other as White Culture. Textbooks were beginning to appear, but there was practically no one trained in the new field. I had gone through eight years of college and graduate school, majoring in literature, without once ever studying a black author in class, and this was a common experience. History majors told me that they had heard of Thaddeus Stevens only as a bogeyman, of John Brown only as a madman, and of David Walker not at all; while to sociologists, the black family was whatever Daniel Moynihan chose to say it was and black beliefs whatever Nathan Glazer chose to say they were.

In addition to black scholarship, there was a clear shortage of black scholars. The vast majority of black academics were employed by the Negro colleges in the South, and with the best will in the world the white academic community could not simply stamp black Ph.D.'s out of the ground now that they needed them. To add to the difficulty, many black scholars did not specialize in black subjects: men and women at Fisk and Howard, Tuskegee and Hampton taught Shakespeare, French, European history, Beethoven, and physics; many of them, having devoted a lifetime of scholarship to their individual interests were reluctant to make a switch from the Congress of Vienna to the Reconstruction now that it was decided that Waterloo was out and the Sea Islands were in.

One thing demonstrated by the introduction of Black Studies was the flexibility of the educational establishment once it was determined to move. Summer seminars, workshops, grants for independent studies suddenly appeared throughout the country. Academic deans suddenly found, doubtless beneath loose boards in the floors of their offices, extra cash with which they could hire qualified black personnel (sometimes, indeed, bribing them away from the poorer, smaller black institutions in the South). Other scholars were shamed or flattered into retooling their disciplines, and where black scholars could not be found, white liberal faculty fleshed out the growing Black Studies Programs, making the same kind of commitment that many of their students had made to the Freedom Summers in Mississippi a few years previously.

It was disorganized, it was sometimes chaotic, and now and again it was dishonest. Instant experts, some of whom had not heard of Phillis Wheatley a few weeks before, suddenly began to file proposals for courses in Black American Poetry. But it worked.

Across the nation the most unlikely collection of jerry-built programs waddled off the ground, and somehow most of them, however erratically, at whatever low altitudes, managed to fly. And they at least began the task of changing the face of American scholarship. Then, in 1968, and within a period of seven months, Martin Luther King was killed, Robert Kennedy was killed, and Richard Nixon was elected President of the United States. The sequence was traumatizing. King had been not only the most articulate, but also the most idealistic of all black leaders, the one most deeply committed to faith in the American dream and to love and reconciliation, and we looked on while his death was greeted by public expressions of dismay and non-too-private expressions of satisfaction. Robert Kennedy, who outlived King by just four months, seemed, apart from the Vietnam-discredited Lyndon Johnson, the only viable politician with any real desire to bring about genuine interracial democracy in the United States. And blacks, having watched Richard Nixon operate over the past two decades, needed neither Watergate nor tapes to gauge his character. We told you in '68 not to buy a used car from him.

The months that followed saw the low-water mark of black faith in America and perhaps the high-water mark of black separatism, and those forces swirled around the new Black Studies Programs like a cyclone. It became a commonplace assertion that no white man was to be trusted, that the only difference between a white conservative and white liberal was the difference between an open enemy and a covert one, the former bent on physical and the latter on cultural genocide. Many of the new programs began a deliberate withdrawal from the mainstream of the academic communities. (Academic, indeed, had come to mean white academic and thus culturally genocidal.) The phrase "Malcolm said" became an infallible means of closing debate, and the programs began to regard themselves not as agents of education but rather as agents of revolution, with no whites wanted.

Some took on deliberately anti-intellectual overtones, their leaders, even those reared in the high schools of Scarsdale, New York, affecting the wearing of overalls, the use of double negatives, and whatever southern dialects they could approximate. Some of the programs scorned intellectualism and the intellectual process, substituting the group therapy/identification process of "rap sessions" for learning. Others maintained intellectual content but narrowed their concern to the modern revolutionists – Malcolm, of course, and Fanon, omitting even DuBois and Douglass from their canon. Others went even further, and in what could only have been gestures of contempt, wrote what Bayard Rustin used to call Chitterlings 100 and Quilting 101 courses into their curricula. The Chitterlings and Quilting courses were once considered a joke. By 1972, one of the largest colleges in the California state system carried in its bulletin a three-credit course entitled "Introduction to the Selection and Preparation of Soul Food."

What the shapers of the courses apparently failed to recognize was the degree to which their contempt was being returned. The acceptance of a Chitterlings 100 course by a faculty senate simply meant that that senate did not care what was happening in the Black Studies Program and did not care what kind of education black students were getting. In justification of the worst fears of the education traditionalists, Black Studies were simply becoming separate, something outside the academic community, located physically on its campus, paid for by its money but divorced from its standards in concerns and in seriousness. It was a program with self-destruct mechanism ticking away. Those who had opposed the institution of Black Studies could say "we told you so," and point to all A's grade lists in Chitterlings 100 to prove their point. Those who had no concern for the welfare of black students could look on complacently while those students compiled totally worthless "academic" records, and those who regarded education as a fiscal matter could reflect that a course in Denunciation might produce as many full-time equivalents as a course in physics – with an instructor drawing a much smaller salary than a physicist.

So a "give them what they want, just keep them quiet" syndrome took over. The programs were moved, bodily in some cases, out of the mainstream of academic life. Even when they remained physically in that mainstream, they were separated psychically. Black Studies was here and the college was there and never the twain met. It was an academic apartheid which would have done Dr. Malan credit.

It was also a situation that could not last and was doomed the moment the colleges and universities of the United States came under economic pressure. The present combination of inflation and depression, of skyrocketing costs and the diminishing returns from alumni and legislators has put every college from the most renowned ivy to the most obscure teachers college in Arkansas into a financial crunch that makes budget-cutting inevitable. When that axe begins to swing, it tends to aim directly at those areas that are least traditional or those that bring least prestige and therefore money to the college. Fads, academic or otherwise, have very short lives, and Black Studies are no longer modish. Women's Studies, Chicano Studies, Indian Studies, Gay Studies, all of which have followed the pattern and avoided some of the pitfalls of Black Studies, are newer and therefore more "progressive." In this sense it is no longer necessary for a college to maintain a Black Studies Program to demonstrate that it is "with it."

But perhaps more important than the lifespan of academic fads is the fact that black students themselves are unwilling to support any longer a course of studies simply because it carries the once-magic word "black." Today's black student is a good deal more sophisticated than his brother of the Class of 1969. He may be no more interested in integration, no more bound to the idea that traditional studies are the be-all and end-all of education, but he has had a chance to see that rhetoric, shucking and jiving, can exist within a black context as well as a white. He has had a chance to see that the wearing of dashiki and the use of Black English does not necessarily lead him toward a real future. He has come to realize that no matter what kind of society he is going to build for himself, no matter where he is going to build it, that he is not likely to be equipped for that building with a Magna Cum Laude degree in the Preparation of Soul Food.

Thus, the black student himself has begun to demand intellectual quality in his Black Studies courses. He has begun to insist that it is not enough that Black Studies be separate and therefore independent, but that they be equal, in content and quality, and stand side-by-side on competitive terms with any course taught in the academic context. This is an interesting development, interesting particularly in what it shows of the long-term validity of student thought. Just as students, black students, in the past have said that they objected to a teaching of literature that ignored them, they are beginning now to say that they object to a teaching of anything that attempts to substitute the adjective black for meaningful content.

In other words, the students are telling us, and I think that we have to trust them, that they *want* to be crowded, that they want the intellectual rigor that pushes them to the level of their potential, that demands from them the best that they have to offer, and will no longer accept the instructor's use of five-letter words and ten-letter words and 12-letter words as substitutes for realistic evaluations of the past, the present, and the future of black people in this country.

If Black Studies courses are going to fulfill those new expectations, and fulfillment is their only means of survival, then Black Studies Programs must be staffed by the best scholarship available, and these scholars must be chosen not on the basis of their ideological values: integration, separatism, liberation, nationalism, revolution, or Pan-Africanism, but must rather be chosen on the basis of their knowledge of their fields, on their ability to transmit that knowledge in a manner that will make it possible for the student on a rational basis to make his own choice. This is all we must do; if we have done this, we have done our job.

But to say that this is all that we must do is to say that all that man must do to conquer cancer is to learn what causes cancer. As long as Black Studies Programs remained outside the parameters of the academic process, there was no need for scholars. There were exceptions, certainly, but far too many Black Studies Programs were staffed by personnel who would scarcely have been admitted as students to any other part of the educational establishment. The nonsensical cry that "the brother in the street" possessed a knowledge denied to the scholar by the very virtue of his scholarship, and that this knowledge was somehow useful in an academic context, was accepted too often, sometimes with a smile, sometimes with a sigh, by bewildered university officials who, simply wanting to be left alone, blithely appointed personnel not only untrained themselves but totally lacking in standards by which to judge their students. This new breed of pseudo-pedagogues could be hired economically, were rarely, if ever, given tenure, and were replaced with a casualness which demonstrated that nobody really cared. For that reason, Black Studies Programs in general (good and bad alike) lost credibility not only in the broad academic perspective but with the very clientele that they were expected to attract.

How do we reverse this situation? The only answer, it seems to me, is the concept of shared resources. Black Studies, and this has been one of its innovative strengths, has in fact cut across the narrow definitions of literature, history, sociology, and political science, and said that we must look at all of these together. We must regard a book such as Richard Wright's *Native Son* not only as a work of literature but also as a work of history and sociology and journalism, utilizing each of these disciplines to see what the particular object under study has to say of the lives of black people. This interdisciplinary process in itself makes it absurd that one should attempt to think of Black Studies as a department in the traditional sense of departments. Instead of attempting to reproduce such departments, those concerned with Black Studies should use their share of faculty allocations to make joint appointments of black scholars in the programs and also in the traditional departments. In this way the concept of the black experience is carried not merely in the fledgling program which is so totally vulnerable, which can be so easily cut off by a turn of fashion or the stock market, but by those departments whose very names – English, History, Government, Anthropology – invoke institutional cachet and permanence. The agent for change will thus be placed where real change takes place. There will be risks, major risks, in spreading Black Studies institution-wide. It is obvious that most of the traditional departments have historically shown no great interest in black subjects, and it is just as obvious that the inclusion in an American Literature course of a book by Langston Hughes may require the exclusion of one by Willa Cather while in a straitened budget and enrollment situation, every course in The Harlem Renaissance may replace one in Restoration Drama.

But the risk must be taken. Carefully but steadily we must move toward abandoning the protected waters of separate Black Studies organizations and launching ourselves upon the seas of the academic world in general. We must attempt to place black scholars on equal terms in any department within the academic field, and we must do this for two reasons – both of them practical. A thorough study of black life in the United States requires scholars in history, literature, art, sociology, government, theater, anthropology, geography, psychology, music, education, economics, and foreign languages. A Black Studies Department employing full-time qualified scholars in all of those fields is talking in terms of a total budget considerably over a quarter of a million dollars per year, a figure that obviously can be sustained only by the largest and wealthiest of colleges. But if a Black Studies Department did in fact swing that kind of economic weight, it would still have difficulties in attracting the type of faculty that it needed. We still may be in the years of the Great Teacher Glut, but qualified black scholars are not yet to be found beneath every bush. Blacks represent better than one-tenth of the American population. But rather than representing ten percent of American Ph.D.s, we represent something like one-tenth of one percent of American doctorates. The qualified black scholar is difficult to find; when such scholars are found, it is only reasonable to assume that, given the choice between a contract with a Black Studies Department and a contract with a History Department, Sociology Department, or Economics Department, they will chose the field in which they have been trained – the traditional academic study.

It is quite pointless to say that this represents the inherent selfishness of the black bourgeoise or that it represents a lack of concern for the "liberation of black people." It is simply that the black man or woman who has, at a cost which all of us should recognize, attained a Ph.D. is far more likely to be attracted to the field of his expertise than he is to the vague and uncertain area of Black Studies. He knows the disciplines of history or political science; he knows the techniques, he knows the literature, and he may well simply not feel as comfortable in the interdisciplinary reaches of Black Studies. Furthermore, he knows that there will, five years hence, *be* a Department of History and a Department of Political Science, and there is no guarantee in any college in the land that there will, five years from now, be a Black Studies Department. If we call this choice selfishness, we are simply ignoring the fact that we are dealing not with heroes out of a blacksploitation film but with the aspirations of human beings who seek steady, settled, and secure lives for themselves. We would all do better to recognize the validity of these aspirations.

Thus, black scholars are most likely to migrate to those institutions that will give them the opportunity to function as they have been taught, as scholars without reference to ideology or to fashion. They are likely to choose the more difficult task of creating equity with their academic colleagues than seeking the "protection of programs where standards of scholarship are vague or disparaged. And this is finally where the job is to be done. Those of us who do not for a moment believe that the destiny of blacks lies in migration to Africa or to an independent state carved out of the United States recognize that our permanent success depends in part on reshaping the total educational framework of the United States.

The continuous cycle of teaching and learning, from students and colleagues alike, is part of every faculty member's life, and a major part of that teaching occurs not in scholarly journals and learned monographs but in the give and take of a faculty coffee room. If a black faculty member is to convince a colleague who has been teaching American literature for the last 30 years that Ralph Ellison belongs in his course, then he must be in a position to cite chapter and verse on Ellison's symbolism, his treatment of the *Bildungsroman* theme, and his use of Shakespearean punning, and to cite them in languages that his colleagues can understand. Some of them will be unwilling to entertain the idea, but others will, and they must be there as a catalytic force if nothing else.

We are back here to the vexed question of "integration," a matter that has always been more important than that "lousy cup of coffee at Woolworth's." This time it is the question of whether it is important to "integrate" the courses of a predominantly white university. The only reasonable answer is, of course, that it is important. One of the disasters of the period of "militant separatism" was the repeated assertion that it is unnecessary for us to talk to the rest of America – much less listen to it   and that it is unimportant whether the rest of American understands us or not.

The idea would be nonsensical even were the separate state to evolve: Canada had better be able to talk to the United

States, particularly if it wants to keep control of its own resources. It is even more nonsensical given the realities: that we and our children and our children's children will live in a multiracial society, and that we cannot do so without communication. It also means that black students, educated in that society to function in that society, cannot live on Black Studies alone. They will be in that American Literature class, and in the same class will be white students.

To announce that we have nothing to say to that class, to withdraw to the shelter of totally separate Black Studies, is to fail in our responsibility to express that unique and valuable image of the United States – what DuBois called our dual vision – to precisely those people who most need a new image. Black scholars therefore, have a dual responsibility in the university. They must be deeply involved in the activity of their traditional departments, but at the same time their relationship to black scholarship as a whole – the Black Studies Program in its essential rather than its organizational meaning – must be intensified rather than diminished. It must be the responsibility of the black faculty to review the degree to which the university is or is not responsive both to the input of blacks into the American experience as a whole and to a transferal of the best of that experience to its students. The black faculty, in addition to its immediate disciplinary needs – meeting as members of the Sociology Department or Anthropology Department or Music Department – must also meet as the black faculty, maintaining a careful view of what is happening to black scholarship and black students from one end of the campus to the other. It must play its role in the traditional table of organization of the college, taking part in the faculty senate and in the various committees, and it must also reach out to other special interest groups, such as Woman's Studies, Native American Studies, Chicano Studies, and reach out as well to those terribly disparaged "white liberals" who are *genuinely* concerned with reforming American education.

It must, too, finally begin to face the task of reassessing the role of whites in the teaching of "black" subjects. In the aftermath of the "revolution" of 1968, an effective cordon was thrown around Afro-American and, even more dubiously, African subjects, declaring them off-limits to whites. Upon cooler examination, however, we must recognize that the policy has certain built-in inconsistencies. On the one hand, it is obvious that a man or woman who has grown up in a culture has a head start toward understanding it. Thus, having been reared in the black church, I "hear" certain covert messages in the religious poetry of Phillis Wheatley that many of my white colleagues seem to miss. On the other hand, it is no less obvious that black drama, black history, and black sociology are human studies and intellectual endeavors, having something to say to all humans, and that all humans have some response to make to them. Enforcement of the parochial view that only blacks may deal with black subjects would, had it been possible, have deprived us of Michael Fabre's study of Richard Wright, a brilliant interpretation of an author who is black and American to his core by a critic who is neither black nor American.

The impulse was understandable; for decades after the "discovery" of the Negro during the Harlem Renaissance, well-meaning big guns like Moynihan, Glazer, and Howe thundered about the intellectual presses, telling us what black life was like, how blacks thought, and how blacks ought to write, just as Jensen has, more recently, begun to inform us that blacks are not really very bright, and Fogel and Engerman have said that slavery wasn't so bad after all. The conclusions of even the well-meaning were often inaccurate and at times insulting.

But correcting those conclusions means engaging in reasoned debate, not refusing debate. The only whites who can be shouted down are those who are liberal, and to silence the liberals is to leave the field to those of more sinister motives. Our task, again, is to educate our white brethren, to see to it that they know the things we know. For, in the final analysis, the black experience is part of the American experience, and any competent teacher of American literature, whatever his color, must be capable of handling Henry James and James Baldwin alike.

The educational role of Black Studies, then, must be twofold: education of both the black and the white college communities, and such an education means willingness to enter into a meaningful dialogue *outside* the perimeters of a separate Black Studies Program, for only such dialogue will bring about resolution of common problems. I feel that I have, as a male, learned within the last five years to understand and to react with a measure of perceptiveness and sensitivity to the concerns of Woman's Issues. But I would not have been able to do so had women not been willing to discuss openly their reasoned objections to the framework in which they are viewed by this society.

We must, then, continue to reshape the educational system, but reshape it from within, on the basis of demonstrated competence, rather than trying to do so from without. We must see that the curriculum deals with truth, as we can best understand truth, and see to it as well that our students approach that curriculum with a sense of searching for truth rather than with the intention of proving preconceptions. And we must recognize that no one (including ourselves) has a monopoly on truth. We must be heard, but we must listen as well; we must state our case, but we must know the cases of others; we must add our gifts to the mosaic of American education, while remembering that there are also gains to be had from that mosaic.

These are the things that we cannot do if we fail to involve ourselves in the educational system at large. Black Studies as a charity case, squatting in one of the dark corners of the institution doing its undefined "thing" and occasionally being thrown a few dollars to keep it from being a nuisance, can serve no practical purpose other than that of providing good salaries and prestigious titles for those connected with it – a more or less genteel ripoff. Black Studies, which meet the traditional standards of scholarship, of intellectual honesty, of mental discipline that were part of man's intellectual striving in the Agora and the University of Timbuctoo alike, can benefit not only black scholarship and black students but their institutions as a whole.

It is only the latter course that makes sense. Black Studies, as presently constituted, is essentially an emergency program, designed to correct as quickly as possible the traditional discriminations of the educational establishment. Such traditions die hard, and perhaps not until the present generation of students or their successors – students who have studied Zora Neale Hurston side by side with Kathleen Anne Porter, students who have studied DuBois side by side with Thoreau, students who have studied Inner City Ward Politics side by side with the New England Town Meeting – fill the faculties of the colleges and universities as well as the elementary and high schools, will it cease to serve a crucial need. That time, like the date at which the NAACP works itself out of the need for existence, lies in the future. To survive the present, Black Studies must demonstrate now that it is an integral part of the academic world. The choice, finally is not between equality and separation. It is between equality and annihilation.

# 10
# *Urbanism, Racism and Class: Futurist Explorations in Black Separatism**

ARLINE SAKUMA McCORD and WILLIAM McCORD

It may well seem odd that two "outsiders" – a WASP and an Oriental – should be given the opportunity to write an article in this extraordinary volume on black separatism. We have the temerity to undertake the task exactly because we are outsiders and possibly have a reasonably objective view of the future of black separatist movements. The best explorations of America's future have been written by Englishmen (Bryce, Dickens, Brogan) and by Frenchmen (de Crevecoeur, Simone de Beauvoir, and most eminently by de Tocqueville). These foreigners observed more of American life and did so more profoundly than the best of our American breed.

In fact, however, we are hardly outsiders to the problems of separatism. During the Second World War, one of us spent four years in a concentration camp: the ultimate form of imposed separatism reserved in those days for Americans of Japanese ancestry. Further, the other author (in spite of his white pigment) stood with black comrades in facing white beatings in Mississippi, police fuselages in Texas, and demonstrations in the North.

Despite common experiences of bigotry such as these, of course, we remain outsiders to black communities. We both recently failed an examination in "black English" administered by two black friends during a trip to Martha's Vineyard, since black English has yet to be adequately translated into common English.

An incident in the life of Malcolm X, who intimately experienced northern ghetto life, further illustrates this separatism in language. Malcolm X once took a leader of the "black movement" to Harlem. A "hustler" approached him and said:

> "Hey baby! I dig you holding this all-originals scene at the track. . . . I'm going to lay a vine under the Jew's balls for a dime – got to give you a play. . . . Got the shorts out here trying to scuffle up some bread. . . . Well, my man, I'll get on, got to go peck a little and cope me some z's. . . ."[1]

The nationally known black leader did not understand the language. Malcolm X had to translate the words even to a fellow black man. The linguistic difference then (which changes from year to year) apparently separates not only the white from the black, but black from black. To truly understand the exact meaning of different black language, one must understand the idioms of Watts or Harlem, Bedford-Stuyvesant or Houston's Third Ward. No person, black or white, has yet mastered this immensely complicated task.

This difference of the black languages in America illustrates only one of the consequences of the long-term segregation and pluralism of a supposedly monolithic community. If one adds class differences, geographical dissimilarities, and educational gaps, it becomes apparent that there is no single black community. The only reality is groups of people who are identified as black, and, because of this identification, suffer in terms of economic, residential, legal, and educational opportunities. It is equally clear, from the various essays in this volume, that there is as yet no one leader who can legitimately claim to speak for *the* black community. The single quality uniting black men is the tragic stigma imposed by the history of slavery, white bigotry, and discrimination.

Under these conditions, we feel that it is as appropriate for any man – "black," "yellow," or "white" – to observe the general situation of the black man in America and to speculate about his future as it was for a Frenchman or Englishman to comment upon the general lot of "Americans."

With this caveat, let us, two outsiders, offer a few observations about the current pattern of urbanism, racism, and class discrimination which has portent for the future of "black separatism."

## URBANIZATION AND SEPARATISM

A few facts should be kept in mind when considering the future of black separatism:

1. Most important, blacks are now predominantly urban dwellers, rather than rural "folk." According to the 1970 census, 73 percent of all blacks lived in standard metropolitan statistical areas. This is the exact reversal of the situation in 1900. At that time, 73 percent of blacks lived in rural areas and were essentially "peasants."

Not only have black people moved from the rural areas to urban centers, they have also migrated from the South to the North. Whereas eight out of ten black persons lived in the 11 states of the Confederacy in 1910, less than one-half of the

*Written especially for this book.

black population lived there by the 1960s.

2. This vast migration of an entire people from the countryside to the cities is unprecedented in history. All Americans have, of course, been increasingly forced into urban areas, but no one except for blacks has had to make this transition so rapidly. Within the space of one man's lifetime, blacks have moved from agricultural occupations (in the South) to industrial areas (in the North). There have been way-stations in this migration – Memphis, Louisville, East Saint Louis – which served as points of entry for later generations to move on to Chicago, Detroit, and New York.

3. Like any people experiencing the transition to urban life, blacks have undergone a number of transformations. As a variety of scholars have illustrated in different contexts, urban life involves:

a. The breakup of organic, village ties and a transition to a highly differentiated, utilitarian style of life.[2]

b. A severe dislocation of social life resulting in high rates of crime, alcoholism, addiction, and other symptoms of social disorganization.[3]

c. A breakdown in family life.[4]

d. An openness to innovation, change, risk-taking.[5]

e. A broadening of horizons, which allows the person to form opinions about complex issues and to recognize differences of opinion.[6]

There can be little doubt that American blacks, like other urban migrants, have undergone many of these transformations in their lives. In certain other respects, however, blacks have not conformed to the usual pattern predicted by urbanologists.

As a group, newly migrated blacks have not benefited from the experience or direct aid of their predecessors in the city. German Jews aided their Russian counterparts in the latter's migrations to the city; the Catholic Church served as an umbrella protecting Irish immigrants; even the Mafia eased the transition of Sicilians to American shores. Newly urbanized blacks have not received such brotherly aid. True, fraternal organizations, storefront churches, and a variety of political organizations proliferate but they have, at best, served as spiritual recompense to black urban migrants. These organizations have never been unified; they have often been ephemeral and plagued by class differences where the upper-class black has often striven to dissociate himself from contact with his recently arrived "peasant" brothers.

Further, because of the pervasive pattern of racial discrimination established early and firmly in American cities, and the particular timing of blacks' arrival to these cities, they have not been allowed to absorb themselves in traditionally white urban organizations. By the time the large number of unskilled black laborers arrived in northern cities, the pressing need for unskilled labor of any color had passed. Earlier floods of immigrants from Europe had already usurped the task of building the cities, using a system of patronage that helped them to weld strong political and economic communities. Thus, labor unions – a major source of support for Irish, Italian, and Jewish migrants – closed their doors to recently arrived black men. For the most part, blacks have also been denied access to traditionally important sources of power that were opened, however reluctantly, to other urban migrant groups. Irishmen, for example, were once treated with the same scorn now reserved for urban blacks. Yet, by acquiring control of the police departments, political machines, and subsidiary agencies in many large American cities, the Irish have now become "lace-curtain" respectables.

Discrimination has forced blacks into jungle-like ghettoes. Previous immigrants also survived terrible housing conditions, but they eventually moved on to more decent accommodations as new floods of immigrants took their place in the slums of the cities. Except for a handful, however, blacks have been forced to remain in the increasingly deteriorated conditions of American cities and to endure the associated social costs of such an existence: uncontrolled crime, rat- and roach-infested housing, economic exploitation, and schools of questionable quality.

Unlike most urban migrants before them, therefore, blacks have flooded American cities, but their hopes have not been fulfilled. While other urban migrants moved on to better and better conditions, the majority of blacks have been forced to admit that their expectations have not been fulfilled.

If one considers the future of America's cities, it is clear that blacks represent a "wave of the future." For good or ill, there is little migration of blacks out of the major urban centers, and the migration of blacks from the South to northern urban cities continues. Thus, in the decade between the census of 1960 and 1970, New York City lost one million people (largely white middle class), but the size of the city remained the same because approximately one million blacks and people of Latin-American origin moved to the "Big Apple."[7] The result of this trend is clearly revealed in New York City's school statistics. In 1973, official figures documented a trend that has been steadily continuing: blacks for the first time became a plurality within the city school system.[8]

In 1973, blacks constituted 36.1 percent of the city's schoolchildren. The number of black students (406,974) increased steadily since 1957 in both absolute and proportional figures. Europeans have steadily been decreasing since 1957. Adding the 259,758 Puerto Rican children and other minority groups in the New York school system, it is clear that a "colored" population dominates the schools.

Chicago schools have followed the same pattern. By 1973, they were more segregated than ever. The proportion of black students in the total system rose to 57.6 percent. Puerto Ricans, another growing minority, accounted for an unprecedented 11.7 percent. The number of all-black elementary schools increased from 1972 from 128 to 144.

The implication of these figures is clear. In New York and Chicago, as well as most other major urban centers, the school systems have become steadily black and Puerto Rican, surrounded by a ring of white schools. Politically, the consequence is equally clear: once these children reach voting age, they can wrest the fruits of political control from presently dominant white groups.

The pattern of current urbanization in America indicates, therefore, that blacks can soon assume control of political power in the cities. With it, they should also gain power over police departments, housing developments, and other crucial city agencies. Yet, it seems equally likely that these urban enclaves of black power will remain isolated from the mainstream of American society. If housing discrimination continues and employment patterns do not change, blacks will rule small urban principalities – but without resources, industries, or a viable tax base. This would indeed be a hollow victory. All current trends, then, appear to point in the same direction: black "separatism," desired or not, will triumph in American cities but black mayors will be left only with the remnants of an urban scene, *blitzkreiged* by racism and poverty.

## RACISM AND SEPARATISM

This dire forecast of bleak, black cities surrounded by lilywhite suburbs *could* be mitigated by a distinct decline in white racism. It is conceivable, for example, that white attitudes toward blacks might lessen in its hostility and that suburban barriers to migration will collapse. It is possible, too, that American businesses in cities as diverse as New York, Houston, Detroit, and Lost Angeles will maintain their headquarters or major facilities in these urban areas. They might do so because of so-called "economies of scale" (savings that accrue from allowing industries and businesses to continue their existence in urban areas which already provide utilities, transportation, and other facilities). In 1974, this option still remains open. In New York, for example, despite black incursions, dire predictions, and an admitted decline in public school quality, the majority of America's 500 biggest corporations maintain their headquarters, or major sub-headquarters, in Manhattan.

Whether this economic trend continues is primarily dependent upon the degree of white racism. If whites perceive black domination of urban centers as inevitably leading to a higher rate of crime, physical dangers in school, and eventual "race-mixing," then they too will flee to the suburbs leaving behind them an urban wasteland. An essential question must, therefore, be faced: is there a discernible decline of white prejudice against blacks?

Unfortunately, no one has provided data as a definitive answer to this question.

On the one hand, Angus Campbell who conducted a study of 15 American cities between 1964 and 1970 concluded, "The evidence shows that on many questions of principle and policy white and black attitudes moved closer together. . . . Reports of cross-racial contacts in various social settings consistently showed increased contact and specifically increased contact as friends."[9] Similarly, a report by the Harris poll concluded, "Despite continuing Negro-Caucasian tensions across the country, Caucasian attitudes toward Negroes have changed significantly. . . . In 1963, 51 percent of all white people objected to the idea of having a Negro family move in next door. Today [1965] this number has diminished to 37 percent."[10] Clearly, too, there has been a massive change in national policy on an official level: since World War II, *de jure* school integration has been ordered, several basic civil rights bills have passed Congress, anti-poverty programs (primarily aimed at blacks) have been instituted, and some political routes to power have been opened. All of this could not have occurred without some change in white racism.

On the other hand, it is quite clear that verbal expressions of white "tolerance" are rarely matched by concrete political or economic actions. When city housing administrations attempt to erect multiracial housing in communities such as New York's Forest Hills, lower-middle-class whites turn out en masse to prevent construction; when Houston blacks begin to assert their power at the ballot box, the white "powers-that-be" redistrict areas to insure the defeat of promising black candidates; just before a black mayor assumes power in Cleveland, a number of formerly appointive jobs suddenly became "tenured" positions; and when urban schools "tip" toward black domination in cities like New York or Atlanta, whites make convenient arrangements to either flee the city, "co-opt" the school administration, or enroll their children in private schools.

The facts about white racism are, therefore, difficult to interpret, and it is even harder to disentangle what white people *say* they believe from what they actually *do*. This is particularly true when whites begin to actually "pay" – economically, politically, or socially for their (verbally expressed) opinions about blacks.

Three studies conducted in different historical periods shed some light on the verbal attitudes held by whites and blacks on "racial" issues. The first is a study of racial attitudes on a cross-national basis conducted by the Harris poll between 1963 and 1965;[11] the second is a study of three cities conducted between 1965 and 1969;[12] and the third is a 15-city study directed by Angus Campbell between 1964 and 1970.[13] These studies reached remarkably similar conclusions:

1. During the 1960s, the majority of white people did not *verbally* express overt racism toward blacks. Campbell found, for example, that:

a. 86 percent of whites would not object to a black supervisor at their job;

b. 69 percent believed that blacks do not get good housing because of landlord discrimination;

c. 67 percent favored laws that would prohibit discrimination against blacks.[14]

2. The degree of virulent racism *appeared* to decline during the 1960s and early 1970s. According to the Harris poll, the short period between 1963 and 1965 marked several major declines in white attitudes about discrimination against blacks:

a. Only 37 percent of whites (as opposed to 51 percent in 1963) objected to a black family living next door to them;

b. while 17 percent of whites objected to working next to a black on a job in 1963, this figure dropped to 10 percent in 1965.[15]

3. During this same period in the 1960s, however, the majority of whites still adhered to stereotypical attitudes about blacks. In the Campbell poll:

a. 67 percent of the white population believed that blacks were pushing too hard for integration;

b. 56 percent of whites believed that blacks brought upon themselves the various disadvantages suffered in jobs, education, and housing;[16]

c. 58 percent believed that blacks had less ambition;[17]

d. 53 percent believed that blacks had looser morals than whites.[18]

4. On basic issues of policy, whites and blacks continued to disagree during the 1960s and early 1970s:

a. only tiny percentages of blacks believed that the speed of integration was moving too fast (four percent in Oakland, two percent in New York, one percent in Birmingham) while, as we have noted, whites consistently believed that integration was moving too swiftly;[19]

b. while overwhelming percentages of blacks believed that

the federal government should insure fair treatment in jobs (84 percent in 1968), only 33 percent of whites agreed with them;[20]

c. in 1970, 78 percent of blacks favored total desegregation vs. 35 percent of whites.[21]

From a variety of different polls, then, it seems clear that the majority of white Americans give lip service to the idea of tolerance and nondiscrimination. Beneath this surface liberalism, however, is a hard core of stereotypes about blacks, a stiff resistance to government policy aimed at changing the balance of power, and a basic disagreement with blacks about which policies ought to be followed.

Whites seem to be saying from one decade to the next that "if blacks were only like us, we would treat them equally." And, indeed, as Gordon Allport pointed out many years ago, there may be a grain of truth to this adage: if people of equal status – educationally, economically, and socially – come together, white racism declines and sometimes disappears.

Unfortunately, life in urban areas is not adequate to the task of aiding in the decline (or disappearance) of racism. Population density is *not* associated with *intimate* contact between people. Rather, urbanization and the concomitant bureaucratic organization of businesses, services, and other points of contact lend themselves to an even greater segmentation of primary and secondary relationships than exists in small towns. Work and leisure are increasingly independent for all, as persons live in one part of the city and work in another. A large proportion of the contacts are hurried and casual, thus increasing the probability of reinforcing stereotyped conceptions of "others." Racism, rationalized on the basis of negative stereotypes, under these conditions can hardly be expected to be undermined. As ethnic identities and loyalties follow not only racial (or national) *but* class differences, even more firmly drawn lines between "we" and "you" than now exist are predictable.

It appears, therefore, that *de facto* separatism will continue (and that various ideological movements among both blacks and whites will glorify it) unless the basic class differences between whites and blacks are eroded. Is there any substantial evidence that the social and economic distance between blacks and whites has lessened or will lessen in the future?

## SOCIAL CLASS AND SEPARATISM

No one could deny that the long-range trend of black economics has been on the upswing. Clearly, the evolution from slave to Pullman porter to black millionaire represents an absolute change in economic welfare. Equally clearly, there has been an upsurge in college-educated blacks and a major increase in the black middle class in recent years. Since 1961, black families earning in excess of $6,000 a year have increased from 20 percent to 25 percent of the black population. Black college enrollment has tripled since 1950. And, as Thomas Pettigrew points out in this volume, the percent of middle-class blacks has increased from 5 to 25 percent of the black population since 1940.[22] In 1973, American blacks earned more than the total national income of Canada.

Why, then, do the Harlems, Bedford-Stuyvesants, and Watts continue to fester in American cities? From our perspective, there are a variety of reasons. First, the *proportional* gain in black income as opposed to whites has been negligible and possibly totally illusory. The Federal Reserve System reported that the median family income of blacks between 1965 and 1967 rose from 44 percent to 59 percent of the median white income. Even this meager proportional gain, however, was wiped out by the unemployment caused by relatively mild recessions in the 1970s. Thus, black families in 1973, while earning more than they ever did in absolute money, were still running 50 percent behind the earnings of whites in equivalent occupations.

Second, both discriminatory patterns in the South and the modernization of agriculture have increasingly forced black farmers to migrate North. In an automated economy, their unskilled labor is not required, and consequently black rates of unemployment have consistently exceeded the white rate by two to one. The old adage of "the last hired and first fired" still applies to the urban blacks.

Third, despite the increase in education attainment, three times the proportion of whites as of blacks had actually completed college in 1973. Again, if it requires underlining, this discrepancy reflects the "apple-pie" tradition of discrimination. Only recently have our northern metropolitan areas made concerted efforts to change the pattern. The "open admissions" policy of the City University of New York, for example, now allows all New York City high school graduates some degree of choice (and free tuition) to any of the public colleges within the city. Although official ethnic statistics have not been publicized, our personal experience indicates that only a few traditional patterns have been uprooted. CCNY, the first free public "Academy" in the United States, formerly drew a large proportion of its students from people of Jewish ethnic background. In 1973, Jews composed much less than 33 percent of the school's enrollment, and "Open Admissions students" brought a flood of black and Latino students to CCNY. Despite some efforts on the part of the college to afford remedial programs, however, New York blacks account for a highly disproportionate number of "dropouts."

We are in full agreement with the policy that allows every person an equal chance at higher education, and we support those programs, however minimal they may be, that attempt to make up for educational deficiencies. Yet, the glaring inadequacies of ghetto high schools and elementary schools retain their impact. An "open admissions" class to CUNY which can boast of a 9th-grade reading level is exceptional. The fault of this discrepancy lies perhaps with the "lower" school system which is, in turn, affected by a downward spiraling of teaching quality, tax base, and ultimately the disappearance of the white middle class who (in spite of their professed "liberalism") continue to desert the city.

Thus, while the economic position as well as the educational status of blacks have improved in absolute terms, the fact is that the majority of urban blacks remains sadly behind their white fellow citizens, continuing to separate black and white.

This opinion is reinforced by several sophisticated studies. The first study tells us that even if discrimination were to disappear today, class differences would persist. This rather pessimistic finding was reached by scholars Stanley Lieberson and Glenn Fuguitt.

Lieberson and Fuguitt, while recognizing that discrimination has caused the difficulties facing blacks today, posed the hypothetical question: what would happen if there were an immediate end to all forms of ethnic discrimination?[23] In this analysis, they posited situations where an employer wished to hire high school graduates on a completely random basis, regardless of ethnic background of the applicants. Using a Markov chain model, the sociologists found that a gap in employment between whites and blacks would persist based upon simple predictions from the father's original occupation. Essentially, they found that "a complete end to discrimination would not mean an immediate end to their [blacks'] social and economic liabilities."[24] On the basis of mathematical predictions, it would require several generations – *after* a total end to discrimination – before blacks could attain the same occupational or educational level as whites. The persistent nature of the class system of American society is, moreover, reinforced by overt discrimination against blacks.

One American institution, the Army has made sustained attempts (under order by President Truman in 1948) to eliminate discrimination in its ranks. Technically, all of the armed services have undergone total desegregation since 1948. Therefore, one would expect them to be the occupations least affected by racial discrimination. Further, the armed services are supposedly the major institutions in American society that are most affected by direct orders.

Some observers of racial integration within the armed services have rendered optimistic conclusions concerning the removal of caste discriminations. One author, Charles C. Moskos, believes that the official lack of discrimination in the armed forces has led to greater black mobility in ranks (although blacks still remain in less skilled positions) and to greater interracial contact in informal associations.[25] In foreign situations, the black crime rate (as defined by the army) dropped. In Vietnam, for example, blacks received 18 percent of disciplinary reports, although they made up 22 percent of the troops. In Germany, blacks made much greater contact with the foreign population than did white soldiers: nearly 15 percent of black soldiers had learned at least some German as opposed to 3.4 percent of the white Americans.

One might very well conclude, therefore, that class integration brought about by edict as in the army might radically reduce the class separatism of blacks and whites. However, a severe cautionary footnote should be added. David Brogi studied the relation between intelligence (as measured by the Army's standard test between 1948 and 1970) and assignment for all draftees. In the white group, as one would predict, the more intelligent men were assigned to "higher" positions in electronics, radio transmission, artillery control, etc. With blacks, however, the correlation was negative: that is, the most intelligent blacks were assigned to the infantry (the lowest "social class" within the army) and were, therefore, killed more often.[26] No one knows exactly why this occurred: possibly, the predominantly southern officers who make up the army's commanders wished to keep intelligent blacks "in their place" – as cannon fodder. Possibly, there were fears that intelligent blacks would disrupt the system if they were placed in higher positions. By the very worst interpretation, army officers wished to decimate the ranks of intelligent blacks by genocide. In any case, the facts stand: even in the most "integrated" social class system of America, blacks were placed at the bottom of the ranks – *particularly* if they were intelligent.

In summation, the most vital change in the black situation has been the unplanned sweep of migration from peasant farms to urban ghettoes. Imposed separatism is a reality within urban areas. It would appear that some facets of racism have been altered and overt discrimination has been lessened by court decision. Nonetheless, one must conclude that the social class barriers separating white and black Americans remain solidly entrenched.

Ironically, it is in these same segregated urban ghettoes that cries for separatism, in one form or another, have been loudly articulated by some members of the black communities. In our opinion, none of the strategies of separatism dissected in this book offers a viable route to black emancipation, which is, after all, the most important issue discussed. Keeping this in mind, let us examine the impact, if any, of such separatist ideology and review them critically in light of the present American scene.

## THE FAILURE OF SEPARATIST IDEOLOGIES

The main obstacle to any type of ideological black separatism – whether in the form of a separate southern nation as the Communists once suggested, or a return to Africa as advocated by Garvey, or militant domination of urban ghettoes desired by the Black Panthers – is simply that the majority of black people in America do not desire it as their long-term goal. In every poll taken, varying only with the specific question posed, black people have consistently rejected the notion of separatism. In one extensive study, Angus Campbell and H. Schuman found that in 1968 from 95 percent to 72 percent of blacks in 15 American cities endorsed integration and rejected separatist ideologies.[27] William Brink and Louis Harris found substantially the same result;[28] and the Center for Urban Education, in its examination of the Bedford-Stuyvesant ghetto, found that fully 80 percent of the black would, if they could, choose to live on an integrated block.[29] Further, the majority of blacks rejected the use of violence as a way of advancing the black cause: in 1969, 64 percent of Houston blacks, 87 percent of the Watts population, and 71 percent of Oakland's blacks opposed violence as a viable means for achieving improvement in their living conditions.[30] These polls were taken during and just after the cresting of ghetto rioting in American cities. Yet the commitment to racial harmony would appear from these research data to be so pervasive in the black communities of America that separatist or militant groups will, no doubt, continue to find it difficult to mount mass support.

Nonetheless, two segments of the American population have given support to the idea of black separatism. On the one hand, young, middle-class, well-educated blacks tend more often to believe that black people should control their own schools, urban communities, and occupations. On the other hand, a significant segment of the least educated, lower class blacks believe in vague propositions such as "blacks should have their own nation." The separatist element in both groups is still a minority, but presumably has lent some substance to the proliferating ideologies of separatism.

In reviewing the various articles in this book, the ideologies of black separatism seem to fall in one or more of the following categories, each by itself containing serious flaws.

The various ideologies of black separatism suggest either physical withdrawal from American society or a partial separatism based on control of specific institutions within the existing community boundaries. The first two subtypes of ideologies supporting black separatism exemplify the former, while the latter is expressed in the remaining four alternatives:

1. A demand that all American blacks should return to Africa and their original heritage.
2. A desire to establish a separate black nation located geographically within the boundaries of the existing United States.
3. A belief that black command over the economic destinies and other institutions of black ghettoes will lead to liberation.
4. The conviction that blacks should unite themselves with the "Third World" in an attempt to overthrow "neo-colonialism."
5. Power, expressed through armed black militancy, particularly in urban centers will lead to liberation.
6. Power, expressed through voting strength, but with a basic commitment to the existing political structure, is the most effective means of altering the deprived condition of American blacks.

With the exception of the solution demanding complete withdrawal of the black population from the United States, each of the other variations on the separatist theme implies the necessity of working out some kind of equitable relationship with the dominant population. Whether or not there is legal recognition of the bounded area inhabited by black people, such a relationship necessitates the development and use of power. How such power can be created would appear, from the summary of ideologies listed above, to be an open question.

On a general level, it can be argued that the expression of separatist ideology and the general approval, if not acceptance of it, by the mass of black Americans, is a necessary step in promoting the semblance of unity in the face of white racism. Further, it can also be argued that unity is imperative to the creation of the power necessary to obtain equitable treatment, regardless of the long-run alternative chosen: integration or geographic separatism. As Dr. Pettigrew points out in his article, however, such a strategy represents only one means of effecting a given desired end. Moreover, such a strategy may have the latent consequence of helping to create even greater differences between the black and white subcultures, thus further exacerbating interactions between them.

Let us examine the assumptions and achievements of each of these ideological movements.

*A Return to Africa.* Beginning with the abolitionist movement and the original migration of a handful of American blacks to Liberia, ranging through the Marcus Garvey movement, a belief that American blacks should return to their "homeland" has, at times, been a major ideological movement. Ironically, the call for a return to Africa has been echoed by "Know Nothing" groups, the KKK, and the White Citizens' Council.

Obviously, this plea for a return to Africa has met with little success. For reasons outlined in this book, the only tangible result of this ideology has been to establish an oligarchy of former American blacks on the coast of Liberia. Like any ruling class, these descendants of ex-slaves run this tiny nation as a closed corporation and regard the indigenous people as "bushmen" with few political rights and no economic power.

The failure of the "Return to Africa" movement can be traced to many causes. First, Afro-Americans are Afro-*Americans.* In poll after poll, the great majority of American blacks reject the option of migration to Africa. The few who have "gone back," such as the distinguished writer Richard Wright, feel alien to the indigenous cultures and seldom remain in Africa. (The only prominent exception to this rule was, of course, W.E.B. DuBois.) Second, African governments do not wish the permanent intrusion of what they regard as a foreign population into their midst. Just as some American black separatists advise white liberals to "convert" their own constituencies, so too do African leaders such as Julius Nyerere recommend that American blacks remain at home and improve the conditions of their own community.

Clearly, therefore, this alternative must be rejected. The attitude of the Afro-American public, the stance of African leaders, and the material obstacles in the path of any such venture remain insurmountable.*

*A Black Nation within America.* From the Communist Party of the 1930s to the more muted demands by contemporary Black Muslims, a small minority of blacks has hoped that some of the originally Confederate states might be carved out of the union to form a new black republic. The official Muslim program proclaims:

> We want our people in America whose parents or grandparents were descendants from slaves, to be allowed to establish a separate state or territory of their own. . . . We believe that our former slave masters are obligated to maintain and supply our needs in this separate territory for the next 20 or 25 years – until we are able to produce and supply our needs. . . . We believe our contributions to this land and the suffering forced upon us by white America justifies our demand for complete separation in a state or territory of our own.[31]

Usually, the locus of this new black state has been placed in Alabama, Mississippi, and Georgia, or perhaps the "black belt" (where there is a black majority), which runs across these three states.

This alternative must be rejected as a chimera. Admittedly, within the framework of coalition politics – a totally different concept – it is possible that blacks will come to dominate parts of the South. The election of 1100 black officials in the South in 1973 and, most prominently, the election of a black as a mayor of Atlanta suggests the potential political clout of southern blacks.

*Rejection of this alternative does not, however, preclude a renaissance of Afro-American culture. It is both appropriate and laudable that American blacks should attempt to regain some historical sense of their original roots. African culture among slaves were systematically and brutally destroyed by the slave traders. While realists must rule out a physical return to Africa as a viable option, a rejuvenation of Afro-American culture – based on historically accurate precedents – would be an important step in achieving a separate, proud identity for black Americans within the context of a culturally pluralistic society.

Yet, a program calling for the establishment of a completely black state has met with total frustration for a variety of reasons:

1. Blacks continue to move out of the South and thus decrease whatever population threat they might have used against southern whites.

2. Blacks have never achieved a level of economic power in the South that would be necessary to reinforce their political demands.

3. Only the blindest of optimists or ethical theorists would believe that whites would willingly relinquish power, status, and economic control over this territory.

***Black Economic Control.*** Advocates of blacks assuming a greater role in controlling their economic destiny have included people as varied as Richard Nixon and Elijah Muhammad. For example, a federally supported program was instituted in the 1960s whereby black capitalists could receive support for their businesses. (Many of the individuals who participated in this program, however, were disabused during 1970 when they were called upon to donate "voluntarily" to the cause of Mr. Nixon's reelection.)

The Black Muslims, under the leadership of Elijah Muhammad, have established black-owned and operated supermarkets, farms, "Shabazz" bakeries, and clothing stores in Chicago and other areas. The assumption underlying the attempts by the Muslims is that these enterprises will eventually make blacks the economic masters of their own destinies. However, since the profit margin in supermarkets – black or white – is a mere 1.5 percent, it is doubtful that such community-based efforts can generate enough capital to provide rapidly enough for the expansion of jobs necessary to make the black community independent of the white economic structure.

The establishment of black control of their economic destiny would appear to require massive support. Federally supported efforts, albeit small to date, have as yet shown few achievements. Attempts to rebuild black businesses in Washington, D.C., after a series of riots, for example, have for the most part failed. Here, the Small Business Administration found that it was profitable to invest only in liquor stores. The owners of these stores reaped some $50,000 a year in profits, but did not produce jobs or income for other ghetto residents.[32]

Attempts to push big business and industries into the ghettoes have also failed, partially due to an inability to guarantee insurance.[33] Even tax incentives to lure big businesses into the ghetto have failed.[34] Reversing the direction of the labor flow, attempts to bring blacks to jobs outside the ghetto have been blocked by various discriminatory practices in the suburbs.[35]

Self-help community programs that attempt to raise capital from ghetto blacks themselves have also met with predictably poor results. There is simply not enough capital in ghetto communities for major investments.

Black economic control over urban ghettoes, then, seems an impossible goal. Duplication of economic structures in the black community requires a kind of aid that is not forthcoming in the foreseeable future; and control of even some small segment of the economy which would allow the development of a symbiotic relationship to the larger structure is unrealistic in view of current economic trends. The trends of the 1960s and 1970s include: (1) movement away from labor-intensive to computerized industries (clearly to the disadvantage of the population of unskilled laborers, largely blacks); (2) a growth of conglomerates, such as ITT, whose huge capital resources allow them to control every economic organization from telephone systems to food chains (again, this is to the marked disadvantage of small businessmen who lack the capital to compete with large semi-monopolies); (3) increasingly close ties between labor unions (seldom noted for their willingness to accept any "outsider" as apprentices) and the existing business establishment and national government.[36]

All three trends suggest that black economic self-sufficiency is an ephemeral goal. Prosperity may spread among blacks, but ultimate control will reside in white-dominated conglomerates, unions, and the federal government. This route to separatism, therefore, also seems doomed: blocked by factors far beyond the control of the American black community.

***A "Separatist" Union with the "Third World."*** Stokely Carmichael, H. Rapp Brown, and the Black Muslims have all envisaged their interests as coinciding with that of the "Third World": the vast masses of peasants living in Asia, Africa, and Latin America.

No one has come up with a concrete plan for such a union, yet spokesmen for some segment of American blacks continue to identify their destiny with those of suppressed populations in other countries. A typical array of headlines in *Muhammad Speaks* (October 12, 1973) rhetorically links blacks with:

> 1. *Pan-Arabism*: "The International Youth Conferences – the largest since World War II – which took place in [East] Berlin went almost unmentioned in the United States Zionist controlled news media. It was a march for world peace, friendship and solidarity – three enemies of the U.S. and Israeli political systems" [p. 2].
>
> 2. *Anti-Imperialism*: "Black people in this country would do well to pay close attention to the way the sophisticated imperialism of the United States programmed failure into Chile's noble attempt to liberate itself from external exploitation" [p. 9].

In the same issue, blacks are encouraged to colonize Belize – formerly British Honduras (p. 16), to support the nationalities' policy of the Soviet Union which supposedly gives autonomy to such former nations as Lithuania (p. 3), and to welcome the newly won (self-proclaimed) independence of Guinea Bissau in Africa.

Perhaps from some point of view blacks may legitimately claim similarity to many "Third World" nations. American blacks may regard themselves as victims of "internal colonialism" (whereby white interests bleed black communities of their labor and resources). Similarly, Third World ideologists frequently portray themselves as subjects of neo-colonialism and view with dismay the export of their resources, labor, and profits to the richer (white) nations of the world.

It is also within the realm of possibility to picture the United States as caught in conflict with the poorer nations of the world. In such a situation, America might well call upon its armed forces for intervention. If, as current trends indicate, the ranks of America's "professional" army become increasingly black, it is quite possible that black troops might refuse to impose an American edict on "recalcitrant" Third World nations. With the end of the draft (combined with continued urban white discrimination), it may well be that the American army will eventually be filled by American blacks. In that event, a powerful military machine within America might put itself at the disposal of elements favorable to Third World interests. Such speculation remains at the "peanuts and talk" stage of cocktail parties but it can not be dismissed as an impossibility.*

A number of trends suggest that the rhetoric linking the fate of American blacks to the Third World populations will remain on the level of bombast. The economic interests of American blacks are so deeply intertwined with those of a (white-dominated) American economy that it is doubtful to expect the average black man to submerge his own interests in an altruistic effort to help Third World nations. Why, for example, should a black laborer sacrifice his own immediate salary and fringe benefits, even such as they are, for such abstract causes as the stabilization of cocoa prices with Ghana, the relief of Chilean copper workers, or gas rationing in support of the Arab cause against Israel? It seems much more likely that black Americans will go along with measures that protect their own economic position rather than engage in efforts to support the rest of the world.

Moreover, on the other side of the ledger, it is doubtful that Third World nations can or will offer more than verbal support for the cause of black liberation in America. Except for extraordinarily oil-rich nations (such as Kuwait or Libya), most of the Third World is devoted to strengthening its own world position; supporting more important causes within its own sphere of influence (such as Saudi Arabian economic support of Pan-Arabism); fighting a civil war (Vietnam, Uganda, Nigeria); maintaining ties with a white-dominated Western world; or, in rare cases such as Tanzania, actually improving the lot of its own masses of poor people. Few resources are left over which are channeled to the use of black Americans.

Thus, neither the tangible economic interests of black Americans nor the political/economic concerns of the Third World appear to dictate, or even suggest, a coalition between the two groups.

## ARMED BLACK MILITANCY

From the Deacons of Self-Defense in Louisiana to the Northern Black Panthers, a small segment of blacks has advocated armed militancy as a means of asserting black control over its own territory. Such groups should not be confused with the rioters of the 1960s who attacked the status quo violently but usually without a specific ideology or general leadership. A typical example of the breed of black militants are "The Black Crusaders," a group that arose in a major Midwestern city. The "Crusaders" have been carefully described by William Helmreich who witnessed their rise and fall.[37]

At its height, the Crusaders probably did not number more than 200 members, most of them in their 20s. They wore distinct uniforms, allocated military titles to each other, firmly rejected any alliance with whites, and advocated the use of weapons by blacks as a means of protecting their own community. The major planks in their program included: "land for all Black people," and "end to policemen patrolling Black communities," and the establishment of a "Black political party which would enable more Black power."[38]

Although typically vague in its particulars, the Black Crusader program specifically avowed hostility to white policemen. They believed that they stood as protectors of the black community and that they were unjustly harassed by police. Indeed, when their headquarters was burned down, many Crusaders believed that police arsonists had done the job.

Simultaneously, the Black Crusaders condemned the entire white establishment (particularly as represented in the police) and had made some abortive attempts to support the candidacy of black-oriented politicians for office. After the resignation of the Crusaders' leader, who was charged with marijuana possession, the organization dwindled in support only to eventually disappear from the American scene. In many ways, the Black Crusaders experienced the same fate as other armed militant organizations in American cities.

Helmreich cites two basic reasons for the disappearance of the Crusaders: a lack of support from urban black masses and the overt hostility of the white establishment. The lack of mass support in this Midwestern city may be attributed to several factors: (1) "Many of the ghetto residents who might have been sympathizers or supporters were impoverished and too concerned with their own problems to be able to become involved very actively with the organization."[39] (2) Police brutality had become a way of life in the ghetto and black residents no longer regarded police attacks on groups like the Black Crusaders as extraordinary. (3) Many ghetto residents may have simply been afraid of displaying any supportive feelings because of feared retaliation from the police.

The opposition of the white establishment (as conveyed directly or through the media) also played an objectively large factor in the demise of the Black Crusaders. The harassment of the organization, arrest of its leaders, and its infiltration by police informers undoubtedly contributed to its eventual death. Other black organizations, more or less dependent on the white establishment, withheld their support. As Helmreich observed:

> "Their [the Crusaders'] office had been burned, many of their leaders were in jail, and the community had, by and large, developed an unfavorable opinion of the organization. Moreover, the Crusaders continued to be followed, stopped, questioned, and, at times, arrested, often on what clearly appeared to be trumped-up charges."[40]

The same fate has more or less befallen most armed militant movements in the United States. Between 1964 and the

*The entire question of America's newly established professional army raises fundamental questions concerning the future of blacks in America. At present, some 25 percent of army ranks are composed of blacks; the officer corps, while technically integrated, is still dominated by whites. Moreover, a disproportionate number of these white officers come from a southern background. One can reasonably project, therefore, a potentially explosive situation where a black rank-and-file, divided (socially, economically, and ideologically) from officers will increasingly come into conflict with white commanders. The high incidence of "fragging" during the Vietnam war (where troops blew up officers who had offended them) may portend a basic division within the American army and lead to a new kind of separatism which could easily erupt into a civil war *within* the army.

1970s, a variety of people – Malcolm X, Stokely Carmichael, Eldridge Cleaver – have taken a militant stand demanding both "black pride" and an armed opposition to repressive white forces.

The Black Panthers took the symbolic lead in advocating community control, rejection of whites, and a semi-Marxist orientation. The Panthers have managed to live a bit longer than the Black Crusaders but their current leader, Huey Newton, had turned, by 1973, to a political (rather than violent) approach to changing the status of blacks. Newton himself came in second in an election for Mayor of Oakland, California, and symbolized the transition of militant blacks from armed conflict to political action. The transformation in groups such as the Black Panthers can be traced to several causes: the killing or imprisonment of more vehement members, the failure of a socialist ideology to appeal to black masses, and the lack of white liberal support (which was, on principle, thrown aside by the original Black Panther leadership).

Whether because of outside pressure, inner divisions, or a lack of broad support, most blacks have rejected the armed Crusader or Panther program as a possible way to achieve improvement in black communities.

Indeed, all programs for black separatism have failed. What path, then, is left?

Clearly, the first step is to accept integration as a necessary step to power within America.

## COALITION POLITICS

Avoiding the pleas for separatism which emotionally swept parts of the black community in the late 1960s and early 1970s, many realistic black leaders have looked to traditional coalition politics as the means for securing power and liberation, Bayard Rustin, for example, has often been called an "accommodationist," "Uncle Tom," and various other epithets. Among black leaders, Rustin has been one of the few to reject separatism and to concentrate on the primary issue: what exact measures might improve the lot of American blacks? He has not been swung by the winds of passion as have his younger comrades. Sometimes alone, this ramrod leader of blacks, carrying with him the memory of Martin Luther King Jr., has consistently tried to forge an alliance with possibly sympathetic white groups. Rustin himself has suffered humiliations ranging from Southern jails to arrest in New York City (he carries a knife-edged cane which some white policemen believe endangers their existence). Yet, he has continued to bear the ideologically unpopular flag of integration. He foresees a time when black political power will join with segments of the white public to achieve a true advancement of the black man's cause in America.

Bayard Rustin, as one of the major "intellectuals" of the black movement, has advanced cogent reasons for discounting black separatism as a major movement in the United States. He correctly believes that trade union movements, the most possible of allies with the blacks, will not contribute to the black movement – unless there is a "quid pro quo." As Rustin points out, separatist black elements have universally been defeated by black trade union groups who have campaigned on a basis of equal economic opportunity and social justice. Black workers, in other words, soundly reject the separatist solution. Further, Rustin argues, class (rather than caste) bases are the only foundation for lasting political alliances. "If the Negro chooses to follow the path of interracial alliances on the basis of class, as almost two million have done today, he can achieve a certain degree of economic equality, which in turn offers a genuine, if not the only, opportunity for self-determination."[41]

Rustin believes that the trade union movement and the Democratic Party in America offer the greatest hope for black advance. Rustin recognizes that there is competition among blacks and whites for scarce jobs and housing; he further acknowledges that trade unions do not ally themselves with blacks out of altruism but rather because of a common recognition of class interests. Blacks, he argues, must recognize that they are a minority in America and must seek out any coalition partner who will aid in the strengthening of their position.

It is clear, as we have already emphasized, that black people will soon dominate many important American cities. They can form a political power base in these urban areas which certainly cannot be ignored by nationally oriented political parties. Further, the political control of the cities will allow blacks the traditional privileges of patronage, control over police and city services, and the granting of contracts. Even if the tax base of America's cities dwindles, these new powers are hardly negligible.

Further, it should be noted that the practice of coalition politics need not be limited to an alliance of blacks with white trade unions. In Houston, liberal whites, rich white conservatives (concerned with the city's image), and blacks joined together to put black candidates into office in positions ranging from school board members to congressmen. In Atlanta, blacks elected a black mayor but simultaneously provided a white candidate (over a black man) with the necessary margin of victory in a city council race. Blacks voted for the white woman on grounds that she had supported the use of revenue-sharing funds for day-care centers.

In Los Angeles, blacks linked themselves with white liberals to overthrow the racist rule of Mayor Sam Yorty. The list could be extended, but two lessons are clear: blacks can be politically astute voters who shift their support to candidates who provide tangible economic gains; and blacks are gaining an increasingly powerful position as a bargaining partner in urban elections.

Nonetheless, over a decade ago, James Q. Wilson issued a most powerful warning of the pitfalls confronting political action by blacks.[42] Many of the same warnings still hold true today:

– Black leadership then as now is fragmented, and it is difficult to organize blacks to back a particular leader.

– Rural-based, less-educated blacks have proven difficult to organize politically. The entry of blacks into the political process has long been delayed in northern cities because of this fact. (Wilson cites a decisive move of blacks into political machines as dating from 1920 in Chicago, 1935 in New York, and 1957 in Detroit.)

– Wilson rightly argued that the interests of blacks and trade unions would become increasingly difficult to reconcile as the particular issue came "closer to home." He cites the relative success of blacks in Detroit politics, for example, as due to a labor-black coalition, which was strong on civil liberties but weak in attempting to pass housing integration laws.

Despite these qualifications, Wilson correctly foresaw a stage in black politics that represents a movement fusing civil action and politics. This he labeled the "new merger." That is, situations where strong, white liberal political movements challenge the existing political status quo. In alliance with blacks, such groups would adhere to the belief that "the natural hostility between the political and civic elites can be ended, and that the civic spirit can dominate the political leader."[43]

Wilson ends his book on a somewhat pessimistic note: "The civic elite has set out to repeal the iron law of oligarchy which it felt had made the political elite unresponsive to the needs of the masses, but in the end they may very well discover that they have only succeeded in amending it."[44]

Developments throughout the nation in the 1970s would seem to have conquered this pessimism. In the North, blacks have organized and voted *en bloc* for causes which they believe will advance their racial or economic interests. This has occurred in cities as diverse as New York and Los Angeles, Cleveland and Newark. In the South, too, a "quiet" revolution has taken place. In 1973, three and one-half million blacks were registered to vote and made the decisive electoral difference in cities as small as Lafayette, Mississippi, and as large as Atlanta, Georgia. John Lewis, a former cotton picker and then head of the Voter Education Project in Atlanta, confidently predicted in 1973 that "within the next eight to ten years, blacks are going to be elected to some of the highest offices. Georgia, Mississippi, the Carolinas are going to be sending several blacks to Congress to join the few who are there now."[45]

Rather than turning inward, as "Black Power" adherents once urged, it appears that blacks are increasingly rejecting separatism and turning to find allies wherever they can. This type of pragmatism can result in strange bedfellows: poor blacks and blue-blood whites voting for the same mayor in Atlanta; "hard-hat" union men and blacks seeking economic security in Detroit; blacks and oil men conspiring to change the nature of Texas.

Of course it can be said that this has always been the way of American politics. Now, having gained a base of urban power, blacks will perhaps learn to use the levers of political influence to push their way to the top – just as the originally "separatist" Irish, Jews, and Italians have done. There will be losses on the way as the uniquely Afro-American culture gradually blends into a uniform American style; storefront churches will pass from the landscape; "soul food" will go the way of corned beef and cabbage. There will be pitfalls and defeats, bribes and betrayals, corrupt deals and lost crusades, but we are convinced that the road of coalition politics is the one viable path for blacks to follow. The idea of separatism is, within this context, only a passing phase in the more important goal of equalizing opportunity and the liberation of all Americans, black and white.

## NOTES

[1] Malcolm X, *The Autobiography of Malcolm X*, (New York: Ballantine, 1973), p. 113.

[2] See, for example, F. Tonnies, *Community and Society* (East Lansing: Michigan State University Press, 1957).

[3] See, for example, Louis Wirth, "Urbanism as a Way of Life," *American Journal of Sociology*, 44 (July 1938).

[4] W.I. Thomas and Florian Znaniecki, *The Polish Peasant in Europe and America* (New York: Dover Publications, 1958).

[5] See Alex Inkeles, "The Modernization of Man," Chapter 10 in *Modernization,* edited by Myron Weiner (New York: Basic Books, 1966).

[6] See William McCord, John Howard, Bernard Friedberg, and Edwin Harwood, *Life Styles in the Black Ghetto* (New York: W.W. Norton, 1969).

[7] See *New York Times*, December 1, 1973.

[8] "A Black Plurality," *New York Times*, October 30, 1973.

[9] Angus Campbell, *White Attitudes Toward Black People* (Ann Arbor: University of Michigan Press, 1969), p. 154.

[10] Louis Harris, *Washington Post,* 1965.

[11] *Ibid.*

[12] McCord, *et al., Life Styles in the Black Ghetto.*

[13] Campbell, *White Attitudes Toward Black People.*

[14] *Ibid.*, p. 4.

[15] Harris, *Washington Post.*

[16] Campbell, *White Attitudes,* p. 4.

[17] Harris, *Washington Post.*

[18] Ibid.

[19] McCord, *et al., Life Styles,* p. 80.

[20] Campbell, *White Attitudes,* p. 129.

[21] *Ibid.,* p. 136.

[22] Thomas Pettigrew, *Racially Separate or Together?* (New York: Anti-Defamation League of B'Nai B'Rith, 1969).

[23] Stanley Lieberson and Glenn Fuguitt, "Negro-White Occupational Differences in the Absence of Discrimination," *American Journal of Sociology,* 73 (1967), 188-200.

[24] *Ibid.*

[25] Charles C. Moskos, "Racial Integration in the Armed Forces," *American Journal of Sociology* (1966), 72.

[26] David Brogi, unpublished Master's Thesis, Department of Sociology, Syracuse University, 1969.

[27] A. Campbell and H. Schuman, "Racial Attitudes in Fifteen American Cities" (The National Advisory Commission on Civil Disorders, 1968).

[28] William Brink and Louis Harris, *The Negro Revolution in America* (New York: Simon and Schuster, 1964).

[29] Center for Urban Education, "Survey of the Residents of Bedford-Stuyvesant" (unpublished paper, 1968).

[30] McCord, *et al., Life Styles.*

[31] "The Muslim Program," *Muhammad Speaks,* October 12, 1973.

[32] Lynn Shepard, "Washington's 14th Street," *Christian Science Monitor,* April 5, 1969.

[33] *Christian Science Monitor,* May 5, 1969.

[34] *Ibid.*

[35] *Christian Science Monitor,* May 9, 1969.

[36] Quotes in *Newsweek*, September 10, 1973.

[37] William B. Helmreich, *The Black Crusaders* (New York: Harper and Row, 1973).

[38] *Ibid.*, pp. 76-77.

[39] *Ibid.*, p. 155.

[40] *Ibid.*, p. 151.

[41] Bayard Rustin, "The Failure of Black Separatism," *Harpers*, January 1970.

[42] James Q. Wilson, *Negro Politics* (New York: Free Press, 1960).

[43] *Ibid.*, p. 314.

[44] *Ibid.*, p. 315.

[45] Quoted in *New York Times,* November 20, 1973.

# 11
# *Racially Separate or Together**

THOMAS F. PETTIGREW

America has had an almost perpetual racial crisis for a generation. But the last third of the 20th century has begun on a new note, a change of rhetoric and a confusion over goals. Widespread rioting is just one expression of this note. The nation hesitates; it seems to have lost its confidence that the problem can be solved; it seems unsure as to even the direction in which a solution lies. In too simple terms, yet in the style of the fashionable rhetoric, the question has become: Shall Americans of the future live racially separate or together?

This new mood is best understood when viewed within the eventful sweep of recent years. Ever since World War I, when war orders combined with the curtailment of immigration to encourage massive migration to industrial centers, Negro Americans have been undergoing rapid change as a people. The latest product of this dramatic transformation from southern peasant to northern urbanite is a second- and third-generation northern-born youth. Indeed, over half of Negro Americans alive today are below 22 years of age. The most significant fact about this "newest new Negro" is that he is relatively released from the principal social controls recognized by his parents and grandparents, from the restraints of an extended kinship system, a conservative religion and an acceptance of the inevitability of white supremacy.

Consider the experience of the 20-year-old Negro youth today. He was born in 1948; he was an impressionable six years old when the highest court in the land decreed against *de jure* public school segregation; he was only nine years old at the time of the Little Rock, Arkansas, desegregation confrontation; he was 12 years old when the student-organized sit-ins began at segregated lunchcounters throughout the South; and he was 15 when the dramatic March-on-Washington took place and 17 when the climactic Selma march occurred. He has literally witnessed during his short life the initial dismantling of the formal structure of white supremacy. Conventional wisdom holds that such an experience should lead to a highly satisfied generation of young Negro Americans. Newspaper headlines and social psychological theory tell us precisely the opposite is closer to the truth.

## RELATIVE DEPRIVATION THEORY

The past three decades of Negro American history constitute an almost classic case for relative deprivation theory (Pettigrew, 1964, 1967). Mass unrest has reoccurred throughout history after long periods of improvement followed by abrupt periods of reversal (Davies, 1962). The pattern derives from four revolt-stirring conditions triggered by long-term improvements: (a) living conditions of the dominant group typically advance faster than those of the subordinate group; (b) the aspirations of the subordinate group climb far more rapidly than actual changes; (c) status inconsistencies among subordinate group members increase sharply; and (d) a broadening of comparative reference groups occurs for the subordinate group (Pettigrew, 1967).

Each of these four conditions typifies the Negro American situation today (Geschwender, 1964; Pettigrew, 1964, 1967). (a) Though the past few decades have witnessed the most rapid gains in Negro American history, these gains have generally not kept pace with those of white America during these same prosperous years. (b) Public opinion surveys document the swiftly rising aspirations of Negro Americans, especially since 1954. Moreover, (c) status inconsistency has been increasing among Negroes, particularly among the young whose educational level typically exceeds the low-status employment offered them. Finally, (d) Negro Americans have greatly expanded their relevant reference groups in recent years; affluent referents in the richest country on earth are now routinely adopted as the appropriate standard with which to judge one's condition. The second component of unrest involving a sudden reversal has been supplied, too, by the Vietnam War. Little wonder, then, that America's racial crisis reached the combustible point in the late 1960s.

The young Negro surveys the current scene and observes correctly that the benefits of recent racial advances have dispro-

*This paper was the author's presidential address to the Society for the Psychological Study of Social Issues, delivered at the annual convention of the American Psychological Association in San Francisco, California, on September 1, 1968. Its preparation was facilitated by Contract No. OEC 1-6-061774-1887 of the United States Office of Education. Reprinted by permission from *Journal of Social Issues*. Vol. xxv, No. 1, 1969.

portionately accrued to the expanding middle class, leaving further behind the urban lower class. While the middle-class segment of Negro America has expanded from roughly five to 25 percent of the group since 1940,[1] the vast majority of Negroes remain poor. Raised on the proposition that racial integration is the basic solution to racial injustice, the young Negro's doubts grow as opportunities open for the skilled while the daily lives of the unskilled go largely unaffected. Accustomed to a rapid pace of events, many Negro youth wonder if integration will ever be possible in an America where the depth of white resistance to racial change becomes painfully more evident: the equivocation of the 1964 Democratic Party Convention when faced with the challenge of the Mississippi Freedom Democratic Party; the Selma bridge brutality; the summary rejection by the 1966 Congress of antidiscrimination legislation for housing; the repressive reaction to riots from the Chicago Mayor's advocacy of police state methods to the New Jersey Governor's suspension of the Bill of Rights in Plainfield; and, finally, the wanton assassinations within ten weeks of two leading symbols of the integration movement. These events cumulated to create understandable doubts as to whether Dr. Martin Luther King's famous dream of equality could ever be achieved.

## SHIFT IN MILITANT STANCE AND RHETORIC

It is tempting to project this process further, as many mass media accounts unhesitantly have done, and suggest that all of Negro America has undergone this vast disillusionment, that Negroes now overwhelmingly reject racial integration for separatist goals. As we shall note shortly, this is emphatically not the case. Nevertheless, the militant stance and rhetoric *have* shifted, and many whites find considerable encouragement in this new Negro mood. Indeed, strictly separatist solutions for the black ghettoes of urban America have been most elaborately and enthusiastically advanced not by Negroes at all but by such white writers as newspaper columnist Joseph Alsop (1967a, 1967b) and W.H. Ferry (1968) of the Center for the Study of Democratic Institutions.[2] Nor should we confuse "black power" ideas as such with separatism, since there are numerous variants of this developing ideology, only a few of which portray a racially separate United States as the desirable end-state. As a presumed intervening stage, black separatism is more concerned with group pride and "local control," more a retreat from whites than an attempt to dominate them. This contrasts with the traditional attempts at racial supremacy of white segregationists. Black separatism and white separatism present the danger that they might well congeal to perpetuate a racially separate nation; but they are otherwise somewhat different phenomena as a cursory examination of their basic assumptions readily reveals.

## SEPARATIST ASSUMPTIONS

White segregationists, North and South, base their position upon three bedrock assumptions. First, they maintain that separation benefits both races in that each feels awkward and uncomfortable in the midst of the other (Armstrong and Gregor, 1964). Whites and Negroes are happiest and most relaxed when in the company of "their own kind." We shall call this "*the comfortable assumption.*"

The second assumption of white segregationists is blatantly racist. The underlying reality of the nation's racial problem, they unashamedly maintain, is that Negroes are inherently inferior to Caucasians. The findings of both social and biological science place in serious jeopardy every argument put forward for "*the racial inferiority assumption,*" and an ever-decreasing minority of white Americans subscribe to it (Pettigrew, 1964). Yet it remains the essential substrata of white segregationist thinking; racial contact must be avoided, according to this reasoning, if white standards are not to be diluted. Thus, Negro attendance at a predominantly white school may benefit the Negro children, but it is deemed by segregationists as inevitably harmful to white children.[3]

The third assumption flows from this presumption of white racial superiority. Since contact can never be mutually beneficial, it will inevitably lead to racial conflict. The White Citizens' Councils in the Deep South, for example, stoutly insist that they are opposed to violence and favor racial separation as the primary means of maintaining racial harmony. As long as Negroes "know their place," as long as white supremacy remains unchallenged, "*the racial conflict assumption*" contends strife will be at a minimum.

Coming from the opposite direction, black separatists fundamentally base their position upon three parallel assumptions. They agree with "*the comfortable assumption*" that both whites and Negroes are more at ease when separated from each other. Some of this agreement stems from the harsh fract that Negroes have borne the heavier burden of desegregation and have entered previously all-white institutions where open hostility is sometimes explicitly practiced by segregationist whites in order to discourage the process. Yet some of this agreement stems, too, from more subtle situations. The demands by a few black student organizations on interracial campuses for all-black facilities have been predicated on "*the comfortable assumption.*"

A second assumption focuses directly upon white racism. Supported by the chief conclusion of the National Advisory Commission on Civil Disorders (1968), black separatists label white racism as a central problem which so-called "white liberals" should confine their energies to eradicating. "*The white-liberals-must-eradicate-white-racism-assumptions*" underlies two further contentions: namely, that "white liberals" should stay out of the ghetto save as their money and expertise are explicitly requested, and that it is no longer the job of black militants to confront and absorb the abuse of white racists.

The third assumption is the most basic of all, and is in tacit agreement with the segregationist notion that interracial contact as it now occurs makes only for conflict. Interaction between Negro and white Americans, it is held, can never be truly equal and mutually beneficial until Negroes gain personal and group autonomy, self-respect, and power. "*The autonomy-before-contact assumption*" often underlies a two-step theory of how to achieve meaningful integration: the first step requires separation so that Negroes can regroup, unify, and gain a positive self-image and identity; only when this is achieved can the second step of real integration take place. Ron Karenga, a black militant leader in Los Angeles, states the idea forcefully:

"We're not for isolation, but interdependence. But we can't become interdependent unless we have something to offer. We can live with whites interdependently once we have black power" (Calame, 1968).

Each of these ideological assumptions deserves examination in light of social psychological theory and findings.

## SOCIAL PSYCHOLOGICAL CONSIDERATIONS OF SEPARATIST ASSUMPTIONS

### The Comfortable Assumption

There can be no denying the reality of initial discomfort and ill-ease for many Negro and white Americans when they encounter each other in new situations. This reality is so vivid and generally recognized that both black and white separatists employ it as a key fact in their thinking, though they do not analyze its nature and origins.

The social science literature is replete with examples of the phenomenon. Kohn and Williams (1956), for instance, studied New York State facilities unaccustomed to Negro patronage. Negro researchers would enter a tavern, seek service, and later record their experiences, while white researchers would observe the same situation and record their impressions for comparison. Typically the first reaction of waitresses and bartenders was embarrassment and discomfort; they turned to the owner or others in authority for guidance. When this was unavailable, the slightest behavioral cue from anyone in the situation was utilized as a gauge of what was expected of them. And if there were no such cues, confusion often continued until somehow the tense situation had been structured. Needless to add, the tension was at least as great for the potential Negro patron.

Other examples arise from small group and summer camp research. Irwin Katz (1964) has described the initial awkwardness in biracial task groups in the laboratory; white partners usually assumed an aggressive, imperious role, Negro partners – a passive role. Similarly, Yarrow (1958) found initial tension and keen sensitivity among many Negro children in an interracial summer camp, much of which centered around fears of rejection by white campers. Not all Negroes and whites, of course, manifest this discomfort. Furthermore, such tension does not continue to pervade a truly integrated situation. Katz noted that once Negroes were cast in assertive roles behavior in his small groups became more egalitarian, and this improvement generalized to new situations. Yarrow, too, observed a sharp decline in Negro anxiety and sensitivity which occurred after two weeks of successful integration at the summer camp. Similar increments in cross-racial acceptance and reductions in tension have been noted in new interracial situations in department stores (Harding and Hogrefe, 1952; Saenger and Gilbert, 1950), the merchant marine (Brophy, 1946), the armed forces (Stouffer *et al.*, 1949), public housing (Deutsch and Collins, 1951; Jahoda and West, 1951; Wilner *et al.*, 1955; and Works, 1961), and even among the Philadelphia police (Kephart, 1957).

### Contact Effects Limited to the Situation

This is not to say that new interracial situations invariably lead to acceptance. As we shall note, the *conditions* of the interracial contact are crucial. Moreover, even under optimal conditions, the cross-racial acceptance generated by contact is typically limited to the particular situation. Thus, white steelworkers learn to work easily with Negroes as co-workers and vote for them as union officers; but this acceptance does not carry over to attitudes and action concerning interracial housing (Reitzes, 1953). A segregated society restricts the generalization effects of even truly integrated situations; and at times like the present when race assumes such overwhelming salience, the racial tension of the larger society may poison previously successful interracial settings.

Acquaintance and similarity theory helps to sort out the underlying process. Newcomb states the fundamental tenet as follows:

> Insofar as persons have similar attitudes toward things of importance to both or all of them, and discover that this is so, they have shared attitudes; under most conditions the experience of sharing such attitudes is rewarding, and thus provides a basis for mutual attraction. (Newcomb *et al.*, 1965)

Rokeach has applied these notions to American race relations with some surprising results. He maintains that white American rejection of Negro Americans is motivated less by racism than by assumed belief and value differences. In other words, whites generally perceive Negroes as holding contrasting beliefs, and it is this perception and not race *per se* that leads to rejection. Indeed, a variety of subjects have supported Rokeach's ideas by typically accepting in a social situation a Negro with similar beliefs to their own over a white with different beliefs (Rokeach *et al.*, 1960; Rokeach and Mezei, 1966; Smith *et al.*, 1967; Stein, 1966; Stein *et al.*, 1965).

Additional work specifies the phenomenon more precisely. Triandis and Davis (1965) have shown that the relative importance of belief and race factors in attraction is a joint function of the interpersonal realm in question and personality. Belief similarity is most critical in more formal matters of general personal evaluation and social acceptance, where racial norms are ambiguously defined. Race is most critical in intimate matters of marriage and neighborhood, where racial norms are explicitly defined. For interpersonal realms of intermediate intimacy, such as friendship, both belief and race considerations appear important. Moreover, there are wide individual differences in the application of belief similarity and race, especially in contact realms of intermediate intimacy.[4]

### Isolation's Negative Effects

Seen in the light of this work, racial isolation has two negative effects, both of which operate to make optimal interracial contact difficult to achieve and initially tense. First, isolation prevents each group from learning of the common beliefs and values they do in fact share. Consequently, Negroes and whites kept apart come to view each other as so different that belief dissimilarity typically combines with racial considerations to cause each race to reject contact with the other. Second, isolation leads in time to the evolution of genuine differences in beliefs and values, again making interracial contact in the future less likely.

A number of pointed findings of social psychological research support this extrapolation of interpersonal attraction theory. Stein *et al.* (1965) noted that relatively racially isolated ninth graders in California assumed an undescribed Negro teenager to be similar to a Negro teenager who is described as being quite different from themselves. Smith *et al.* (1967) found that belief similarity relative to racial similarity was more critical in desegregated settings, less critical in segregated settings. And the U.S. Commission on Civil Rights (1967), in its study of *Racial Isolation in the Public Schools*, found that both Negro and white adults who as children had attended interracial schools were more likely today to live in an interracial neighborhood and hold more positive racial attitudes than comparable adults who had known only segregated schools. Or, put negatively, those Americans of both races who experienced only segregated education are more likely to reflect separatist behavior and attitudes as adults.

Racial separatism, then, is a cumulative process. It feeds upon itself and leads its victims to prefer continued separation. In an open-choice situation in Louisville, Kentucky, Negro children were far more likely to select predominantly white high schools if they were currently attending predominantly white junior high schools.[5] From these data, the U.S. Commission on Civil Rights concluded: "The inference is strong that Negro high school students prefer biracial education only if they have experienced it before. If a Negro student has not received his formative education in biracial schools, the chances are he will not choose to enter one in his more mature school years" (U.S. Commission on Civil Rights, 1963).

Similarly, Negro adult products of segregated schools, the Civil Rights Commission (1967) finds, are more likely to believe that interracial schools "create hardships for Negro children" and less likely to send their children to desegregated schools than Negro products of biracial schools. Note that those who most fear discomfort in biracial settings are precisely those who have experienced such situations least. If desegregation actually resulted in perpetual and debilitating tension, as separatists blithely assume, it seems unlikely that children already in the situation would willingly opt for more, or that adults who have had considerable interracial contact as children would willingly submit themselves to biracial neighborhoods and their children to biracial schools.

### A Social Cost Analysis is Needed

A social cost analysis is needed. The question becomes: What price comfort? Racially homogeneous settings are often more comfortable for members of both races, though this seems to be especially true at the start of the contact and does not seem to be so debilitating that those in the situation typically wish to return to segregated living. Those who remain in racial isolation, both Negro and white, find themselves increasingly less equipped to compete in an interracial world. Lobotomized patients are more comfortable, too, but they are impaired for life.

There is nothing inevitable, then, about the tension that characterizes many initial interracial encounters in the United States. Rather it is the direct result of the racial separation that has traditionally characterized our society. In short, separation is the cause, not the remedy, for interracial awkwardness.

## THE ASSUMPTIONS OF RACIAL INFERIORITY AND WHITE-LIBERALS-MUST-ERADICATE-WHITE-RACISM

The second set of separatist assumptions raises related issues. Indeed, both of these assumptions also afford classical cases of self-fulfilling prophecies. Treat a people as inferior, force them to play subservient roles,[6] keep them essentially separate, and the products will necessarily support the initial racist notions. Likewise, assume whites are unalterably racist, curtail Negro efforts to confront racism directly, separate from whites further, and the result will surely be continued, if not heightened, racism.

The core of racist attitudes, the assumption of innate racial inferiority, has been under sharp attack from social science for over three decades.[7] Partly because of this work, white American attitudes have undergone massive change over these years. For example, while only two out of five white Americans regarded Negroes as their intellectual equals in 1942, almost four out of five did by 1956 – including a substantial majority of white Southerners (Hyman and Sheatsley, 1956, 1964). Yet a sizable minority of white Americans, perhaps still as large as a fifth, persist in harboring racist attitudes in their most vulgar and naive form. This is an important fact in a time of polarization such as the present, for this minority becomes the vocal right anchor in the nation's social judgment process.

Racist assumptions are not only nourished by separatism but in turn rationalize separatism. Equal status contact is avoided because of the racist stigma branded upon Negro Americans by three centuries of slavery and segregation. Yet changes are evident in social distance attitudes, too. Between 1942 and 1963, the percentage of white Americans who favored racially desegregated schools rose from 30 to 63; and those with no objections to a Negro neighbor from 35 to 63 (Hyman and Sheatsley, 1964; Sheatsley, 1965). Nor has this trend abated during the recent five years of increasing polarization – a period which the mass media misinterpreted with the vague label of "backlash".[8] The most dramatic shifts have occurred in the South; the proportion of white southern parents who stated that they would not object to having their children attend classes with "a few" Negro children rose from only 38 percent in 1963 to 62 percent by 1965 (American Institute of Public Opinion, 1965). Consistently favorable shifts also characterized white opinion in the North. Here, a school with "a few" Negro children was declared objectionable by 87 percent of white parents in 1963, by 91 percent in 1965; a school where the student body was one-half Negro was acceptable to 56 percent in 1963, to 65 percent in 1965; and a school with a majority of Negro students found no objection among 31 percent in 1963, among 37 percent in 1965. Similar changes are evident in white attitudes in other realms and in more current surveys, though shifts in attitudes toward intimate contact have remained limited.

This slow but steady erosion of racist and separatist attitudes among white Americans has occurred during years of confrontation and change. To be sure, the process has been too slow to keep pace with the Negro's rising aspirations for full justice and complete eradication of racism. Yet this relentless trend parallelling the drive for integration should not be overlooked.

### In a Period of Confrontation

Thus, in a period of confrontation, dramatic events can stimulate surprisingly sharp shifts in a short period of time. Consider the attitudes of white Texans before and after the tragic assassination of Martin Luther King, Jr., the riots that followed his murder, and the issuance of the forthright Report of the National Advisory Commission on Civil Disorders (1968). Table 1 shows the data collected prior to the assassination in November 1967 and February 1968 and following the assassination in May 1968.

**Table 1 Percent of White Texans Who Approve***

| Area of Desegregation | Nov. 1967 | Feb. 1968 | May 1968 | May – (Nov. + Feb.)/2 Change |
|---|---|---|---|---|
| Same buses | 65.6 | 66.6 | 75.6 | + 9.5 |
| Same jobs | 68.5 | 70.7 | 77.3 | + 7.7 |
| Same restaurants | 60.7 | 62.5 | 69.2 | + 7.6 |
| Same hotels | 55.2 | 55.4 | 62.5 | + 7.2 |
| Same schools | 57.1 | 60.4 | 64.3 | + 5.6 |
| Teach your child | 53.1 | 53.6 | 57.7 | + 4.4 |
| Same churches | 61.5 | 62.9 | 66.2 | + 4.0 |
| Same social gatherings | 42.1 | 42.4 | 45.3 | + 3.1 |
| Live next door | 34.2 | 36.2 | 36.8 | + 1.6 |
| Same swimming pools | 35.1 | 30.9 | 34.2 | + 1.2 |
| Same house party | 29.4 | 30.0 | 30.3 | + 0.6 |
| College roommate of your child | 21.4 | 21.5 | 21.4 | – 0.1 |

*These results are taken from R.T. Riley and T.F. Pettigrew, "Dramatic events and racial attitude change." Unpublished paper. Harvard University, August 1968. The data are from probability samples of white Texans drawn and interviewed by Belden Associates of Dallas, Texas, specifically for the U.S. Office of Education Contract No. OEC 1-6-061-774-1887 to Harvard University.

Observe the especially large change in the four realms of relatively formal contact – desegregation in buses, jobs, restaurants, and hotels: the moderate change in realms of relatively informal contact – the desegregation of schools and churches; and the lack of significant change in realms of intimate contact – desegregation of social gatherings, housing, swimming pools, house parties, and college dormitories. Despite the ceiling effect, approval increased greatest for those items already most approved. One is reminded of the Triandis and Davis (1965) breakdown of racial realms by degree of intimacy. The attitude change also varied among different types of white Texans; the young and the middle class shifted positively the most, again despite ceiling effects.[9] The tentative generalization growing out of these data is: In times of confrontation, dramatic events can achieve positive attitude changes among those whites and in those realms least subject to separatist norms.

### Contact Studies

The most solid social psychological evidence of racial attitude change comes from the contact studies. Repeated research in a variety of newly desegregated situations discovered that the attitudes of both whites and Negroes toward each other markedly improved. Thus, after the hiring of Negroes as department store clerks in New York City, one investigation noted growing acceptance of the practice among the white clerks (Harding and Hogrefe, 1952) and another noted rapid acceptance among white customers (Saenger and Gilbert, 1950). And a series of studies concentrating on public housing residents found similar results (Deutsch and Collins, 1951; Jahoda and West, 1951; Wilner *et al.*, 1955; and Works, 1961), as did studies on servicemen (MacKenzie, 1948; Stouffer *et al.*, 1949), the merchant marine (Brophy, 1946), government workers (MacKenzie, 1948), the police (Kephart, 1957), students (MacKenzie, 1948), and general small town populations (Williams, 1964). Some of these results can be interpreted not as the result of contact, but as an indication that more tolerant white Americans seek contact with Negro Americans. A number of the investigations, however, restrict this self-selection factor, making the effects of the new contact itself the only explanation of the significant alterations in attitudes and behavior.

A major study by Deutsch and Collins (1951) illustrates this important literature. These investigators took ingenious advantage of a made-to-order natural experiment. In accordance with state law, two public housing projects in New York City were desegregated; in all cases, apartment assignments were made irrespective of race or personal preference. In two comparable projects in Newark, the two races were assigned to separate buildings. Striking differences were found between the attitudes toward Negroes of randomly selected white housewives in the desegregated and segregated developments. The desegregated women held their Negro neighbors in higher esteem and were considerably more in favor of interracial housing (75 percent to 25 percent). When asked to name the chief faults of Negroes, they mentioned such personal problems as feelings of inferiority and oversensitivity; the segregated women listed such group stereotypes as troublemaking, rowdy, and dangerous.

As discussed earlier, however, improvements in social distance attitudes are often limited to the immediate contact situation itself. Yet basic racist stereotypes are often affected, too. One white housewife in an interracial development put it bluntly: "Living with them my ideas have changed altogether. They're just people . . . they're not any different." Commented another: "I've really come to like it. I see they're just as human as we are" (Deutsch and Collins, 1951). And a Negro officer on an interracial ship of Korea summed it up candidly: "After a while you start thinking of whites as people."

### On a National Scale

Recent surveys bear out these contact findings on a national scale. Hyman and Sheatsley (1964) found that the most extensive racial attitude changes among whites have occurred where extensive desegregation of public facilities had already taken place.[10] And data from the Equal Educational Opportunity Survey – popularly known as "the Coleman Report" – indicate that white students who attend public schools with Negroes are the least likely to prefer all-white classrooms and all-white "close friends," and this effect is strongest among those who began their interracial schooling in the early grades (Coleman *et al.*, 1966, p. 333). Recall, too, the similar findings of the U.S. Commission on Civil Rights (1967) for both Negro and white adults who had attended biracial schools as children.

Not all intergroup contact, of course, leads to increased acceptance; sometimes it only makes matters worse. Gordon Allport (1954), in his intensive review of this research, concluded that four characteristics of the contact situation are of the utmost importance. Prejudice is lessened when the two groups: (a) possess equal status in the situation, (b) seek common goals, (c) are cooperatively dependent upon each other, and (d) interact with the positive support of authorities, laws, or custom. Reviewing the same work, Kenneth Clark (1953) came to similar conclusions, and correctly predicted one year prior to the Supreme Court ruling against *de jure* public school segregation that the process would be successful only to the extent that authorities publicly backed and rigorously enforced the new policy.

The Allport statement of contact conditions is actually an application of the broader theory of interpersonal attraction. All four of his conditions maximize the likelihood of shared values and beliefs being evinced and mutually perceived. Rokeach's belief-similarity factor is apparently, then, a key agent in the effects of optimal contact. Thus, following the Triandis and Davis (1965) findings, we would anticipate the attitude alterations achieved by intergroup contact, at least initially, to be greatest for formal realms and least for intimate realms – as with the changes wrought in white Texan attitudes by the dramatic events of early spring 1968.

Accordingly, from this social psychological perspective, the black separatist assumption that "white liberals" should eliminate white racism is an impossible and quixotic hope. One can readily appreciate the militants' desire to avoid further abuse from white racists; but their model for change is woefully inadequate. White liberals can attack racist attitudes publicly, conduct research on racist assertions, set the stage for confrontation. But with all the will in the world they cannot accomplish by themselves the needed Negro push, the dramatic events, the actual interracial contact which has gnawed away at racist beliefs for a generation. A century ago the fiery and perceptive Frederick Douglass (1962, pp. 366-367) phrased the issue pointedly:

> I have found in my experience that the way to break down an unreasonable custom is to contradict it in practice. To be sure in pursuing this course I have had to contend not merely with the white race but with the black. The one has condemned me for my presumption in daring to associate with it and the other for pushing myself where it takes it for granted I am not wanted.

## THE ASSUMPTIONS OF RACIAL CONFLICT AND AUTONOMY-BEFORE-CONTACT

History reveals that white separatists are correct when they contend that racial change creates conflict, that if only the traditions of white supremacy were to go unchallenged racial harmony might be restored. One of the quietest periods in American racial history, 1895-1915, for example, witnessed the construction of the massive system of institutional racism as it is known today – the nadir of Negro American history as Rayford Logan (1957) calls it. The price of those two decades of relative peace is still being paid by the nation. Even were it possible in the late 20th century, then, to gain racial calm by inaction, America could not afford the enormous cost.

But if inaction is clearly impossible, the types of action called for are not so clear. Black separatists believe that efforts to further interracial contact should be abandoned or at least delayed until greater personal and group autonomy is achieved by Negroes. This is the other side of the same coin that leaves the struggle against attitudinal racism completely in the hands of "white liberals." And it runs a similar danger. Racism is reflected not only in attitudes but more importantly in institutionalized arrangements that operate to restrict Negro choice. Both forms of racism are fostered by segregation, and both have to be confronted directly by Negroes. Withdrawal into the ghetto, psychologically tempting as it may be for many, essentially gives up the fight to alter the racially discriminatory operations of the nation's chief institutions.

The issues involved are highlighted in the schematic diagram shown in Fig. 1. By varying contact-separation and an ideologically vague concept of "autonomy," four cells emerge that represent various possibilities under discussion. Cell "A" – true integration – refers to institutionalized biracial situations where there is cross-racial friendship, racial interdependence, and a strong measure of personal autonomy (and group autonomy, too, if group is defined biracially). Such situations do exist in America today, but they are rare embattled islands in a sea of conflict. Cell "B" represents the autonomous "black power" ghetto, relatively independent of the larger society and with a far more viable existence than is commonly the case now. This is an ideologically derived hypothetical situation, for no such urban ghettoes exist today. Cell "C" stands for merely desegregated situations. Often misnamed as "integrated," these institutionalized biracial settings include both races but little cross-racial acceptance and often patronizing legacies of white supremacy. Cell "D" represents today's typical Negro scene – the highly separate urban ghetto with little or no personal or group autonomy.

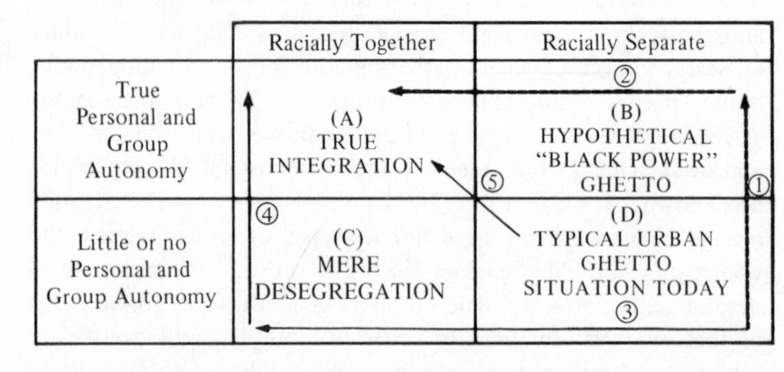


**Fig. 1 Schematic Diagram of Autonomy and Contact-Separation***

*The author is indebted to Professor Karl Deutsch, of Harvard University, for several stimulating discussions out of which came this diagram. Dotted lines denote hypothetical paths, solid lines actual paths.

### To Get From "D" to "A" . . .

Save for white separatists, observers of diverse persuasions agree that the achievement of true integration (cell "A") should be the ideal and ultimate goal. But there are, broadly speaking, three contrasting ways of getting there from the typical current situation (cell "D"). The black separatist assumes only one route is possible: from the depressed ghetto today to the hypothetical ghetto of tomorrow and then, perhaps, on to true integration (lines numbered 1 and 2 on Fig. 1). The desegregationist assumes precisely the opposite route: from the present-day ghetto to mere desegregation and then, hopefully, on the true integration (lines numbered 3 and 4 in Fig. 1). Experience to date combines with a number of social psychological considerations to favor the last of these possibilities.

The black separatist route has a surprising appeal for an untested theory; besides those whites who welcome any alternative to integration, it seems to appeal to cultural pluralists (white and black), to militant black leaders searching for a new direction to vent the ghetto's rage and despair, and to Negroes who just wish to withdraw as far away from whites as possible. Yet on reflection, the argument involves the perverse notion that the way to bring two groups together is to separate them further. One is reminded of the detrimental consequences of isolation in economics, through "closed markets," and in genetics, through "genetic drift." In social psychology, isolation between two contiguous groups generally leads to: (a) diverse value development, (b) reduced intergroup communication, (c) uncorrected perceptual distortions of each other, and (d) the growth of vested interests within both groups for continued separation. American race relations already suffer from each of these conditions; and the proposal for further separation even if a gilded ghetto were possible, aims to exacerbate them further.

### No Access to the Tax Base . . .

Without pursuing the many economic and political difficulties inherent in the insulated ghetto conception, suffice it to mention the meager resources immediately available in the ghetto for the task. Recognizing this limitation, black separatists call for massive federal aid with no strings attached. But this requires a national consensus. Some separatists scoff at the direct path to integration (line 5 in Fig. 1) as idealistic dreaming, then turn and casually assume the same racist society that resists integration will unhesitantingly pour a significant portion of its treasure exclusively into ghetto efforts. Put differently, "local control" without access to the necessary tax base is not control. This raises the political limitations to the black separatist route. The Irish-American model of entering the mainstream through the political system is often cited as appropriate to black separatism – but is it really? Faster than any other immigrant group save Jewish-Americans, the Irish have assimilated via the direct diagonal of Fig. 1. Forced to remain in ghettoes at first, the Irish did not settle for "local control" but strove to win city hall itself. Boston's legendary James Michael Curley won "Irish power" not by becoming mayor of the South Boston ghetto, but by becoming mayor of the entire city. There are serious problems with immigrant analogies for Negroes, since immigrants never suffer from slavery and legalized segregation. But to the extent an analogy is appropriate, Mayor Carl Stokes of Cleveland and Mayor Richard Hatcher of Gary are far closer to the Irish-American model than are black separatists.

### Fate Control . . .

A critical part of black separatist thinking centers on the psychological concept of "fate control" – more familiar to psychologists as Rotter's (1966) internal control of reinforcement variable. "Until we control our own destinies, our own schools and areas," goes the argument, "blacks cannot possibly achieve the vital sense of fate control." And Coleman Report (Coleman *et al.*, 1966) data are cited to show that fate control is a critical correlate of Negro school achievement. But no mention is made of the additional fact that levels of fate control among Negro children were found by Coleman to be significantly higher in interracial than in all-Negro schools. Black separatists brush this important finding aside on the grounds that all-Negro schools today are not what they envision for the future. Yet the fact remains that interracial schools appear to be facilitating the growth of fate control among Negro students now, while the ideological contention that it can be developed as well or better in uniracial schools remains an untested and hypothetical assertion.

Despite the problems, black separatists feel their route (lines 1 and 2 in Fig. 1) is the only way to true integration in part because they regard the indirect desegregation path (lines 3 and 4 in Fig. 1) as an affront to their dignity. One need only know the blatantly hostile and subtly rejecting racial acts that typify some interracial situations to know to what this repudiation of nonautonomous desegregation refers (Cell "C" in Fig. 1; Chessler, 1967). But it is conceptionally and practically useful to make a clear distinction between true integration (Cell "A" in Fig. 1) and mere desegregation (Cell "C" in Fig. 1). The U.S. Commission on Civil Rights (1967), in reanalyzing Coleman's data, found this distinction provided the tool for separating empirically between effective and ineffective biracial schools where whites form the majority. Negro student achievement, college aspirations, and sense of fate control proved to be highest in truly integrated schools when these schools are independently defined as biracial institutions characterized by no racial tension and widespread cross-racial friendship. Merely desegregated schools, defined as biracial institutions, typified by racial tension and little cross-racial friendship have scant benefits over segregated schools.

### Allport Conditions for Optimal Contact

This civil rights commission finding reflects the Allport (1954) conditions for optimal contact. Truly integrated institutions afford the type of equal-status, common goal, interdependent, and authority-sanctioned contact that maximizes cross-racial acceptance and Rokeach's belief similarity.[11] They apparently also maximize the positive and minimize the negative factors which Katz (1964, 1967) has carefully isolated as important for Negro performance in biracial task groups. And they also seem to increase the opportunity for beneficial cross-racial evaluations which may well be critical mediators of the effects of biracial schools (Pettigrew, 1967). Experimental research following up these leads is now called for to detail the precise social psychological processes operating in the truly integrated situation (Pettigrew, 1968).

The desegregation route (lines 3 and 4 in Fig. 1) has been successfully navigated, though the black separatist contention that Negroes bear the principal burden for this effort is undoubtedly true. Those southern institutions that have attained integration, for example, have typically gone this indirect path. So it is not as hypothetical as the black separatist path, but it is hardly to be preferred over the direct integrationist route (line 5 in Fig. 1).

### The Self-Fulfilling Prophecy

So why not the direct route? The standard answer is that it is impossible, that demographic trends and white resistance make it out of the question in our time. The self-fulfilling prophecy threatens once more. Secretary of Health, Education and Welfare, Wilbur Cohen, insists that integration will not come in this generation – hardly a reassuring assertion from the chief of the federal department with primary responsibility for furthering the process.[12] The Secretary adopts the Alsop separatist argument and opts for programs exclusively within the ghetto, a position that makes extensive integration unlikely even a generation hence. One is reminded of the defenders of slavery who in the 1850s attacked the Abolitionists as unrealistic dreamers and insisted slavery was so deeply entrenched that efforts should be limited to making it into a benign institution.

If the nation acts on the speculations of Cohen, Alsop, and Ferry, then, they will probably be proven correct in their pessimistic projections. For what better way to prevent racial change than to act on the presumption that it is impossible?

### Urban Racial Demography

The belief that integration is impossible is based on some harsh facts of urban racial demography. Between 1950 and 1960, the average annual increment of Negro population in the central cities of the United States was 320,000; from 1960 to 1966, the estimated annual growth climbed to 400,000. In the suburbs, however, the average annual growth of the Negro population has declined from 60,000 between 1950 and 1960 to an estimated 33,000 between 1960 and 1966. In other words, it would require about 13 times the present trend in suburban Negro growth just to maintain the sprawling central city ghettoes at their present size. In the nation's largest metropolitan areas, then, the trend is forcefully pushing in the direction of ever-increasing separatism.

But these bleak data are not the whole picture. In the first place, they refer especially to the very largest of the metropolitan areas – to New York City, Chicago, Los Angeles, Philadelphia, Detroit, Washington, D.C., and Baltimore. Most Negro Americans, however, do not live in these places, but reside in areas where racial integration is in fact possible in the short run were a good faith attempt to be made. The Harlems and Wattses, especially during this period of urban riots, have blinded some analysts into thinking of the entire Negro population as residing in such ghettoes. Put differently, there are more areas such as Berkeley and White Plains – small enough for school integration to be effectively achieved – than there are New York Cities.

In the second place, the presumed impossibility of reversing the central city racial trends are based on anti-metropolitan assumptions. Without metropolitan cooperation, central cities – and many suburbs, too – will find their racial problems insoluble. So need we assume such cooperation impossible? Effective state and federal incentives are being proposed, and a few established to further this cooperation. Moreover, some large Negro ghettoes are already extending into the suburbs (e.g., Pittsburgh and soon Chicago); the first tentative metropolitan schemes to aid racial integration are emerging (e.g., Boston, Hartford, and Rochester); and several major metropolitan areas have even consolidated (e.g., Miami-Dade County and Nashville-Davidson County). Once the issue is looked at in metropolitan terms, its dimensions become more manageable. Negro Americans are found in America's metropolitan areas in almost the same ratio as white Americans; about two-thirds of each group resides in these 212 regions, so that on a metropolitan basis Negroes are not significantly more metropolitan than their one-ninth proportion in the nation as a whole.

## POLICY IMPLICATIONS

Much of the policy confusion seems to be derived from the assumption that since *complete* integration in the biggest cities will not be possible in the near future, present efforts toward opening integration opportunities for both Negro and white Americans are premature. This thinking obscures two fundamental issues. First, the democratic objective is not total racial integration and the elimination of the ghetto; the idea is simply to provide an honest choice between separation and integration. This separation side of the choice is available today; it is integration that is closed to Negroes who would choose it. The long-term goal is not a complete obliteration of cultural pluralism, of distinctive Negro ghettoes, but rather the transformation of these ghettoes from today's racial prisons to tomorrow's ethnic areas of choice. Life within ghettoes can never be fully satisfactory as long as there are Negroes who reside within them only because discrimination requires them to.

Second, the integrationist alternative will not become a reality as long as we disparage it, as long as we abandon it to future generations. Exclusive attention to within-ghetto enrichment programs is almost certain, to use Kenneth Clark's pointed word, to "embalm" the ghetto, to seal it in even further from the rest of the nation (making line 2 in Fig. 1 less likely yet). This danger explains the recent interest of conservative whites in exclusive ghetto enrichment programs. The bribe is straightforward: "Stop rioting and stop demanding integration, and we'll minimally support separatist programs within the ghetto." Even black separatists are understandably ambivalent about such offers, as they come from sources long identified with opposition to all racial change. Should the bargain be struck, however, American race relations will be dealt still another serious blow.

### What is Possible

The outlines of the situation, then, are these: (a) widespread integration is possible everywhere in the United States save in the largest central cities; (b) it will not come unless present trends are reversed and considerable resources are provided for the process; (c) big central cities will continue to have significant Negro concentrations even with successful metropolitan dispersal; (d) large Negro ghettos are presently in need of intensive enrichment; and (e) some ghetto enrichment programs run the clear and present danger of embalming the ghetto further.

Given this situation and the social psychological considerations of this paper, the overall strategy needed must contain the following elements:

(a) A major effort toward racial integration must be mounted in order to provide genuine choice to all Negro Americans in all realms of life. This effort should envisage by the late 1970s complete attainment of the goal in smaller communities and cities and a halting of separatist trends in major central cities with a movement toward metropolitan cooperation.

(b) A simultaneous effort is required to enrich the vast central city ghettoes of the nation, to change them structurally, and to make life in them more viable. In order to avoid embalming them, however, strict criteria must be applied to proposed enrichment programs to insure that they are productive for later dispersal and integration. Restructuring the economics of the ghetto, especially the development of urban cooperatives, is a classic example of productive enrichment. The building of enormous public housing developments within the ghetto presents a good illustration of counterproductive enrichment. Some programs, such as the decentralization of huge public school systems or the encouragement of Negro business ownership, can be either productive or counterproductive depending upon how they are focused. A Bundy Decentralization Plan of many homogeneous school districts for New York City is clearly counterproductive for later integration; a Regents Plan of a relatively small number of heterogeneous school districts for New York City could well be productive. Likewise, Negro entrepreneurs encouraged to open small shops and expected to prosper with an all-Negro clientele are not only counterproductive but are probably committing economic suicide. Negro businessmen encouraged to pool resources to establish somewhat larger operations and to appeal to white as well as Negro customers on major traffic arteries in and out of the ghetto could be productive.

### A Mixed Integration-Enrichment Strategy

In short, a mixed integration-enrichment strategy is called for that contains safeguards that the enrichment will not impede integration. Recent survey results strongly suggest that such a mixed strategy would meet with widespread Negro approval. On the basis of their extensive 1968 survey of Negro residents in 15 major cities, Campbell and Schuman (1968, p. 5) conclude:

> Separatism appeals to from five to eighteen percent of the Negro sample, depending on the question, with the largest appeal involving black ownership of stores and black administration of schools in Negro neighborhoods, and the smallest appeal the rejection of whites as friends or in other informal contacts. Even on questions having the largest appeal, however, more than three-quarters of the Negro sample indicate a clear preference for integration. Moreover, the reasons given by respondents for their choices suggest that the desire for integration is not simply a practical wish for better material facilities, but represents a commitment to principles of nondiscrimination and racial harmony.

Young men prove to be the most forthright separatists, but even here the separatist percentages for males 16-19 years of age ranged only from 11-28%. An interesting interaction between type of separatism and educational level of the respondent appears in the Campbell and Schuman (1968, p. 19) data. Among the 20-39-year olds, college graduates tended to be the more separatist in those realms where their training gives them a vested interest in competition-free positions – Negro-owned stores for Negro neighborhoods and Negro teachers in mostly Negro schools; while the poorly educated were most likely to believe that whites should be discouraged from taking part in civil rights organizations and to agree that "Negroes should have nothing to do with whites if they can help it" and that "there should be a separate black nation here."

### Negroes Want Both Integration and Black Identity

But if separatism draws little favorable response even in the most politicized ghettoes, positive aspects of cultural pluralism attract wide interest. For example, 42 percent endorse the statement that "Negro schoolchildren should study an African language." And this interest seems rather general across age, sex, and education categories. Campbell and Schuman (1968, p. 6) regard this as evidence of a broadly supported attempt ". . . to emphasize black consciousness *without* rejection of whites . . . A substantial number of Negroes want *both* integration and black identity."[13] Or in the terms of this paper, they prefer cell "A" in Fig. 1 – "true integration."

The Campbell and Schuman data indicate little if any change from the pro-integration results of earlier Negro surveys (Brink and Harris, 1964, 1967). And they are consistent with the results of recent surveys in Detroit, Miami, New York City, and other cities (Meyer, 1967, 1968; Center for Urban Education, 1968). Data from Bedford-Stuyvesant in Brooklyn are especially significant, for here separatist ideology and a full-scale enrichment program are in full view. Yet when asked if they would prefer to live on a block with people of the same race or of every race, 80 percent of the Negro respondents chose an interracial block (Center for Urban Education, 1968). Interestingly, the largest Negro segment choosing integration – 88 percent – consisted of residents of public housing where a modest amount of interracial tenancy still prevails.

A final study from Watts links these surveys to the analysis of this paper. Ransford (1968) found that Negro willingness to use violence was closely and positively related to a sense of powerlessness, feelings of racial dissatisfaction, and limited contact with whites. Respondents who indicated that they had no social contact with white people, "like going to the movies together or visiting each other's homes," were significantly more likely to feel powerless and express racial dissatisfaction as well as to report greater willingness to use violence. The personal, group, and national costs of racial separatism are great.

## A FINAL WORD

Racially separate or together? Our social psychological examination of separatist assumptions leads to one imperative: the attainment of a viable, democratic America, free from personal and institutional racism, requires extensive racial integration in all realms of life. To prescribe more separation because of discomfort, racism, conflict, or autonomy needs is like getting drunk again to cure a hangover. The nation's binge of *apartheid* must not be exacerbated but alleviated.

## REFERENCES


Allport, G.W. *The Nature of Prejudice.* Cambridge, Mass.: Addison-Wesley, 1954.

Alsop, J. No More Nonsense About Ghetto Education! *The New Republic,* July 22, 1967, **157**, 18-23. (a)

Alsop, J. Ghetto Education. *The New Republic* November 18, 1967, **157**, 18-23. (b)

American Institute of Public Opinion, press release, May 22, 1965.

Armstrong, Clairette P., and Gregor, A.J. Integrated Schools and Negro Character Development: Some Considerations of the Possible Effects. *Psychiatry,* 1964, **27**, 69-72.

Brink, W., and Harris, L. *The Negro Revolution in America.* New York: Simon and Schuster, 1964.

Brink, W., and Harris, L. *Black and White: A Study of U.S. Racial Attitudes Today.* New York: Simon and Schuster, 1967.

Brophy, I.N. The Luxury of Anti-Negro Prejudice. *Public Opinion Quarterly,* 1946, **9**, 456-466.

Calame, B.E. A West Coast Militant Talks Tough But Helps Avert Racial Trouble. *The Wall Street Journal* July 26, 1968, **172**(1), 15.

Campbell, A., and Schuman, H. Racial Attitudes in Fifteen American Cities. In The National Advisory Commission on Civil Disorders, *Supplemental Studies.* Washington, D.C.: U.S. Government Printing Office, 1968.

Center for Urban Education. Survey of the Residents of Bedford-Stuyvesant. Unpublished paper, 1968.

Chessler, M. *In Their Own Words.* Atlanta, Ga.: Southern Regional Council, 1967.

Clark, K.B. Desegregation: An Appraisal of the Evidence. *Journal of Social Issues,* 1953, **9**, 1-76.

Coleman, J.S., Campbell, E.Q., Hobson, C.J., McPartland, J., Mood, A.M., Weinfeld, F.D., and York, R.L. *Equality of Education Opportunity.* Washington, D.C.: U.S. Government Printing Office, 1966.

Davies, J.C. Toward a Theory of Revolution. *American Sociological Review,* 1962, **27**, 5-19.

Deutsch, M., and Collins, Mary. *Interracial Housing: A Psychological Evaluation of a Social Experiment.* Minneapolis: University of Minnesota Press, 1951.

Douglass, F. *Life and Times of Frederick Douglass: The Complete Autobiography.* New York: Collier Books, 1962 (original edition in 1892).

Ferry, W.H. Black Colonies: A Modest Proposal. *The Center Magazine,* January 1968, **1**, 74-76.

Geschwender, J.A. Social Structure and the Negro Revolt: An Examination of Some Hypotheses. *Social Forces,* 1964, **43**, 248-256.

Harding, J., and Hogrefe, R. Attitudes of White Department Store Employees Toward Negro Co-workers. *Journal of Social Issues,* 1952, **8**, 18-28.

Hyman, H.H., and Sheatsley, P.B. Attitudes Toward Desegregation. *Scientific American,* December 1956, **195**, 35-39.

Hyman, H.H., and Sheatsley, P.B. Attitudes Toward Desegregation. *Scientific American,* July 1964, **211**, 16-23.

Jahoda, Marie, and West, Patricia. Race Relations in Public Housing. *Journal of Social Issues,* 1951, **7**, 132-139.

Jordan, R.A. Go-slow Integration Draws Retorts. *The Boston Globe,* August 8, 1968, **194**, 2.

Katz, I. Review of Evidence Relating to Effects of Desegregation on the Performance of Negroes. *American Psychologist,* 1964, **19**, 381-399.

Katz, I. The Socialization of Competence Motivation in Minority Group Children. In D. Levine (Ed.), *Nebraska symposium on motivation, 1967.* Lincoln: University of Nebraska Press, 1967.

Kephart, W.M. *Racial Factors and Urban Law Enforcement.* Philadelphia: University of Pennsylvania Press, 1957.

Klineberg, O. *Negro Intelligence and Selective Migration.* New York: Columbia University Press, 1935.

Kohn, M.L., and Williams, R.M., Jr. Situational Patterning in Intergroup Relations. *American Sociological Review,* 1956, **21**, 164-174.

Logan, R.W. *The Negro in the United States: A Brief History.* Princeton, N.J.: Van Nostrand, 1957.

MacKenzie, Barbara. The Importance of Contact in Determining Attitudes Toward Negroes. *Journal of Abnormal and Social Psychology,* 1948, **43**, 417-441.

Meyer, P. *Miami Negroes: A Study in Depth.* Miami, Florida: *The Miami Herald,* 1968.

Meyer, P. *A Survey of Attitudes of Detroit Negroes After the Riot of 1967.* Detroit, Mich.: Detroit Urban League, in press.

National Advisory Commission on Civil Disorders. *Report.* Washington, D.C.: U.S. Printing Office, 1968.

Newcomb, T.M., Turner, R.H., and Converse, P.E. *Social Psychology: The Study of Human Interaction.* New York: Holt, Rinehart and Winston, 1965.

Pettigrew, T.F. Parallel and Distinctive Changes in anti-Semitic and anti-Negro attitudes. In C.H. Stember (Ed.), *Jews in the Mind of America.* New York: Basic Books, 1966.

Pettigrew, T.F. Social Evaluation Theory: Convergences and Applications. In D. Levine (Ed.), *Nebraska Symposium on Motivation, 1967.* Lincoln: University of Nebraska Press, 1967.

Pettigrew, T.F. Race and Equal Educational Opportunity. *Harvard Educational Review,* 1968, **38**, 66-76.

Ransford, H.E. Isolation, Powerlessness, and Violence: A Study of Attitudes and Participation in the Watts Riot. *American*

*Journal of Sociology,* 1968, **73**, 581-591.

Reitzes, D.C. The Role of Organizational Structures: Union versus Neighborhood in a Tension Situation. *Journal of Social Issues,* 1953, **9**, 37-44.

Riley, R. and Pettigrew, T.F. Dramatic Events and Racial Attitude Change. Unpublished paper, Harvard University, 1968.

Rokeach, M. Belief versus Race as Determinants of Social Distance: Comment on Triandis' Paper. *Journal of Abnormal and Social Psychology,* 1961, **62**, 187-188.

Rokeach, M., and Mezei, L. Race and Shared Belief as Factors in Social Choice. *Science*, 1966, **151**, 167-172.

Rokeach, M., Smith, Patricia W., and Evans, R.I. Two Kinds of Prejudice or One? In M. Rokeach (Ed.), *The Open and Closed Mind.* New York: Basic Books, 1960.

Rotter, J.B. Internal versus External Control of Reinforcement. *Psychological Monographs,* 1966, **80**, Whole no. 609.

Saenger, G., and Gilbert, Emily. Customer Reactions to the Integration of Negro Sales Personnel. *International Journal of Opinion and Attitude Research,* 1950, **4**, 57-76.

Schwartz, R., Pettigrew, T., and Smith, M. Fake Panaceas for Ghetto Education. *The New Republic,* September 23, 1967, **157**, 16-19.

Schwartz, R., Pettigrew, T., and Smith, M. Is Desegregation Impractical? *The New Republic,* January 6, 1968, **157**, 27-29.

Sheatsley, P.B. White Attitude Toward the Negro. In T. Parsons and K.B. Clark (Eds.), *The Negro American.* Boston: Houghton Mifflin, 1966.

Smith, Carole R., Williams, L., and Willis, R.H. Race, Sex and Belief as Determinants of Friendship Acceptance. *Journal of Personality and Social Psychology,* 1967, **5**, 127-137.

Stein, D.D. The Influence of Belief Systems on Interpersonal Preference. *Psychological Monographs,* 1966, **80**, Whole no. 616.

Stein, D.D., Hardyck, Jane A., and Smith, M.B. Race and Belief: An Open and Shut Case. *Journal of Personality and Social Psychology,* 1965, **1**, 281-290.

Stember, C.H. Evaluating Effects of the Integrated Classroom. *The Urban Review,* June 1968, **2** (3-4), 30-31.

Stouffer, S.A., Suchman, E.A., DeVinney, L.C., Star, Shirley, A., and Williams, R.M., Jr. *Studies in Social Psychology in World War II,* Vol. 1, *The American Soldier: Adjustment During Army Life.* Princeton, N.J.: Princeton University Press, 1949.

Triandis, H.C. A Note on Rokeach's Theory of Prejudice. *Journal of Abnormal and Social Psychology,* 1961, **62**, 184-186.

Triandis, H.C., and Davis, E.E. Race and Belief as Determinants of Behavioral Intentions. *Journal of Personality and Social Psychology,* 1965, **2**, 715-725.

United States Commission on Civil Rights. *Civil Rights USA: Public Schools, Southern States, 1962.* Washington, D.C.: U.S. Government Printing Office, 1963.

United States Commission on Civil Rights. *Racial Isolation in the Public Schools.* Vols. I and II. Washington, D.C.: U.S. Government Printing Office, 1967.

Williams, R.M., Jr. *Strangers Next Door: Ethnic Relations in American Communities.* Englewood Cliffs, N.J.: Prentice-Hall, 1964.

Wilner, D.M., Walkley, Rosabelle, and Cook, S.W. *Human Relations in Interracial Housing: A Study of the Contact Hypothesis.* Minneapolis: University of Minnesota Press, 1955.

Works, E. The Prejudice-Interaction Hypothesis from the Point of View of the Negro Minority Group. *American Journal of Sociology,* 1961, **67**, 47-52.

Yarrow, Marian R. (Ed.) Interpersonal Dynamics in a Desegregation Process. *Journal of Social Issues,* 1958, **14**(1), 3-63.

## NOTES

[1] These figures derive from three gross estimates of "middle class" status: $6,000 or more annual family income, high school graduation, or white-collar occupation. Thus, in 1961, roughly a fifth of Negro families received in excess of $6,000 (a percentage that now must approach a fourth even in constant dollars), in 1960, 22 percent of Negroes over 24 years of age had completed high school, and in 1966, 21 percent of employed Negroes held white-collar occupations.

[2] See, too, replies to Alsop by Schwartz *et al.* (1967, 1968). Alsop eagerly calls for giving up the effort to integrate schools racially in order to put all efforts into achieving separate but improved schools in the ghetto. Ferry goes further and advocates "black colonies" be formally established in American central cities, complete with treaties enacted with the federal government. Black militants, in sharp contrast, complain of being in a colonial status now but do not endorse it as a desired state of affairs.

[3] Analysis specifically directed at this point shows this contention not to be true for predominantly-white classrooms as contrasted with comparable all-white classrooms (U.S. Commission on Civil Rights, 1967, Vol. 1, p. 160).

[4] This resolution of the earlier Triandis (1961) and Rokeach (1961) controversy takes on added weight when the data from studies favorable to the Rokeach position are examined carefully. That different interpersonal realms lead to varying belief-race weightings is borne out by Table 4 in Stein *et al.* (1965); that intensely prejudiced subjects, particularly in environments where racist norms even extend into less intimate realms, will act on race primarily is shown by one sample of whites in the Deep South of Smith *et al.* (1967).

[5] For 12 junior highs, the Spearman-Brown rank order correlation between the white junior high percentage and the percentage of Negroes choosing predominantly white high schools is +.82 (corrected for ties) – significant at better than the one percent level of confidence.

[6] For a role analysis interpretation of racial interactions in the United States, see Pettigrew (1964).

[7] One of the first significant efforts in this direction was the classic intelligence study by Klineberg (1935). For a summary of current scientific work relevant to racist claims in health, intelligence, and crime, see Pettigrew (1964).

[8] The incorrect interpretation of present white animosities toward the Negro as a "backlash" is a classic case of the ecological fallacy; see Pettigrew (1966).

[9] That the post-King murder data do not reflect merely temporary shifts is demonstrated by further data collected in Texas in August of 1968. Similar to these results was an overall shift of approximately five percent toward favoring the racial

desegregation of public schools noted among white Texans between two surveys taken immediately before and after the 1957 crisis in Little Rock. And, once again, the most positive shifts were noted among the young and the middle class (Riley and Pettigrew, 1968).

[10]This is, of course, a two-way causal relationship. Not only does desegregation erode racist attitudes, but desegregation tends to come first to areas where white attitudes are least racist to begin with. The Hyman-Sheatsley (1964) finding cited, however, specifically highlights the former phenomenon: "In those parts of the South where some measure of school integration has taken place official action has *preceded* public sentiment, and public sentiment has then attempted to accommodate itself to the new situation.

[11]Another white observer enthusiastic about black separatism even denies that the contact studies' conclusions are applicable to the classroom and other institutions which do not produce "continual and extensive equal-status contact under more or less enforced conditions of intimacy." Stember (1968) selectively cites the public housing and armed forces contact investigations to support his point; but he has to omit the many studies from less intimate realms which reached the same conclusions – such as those conducted in schools (Pettigrew, 1968), employment situations (Harding and Hogrefe, 1952; Kephart, 1957; MacKenzie, 1948; Williams, 1964), and even one involving brief clerk and customer contact (Saenger and Gilbert, 1950).

[12]Consistent with the thesis of this paper, a number of leading black separatists attacked the Cohen statement. For example, Bryant Rollins, separatist spokesman in Boston, called Cohen's statement "a cop-out" and described it as typical of "white bureaucratic racists who don't want to do anything" (Jordan, 1968).

[13]This is not a new position for Negro Americans, for their dominant response to Marcus Garvey's movement in the 1920s was essentially the same. Garvey stressed black beauty and pride in Africa and mounted a mass movement in the urban ghettoes of the day, but his "back to Africa" separatist appeals were largely ignored.

# 12
# *The Failure of Black Separatism**

BAYARD RUSTIN

We are living in an age of revolution – or so they tell us. The children of the affluent classes pay homage to their parents' values by rejecting them; this, they say, is a youth revolution. The discussion and display of sexuality increases – actors disrobe on stage, young women very nearly do on the street – and so we are in the midst of a sexual revolution. Tastes in music and clothing change, and each new fashion too is revolutionary. With every new social phenomenon now being dubbed a "revolution," the term has in fact become nothing more than a slogan which serves to take our minds off an unpleasant reality. For if we were not careful, we might easily forget that there is a conservative in the White House, that our country is racially polarized as never before, and that the forces of liberalism are in disarray. Whatever there is of revolution today, in any meaningful sense of the term, is coming from the right.

But we are also told – and with far greater urgency and frequency – that there is a black revolution. If by revolution we mean a radical escalation of black aspirations and demands, this is surely the case. There is a new assertion of pride in the Negro race and its cultural heritage, and although the past summer was marked by the lack of any major disruptions, there is among blacks a tendency more pronounced than at any time in Negro history to engage in violence and the rhetoric of violence. Yet if we look closely at the situation of Negroes today, we find that there has been not the least revolutionary reallocation of political or economic power. There is, to be sure, an increase in the number of black elected officials throughout the United States and particularly in the South, but this has largely been the result of the 1965 Voting Rights Act, which was passed before the "revolution" reached its height and the renewal of which the present administration has not advocated with any noticeable enthusiasm. Some reallocation of political power has indeed taken place since the presidential election of 1964, but generally its beneficiaries have been the Republicans and the anti-Negro forces. Nor does this particular trend show much sign of abating. Nixon's attempt to reverse the liberal direction of the Supreme Court has just begun. Moreover, in the 1970 Senate elections, 25 of the 34 seats to be contested were originally won by the Democrats in the great liberal surge of 1964, when the political picture was quite different from that of today. And if the Democrats only break even in 1970, the Republicans will control the Senate for the first time since 1954. A major defeat would leave the Democrats weaker than they have been at any time since the conservative days of the 1920s.

There has been, it is true, some moderate improvement in the economic condition of Negroes, but by no stretch of the imagination can it be called revolutionary. According to Andrew Brimmer of the Federal Reserve System, the median family income of Negroes between 1965 and 1967 rose from 54 percent to 59 percent of that for white families. Much of that gain reflected a decrease in the rate of Negro unemployment. But between February and June of 1969, Negro unemployment rose again by 1.3 percent and should continue to rise as Nixon presses his crusade against inflation. The Council of Economic Advisers reports that in the past eight years the federal government has spent $10.3 billion on metropolitan problems while it has spent $39.9 billion on agriculture, not to mention, of course, $507.2 billion for defense. In the area of housing, for instance, New York City needs at the present time as many new subsidized apartments – 780,000 – as the federal housing program has constructed *nationally* in its entire 34 years. Appropriations for model cities, rent supplements, the Job Corps, the Neighborhood Youth Corps, and other programs have been drastically reduced, and the Office of Economic Opportunity is being transformed into a research agency. Nixon's welfare and revenue-sharing proposals, in addition to being economically stringent, so that they will have little or no effect on the condition of the Northern urban poor, are politically and philosophically conservative.

Any appearance that we are in the grip of a black revolution, then, is deceptive. The problem is not whether black aspirations are outpacing America's ability to respond but whether they have outpaced her willingness to do so. Lately it has been taken almost as axiomatic that with every increase in Negro demands, there must be a corresponding intensification of white resistance. This proposition implies that only black complacency can prevent racial polarization, that any political action by Negroes must of necessity produce a reaction. But

*Reprinted by permission of the author who reminds the reader that this paper was written in the climate of 1969.

such a notion ignores entirely the question of what *kind* of political action, guided by what *kind* of political strategy. One can almost assert as a law of American politics that if Negroes engage in violence as a tactic they will be met with repression, that if they follow a strategy of racial separatism they will be isolated, and that if they engage in anti-democratic activity, out of the deluded wish to skirt the democratic process, they will provoke a reaction. To the misguided, violence, separatism, and minority ultimatums may seem revolutionary, but in reality they issue only from the desperate strivings of the impotent. Certainly such tactics are not designed to enhance the achievement of progressive social change. Recent American political history has proved this point time and again with brutal clarity.

The irony of the revolutionary rhetoric uttered in behalf of Negroes is that it has helped in fact to promote conservatism. On the other hand, of course, the reverse is also true: the failure of America to respond to the demands of Negroes has fostered in the minds of the latter a sense of futility and has thus seemed to legitimize a strategy of withdrawal and violence. Other things have been operating as well. The 15 years since *Brown vs. Topeka* have been for Negroes a period of enormous dislocation. The modernization of farming in the South forced hundreds of thousands of Negroes to migrate to the North where they were confronted by a second technological affliction – automation. Without jobs, living in cities equipped to serve neither their material nor spiritual needs, these modern-day immigrants responded to their brutal new world with despair and hostility. The civil rights movement created an even more fundamental social dislocation, for it destroyed not simply the legal structure of segregation but also the psychological assumptions of racism. Young Negroes who matured during this period witnessed a basic challenge to the system of values and social relations which has presumed the inferiority of the Negro. They have totally rejected this system, but in doing so have often substituted for it an exaggerated and distorted perception both of themselves and of the society. As if to obliterate the trace of racial shame that might be lurking in their souls, they have embraced racial chauvinism. And, as if in reply to past exclusions (and often in response to present insecurities), they have created their own patterns of exclusiveness.

The various frustrations and upheavals experienced recently by the Negro community account in large part for the present political orientation of some of its most vocal members: seeing their immediate self-interest more in the terms of emotional release than in those of economic and political advancement. One is supposed to think black, dress black, eat black, and buy black without reference to the question of what such a program actually contributes to advancing the cause of social justice. Since real victories are thought to be unattainable, issues become important insofar as they can provide symbolic victories. Dramatic confrontations are staged which serve as outlets for radical energy but which in no way further the achievement of radical social goals. So that, for instance, members of the black community are mobilized to pursue the "victory" of halting construction of a state office building in Harlem, even though it is hard to see what actual economic or social benefit will be conferred on the impoverished residents of that community by their success in doing so.

Such actions constitute a politics of escape rooted in hopelessness and further reinforced by government inaction. Deracinated liberals may romanticize this politics, nihilistic new leftists may imitate it, but ordinary Negroes will be the victims of its powerlessness to work any genuine change in their condition.

The call for black power is now over three years old, yet to this day no one knows what black power is supposed to mean and therefore how its proponents are to unite and rally behind it. If one is a member of CORE, black power posits the need for a separate black economy based upon traditional forms of capitalist relations. For SNCC, the term refers to a politically united black community. US would emphasize the unity of black culture, while the Black Panthers wish to impose upon black nationalism the philosophies of Marx, Lenin, Stalin, and Chairman Mao. Nor do these exhaust all the possible shades and gradations of meaning. If there is one common theme uniting the various demands for black power, it is simply that blacks must be guided in their actions by a consciousness of themselves as a separate race.

Now, philosophies of racial solidarity have never been unduly concerned with the realities that operate outside the category of race. The adherents of these philosophies are generally romantics, steeped in the traditions of their own particular clans and preoccupied with the simple biological verities of blood and racial survival. Almost invariably their rallying cry is racial self-determination, and they tend to ignore those aspects of the material world which point up divisions within the racially defined group.

But the world of black Americans is full of divisions. Only the most supine of optimists would dream of building a political movement without reference to them. Indeed, nothing better illustrates the existence of such divisions within the black community than the fact that the separatists themselves represent a distinct minority among Negroes. No reliable poll has ever identified more than 15 percent of Negroes as separatists; usually the percentage is a good deal lower. Nor, as I have already indicated, are the separatists unified among themselves, the differences among them at times being so intense as to lead to violent conflict. The notion of the undifferentiated black community is the intellectual creation both of whites – liberals as well as racists to whom all Negroes are the same – and of certain small groups of blacks who illegitimately claim to speak for the majority.

The fact is that like every other racial or ethnic group in America, Negroes are divided by age, class, and geography. Young Negroes are at least as hostile toward their elders as white new leftists are toward their liberal parents. They are in addition separated by vast gaps in experience, northern from southern, urban from rural. And even more profound are the disparities in wealth among them. In contrast to the white community, where the spread of income has in recent years remained unchanged or has narrowed slightly, economic differentials among blacks have increased. In 1965, for example, the wealthiest five percent of white and nonwhite families each received 15.5 percent of the total income in their respective communities. In 1967, however, the percentage of white income received by the top five percent of white families had dropped to 14.9 percent while among nonwhites the share of income of the top five percent of the families had risen to 17.5 percent. This trend probably reflects the new opportunities which are available to black professionals in industry, government, and academia, but have not touched the condition of lower class and lower middle class Negroes.

To Negroes for whom race is the major criterion, however, divisions by wealth and status are irrelevant. Consider, for instance, the proposals for black economic advancement put forth by the various groups of black nationalist. These proposals are all remarkably similar. For regardless of one's particular persuasion – whether a revolutionary or a cultural nationalist or an unabashed black capitalist – once one confines one's analysis to the ghetto, no proposal can extend beyond a strategy for ghetto development and black enterprise. This explains in part the recent popularity of black capitalism and, to a lesser degree, black cooperatives: once both the economic strategy and goal are defined in terms of black self-determination, there is simply not much else available in the way of ideas.

There are other reasons for the popularity of black capitalism, reasons having to do with material and psychological self-interest. E. Franklin Frazier has written that Negro business is "a social myth" first formulated toward the end of the 19th century when the legal structure of segregation was established and Negro hopes for equality destroyed. History has often shown us that oppression can sometimes lead to a rationalization of the unjust conditions on the part of the oppressed and, following this, to an opportunistic competition among them for whatever meager advantages are available. This is, according to Frazier, exactly what happened among American Negroes. The myth of Negro business was created and tied to a belief in the possibility of a separate Negro economy. "Of course," wrote Frazier, "behind the idea of the separate Negro economy is the hope of the black bourgeoisie that they will have the monopoly of the Negro market." He added that they also desire "a privileged status within the isolated Negro community."

Nor are certain Negro businessmen the only ones who stand to gain from a black economy protected by the tariff of separatism. There are also those among the white upper class for whom such an arrangement is at least as beneficial. In the first place, self-help projects for the ghetto, of which black capitalism is but one variety, are inexpensive. They involve no large-scale redistribution of resources, no "inflationary" government expenditures, and, above all, no responsibility on the part of whites. These same upper class whites may have been major exploiters of black workers in the past, they may have been responsible for policies which helped to create ghetto poverty, but now, under the new dispensations of black separatism, they are being asked to do little more by way of reparation than provide a bit of seed money for a few small ghetto enterprises.

Moreover, a separate black economy appears to offer hope for what Roy Innis has called "a new social contract." According to Innis' theory, the black community is essentially a colony ruled by outsiders; there can be no peace between the colony and the "mother country" until the former is ruled by some of its own. When the colony is finally "liberated" in this way, all conflicts can be resolved through negotiation between the black ruling class and the white ruling class. Any difficulties within the black community, that is, would become the responsibility of the black elite. But since self-determination in the ghetto, necessitating as it would the expansion of a propertied black middle class, offers the advantage of social stability, such difficulties would be minimal. How could many whites fail to grasp the obvious benefit to themselves in a program that promises social peace without the social inconvenience of integration and especially without the burden of a huge expenditure of money? Even if one were to accept the colonial analogy – and it is in many ways an uninformed and extremely foolish one – the strategy implied by it is fatuous and unworkable. Most of the experiments in black capitalism thus far have been total failures, as, given the odds, they will continue to be. For one thing, small businesses owned and run by blacks will, exactly like their white counterparts, suffer a high rate of failure. In fact, they will face even greater problems than white small businesses because they will be operating in predominantly low-income areas where the clientele will be poor, the crime rate and taxes high, and the cost of land, labor, and insurance expensive. They will have to charge higher prices than the large chains, a circumstance against which "Buy Black" campaigns in the long or even the short run will have little force. On the other hand, to create large-scale black industry in the ghetto is unthinkable. The capital is not available and, even if it were, there is no vacant land. In Los Angeles, for example, the area in which four-fifths of the Negroes and Mexican-Americans live contains only 0.5 percent of all the vacant land in the city, and the problem is similar elsewhere. Overcrowding is severe enough in the ghetto without building up any industry there.

Another current axiom of black self-determination is the necessity for community control. Questions of ideology aside, black community control is as futile a program as black capitalism. Assuming that there was a cohesive, clearly identifiable black community (which, judging by the factionalism in neighborhoods like Harlem and Ocean Hill-Brownsville, is far from a safe assumption), and assuming that the community was empowered to control the ghetto, it would still find itself without the money needed in order to be socially creative. The ghetto would still be faced with the same poverty, deteriorated housing, unemployment, terrible health services, and inferior schools – and this time perhaps with the exacerbation of their being entailed in local struggles for power. Furthermore, the control would ultimately be illusory and would do no more than provide psychological comfort to those who exercise it. For in a complex technological society there is no such thing as an autonomous community within a large metropolitan area. Neighborhoods, particularly poor neighborhoods, will remain dependent upon outside suppliers for manufactured goods, transportation, utilities, and other services. There is, for instance, unemployment in the ghetto while the vast majority of new jobs are being created in the suburbs. If black people are to have access to those jobs, there must be a metropolitan transportation system that can carry them to the suburbs cheaply and quickly. Control over the ghetto cannot build such a system nor can it provide jobs within the ghetto.

The truth of the matter is that community control as an idea is provincial and as a program is extremely conservative. It appears radical to some people because it has become the demand around which the frustrations of the Negro community have coalesced. In terms of its capacity to deal with the social and economic causes of black unrest, however, its potential is strikingly limited. The call for community control in fact represents an adjustment to inequality rather than a protest against it. Fundamentally, it is a demand for a change in the racial composition of the personnel who administer community institutions: that is, for schools, institutions of public and social service, and political organizations – as all of these are presently constituted – to be put into the keeping of a new class of black officials. Thus, in a very real sense, the notion of community control bespeaks a fervent hope that the poverty-stricken ghetto, once thought to be a social problem crying for rectification, might now be deemed a social good worthy of acceptance. Hosea Williams of SCLC, speaking once of community control, unwittingly revealed the way in which passionate self-assertion can be a mask for accommodation: "I'm now at the position Booker T. Washington was about 60 or 70 years ago," Williams said. "I say to my brothers, 'Cast down your buckets where you are' – and that means there in the slums and ghettoes."

There is indeed profound truth in the observation that people who seek social change will, in the absence of real substantive victories, often seize upon stylistic substitutes as an outlet for their frustrations.

A case in point is the relation of Negroes to the trade union movement. In their study *The Black Worker*, published in 1930, Sterling D. Spero and Abram L. Harris describe the resistance to separatism among economically satisfied workers during the heyday of Marcus Garvey:

> . . . spokesmen of the Garvey movement went among the faction-torn workers preaching the doctrine of race consciousness. Despite the fact that Garveyism won a following everywhere at this time, the Negro longshoremen of Philadelphia were deaf to its pleas, for their labor movement had won them industrial equality such as colored workers nowhere else in the industry enjoyed.

The inverse relation of black separatism and anti-unionism to the quality of employment available to Negroes holds true today also. In the May 1969 UAW elections, for example, black candidates won the presidency and vice-presidency of a number of locals. Some of the most interesting election victories were won at the Chrysler Eldon Gear and Axle Local 961 and at Dodge #3 in Hamtramck where the separatist Eldon Revolutionary Union Movement (ELRUM) and Dodge Revolutionary Union Movement (DRUM) have been active. At both locals, the DRUM and ELRUM candidates were handily defeated by black trade unionists who campaigned on a program of militant integrationism and economic justice.

This is not to say that there are not problems within the unions which have given impetus to the separatist movements. There are, but in the past decade unions have taken significant steps toward eliminating discrimination against Negroes. As Peter Henle, the chief economist of the Bureau of Labor Statistics, has observed:

> Action has been taken to eliminate barriers to admission, abolish discrimination in hiring practices, and negotiate changes in seniority arrangements which had been blocking Negro advances to higher paying jobs. At the same time, unions have given strong support to governmental efforts in this same direction.

Certainly a good deal is left to be done in this regard, but just as certainly the only effective pressure on the unions is that which can be brought by blacks pressing for a greater role *within* the trade union movement. Not only is separatism not a feasible program, but its major effect will be to injure black workers economically by undermining the strength of the union. It is here that ignorance of the economic dimension of racial injustice is most dangerous, for a Negro, whether he be labeled a moderate or a militant, has but two alternatives open to him. If he defines the problem as primarily one of race, he will inevitably find himself the ally of the white capitalist against the white worker. But if, though always conscious of the play of racial discrimination, he defines the problem as one of poverty, he will be aligned with the white worker against management. If he chooses the former alternative, he will become no more than a pawn in the game of divide-and-conquer played by, and for the benefit of, management – the result of which will hardly be self-determination but rather the depression of wages for all workers. This path was followed by the "moderate" Booker T. Washington who disliked unions because they were "founded on a sort of enmity to the man by whom he [the Negro] is employed" and by the "militant" Marcus Garvey who wrote:

> It seems strange and a paradox, but the only convenient friend the Negro worker or laborer has in America at the present time is the white capitalist. The capitalist being selfish – seeking only the largest profit out of labor – is willing and glad to use Negro labor wherever possible on a scale reasonably below the standard union wage . . . but if the Negro unionizes himself to the level of the white worker, the choice and preference of employment is given to the white worker.

And it is being followed today by CORE, which collaborated with the National Right to Work Committee in setting up the Black Workers Alliance.

If the Negro chooses to follow the path of interracial alliances on the basis of class, as almost two million have done today, he can achieve a certain degree of economic dignity, which in turn offers a genuine, if not the only, opportunity for self-determination. It was this course which A. Philip Randolph chose in his long struggle to build a Negro-labor alliance, and it was also chosen by the black sanitation workers of Memphis, Tennessee, and the black hospital workers of Charleston, South Carolina.

Not that I mean here to exonerate the unions of their responsibility for discrimination. Nevertheless, it is essential to deal with the situation of the black worker in terms of American economic reality. And as long as the structure of this reality is determined by the competing institutions of capital and labor (or government and labor, as in the growing public sector of the economy), Negroes must place themselves on one side or the other. The idea of racial self-determination within this context is a delusion.

There are, to be sure, sources beyond that of economic discrimination for black separatism within the unions. DRUM, ELRUM, and similar groups are composed primarily of young

Negroes who, like whites their age, are not as loyal to the union as are older members, and who are also affected by the new militancy which is now pervasive among black youth generally. This militancy has today found its most potent form of expression on campus, particularly in the predominantly white universities outside the South. The confusion which the movement for programs in black studies has created on campus almost defies description. The extremes in absurdity were reached this past academic year at Cornell, where, on the one hand, enraged black students were demanding a program in black studies which included Course 300c, Physical Education: "Theory and practice in the use of small arms and combat. Discussion sessions in the proper use of force," and where, on the other hand, a masochistic and pusillanimous university president placed his airplane at the disposal of two black students so that they could go to New York City and purchase, with $2,000 in university funds, some bongo drums for Malcolm X Day. The foolishness of the students was surpassed only by the public relations manipulativeness of the president.

The real tragedy of the dispute over black studies is that whatever truly creative opportunities such a program could offer have been either ignored or destroyed. There is, first, the opportunity for a vastly expanded scholastic inquiry into the contribution of Negroes to the American experience. The history of the black man in America has been scandalously destroyed in the past, and as a field of study it has been relegated to a second-class status, isolated from the main themes of American history and omitted in the historical education of American youth. Yet now black students are preparing to repeat the errors of their white predecessors. They are proposing to study black history in isolation from the mainstream of American history; they are demanding separate black studies programs that will not be open to whites, who could benefit at least as much as they from a knowledge of Negro history; and they hope to permit only blacks (and perhaps some whites who toe the line) to teach in these programs. Unwittingly they are conceding what racist whites all along have professed to believe – namely, that black history is irrelevant to American history.

In other ways black students have displayed contempt for black studies as an academic discipline. Many of them, in fact, view black studies as not an academic subject at all, but as an ideological and political one. They propose to use black studies programs to create a mythologized history and a system of assertive ideas that will facilitate the political mobilization of the black community. In addition, they hope to educate a cadre of activists whose present training is conceived of as a preparation for organizational work in the ghetto. The Cornell students made this very clear when they defined the purpose of black studies programs as enabling "black people to use the knowledge gained in the classroom and the community to formulate new ideologies and philosophies which will contribute to the development of the black nation."

Thus, faculty members will be chosen on the basis of race, ideological purity, and political commitment – not academic competence. Under such conditions, few qualified black professors will want to teach in black studies programs, not simply because their academic freedom will be curtailed by their obligation to adhere to the revolutionary "line" of the moment, but because their professional status will be threatened by their association with programs of such inferior quality.

Black students are also forsaking the opportunity to get an education. They appear to be giving little thought to the problem of teaching or learning those technical skills that all students must acquire if they are to be effective in their careers. We have here simply another example of the pursuit of symbolic victory where a real victory seems too difficult to achieve. It is easier for a student to alter his behavior and appearance than to improve the quality of his mind. If engineering requires too much concentration, then why not a course in soul music? If Plato is both "irrelevant" and difficult, the student can read Malcolm X instead. Class will be a soothing, comfortable experience, somewhat like watching television. Moreover, one's image will be militant and, therefore, acceptable by current college standards. Yet one will have learned nothing, and the fragile sense of security developed in the protective environment of college will be cracked when exposed to the reality of competition in the world.

Nelson Taylor, a young Negro graduate of Morehouse College, recently observed that many black students "feel it is useless to try to compete. In order to avoid this competition, they build themselves a little cave to hide in." This "little cave," he added, is black studies. Furthermore, black students are encouraged in this escapism by guilt-ridden new leftists and faculty members who despise themselves and their advantaged lives and enjoy seeing young Negroes reject white middle-class values and disrupt the university. They are encouraged by university administrators who prefer political accommodation to an effort at serious education. But beyond the momentary titillation some may experience from being the center of attention, it is difficult to see how Negroes can in the end benefit from being patronized and manipulated in this way. Ultimately, their only permanent satisfaction can come from the certainty that they have acquired the technical and intellectual skills that will enable them upon graduation to perform significant jobs competently and with confidence. If they fail to acquire these skills, their frustration will persist and find expression in ever newer forms of antisocial and self-destructive behavior.

The conflict over black studies, as over other issues, raises the question of the function in general served by black protest today. Some black demands, such as that for a larger university enrollment of minority students, are entirely legitimate; but the major purpose of the protest through which these demands are pressed would seem to be not so much to pursue an end as to establish in the minds of the protesters, as well as in the minds of whites, the reality of their rebellion. Protest, therefore, becomes an end in itself and not a means toward social change. In this sense, the black rebellion is an enormously *expressive* phenomenon which is releasing the pent-up resentments of generations of oppressed Negroes. But expressiveness that is oblivious to political reality and not structured by instrumental goals is mere bombast.

James Forman's *Black Manifesto*, for instance, provides a nearly perfect sample of this kind of bombast combined with positive delusions of grandeur. "We shall liberate all the people in the U.S.," the introduction of the *Manifesto* declares, "and will be instrumental in the liberation of colored people the world around. . . . We are the most humane people within the U.S. . . . Racism in the U.S. is so pervasive in the mentality of whites that only an armed, well-disciplined, black-controlled government can insure the stamping out of racism in this country. . . . We say think in terms of the total control of the U.S."

One might never imagine from reading the *Manifesto* that Forman's organization, the National Black Economic Development Conference, is politically powerless, or that the institution it has chosen for assault is not the government or the corporation, but the church. Indeed, the exaggeration of language in the *Black Manifesto* is directly proportional to the isolation and impotence of those who drafted it. And their actual achievements provide an accurate measure of their strength. Three billion dollars in reparations was demanded – and $20,000 received. More important, the effect of this demand upon the Protestant churches has been to precipitate among them a conservative reaction against the activities of the liberal national denominations and the National Council of Churches. Forman's failure, of course, was to be expected: the only effect of an attack upon so organizationally diffuse and nonpolitical an institution as the church can be the deflection of pressure away from the society's major political and economic institutions and, consequently, the weakening of the black movement for equality.[1]

The possibility that his *Manifesto* might have exactly the opposite effect from that intended, however, was clearly not a problem to Forman, because the demands he was making upon white people were more moral than political or economic. His concern was to purge white guilt far more than to seek social justice for Negroes. It was in part for this reason that he chose to direct his attack at the church, which, as the institutional embodiment of our society's religious pretensions, is vulnerable to moral condemnation.

Yet there is something corrupting in the wholesale release of aggressive moral energy, particularly when it is in response to the demand for reparations for blacks. The difficulty is not only that as a purely racial demand its effect must be to isolate blacks from the white poor with whom they have common economic interests. The call for three billion dollars in reparations demeans the integrity of blacks and exploits the self-demeaning guilt of whites. It is insulting to Negroes to offer them reparations for past generations of suffering, as if the balance of an irreparable past could be set straight with a handout. In a recent poll, *Newsweek* reported that "today's proud Negroes, by an overwhelming 84 to 10 percent, reject the idea of preferential treatment in hiring or college admissions in reparations for past injustices." There are few controversial issues that can call forth a greater uniformity of opinion than this in the Negro community.

I also question both the efficacy and the social utility of an attack that impels the attacked to applaud and debase themselves. I am not certain whether or not self-flagellation can have a beneficial effect on the sinner (I tend to doubt that it can), but I am absolutely certain that it can never produce anything politically creative. It will not improve the lot of the unemployed and the ill-housed. On the other hand, it could well happen that the guilty party, in order to lighten his uncomfortable moral burden, will finally begin to rationalize his sins and affirm them as virtues. And, by such a process, today's ally can become tomorrow's enemy. Lasting political alliances are not built on the shifting sands of moral suasion.

On this part, the breast-beating white makes the same error as the Negro who swears that "black is beautiful." Both are seeking refuge in psychological solutions to social questions. And both are reluctant to confront the real cause of racial injustice, which is not bad attitudes but bad social conditions. The Negro creates a new psychology to avoid the reality of social stagnation, and the white – be he ever so liberal – professes his guilt precisely so as to create the illusion of social change, all the while preserving his economic advantages.

The response of guilt and pity to social problems is by no means new. It is, in fact, as old as man's capacity to rationalize or his reluctance to make real sacrifices for his fellow man. Two hundred years ago, Samuel Johnson, in an exchange with Boswell, analyzed the phenomenon of sentimentality:

> Boswell: "I have often blamed myself, Sir, for not feeling for others, as sensibly as many say they do."
> Johnson: "Sir, don't be duped by them any more. You will find these very feeling people are not very ready to do you good. They *pay* you by *feeling*."

Today, payments from the rich to the poor take the form of "giving a damn" or some other kind of moral philanthropy. At the same time, of course, some of those who so passionately "give a damn" are likely to argue that full employment is inflationary.

We are living in a time of great social confusion – not only about the strategies we must adopt but about the very goals these strategies are to bring us to. Only recently whites and Negroes of good will were pretty much in agreement that racial and economic justice required an end to segregation and the expansion of the role of the federal government. Now it is a mark of "advancement," not only among "progressive" whites but among the black militants as well, to believe that integration is passé. Unintentionally (or as the Marxists used to say, objectively), they are lending aid and comfort to traditional segregationists like Senators Eastland and Thurmond. Another "advanced" idea is the notion that government has gotten too big and that what is needed to make the society more humane and livable is an enormous new move toward local participation and decentralization. One cannot question the value or importance of democratic participation in the government, but just as misplaced sympathy for Negroes is being put to use by segregationists, the liberal preoccupation with localism is serving the cause of conservatism. Two years of liberal encomiums to decentralization have intellectually legitimized the concept, if not the name, of states' rights and have set the stage for the widespread acceptance of Nixon's "New Federalism."

The new anti-integrationism and localism may have been motivated by sincere moral conviction, but hardly by intelligent political thinking. It should be obvious that what is needed today more than ever is a political strategy that offers the real possibility of economically uplifting millions of impoverished individuals, black and white. Such a strategy must of necessity give low priority to the various forms of economic and psychological experimentation that I have discussed, which at best deal with issues peripheral to the central problem and at worst embody a frenetic escapism. These experiments are based on the assumption that the black community can be transformed from within when, in fact, any such transformation must depend on structural changes in the entire society. Negro poverty, for example, will not be eliminated in the absence of a total war on poverty. We need, therefore, a new national economic policy. We also need new policies in housing, education, and health care which can deal with these problems as they relate to Negroes within the context of a national solution. A successful strategy, therefore, must rest upon an identification of those central institutions which, if altered sufficiently, would transform the social and economic relations in our society; and it must provide a politically viable means of achieving such an alteration.

Surely the church is not a central institution in this sense. Nor is Roy Innis' notion of dealing with the banking establishment a useful one. For the banks will find no extra profit – quite the contrary – in the kind of fundamental structural change in society that is required.[2]

Moreover, the recent flurry of excitement over the role of private industry in the slums seems to have subsided. A study done for the Urban Coalition has called the National Alliance of Businessmen's claim to have hired more than 100,000 hard-core unemployed a "phony numbers game." Normal hiring as the result of expansion of turnover was in some cases counted as recruitment. Where hard-core workers have been hired and trained, according to the study, "The primary motivation . . . is the need for new sources of workers in a tight labor market. If and when the need for workers slackens, so will industry's performance." This has already occurred. The *Wall Street Journal* reported in July of 1969 that the Ford Motor Company, once praised for its social commitment, was forced to trim back production earlier in the year and in the process "quietly closed its two inner-city hiring centers in Detroit and even laid off some of the former hard-cores it had only recently hired." There have been similar retrenchments by other large companies as the result of a slackening in economic growth, grumblings from stockholders, and the realization by corporate executives that altruism does not make for high profits. Yet even if private industry were fully committed to attack the problem of unemployment, it is not in an ideal position to do so. Private enterprise, for example, accounted for only one out of every ten new jobs created in the economy between 1950 and 1960. Most of the remainder were created as the result of expansion of public employment.

While the church, private enterprise, and other institutions can, if properly motivated, play an important role, it is the trade union movement and the Democratic Party which offer the greatest leverage to the black struggle. The serious objective of Negroes must be to strengthen and liberalize these. The trade union movement is essential to the black struggle because it is the only institution in the society capable of organizing the working poor, so many of whom are Negroes. It is only through an organized movement that these workers, who are now condemned to the margin of the economy, can achieve a measure of dignity and economic security. I must confess I find it difficult to understand the prejudice against the labor movement currently fashionable among so many liberals. These people, somehow for reasons of their own, seem to believe that white workers are affluent members of the Establishment (a rather questionable belief, to put it mildly, especially when held by people earning over $25,000 a year) and are now trying to keep the Negroes down. The only grain of truth here is that there *is* competition between black and white workers which derives from a scarcity of jobs and resources. But rather than propose an expansion of those resources, our stylish liberals underwrite that competition by endorsing the myth that the unions are the worst enemy of the Negro.

In fact it is the program of the labor movement that represents a genuine means of reducing racial competition and hostility. Not out of a greater tenderness of feeling for black suffering – but that is just the point. Unions organize workers on the basis of common economic interests, not by virtue of racial affinity. Labor's legislative program for full employment, housing, urban reconstruction, tax reform, improved health care, and expanded educational opportunities is designed specifically to aid both whites and blacks in the lower and lower middle classes where the potential for racial polarization is most severe. And only a program of this kind can deal simultaneously and creatively with the interrelated problems of black rage and white fear. It does not placate black rage at the expense of whites, thereby increasing white fear and political reaction. Nor does it exploit white fear by repressing blacks. Either of these courses strengthens the demagogues among both races who prey upon frustration and racial antagonism. Both of them help to strengthen conservative forces – the forces that stand to benefit from the fact that hostility between black and white workers keeps them from uniting effectively around issues of common economic interest.

President Nixon is in the White House today largely because of this hostility; and the strategy advocated by many liberals to build a "new coalition" of the affluent, the young, and the dispossessed is designed to keep him there. The difficulty with this proposed new coalition is not only that its constituents comprise a distinct minority of the population, but that its affluent and youthful members – regardless of the momentary direction of their rhetoric – are hardly the undisputed friends of the poor. Recent Harris polls, in fact, have shown that Nixon is most popular among the college educated and the young. Perhaps they were attracted by his style or the minimal concessions he has made on Vietnam, but certainly their approval cannot be based upon his accomplishments in the areas of civil rights and economic justice.

If the Republican ascendancy is to be but a passing phenomenon, it must once more come to be clearly understood among those who favor social progress that the Democratic Party is still the only mass-based political organization in the country with the potential to become a majority movement for social change. And anything calling itself by the name of political activity must be concerned with building precisely such a majority movement. In addition, Negroes must abandon once and for all the false assumption that as ten percent of the population they can by themselves effect basic changes in the structure of American life. They must, in other words, accept the necessity of coalition politics. As a result of our fascination with novelty and with the "new" revolutionary forces that have emerged in recent years, it seems to some the height of conservatism to propose a strategy that was effective in the past. Yet the political reality is that without a coalition of Negroes and other minorities with the trade union movement and with liberal groups, the shift of power to the Right will persist and the democratic Left in America will have to content itself with a well-nigh permanent minority status.

The bitterness of many young Negroes today has led them

to be unsympathetic to a program based on the principles of trade unionism and electoral politics. Their protest represents a refusal to accept the condition of inequality, and in that sense it is part of the long, and I think, magnificent black struggle for freedom. But with no comprehensive strategy to replace the one I have suggested, their protest, though militant in rhetoric and intention, may be reactionary in effect.

The strategy I have outlined must stand or fall by its capacity to achieve political and economic results. It is not intended to provide some new wave of intellectual excitement. It is not intended to suggest a new style of life or a means to personal salvation for disaffected members of the middle class. Nor is either of these the proper role of politics. My strategy is not meant to appeal to the fears of threatened whites, though it would calm those fears and increase the likelihood that some day we shall have a truly integrated society. It is not meant to serve as an outlet for the terrible frustrations of Negroes, though it would reduce those frustrations and point a way to dignity for an oppressed people. It is simply a vehicle by which the wealth of this nation can be redistributed and some of its more grievous social problems solved. This in itself would be quite enough to be getting on with. In fact, if I may risk a slight exaggeration, by normal standards of human society I think it would constitute a revolution.

## NOTES

[1] Forman is not the only militant today who fancies that his essentially reformist program is revolutionary. Eldridge Cleaver has written that capitalists regard the Black Panther Breakfast for Children program (which the Panthers claim feeds 10,000 children) "as a threat, as cutting into the goods that are under their control." He also noted that it "liberates" black children from going to school hungry each morning. I wonder if he would also find public school lunch programs liberating.

[2] Innis' demand that the white banks deposit $6 billion in black banks as reparations for past injustices should meet with even less success than Forman's ill-fated enterprise. At least Forman had the benefit of the white churchman's guilt, an emotion not known to be popular among bankers.

# Part IV
# The Leftist Side of The Separatist/Nationalist Question

Black separatism is frequently a reaction against systemic exclusion and consequently often attempts to promote liberal social change alternatives. In this sense, separatism itself is regarded by many as leftist – "conservatives" and "reactionaries" label any form of black militancy (even the integration-oriented variety) as "red" or "Communist-inspired." For example, the late Reverend Martin Luther King, Jr., was labeled a "Communist"!

Beyond how some people fuzzy-mindedly and wrongly equate all forms of black aggressiveness with left-wing activity, black nationalism and avowedly leftist organizations have, in the past and even today, had a rather strange and precarious relationship. Generally most socialist-oriented movements and organizations eschew black nationalism/separatism, contending that racism is merely the by-product of capitalism; that capitalism encourages class divisions and consequently racism where it ordinarily might not exist. Black nationalism, the argument goes, is essentially the reverse of white racism, and black separatism is extreme race "chauvinism." Black separatists may also regard capitalism and its attendant class dichotomies as having a deleterious effect on race relations, but they generally believe that *race* rather than *class* is the most significant factor in race relations in the United States.

These different emphases thus create a dilemma for "radical" separatists who would like to join forces with leftists in their struggle against racism and capitalism. And they have tried.

In 1928, at its Sixth International Congress, the Communist International (Comintern), impressed with Garvey's successful appeal to the black masses, fashioned a program for the black masses called "Self-Determination in the Black Belt" and commanded the Communist Party in the United States to implement it. Understandably, the party was reluctant to attempt implementation, mainly because it had no idea of how to do so, in addition to its past ideological opposition to Garvey and the African Blood Brotherhood's nationalism/separatism. The party particularly excoriated Garvey's Back-to-Africa program as "Black Zionism" and "race chauvinism," because, if successful, it meant the eventual separation of black and white workers. The Comintern also launched an international black recruitment campaign centered around "nationalism." George Padmore and C.L.R. James, among others, were significant figures in international Communist circles.

In fact, Marcus Garvey preferred white capitalists over Communists, arguing that a white Communist is no different from any other white man – beneath all his "liberalism" lurked a white racist. The white capitalist, contended Garvey, would at least hire black workers if they worked at a lower wage level than white workers.

But, closer to home, the party's Self-Determination policy did not meet with much success. Blacks in the "Black Belt" as well as in the North were caught up in the Depression and chose New Deal here-and-now-meat-to-eat over Communist ideological pie-in-the-sky-bye-and-bye. However, what the American Communists already knew, particularly the black ones, and what the Comintern eventually came to realize, was that their call for equality in the system was more appealing to the black masses than their separatist appeal. Around 1933, the Self-Determination policy was formally deemphasized.

Beyond the dilemma black separatism presented to the Party, its attempt to increase its black membership was not very successful. Evidently the Party itself suffered from the same malaise it accused the separatists of having – "race chauvinism." Examples of the bitter disappointment experienced by some black Party members may be seen in their fictional and nonfictional works: Richard Wright's *Black Boy*, Ralph Ellison's *Invisible Man,* Langston Hughes' *I Wonder As I Wander,* Angelo Herndon's *Let Me Live,* and most recently Harold Cruse's *The Crisis of the Negro Intellectual*. To a man, these artists become disenchanted with the Party and eventually quit it, denouncing Communists as being just as racist as the average noncommunist racist "red-neck."

These disenchantments notwithstanding, other blacks embraced the party, quickly adding that they articulated no permanent allegiance to separatism. Some of the early black members of the party included James W. Ford (who was the Communist Party's vice-presidential candidate in 1932), Harry Haywood, and Benjamin Davis, Jr.

Contemporary separatism and leftist organizations still exhibit distrust and skepticism toward each other. One outstanding example of this uneasiness may be seen in the Black Panther Party. Originally a black nationalist organization, the

Panther leadership moved to Marxism-Leninism, basing its ideology on the class struggle, but adding that *class* and *race* must be simultaneously attacked. It allowed no white members in the Party, but it did encourage allegiances with other "radical" and leftist groups. There even emerged at one time the White Panther Party, headed by John Sinclair. But the Panther rank-and-file became disenchanted with Marxism-Leninism, "communalism," and, finally, "intercommunalism," based on a class analysis, and turned to plain old black nationalism based on racial oppression. The Black Panther Party now operates not unlike a ghetto-improvement association, with its former all-encompassing universal ideological preachments firmly rooted in practical problems of the black community,

# 13
# *A Transitional Program for Black Liberation* *

SOCIALIST WORKERS PARTY

It is becoming more and more clear to increasing numbers of Afro-Americans that nothing less than a revolution in this country will bring about the liberation of black people. As a result, a great deal of mass struggle – and organizing a mass political party around militant action on that program.

How can these lessons best be applied at the present stage of the struggle for black liberation in the United States? That is the all-important question this document proposes to discuss and answer.

What do the developments of the past 15 years demonstrate? The struggle for black liberation has taken giant steps forward since the 1955 Montgomery bus boycott touched off the contemporary phase of the movement. It has given Afro-Americans a heightened sense of dignity, worth, and destiny as a people. It has made the claims of the black masses into a paramount and unpostponable issue in American life and politics. It has acquainted the whole world with the intolerable conditions of the more than 22 million Afro-Americans and their determination to end the racist system and to win self-determination.

More recently, it has propelled black nationalism from deeply felt resentment against injustice and inequality into a powerful and ascending force in the Afro-American communities.

In the conclusion to his biography of Sammy Younge, Jr., the first black college student to die in the black liberation movement, SNCC leader James Forman summed up the situation in the following terms:

> "The history of resistance to the most unique colonization experience known to mankind shows that the '60s must be recorded as an accelerating generation, a generation of black people determined that they will survive, a generation aware that resistance is the agenda for today and that action by people is necessary to quicken the steps of history."

*This document was adopted, after a three-month preconvention discussion, by the 23rd National Convention of the Socialist Workers Party held in New York City, August 29 – Sept. 1, 1969. New York, Merit Publisher.

Black Americans have participated in plenty of actions since 1955 – and these struggles have been responsible for whatever advances have been achieved. But it is painfully evident that all the struggles over the past decade and a half have not succeeded in improving the living and working conditions of the masses of black people or eliminating the worst abuses inflicted daily upon them. Only a few favored individuals from the black upper crust have benefited from the tokenism through which the white possessors of power and wealth have tried to dampen or buy off the militancy of the masses.

A pile of economic statistics confirms what almost every Afro-American knows from personal experience. Blacks are subjected to many forms of discrimination, have much lower incomes and fewer job opportunities, get lower wages, live in rotten housing, have bigger rates of unemployment, and receive inferior education. Just one figure from the bottom of the heap shows what the score is. Forty percent of the nation's 9,500,000 citizens on welfare are black. In some states monthly welfare payments amount to as little as $40 for a family of four. In New York City, 80 percent on welfare are blacks or Puerto Ricans.

Despite the heightened consciousness of the nature of this oppression and the awareness of the failure of the policies pursued in the past, no clear alternative conception has yet emerged from the black community on what has to be done to bring better results. Although repeated uprisings in the black communities have indicated time and again the existence of a deep-going mass radicalization, little headway has been made in organizing the ghetto masses into an effective force for struggle. Instead, the gunning down of black leaders, the assassination of Malcolm X and Martin Luther King, Jr., the repression of the Blank Panther Party and the lack of mass agencies of struggle have bred a widespread feeling of frustration which exists in the black community on all levels.

### THE FRAUD OF BLACK CAPITALISM

Meanwhile the chief political representatives of American capitalism are not silent or inactive. They have no intention of removing the causes of discrimination, poverty, and misery. These are built into their system of racist oppression and economic exploitation. They have shown by the use of police, state, and federal troops over the recent years that they are ready to resort to the most brutal and bloody repression to put down black protest. In order to maintain their rule they strive to keep blacks divided amongst themselves and separated from potential allies among the whites. They expect to keep blacks in their place by alternating cheap concessions ("tokenism") with repressions.

The Kennedy and Johnson administrations banked on the passage of a few civil rights bills and a fake war-on-poverty to calm and appease the growing militancy. These have not worked. Now the more conservative Nixon administration has announced the development of a "black capitalism."

The essence of this program is that the principal lending institutions, backed by government loan guarantees, are supposed to help set up and encourage different sorts of small business enterprise by black individuals or groups. Not much has yet been done along this line. But the idea of creating a puny black capitalism alongside the gigantic edifice of white capitalism and in competition with it is a pure fantasy and a cruel hoax. While it may benefit a few black businessmen, it will fool very few black people.

Today almost all black businesses are tiny family operations, catering to a ghetto clientele and providing a meager income for their owners and a few jobs for others. About 25 percent of black firms are barber shops and beauty parlors. One out of every 40 Americans is a proprietor, while only one black in 1,000 is.

For show-window purposes, Nixon and his henchmen may aid and establish a few more black-operated enterprises – which will remain in debt to their financiers. But they will not narrow the colossal discrepancy between white capitalist ownership and the layer of black proprietors. The predominant trend of American economy is toward accelerated concentration of business and industry in fewer and bigger monopolies. This cuts down small white business as well as blocking the growth of black business. A sprinkling of new black firms cannot alter or reverse this process. They will remain petty and shaky marginal enterprises while the major banks, industries, insurance companies, chain stores, and real estate interest stay in white hands and keep on fleecing the black communities.

Nor do the corporations which control the job market have any compelling reasons to better wages or working conditions for their black wage-slaves or eliminate the higher rate of unemployment among black workers and youth.

So long as the capitalist system prevails, Afro-Americans have the right to demand equal, if not greater, access to capital resources, credits, and loans so they can go into business on their own as well as into factories, offices, and government positions. Cooperatives may help some black communities to lessen the parasitic grip of the white bloodsuckers and acquire a larger measure of autonomy over minor aspects of their economic life. But this is quite different from expecting that the present owners and controllers of the United States will satisfy the needs of the black community or that black capitalism will solve or even alleviate the most pressing problems of black people, such as housing, education, employment, and poverty. A fundamental transformation of the whole economic, social, and political system is required for this.

## THE LIBERAL APPROACH

The liberal black leaders, from Whitney Young and Roy Wilkins to Ralph Abernathy and Bayard Rustin, advocate extensive reforms for the benefit of black people. The trouble is that they expect to see these concessions come from Democratic and Republican party politicians, the very agents of the capitalist ruling class which has bred racism for centuries, upholds it, and is its main beneficiary at home and abroad.

These gradualists and reformists keep their ideas and activities within the limits of the established order which they are committed to serve. They resemble the house-slaves and handkerchief-heads who came, cap in hand, begging "massa" for favors.

The more astute white capitalist politicians and their black stooges are aware that any breakaway from the two-party system to the left is a danger to them. That is why they back the campaigns and build up the reputations of black Democrats like Mayor Carl Stokes of Cleveland and Mayor Richard Hatcher of Gary. Such black men are nominated and put in office, not to serve the welfare of the black community, but to head off the mounting demands for change, to coopt and corrupt black nationalist sentiment if possible, and turn it back into channels which are safe and secure for the white supremacists.

The first major action of Mayor Stokes was to increase payroll taxes to raise money so that more cops could be hired to maintain control over the black community. And Mayor Hatcher admitted his administration has little control over what happens to black people in Gary. "There is much talk about black control of the ghetto," he said. "What does it mean? I am mayor of a city of roughly 90,000 black people – but we do not control the possibilities of jobs for them, of money for their schools, or state-funded social institutions. These things are in the hands of U.S. Steel Corporation, the county department of welfare, and the State of Indiana."

## THE POSITIONS OF THE REVOLUTIONARY NATIONALISTS

To one degree or another almost every Afro-American shares the sentiments if not the ideology of black nationalism. The spectrum of the black nationalist movement comprises a wide variety of political positions and trends, ranging from those on the extreme right, who want to build black business, through the purely cultural nationalists, to the revolutionary left wing.

Today hundreds of thousands of black men and women look forward to the black revolution as the road to liberation. In the vanguard are the rebellious black youth in the ghettoes, the streets, and the campuses who are absorbing ideas and inspirations from the "Third World" revolutions, the teachings of Malcolm X, and their own experiences in struggle. The most advanced recognize that capitalism is the source and support of racism and that it is necessary to abolish capitalism in order to attack racism at its roots.

This rapidly growing revolutionary consciousness means that increasing numbers of black people, especially among the youth, are ready to devote their lives to the building of a revolutionary movement to win power for the masses and overturn this system. They are now forced to grapple with the extremely complex problem of how this can be done. Without a correct and realistic perspective for carrying on the liberation struggle, based on a clear understanding of the objective conditions in the United States today, thousands of excellent revolutionary cadres run the risk of disorientation or wasting time and energy while trying to reach the goal of emancipation.

Numerous revolutionaries see the necessity and desirability of breaking away, once and for all, from both the Democratic and Republican parties and forming an independent black party which will not only enter candidates in election campaigns but mobilize the Afro-American communities in actions to attain community demands.

However, they do not yet see clearly how to link struggles for the pressing immediate needs of the black people with the revolutionary goal of overturning the whole racist capitalist system. In their search for an answer to this difficult problem they swing from one extreme to the other without finding a logical and practical connection between the two ends. Thus at one time they talk about armed struggle by small, highly disciplined and trained groups of militants as the only really revolutionary method of action. When they run up against the unrealism of guerrilla-type actions in the United States, where the scale of revolutionary struggles demands huge and much more complex commitments of forces, they fall back to spasmodic and uncoordinated activities associated with the largely spontaneous struggles that flare up in the community over issues that often do not appear to be far-reaching. Many militants who have grasped the need to overturn the system as a whole feel that in participating in such battles they are merely marking time while they search for the formula that will put a successful revolution on the agenda in the United States.

In order to work out a strategy and tactics that can realistically hasten a revolutionary showdown, it is necessary first of all to understand where the black liberation struggle actually stands today. What stage is it in?

In the country as a whole, a struggle for government power by the working class is not an immediate perspective. This obviously holds true for the white workers, who remain relatively quiescent politically and still tied in with the Democratic Party machinery through the union bureaucracy.

Without the white workers, the movement for black liberation cannot realistically pose an immediate struggle for government power. It is true, of course, as the mass uprisings indicate, that the black masses are more ready to fight for their rights against the authorities than any other sector of American society. But it requires the active backing and participation of the majority of the population to achieve government power. This stage has not yet been reached in the United States. Moreover, the political understanding of the black masses today is far less advanced than their combative frame of mind. Despite their bitterness, nine-tenths of the black voters cast a ballot for the Democratic candidates for president in 1968, as they did in 1964.

The truth is that we stand in a preparatory period. Once this is thoroughly understood, the problems begin to fall into place.

The first big problem is how to break the hold of the white supremacist capitalist politicians upon Afro-Americans. The solution lies in promoting the formation of an independent mass black political party.

The second big problem is how to get Afro-Americans in their majority to move faster and farther along the road to revolution. The solution lies in formulating and fighting for a program that can help transform the general discontent and general militancy of the black masses into an organized, cohesive, consciously revolutionary force. By presenting and fighting for such a program, a small vanguard can transform itself into an influential power among the masses.

The next section of this document presents proposals along this line, many of which have already been brought forward by various elements in the movement.

## SUGGESTED PROGRAM OF MASS STRUGGLE

The motivation for a program of revolutionary mass struggle must be the self-determination of Afro-Americans. Like all oppressed nationalities, black people can achieve their freedom only by taking their destiny in their own hands: "Who would be free, themselves must strike the blow."

This means that black people must form and unify their own organizations of struggle, take control of the black communities and all the institutions within them, and conduct a consistent fight to overcome every form of economic, political, and cultural servitude and inequality generated and enforced by the decadent, racist capitalist society.

### A. Black control of the black community

It is a basic democratic principle that a people should have the right to decide its own affairs. Therefore, the central demand of the liberation forces is for black control of the black community. This is an indispensable step toward freeing the black masses from domination by the white racists who benefit from their exploitation.

The demand for black control of the black community has a number of attributes which give it an extremely powerful potential for mobilizing the masses in a revolutionary direction.

The demand for black control has been raised spontaneously in thousands of struggles across the country. It is obviously a demand that speaks directly to the needs and present understanding of black people. At the same time, black control of the black community is a democratic demand. It is based on something that even the ruling class says it believes in – the right of people to have democratic control over their own lives and communities. Thus, the resistance the power structure puts up against this struggle will help to expose the hypocrisy of the ruling class on one of the central issues which it uses to brainwash and enslave the masses – its proclaimed adherence to democracy.

At the same time, the struggle for black control is profoundly revolutionary, because it poses the question of who will have decision-making power over black people: they or the capitalist rulers. The realization of this aim can build black fortresses which will be centers of black counterpower to the white power structure in the principal cities of the United States.

As they develop within the black communities, struggles

targeted to win control over specific institutions and agencies can pave the way and prepare increasing numbers of people for the all-inclusive goal of total control of their community. These partial struggles, carried out around issues such as black control of the schools, can be extremely important because, through them, encouraging victories can be won. These victories, even if limited to specific areas, can help to raise the confidence of the community in its own power and lay the basis for broader future struggles.

The following demands can help promote this process:

1. Replacement of police occupation of the black community with a community-controlled police force drawn from residents of the community.

2. Black control of all government funds allocated to the black community and control over all plans for renovating and constructing housing and other communal facilities and improvements.

3. Community control over all institutions in the black community, such as hospitals, welfare centers, libraries, etc.

4. Establishment of community councils to make policy decisions and administer the affairs of the black community. These councils should be composed of representatives elected by workers in various hospitals, educational institutions – as well as delegates elected on a block basis.

The local councils or boards of control should be joined together on regional, state and national levels, the aim being to create a National Council of Black Communities. This should be composed of elected, not appointed, delegates representing the local constituencies.

Such a National Council could work out common policies and speak with one voice on all matters affecting the communities as a whole and their relations with all other forces and agencies. It would thus exercise far more authority than any single community could. To prevent the National Council from bureaucratic usurpation of power, elections should be held regularly and delegates should be subject to recall at any time so that they remain under the control of the local committees they represent.

### B. Formation of a black political party

The indispensable instrument for organizing and carrying on effective struggle for such demands, achieving complete control over the black community, and moving forward to black liberation is an independent black political party. Its program would be designed to use the immense wealth created by working people, black and white, not for imperialist war and the enrichment of a few but for the needs of the majority.

The main purpose of a black party is to lead Afro-Americans in political and mass action. But its progressive proposals would attract support from other sections of the population which suffer from the evils of capitalist rule.

A black party would expose and challenge the do-nothing policies of the Democrats and Republicans and present an alternative to them not only by participating in elections but by organizing effective community actions. It would take the initiative in promoting the self-mobilization of the black people and forming alliances with students, poor white people, workers and all other forces interested in radical change. It could play a vanguard role in bringing revolutionary ideas to all sections of the country.

### C. Key planks in a party program

#### *Domestic policy*

1. It is the duty of society to provide well-paid jobs for all. A shorter work week with no loss in pay to spread the available work. Unemployment insurance at full wages for everyone 18 or over whether or not they have held jobs before.

2. Transfer the funds from the war budget to launch a multi-billion-dollar crash program of public works to build schools, hospitals, better public transport, parks and recreation facilities, nurseries, libraries, and housing. Give black workers priority on all jobs connected with the construction program.

3. Enact a $3-an-hour minimum wage with guaranteed protection of this minimum against increases in the cost of living.

4. Put an immediate end to hunger and malnutrition through a guaranteed annual income which can assure everyone – including the old, sick and disabled – adequate living standards.

5. Abolish all taxes on incomes of $7,500 and under. Abolish all sales taxes which discriminate against the poor.

6. Make free quality medical care available to all citizens. Expropriate the drug monopolies and medicine profiteers. Undertake a large-scale program to train black people as doctors and nurses.

7. Organize self-defense units to protect the black community and its organizations. Oppose guns laws which leave black people defenseless and unarmed while white cops and racists assault members of the black community.

8. Investigate the financial records of all landlords and businesses operating in the black community and tax their superprofits to help finance improvement projects for the community.

9. Extend credits to black cooperatives and small businesses.

10. Enforce and tighten all existing housing codes. No tenant to pay rent exceeding ten percent of his total income.

11. Expropriate any firm which discriminates against black people.

12. Elect price committees to inspect and police prices in the neighborhoods.

13. Review the cases of, and release all, black prisoners because they have not received fair trials. All black people to be tried by a jury of their peers as guaranteed by the Constitution – that is, by other black people.

#### *Military and foreign policy*

1. End the draft. Exempt black youth from military service.

2. Bring the GIs home from Vietnam immediately. The black man's struggle is here at home.

3. Take a referendum on the attitude of the black community toward the Vietnam war and all foreign wars.

4. Support the constitutional right of GIs to speak out against the war and discrimination in the armed forces. An immediate end to all discrimination in the armed forces.

5. Self-determination for the Vietnamese and all Third World peoples. Solidarity with the liberation struggles of all oppressed nationalities.

6. End government assistance to all oppressive regimes from South Africa to South Vietnam. Dismantle all foreign military bases.

***Black education***

The black community should have control of its entire educational system from the nursery school through college. This can be accomplished in the following ways:

*The educational system*

1. Election of community control boards to supervise schools in the black community.

2. The establishment of an educational system and curriculum which meets the needs of black children, prepares them for future economic security, gives them a knowledge of themselves and an understanding of the true history and culture of black people.

3. Parent involvement in every phase of school life.

4. Institute a crash program to train black administrators and teachers. Preferential hiring of black teachers and administrators.

5. Community groups entitled to use school facilities to promote activities of benefit to the community and the black liberation struggle.

6. Offer a full program of adult education.

7. Dismiss all school officials who victimize or insult students on racial grounds.

8. Introduce special tutoring programs for all students who have fallen behind in their studies.

*High Schools*

1. Establish student policy-making boards to run student activities in the high schools, handle disciplinary problems, and participate in the general supervision of the schools.

2. Hold regular full assemblies to discuss school problems and ascertain the will of the students.

3. Maintain the rights of all students and teachers. These should include: freedom of expression, freedom to organize, to pass out literature, freedom from censorship of school newspapers, freedom of assembly, and the right to invite any outside speakers regardless of their political views.

4. An end to disciplinary expulsions.

5. An end to the tracking system – special tutoring for all students who fall behind.

6. A rounded black studies program which will teach Afro-American history and literature truthfully and throw light on the real nature of capitalist racism.

7. Upgraded job training programs. Adequate preparation for all students desiring to attend college.

8. A guaranteed job for all high school graduates.

*A black university*

The black community should have universities which are related to the needs of black people, to their struggle against oppression, and to their development as a nationality. Third World university students and faculty should be able to shape their own educational destiny and provide training in all the skills and professions required by the black community. The following demands to accomplish these ends have already been raised in the campus struggles:

1. Autonomous black studies and Third World studies departments, adequately financed and with complete control of curriculum, facilities, and policies in the hands of Third World students and faculty.

2. Representatives of Third World groups on all policy-making bodies.

3. Availability of university facilities for use by the community and their expansion in the black community.

4. Free university education for all Third World students who desire it, with full expenses paid by the government and scholarships available to all who need them.

5. Guaranteed jobs for all graduates.

***The black workers***

Because of the role they play in production, black workers are potentially the most powerful sector of the black community in the struggle for liberation. As the victims of inequality in the economy, black workers have already begun to organize separately on the job to advance their interests and protect their rights.

The unity of black and white workers is indispensable to combat and overthrow capitalism. But where white workers are privileged and black workers are penalized, black unity in action must precede and prepare the ground for black-white unity on a broad scale. Black caucuses in the unions can fight against discrimination in hiring, firing, and upgrading and for equality of treatment in the unions themselves, as DRUM and other black caucuses in Detroit and elsewhere are undertaking to do. Where they are part of organized labor, they should strive to democratize the unions, regenerate their progressivism, and eliminate white job-trust conceptions and practices.

These aims can be furthered through the following demands.

1. Rank and file democratic control of the unions. Elimination of all racist practices in the labor movement.

2. Preferential hiring, advancement of black workers, and free access to apprentice training programs, the skilled trades, and higher paying supervisory posts.

3. An escalator clause in all union contracts to assure automatic wage adjustments to keep up with the rising costs of living.

4. A 30-hour week with no reduction in pay.

5. Speedier grievance procedures. No restrictions on the right to strike.

6. Equal rights and treatment for all black union members.

7. Complete independence of the unions from government interference. Repeal of all anti-labor laws.

8. Workers control of industry through factory committees elected by the workers on the job.

Most of the proposals listed above have been brought forward at one time or another in the course of the black liberation struggle over the past years; others are taken from the experiences of the masses elsewhere in fighting against capitalist domination. A program of this sort cannot be fully finalized or frozen. It has to remain flexible and open-ended with plenty of room for additions and improvements as the struggle develops and new problems come to the fore.

The whole point of the program is to provide a guide for the organization and action of the Afro-American masses, which can lead the goal of black liberation with the maximum of gains en route.

The black liberation movement is bound to play a vanguard role in the coming American socialist revolution both by its example of combativeness against the racist power structure and by the stimulus its struggles will give to actions of other sectors thrown into opposition to the ruling capitalist class.

The strategy of the black liberation movement hinges on the achievement of two tasks. One is the unification and mobilization of the black masses for revolutionary action. The other is the weakening of the enemy forces.

Since Afro-Americans constitute a minority of the population in the United States, it will be necessary to find ways and means to take advantage of potential social divisions among the whites and thereby reduce the original unfavorable odds. This can be done by drawing one part of the poor and working class whites, as well as sympathetic students and intellectuals, into an alliance of action while some other sections of the white population are neutralized. Those parts of the program suggested above which not only correspond to the needs of the blacks but will likewise benefit prospective political allies among the white majority can serve to further these long-range aims of a realistic revolutionary strategy.

## REVOLUTIONARY STRATEGY AND TACTICS

How does the program outlined above fit into the strategy and tactics of a socialist revolution in the United States?

At first sight most of the points appear limited in nature. Many of them concern rights and liberties guaranteed to every citizen by the Constitution. Or they propose broadening these rights – for example, establishing the right of black control of the black community. They can be defined as "democratic demands."

Other points concern guaranteeing jobs, hourly wages, annual income, a 30-hour week, social benefits such as adequate medical care. Others involve independent political action, the defense of the black community, organization of black power. For reasons which will be explained below, these can be defined as "transitional demands."

Taken point by point, the program can seem modest, perhaps even feasible under capitalism if one were to take at face value the propaganda about capitalism standing for democracy, a good living, and a free world.

Particularly to be noted about the demands is that they have either already appeared in the black communities, in some instances with quite broad backing, or they are easily understood and appeciated by wide groups and, with correct leadership, could serve as rallying slogans for very massive struggles. This is a first prerequisite for any program for revolutionary struggle. That is, above all, the program must be based on the objective needs of black people.

But how does such a program tie in with the struggle to overturn capitalism and build a socialist society in America?

To understand this, it is necessary to bring in some general considerations. On a world scale, capitalism as an internationally integrated system for the production and distribution of basic necessities is in its death agony. It offers little to most of humanity but grinding poverty, hopeless insecurity, declining opportunities, increasingly repressive regimes, and endless wars, each more horrifying than the last.

A number of countries have already torn loose and set out on the road to building socialism, whatever the difficulties, hardships, and setbacks caused in the final analysis by the poverty-stricken level at which they had to begin and the efforts of the capitalist powers to injure and destroy them. The relationship of forces between capitalism and socialism on a world scale has changed to such a degree in the past 50 years since the first successful socialist revolution in Russia that even the United States is, at bottom, on the defensive. This is the basic reality despite the decades of prosperity arising out of the victory in World War II and the preparations for World War III, and despite the colossal military force at the command of the American capitalist rulers.

What is to be observed all over the world is that mass struggles of any considerable scope now tend to collide with the capitalist system and, with proper leadership, have the potential to break through the barriers of capitalism and cross over into struggles for socialism.

This tendency is so strong, so deeply imbedded, that examples can be cited throughout the Third World where a struggle for such democratic demands as national independence and a thoroughgoing agrarian reform has moved in the direction of a struggle for socialism. In Cuba, Vietnam, and China these struggles have culminated in actual revolutionary overturns of the capitalist system.

While the tendency for mass struggles to move toward socialism is especially striking in the Third World, it is also operative – with certain modifications – in the industrially advanced capitalist countries. Under the impulse of serious problems affecting their lives in general and standard of living, masses of working people can become engaged in struggles of a militant nature, the logic of which is to disregard the limitations of capitalism and to seek solutions that can actually be worked out only if socialism is instituted.

This gives these struggles a "transitional" nature. Beginning with a limited challenge to the rule of capitalism, they move logically toward the creation of a new revolutionary power in opposition to the capitalist government.

The key demands being raised in the black liberation struggle today, such as black control of the black community, jobs for all, and self-determination of Third World peoples have this quality of being transitional in nature. They are rooted in the needs and present understanding of the black community, yet they have a revolutionary logic because the capitalist system does not have the capacity to meet them. A new, more rational, more productive system is required.

On the ideological level, such transitional demands constitute a means of bringing the level of understanding of the broad masses under capitalism to the higher level required to understand consciously the need for socialism. The present-day struggles around these demands for changes in the system can lead to and become part of the overall struggle for power. The mobilization of the masses thus takes place as a process, with each struggle awakening, educating, inspiring, and organizing new layers toward revolutionary consciousness and action.

Several examples will suffice to show this logical development.

Unemployment is a familiar enough phenomenon in the black communities. It is easy for a black youth, for instance, to understand why he should have a guaranteed job opportunity. When great numbers of youths face the same situation, a point can be reached where they can engage with some militancy in common action in support of jobs for all.

The problem is obviously no longer an individual problem, as the capitalists seek to picture it and to maintain it. Its true nature has come to the surface. It is a problem involving society as a whole, demanding an overall solution.

Where are the jobs to be found? One possibility is to take all the current jobs and reduce the hours on each job sufficiently to make room for everyone seeking employment. To maintain living standards, however, current yearly incomes must be guaranteed despite the reduced work week.

What power can enforce such a solution? Quite clearly, only the government can do this. Since the present government will resist this collective way of solving the problem, the question arises as to who it really represents and why it should not be removed to make way for a government that will guarantee jobs for all.

More questions arise. The solution demands economic planning on a national scale and the placing of human needs above profit-making. Consideration of the socialist alternative to capitalism has thus been placed on the agenda.

Thus, the demand for jobs, can, under certain circumstances, have very far-reaching consequences.

The actions spearheaded by black students on campuses across the country give another indication of the potential role of struggles around transitional demands. The demand for increased or open enrollment of Third World students has already been shown to have far-reaching implications. Significant gains towards increasing black enrollment can and have been made within the present educational structure, but the struggle for open enrollment – that is, for college education for all who want it – will not be so easy for the system to fulfill.

Certain key questions are immediately raised by this demand: Where are the resources for such a vast expansion of educational facilities to come from? How will adequate jobs be found for all the students upon graduation?

If persistently pursued, struggles around this demand call into question the capitalist economic structure itself. Because of its built-in need for large pools of low-paid, unskilled labor, capitalism is not constructed to absorb the costs and consequences of higher education for the most exploited sector of the working force.

From the standpoint of moving the revolution forward, struggles such as those that have been taking place on the campuses – whether they end in victories or not – can inspire and lead to demands with more far-reaching implications than was apparent in the original issues. The black community as a whole has supported and received inspiration from the example set by the black students in struggles for self-determination.

The fight for autonomous black studies departments, for example, has helped pave the way for struggle for control of other institutions in the black community. If there can be black control of black studies departments in the universities, why not black control of the public schools, black control of the police, and black control of the community?

The impact which these black student struggles have already had can be seen in the fact that they have succeeded in bringing about unprecedented unity in action between blacks and other national minorities including Chicanos, Oriental-Americans, Puerto Ricans, and Indians. They have likewise attracted support from many radical white students and even, in one small but significant instance, from a progressively-led union local of oil workers in the Bay Area.

The movement of black and Third World students is a clear example of how a struggle in a limited arena under present conditions can help to expose the system and lead to bigger and broader efforts. Struggle is the school of the masses and the means for clarifying their consciousness of what has to be done. All the demands that bring them into action for their own aims are worth raising, fighting for, and incorporating into an overall revolutionary strategy and program.

The strategy of advancing the black liberation struggle through the development of transitional demands is fundamentally different from both the reformist and ultraleftist concepts of what to do.

The reformists view capitalism as so powerful and entrenched that it cannot be overturned, at least for a long time to come. From this pessimistic outlook, they conclude that the best that can be accomplished is to improve the lot of the poverty-stricken masses a little, either by persuading or pressuring the rulers.

The ultralefts see capitalism as completely finished, not only as to perspectives but in capacity to survive. They see it as standing by inertia, requiring only a slight push to make it collapse. They dream of bringing this about by galvanizing the masses through clever or extremely revolutionary propaganda – which often turns out to be mere rhetoric – or by a small heroic group undertaking a spectacular action which, by setting an example, will prove contagious, setting the masses in motion in some kind of spontaneous way.

Against both the reformists and ultralefts, revolutionary Marxists view capitalism as having entered the epoch of its death agony, yet as still retaining considerable capacity to defer the final showdown through violent means, through a few concessions in some instances, through keeping the masses from gaining an understanding of politics, and through blocking the organization of a revolutionary party deeply rooted among the masses and endowed with a competent leadership.

As against both the reformists and ultralefts, the revolutionary Marxists seek to take advantage of the basic weakness in the position of the ruling class. This lies in the deep-going tendency of all serious social struggles in this epoch to involve government power and to raise the question of who should exercise this power, no matter how limited these struggles may be or may appear to be, at the beginning.

The revolutionary Marxists propose a strategy based on this fact. The succession of transitional demands suggested above corresponds to the course of struggle repeatedly observed in the world today. To pose these demands in their logical succession, to try to organize battles along this line, helps to develop an understanding of the main existing tendency in the class struggle, thereby advancing the political understanding of the masses and hastening the stage when a final showdown with the racist capitalist system becomes a realistic possibility.

## THE GOAL OF LIBERATION: CAPITALISM OR SOCIALISM?

The program of a movement or a party is a means to an end – and for a revolutionary movement that end means the replacement of the prevailing system of racist oppression by a free and equal society. What kind of socioeconomic organization can enable the black liberation movement to achieve self-determination and a better life for all Afro-Americans?

Black nationalists have very varying attitudes on this crucial question. On the right are some who believe in building up black capitalism. To the left are those revolutionaries who have come to understand that only a socialist society can solve the fundamental problems of the black masses. Many nationalists are disinclined to take any definite position on this matter. We will settle that when we come to it, they say. However, this is not the sort of issue that a movement seriously committed to the abolishment of racist oppression can evade or leave indefinitely hanging in midair.

A realistic decision on what kind of economy can succeed the present system of exploitation in the United States cannot be made in an arbitrary manner. The possibilities have been restricted by great historical factors which have been at work over a long stretch of time. Foremost among these factors is the level of economic development which determines the character and the goals of the contending forces.

This point can be made clearer by comparing the situation which confronted the movement for black emancipation in the mid-19th century with that of today. At that time, the main immediate oppressors of the black people were the southern slaveholders, while the Afro-Americans in bondage were mostly cultivators of the soil. The objectives of that revolution were to destroy chattel slavery and to provide the freedmen with the economic, social, and political means for their liberation and advancement.

What happened, as everyone knows, was that the slave power was smashed during the Civil War and Reconstruction and the slaves given their formal freedom. But since the northern capitalist conquerors denied them the promised "40 acres and a mule" and other prerequisites for their economic independence and the exercise of political power, the blacks could be thrust back into a new state of servitude from which they suffer to the present day.

Today, the main oppressor of the Afro-American is the capitalist class. The vast majority of black people no longer live on plantations in the rural South or work in the fields. They are packed into city slums where they make their living – if they are not thrown on welfare – by working in capitalist enterprises. They are surrounded on all sides by the capitalist owners who fleece them as employers, loansharks, bankers, landlords, and merchants.

In order to win liberation, the revolutionary movement must overthrow these exploiters whose system breeds and sustains racism and oppression. Because Afro-Americans are both an oppressed nationality and the most heavily exploited segment of the American working class, the black liberation movement has a twofold character. It is at one and the same time a nationalist movement for self-determination and a proletarian struggle against the capitalist possessors of wealth and power.

Afro-Americans have been the principal victims of the profit system at all stages of its development in North America over the past 400 years. They were enslaved and shipped across the Atlantic to raise staple crops to enrich the planters. They are still laboring for the profits of others today, although in the cities rather than the countryside and for capitalists rather than slaveholders.

The hour has struck when an end must be put to all forms of exploitation and servitude. Full and definitive liberation cannot be achieved except by abolishing the private ownership of the means of production by the corporations and banks.

This measure is mandatory whether Afro-Americans decide to exercise their right of self-determination through the creation of a separate black nation or within the context of the creation of a single socialist republic along with insurgent white workers and other anti-capitalist forces.

The transitional program of a genuinely revolutionary movement must have a clear and conscious goal which guides all its activities and lights the way for its followers. It must be designed to satisfy the needs of the working masses and place them in control of their own affairs. While promoting a transition from national oppression to self-determination, it will of necessity advance the transition from capitalism to socialism.

Through this second emancipation, black America will not only have effected its own liberation, but promoted the liberation of all oppressed peoples from racism, capitalism, and imperialism.

# 14
# *The Communist Party, Always Out of Step* *

BRUNETTA R. WOLFMAN

Georgia USSR and Georgia USA are thousands of miles apart in fact but were drawn close together for a small band of "true believers" by Joseph Stalin. He elaborated on Lenin's formulation of the national and colonial question and, with its acceptance by the Communist International in 1928, the treatise became doctrine and manifesto for the infinitesimal American Communist Party (Record, 1951, p. 59). A Georgian-born Bolshevik, Stalin defined a nation as a community of people, historically constituted, stable, with a common language, community of territory, economic cohesion, and a psychological make-up which manifests itself in a common culture (Stalin; 1944, pp. 5-8). He also declared the right of nations to self-determination and to protect their institutions and customs while he attacked separatism as detrimental to the interests of the proletariat and the Party.

For approximately 30 years, the Stalinist doctrine of the national question with its American analogue of the Negro nation determined the policy of the CPUSA. The formulation did not contribute to any great political or organizational successes in this country (though Elijah Muhammad's Muslim group and the Republic of New Africa may have been influenced directly or indirectly by the Party's program). At the 17th National Convention of the CPUSA, the concept of the Negro nation was dropped in favor of the definition of a racially distinctive people who are a part of the American whole and who differ from other minority groups because of the "revolutionary import of their struggle" (CPUSA, 1960).

"Self-determination of the Negro people in the Black Belt," "struggles against white chauvinism," "organizing the unorganized" – slogans reflecting programmatic efforts and the campaigns for justice for Angelo Herndon, the Scottsboro Boys, the Trenton Six, Willie McGee, and Angela Davis should have provided a basis for mass Black memberships and identification. However, the Communist Party has succeeded in attracting only a few intellectuals and workers and never the Black masses. This failure might be attributed to factors such as the Party's identification with a foreign power and ideology and the strong element of nativism which pervades American Black life and thought, reaction against the Party's program and identification with the working class, dislike for the concept of the Negro nation, and reaction against the Party attacks on the basic institutions, cultural forms, and social structure of the Black community.

Perhaps the Party's lack of success with the Black masses may be placed in perspective if its appeal to Black intellectuals is examined first. The latter group seldom has moved too far away from its racial origins, which have offered nurture, impetus, inspiration, while the intellectuals have given expression to the group hopes, fears, frustrations, and aspirations. The Black intelligentsia has not allowed or permitted itself to stray far from its roots; most of its artistic and literary creations have been based on the Black experience and the despair of the Black masses.

Those intellectuals who have been involved with the Communist Party tended to find the Party accidently while searching for solutions to the problems of inequality or Black identity. Their initial encounters with Communist members or publications were exhilarating and appealing to them, because the attitudes and ideas appeared to be devoid of the normal American taint of race prejudice. Richard Wright (1950; p. 118) noted with pleasant surprise that the Communist intellectuals whom he met were not condescending and offered him the "first sustained relationships" in his life. He found that he could discuss ideas and societal problems without self-consciousness and with people who shared his views. He and others have felt a sense of joy and relief at finding a compatible and empathetic group with an inclusiveness based on ideology. Wright stated with a sense of relief:

> It seemed to me that here at last, in the realm of revolutionary expression, Negro experience could find a home, a functioning value and role . . . It urged life to believe in life. (1950; p. 118)

The sense of release came with the discovery that there were Americans who cared about Blacks and discrimination and had a sense of mission and desire to correct the situation. The Communist literature, full of slogans and strategies for involving the Black masses and the working class in the "struggle for liberation," was intoxicating, inspiring Black intellectuals to rhapsodies of brotherhood and comradeship.

The Party membership and apparatus were programmed to view Blacks as special because the Party platform singled out the "Negro liberation" as an area for intense work. The low per-

*Written especially for this book.

centage of the Black members was a source of constant concern. The sense of specialness had great appeal to some Blacks since they were more accustomed to being treated as pariahs rather than as favored persons. For example, William L. Patterson (1971) was flattered by the attention given him by Party officials along with special attention and favors; he was selected to attend the University of the Toiling People of the Far East in the Soviet Union – a training school for Third World Party functionaries. This was done because he was a young lawyer with great potential and promise for Party work; he repaid with life-long dedication and service to Party causes. A common practice with the Black intellectuals or labor militants who became involved with the Party was to quickly promote them to positions of authority, bypassing Caucasians who were long-time members of the Party. Any incipient leadership qualities or organizational ability possessed by Black recruits were seldom nurtured or given time to develop because of the need to have Blacks in visible Party positions. However, since the national convention and the Central Committee developed the Party program and platform, the leadership, operating under the concept of democratic centralism, was not obliged to be creative; they had the responsibility for the implementation of the slogans and policies on the local or state level. This method of functioning consistently caused difficulties for many Black intellectuals who were inclined to operate independently and not in concert with dictums or manifestoes. Even though Blacks were given special favors and encouraged to assume leadership roles, they were still subject to the rigid discipline of the Party and the mechanical assumptions of the Communist faith.

Doctrines relating to the "Negro nation" and the sins of "white chauvinism" were a source of emotional satisfaction to the Black membership, because the tenets not only corroborated the specialness of Blacks but provided an outlet for acting out racial hostilities and antagonisms. All Caucasians were likely to be guilty of prejudicial acts, comments, or thoughts; such sins of commission and omission were then subject to criticism and self-criticism – in extreme cases, a Communist trial. Black members often charged their white comrades with "white chauvinism," triggering long discussions, usually in the presence of a Party functionary. The charges would be examined during the course of the discussions with careful attention given to the bourgeois roots of chauvinism; the accused member, an active participant in the discussion, was expected to analyze the deed, accept the guilt, and help formulate ways in which to absolve himself of chauvinism to avoid a repetition of the act. The opportunity to charge one's white comrades with such a dreadful sin gave considerable power to the black comrades, though they could in turn be accused of "bourgeois nationalism" and subjected to the same type of intensive political examination. There was a cathartic quality about these discussions which helped bind the membership to the Party program and discipline while creating an illusion of accomplishment and action. The discussions of white chauvinism and the trials were seen by the Party leadership as a means of impressing the Black masses with the sincerity of the Party and with the message that the Communists were the only political group concerned with the Negro liberation struggle. Though the Yokinen trial in 1931 (Browder; 1935, p. 291) was public, most trials or criticism and self-criticism sessions were confined to Party members. However, Party members managed to let the Black community know that it was constantly engaged in correcting the racist behavior of its membership and it expelled those who were recalcitrant or intransigent.

The glorification of Black history and culture by the Party was another way in which intellectuals and militants were attracted. This again was counter to accepted American behavior and belief and offered assurance to those intellectuals who had rejected concepts of Black inferiority. American Communist revisionists interpreted the historical and cultural development of the Black people in terms of the Marxist-Leninist world view, in the context of the revolutionary development of the working class and an oppressed people. A sense of grandeur, goodness, and militance permeated the interpretations, essays, fiction, and art. Even though the Party's approach was simplistic, it appealed to some intellectuals who were more accustomed to fighting the "establishment" in order to assure that dignity and recognition be granted the contribution of Blacks to American history and culture. Within the Communist movement, there was encouragement for Black intellectuals to work on some of their interests and concerns, but the Party was generally more interested in propaganda and material that could be used to help organize the Black masses. This doctrinaire approach to culture and creation was usually a cause for the disaffection of the creative intellectuals who could not and would not follow the dicta of Party functionaries.

Since Black intellectuals have always been somewhat estranged from the Black community, though serving as interpreters, the infatuation of some intellectuals with the Communist Party has not been a reflection of the interests of the masses. The sense of relief and empathy with Party members, the discovery of a concerned group of whites, the acting-out of hostile feelings, and a sense of superiority resulting from special attention and revisionist writings which attracted intellectuals to the Party have not had the same appeal to the Black masses.

The Communist program and activities have won few converts in Black communities for many complex reasons. The very things which make the Communist Party unique and constitute the core of its program and structure are the very things which have made it unappealing to the Black masses. The identification with a foreign country, an ideology rooted in European philosophy, democratic centralism and the tight organizational structure, identification with the American working class, concepts of the Negro nation and white chauvinism, antipathy to indigenous Black organizations and culture, close social contacts between white and Black members, and the risk involved in Party membership are some of the factors that have repelled Blacks.

The slavish reliance of the American Communist Party on first the Comintern and then the Communist Party of the USSR has contributed to its lack of independence and development of a nationalistic program. Under Browder, there was an abortive attempt made to revise the platform and activities to conform to American patterns, but the international Communist leadership was less tolerant of deviation in the post-World War II era than they were to be later. It was this close identification with the Soviet Communist Party and its satellite Parties that helped create a great barrier between the American Party and the Black community. Even though the status of Blacks has been a subordinate one, Blacks take great pride in the long period of time in which they have been in America and the extent to which they are entwined in the fabric of the country.

Strong nativist sentiments are to be found in the Black community because of the close identification with America. The prideful association with Africa is of recent origin and dates to the independence of the Black African nations; for centuries, colonialism and acceptance of stereotypes affected Black perceptions of Africa and Africans, creating shame and hostility, which prevented a positive identification. There had been acceptance of the white supremacist myth that Blacks had no past before their arrival in the American hemisphere. Blacks take pride in being in America since the early 17th century and in having provided the labor to build the country. They have resented the importation of unskilled European and Asian laborers and the subsequent mobility of these immigrants. Though there is a recognition of the racial barriers preventing the integration of Blacks into American society, there is nonetheless hostility to newer groups who have quickly adopted the American racial mores and modes. The immigrant groups have utilized the existence of an oppressed racial group in order to gain economic and social status. Their own position in the society has been much more fluid as a result of a permanent lower caste which immediately elevated the immigrants' social position and provided the impetus for mobility. If they had not achieved some measure of material success, they might have been equated with Blacks and consigned to a permanent depressed economic and social position. Each successive group of immigrants provided competition for Blacks, since the foreigners were recruited for the lowest level of unskilled jobs, and even during the era of great industrial growth, the rivalry for employment was intense and sometimes violent.

Not only have Blacks identified with America as a homeland, but they have espoused and believed in the egalitarian democratic ideals of the nation. Since these beliefs are considered to be unique to the American nation, there is suspicion of foreign ideologies which might not be egalitarian or in the interests of the Black people. Though the American Communist Party was formed out of indigenous socialist groups, it was inspired by the Bolshevik Revolution and dominated by a foreign-born membership. The Palmer Raids, McCarran Act, and deportation proceedings were constant threats and obstacles to Party participation, something noted by the Black community. The large number of foreigners in the Party was an asset in organizing some industries in which there were many immigrant workers but did create barriers to the recruitment of native-born workers. There were nationality lodges and clubs at which the meetings were conducted in the mother tongue of the members; this helped set the Communists apart as foreign and alien to the American environment.

Marxist-Leninist and later Stalinist economic determinism and philosophy were also alien to the American faith in the free enterprise capitalist system. Blacks along with the rest of the society believe in individualism and the American economy. Though they understand the societal roots of economic and social discrimination, Blacks also have faith in the system and believe that success will follow diligence and determination. In addition to the disagreement with the economic philosophy of Marxism-Leninism, another fundamental difference would be related to the Communist view of religion. Since religious faith and activities have played such a major role in the development of Black society, any group opposing religion and the churches would be *a priori* in opposition to Black interests. Black Christianity was for many years and still is personalized and oriented to the other world so that many secular or political concerns have been generally considered to be ungodly. This would mean that a secular political group that considered religion to be an opiate would come into direct or covert conflict with a racial group for whom religion has been one of the motivating forces in life.

The language and organizational structure of the Communist movement would also tend to mark it as foreign and outside the American mainstream. The stiff sloganistic speeches and writings of the Communist leadership, much of which has sounded as if it was poorly translated from a foreign language, has held no appeal for Blacks who have a strong oral tradition. The ability to speak eloquently, with great flair, to turn a phrase, play on words, and entertain the listeners is an important attribute in Black society. Verbal ability and command of language, whether through street games like "The Dozens" or in the pulpit, are necessary to win the respect and admiration of the Black masses. Though the Communists have admired speakers who could thrill and captivate crowds, it has been important to articulate the Party line or Marxist-Leninist doctrine, not exactly crowd stoppers in and of themselves. Phrases like "Negro liberation, petty bourgeois nationalism, proletariat, revolutionary forces, bearer of the banner of freedom, struggling masses, Negro masses, oppressed people, hero of the working class, vanguard of the working class, international solidarity," etc. were seldom heard or read by the general public until the students of the 1960s were radicalized. Indeed, these expressions were the sole property of the left wing and even in their original context sounded foreign to Blacks whose only slogans related to equality.

The organizational structure of the Party, based on the Soviet model of democratic centralism, was another obstacle to Black participation. The way in which the concept was carried out was in contrast to the American ideal of democratic participation and involvement because of the important role of the Central Committee. Supposedly, decisions on program and policy were initiated within the Central Committee with discussion throughout the structure, down to the smallest club and back to the Central Committee and Convention. Once a policy or program was set, the membership was bound by the decision until the process to revise or revoke the particular decision had been completed. Discipline was imposed on members to support the policies, and there was little allowance for individual interpretations or disagreements. Though Blacks have limited individual freedom within the context of the American society, they strongly believe in all the idealized freedoms and, indeed, place great stress on individualism. Churches and organizations in the Black community are constantly hit by schisms caused by individual differences and disagreements.

Small Communist cells and clubs centered around an industry or neighborhood tended to be segregated by race, partially intentional and partially for functional reasons. These groups were given responsibility for organizing in the industry, shop, or neighborhood, and they were only bound to similar groups by policy, program, and Party functionaries. There was infrequent contact between cells or clubs, though fund-raising parties or celebrations might provide opportunities for expanded social contact between Party members. A puritanical interpretation of Leninism and an almost fanatical devotion to duty kept the meetings from being fun and gave a somber quality to the organizational life of the Party. Richard Wright (1950) noted the dour passive nature of the meetings of the club to which he was assigned and was puzzled by the sheeplike behavior of the Blacks. The closed nature of the clubs and the Party tended to be a poor contrast to the majority of the organizations within the Black community which were open to all and welcomed new membership.

Perhaps one of the biggest obstacles to Black involvement in the Communist Party was one which was insurmountable – the Party was built on and dedicated to the working class and to its eventual accession to the power of the state. Workers were glorified and considered to be the source of strength, wisdom, and hope – something not within the experience of American Blacks. The latter had little positive contact with the working class until the CIO was organized, and only in rare instances were in leadership positions until the end of the 1960s. Since Blacks and the white working class were in competition with one another, a natural antagonism developed, which was intensified by the anti-Black policies of organized labor. The skilled trades and crafts early in the 20th century developed policies and practices which forced Blacks out of many areas of employment in which they had achieved some security and numbers.

Blacks have had hostile encounters with the white working class not only over the matter of jobs but over issues involving housing and schooling as well. As Blacks moved into urban areas from the rural South, they tended to displace the white lower and working classes; often, this was done at the instigation of real estate interests and met with violent opposition from low-income whites. Often this group was composed of the foreign born and the intrusion of Blacks into their neighborhoods violated not only their mores but the patterns of community organization and activities. The ethnic national associations, shops, or religious centers depended on a clientele which lived in close proximity.

Since the white working class has benefited from the lower social and economic status of Blacks, they have attempted to protect their position through the maintenance of segregated neighborhoods and racially homogeneous schools. As a result, the two groups have remained separate and ignorant of any common problems or concerns.

Though the Communist Party attempted to represent the mutual interests of Black and white workers, it was never successful in overcoming the natural antipathy and distrust which has existed between the two. Since the Communist "working class" ideology is incompatible with a free enterprise ideology, it has not found favorable reception in Black circles where there is strong faith in success in the American way, if not for one's self then for one's children. The belief in hard work – that the meek shall inherit the earth and that right will prevail – though filtered through the consciousness of color, still provides the basic foundation for Black America's allegiance to the USA. Therefore, the Marxist doctrines, particularly those stressing the dominance of the working class, would find little support.

Another basic tenet of American Communism, that of the Negro nation, has not found favor with Blacks. A strong belief in racial integration pervades the thinking and hopes of Black Americans, and any concept that stresses separation and differences is not likely to be accepted. In this country, separateness has always been associated with inequality and inferiority rather than with ideas of self-determination. Even though the majority of the Black population was in the southeastern United States, the desire was not to create a nation there but to move to the North where there was a promise of freedom. The concept of white chauvinism provided some amusement and was of some interest because Blacks delighted in being able to openly chastise whites for acts of bigotry. However, Blacks were also very realistic and aware that the Communist trials for chauvinism, etc. would not affect the basic relationships between the races.

The social life of the Party and front groups was another detriment to the recruitment of Black members. Since the Party demands a great portion of a member's time for meetings, fund raising, political organizing, and social events, there was little time left for individual social interests. Many of the Party activities were carried out in interracial groups with distinct Bohemian overtones. This has had little appeal to Blacks who prefer to socialize with other Blacks without the tensions inherent in interracial contacts.

Another reason for the Party's lack of popularity with Blacks was closely linked to problems of security and the fact that the Communists have always been considered subversive and un-American. The Palmer Raids and early attacks on Party members, arrests, deportations, red-listings, and firings were effective deterrents for a racial group faced with other barriers to economic and social security. The threats to civil service or government-related employment caused many Blacks to fear the consequences of involvement with the Party. Since the economic position of the black population is a tenuous one, there is an unwillingness to take chances and make the position even more precarious. There is a tendency to feel that whites have less to risk since they can find jobs if they are fired because of Communist affiliations. This cautious approach is the result of the insecure position and desire to achieve economic success within the American system.

This same discreet, perhaps wary, approach has been characteristic of Black political involvement and a pragmatic allegiance to the traditional parties. There appears to be little faith in those candidates or parties that are too far to the left; Blacks did not follow Wallace or the Progressive Party even when a Black woman, Mrs. Carlotta Bass, was the vice-presidential candidate. The Black community has been hospitable, respectable, and cordial to Black spokesmen of the left, but they have stayed with the conventional choices. Men like Ben Davis, Paul Robeson, and W.E.B. DuBois did not lose any respect because of their political stands or affiliations, but they did not win over the Black masses or even a sizable portion of the intellectuals.

The Communist Party probably made its most serious mistake by its opposition to the basic institutional supports within the Black community – the churches, social and civil rights organizations, and culture. The Marxist contention that religion and the organized church were opiates and robbed the working class of potential strength and power because of their reliance on the status quo has prevented the Party from becoming a force in the Black community. Since the Black church provides a sustaining strength and continual training for indigenous leaders, it offers Blacks an organization with social and morale-building activities. The preacher is a source of advice and leadership, while able to interpret the meaning of life and death. He is a source of comfort as well. He often is the mediator between the majority community and the oppressed minority, sometimes privy to job information or advice about ways in which survival can be insured. He provides, along with the few doctors, lawyers, and teachers, the core of community leadership and knowledge and represents a continuity of tradition which has helped perpetuate and propel the group.

Since churches and ministers were antithetical to the interests of the Communist Party, it was only under the aegis of the united front that any attention was paid to Black ministers. Then it was only in a manipulative sense that they were judged to be important to the cause. The civil rights movement was probably an impetus to recognition of the role of the ministers, though they were still distrusted by the Party and considered to be misleaders of the people. Any Black leader who did not espouse the Communist line was berated and considered to be a petty-bourgeois or, perhaps worse, a petty-bourgeois nationalist. Since nationalism was almost as dangerous as heresy and chauvinism, any militant pro-Black leader was considered to be a potential ideological enemy.

The Black church was never fully appreciated as anything other than a place to hold meetings and identify with the community; it was not fully appreciated in its historical setting and within the context of its role as a force that sustained Blacks. This was true of other groups within the community, such as the NAACP or Urban League, which were regularly attacked by the Party functionaries in articles and speeches. Black Communist leaders consistently attacked the civil rights organizations for considering the Negro question to be one of race (Haywood; 1930, p. 699) rather than one of class or national oppression. These organizations were also attacked because their boards of directors included philanthropists and industrialists who represented the ruling class (Haywood, 1931, p. 332). It was also stated that these groups encouraged nationalism, which was in opposition to the spirit of international working class solidarity and that they also encouraged a segregated group economy. In fact, campaigns to only buy where Blacks could work were opposed by the Party for this reason.

However, when the NAACP celebrated its 50th anniversary, the official organ of the Party, *Political Affairs,* had an article urging reassessment of the organization. Though the NAACP was still characterized as a reformist group, Party members were urged to join in the interests of the united front and fight for a more militant program (Strong, 1950, p. 32). Communists were exhorted to oppose the policies and actions of leaders like Roy Wilkins but to work to make the NAACP a fighting organization and build a movement to realize such things as fair employment practices. In many branches, there were unsuccessful attempts to take over the leadership of the Association; the national convention repudiated such efforts in 1950 and authorized its national office to oust any branches which were under the control of Communists (Record, 1964, pp. 163-164).

The Communists did not recognize that the Association not only carried on a civil rights activity but also provided a social outlet for its membership. The latter is of utmost importance because it contributes to the fulfillment of the membership, provides time-consuming activity, and helps keep the organization from insolvency. Social activities assume major proportions for the Association in the same way that it does for Party membership. A difference is that the status and visibility of the Black bourgeoisie is enhanced through NAACP participation, which helps them maintain ties with the Black community.

Over the years, the Party's Negro program and tactics seemed to vacillate and change directions. However, they were really following the changes in the international and national directives of the Central Committees. On the other hand, the "revisionist" organizations like the NAACP, the Urban League, and the Southern Christian Leadership Conference have rigidly followed legalistic or conciliatory methods with goals that have been undeviatingly directed toward the integration of Blacks into American society. The organizational structures and activities are secularized versions of forms developed within the Black church and have comfortable and familiar associations for the membership, particularly those with status aspirations. These Black civil rights organizations have helped Blacks achieve mobility, given them opportunities to learn organizational skills, and provided power bases for political activities.

The leadership of these indigenous though nominally interracial groups has generally been castigated by the Party and accused of misleading the Black population. Here again is a serious misunderstanding of the petty bourgeois aspirations of Black America; there is a great reservoir of pride in Blacks who have achieved a semblance of success, inside or outside the community. Those Blacks who have managed to obtain an education, profession, or business are considered to have not only overcome great obstacles, but to be self-made, and a "credit to the race." They serve as models to be emulated and as spokesmen for the masses whose concerns are seldom of interest to the majority population. An inherent hostility is accorded by the masses to any outsiders who denigrate the role and contributions of those in the leadership of Black organizations.

Another source of Black pride is the culture of the people, born of privation, suffering, and hope, and unique to American Blacks though reflecting African origins. The American Communist Party gave lip service to the value and place of Black culture but found itself at odds with the cultural theoreticians of international Communism. The latter could never tear itself away from the belief that such important aspects as jazz, dancing, and preaching were decadent and reflected incorrect orientations since the only true culture was socialist realism, which advanced the ideology of Marxism. Black culture evolved as a survival mechanism under specific circumstances, and the Communists only expressed appreciation of those aspects which they interpreted as expressions of revolutionary aspirations. This meant reinterpreting some aspects – such as spirituals and folk tales – and ignoring others – jazz, blues, and dance; often this contradicted the meaning and importance given to the same aspects by Black people.

In summary, one might conclude that American Blacks and Reds have marched to different drummers and that the Communists have almost always been out of step with the Black masses. While the folk followed Garvey and the preachers, the Party castigated them as petty bourgeois nationalists. While the Party preached the doctrine of the Negro nation, Blacks strove for integration. When Black intellectuals and radical polemicists used the rhetoric of Negro nationhood, and just as Black politicians began to achieve electoral victories in cities and Congressional districts with Black majorities, the Party abandoned the idea of the nation in the Black Belt and self-determination. When Blacks marched on Washington and campaigned for victory over Jim Crow, the Communists were enjoining the masses to work for victory overseas first. While the Black organizations and communities supported economic boycotts in order to get jobs where they spent money, the Reds were inveighing against such campaigns because they smacked of "Jim Crow's nationalism" and a segregated group economy. Support of the Communist Party, even if the ideology and tactics had appealed, was not desirable for American Blacks who rejected the possibility of double jeopardy. Being Black was cause for enough insecurity without the risk inherent in being Red as well.

## REFERENCES


Browder, Earl. *Communism in the United States.* New York: International Publishers, 1935.

CPUSA. *Proceedings of the 17th National Convention, Political Affairs,* Vol. XXX 19, No. 2, February 1960.

Ford, James W. *The Negro and the Democratic Front.* New York: International Publishers, 1938.

Haywood, Harry. "Against Bourgeois-Liberal Distortions of Leninism on the Negro Question in the United States." *The Communist,* Vol. IX, No. 8, August 1930.

Howe, Irving, and Coser, Lewis. *The American Communist Party: A Critical History (1919-1957).* Boston: Beacon Press, 1957.

Patterson, William L. *The Man Who Cried Genocide: An Autobiography.* New York: International Publishers, 1971.

Perry, Pettis. "Lessons on Civil Rights Mobilization," *Political Affairs,* Vol. XXIX, No. 3, March 1950.

Record, Wilson. *The Negro and the Communist Party.* Chapel Hill: University of North Carolina Press, 1951.

Stalin, Joseph. *Marxism and the National and Colonial Question.* New York: International Publishers, 1944.

Strong, Edward E. "On the 40th Anniversary of the NAACP," *Political Affairs,* Vol. XXIX, No. 2, February 1950, pp. 23-32.

Wright, Richard. In *The God That Failed,* edited by Richard Crossman. New York: Harper and Brothers, 1950.

# 15
# *Black Marxist-Leninist Worker Movements: Class or National Consciousness?**

JAMES A. GESCHWENDER

The dilemma of integration or separatism is not necessarily resolved with the development of a Marxist-Leninist perspective. Politically conscious black workers still have a range of options: they may see themselves as part of an oppressed nation and struggle for national liberation, setting aside the question of socialism until after independence; they may identify as part of an oppressed class and struggle for a socialist revolution in the anticipation that racism will disappear when capitalism is destroyed; or they may reject both of these simplistic notions and attempt to wage a simultaneous struggle against capitalism and racism. There are no easy formulas which blend the concepts of nation with class and provide a blueprint for struggle. It will be instructive to examine the ideological perspectives of one organization which attempted this task – The League of Revolutionary Black Workers.

## THE LEAGUE OF REVOLUTIONARY BLACK WORKERS

League activities centered around the Detroit auto industry from 1968 to 1972.[1] Detroit has always had a large number of political activists and organizations. Among the more significant for young blacks achieving maturity in the early 1960s were James Boggs, Grace Lee Boggs, the Communist Party, and Socialist Workers Party, and a group of followers of C.L.R. James, who were often referred to as Facing Reality or Friends of Facing Reality. Each of these groups espoused one or more varieties of Marxist-Leninist thought; each wrote political tracts which were circulated, read, and discussed in Detroit's ghetto. This political stimulation was enriched by the national media and book distributors which exposed Detroiters to the ideas of Mao, Che, Fanon, Malcolm X, and many others.

Many young Detroit blacks read and discussed various political theses in an attempt to work out an ideology which they considered appropriate to blacks in 20th-century America. The 1967 Detroit insurrection developed in this context and left a legacy of pride and anger to combine with the continuing political ferment. A black Marxist-Leninist newspaper, *The Inner City Voice,* began operations in the Fall of 1967. A spontaneous interracial wildcat strike took place at Hamtramck Assembly (Dodge Main) on May 2, 1968. Disciplinary action was disproportionately administered to black workers, and as a result a group of black workers joined together with the editors of *The Inner City Voice* and formed the Dodge Revolutionary Union Movement (DRUM).

DRUM engaged in a wide range of political activities. It started a weekly newsletter designed to provide political education for black workers. It included discussions of health and safety factors in the plant, racism in job assignments, use of bigotry in personal relations between white and black workers, the relationship between these conditions and the nature of capitalism, and the union-management collaboration designed to maintain the system in operation. DRUM leadership launched a series of political actions aimed at simultaneously achieving improvements in objective conditons, mobilizing additional support, and educating black workers to the nature of the opposition.

DRUM actions included rallies, demonstrations, a boycott of a worker-patronized bar accused of racist practices, and a wildcat strike which cost Chrysler the production of over 1900 cars. These activities stimulated the formation of more Revolutionary Union Movements in other Detroit-area plants, each of which engaged in a similar series of political activities. Confrontation tactics were supplemented by running candidates for various local union posts with variable success. The electoral activities stimulated a type of oppositional response on the part of local union leadership, management, international union leadership, police, and newspapers, which aided the campaign of political education. The League of Revolutionary Black Workers was formed to aid the development of coherent lines of activity among the various revolutionary union movements.

## IDEOLOGY

A detailed recitation of the activities of the League is less relevant to the purpose of this paper than is an examination of

*An original piece abstracted especially for this volume from James A. Geschwender, *Black Marxist-Leninist Worker Movements* (mimeo, Copyright 1973). This research has been supported by grants from The Research Foundation of the State University of New York.

the structure and content of the League's ideology and a consideration of the implications that the ideology had for League development. No single statement exists which presents the League's ideology in a unified, concise form. There are three documents that may be combined to arrive at a reasonably complete understanding of the position developed by the League: a 38-page pamphlet incorporating the League's general policy statement and labor program, the initial publication of a portion of this document in *The Inner City Voice,* and a republication of a revised version.[2] Part of the League leadership felt that the initial formulation was inadequate because it failed to include sufficient labor history to provide a complete understanding of the relationship of blacks to capitalism and of blacks to organized labor. This discontent surfaced after a portion of the original statement was published in the newspaper, leading to the publication of a revised version.

**Basic Premises**

This presentation of League ideology is a summary description of a hypothetical document resulting from an integration of the separate statements. The introductory section is titled, "Here's Where We're Coming From." It begins:

> The League of Revolutionary Black Workers is dedicated to waging a relentless struggle against racism, capitalism, and imperialism. We are struggling for the liberation of black people in the confines of the United States as well as to play a major revolutionary role in the liberation of all oppressed people in the world.[3]

A small, all-white capitalist class is seen as owning the basic means of production in the United States. Most whites and virtually all blacks are workers. All Americans gain from imperialism and all whites gain from racism. The dual set of privileges gives white workers an investment in the status quo and encourages them to collaborate with the United States government to perpetuate imperialism abroad and racism at home. These systems of privilege were expected to create the environment in which the League would grow and attract members inspired by internal struggles for black liberation and international revolutionary struggles. League goals were threefold: liberate blacks in America, lead workers' struggles, and aid all struggles against imperialism. These efforts would be guided by the principles of Marxism-Leninism and would be led by a Marxist-Leninist political party. The League program for building a party included: organizing black workers on a broad scale; politicizing and educating blacks to the nature of racism, capitalism, and imperialism; supporting black efforts to develop a broad economic base in the community; developing a community self-defense organization; conducting struggles on behalf of black workers and the total community; and forming principled alliances and coalitions with others who struggle against racism, capitalism, and imperialism.[4]

**Labor History**

The League analysis of American labor history interpreted slavery as both a set of economic relations and a set of social relations. The restriction of slave status to black Africans transformed class into race. Labor was divided between free whites and unfree blacks. Both were exploited, but whites retained white skin privilege. This difference prevented either white or black labor from becoming fully proleterianized.

League analysis concluded that historically white working class struggles have been a mixture of race and class struggles. White workers opposed slavery because they did not wish to compete with slave labor, but they did not favor abolition because they were opposed to racial equality. White workers fought for worker's rights, but they also fought to restrict black civil and work rights. White skin privilege sometimes hurt the white worker when blacks were used as strikebreakers, but organized labor – including many of the early socialists – did not sympathize with the black struggles. Organized labor often supported American imperialism. The League concluded that the organized labor movement was the enemy of black freedom and that white labor had to be considered hostile because of the support that it gave to American imperialism.[5]

The League presentation of labor history was less hostile toward the white worker than toward organized labor. White skin privilege accrued from the development of imperialism during the late 19th century, but was eroded during its decline in the 20th century. The erosion of privilege removed the major motivation for white workers to be racist. Capitalism was under attack from revolutionary groups around the world but it was buttressed by organized labor. It is at this point that the role of the white worker was viewed as significant but problematic:

> . . . as long as white workers think of themselves as white workers or white middle or lower class, they will be counter to the struggle, and will retain White consciousness as opposed to class consciousness. To think in those terms means a struggle for the decaying privileges that buttress the system of racism and exploitation instead of for the liberation of all working people.
>
> It is without question that white labor will be forced to shift gears. Currently, however, the liberation struggle of blacks is moving at a quickening pace. It is our contention that the key to the black liberation struggle lies with the black workers.[6]

The League argued that the black liberation struggle is part of a worldwide struggle of oppressed against oppressor, but not all elements are strategically located to exert leverage toward change. The black worker is singled out as the most crucial for the struggle, but not all black workers occupy equally strategic positions. It is primarily black workers in mines and factories who were expected to form the nucleus of the revolutionary struggle. This is a result of the high proportion of blacks in these occupational locations, the high proportion of persons in these locations who are black, and the key position of factories and mines in the capitalist extraction of profit.

**Position of Black Workers**

The League noted that, when compared to whites, blacks had higher rates of labor force participation, were over-represented in blue-collar and service occupations and under-represented in craftsmen, foremen, and upper white-collar occupations. It asserted that blacks were also disproportionately concentrated in the harder, dirtier, less desirable jobs within occupational categories. The virtual exclusion of blacks from decision-making posts in American society was stressed.

### Economic Situation of Black Workers

The League demonstrated that black workers are concentrated in occupations receiving the lowest pay rates. It was argued that the American economy requires poverty in order to discipline the work force and inhibit the development of revolutionary political movements. The spiral of low wages, inflationary prices, and increased taxes was portrayed as keeping many black families hungry despite having one or more members employed.

### Working Conditions for Blacks

Black workers work in the sector of the economy characterized by the hardest, dirtiest, and most dangerous jobs. The jobs are dangerous both in terms of possibility for industrial accidents and in terms of exposure to disease-producing and debilitating conditions. Accidents were seen as resulting from speedups in pursuit of higher profits. Industries with a high proportion of blacks have a high degree of regimentation and control over the worker. The League viewed struggles over these conditions as especially significant:

> The struggle of black workers in industry over working conditions, organized and consciously led, or unorganized and undirected, is primarily the struggle to control the process of production. It is the responsibility of the revolutionary workers movement to provide leadership to this struggle and to clearly demonstrate to the masses of workers that to control and improve conditions, to control the process of production, we must control the instruments of production themselves. It is the transformation of the struggle against the excesses of production into a movement to seize control of these instruments which will lead to the organized, consciously led struggle of all people to own and control the instruments of power in this society up to and including the state.[7]

### The Position of Black Workers in Organized Labor

It was charged that organized labor is corrupt and racist. The League chronicled the long battle for black representation at decision-making levels in the UAW and the exclusion of blacks from the skilled trades. Management and the UAW claimed that DRUM, FRUM, ELRUM, etc. constituted racist attempts to racially divide a labor force which the League claimed was already divided. The UAW was charged with using a number of subterfuges, including retiree voting, in order to exclude blacks from power even in those areas where they had numerical concentrations. The UAW was seen as opposing the revolutionary union movements because the latter might disrupt the union's pattern of influence over the social, political, and economic life of black communities.

### Unorganized Black Workers

Large numbers of black workers are employed in sectors of the economy which are not yet organized and which have even worse conditions of employment than exist in the organized sector. The League believed that it was its task to reach out to unorganized black workers and aid in the creation of a new militant organization. Unorganized workers were seen as constituting a potentially potent revolutionary force.

### Black Women Workers

Black women constitute a significant segment of the reserve labor force which is called upon in times of need. They are subject to both sexual and economic exploitation when active in the labor force and are the producers of the next generation of workers when not directly in the labor force. The League did not do much to organize black women qua women, but it recognized a special need and believed that a special program was required. Highest priority was placed upon the organization of workers. Black women were recruited as black workers and they did play a significant role in League activities.

### Economic Conditions

Black workers occupy a precarious position in which slight economic fluctuations have a major impact in the black community. The "speedup" often remains, despite unemployment. It is not unusual to find black automobile workers required to work a 56-hour week while many of their co-workers are unemployed. High employment rates do not diminish management's desire to "rationalize" production and increase output per man-hour of labor.

### Blacks In The Auto Industry

The League argued that an internal revolution was needed in the UAW. It had been involved in civil rights activities but it also tolerated racist conditions in the plants. The League charged that the UAW had only token integration at decision-making levels. The UAW collected dues from black workers who were subjected to unsafe working conditions. The League demanded that dues collected from black workers be turned over to them so that they could establish a black "United Foundation."

### The Union as a Political Force

The League recognized that a large labor union is a major political force, controlling large numbers of workers who can strike and who pay dues which may be used to influence societal affairs. It charged that the UAW failed to do all that it could to improve conditions of life for blacks, end the Vietnam war, improve working conditions, slow down the pace of production (end the speedups), prevent harrassment of black workers – particularly those of either a nationalist or revolutionary inclination – and help end umemployment by reducing the work week.

### Revolutionary Organization in Organized Industry (The DRUM Experience)

This was the most important section of the League's position statement because it incorporated self-criticism of past practice as well as developing the correct line for the future. Struggles against racism were seen as contributing to the development of class consciousness among black workers. This was often expressed in the development of black caucuses within unions – caucuses that were doomed to fail as long as they restricted their activities because of loyalty to the dominant union leadership. DRUM-type structures are needed because they are free to wage an unlimited struggle against both management and the union. Struggles for DRUM-type organizations had both important successes and important failures. Strike actions produced some worker political education and improved some working conditions. The League felt that its challenges forced the union leadership "to expose its basic racist, class collaborationist nature in the most open and brutal manner to the masses of black workers."[8]

Past struggles were not seen as having eliminated racism and exploitation in the plants but as having pointed the direction for future struggles. The basic lessons emerging out of past struggle were seen to be:

> 1. In-plant organizations must be well organized and disciplined. We must have a division of labor within the organization. Decisions of the organization must be carried out in accordance with the rules of the League. . . . The organization must hold its loyalty to the League particularly and black workers in general, and must be free from political and financial ties to the union hierarchy which prevents independent action on the part of the rank and file.
>
> 2. Isolation of workers in a single plant is a major cause of failure of strike or other actions on a local level. The struggle is not an individual struggle for higher wages and better working conditions for workers in a particular plant; it is a class struggle to free all workers. . . . When workers engage a corporation in a struggle for power, the ruling class inevitably brings in outside forces such as the police and courts to repress the workers' struggle. In such instances, we must be able to meet increasing force with equal or greater power. This may mean expanding the struggle to other plants, eventually to the point of general strike. . . .
>
> 3. To prevent isolation and solidify the black working class, the League of Revolutionary Black Workers must be developed as a broadly based labor organization. The League must unite Black workers from all plants and in the common struggle to overcome the drawbacks of isolation, lack of skilled organizers and resources . . . any member of the League must aid and defend the struggles of any other member or any other organization when called upon to do so. . . .
>
> 4. The League must increase its capacity to educate, organize, and lead workers in industries where we are already active, and must develop new DRUM-type movements throughout the ranks of organized labor. . . . The organization of workers is not a one-shot affair. . . . It requires fortitude, determination, planning, discipline, correct political direction, sophisticated administration, material resources, and capable, unselfish, educated, and experienced leadership. These qualities can only come from a thoroughly organized base within the black working class itself. . . .
>
> 5. The DRUM experience indicates the necessity of engaging workers inside the plants in constant struggle with the company and union leadership. Struggle is necessary to increase the unity, strength, and level of consciousness of the workers. The process of struggle itself unites workers as a powerful force against their enemies. . . .
>
> 6. The involvement of workers in protracted struggles inevitably leads to serious mass action such as wildcat strikes. The DRUM experience shows that we must protect and provide for workers engaged in open conflict with the company. We must be able to support the families of striking workers, to provide for workers who are fired, lawyers when necessary, etc. To provide the supportive base for struggles in which workers face economic or legal reprisal, the League of Revolutionary Black Workers must develop the National Black Labor Strike and Defense Fund, Workers and the community will be asked to contribute to the LSDF.
>
> 7. To win struggles, leaders must be familiar with labor laws, union contracts, history of blacks in labor, the internal policies of the union, history of union leadership, union procedure etc. – for instance, few workers in organized labor know that safety strikes are legal.
>
> 8. Attempts to seize control of unions at the local level are concrete means of engaging workers in struggle against local union tyrants. It is theoretically possible, in many cases, to win local elections. Often victory is lost only when union bureaucrats are willing to totally and openly expose the corrupt and undemocratic nature of the union to its rank and file.
> The DRUM experience shows that even when elections are stolen, the bureaucrats still lose. The consciousness of the workers is raised, their aggressiveness is heightened, and their determination to join DRUM-type organizations and resolutely fight the union pirates is strengthened. . . .
>
> 9. The League will struggle to win rank and file union positions of stewards, committeemen, convention delegates, etc. Where union cheating prevents assumption of such positions, we will use every available method to struggle (i.e., appointment of blue ribbon [blue button?] stewards).
>
> 10. The League and its membership shall struggle against union leadership at union conventions, conferences, and meetings.
>
> 11. The League will regularly hold local, regional, and national level conferences, conventions, and congresses for the purpose of expansion of the organization of black workers.
>
> 12. The League organizers shall use public denunciation and demonstrations against racist union bureaucrats and corporations, using community and student support in these efforts.

13. The League will use the courts, NLRB, and other "legal" devices as offensive tools of struggle wherever possible. This is "legal" struggle against election cheating, violations of workers' rights under NLRB, etc.

14. The League will oppose the influence of the racist labor bureaucrats and corporations in the black community.

15. The League organization will organize workers for self-defense against the white racist corporations and unions.

16. The League organization will conduct social and cultural activities for the recreation of black workers as respite from the total alienation of work (i.e., rallies, raffles, cabarets, dances, picnics, parties, etc.).

17. League organizations will develop programatic demands based on the general League program and the specific problems of local workers. These demands must relate in such a manner as to rally the support of black workers in terms of their general and specific characteristics.[9]

## LEAGUE ORGANIZATIONAL ACTIVITIES

The League organized demonstrations, conducted wildcat strikes, and mounted challenges in local union elections. None of these activities were pursued because of their intrinsic value. All were designed as steps toward building a revolutionary black Marxist-Leninist organization. It is, therefore, important to examine the organizational theory which provided the underpinnings for League organizational activities and to contrast the theory with actual practice.

### The Workplace is the Focus for Organization

The prime focus of the League's organizing activities has always been the black worker at the point of production. All other organization practices have been secondary and designed, at least in principle, to stimulate support for worker organizations and worker organizing activities. John Watson states the theoretical rationale for this focus as follows:

> We have a certain program, a certain understanding of the dynamics of American capitalist society and we're acting on the results of our analysis. This doesn't mean that we're against those people who are involved in community organization. Our analysis tells us that the basic power of black people lies at the point of production, that the basic power we have is the power as workers.
> As workers, as black workers, we have historically been and are now an essential element in the American economic scene. Without black slaves to pick the cotton on the Southern plantations, the primitive accumulation of capital which was necessary to develop industry in both Europe and America would never have been accomplished. Without black workers slaving on the assembly lines in automobile plants in the city of Detroit, the automobile companies would not be able to produce cars in the first place, and therefore, wouldn't be able to make the tremendous profits which they have been making.
> Therefore, we feel that the best way to organize black people into a powerful unit is to organize them in the factories in which they are working. We feel that black workers, especially, have the power to completely close down the American economic system. In order to implement that power, we have to become organized.[10]
> ... white workers enjoy a privileged position within the proletariat. They have time and time again chosen to defend their position of privilege rather than to move in conjunction with black workers to overthrow all inequities. This has demonstrated to us the necessity of developing a strong independent black organization. At the same time, we clearly understand white workers are oppressed and exploited. They face many of the same problems and contradictions that black workers face. We feel that as revolutionary development takes place within the white proletariat, and as white workers begin to move to overthrow racism, capitalism, and imperialism, then principled alliances are possible.[11]

This theoretical analysis led the League to conclude that its main thrust had to be toward the worker at the point of production. However, the dual nature of black oppression in America – as members of the working class and as members of a race – could not be ignored. Organization of blacks qua blacks as well as blacks qua black workers was conceivable. Numerous groups all over the United States were pursuing a variety of programs aimed at the black community. Nevertheless, the League believed that its major organizing thrust should be aimed at the factories for reasons of pragmatic effectiveness as well as for reasons derived from theory. They believed that the best way to organize the community was to first organize the factory:

> In one factory we have 10,000 people who are faced with the same brutal conditions ... When you go out into the community, the interests of the people ... are going to be much more greatly dispersed.... Just in terms of expediency there are greater possibilities in the organization of the plant ... The kinds of actions which can be taken [in the community] are not as effectively damaging to the ruling class as the kinds of actions which can be taken in the plant.... It's almost an inevitable and simultaneous development that as factory workers begin to get organized, support elements within the community are also organized.[12]

### The League and Community Organizing

The League did not confine its activities to the work place.[13] Many League members had histories of participation in the civil rights movement. Many had also been active in community organizing. John Watson had been a staff organizer for the West Central Organization (WCO) and later became its director. John Williams was formerly a community organizer for the North

Woodward Interfaith Organization and later headed up the Santa Maria Schools. Ken Cockrel successfully participated in the legal defense of the members of the Republic of New Africa charged in the shootout with police at the Bethel Baptist Church.[14] He also participated in the successful defense of a black automobile worker charged with murdering his foreman and shooting two others.[15] The latter defense was based primarily on the claim that the conditions of work in the automobile plant were responsible for causing a state of temporary insanity. Subsequent court action won workmen's compensation rights, back pay, and medical costs. Ken Cockrel had also previously worked as research director for the North Woodward Interfaith Organization.

### The Organization of the Detroit Branch of the Black Panther Party

The notion that community organization should primarily be designed as a vehicle for generating support for black workers' activities also played a role in the establishment of a Detroit branch of the Black Panther Party.[16] The same period of ferment and struggle which produced the League in Detroit also produced the Black Panther Party in Oakland.[17] The Black Panthers had a great deal of romantic appeal for black youth. The national media gave them extensive publicity as a result of their confrontations with the police. There was a great deal to the style of confrontation, to the "machismo" involved in carrying guns and "policing the police," and to the dressing in berets and leather jackets which was likely to attract imitators and recruits.

The League was aware of this appeal and felt a certain degree of empathy with the Panthers as fellow black revolutionaries, fellow self-identified Marxists-Leninists. However, the League officers were concerned with what they believed to be fundamental errors in the Panthers' theoretical analysis, particularly as it related to organizing the lumpen elements of the black community. The League was convinced that no successful revolutionary movement could be built with the lumpen as its base. The League believed that the lumpen lacked a basic source of power, whereas black workers had potential power through their relation to production. John Watson believed that some of the problem resulted from a failure to distinguish between the role of the lumpen in the type of society analyzed by Fanon and the role of the lumpen in the United States:

> . . . in discussing the lumpen proletariat. In Fanon's case, he was describing the landless peasants, the peasants in Algeria who were kicked off the land and forced to come to the cities. These peasants presented a certain kind of militant rebellious class – as opposed to the lumpen proletariat as it exists in America. Now even the lumpen proletariat . . . as it exists in the third world countries is a class which many times does go over to the side of the oppressors. . . . it was Fanon's position that this particular class would be willing to fight with the liberation forces. However, they would only be willing to fight if they were properly politically educated, if they were properly engaged in struggle. . . . That was a point of great debate within the black movement; that is, especially when the development of the League began to take place at the same time the Panthers came into national prominence. . . . When they developed the line that the lumpen proletariat is the vanguard of the revolution, it became a line which was being espoused . . . throughout the country by all kinds of elements which described themselves as political revolutionaries. It was a question with which we had to struggle. From our experience and our struggle, we could emphasize that the working class is the vanguard of the major force within the revolutionary struggle, and that the lumpen proletariat is in and of itself a class which generally splits. . . . There are . . . sectors of that class which can become revolutionaries . . . if you . . . have a very intensive program of political education. . . . A lot of the experience of the Panthers has come precisely from that analysis – the analysis that the lumpen proletariat . . . is going to be in the vanguard of the revolution. That is precisely why the Panthers have been led into so many adventuristic actions over the past three years, and have been engaged in so many of these shoot-outs in which they essentially came out on the losing end. It's precisely why the Panthers have been unable to prevent their organization from being infiltrated with agents.[18]

The League officials recognized that it was inevitable that there would be a Detroit branch of The Black Panther Party. They also recognized that it would be highly successful in attracting members, including many potential League members. They were afraid that the romantic appeal of the Black Panther Party would lead to the dissipation of youthful enthusiasm and energy in unproductive directions. The League wished to prevent this and sought to harness such enthusiasm for more viable programs. League members decided to be the first to organize a Detroit branch of the Panthers. Several League members were involved in this attempt, but the prime role was carried out by Luke Tripp. A chapter was organized and its activities were directed toward supporting working organizations – that is, toward carrying out the League program.

A revolutionary group may enter into reformist activities as a vehicle for attracting recruits to their revolutionary program, but reformist activities may become ends in themselves and hinder the development of a revolutionary program. It is equally true that community organizing programs may be initiated as a means of generating support for worker-centered activities. It is also possible that these community programs may have value in themselves and may become sufficiently attractive that energies will be distracted from the prime focus – workers – to more peripheral concerns. Both the revolutionary rationale for community organizing and its seductive nature may be seen in the following statements made by Cockrel and Hamlin:

> . . . when you talk about the League expanding into what is called community work . . . it simply recognized . . . a broader political definition of . . . workers. And it was also an objective understanding of the fact that workers leave the plant and have to go somewhere. They live where we live so it become(s) eminently sensible, as well as objectively desirable, to have organizations that relate to workers within a context outside of the plant so that we can generate the kind of support that we need in order to support the struggles inside the plant.[19]

> . . . most of the organizing areas that we have gotten into we were kind of dragged into reluctantly. We always had an impulse to stay with the plants and organize the plants because that's where the power was. That's where the blacks have power, they are the producers, they can close down the economy. And so our impulse was to stay there. But after we recognized that we had to involve all our people in supporting the struggles in the plants, we began to look beyond factories. Plus certain situations became so critical that we had to move in to begin to organize to avert disaster, and to try to provide some kind of help and leadership. The most obvious one was the schools. What had happened was that the League represents a merger of various elements in the black community and students. . . . The reason we first got involved with students and the lumpen proletariat, the brothers from the street, was because the workers themselves could not go out to the plant to pass out literature. If they did, they obviously would get fired. And so to protect them from that, we allowed them to remain anonymous when we first began. And we now do that in every new place we go into.[20]

Thus, all community activity was primarily designed to support the main thrust – organizing black workers at the point of production. Sometimes this paid off in somewhat unexpected ways. An influential interdenominational organization of black ministers (IMA) announced its support of DRUM during its battle with Chrysler in August of 1968.[21] They announced their support of black workers at Dodge Main, their sympathy with the goals of DRUM, and they called for an investigation of both the plant medical practices and the grievance procedures. While the IMA did not have any direct power base to use as a lever with Chrysler, their appeal lent respectability to DRUM's cause and made it more difficult for Chrysler to write off their problems as the result of irresponsible agitators.

### The National Black Economic Development Conference

Several League members joined with James Forman in the preparation of the Black Manifesto calling for reparations which he presented to the National Black Economic Development Conference (BEDC) held in Detroit from April 25 to April 27, 1969.[22] The manifesto was adopted and, backed by militant demands, raised a relatively large amount of money in Detroit and nationwide. Some of these funds were made available to The League of Revolutionary Black Workers and were used to facilitate getting their message to a larger audience. This was a direct result of their activities in and on behalf of BEDC.

These funds were put to effective use. The League established its own print shop (The Black Star Press), its own publishing concern (Black Star Publishing), its own film production unit (Black Star Productions), and set up its own book store (Black Star Book Store). These facilities enabled the League to print and distribute its own materials, thus reducing the need to rely on the goodwill of outsiders. It had previously had difficulty in getting material published because of reactions of some white printers. The ability to publish material freed the league from the restrictions that this caused, reduced the degree of vulnerability to outside pressures, and enabled expansion of the political education program. Other significant accomplishments included the making of a movie on the League history, *Finally Got the News*, a second film dealing with drugs in the ghetto, and the distribution of films produced about other revolutionary groups such as Al Fatah. Also published were an important theoretical pamphlet by Ernie Mkalimoto and a significant book by James Forman, who was by that time a League officer.[23]

### The International Black Appeal

Another outgrowth of the Black Economic Development Conference which had potential significance was the International Black Appeal (IBA) modeled after the United Jewish Appeal, Catholic Charities, and the Community Chest.[24] All funds raised by the IBA were to be dispersed in the black community. A series of programs were planned to establish emergency food and health centers, a labor defense fund, legal defense services, a black-controlled welfare system, and housing and recreation programs. The labor defense fund was given especially high priority because of the experiences of an ELRUM strike:

> It happened that in that particular strike 26 workers were discharged. Many of them were not members of ELRUM but were people that management wanted to get rid of. But we felt a degree of responsibility to all the men because what happened was that naturally management and UAW was trying to make us the villains in this case: they wanted to make us the ones responsible for those workers losing their jobs. So we tried to do what we could to support them in terms of raising funds and we tried to arrange jobs for them. A number of them got back to work some six or seven months later without back pay.[25]

It was generally acknowledged that one could not ask workers, especially family men, to risk their jobs unless some alternative source of support was insured. The defense fund could provide that insurance and strengthen the League in the factories. The fund was designed to be supported entirely by black donations. Campaigns were conducted throughout the black community, and attempts were made to get the IBA established as a "check-off" charitable contribution in the factories. It is not surprising that the auto companies and the union noted the association between the League and the IBA and viewed the fund with a jaundiced eye.

The IBA was unsuccessful in its attempt to get accepted as a regular part of the check-off contribution system in the factories. This greatly curtailed its fund-raising ability. Nevertheless, some funds were raised, and a very limited start was made on some of the programs. This occurred primarily in the realm of sponsoring social events and athletic competitions, and provided limited support to blacks who had lost their jobs through militant activities.

### Non-Worker-Oriented Activities

These activities deviated from the general League policy of concentrating major efforts on the workplace and limiting community activities to the development of support. It is true that one intended function of the fund was to provide financial security for persons losing their jobs as a result of militancy in the workplace, but the fund also supported other community activities. There was an additional League activity which appeared to conflict with their stated objective of organizing black workers at the point of production.

### Control, Conflict, and Change Book Club

The "Control, Conflict, and Change" book club was organized in the Fall of 1970 by the Motor City Labor League.[26] It grew to a membership in excess of 700 but it was primarily white middle-class liberals with a sprinkling of radicals. Less than two percent of its membership was black. The book club sought to socialize this population to a radical perspective. League members cooperated with the Motor City Labor League in an attempt to develop a broader base of community support for their activities. They aided in the selection of books and provided most of the club speakers and many of the discussion leaders. These activities were justified in that they represented principled cooperation with white radicals as part of the larger struggle against capitalism and imperialism. Nevertheless, these activities did not further the prime objective of organizing black workers at the point of production and were costly in terms of time and energy.

## STRAINS IN THE IDEOLOGY

League ideology incorporated internal contradictions which produced strain and tactical inconsistencies. League ideologues implicitly attempted to merge two models of racial stratification without full articulation and development of strategic and tactical implications. Part of the League's ideology was derived from the *Capitalist Exploitation Model*, one version of which was developed by Oliver Cox.[27]

### Capitalist Exploitation Model

The model includes the following premises:

> . . . [that] racial exploitation and race prejudice developed among Europeans with the rise of capitalism and nationalism, and that because of the worldwide ramifications of capitalism, all racial antagonisms can be traced to the policies and attitudes of the leading capitalist people, the white people of Europe and North America.[28]
>
> . . . racial exploitation is merely one aspect of the problem of the proleterianization of labor, regardless of the color of the laborer. Hence, racial antagonism is essentially political class conflict. The capitalist exploiter . . . will utilize any convenience to keep his labor and other resources freely exploitable. He will devise and employ race prejudice when that becomes convenient.[29]
>
> Although both race relations and the struggle of the white proleteriat with the bourgeoise are part of a single social phenomena, race relations involve a significant variation. In the case of race relations the tendency of the bourgeoise is to proleterianize a whole people.[30] Race prejudice, then, constitutes an attitudinal justification necessary for an easy exploitation of some race . . . race prejudice is the social-attitudinal concomitant of the racial exploitative practice of a ruling class in a capitalist society. The substance of race prejudice is the exploitation of the militarily weaker race.[31]

The model begins with the exploitation of all workers under capitalism. Race prejudice develops to justify the exploitation of entire racial groups and is used to divide the work force into mutually distrustful and hostile camps. This prevents the development of solidarity and class consciousness and keeps the proleteriat weak and exploitable. Race prejudice harms both majority and minority segments of the proleteriat. Cox does not claim that race prejudice always has an immediate economic explanation. Once it is introduced into a society it takes a meaning and a life independent of its original cause.

The League accepted most premises of the Capitalist Exploitation Model and believed capitalism to be the major source of the exploitation of blacks in America and imperialism to be the major source of the exploitation of blacks in the Third World. The League recognized that the capitalist class was primarily white and that it had been quite successful in selling racism to the white worker, partially by insuring a skin color advantage. The League believed that white skin privilege was a capitalist ploy designed to split the working class, but many white workers bought it hook, line, and sinker. The only hope for the black American was seen to be a socialist revolution which could only be brought about by workers. A multiracial workers' revolution was made unlikely by white racism; thus, the role of revolutionary vanguard had to be assumed by black workers.

The League saw the role to be played by black workers as more active than had Cox, who thought that socialism could only be achieved by a white-led worker revolution. Black gains would be a by-product of worker gains. The League saw black workers as the most significant element in that revolution, since they are more responsive than white workers to organizational attempts because of their superexploited position in American society. Organizing attempts would initially have to be along national (racial) lines and focused on racism and concrete working conditions. Successes should stimulate further organizational efforts and facilitate political education. Political education would not be effective in a vacuum but must be combined with meaningful action. White radicals could be accepted as allies provided that they could relate to the political orientations and objectives of the League. It was believed that white workers would become radicalized by the black workers' example of successful class action on behalf of proleterian objectives. The populist movement of the late 19th century demonstrated that white workers can overcome their racism when they perceive it to be in their interest to do so, but it also demonstrated that latent racism is a weak point which may be exploited to destroy such movements.[32] One League spokesman cited the experience of the Populist Party as the basis for the League decision to restrict its membership to blacks.[33]

### The Colonial Model

The League also derived a portion of its ideology from the *Colonial Model*, which is probably best described in the works of Wilson, Tabb, and Blauner.[34] Five major aspects of the colonization process may be applicable to the black experience in America: (1) black entrance into America was involuntary,

(2) whites control black institutions, (3) black culture was destroyed, (4) white racism persists, and (5) cultural nationalism and ghetto revolts parallel the early stages of colonial revolutions. The model must be modified to account for results of a shift in exports from raw materials in the traditional colonies to labor power in the black internal colony.

The League attempted to merge the Cononial Model with the Capitalist Exploitation Model. It accepted as a basic premise the nature of capitalism as an intrinsically expoitative system which used race prejudice to justify the exploitation of an entire race and as a tool to divide the proleteriat. Capitalists were believed to create the perception of opportunities for individual mobility in order to hinder the development of class consciousness. The League believed that encouragement for black capitalism was designed to introduce a cleavage into the black community analagous to the split in the proleteriat. These two programs for domination combine to produce a small black bourgeoisie, incorporating minor capitalists and individual blacks who have been placed in visible but minor positions in the establishment. This black bourgeoisie may be expected by the capitalists to play a role corresponding to that of the colonial bourgeoisie described by Fanon.[35]

### Ideological Implications for Strategy

Different racial stratification models imply different lines of tactical endeavor. The Capitalist Exploitation Model suggests the pursuit of a socialist revolution. The Colonial Model implies cultural and revolutionary nationalism aimed at establishing a separate black state. A combined Capitalist Colonial Exploitation Model contains internal contradictions. Black workers are unlikely to be able to carry out a socialist revolution without white allies, but white workers are seen as enemies. Wars of national liberation require the unified actions of all blacks, but a socialist revolution requires that black workers overthrow black along with white capitalists.[36]

The contradictions in the League version of the Capitalist Colonial Exploitation Model suggested incompatible tactical lines which were a constant source of strain in the organization. It is difficult to engage in principled cooperation with white radicals if all whites are defined as exploiters and enemies. It is also difficult to build a strong community support movement if all members of the black bourgeoisie are defined as exploiters, collaborationists, and enemies. These contradictions may be resolved, but the League did not succeed in resolving them.

## WHY DID THE LEAGUE DIE?

The League of Revolutionary Black Workers generated a great deal of opposition. Local union officials were usually older white (often Polish) workers who might be expected to resist the Revolutionary Union Movements for a number of reasons. There was a clash between young and old, white and black, entrenched and challenged, as well as between conservative and radical. The League rhetoric was not geared to win friends. Older workers may be expected to resent terms like pig, pollack, racist, etc., especially if they believed that their present positions were earned by reason of seniority. They might reasonably be expected to resist the demands of the younger black workers with less seniority.

The international UAW leadership was largely comprised of persons who had demonstrated a commitment to workers' rights and civil rights. The rhetoric would be especially galling to them. However the international leadership had a more compelling reason for resisting the League. Unions cannot negotiate contracts with management unless they can insure that contract provisions will be adhered to by all union members. Any group that foments wildcat strikes is a threat to the entire collective bargaining process.

No extended explanation is required to explain why auto manufacturers and police might feel unhappy about having in their midst a black Marxist-Leninist revolutionary group, dedicated to the destruction of capitalism by any means necessary. The League found that the local union leadership fought it at every turn. It was charged that elections were rigged against League candidates. The international leadership did not appear to play a neutral role. Statements released to the newspaper and letters sent to union members were hostile to the League. League members were arrested and they clashed with police on several occasions. This combination of circumstances led the League to believe that a conspiracy to destroy it existed among union, management, and the police.

Not all League difficulties came from the outside. There were differences in ideological emphasis within the League which led to inconsistent and contradictory lines of behavior. Some League members were more inclined toward the Capitalist Exploitation Model and others were more inclined toward the Colonial Model. This produced problems in several areas. Political education was hindered by nationalist-oriented members who believed that Marx and Lenin had nothing to offer because they were white. Principled cooperation with white radicals was similarly hampered. At the same time, some nationalistically inclined recruits were repelled by an approach that appeared to "put down" cultural nationalism.

It is difficult to assess the relative importance of external and internal enemies. It is quite possible that the solid opposition to the League coming from outside forces may have destroyed it even if there had been internal ideological harmony. It is also possible that the internal difficulties may have destroyed it even if there were no external enemies. However, it is clear that the League was weakened by its internal problems. The external enemies are to be expected. A revolutionary group that is not opposed is not taken seriously.

The experience of the League of Revolutionary Black Workers provides important lessons for all – but especially for those who wish to pick up the beat where DRUM left off. The League suffered because it did not have an integrated Capitalist Colonial Exploitation Model which adequately integrated class with nation and which implied a consistent line of struggle. This is not a weakness unique to the League. No such model existed at that time. However, such a model can be constructed. Serious study of the League experience may provide clues that could aid the process.

## NOTES

[1] For a more extended description of League activities, see James A. Geschwender, "The League of Revolutionary Black Workers: Problems Confronting Black Marxist-Leninist Organizations," *The Journal of Ethnic Studies,* 2 (Fall, 1974), pp. 1 - 23, and James A. Geschwender, *Black Marxist-Leninist Worker Movements* (mimeo, 1973).

[2] League of Revolutionary Black Workers, "The General Policy Statement and Labor Program of the League of Revolutionary Black Workers," pamphlet, no date or publisher listed; *Inner City Voice,* 2 (October 1970); pp. 11-12; 2. (November-December 1970); pp. 11-13; 3 (February 1971); pp. 11-13.

[3] *Inner City Voice,* 2 (November-December 1970); p. 10.

[4] *Ibid.,* pp. 10-11.

[5] *Inner City Voice,* 3 (February 1971); p. 10.

[6] *Ibid.,* pp. 10-11.

[7] "The General Policy Statement . . .," p. 15.

[8] *Ibid.,* p. 29.

[9] *Ibid.,* pp. 30-33.

[10] "To the Point of Production: An Interview with John Watson of the League of Revolutionary Black Workers," *Fifth Estate.* Reprinted as a Bay Area Radical Education Project Publication, *The Movement,* June 1969.

[11] Dan Georgakas, "League of Revolutionary Black Workers: Interview with John Watson," *Liberated Guardian,* 2 (1), (May 1, 1971), p. 12.

[12] *Fifth Estate,* pp. 6-7.

[13] Interview with John Watson, July 7, 1971. Ken Cockrel quoted in Jim Jacobs and David Wellman, "An Interview with Ken Cockrel and Mike Hamlin of the League of Revolutionary Black Workers," *Leviathon,* June 1970. Reprinted as *Our Thing is DRUM.*

[14] *Detroit News,* June 11, 1969; Jan. 5, 1970; June 16, 1970.

[15] *Time,* June 7, 1971.

[16] Interview with Luke Tripp and John Williams, July 1971.

[17] See Gene Marine, *The Black Panthers,* New York; New American Library, 1969.

[18] John Watson, "Perspectives: A Summary Session," the final presentation of the first year of the Control, Conflict, and Change Book Club, June 8, 1971.

[19] Ken Cockrel quoted in Jacobs and Wellman, p. 19.

[20] Mike Hamlin quoted in Jacobs and Wellman, p. 22.

[21] *Detroit Free Press,* August 18, 1968.

[22] Black Star Publishing (Eds.), *The Political Thought of James Forman,* Detroit; Black Star, 1970, pp. i-ii, 1-69; Jim Jacobs, "The Midwest and the League," in Jacobs and Wellman, p. 10; and Robert S. Lecky and H. Elliott Wright (Eds.), *Black Manifesto,* New York; Sheed and Ward, 1969.

[23] Interview with John Williams and Luke Tripp, late July 1971. The book was *Political Thought of James Foreman,* and the pamphlet was, "Revolutionary Nationalism and Class Struggle."

[24] Pamphlets on the IBA in my collection and interview with John Williams and Luke Tripp, July 1971.

[25] Mike Hamlin quoted in Jacobs and Wellman, pp. 15-16.

[26] Watson, "Perspectives. . . ."

[27] Oliver C. Cox, *Caste, Class and Race,* New York, Monthly Review Press, 1948.

[28] *Ibid.,* p. 322.

[29] *Ibid.,* p. 333.

[30] *Ibid.,* p. 344.

[31] *Ibid.,* p. 476.

[32] For a description of the populist movement, see C. Vann Woodward, *The Strange Career of Jim Crow,* New York; Crowell, 1961.

[33] Watson presents a well-reasoned discussion of the populist movement, including an analysis of the role of racism in its ultimate demise. This is quoted in Fifth Estate, pp. 12-13.

[34] William J. Wilson, "Race Relation Models and Explanations of Ghetto Behavior," pp. 259-275 in Peter I. Rose (Ed.) *Nation of Nations,* New York, Random House, 1972; William K. Tabb, *Political Economy of the Black Ghetto,* New York, Norton, 1970; Robert Blauner, *Racial Oppression in America,* New York, Harper & Row, 1972.

[35] Frantz Fanon, *The Wretched of the Earth,* New York, Grove Press, 1968.

[36] John Williams stated this point in an interview on Nov. 11, 1971.

# 16
# *Nineteen Theses: Black Nationalism and the Liberation Movement in the Third World*[*]

C.J. MUNFORD

## THE THIRD WORLD

1. Contemporary *imperialism* has transcended the empire-building and empire-tending of the imperialist powers of the 19th and early 20th century. It has undergone a change, in essence, transforming it from the colonial administration of the now-weakened imperial powers of the past into a universal system of oppression weighing with especial crudity on all the peoples of the Third World who are still integrated in the capitalist world system. The system is maintained and constantly revitalized by the pervasive presence and activity of the United States – the supreme imperialist power of the contemporary world. As a phenomenon with "totalist" pretensions, it includes within its compass the old forms of colonialism along with all the repercussions of past and continued colonization of subjugated "minorities" at home (e.g. American Blacks) and "backward natives" abroad, and more "refined" political manipulations and "modernized" exploitation of neo-colonialism. An essential element of contemporary imperialism, *racism* is double edged. The term racism describes the peculiar manner in which a group of people is systematically colonized, dehumanized, and oppressed as a group while being subjected to super-exploitation by the bourgeoisie. At the same time, as a justification for the brutalization of colonized peoples, racism in all its psycho-social guises is the only authentic ideology peculiar to imperialism. Now that the non-white Third World (including the Black colony within the United States) has become the chief object of imperialist rapacity, *racial discrimination* is the essential mode of imperialist exploitation. In America, capitalism was racist from its inception, and today's monopoly capitalism is rapaciously racist.

2. Though it functions independently of any direct foreign guidance or tutelage, the Black liberation movement in the USA is nevertheless an expression of the worldwide surge of autonomous revolutions and wars of national liberation which form part of the worldwide transition from capitalism to socialism. Like the South Vietnamese National Liberation Front and the freedom fighters of Africa, the Black liberation movement in the U.S. has dared to strike real blows at racism and imperialism wherever they are to be found. The struggle for Black liberation in America creates both the required "objective and subjective conditions" for national liberation. It refuses to sit back in inactive suspense waiting either for "ripened conditions" or for the cajolings of bourgeois reformers. To the extent that the national liberation movement of American Blacks asserts its autonomy and inclination to real combat, it can be regarded as having inserted itself in the framework of the new worldwide *revolutionary international* which unites the great socialist world system, the national liberation movement, and the anti-capitalist struggles of working class forces in the advanced capitalist countries. Thus, there are ties binding the struggle of American Blacks with other liberating movements and with the socialist countries. Acquiring greater and greater proportions as the vanguard revolutionary force in contemporary U.S. history, the Black liberation movement is now directed towards the root and branch destruction of the imperialist-racist dehumanization of Black people in America through the overthrow of the capitalist system and the exercise of the right of self-determination.

3. All the fraternal movements and revolutionary forces of the socialist camp and the turbulent African, Asian, and Latin American "Third World" must be made to understand that the fate of their own liberation struggle is tied to the Afro-American struggle for national liberation within the confines of the parent state of world imperialist exploitation and neo-colonialism. For the latter movement strikes at the vitals of Yankee imperialism and racism, at the soft underbelly of the beast. The direct and fundamental interests of national liberation and socialist revolution on a worded scale require that the revolutionary peoples of Asia, Africa, and Latin America join the socialist world system in aiding Black revolution in America. It needs their solid support and solidarity.

4. The radically new elements in U.S. economic life are the automation, cybernation, and technical efficiency that are finally making it possible for American monopoly capitalism

*Written especially for this book.

to dispense with some of its super-exploited, but now redundant Black wage laborers. The fate of many Black youths· has become one of perpetual unemployment and misery in the United States' "native reserves" known as ghettoes. Or, when they are temporarily reprieved from immediate exclusion from the economy, Black workers are increasingly restricted to the semi-servitude of unskilled menial positions desired by no one else. The process of sub-proletarianization of large masses of Black people has already passed the point where it could have been reversed.

5. There is a class contradiction within the framework of the United States between the artificially inflated "affluence" of an intermediate class of white labor aristocrats (straw bosses, foremen and underforemen, union bureaucrats, etc.) and the super-exploited Black Lazarus-stratum of the working class. The class of labor aristocrats is not to be confused with the vast majority of ordinary white workers. There is no class contradiction between the latter group and the Black "race-class" of workers. Because of the labor aristocracy, racial hatred of Blacks and white racism in organized labor cannot be dismissed as mere "irrational" atavisms preventing "the reign of good will and harmony between Black and white Americans." Rather they are component blocks in the edifice of the U.S. economic system. Racial discrimination is used as a criterion by which to exclude American Blacks from competing equally for employment with whites, thereby perpetuating the super-exploitation of a specially marked "caste," a caste consisting of one-tenth of the population. The heavy burden of misery borne by Blacks spares the white lower classes from the graver effects of the indigency and exploitation inherent in the capitalist system. The U.S. imperialist system reclines on the pillar of white racism as one of the fundamental guarantees for its continued existence. Thus to attack white racism is to attack U.S. imperialism; obversely, to destroy the "American way of life," the capitalist way of life, is to eradicate racism. Since racial prejudice and hatred guarantees the status of some white wage earners as a *labor aristocracy* in the U.S., it is utopian and self-deceiving in the extreme to expect the growth of a sense of class solidarity between Black and white workers without a bitter struggle against racism by white workers.

6. The scientific and technological revolution has changed the economic atmosphere of the United States. It is rapidly freeing certain high "growth-rate" industries from dependency on mass unskilled labor. Since the advent of automation in the United States – an unprecedented success in imitating and replacing the skill of man-the-organism with the mechanistic complexities of the machine – some corporations have discovered that they can do very well without the menial labor of their Black beasts of burden. They no longer feel any need for Black hands, both because unskilled muscle power is increasingly obsolete on automated sections of the production line, and because white labor aristocrats – accomplices in the crime of racial discrimination – are more politically reliable and less likely to sabotage or destroy costly machinery. The growing exclusion of young Blacks from certain sensitive industries due to automation can even be expected to further accelerate as fear of damage caused by malingering and sabotage to industrial plants and the production process in general swells in the hearts of the monopoly bourgeoisie, frightened by the spectre of Black workers' militancy. Seeing the hatred burning in the eyes of Black workers, the big corporations will move to protect their production apparatus from Black anger and disruption by becoming ever more independent of Black labor – at least at the sensitive factory-technical level. Black political strategists must reckon with the prospect that their people will occupy fewer of the factory-technical positions from which to exercise economic pressure on production. Anyone who becomes by definition "unemployable" for and in a given social system, or who is regarded as employable only at the rates fixed by the oppressor who has deprived him of all belongings and property rights (i.e., as abnormally cheap labor) has been socially relegated to *subhumanity*, a status in this connection defined as man as a producing or laboring animal, but not as a consuming – or at most only a sub-consuming – figure. Its labor "saved" or made superfluous by the analytical invention of automation, the Black proletariat is swiftly becoming sub-proletarianized. This sub-proletarianization of American Blacks is yet another of the many phases of the long and continuing history of dehumanization at the volition and hands of capitalists. But this is a process of tremendous *revolutionary potential,* for we have learned to expect explosive outbursts from this disinherited "sub-class" of modern "have-nots."

7. Even if by some strange, improbable mutation of history the Black community would succeed in transforming the existing ghettoes into real citadels of independent Black cultural creativity expressed through institutions controlled by the people, and with a viable economy organized in the "cooperative form" advocated by some Black leaders, a dispersed Black socialist nation, locked away in more or less sealed "wards," surrounded by a monopoly capitalist economy, would remain woefully vulnerable to the aggressive outbursts of the monopoly bourgeoisie. In fact, the existence of prosperous, privileged Black islands in a capitalist sea would provide a focus for constantly reviving surges of white racist envy and jealousy. Renovated ghettoes would guarantee continued life to white racial hatred and even lend plausibility to a new "social" interpretation of racist ideology. The spectacle of Blacks enjoying culturally confident, successful lives under forms of socialism in isolated Black wards would open the door for those racists in any way personally or socially frustrated or economically insecure to create the myth of "a foreign, privileged incubus" in the body politic, of "strangers" without real connection or loyalty to the state. No matter how affluent, continued life for Afro-Americans in the separate ghettoes of a capitalist United States would only reduce the nation to the permanent status of "ghetto Jews," forever menaced by murderous pogroms, whether spontaneous in origin or deliberately fomented by white racist ideologues and the mass media. The only sure means to efface the pernicious effects of institutionalized racism in North America is to found a socialist society under the dictatorship of a multinational American proletariat.

The contention made by the Pan-Africanists that the Black community should satisfy itself with gaining total control over "its" ghettoes and neighbourhoods is not only erroneous from the revolutionary point of view, but downright dangerous and self-defeating. Granted that right now Black sway even over artificially isolated, insulated centers of the colonial population is presently intolerable in the view of the bloc-in-power, nevertheless under pressure it is a concession that the monopoly bourgeois regime could conceivably come round to if this crumb promised to nullify the revolutionary demand for socialism. Recently certain Black Pan-Africanists have spoken in favour of the creation of a so-called "non-capitalist" economy in Black ghettoes, an economy animated by a "communal and humanistic spirit." It is realistic to imagine that a socialist, communal economy would be allowed to exist as a kind of fetus curled in the womb of capitalist white America, within the confines of the very citadel of world imperialist exploitation? In any case, self-contained neighborhood fastnesses, Black islands in a vast capitalist sea, could no more banish racist oppression than "Black capitalism" can alleviate white exploitation of Black people. "Autonomous" Black control of communities encircled by capitalist surrounding territory leaves intact that racist capitalism, the very existence of which is incompatible with Black liberty. There is no place for the pursuit of an equilibrium between the exploited Black people and the forces of racist capitalist superordination.

The confusion is engendered by the failure of many to understand either the essence or the concrete economic possibilities of the new "communalism" which rejects capitalism as an acceptable "lifestyle" for Black people. The opposition to the egoistic individualism of the "Negro middle class" which differentiates itself in "success" in the "white man's world" from the mass of the Black community, and the resistance of Black nationalists to the penetration of the interests and values of "*white* capitalism" are fundamentally analogous to the African "socialisms" of Nkrumah and Nyerere, and theoretically related to such Latin American populist movements as the Gétulism of Brazil and the Peronism of Argentina. The Black colony's embryonic or incipient Pan-African "socialism"/communalism shares with the former movements a social character rooted in the mass support of urban plebeians of *recent rural origin* (the great majority of American Blacks have only recently migrated to metropolitan ghettoes from southern rural subjugation). Like other populisms, Pan-African communalism is a "have-not" collectivism of the propertyless – a sentimental, non-scientific egalitarianism geared rather to the utopian universal possession of equal shares of property than to the abolition of private property in the means of production. Without the direction of a state-controlled programme of systematic socialist construction, this communalism is no more a reliable basis for future American socialism than the communalism of the African village with its collective ownership of land is a sufficient point of departure for the development of a modern "African socialism." The widely prevalent misconception of the Black colony's ability to capture control of and exploit its "own economy" *within* the broader national economic framework of the United States thus entails the menace that such an appeal could be misused for subjugation-perpetuating reformist ends. Even when disguised as a humanist communalism, no "living standard" worshipping reformist "economism" can be allowed to derail the locomotive of class struggle against the monopoly capitalist class, all of whose members happen to be white. The only way to open the door to "control of one's economic life," to "Black economic power," is to deliver telling blows relentlessly to the ruling class. For racist capitalism is the vampire draining the life blood, the "monkey" on the backs of Afro-Americans.

9. *Bourgeois* revolution – the epitome of which was the French Revolution of 1789-1795 – left the basic right of private property in the means of production intact, adversely affecting only feudal property and feudal forms of appropriation, distribution, and consumption. But a proletarian dictatorship in the United States will use the power of the State to establish a socialist mode of production, appropriation, and distribution of goods. As a consequence, the *national liberation struggle* of the Afro-American people can under *no* circumstances be counted as a bourgeois-democratic nationalist movement (such as that which triumphed in India under Ghandi and Nehru), but rather as the indispensable prelude to socialist revolution in the United States, and the *bearer of an embryonic socialism* destined to grow to maturity in a transformed American republic of nationalities.

10. The life options available to the people in the Black colony in the contemporary United States have been reduced to the following sociopolitical alternatives:

    a. Continued destitution in black ghettoes until such time when the white power structure decides upon and finalizes plans for eventual genocide – i.e., the extermination of Blacks and their retaliatory destruction of millions of whites and of civilization in the U.S.

    b. Integration – this is the goal of the "Negro middle class" and, increasingly, of upper class, securely buffered, compromise-oriented, and formally educated whites who are tranquilized by the spectacle of a carefully selected corps of domesticated Black "screens" striving frantically to "defuse" the Afro-American community. But the implications of this alternative are too contrary to white supremacy (i.e., full politicoeconomic egalitarianism) to ever be applied in any large scale manner in racist America, and are too far removed from Black national aspirations to be accepted by the Afro-American people.

    c. Socialist revolution inspired by Marxism-Leninism and allowing the Black popular masses to exercise the right of self-determination for the first time in their history.

## POLITICAL STRATEGY AND TACTICS OF THE MOVEMENT IN NORTH AMERICA

11. In the vocabulary of social revolution, a *stage* or *phase* is defined as a specific order of the constituent elements of a given social formation expressed as an unstable equilibrium of antagonistic forces. The nature of the stage of any revolution is determined by the principal contradiction in society. In the 20th century the principal contradiction manifests itself in increasing socialization of production and continuing private appropriation of the fruits of production. This contradiction manifests itself in heightened form in the racist super-exploitation of Black labor power by the monopoly bourgeoisie. Particular to each stage is a type of action designed to accelerate the dynamics of political development in a certain direction, to replace the balance of forces with a new equilibrium favourable to victory over the social or national enemy. For that reason, the only movement in the life of Afro-Americans that can justifiably be termed revolutionary is the anti-racist struggle of the Black community for national liberation and self-determination for an end to white supremacy. The only chain of action pertinent to the stage of national liberation of the Black community is anti-racist, anti-monopoly class struggle.

12. Distinct from the principal contradiction in North American society, two sets of other contradictions function in dialectical tension as the historic and social matrix within which the task of national liberation of blacks must be accomplished. The latter contradictions are of a major and minor nature. Fundamental, of major character, is the antagonistic contradiction between the demand for control by Black people of the means to fulfill their basic socio-political, economic, and cultural needs and continued white supremacy. The lesser contradiction – whose resolution, however, is of no less importance in steering the Black liberation movement surely along the road to emancipation – is the clash between the interests of a small group of "traditional Negro leaders" at the head of the tiny "Negro middle class" and the vast majority of the slum-dwelling Black popular masses. As a consequence, the task of Black revolutionaries is twofold:
    a. the achievement of national liberation by overthrowing the capitalist system and
    b. the effective mobilization of the Black masses against weak-kneed vacillation and collaborationism of the Black service class.

    Mobilization of the masses implies a programme of education, propaganda, organization, encouragement, and enlightenment centering around the goal of national liberation. But such action cannot be taken as a substitute for direct assaults on racist capitalism.

13. Careful analysis of the economic implications of the socio-historical phenomenon of "Negro" collaborationism results in a double-edged definition of the Black "bourgeoisie" or "Black service class," and dictates the Black national liberation movement's political attitude towards that "middle class":
    a. Not only is it a numerically insignificant segment of the whole Black population, but economically it is essentially different from the white or true bourgeoisie, for the Black middle class owns none of the means of production. Black capitalism is a ridiculous hoax. It is the stalking horse of Richard Nixon and the financial oligarchy. The Blacks who fancy themselves as capitalists are fools – the tools of white supremacy. Exclusion of Blacks from ownership of major means of production signifies that the Negro service class holds no capital and never will be allowed to accumulate any and therefore can never ascend to real economic and social power. Both in the South and the North the business activity of Black capitalists is marginal at best and in most cases vegetates in a tiny, arbitrarily restricted, separate "economy." Forever starved of capital, "Black business" has only managed to survive where tolerated by dominant white monopoly capital, where it is allowed to exploit a completely Black clientele on a segregated basis.
    b. It is spiritually identified with racist capitalist society in social aspirations – i.e., with full integration as its paradoxical goal, it has submitted to the psychological rape of racist America.

    The political assessment that must follow then is that the Black "bourgeoisie" – in social content – is as parasitic upon the whole Black community as Frantz Fanon's colonial middle class was upon the colonial economy. As a *service stratum* of the Black populace ministering to the variegated needs of the white power structure in the same spirit as the colonial bourgeoisie acts as middlemen in the colonial and neo-colonial worlds, the "Negro bourgeoisie" occupies an ambiguous intermediary and parasitic position between the dominant white bourgeoisie on the one hand and the oppressed majority of Black people on the other.

14. The sanguinary repression now being unleashed against the forces of Black revolution is a sure sign of the crisis of the white racist system of domination. Fascist repression of the ghettoes is symptomatic of the ruling class' inability to banish the threat, to overcome the contradiction to its power posed by the stride toward Black liberation. The defeat of facism, like the eventual overthrow of monopoly capitalism in the United States, will be the product – direct or indirect – of a successful struggle for Black self-determination.

15. Recently the group around Stokely Carmichael has contended that the fate of American Blacks is dependent upon the creation of a "revolutionary base" in a completely liberated and unified Africa. Not until power has been seized by socialist revolutionaries throughout the Black continent and a base established in which all Africans will speak a *single language* and respond to the commands of a single government is it considered possible to extend emancipation to the embattled African people of North America. At the very least, this thesis is a fallacious interpretation and a misapplication of the doctrine of the "revolutionary base area" developed by Mao Tse-tung and General Vo Nguyen Giap from their concrete experiences

with guerrilla warfare – one in huge, semi-colonial, semi-feudal China; the other in tiny, colonial Vietnam – *national* experiences which by no stretch of the imagination correspond with the reality of the relationship between a *colonized people in North American captivity* and its *mother continent.* In a positive sense, this thesis represents a kind of Pan-African doctrine of "socialism in one country" metamorphosed and distorted to apply to a whole continent suffering from the ills of continued white rule and neo-colonial reaction. The sad result of its general adoption by American Blacks, however, would be the indefinite postponement of the struggle for socialism and Black national liberation in the United States, and the diversion of the attention of promising young Black cadres away from the problems of America's ghettoes to engagement in an African adventurism. In Vietnam a sound lesson is being taught the Black men of both Africa and America – if they will only both to learn it: the heroic Vietnamese people's victorious armed struggle against white American imperialism is proof positive that each people must rely on its *own* forces and on the solidarity of the socialist camp and must fight without ceasing until final victory, no matter what the sacrifice. Vietnam showed that a determined revolutionary force, though outnumbered, can defeat the onslaught of the mightiest reactionary class. The best expression of the mutual solidarity of Black Africans and Afro-Americans is the joint resolve to expand and deepen *independently* the national liberation and anti-imperialist struggles now underway on the African continent and in the northern half of the western hemisphere.

16. The advisability of an alliance (permanent or temporary), or at least of parallel, mutually supporting actions between the Black national liberation movement on the one side and white revolutionaries and militant organized labor on the other, has become a problem of burning urgency requiring immediate solution. Owing to their sometimes superior knowledge of the works of revolutionary thinkers, and due also to a general altruism, some white youths often appear to be considerably ahead of Blacks in the understanding of Marxism-Leninism. This has bred a kind of inferiority complex in the minds of some Black militants. The unwillingness of some white progressives to combat their own racism and the racism of other whites, especially of white workers, has also put Blacks off. The same is true for other traits of some of the younger white radicals who appear to be condemned without reprieve to permanent instability, to constant dissolution. As they grow older, graduate from university, marry, seek employment, and acquire a stake in bourgeois society, will not many succumb to the siren-like attractions of anti-Black liberalism? Now, undue suspicion can deprive the Black emancipation movement of valuable allies and thus should be avoided. But the class composition of white petty bourgeois radicalism is suspect, to say the very least. One wonders what grounds there are for expecting the white *middle* and *lower middle classes* – the social strata from which most of the radical college youth are recruited – to be more resolute than their parents. Certainly it has been clear since Marx and Lenin that individual revolutionaries and intellectuals can and often do overcome social position, slipping through the tight bonds of inherited caste prejudices and class status, escaping "white skin privilege" to betray the oppressors for the benefit of the oppressed. But it is by no means certain that the rigors of the struggle against the monopoly bourgeoisie would not act traumatically upon many, if not most, petty bourgeois radicals, causing them to draw back, hesitate, fall into stupified inertia or passive contemplation. Or perhaps drive many into the ranks of fascism and overt racism. It is true that petty bourgeois radicalism at times is capable of trenchant political analysis, including support – as an ideal – of the struggles of the revolutionary peoples of Africa, Latin America, Vietnam, and Palestine, and acceptance of the right of self-determination for the Black people of America. But even then petty bourgeois revolutionaries cannot bring themselves to admit the political independence and vanguard role of the Blacks at home, instead insisting that the initiative must come from outside, either from the Third World or from alienated white youths. Turning to the political role of organized labor under the leadership of the likes of George Meany and the AFL-CIO bureaucracy, it has always been proverbial for its lack of anything resembling a revolutionary class consciousness. Rather, its distinguishing ideological feature has been its steadfast devotion to an ideal of white racial solidarity with "management" *against* Blacks. This white supremacist ideology nullified or stunted the growth of real class solidarity among proletarians in the United States – i.e., between white and Black workers – and grossly facilitated the super-exploitation of the long-suffering "sub"-proletarians originally stolen from Africa as slaves. It also resulted in the hopeless opportunist degeneracy and gangsterism of the rightwing labor movement in the U.S. Thus it is imperative for theorists of the Black revolution not to be paralyzed by all this. Black revolutionaries must seek their allies among reliable white class elements – i.e., among real Marxist-Leninists and proletarians. For these reasons, the problem of Black revolutionary alliance with white revolutionaries is one which requires constant solution and permanent re-evaluation. An ally at one moment in history – and historical moments are very brief nowadays, sometimes lasting no more than several months – can be transformed into an enemy at the next. Any real, effective political alliance between progressive forces in society must operate on the basis of carefully considered and established priorities. If they are to both prove their *bona fides* and deliver effective blows to U.S. imperialism and racism, all white revolutionaries hoping to unite in alliance with the forces of Black militancy must subordinate their political activities to expanding and supporting the Black colony's struggle against racism. Only such a struggle will create the proper conditions to begin the accelerated democratization and socialization of society.

17. One of the most crucial tasks for the Black liberation movement is the *internationalization* of the struggle of the Black domestic colony for self-determination. Here the prime aims must be the procurement of reliable foreign support expressed in terms of diplomatic support, refuge

for persecuted representatives of Black liberation movements, and a steadily swelling volume of sympathetic propaganda. Early fraternal recognition of the American Black liberation movement by the revolutionary governments and liberation movements of fraternal peoples is a goal of major importance, comparable to the early establishment of fraternal ties linking socialist Cuba, the Soviet Union, and People's China with the embattled South Vietnamese National Liberation Front and Provisional Revolutionary Government. However, it should be understood that internationalization must mean something must more trustworthy and significant than a "plebiscite in the ghettoes" supervised by the American-dominated U.N. (remember Lumumba)! Moreover, a realistic assessment of the present balance of forces in the diplomatic world – no matter how temporary and unstable an equilibrium it represents – makes it incumbent upon the planners of Black revolution to recognize the tremendous power to intimidate still curled meancingly in the mailed fist of U.S. imperialism, an intimidating force certain to cause many of the more timid or client neo-colonial states – despite the privately or publicly expressed preferences of their peoples – to temporize, to invent endless pretexts to excuse their failure to support the Black struggle for self-determination in America, and to shrink from taking concrete steps to open the debate of "an internal affair of the United States" in the international arena. Under these circumstances, in order to merit fraternal support, focus the attention of mankind on the brutal repression in the United States, and win the sympathy of world opinion, the Black national liberation movement in particular and the Black domestic colony in general must increase their sensitivity and sympathy for the struggles of the world's other oppressed peoples. In their own interest, Black men in America must be much more assiduous in feeling and expressing solidarity with the heroic fighters of Vietnam, Africa, North Korea, and Palestine, and especially for the ubiquitous guerrilla campaigns and inextinguishable revolutionary "brushfires" in nearby Latin America.

18. Black people in America have long had recourse to organize self-defense to protect themselves from the aggression of white racists. During Black Reconstruction, the response to wanton brutality, lynching, and live immolation was the now-famed organized resistance of Black communities. Following World War I, the pogroms of northern white mobs crazed by the racism endemic in the "American way of life" was checked by the widespread movement in the new ghettoes of the North to establish systematic armed self-defense against white attacks. Now the crimes committed daily in Black ghettoes throughout the United States by foreign occupation forces consisting of white police, national guard and regular troops, and Black mercenaries have aroused a cry for "community control" and stimulated a movement to provide armed defense of the community against *pig* outrages. These movements, which span a century, these self-defense institutions and measures, are justified and deserving of the unflagging support of all American revolutionaries.

19. Like other colonized people who have been suppressed for centuries, the Black domestic colony in the United States constitutes a *nation*. It is different from other emergent nations in that it consists of forcibly transplanted colonized subjects who have acquired cohesive identity in the course of centuries of struggle against enslavement, cultural alienation, and the spiritual cannibalism of white racism. It differs more substantially from other emergent nations in that its people are dispersed across the continental United States and are thoroughly integrated in the monopoly capitalist economy as workers or as members of the reserve army of dirt cheap labor. The common history which the Black people of America share is manifested in a concrete national culture with a peculiar "spiritual complexion" or psychological temperament. Though the Black nation expresses its thoughts, emotions, and aspirations in the same tongue as American whites, the different conditions of existence, the long trial of super-exploitation and dehumanization at the hands of white capitalist overlords, and heroic resistance have, from generation to generation, welded the bonds of a specific Black experiences. The only way to resolve the antagonistic contradiction between the colonized Black "minority" nation and the American imperialist-racist system is to overthrow capitalism and give Black people the opportunity to exercise their right of self-determination. An absolute impasse has been reached in the development of American Blacks; the obstacles to national self-determination raised by racist capitalism must be swept away.

# 17
## *Marxism-Leninism and the Black Revolution: A Critical Essay**

RONALD W. WALTERS

### INTRODUCTION

#### The Rise of the Black Neo-Marxian Ideology

One of the more important developments in the ongoing dynamic of the black political movement as reflected in the style of its ideology is the rise of Black neo-Marxism. Although a precise history of this development is not necessarily germane to our discussion, suffice it to say that for nearly a year there has been a slow development of the popularity of Marxist-Leninist thought among many former black nationalist or Pan-Africanist spokesmen and students in the black community. The resulting struggle, bitterness, and confusion has been so great as to produce serious division in the increasing unity which the movement had begun to achieve in the early 1970s about the nature of the black struggle in the United States.

Increasingly, the speeches and activities of the leaders of the black movement have exemplified a turning away from those of the late 1960s and early 1970s to ideas which pinpoint the nature of the capitalist system and its attendant imperialist tendencies as the enemy of black and oppressed people, and, therefore, the need to engage in revolutionary struggle to establish a national and international socialist system to alleviate their ills. Many black students on the college campuses of both black and white institutions who formerly conceived of the ideas of Malcolm X and Nkrumah as the revolutionary ideological standard now view these works from the perspective of classical Marxism-Leninism in an effort to arrive at the most "scientifically correct" mode of waging a struggle against those who oppress them, whether they be black or white.

One of the most telling indications of this trend, which perhaps may be viewed as the recent high water mark in the development of black neo-Marxian thought, is the recent African Liberation Day celebration. This year, the celebration was preceded by a two-day conference which centered on the theme of imperialism and was designed to promote ideological debate and analysis over the condition of black and oppressed people. This symposium, held at Howard University, was not to reach a synthesis of opinion from the varying views of Nkrumahists, Pan-Africanists, Black Nationalists, and Marxists, but was to reflect the deep split in the activist community concerning how and under what prevailing philosophy the struggle against racism and imperialism should be organized.

This split, now mature, was to reflect itself in the June session of the Sixth Pan-African Conference in Dar es Salaam, Tanzania, where it has been reported there were again serious differences of opinion among the delegates from various parts of the African world as regards the applicability of the race or class analysis program of action to the struggles of African peoples under different conditions in the black world. The report of the Political Committee of the Congress urged working class solidarity in the confrontation with capitalism, and was objected to by spokesmen from the American delegation who urged that a strict application of the report could not be effectuated in America, where the white working class did not perceive an identity of interest with the black working class because of its racism and privilege relative to black workers. Even on this point, there was not unanimous consensus by members of the American Delegation.

This brief sketch of events should be enough to suggest that there has indeed been a development of significance among black activists ideologically. But the greater importance of such a fact is that, if followed in terms of programs, there will not only be a different rhetoric but an attempt at different types of programs of action surfacing in the black urban landscape of America. This paper will attempt to look critically at this development, not from within the perspective of Marxist thought itself, but questioning the relationship of it to the black struggle in America. This is an important distinction because it says that we will not be so much concerned with the complex development of Marxist thought from the point of view of its supporters and detractors, but to what extent the essential principles as they have been expounded by the neo-Marxists are or are not grounded in the perceived reality of the black condition.

#### The Neo-Marxian Argument and its Roots

Boiled down to its essential tenets, the black neo-Marxian argument can be illustrated as follows:[1]

1. Imperialism and racism are the twin evils which generally oppress poor and black peoples in the world with the major

*Written especially for this book.

emphasis on imperialism as the more comprehensive rationale.

2. The source of this imperialism is the Leninist notion of monopoly capital. Capitalism then becomes the driving force of oppression and, as it relates to America, it was the motivating force for slavery – racism being one of its most ominous consequences.

3. The workings of capitalism have produced distinct classes, which have defined relationships to the productive forces of the society – the main classes being those who do not (workers or proletariat) and those who do (bourgeois) control the means of production. This forms the objective condition for the definition of international and national class relationships.

4. Capitalism, therefore, must be destroyed, and the mechanism must be class conflict spurred on by the formation of militant workers' movements. Blacks are part of the working class, therefore, this becomes their main identity in the struggle for the establishment of a new order. Their duty is similarly to wage class struggle (regardless of race) with the capitalists and their supporters, and the ideological concepts which surface will be a manifestation of that struggle.

5. The objective is a socialist transformation of the state, and, in the attempt to bring about such transformation, the mechanism will be a United Front of all progressive (anti-capitalist, anti-imperialist, anti-racist) forces. In this struggle, racial chauvinism or nationalism cannot be tolerated because it is a detraction from the Front and from the solidarity of the worker coalitions across race lines.

6. Because the white working class is not yet at the stage of consciousness where it can wage class struggle, it will be the duty of the black politically aware to educate the black masses (workers) and the duty of the black workers to educate and politicize the white working class into an understanding of their class interest and their interracial class interests. In this sense, black workers thus become the vanguard of the movement. If this movement for socialist transformation is successful, it will destroy racism and bring about a more equitable distribution of material resources and, therefore, direct benefit to the black working classes.

This is a rational ideology in the sense that it is an orderly construct for the way in which society might be changed; certain aspects of it will be examined below in some detail. Nevertheless, one is bound to wonder why there is the need for the adoption of such a construct at this time, considering previous attempts on the part of socialists and communists to apply this theory to the black community. The answer to this might be found in four factors, all of which together provide an environment for a shift in ideological focus.

The first factor might be called the "Gordian knot of black liberation." It is a recognition that historically there were only two roads open, conceptually and programmatically, by which it was possible for blacks to achieve that complete sense of self-determination and freedom that is enjoyed by others who are not enslaved and oppressed. One road has traditionally led "back to Africa," and with the increasing integration of blacks into the economic structures of American life, it has become only a theoretical option for the majority of the black community, although some have indeed returned to Africa. The other road has been within the United States, and here the theories have ranged from complete societal integration to the formation of separate states within the country. The knot is that neither of these options has been wholly successful nor embraced by the masses. Hence, although the two roads have been traveled together, the cycles of ideology have shifted between them according to other empirical factors in the society. The movements of the early and mid-1960s were predominantly nationalist in character with a heavy Pan-African content, but by the early 1970s the Pan-African movement was paramount. Now, nearing the mid-1970s, there is a turning away from the heavy focus on Africa to a more nativistic set of concerns. Some feel that the Marxist philosophy makes it possible for the shift to occur while maintaining the essential theoretical linkage to the international dimensions of the movement.

Secondly, although there was and has been a high outpouring of writings on the theory and practice of black nationalism and Pan-Africanism, there never developed the clarity and the pseudoscientific quality of dogma that would be satisfactory to many in its illumination of the social forces that have plagued the black community. The explanatory power of black nationalist theory has been so limited, as some point out, that it has had to borrow from the theory of colonialism in order to arrive at an explanation of the way in which forces of oppression manifest themselves politically. Marxists argue, however, that the structure of colonialism was merely the result of more fundamental economic forces brought on by the imperialist impulses and by the workings of monopoly capital. Here, again, there was already an elegant, comprehensive, and complex critique of capitalism which seemed to provide some answers to both the question of economic exploitation and the resulting political social structures that developed.

Perhaps the most telling criticism of Marxism here, however, is that there has not been sufficient critique of the Western intellectual tradition which forms the basis from which theories about society are derived. This Western tradition, both in theory and method, sets limits to the ability of black and other oppressed peoples to devise alternative realities about Western societies because blacks (particularly the intellectual) and others are unable to break free from the bourgeois process into which they have been socialized.

Thirdly, the failure or perceived failure of blacks to have developed systematic theory from black nationalism and Pan-Africanism has been reflected in the failure of blacks to develop viable programs based on these ideologies. Thus today there are few Pan-Africanist or black nationalist programs that would stand as concrete illustrations of the theory. Perhaps here the greatest problem was that the plethora of organizations that sprang up in the period 1965-1970 possessed only a vague appreciation of the common elements of the theory which formed parts of their separate efforts, and thus, the opportunity of building a comprehensive set of institutions out of a comprehensive philosophy was lost.

Finally, the sense that the black power movement is over has led to a new period of the subordination of blackness. There are many who have said that the movement is over because it failed and others who would say that its successes have run their course and we are now at a new, pragmatic, stage in history. The character of this stage is probably best illustrated by the strange quiescence of active protest on the campuses and in the community, by the exchange of a black identity for a "minority" or "poor" or "oppressed" objective identity, and by the rhetoric of "sophisticated" leadership which says that black initiatives must now be couched in terms that have appeal and identity of interest with wider, non-black audiences. Whatever the reasons, and despite the occasional remnants of a symbolic nature that one recognizes from the black nationalist period in our history, it just "ain't hip" to project blackness any more.

As we shall see below, these factors have been exaggerated somewhat in order to spell out clearly the mood which has brought many to the point where they feel that the ideologies of the past few years are no longer functional. It is equally true that they have been developed with an eye to those things that the neo-Marxists have identified as salient reasons for their conversion to a new religion. Yet, whether or not the reasons are valid for the partial transformation of black ideology, one must still ask whether the transplanted Marxism-Leninism is an improvement in theory and practice or whether it is simply another frantic search for the key that unlocks the door to the long sought after goal of complete black liberation.

### The Non-Empirical Reality of Black Neo-Marxist Thought

One of the fundamental questions that must be asked of those factors providing a basis for a transformation of ideology is to what extent they are transitory phenomena or consistent with the empirical realities of black life in America. This would appear to be a fair question because of the Marxist preoccupation with scientific theory, although it is also understood that some would attack this question as being within the framework of bourgeois social science. The writer means, by the use of the term "empirical," simply whether or not the applicability of Marxist-Leninist theory is able to be realized because it falls within the capability and reflects the experience of the black community. In order to discuss this point, the writer will posit several aspects of the black experience as "empirical" and relate parts of the neo-Marxist argument which apply to them.

One aspect of this empirical experience is the "cyclical" nature of black ideology as it swings from one dominant theme to another in varous periods of black history. It might appear that the causes are entirely capricious – that is to say, that they lend themselves to the whims of the perpetrators. But it equally might be that there is an element of "fadism" in the shifts, for no community in America is as responsible for the development of rapidly changing social styles as blacks. To this extent, we may have become socialized to the American need for a new car, a new house, a new dress, and, yes, even a new ideology, as soon as we grow tired of the old one. But there is another factor as important which resides in the dimension of our powerlessness to control the total range of social forces to which we are subjected. The question this raises is how we can have a consistently viable theory and set of programs when confronted by white power in the form of the Houston Plan, the FBI surveillance and destruction of black organizations and leaders, and the neglect or refusal of the government to provide resources for social development of our communities upon which such consistency must ultimately rest. This is perhaps another way of saying that these shifts are a response, in part, to the dominant forces in the society and to the lack of a consistent base from which to keep black programs and theories alive in the "laboratory' of the black experience.

Even if these things are true, however, one must still account for the particular nature of a movement which arises to take over its place in the cycle, and though we have made a feeble attempt to do so above, still it strikes this writer that the instinct which guides this recent attempt at the construction of ideology smacks of "naive realism." It is *real* in the sense that it seeks to deal with practicality, but *naive* because the range of the application of the theory extends to the total society. Most of the other black theories have argued that the nature of society would be changed if the black condition were dealt with realistically. This is the first serious group in modern times in addition to the Panther Party to suggest that the society itself must be the battleground for change and that thereby the black condition would be improved.

Secondly, this movement is ahistorical in the sense that it, by inference, negates the experiences of those blacks who in the 1930s had flirtations with Marxist-Leninist thoughts and withdrew. I have spoken of the current movement as a "neo" movement, and it is in this sense that the meaning takes on form. The major difference this writer perceives is that the black experience with Marxists in the 1930s was developed as a direct outgrowth of policy fostered by white Marxists. Many of the lines of thought and the programs that developed, therefore, may only inferentially be ascribed to blacks. The writer feels that this new event is unique because it arises primarily from within the black community, devoid of known significant participation by whites. Nevertheless, because of the substance of the ideology, and in particular its "working class solidarity" integrationist bias, this new movement is seen to be no more insulated from the lessons of that period of history than any other.

Perhaps the most dangerous lesson of the 1930s was that of white co-optation of black organizations, individuals, and goals. One simply must not come away from a reading of Harold Cruse's *Crisis of the Negro Intellectual,* or the last hundred pages of George Padmore's *Pan Africanism or Communism,* or Wilson Record's *Race and Radicalism* without an overwhelming understanding of the betrayal and exploitation of the black community by the white left. And although a review of that period is beyond the scope of this brief essay, there is nothing that has happened over the last four decades to suggest the imperfection of that understanding for all time.

In addition, should this period be looked upon as ancient history, we have only to understand the trauma which Frantz Fanon experienced when he discovered that the white left in Paris was incapable of materially relating to the Algerian Revolution, and that the white left in America (predominantly non-Marxist) abandoned the black revolutionary movement of the '60s when it became clear that they could not co-opt it. What strange magic is there today to keep the neo-Marxian movement from being co-opted by the white left? If the answer is that they will be kept out of the leadership of its black coalition, then how will this position set with the pure Marxists in the ranks who are opposed to racial nationalism?

The next aspect of our empirical condition is that we are a black minority in a highly urban technologically oriented society, and no revolution has yet been made in such a place, especially by a highly identifiable minority of its citizens without significant control of the mechanisms of force. For the writer, this raises the serious question of the utility of the entire theory of Marxism-Leninism to such a society, and suggests that we do not yet have a theory of liberation *tailored to the conditions of black people in America.*

Marx and Lenin wrote basically for agrarian societies as is true from their characterization of social classes and the nature of the revolution they sought to make. Most of the world at that time (and even now) fitted that condition, not to mention Russia. So profound is this fact that it is almost a cliche to say that Marx never envisioned the dimension of the American race problem (although he and Engels wrote on the Civil War), that the capitalist system has, thus far, overcome its internal contradiction (and external contradictions) by force and oppression, and that it now has reached a "post-industrial" stage.

How then, does the Marxist theory, which is tailored to the production of *goods,* fit a society which is tailored to the production of *services,* having clearly passed the point where such feudalistic notions as land redistribution and control of plants (there will shortly be no one in the plants except computers) are objects for the *future* viability of a nation. It is obvious that those who make a religion out of Marx must grapple with problems of national structure at the expense of the internal groups comprising it. It is also clear that Lenin never understood the internally multinational politics of America and the way in which political alleigance was based on a system of distribution of powers to ethnic groups who supported the state. Why else is it possible that the nation is about to emerge from an internal "contradiction" – i.e., "The Watergate Affair" – which would cripple any other nation irrevocably, with its system of politics intact? Certainly there is a brand of logic which dictates that if we are to give alleigance to a theory it must fit the peculiar conditions of the state in which we find ourselves if we make an argument for the power of theory to lead to correct solutions to the problem of black liberation in America.

Finally, it is the most reasonable of statements to say that "blacks in America must analyze the examples of any people who have ever beat capitalism," and that in this we must not suppose that those examples can be transported here. For, besides the empirical fact of the degree of American industrialization, there is the persistence of black-white race conflict which mitigates against the mindless adoption of revolutionary prescriptions from exotic places. The examples that come to mind – France, Russia, China, Cuba, Algeria, and others – where successful transfer of power has been accomplished, had societies that were agrarian and people who were nearly *ethnically homogeneous.* If one conceives of change methods in essentially violent or paramilitary terms, then this has great significance. One is startled to find that after nearly two years, three of the people on the FBI's Ten Most Wanted List are young women wanted for bombings, and many members of the SLA are still at large. By contrast, nearly every member of the Black Liberation Army, a group of nearly 35 people, is behind bars. Is the lesson here simply that black skin is visible, or is it that the racist systems of control, which have been amassed upon black people by thousands of agencies in the society, has made us vulnerable to almost instant identification and documentation.

The simple identification of a militant organization with the surrounding community is not enough to make it secure if its methods are not tailored to the empirical situation. The Black Panther Party is the first to admit this. They offered valuable programs to the communities in which they located, yet their methods were such in confronting the white power structure that it was determined that they must be physically destroyed, as evidenced by the attacks on their headquarters in the winter of 1970.

The question raised for the writer, besides the problem of violent confrontation with the system of white power from a base of powerlessness, is not that of violence at all, but that, given the hostility of the society to blacks, how will it be possible to make a radical ideology viable across race lines with blacks in the leadership? The questions are ultimately simple: Will they listen? If they listen, will they follow? *Doubts abound!* Otherwise, if one bypasses race-conflict and racism in the application of Marxist ideology and if one takes the view that the application will only be in terms of blacks, one is not serious about a confrontation with the *state* as the repository of racism and imperialism using their theoretical foundation.

Having posited the empirical reality of the black community in conceptual terms, having to do with its powerlessness as the basis of shifting ideology, with the lessons of confrontation and co-optation from the white left in the 1930s, with the urban-technological definition of black environment, and with a pervasive race conflict-racism producing social reality, we are now prepared for a more specific discussion of the Marxist principles which underpin their argument.

## A FEW POPULAR MARXIST CONCEPTS

### The Scientific Character of Marxist Thought.

We have made the observation that the neo-Marxists have criticized the bourgeois tradition of Western scholarship as a limiting factor in the development of alternative theory for black liberation; in this they may be entirely right. This is not to say, however, that they do not suffer from the same malady, or pseudo-scientific fantasy as it were, of explaining social phenomena with the use of a prefabricated set of assumptions. For they are just as avid users of "clear" and "concrete" formulations which lend themselves to logic (Western), consistency, and verifiability. Yet the puzzle (contradiction here is that Marxist concepts such as "dialectic," "materialism," the notion of "classes" and others are not, as such, scientific, in that, as they are defined in the literature, they do not lend themselves to consistency or verifiability in their application to the black community.

For example, the principle of the "dialectic" is built upon the notion of "contradictions" – that for each contradiction there will be a "thesis" and an "anti-thesis" from which there emerges a "synthesis." Thus, the synthesis of opposing forces becomes a new creation, a mode of development. Marx's notion of dialectical materialism had been perhaps most applied in the natural sciences where the principle, as it has existed in physics, of "action-reaction" was well known. Marx, however, took this principle and sought to apply it to social reality. Thus, his concept of dialectical materialism seeks to explain human history and the development of society when applied as historical materialism.

It should not go unnoticed that this attempt to apply an

essentially natural science concept involving the behavior of matter is strikingly similar to the attempt by modern "systems theorists" to apply principles of physics to the description of social behavior. Yet they are soundly criticized by Marxists as applying bourgeois social science. In any case, the use of a one-factor modality such as materialism to explain history momentarily enhances the power of the Marxists' analysis. I use the term "momentarily" because the power of this analysis is undeniablly persuasive in its explanation of *certain events* in history and *certain epochs.* It does not explain *all* human history as it claims to do without stretching the implications of the analysis ad infinitum as its users are prone to do. It does not explain the origins of World War I or World War II, nor many other phenomena that will be discussed below.

Economic determinism is only *one kind* of determinism useful in the explanation of historical phenomena, any one of which, if stretched to be comprehensive, would lose all claim to scientific application, as does the Marxist concept. In this sense, phenomenology is perhaps a more scientifically comprehensive tool for viewing history than any one brand of determinism, whether it be economic, political, or cultural.

**Imperialism**

The black neo-Marxists have claimed that this concept was comprehensive enough to serve as the focus around which all struggle should be organized. Since they are against capitalism, and imperialism is the highest stage of capitalism according to Lenin,[2] then it must be the overall conceptual tool. But if we have suggested that such economic determinism is not a comprehensive rationale for either historical or contemporary events, *then it should be clear that imperialism is not the highest stage in the development of capitalism, but the highest stage in the development of European civilization.* I believe, with Samir Amin, that a nation (and the range of national and international problems which it faces) cannot be classified solely according to its mode of production.[3] The impulse to imperialism likewise cannot be ascribed solely to economic causes. If so, how then does one justify American imperialism for nearly two decades in Vietnam, a poor country where the U.S. has spent many times over what it has received, by this concept. One might argue that the military-strategic infrastructure of the Western world was created only to serve the security interests of the monopoly capitalist, but it is equally true that one major impulse to imperialism of a large power is that it seeks to create other systems in its likeness, not only to serve its economic interest but to reflect its particular brand of political philosophy as right and virtuous by the establishment of similar institutions.

One great failing of the Marxist philosophy is that it underestimates the extent to which there are nations whose people believe in their national myths and in the philosophical bases which undergird the form and content of their political (and cultural) institutions. How else could it have been that a President of the United States who had so faithfully served the capitalist class was turned out of power by at least the rhetoric and processes of the political system? This is not a naive view of the reality of the American system, but one that recognizes the power and importance of its economy yet does not seek to ascribe all social and international causation to it.

No, the real question here is one of *civilization.* That human history does not lend itself to a piecemeal, one-factor model of causation but, depending upon the phenomenon, it embraces economics, politics, culture, and other aspects of human behavior – the sum total of which is a particular civilization. *It is the conflict* of civilizations which is central, and the internal conflict between American and European peoples is *simply a manifestation of that age-old struggle for supremacy in the world.* What Marx meant by bourgeois was culturally Western – those who had inherited the fruits of the Industrial Revolution (which had Western origins) and controlled its application to Soviet society. To miss the problem of culture within the Western European style of industrialization (which Lenin did not separate from technique) is not to understand the faults in Marxist-Leninist thought. For it is not simply that the political elites of many poor nations are tied to larger powers by economics, but that they have gone through a process of "bourgeoisification" (or Westernization) which they did not get in the corporation but in the Western centers of culture – most often the university. Thus, the control exercised by Western civilization over such individuals is more important as an indication of their *values* and *behavior* than their ties to the system of economics alone. The struggle in this sense therefore, is not so much against a capitalist class as it is to develop a process of reindegenization for the political, economic, and intellectual elite within the framework of the goals of the people, whether they are revolutionary or not.

**Class and Class Struggle**

The previous discussion brings us to the question of classes as propounded by Marx and as seen by the neo-Marxists. Implicit in what was said above is the fact that the Marxist definition of classes again is a unidimensional aspect which is inaccurate, sloppy and nonfunctional for use in a modern society. This is to say that one's relationship to the mode of production is only *one way* of defining social classes. But class consciousness is not always a coherent product because of its *diverse* origins. Some may be identified (or more importantly, may identify themselves) by their occupational relationship, but does the Marxist logic reconcile the often differing status (and thus class-conscious) relationship between one's occupation and one's income? Further, for many in the black community the usual indications of class often did not, and many times still do *not*, reflect status accurately because, due to the low status of jobs, one achieved community status (and, therefore, presumably class consciousness) from other things such as membership in social clubs and the varied activities in social life.

The low-status occupations of most members of the black community only hint at the fact that our general relationship to the means of production is minimal. Former Federal Reserve Board Member, Andrew Brimmer, has calculated that black business represents only 0.24 percent of the total revenue produced by the business sector, or one-quarter of one percent.[4] Can anyone seriously claim that there is a real relationship of the black business community to the societal means of production? In fact, there is some evidence to show that as one descends the scale of income, the incidence of materialist values grows stronger among the masses. Perhaps this is a key to why some revolutions have been led by a few alienated intellectuals who have been able to rationalize their deemphasis on materialistic values.

The concept, therefore, has very little meaning as an indicator of materialistic values or of the behavior of individuals – a more fruitful indicator is race. Perhaps it may be explained in this manner. In a recent symposium (April 1974) on imperialism within the framework of the Annual African Heritage Studies Association Conference, James Turner made the observation that a strategy which attacked the corporate structure either within the United States or outside it would mean sacrificing blacks' jobs and income most immediately. This was an irritating observation to the black neo-marxists, but profound in the sense that he realized that because of racism (*not classism*) in any significant retrenchment of the economy, blacks were the first let go from employment. This crisis construct, as all similar situations, is perhaps the best way to get a clear picture of how blacks are *actually* defined in this society in relation to the forces of production. It would not be amiss to extend his analysis to say that before the economic system would crumble, even those blacks who were self-employed would face expropriation of their resources, foreclosure on their loans, etc., before white industry would be allowed to die – because they are black in a white survival-oriented society.

Thus, it is not an academic argument to those in the black community whether they are defined most primarily because of race or class, since they have always faced the prospect of vulnerability – economic and otherwise – because of race *first*. This primary definition has not only kept them in the poor classes but away from the actual means of production for the society. Small wonder then that the doctrine of class struggle is doomed to failure – no one would know whom to struggle against! More importantly, unnecessary internally fictitious divisions would be developed among black people which would have little resemblance to reality and would only serve to further confuse us rather than to unite us. For just as there is no guarantee that out of the dialectical process of ideological struggle the "truth" would come, there is no assurance that out of class struggle within an advanced industrial country where race conflict is dominant would classlessness develop. There is more strength in a largely unified community than there is in an infinitesimally correct minority in the struggle for significant change by people who are already a black minority in a majority white country. The error of an incorrect classification of the black community by such things as income (see Scammon and Wattenberg, *Commentary,* April 1973) is as bad as it is coming from the black left and such fictions should not be allowed to go unchallenged.

***United Front Strategy***

Much of what has been said before mitigates against a United Front strategy aimed at the overthrow of capitalism largely because the balance of the energies of the oppressed groups are programmed around their ethnic (not class) interests, and an almost complete reorientation of the basic self-interest of other groups will be nearly impossible to achieve. Objectively, however, such an idea does not appear to be a bad one, but here again it is remarkable how the technique fails to take advantage of the need for black organization. Is it really the case that other groups (non-black) might actually perceive their self-interest in terms of their potential progress in America to be the same as blacks? And what will the form of leadership of such a United Front be? Will blacks be in the lead, or do we still have to follow the dictates of a coalition which in the end might either co-opt us or sell us out? What history of information do we have that leads us to believe that they can genuinely be trusted and are not in fact front groups for the agents of repression? We take a great deal on faith and it all succumbs to the rush of our historical experience with such groups when black self-determination is the issue. But perhaps this is not the issue any more if one is interested primarily in the character of the state.

There is and has been a history of coalition of a temporary nature, with groups in the black community. Yet no such coalition has prevented, for example, the Jewish community, out of their own ethnic interests, from taking a negative position on the question of quotas against the interests of blacks. The Civil Rights Coalition and the religious coalitions are still active on some questions of the rights of blacks as citizens in America and on the question of support for African freedom. But these coalitions arose not out of any theory but out of the realization that all of the resources needed to move the black community forward did not reside within it. This understanding as it operated was then a manifestation of our empirical condition and not a product of naive realism. Perhaps the real difference between the structuring of such coalitions is that one seeks to work within the framework of the existing system and the other to overthrow it. It remains to be seen which groups will come forward to join in the latter task and which do not seek to use the dynamism of the black movement for their own ends.

**The Position of Workers in a Revolutionary Struggle**

One of the slogans one hears frequently from the neo-Marxists is that workers must "take the lead" in fomenting the revolutionary struggle to destroy American capitalism. This writer would submit again that the use of classes in this way is confusing because the history of revolutions does not show where the workers have *ever* taken the lead in the development of a revolutionary movement. The lead has come from mostly intellectual and military elites. Therefore, in the face of the lack of clear precedent (and only with the prescription of theory) together with the lack of allies and their position of economic and social vulnerability, it is *immoral* to ask black workers to commit *revolutionary suicide.*

No one is clearer than James Boggs in his work *Racism and the Class Struggle* on the impossibility of black workers obtaining "class" allies among white workers in order to challenge the capitalist. The primary reason for this, Boggs says, is not only racism, but that the white worker has attained a level of affluence which allows him to perceive his interests as different from those of blacks. Even the labor unions, which support him, have attained the same level of affluence, appearing little different in substance and style than the management which they "oppose." Some unions have even developed a pattern of contract settlements which contain "no-strike" provisions in exchange for having graduated salary increases which are tied automatically to changes in the cost of living. There is hardly any "class" difference here, and in any serious showdown, even where the interest of the black and white workers are identical, what will prevent the emergence of a scapegoat syndrome where blacks are blamed for joint actions taken by blacks and whites on behalf of their common interests? It happens today with startling regularity.

If we lived in a revolutionary situation – i.e., where the *white* working class was alienated and ready to move on the system – then the black worker's role would be a little more than marginal. Even there, however, the role of the vanguard position would have to be defined to mean that blacks had an *indirect* responsibility to "trigger" the revolutionary activity of white workers because of their experience with oppression and political mobilization. But given the inability of the black workers to perform the role which Marxist theory directs because of the lack of a revolutionary situation, their assumption of a *vanguard* position makes them clear cannon fodder for what should be a white revolutionary role.

**Socialist Transformation**

This is perhaps the weakest part of the theory of Marx because he left no detailed understanding of what form the future would take, particularly when he appeared bold enough to predict the future course of capitalism. One might counter that it was outside of the obligation of Marx to predict the shape of future socialist-oriented society, but if this is so, then how is it that we know that the changes a revolution might make will be any better than those conditions that currently exist. Are we to go on faith? If so, then this smacks of religion, not science. Is it necessary for us to agree with classical Marxist theory concerning the "withering away of the state," for example, or should we make a calculation of our own interests with regard to it?

At the present time, it appears that there are many who have identified part of the problem of black people in America as stemming from the structure of the economy; they have come to an appreciation of Marxist principles because it advocates the redistribution of the wealth. All of us would agree with this, but what lies beyond, since most people would not follow the dogma of material sufficiency as the total definition of their well-being, is a valid question. As we stated above, human beings have needs which transcend the material level, and part of the tragedy of the black assent to the Marxist emphasis on materialism is that we abdicate a culturally historical obligation to put materialism into proper perspective. Sharing material goods will be impossible, will mean little, unless the importance of material goods is addressed first. One suspects that when this problem is addressed, one will discover that it is the material goods that are a direct product of the productive forces of the society, making possible the creation and appreciation of other aspects of culture, not the other way around. By having it the other way around, the Marxist have engaged in the mystification of materialism. Materialism may, in fact, be inescapable in a highly technological society.

The American Constitution does not mention capitalism, and only in an oblique way does it deal with the definition of rights to private property, although this is *well understood* as its basis. As a result of the gentlemen's agreement on the nature of capitalism in America, it has been left to business-oriented regulatory agencies and commissions established to protect civil rights to launch an occasional challenge to isolated inequitable practice. A corporation is free, however, to raise its prices with impunity in an effort to derive what profits it can, with the "market" as the only real check and balance. The market as it exists in America is anything but free because the "gentlemen's agreement" often extends to the nature of prices for products, thus, pricing many individuals who cannot pay out of its essential goods and services.

What is clearly needed is a new system, or at the least an understanding that although the political promise of the right to life, liberty, and the pursuit of happiness is an established principle, it will continue to be meaningless without a guarantee by the state that there will be such material goods available to make this pursuit a real possibility. In short, this may be the only reason why man should continue to tolerate the existence of the state.

Black people have just as great a need for the fulfillment of such a promise of happiness, but for us it also must come free of racism and with a substantial measure of our own history and culture. For we must answer the ultimate question of whether or not a culture that only reflects a shared materialism is sufficient and desirable if it is devoid of the dynamic blackness of our past. We should be able to recognize our future even in a revolutionary new order.

A central question is who the revolutionary new order will benefit most, and the answer is undoubtedly the white workers and poor unemployed whites, since this is their country, they are in the majority, and there are more of them exploited, on welfare, and unemployed than blacks. Our oppression can be summed up in different numbers and by its total quality. But in this regard, the National Question, as it has been used by some to refer to blacks, is probably more appropriate to be applied to the Irish, Italian, or Slavic American who forms the bulk of the working class whites with the greatest stake in this system. The revolution should be made by them, for *only they can sustain it*. Only they have real power in the board rooms, in the military, in the Congress, and in the White House.

What is not well understood by many is that the act of seizing power is not revolution, it is merely a violent act. If the act is sustained and legitimized, then a transfer of power will have been accomplished, but even this is not revolution. Revolution only comes when it can be demonstrated that radical social changes have occurred within the society as a result of the seizure of power. Thus, the act of rebellion of seizing power must be sustained, and this writer would argue that in terms of the technology it would require to both sustain the gains of power and to effect radical social changes in America, it would be beyond the power of the black community to execute on behalf of 270 million people. The realization of this (which is also incidentally the rationale for a revolutionary United Front) still means that legitimate government would be substantially under the control of whites. Thus, there can be no black revolution which would have the effect of revolutionizing America or controlling it. This is why the best use of black resources, as we shall see below, must be according to *scale* because the National Question in America is about the liberation of white people, with black liberation a questionable by-product.

The point here is relatively simple; *a white revolution in a white country needs white revolutionaries to be successful.*

## THE RACE-CLASS SYNTHESIS

Although we have tried to point out a few of the flaws in the thinking of black neo-Marxists derived from Marxist-Leninist philosophy, it does not mean for one moment that it has not made an important contribution to the clarification and raising of major issues of black liberation. This attempt was to demystify Marx, to call attention to the fadish nature of the neo-Marxists, and to urge a serious attempt at a synthesis of these ideas with those of the past that have served black people so well. It has been an attempt to put Marxism into another kind of black perspective.

In this attempt to find perspective, one can agree with the thesis of Brother Bill Strickland, who said, in May 1974 at the annual meeting of the National Conference of Black Political Scientists, that in a national liberation struggle it is race that is paramount, and afterward it is class. He did not elaborate greatly upon this thesis but let us presume that he meant that in the initial stages of a struggle for national liberation, the leading edge of the revolutionary movement is the group that has been most oppressed and usually because of race conflict within nonhomogeneous societies where the oppressor race is different than the oppressed. After the majority race comes to power and the race oppressors have been thrown out, if the government assumes the same capitalist form, the major contradictions will be class contradictions. This situation does not fit the empirical situation in the United States, but it is precisely the reason why the writer has come to feel that the application of Marxist class analysis is most powerful in *racially homogeneous societies* where class antagonisms may perhaps be easier to isolate and where the focus of conflict is clearly on systemic change.

The paradox in the application of Marxism is that mere systemic change will not be enough to guarantee racial justice without a major struggle against racism. But we do need systemic change.

If Lenin is correct in his view that Marxism is a flexible instrument meant to be applied according to the circumstances, then perhaps there might be some room for blending perspectives. For example, there is the question of culture, although since Marx said that it was *material* which determined *consciousness* this is difficult to take as a law of nature. It is especially true that when one considers the process of dialectics, there must be an interactive relationship between the two, neither eternally dominant but each having the ability to influence the other. Likewise the definition of the "concrete," if one implies by that materialism, is always elusive and misses the power which social symbols often exercise over matter. If these things were understood well, then the basis might be laid for the projection of African-American culture, rather than its subservience to a classless, raceless revolution.

In a way, our argument for the inclusion of blackness as a major dimension of the revolutionary movement is a foregone conclusion. For there has never been a revolutionary movement without a heavy nationalist content. What then is this new revolution to be made in the name of – American Nationalism? For those who have been alienated from the American system, it must be in the name of something else more immediately meaningful than that. This is why "Imperialism and Racism" has become the new slogan against which to fight. Yet, to repeat, the danger is that imperialism can vanish, systems may change, and racism may remain a constant. It has happened in the Soviet Union, in Cuba, and in the so-called socialist countries of Scandinavia. It is also why in the 1930s the Soviet theorist who directed the flirtation of the white left with the black community found it so hard to apply those programs coming from a consideration of the National Question. Those who support Marxism-Leninism talk as though, in considerations of the National Question, there is some blueprint for black liberation. There is not – only failure. The seeds of this failure are that the National Question was meant to apply to places where *classic* imperialism and *classic* colonialism exist, not a unique situation like that in the U.S. Our own understanding of this situation, then, must be substituted for the rhetoric of the National Question, which was geared mainly to the nations of eastern and western Europe.

We must welcome the emphasis on criticism if it does not mean that individuals and groups will be criticized on the basis of their Marxist deviationism. But there are reactionary actions which are just as patent to black nationalists as to Marxists and others, which include the acceptance of money from Gulf Oil by the Southern Christian Leadership Conference at a time when we were struggling to cause them to change colonial policies in southern Africa; or visiting South Africa as a guest of the Government, thereby being used to show the world that everything is alright; or becoming a mouthpiece for the oppressive policies of American corporations; or having a black man hug a white President to prove that some prominent blacks back him; or condoning the police "sweep" of black people on the streets of San Francisco in an effort to find the Zebra Killer; and others. Such acts are committed by blacks in all income, occupational, and value categories, and as such, because of the ambiguities of class, such criticism must be *classless.*

The Marxist tradition has also helped us to identify a very important source of black oppression – capitalism and imperialism. It is true that the problem of race analysis has difficulty because it does not immediately identify something concrete for those who want to struggle – it counsels universal vigilance. This is why the black nationalist movement degenerated into breast-beating sessions or turned the whole focus of its attention to Africa. But the systemic aspects of racial oppression can be overdone to the point where individuals will think that everything is a system of oppression when it is not. Even the economic system has less the earmarks of a System than it does of loose cooperation between several major types of economic activities which are not necessarily organically linked. If they were, much greater control over such things as inflation would be possible. As it is, no one claims to know what to do nor, by inference, do they know then exactly how the economic system works.

It is, therefore, clear that the challenge to the system of economy by the Marxist needs much greater sophistication because the terms both descriptive and analytical are crude and often have an 18th-century agrarian ring. This is the 20th century and a great deal has happened in the process of, if you will, "bourgeoisification" of economic activity; come the revolution, it will still be necessary to carry on a great part of that activity. For even though Marx wrote of a socialist international, and thereby could be presumed to have had strong international consciousness, the world has come closer today than it was then to being a genuine international community.

As a result, in the regulation of economic activity, problems that concern themselves with the balance of trade, international inflation, the terms of trade, the costs of international lending and borrowing, the existence of international cartels or commodity agreements, economic communities and special customs or tariff areas, laws of the sea and many, many other things will continue to exist and the bourgeois terms developed for handling them will be useful even if they are handled in different ways.

But the point is that these issues are very complex, and it does little good to think of or describe modern economic phenomena in terms of land, labor, and capital when many of the relationships which Marx assumed between them have eroded or have been transcended by the pace of technological transformation of this advanced post-industrial society. More competence in economic analysis could more successfully identify the contradictions in the system, thus exposing additional areas for struggle.

## THE MAINTAINANCE OF THE BLACK NATIONALIST TRADITION

We have suggested above that there are areas that have been important to black neo-marxists to explore because they have helped to provide interpretations and to pinpoint other areas for struggle against racism and imperialism. But this does not mean that the dominance of racism does not need the maintenance of a strong black nationalist tradition as its antithesis, just as the oppression of capitalism needs a strong anti-capitalist, anti-imperialist force to confront it.

Lerone Bennett, Jr., has given us an eloquent, "true to the bone" statement in his work "The Challenge of Blackness," which exhorts us to understand and be true to our history. Clearly implied in this work is the fact that if we do not understand the meaning of our history, we are doomed to repeat its mistakes. One of the most profound aspects of our history for which this writer has the greatest respect is that in times of adversity there were always groups and individuals who would keep their eye on the preservation of the race, who would stand up and be counted on behalf of its problems and its progresses. If you did this, you were known as a "race" man or woman, and if a group did this, it was called race conscious or, in the words of our new history, black nationalist. We should not bore you with a recitation of the names and organizations, you know them well by now. The question is, has America changed so much or will it change so much that this ethic is not now necessary? What has happened to make it so?

*What we need are the long distance runners of ideology.* Those who have understood the consistent basis of our historical dilemma with white power, who know our needs, and who help to consolidate the lessons of history, rather than shift from theory to theory based on an attractive hunch. Our history gives us the most scientific basis for predicting the behavior of white America and the nature of our response because of the many experiences which form the basis for such judgments. Marx himself said that the best theory was a reflection of praxis and that there was a dialectical relationship between the two. Would it not be a violation of even the Marxist thought to ignore the scientific basis of the development of black nationalism as a *permanent* ethic of the black community?

Why have we changed our scale of focus from the black community to the reformation of the nation and the world? Out of theory? There is no theory that would support the liberation of a nation by its poor, oppressed, powerless, and racial minority. Even if we are comfortable with the point of view that the problems of the black community are tied up to the systemic conditions of America represented by capitalism, this understanding does not change our role and our obligation to keep the scale of our own political activity "plugged-in" to the needs of our people both in the immediate and long-range sense. Clearly, a revolution in America is a long-range proposition and, as we have shown, the ultimate and major responsibility of whites.

This sudden shift in emphasis has all the earmarks of the most formal kind of intellectualism in the sense that even though the environment for ideological change has been ripe, it still requires an almost coldly calculated analysis to arrive at the direction of such change. In addition, it is conceivable that one of the elements that has forced a shift in ideology is the feeling that social progression to new stages requires a new ideology at each age to deal with social problems. This is a very sophisticated notion, almost bourgeois in its formulation because it fits so neatly into the Western notion of progress. Nothing in this new stage of history has changed so radically that we need to abandon the past, certainly nothing has convinced this writer that America is any closer, or any segment of America is more ready for revolution than in the past.

An American revolution, as we have said, will have to be made by American whites. Meanwhile, the black revolution must proceed even if it is viewed as reactionary by some. The black revolution is a change in the total relative position of black people within American society regardless of the form of government. Andrew Billingsley has been helpful in pointing out that one aspect of that change is a change in positions of leadership, but that symbolic reasons are not sufficient unless such positions can be translated into real instruments of power so that they produce changes in total relative position of the black group. We needn't argue over whether or not a change in position will mean a change in the condition of the black community; how can it be otherwise? The problem is that the relative position between blacks and whites in American society has worsened to the point where increasing numbers of young blacks are beginning to think that what is needed is a total revolution. We may all believe this but that does not mean that we live in an *objective* revolutionary situation which lends itself to black leadership and control. *Subjective* revolution is fantasy.

So, the black revolution must continue to wage a protracted struggle for the breakthroughs, recognizing the continuation of black-white conflict on the whole. Yet, because of its empirical situation, it must engage in temporary coalitions, using the resources of all who would help *better its cause,* but fundamentally organizing on our own. This is not narrow or chauvinist. The external aspect of chauvinism is racism, and few would advocate black racism as a part of black nationalism, because it is fundamentally a rationale for *internal* cohesion and organization. Nor is it narrow when it is all you can afford; the quest for black power would be a narrow-minded quest if blacks had the resources to acquire significant other power over society.

On the other hand, if we look at the examples of the Jews, the Chinese, and other ethnic minorities, it appears to be possible for everyone else but us to change positions within American society without the position of everyone else changing. We have assumed that because of racism the structural makeup of the system required that we remain at the bottom. Perhaps this is true, and perhaps it is not, particularly if we emphasize the elimination of racism. The question must be faced squarely of whether or not we would want to revolutionize an evil system if our material condition was radically altered upward within the system as it now stands. If our judgment is correct that the system is incapable of fulfilling the promises of justice, then it has given us no choice. Despite Oliver Cox's protestations, racism does not appear to be endemic to capitalism because there are more whites unemployed than blacks and since racism preceded the development of either capitalism or imperialism. There, thus, appears to be even stronger grounds for keeping the scale of the black revolution manageable within the framework of black interests.

Many people have been dismayed that the pace and style of the black revolution is not the same as it was in the late 1960s. Here, again, if we understand our history, we would know that the style of struggle changes but that does not mean that there are no gains possible in a given period because of changes in style. The style now has become one of political, economic, and educational preparation and pragmatic struggle and many young people have welcomed this change in the style of the movement because they sense a realization of the fruits of the past era of struggle.

In addition, it is important to develop this base of trained individuals because many of them will become the material for the continued development of black institutions. The black revolution has not deemphasized the development of black institutions, and much of the previous style of the movement has changed because so many people have begun to deal seriously with developing black institutions of all kinds. James Boggs gives us an added rationale for developing black institutions when he says that, "the more these institutions inside the black community become liberated from white control and reorganized to meet the needs of black people, the more they become bases for expanded struggle. . . ." Every revolution needs a base from which it can develop. We have learned from the struggles of the 1960s that a group of disparate organizations will be ineffective until they have a higher level of organization, for only then can they become institutionalized. Many have emerged from a period in which we thought that universities or black studies programs would provide a base, but they cannot because of their structural relationship to white power, though they can contribute to the base. This is why such institutions as the National Black Political Assembly are so important; they provide a unifying base as an instrument to institutionalize black politics on an independent level. No attempt should be made to turn it into one kind of organization or other because it is the embodiment of many kinds of political traditions in the black community.

The struggle to build institutions identifies our scale of struggle, and the attempt to revolutionize the entire American system may turn out to be a wasteful aberration, a mistake of black history. Again, one must admit perhaps to having identified the wrong struggle for the Marxists, it may be that they are not about black struggle. But there once was a time when it was felt that the essence of the black revolution was to bring about the fruition of black power – the power of blacks to decide who would govern the community, who would teach their children in it, who would build the houses, etc. These are still worthy objects of black self-determination, but the neo-Marxists seem now to be saying that black is not sufficient, that black people are exploiting each other just as much as whites are, that what becomes important is the ideological orientation, not the color.

On one level, it is possible to agree with this logic. For in this morning's paper there were two stories – one about a white man, challenged by the Maryland NAACP, who represented a private Democratic social club and was saying that he would work with Negroes but not dance with them; that if one asked a white woman to dance, there would be a riot, and so on. But on another page, there was the story of a young black woman who had been brutally murdered by four young blacks. So that we should be willing to accept the major premise – that black is not sufficient as a guide to the goodness or correctness of a person.

Nevertheless, the struggle for black power historically has given us some indication that race is more a salient basis for organized struggle than class. True, we have had our traitors in the slave revolts and our uncle toms after slavery, but we have always had at least a moral claim of blackness on each other which has acted as a sanction and a unifying force, largely responsible for whatever victories we have won. Thus, it is not only that ideological solidarity which springs from the same racial group is likely to be stronger, but it is likely to be stronger because the major premises of that ideology are rooted in the empirical condition of the people – there are certain truths that analysis cannot reveal to people about their own history; they just know what is right.

Thus the struggle for the development of black power to higher levels makes sense because we know that, *on the whole*, black policemen are more humane, that black teachers do care more for our children, that a black mayor will care more for black citizens, etc., and these are the dividends of struggle to lift the base of the entire community through its empowerment – politically, economically, culturally.

## CONCLUSION

As one looks at this series of questions raised about the place of Marxism-Leninism within black liberation, but more closely at the notion of the "cyclical" phenomena of ideological change and development, one should then expect that this ideological development will be short-lived. It will probably be replaced by another ideology in the cycle such as integrationism or black nationalism. Although we cannot work it out here with much precision, the ebb and flow of thought in the cycle seems to be based on that combination of forces in the society which gives the most or least hope to achievement of black goals in any one period of history. Given the nature of American society, therefore, one should not have to explain why neo-Marxist-Leninist ideology (which is at once neo-integrationist) will disappear when its allies have forsaken it. Our argument about the empirical nature of the black situation in the United States, then, means that we may not have to fear for the loss of either the black nationalist or Pan-Africanist ethic because they are part of that real reserve of energy which we use to refuel our challenges to racism and imperialism periodically.

Since we have not said much about Pan-Africanism, let this writer make the observation that a recent article by Lerone Bennett ("Pan Africanism at the Crossroads," *Ebony*, August 1974) incisively discusses the Sixth Pan-African Conference and shows how clearly the philosophy of Pan-Africanism is being either misunderstood or deliberately misinterpreted by some brothers and sisters on the Continent. For they have, according to Brother Bennett, castigated the theory of Pan-Africanism based on its tendencies toward what was called "racialism" and because of their feeling that a "back to Africa Movement" was unrealistic.

To begin with, this view shows how completely some of the delegates have been socialized into the acceptance of European ideas which may be as dysfunctional as those bourgeois ideas which they despise. Their opposition to Negritude is puzzling all the more in this regard, simply because Negritude only asserts the uniqueness and the commonalities of black people all over the world. Granted, there are problems to the theory (indeed to any theory) if taken too literally, but would they substitute in its place the fraudulent theory of racelessness as the basis for world civilizations? What gains do we make, why is it better, why should we substitute racelessness for the varieties of African culture? Negritude is racial but not racist (in the American usage of the word) because it does not raise the other fraud that black people or their civilization have been the best in the world. If anything, the record shows that perhaps we have been more tolerant of other peoples than many, but that does not amount to cultural superiority. Could it be that what people really object to is the heavy overtone of *French cultural expression* of the concept rather than the concept itself? In this sense, the real objection is political, not intellectual, and it is rooted in the politics between nations. And that is another matter.

It is also puzzling that some Africans refuse to recognize the racial roots of their oppression even though they may not be in daily contact with whites. This myopia is just as dangerous an illusion as that which fails to see the systemic features of oppression when whites are present in the daily scheme of oppression. Perhaps this is a clear perspective which one can only have outside of the Continent, where there is the opportunity to see daily those things that point to the disdain which many Europeans have for the African. Why else has the response to the drought in the Sahel been so slow and ineffective compared to those in India or Bangladesh? Why else have the Europeans been so close to the white minority regimes of southern Africa? Why has there been such a differential response by the British to violence against them in Africa and violence against them in Southern Ireland (where the Irish have not been brutally oppressed, and the English have allowed rebellion to go on for years, even reaching London itself!)? These are complex matters which could be extended considerably and there are other causes for them, yet the arrogance and dominance of European culture beg for a central place in the rationale of them all.

Secondly, there cannot be another "back to Africa movement" of any consequence because of the Americanization of the Africans here and the Nationalization of Africans on the Continent. So, that is not the basis for a modern formulation of the theory of Pan-Africanism. It is that in those places where the African world has extended itself considerably outside of the Continent, African communities are maturing and provide a permanent base of interaction with the motherland. This process of interaction has been historically recognized to rest on the assumption that there are a mutual set of needs which must be satisfied based upon a common recognition of the African experience in the world.

Outside the Continent, these needs will be for a people to dip periodically in the wellspring of their African identity, and at least the vision of Africa in the scheme of black liberation has been important as a motivation for community mobilization. This mobilization has brought a sense of togetherness and shared purpose to many without other viable objectives. But there is also a need on the continent for the recognition of a role of all African peoples in the future of the Continent and its development. Many of the progressive ideas which have found their germination on the Continent have and will come from the diaspora. This is why the concept of Pan-Africanism must embrace, but include, other levels than the OAU (the governmental expression of the concept), because as was demonstrated at the Sixth Pan-African Conference, there are many places in the African world where mutual interaction of African peoples will be beneficial outside of the framework of "official" affairs and governmental relations. It is not that the OAU is inherently evil, but that it does not accurately reflect a functional concept of Pan-Africanism.

Much of what has been said about Pan-Africanism can be related to Black Nationalism because it has been the impulse which has caused blacks in their communities in diaspora to stretch out their hand to Africa. The nationalist movement in the United States and all over the world has been the main repository of Pan-Africanism. It was indeed this movement which became dissatisfied with the simple glorification of Africa and began to arrive at pragmatic programs of action to support continental initiatives such as the liberation movements, Rhodesian sanctions, the behavior of multinational corporations and other programs. Black nationalism should be supported by brothers and sisters on the Continent, therefore, because it is the main force which keeps the consciousness of those outside the continent focused on Africa and its progress. *But whether or not it is supported on the Continent, the needs of the black communities outside it will not change because there are Africans outside of the continent, and that extension constitutes an umbilical cord which cannot be cut by theory. We too are an African people!* But our special location means that we must reject African continental chauvinism and incorrect political strategies for the view that we are equal Africans, and there must be mutual respect for the nature of our special struggles in the diaspora!

The other half of the attention of black nationalists is in the countries of their residence. And although it was not the purpose of this essay to expand the empirical determinants of the black condition into a full-blown concept or program of black nationalism, still it is seen to be necessary. Perhaps this has been too difficult before because the movement itself has been caught up in cultism and the many petty side-issues that have hampered it from "seeing the thing whole." But part of the task of beginning is to recognize that this generation did not create the race self-determination ethic, that it exists in various forms in the black community as it has throughout our existence in diaspora. This writer has consistently attempted to demystify the ethic (see, "African American Nationalism: A Unifying Ideology," *Black World,* Vol. 22, No. 12, October 1973) by showing that it has not so much to do with how you look, or where you live, or whether or not you can speak Swahili, or where you go to school, or what kind of job you have, but what you *think and do.* Is it that what you think and do are related to the development and preservation of the race, or yourself? This is the central question, and the problem is that there have been many answers defining how one should think and act, and the black neo-Marxist answer may be seen as another contribution to the many which exist.

In a way, we owe our brothers and sisters who are the black neo-marxists a great deal of credit because they have exposed much that is true about America and about our struggle. In particular they have exposed the lack of serious work on the development of a systematic black theory of politics. But some of our brothers and sisters in the movement are also lazy because, rather than engage in the hard work of developing indigenous theory, they have borrowed a ready-made alien set of conceptualizations to apply to our struggles. We will have a dialogue in the coming years, but it can only begin in earnest if we agree that the primary consideration is that our people's freedom is the only central issue, not the fulfillment of any grand ideology. If this be so, then let it begin again.[5]

## NOTES

[1] In fact these views are not those of blacks but have been taken from the ideology of Karl Marx and V.I. Lenin. For a reference to introductory material on these concepts, see Karl Marx and Friedrich Engels, *Selected Works*, 2 vols., Foreign Languages Publishing House, 1958, or Karl Marx and Friedrich Engels, *The German Sociology*, New York, 1947; T.B. Bottomore and M. Rubel, Eds., *Selected Writings in Sociology and Social Philosophy,* New York, 1964. Also, V.I. Lenin, *Imperialism – The Highest Stage of Capitalism,* International Publishers, 1969, and V.I. Lenin, *Selected Works,* International Publishers, New York, 1971.

[2] V.I. Lenin, *Imperialism the Highest Stage of Capitalism,* New York, International Publishers, 1969.

[3] Samir Amin, "The Class Struggle in Africa," Africa Research Group Reprint No. 2.

[4] *Black Enterprise Magazine,* June 1974, p. 28, 1973 data.

[5] One cannot help but be struck by the fact that ideological reoccurrence in the black community is indeed cyclical after reading *Voices of a Black Nation: Political Journalism in the Harlem Renaissance,* Theodore G. Vincent (Ed.), San Francisco, Ramparts Press, 1973. These pages are replete with the Marxist and anti-Marxist views of George Padmore, W.E.B. DuBois, Langston Hughes, Cyril Briggs, and others of the 1930s. We have indeed been here before and it is in a sense of tragedy that we are here again.

## REFERENCES


Allen, Robert L. *Black Awakening in Capitalist America.* New York: Doubleday-Anchor, 1969.

Amin, Samir. "Class Struggle in Africa," Cambridge, Mass.: Africa Research Group, 1970.

Bailey, Ronald. "Imperialism and Black People in the 1970's." Paper delivered at the National Conference of Black Political Scientists, 1974 Annual Meeting, Atlanta, Georgia, May 2-4, 1974.

Bell, Daniel. *The End of Ideology.* New York: Free Press-Macmillan, 1962.

Bennett, Lerone, Jr. *The Challenge of Blackness.* Chicago: Johnson Publishing, 1972.

Boggs, James. *Racism and the Class Struggle.* New York: Monthly Review Press, 1970.

Carmichael, Stokeley, and Hamilton Charles. *Black Power: The Politics of Liberation in America.* New York: Vintage Random House, 1967.

Cox, Oliver C. *Capitalism as a System.* New York: Monthly Review Press, 1964.

Hagopian, Mark. *The Phenomenon of Revolution.* New York: Dodd and Mead, 1974.

Lenin, V.I. *Imperialism – the Highest Stage of Capitalism.* New York: International Publishers, 1969.

Lenin, V.I. *Selected Works.* New York: International Publishers, 1971.

Parkin, Frank. *Class Inequality and Political Order.* New York: Praeger, 1971.

# Part V
# Views on Black Separatism from other Areas of the African Diaspora

This section gives examples of how other blacks in the African Diaspora view the black struggle in the United States. These views are important because in a world made finite by instant communications, what happens to groups in any part of the world is immediately known by others almost everywhere else. In recent years, there has emerged a more acute awareness of and identification with racial and ethnic kinspeople across national and international boundaries. This awareness may be seen historically in Zionism and also in the identification of American ethnics with their counterparts in Europe – Polish Clubs, German Bunds, Italian Leagues, etc.; presently the concepts of the Third World (or the "underdeveloped" nations) and the "developed world" are euphemisms for non-white and white peoples, respectively (except for the Japanese, Taiwanese, and a few other "colored" peoples who also comprise "developed" nations). The term "Afro-Asian Bloc" in the United Nations also denotes "Third World Peoples." A lack of ethnic or racial identification these days seems to be the exception rather than the rule. Therefore, examining how other blacks view black separatism in the United States can be instructive and potentially beneficial for all concerned.

African and black American views of each other, of course, are not new. These reciprocal views have, over time, ranged from negative stereotypes to exaggerated and overromantized myths. Part V begins with Helmreich's bibliographic exploration and evaluation of some "historical articles and books that have appeared on the subject [of the continental African and black American nationalist relationship] in recent years and which are of sufficiently high quality to be useful for . . . scholars and educators" and informed lay people. In a second chapter, he continues his bibliographic explorations and evaluations, covering anthropological and sociological works on African and black American relationships. These two chapters should provide an overview of the relationship between African and Afro-American communications over time.

In a broader context, Africa's importance in the present world context is significant in that she possesses a significant portion of the world's resources. Hence, as a potential international powerbroker, she will play an important role in world affairs and her opinion of the black condition in America and elsewhere must be respected – now or later.

Anise, a political scientist from Nigeria, one of the largest and richest countries in Africa, offers an exceptionally analytic and insightful assessment of black American liberation strategies. He points out that his intention "is not to challenge the general validity of the prevailing style of black [American] analysis, but to call for the abandonment of that style of analysis that is preoccupied with white-determined definitions of black alternatives and strategies."

Turning to some West Indian's views on the black American liberation struggle, it should be remembered that as early as the 1880s, Blyden (a native of the West Indies who settled in West Africa) urged "pure" black Americans to emigrate to Africa. Later in the 1920s, Marcus Garvey (a Jamaican) organized the largest mass movement among black Americans up to that time and made the Back-to-Africa idea part and parcel of his program. Forsythe discusses radicalism and separatism among W.A. Domingo, C.L.R. James, Marcus Garvey, and Claude McKay. Edmondson continues with a broad sociopolitical and historical comparative analysis of Black Power as it relates to transnational aspects of "the black situation in black America, Africa, and the Caribbean, which may condition the future prospects of Pan-Negro ideological initiation and diffusion." In the final chapter in this section, Forsythe (a sociologist) examines black separatism from a sociopsychological perspective, arguing that "separatism is . . . a necessary element for black survival and black advancement."

# 18
# *Africa and Black Nationalism in America: Review Essay**

WILLIAM B. HELMREICH

## INTRODUCTION

Probably no other period in American history can compare to that of the 1960s insofar as the development of black pride and identity is concerned. During these years, Afro-Americans became involved in a host of programs and activities ranging from revolutionary socialism and community control to black capitalism. Among the important developments during this era was a considerable increase of identification with Africa. This interest manifested itself in many areas including the spread of black studies programs emphasizing African history, politics, and culture, the adoption of African modes of dress, and visits to Africa by more and more black Americans.

One indication of the growing interest in this topic has been the tremendous increase, within the last decade or so, of books and articles, both scholarly and popular, that deal with the relationships of Afro-Americans in the United States to Africa. Unfortunately, the work in this area has not been systematically brought together and evaluated in a comprehensive and thorough manner. This essay constitutes a beginning effort at filling this gap by evaluating research done in the last decade or so on historical aspects of this relationship.* Its purpose, however, is not to offer a critique of the literature but rather to serve as a useful guide to interested scholars and educators by presenting the best material available in this area. Specifically, the period covered is from 1960 to 1973, a period that saw millions of black people actively engaged in a struggle to improve the quality of their lives in every possible way. Insofar as it served to enhance black pride, awareness, and identity, the increased interest in Africa that developed during these years must be seen as a direct and important result of that struggle.

*Interest in Africa has increased tremendously in the past ten or 15 years both in terms of scholarly research and in the popular press. This article, written especially for this book, evaluates historical articles and books that have appeared on the subject in recent years and that are of sufficiently high quality to be useful for both scholars and educators. Among the topics covered are works dealing with Liberia, Sierra Leone, Ethiopia, Edward Blyden, Marcus Garvey, W.E.B. DuBois, and Malcolm X. A complete bibliographical listing of work on this topic appears at the end of the essay.

## GENERAL WORKS

Although no book has yet been written that fully describes and assesses the history of the Afro-American's involvement with the African continent, a number of excellent articles summarizing such interest have appeared in recent years. Two of the best such articles have been written by E.P. Skinner and St. Clair Drake.[1] Both writers do a thorough job of tracing the history of the black community's involvement with Africa and are therefore excellent starting points for the reader interested in this topic.

Turning to edited works, a very good collection compiled by Martin Kilson and Adelaide Hill presents many important documents which graphically demonstrate the important role played by Africa over the years in the black community.[2] Included are selections from the works of Martin Delany, Alexander Crummell, Paul Robeson, Alain Locke, and many others. This is a comprehensive and well-balanced collection, although it could have benefited considerably from the inclusion of more selections reflecting the recent upsurge of interest in this subject. Another useful collection has been edited by John A. Davis, former Executive Director of the American Society for African Culture (AMSAC).[3] The first two portions of this reader deal with African society and culture, while the third section is devoted to an examination of attitudes toward Africa. Among the topics discussed are an evaluation of the role played by the NAACP in advancing knowledge about Africa,[4] an article by E. Franklin Frazier concerning the role that Afro-Americans can play in Africa,[5] and two interesting contributions on Liberia.[6] A third reader by Okon E. Uya, while it contains a few good selections, consists mostly of articles that are well-known and already widely published.[7]

## THE 19th CENTURY

When we think of migration to Africa, Liberia is often the first country that comes to mind. Interest in Sierra Leone, however, while not as great as that shown in Liberia, preceded the interest that developed in Liberia. Among those from the New World who migrated to Sierra Leone was a group of 1190 ex-slaves who had been freed by the British, had resettled in Nova Scotia, and who had eventually gone to Sierra Leone. Other emigrants to Sierra Leone came from the United States via England. These migrations are detailed in an authoritative history of Sierra Leone, written by Christopher Fyfe.[8] One American who left the United States in 1815 for Sierra Leone was the well-known black merchant, Paul Cuffe. One of the best biographies of this individual has been written by Sheldon H. Harris, whose book includes a record of Cuffe's diary and his letters.[9]

The emigrationist, Martin R. Delany was probably one of the most important black leaders of the 19th century. While the reader has much to choose from here, perhaps the two best (and most readable) works on this figure are the ones by Victor Ullman and Dorothy Sterling.[10] Those interested only in Delany's trip to the Niger Valley are directed to articles by A.H.M. Kirk-Greene and by Howard H. Bell.[11] Bell makes a number of interesting points in his evaluation of sentiment for emigration during the 1858-61 period, particularly in assessing the attitudes of Delany and Frederick Douglass. He argues that had it not been for the outbreak of the Civil War, Douglass would probably have become a strong supporter of emigration as a solution to the problems then facing black people in the United States.

Another articulate spokesman for black emigration was Bishop Alexander Crummell. Good overviews of Crummell's life and ideas may be found in an article by Katherine O. Wahle and in a Ph.D. dissertation by O.M. Scruggs.[12] It is unfortunate that relatively little attention seems to have been paid to this important 19th-century leader and his contributions to the development and awakening of black consciousness in America.

By way of contrast, a good deal of solid research is available on the life and work of Edward Wilmot Blyden. The best book-length work has been written by Hollis R. Lynch and is a valuable source of information for both the beginner and the scholar.[13] Another good book on Blyden has been done by Edith Holden although, as the author acknowledges, it is not so much an analysis of Blyden's life and work as it is a straightforward factual biography.[14] An intriguing article by Thomas H. Henriksen examines Blyden's writings in terms of how they influence blacks today.[15] In it Henriksen asserts that Blyden's ideas on "Pan-Negroism" were the basis for what later became Pan-Africanism (as Lynch has also noted) and that his ideas on black pride were actually the precursors of the "Black is beautiful" idea.

Yet another important leader of the 19th Century was Bishop Henry M. Turner. In a well-written and documented book, Edwin S. Redkey chronicles the life of Turner and the involvement of the American Colonization Society with emigration to Africa.[16] Redkey's thought-provoking work does an excellent job of covering the crucial period between 1890 and 1910, a period that witnessed the emergence of two of the most important leaders in the history of the Afro-American experience – Booker T. Washington and W.E.B. DuBois.

## THE 20th CENTURY

Probably the best introductions to interest in Africa during the 20th century have been written by St. Clair Drake and Robert G. Weisbord.[17] Drake discusses the concepts of Negritude, cultural and political Pan-Africanism, and the effects these movements have had and are likely to have upon Afro-Americans in the future. He seems to feel that Africa's significance for the Afro-American lies primarily in its ability to fulfill the psychological needs of black people in terms of developing pride in their history and culture. Drakes observes that while Africa will probably be hospitable to those few who come to Africa to settle, it is unlikely that Africa will actively solicit emigration from the United States. Considering that Drake's article first appeared in 1963, it was almost prophetic in predicting the current increase of interest in Africa and the attitudes that have come to be associated with such interest.

Weisbord's book contains an excellent discussion of interest in Africa from the beginning of the 20th century to the present. In addition, Weisbord presents in-depth analyses of pro-Ethiopian sentiment in the black community, the Garvey Movement, and a fascinating chapter describing the many, yet little-known Africanist groups that sprang up in the years following Garvey's demise. Weisbord also evaluates current interest in Africa and the attitudes of Africans toward such interest. Another useful introduction to the subject of expatriation in recent times may be found in an article by Leonard E. Collins, Jr., in which the author focuses on contemporary interest in Africa and the expectations of blacks who have recently gone there.[18]

One of the focal points in the black community's involvement with things African has been Ethiopia. In a highly readable, informative, and well-documented article, Weisbord presents a detailed account of this involvement, discussing not only the interest evinced in Ethiopia during its war with Italy, but also the important place occupied by Ethiopia in the Afro-American community *before* the 1930s.[19] Weisbord observes that this interest was due mainly to two factors – Ethiopia's long cultural tradition and its resistance to European colonization and domination.

Thoughts about black leaders who stressed ties with Africa often lead to Marcus Garvey and W.E.B. DuBois rather than to Booker T. Washington. Therefore, Louis R. Harlan's excellent article detailing Washington's involvement with Africa is most welcome and worthwhile.[20] In his essay, Harlan touches upon various aspects of this relationship including Washington's efforts to convince President Theodore Roosevelt to improve the conditions of black people living in the Congo, his attempts to prevent Liberia from being swallowed up by European colonialists, and the sending of Tuskegeeans to Togo as farmers in the beginning of the 20th century. Harlan asserts, however, that Washington's conservatism was reflected in his views on Africa and that, in principle at least, he supported colonialism by encouraging American investment in Africa.

One of the most important centers for black culture in America during the early part of the 20th century was, of course, Harlem, and a great deal has been written on that community.[21] These works all deal, to some extent, with interest in Africa as it was expressed by leaders and members of the Harlem community. Nathan I. Huggins, in particular, portrays the Harlem community in terms of its personality, including in this portrayal a discussion of how various Harlem Renaissance figures such as Alain Locke, Aaron Douglas, Countee Cullen, and Langston Hughes viewed the African continent.[22] In an article published in 1963, Richard B. Moore has also given us a vivid picture of the role played by Africa in the minds of Harlemites from the turn of the century to today's times.[23] In addition to discussing Garvey, DuBois, and Ethiopia, Moore also talks about the reaction in Harlem to the 1956 Arab-Israeli War and gives us a good description of the various Africa-oriented groups that have flourished in Harlem from the 1920s until today.

In response, perhaps, to the renewed interest in Marcus Garvey during the 1960s, a good deal of material has appeared recently on the life and activities of this pivotal and controversial leader. No less than three solid biographies and a number of excellent articles were published in this period. While some may question the seriousness of Garvey's intentions regarding African settlement, a careful reading of Amy Jacque Garvey's book leaves little doubt as to Garvey's contributions in giving publicity to Africa and in making black people prouder of their African heritage.[24] Theodore G. Vincent's account, in addition to its careful description of Garvey's life, contains an especially interesting section on the Universal Negro Improvement Association's influence on later nationalism.[25] Vincent talks about what happened to the Garveyites and the leaders of the U.N.I.A. after the Movement collapsed, what groups they joined, and how effective they were. Elton Fax' biography treats Garvey's life in the context of West Indian, particularly Jamaican, history.[26] Written in an interesting style, Fax draws heavily upon earlier works by Edmund David Cronon and others in interpreting various aspects of Garvey's life and career.[27] For those interested in a first-hand examination of Garvey's writings, the standard work is Amy Jacque Garvey's *Philosophy and Opinions of Marcus Garvey,* which was originally published in two separate volumes, the first appearing in 1923 and the second in 1925.[28] The second edition of this work, published in 1967, is prefaced by an excellent introduction summarizing Garvey's life, and written by E.U. Essien-Udom.

A well-documented article by M.B. Akpan presents a detailed discussion of Garvey's plan to settle Afro-Americans in Liberia with special emphasis upon the reasons for Liberia's negative response to his efforts.[29] In a thought-provoking article critical of Garvey, Wilson Moses asserts that Garvey merely capitalized on black pride, displayed an elitist view toward Africa, and was uninterested in "uncivilized areas" there except for the purpose of "redeeming" them.[30] In arguing that W.E.B. DuBois and Malcolm X were far more important for the development of black nationalism, Moses also suggests that the disillusionment that followed Garvey's conviction may have been responsible for the expansion of a generally negative attitude toward black nationalism that prevailed in the black community for a number of years after the Garvey era.

Turning to the crucial role W.E.B. DuBois played in promoting interest in Africa, we have an article written by Harold R. Issacs which argues that although DuBois was "a romantic racist," he never urged mass migration to Africa.[31] Rather, asserts Isaacs, he concentrated on promoting the freedom of Africa for *Africans.* The article is based on an interview conducted with DuBois. A number of articles have appeared in recent years assessing DuBois' involvement in Pan-Africanism.[32] These essays, most of which focus on his participation in the various Pan-African Congresses held between 1900 and 1945, leave no doubt as to the political and ideological importance of DuBois' activities in this area. William L. Hansberry has written a fine article evaluating DuBois' scholarly contributions to an understanding of Africa's past.[33] Hansberry's article is lucid and informative, particularly in his discussion of how he and other black scholars were influenced by DuBois' interest in this topic. In understanding why there is not a great deal of information on DuBois' views concerning the relationship between Afro-Americans and Africa, it must be taken into account that when DuBois died in 1963 the militant and nationalist phase of the Black Movement was not yet really underway. Moreover, although DuBois was an advocate of closer ties between black people in the United States and in Africa, this was only one of his many interests.

For a complete and accurate assessment of the role of Malcolm X in history, we will probably have to wait until the passage of time allows historians to place his contributions into a proper perspective. Nevertheless, it is already abundantly clear that Malcolm X played a central role in the development of black nationalism and pride during the 1960s and that his influence continues to be felt in the black community. Those interested in a general picture of his life are, of course, referred to the well-known *Autobiography of Malcolm X* and to the biography by Peter Goldman.[34] Although Malcolm X' own account presents a fascinating picture of his experience while in Africa, Goldman's book is also very useful because it gives us a sensitive and vivid portrayal of this great leader's ambivalences and doubts on the question of just how black people in the United States ought to develop their ties with their brothers throughout the world.

Finally, we have an excellent collection of interpretive essays, interviews, speeches, etc., concerning Malcolm X,[35] edited by John Henrik Clarke. Of particular interest for our topic are some of the speeches given by Malcolm X in which he talks about the importance of the African heritage, his attempts to forge a common black front, and his plans for the organization which he founded – the Organization of Afro-American Unity.[36]

As this essay and the bibliography that follows demonstrate, a good deal of research has been carried out in recent years on the historical aspects of the Afro-American's relationship to Africa. It is important that such research continue, not only because of its scholarly value, but because Africa is today an important factor in the self-perception of many members of the black community. Thus, developing a better understanding of the Afro-American's past concern with Africa has important ramifications for the present as well.

## NOTES

[1] E.P. Skinner, *African, Afro-American, White American: A Case of Pride and Prejudice*, New York, The Trustees of Columbia University, 1973, pamphlet; S.C. Drake, "Negro Americans and the Africa Interest," in J.P. Davis (Ed.), *The American Negro Reference Book*, Englewood Cliffs, Prentice-Hall, 1966, pp. 662-705.

[2] M. Kilson and A.C. Hill (Eds.), *Apropos of Africa,* New York, Anchor, 1971.

[3] J.A. Davis (Eds.), *Africa Seen by American Negro*

*Scholars,* New York, American Society of African Culture, 1963.

[4] J.W. Ivy, "Traditional NAACP Interest in Africa (as reflected in the pages of *The Crisis*)," in Davis, pp. 229-246.

[5] E.F. Frazier, "Potential American Negro Contributions to African Social Development," in Davis, pp. 263-278.

[6] W.E.B. DuBois, "Liberia, the League and the United States," in J.A. Davis, *Ibid.,* pp. 329-344, J.W. Davis, "Liberia, Past and Present" in *Op. cit.* pp. 344-359.

[7] O.E. Uya (Ed.), *Black Brotherhood: Afro-Americans and Africa,* Lexington, Mass.: D.C. Heath, 1971.

[8] C. Fyfe, *A History of Sierra Leone,* London, Oxford University Press, 1962.

[9] S.H. Harris, *Paul Cuffe: Black America and the African Return,* New York, Simon and Schuster, 1972.

[10] V. Ullman, *Martin R. Delany: The Beginnings of Black Nationalism,* Boston, Beacon Press, 1971; D. Sterling, *The Making of an Afro-American: Martin Robison Delany, 1812-1885,* New York, Doubleday, 1971.

[11] A.H.M. Kirk-Green, "America in the Niger Valley: A Colonization Centenary," *Phylon,* 23, Fall 1962, 225-239; H.H. Bell, "Negro Nationalism: A Factor in Emigration Projects 1858-1861," *J. of Negro Hist.* 47, January 1962, 42-53.

[12] K.O. Wahle, "Alexander Crummell: Black Evangelist and Pan-Negro Patriot," *Phylon* 24 (4), 1968, 388-395; O.M. Scruggs, *We the Children of Africa in this Land: Alexander Crummell,* Washington, D.C., Howard University, 1972; Ph.D. dissertation.

[13] H.R. Lynch, *Edward Wilmot Blyden: Pan-Negro Patriot, 1832-1912,* New York, Oxford University Press, 1967.

[14] E. Holden, *Blyden of Liberia: An Account of the Life and Labor of Edward Wilmot Blyden, L.L.D., as Recorded in Letters and in Print,* New York, Vantage Press, 1966.

[15] T.H. Henriksen, "Edward W. Blyden: His Influence on Contemporary Afro-Americans," *Pan-African Journal,* 4, Summer 1971, 255-265.

[16] E. Redkey, *Black Exodus: Black Nationalism and Back to Africa Movements 1890-1910,* New Haven, Yale University Press, 1969.

[17] S.C. Drake, " 'Hide my Face?' On Pan-Africanism and Negritude," in H. Hill (Ed.), *Soon One Morning* New York, Knopf, 1963, pp. 78-105; R.G. Weisbord, *Ebony Kinship: Africa, Africans, and the Afro-American,* Westport, Conn.; Greenwood Press, 1973.

[18] L.E. Collins, Jr., "The Afro-American Return to Africa in the Twentieth Century – Illusion and Reality," *Afro-American Stud.* 3 (2), 1972, 103-109.

[19] R.G. Weisbord, "Black America and the Italian-Ethiopian Crisis: An Episode in Pan-Negroism," *The Historian,* 34 (2), 1972, 230-241.

[20] L.B. Harlan, "Booker T. Washington and the White Man's Burden," *Am. Hist. Rev.,* 71, January 1966, 441-467.

[21] See J.W. Johnson, *Black Manhattan,* New York, Atheneum, 1930; C. McKay, *Harlem: Negro Metropolis,* New York, Dutton, 1940; G. Osofsky, *Harlem: The Making of a Ghetto,* New York, Harper & Row, 1963; S.M. Scheiner, *Negro Mecca: A History of the Negro in New York City, 1865-1920,* New York, New York University Press, 1965; N.I. Huggins, *Harlem Renaissance,* New York, Oxford University Press, 1971.

[22] Huggins, pp. 79-81, 137-189.

[23] R.B. Moore, "Africa Conscious Harlem," *Freedomways,* 3, Summer (1963, 315-334.

[24] A.J. Garvey, *Garvey and Garveyism,* Kingston, Jamaica, 1963.

[25] T.G. Vincent, *Black Power and the Garvey Movement,* Berkeley, Ramparts Press, 1970.

[26] E. Fax, *Garvey: The Story of a Pioneer Black Nationalist,* New York, Dodd, Mead, 1972.

[27] E.D. Cronon, *Black Moses: The Story of Marcus Garvey and the Universal Negro Improvement Association,* Madison, Univ. of Wisconsin Press, 1955.

[28] A.J. Garvey, *The Philosophy and Opinions of Marcus Garvey,* London, 1967, Frank Cass, 2 Volumes.

[29] M.B. Akpan, "Liberia and the Universal Negro Improvement Association: The Background to the Abortion of Garvey's Scheme for African Colonization," *J. of African Hist.* 14 (1), 1973, 105-127.

[30] W. Moses, "Marcus Garvey: A Reappraisal," *Black Scholar* 4, November-December 1972, 38-49.

[31] H.R. Isaacs, "DuBois and Africa," *Race,* 2, November 1960.

[32] See B. Fonlon, "The Passing of a Great African," *Freedomways,* 5, Winter 1965, 195-206; R.B. Moore, "DuBois and Pan Africa," *Freedomways,* 5, Winter 1965, 166-187; D. Walden and K. Wylie, "W.E.B. DuBois: Pan-Africanism's Intellectual Father," *J. of Human Rel.,* 14 (1), 1966, 28-41; C.G. Contee, "The Emergence of DuBois as an African Nationalist," *J. of Negro Hist.,* 54, January 1969, 48-63.

[33] W.L. Hansberry, "W.E.B. DuBois' Influence on African History," *Freedomways,* 5, Winter 1965, 73-87.

[34] Malcolm X (with the assistance of A. Haley), *The Autobiography of Malcolm X,* New York, Grove Press, 1965; P. Goldman, *The Death and Life of Malcolm X,* New York, Harper & Row, 1973.

[35] J.H. Clarke (Ed.), *Malcolm X: The Man and his Times,* New York, Collier, 1969.

[36] *Ibid.,* pp. 321-332, 388-301, 335-342.

## BIBLIOGRAPHY OF WORKS ON AFRO-AMERICANS AND AFRICA

### General Works

Akiwowo, A. "Racialism and Shifts in the Mental Orientation of Black People in West Africa and in the Americas, 1856 to 1956." *Phylon,* 31, Fall 1970, 256-264.

Bell, H.H. "Negro Nationalism: A Factor in Emigration Projects 1858-1861," *J. of Negro Hist.,* 47, January 1962, 42-53.

Bracey, J., A. Meier, and E. Rudwick (Eds.) *Black Nationalism in America,* Indianapolis, Bobbs-Merrill, 1970, esp. pp. 38-48, 77-86, 114-120, 156-210.

Davis, J.A. (Ed.) *Africa Seen by American Negro Scholars,* New York, American Society of African Culture, 1963.

Drake, S.C. "Negro Americans and the Africa Interest," in J.P. Davis (Ed.), *The American Negro Reference Book* Englewood Cliffs, N.J., Prentice-Hall, 1966, pp. 662-705.

Draper, T. *The Rediscovery of Black Nationalism.* New York, Viking, 1969.

James, C.L.R. *A History of Pan-African Revolt.* Washington, D.C., Drum and Spear Press, 1969, 2nd ed. rev.

Kilson, M., and Hill, A.C. (Eds.) *Apropos of Africa: Afro-American Leaders and the Romance of Africa.* New York, Anchor, 1971.

Shepperson, G. "Notes on Negro American Influences on the Emergence of African Nationalism." *J. of African Hist.*, 1 (2), 1960, 299-312.

Shepperson, G. "Pan-Africanism: Some Historical Notes." *Phylon*, 23, Winter 1962, 346-358.

Shepperson, G. "The African Diaspora – Or the African Abroad," *African Forum*, 2 (1), 1966, 76-93.

Skinner, E.P. *Afro-Americans and Africa: The Continuing Dialectic.* New York, The Trustees of Columbia University, 1973, Pamphlet.

Stuckey, S. *The Ideological Origins of Black Nationalism.* Beacon Press, Boston, 1972.

Uya, O.E. (Ed.) *Black Brotherhood: Afro-Americans and Africa.* Lexington, Mass., D.C. Heath, 1971.

**Slavery**

Blassingame, J.W. *The Slave Community: Plantation Life in the Ante-Bellum South.* New York, Oxford Univ. Press, pp. 1-40.

Genovese, E.D. "The Negro Laborer in Africa and in the Slave South," *Phylon*, 21, Winter 1960, 343-350.

Levine, L. "Slave Songs and Slave Consciousness: An Exploration in Neglected Sources," pp. 99-126, in T.K. Hareven (Ed.). *Anonymous Americans: Explorations in Nineteenth Century Social History.* Englewood Cliffs, Prentice-Hall, 1971.

Rawick, G.P. *The American Slave: A Composite Autobiography.* Vol. 1; *From Sundown to Sunup: The Making of the Black Community.* Westport, Conn., Greenwood, 1972.

Reed, H.A. "Slavery in Ashanti and Colonial South Carolina," *Black World*, 20, February 1971, 37.

Stuckey, S. "Through the Prism of Folklore: The Black Ethos of Slavery," pp. 172-191, in J. Chametzky and S. Kaplan (Eds.), *Black and White in American Culture: An Anthology From the Massachusetts Review.* Amherst, Univ. of Mass., 1969.

Stuckey, S. "Slave Resistance as Seen Through Slave Folklore," pp. 51-60, in I.S. Reid (Ed.), *Black Prism: Perspectives on the Black Experience.* New York, Faculty Press, 1969.

**Religion**

Coan, J.R. *The Expansions of Missions of the A.M.E. Church in South Africa, 1896-1908.* Hartford, Hartford Seminary, 1961, Ph.D. Dissertation.

Drake, S.C. *The Redemption of Africa and Black Religion.* Chicago, Third World Press, 1970.

Epps, A. "A Negro Separatist Movement of the Nineteenth Century." *Harvard Rev.* 4, Summer 1969, 69-87.

**American Colonization Society**

Redkey, E.S. *Black Exodus: Black Nationalism and Back to Africa Movements 1890-1910.* New Haven, Yale University Press, 1969.

Staudenraus, P.J. *The African Colonization Movement, 1816-1865.* New York, Columbia University Press, 1961.

**Negro Convention Movement**

Bell, H.H. (Ed.) *Minutes of the Proceedings of the National Negro Conventions 1830-1864.* New York, Arno Press, 1969.

Pease, W.H., and Pease, J.H. "The Negro Convention Movement," in N.I. Huggins, M. Kilson, and D.M. Fox (Eds.), *Key Issues in the Afro-American Experience,* (Vol. 1), New York, Harcourt, Brace, Jovanovich, 1971, pp. 191-205.

**Liberia and Sierra Leone**

Akpan, M.B. *The African Policy of the Liberian Settlers 1841-1932:* A Study of the Native Policy of a Non-Colonial Power in Africa. Ibadan, Nigeria, Univ. of Ibadan, 1968, Ph.D. Dissertation.

Akpan, M.B. "Liberia and the Universal Negro Improvement Association: The Background to the Abortion of Garvey's Scheme for African Colonization." *Jour. of African Hist.*, 14 (1), 1973, 105-127.

Balfit, S. "American-Liberian Relations in the Nineteenth Century." *J. of Human Rel.*, 10, Summer 1962, 405-418.

Chalk, F. "DuBois and Garvey Confront Liberia: Two Incidents of the Coolidge Years." *Can. J. of African Stud.* 1 (2), 1967, 135-141.

Fyfe, C. *A History of Sierra Leone.* London, Oxford Univ. Press, 1962.

Hargreaves, J.D. "African Colonization in the Nineteenth Century – Liberia and Sierra Leone," pp. 55-76, in J. Butler (Ed.), *Boston University Papers in African History,* Vol. 1. Boston, Boston University Press, 1964.

Harris, S.H. "An American's Impressions of Sierra Leone in 1811," *J. of Negro Hist.*, 47, January 1962, 35-41.

Harris, S.H. *Paul Cuffe: Black America and the African Return.* New York, Simon and Schuster, 1972.

Jones, H.A.B. *"The Struggle for Political and Cultural Unification in Liberia, 1847-1930,"* Evanston, Ill., Northwestern Univ., 1962, Ph.D. Dissertation.

West, R. *Back to Africa: A History of Sierra Leone and Liberia.* London, 1970.

**Martin R. Delany**

Bell, H.H. "Introduction," in M.R. Delany and R. Campbell, *Search For a Place: Black Separatism and Africa, 1860.* Ann Arbor, Univ. of Mich. Press, 1969, 1-22.

Kirk-Greene, A.H.M. "America in the Niger Valley: A Colonization Centenary." *Phylon*, 23, Fall 1962, 225-239.

Sterling, D. *The Making of an Afro-American: Martin Robison Delany, 1812-1885.* New York, Doubleday, 1971.

Ullman, V. *Martin R. Delany: The Beginnings of Black Nationalism.* Boston, Beacon Press, 1971.

**Alexander Crummell**

Scruggs, O.M. *We the Children of Africa in this Land: Alexander Crummell.* Washington, D.C., Howard Univ., 1972, Ph.D. Dissertation.

Wahle, K.O. "Alexander Crummell: Black Evangelist and Pan-Negro Patriot," *Phylon*, 29 (4), 1968, 388-395.

**Edward Wilmot Blyden**

Billingsley, A. "Edward Blyden: Apostle of Darkness." *Black Scholar*, 2, December 1970, 3-12.

Henriksen, T.H. "Edward W. Blyden: His Influence on Contemporary Afro-Americans." *Pan-African, J.*, 4, Summer 1971, 255-265.

Holden, E. *Blyden of Liberia: An Account of the Life and Labor of Edward Wilmot Blyden, L.L.D., as Recorded in Letters and in Print.* New York, Vantage Press, 1966.

Jones, W.D. "Blyden, Gladstone, and the War." *J. of Negro Hist.*, 49, January 1964, 56-61.

Lynch, H.R. "Edward Wilmot Blyden: Pioneer West African Nationalist." *J. of African Hist.*, 6 (3), 1965, 373-388.

Lynch, H.R. *Edward Wilmot Blyden: Pan-Negro Patriot, 1832-1912.* New York, Oxford Univ. Press, 1967.

**Henry M. Turner**

Redkey, E.S. "Bishop Turner's African Dream." *J. of American Hist.*, 54 (2), 1967, 271-290.

Redkey, E.S. *Black Exodus: Black Nationalist and Back to Africa Movements, 1890-1910.* New Haven, Yale University Press, 1969.

Redkey, E.S. "The Flowering of Black Nationalism: Henry McNeal Turner and Marcus Garvey," in N.I. Huggins, M. Kilson, and D. Fox (Eds.), *Key Issues in the Afro-American Experience* (Vol. 2). New York, Harcourt, Brace, Jovanovich, 1971, 107-124.

**Booker T. Washington**

Harlan, L.R. "Booker T. Washington and the White Man's Burden." *Amer. Hist. Rev.*, 71, January 1966, 441-467.

Mabata, J.C. "Booker T. Washington and John Tengo Jabavu: A Comparison." *Afro-American Stud.*, 2 (3), 1971, 181-186.

**Alfred Charles Sam**

Bittle, W.E., and Geis, G.L. "Alfred Charles Sam and an African Return: A Case Study in Negro Despair." *Phylon*, 23, June 1962, 178-194.

Bittle, W.E., and Geis, G.L. *The Longest Way Home.* Detroit, Wayne State Univ. Press, 1964.

**Ethiopia**

Contee, C.G. "Ethiopia and the Pan-African Movement Before 1945." *Black World*, 21, February 1972, 41.

Ross, R. "Black Americans and Italo-Ethiopian Relief." *Ethiopian Observer*, 15 (2), 1972, 122-131.

Weisbord, R.G. "Black America and the Italian Ethiopian Crisis: An Episode in Pan-Negroism." *The Historian*, 34 (2), 1972, 230-241.

**W.E.B. DuBois**

Aptheker, H. "DuBois on Africa and World Peace: An Unpublished Essay." *Political Affairs*, 47, February 1968, 81-89.

Blair, T.L. "DuBois and the Century of African Liberation," pp. 8-14, in A. Berrian and R. Long (Eds.), *Negritude: Essays and Studies.* Hampton, Va. Hampton Institute Press, 1967.

Chalk, F. "DuBois and Garvey Confront Liberia: Two Incidents of the Coolidge Years." *Can. J. of African Stud.*, 1 (2), 1967, 135-141.

Clark, J.H., E. Jackson, E. Kaiser, and J.H. O'Dell (Eds.) *Black Titan: W.E.B. DuBois.* Boston, Beacon Press, 1970.

Contee, C.G. "The Emergence of DuBois as an African Nationalist." *J. of Negro Hist.*, 54, January 1969, 48-63.

DuBois, S.G. *His Day is Marching On.* Philadelphia, Lippincott, 1971, esp. pp. 298-378.

DuBois, W.E.B. "Ghana Calls." *Freedomways*, 2, Winter 1962, 71-74.

Fonlon, B. "The Passing of a Great African." *Freedomways*, 5, Winter 1965, 195-206.

Hansberry, W.L. "W.E.B. DuBois' Influence on African History." *Freedomways*, 5, Winter 1965, 73-87.

Isaacs, H.R. "DuBois and Africa." *Race*, 2, November 1960, 3-23.

Lacy, L.A. *The Life of W.E.B. DuBois: Cheer the Lonesome Traveler.* New York, Dial Press, 1970.

Moore, R.B. "DuBois and Pan-Africa." *Freedomways*, 5, Winter 1965, 166-187.

Paschal, A.G. "The Spirit of W.E.B. DuBois," (Part I). *Black Scholar*, 2, October 1970, 17-28.

Paschal, A.G. "The Spirit of W.E.B. DuBois," (Part II). *Black Scholar*, 2, February 1971, 38-50.

Walden, D., and Wylie, K. "W.E.B. DuBois: Pan Africanism's Intellectual Father." *J. of Human Rel.*, 14 (1), 1966, 28-41.

**Marcus Garvey**

Akpan, M.B. "Liberia and the Universal Negro Improvement Association: The Background to the Abortion of Garvey's Scheme for African Colonization." *J. of African Hist.*, 14 (1), 1973, 105-127.

Bennett, L. "The Ghost of Marcus Garvey." *Ebony*, 15, March 1961, 53-61.

Chalk, F. "DuBois and Garvey Confront Liberia: Two Incidents of the Coolidge Years," *Can. J. of African Stud.*, 1 (2), 1967, 135-141.

Edwards, A. *Marcus Garvey, 1887-1940.* London and Port-of-Spain, Beacon Publications, 1967.

Elkins, W.F. "The Influence of Marcus Garvey on Africa: A British Report of 1922." *Science and Society*, 32, Summer 1968, 321-323.

Essien-Udom, E.U. "Introduction," in *Philosophy and Opinions of Marcus Garvey.* London, Frank Cass, 1967, 2nd ed., 2 Vol.

Fax, E. *Garvey: The Story of a Pioneer Black Nationalist.* New York, Dodd, Mead, 1972.

Garvey, A.J. *Garvey and Garveyism.* Kingston, Jamaica, 1963.

Garvey, A.J. *The Philosophy and Opinions of Marcus Garvey.* London, Frank Cass, 1967, 2nd ed., 2 Vol.

Garvey, A.J. "Marcus Mosiah Garvey." *Negro Digest*, 18, May 1969, 42.

Garvey, A.J. "Garvey and Pan-Africanism: A Wife's Footnote to Black History." *Black World*, 21, December 1971, 15-18.

Hart, R. "The Life and Resurrection of Marcus Garvey." *Race*, 9 (2), 1967, 217-237.

Langley, J.A. "Marcus Garvey and African Nationalism." *Race*, 10 (2), 1969, 157-172.

Moses, W. "Marcus Garvey: A Reappraisal." *Black Scholar*, 4, November-December 1972, 38-49.

Redkey, E.S. "The Flowering of Black Nationalism: Henry McNeal Turner and Marcus Garvey," in N.I. Huggins, M. Kilson, and D.M. Fox (Eds.), *Key Issues in the Afro-American Experience.* New York, Harcourt, Brace, Jovano-

vich, 1971, Vol. 2, 107-124.
Sundiata, T. "A Portrait of Marcus Garvey." *Black Scholar,* 2, September 1970, 7-19.
Vincent, T.G. *Black Power and the Garvey Movement,* Berkeley, Ramparts Press, 1970.

**Malcolm X**
Clarke, J.H. (Ed.) *Malcolm X: The Man and his Times.* New York, Collier, 1969.
Epps, A. "The Theme of Exile in Malcolm X' Harvard Speeches." *The Harvard J. of Negro Affairs,* 2 (1), 1968, 40-54.
Goldman, P. *The Death and Life of Malcolm X.* New York, Harper & Row, 1973.
X, Malcolm (with the assistance of A. Haley). *The Autobiography of Malcolm X.* New York, Grove Press, 1965, esp. pp. 343-363.

**Miscellaneous**
Hooker, J.R. "The Negro American Press and Africa in the Nineteen Thirties." *Can. J. of African Stud.,* 1, March 1967, 43-50.
King, K.J. "Africa and the Southern States of the U.S.A.: Notes on J.H. Oldham and American Negro Education for Africans." *J. of African Hist.,* 10 (4), 1969, 659-677.
Shaloff, S. "William Henry Sheppard: Congo Pioneer." *African Forum,* 3 (4), 1968, 51-62.
Stuckey, S. "The Cultural Philosophy of Paul Robeson." *Freedomways,* 11 (1), 1971, 78-90.

# 19

# *Afro-Americans and Africa: Anthropological and Sociological Investigations* *

WILLIAM B. HELMREICH

## INTRODUCTION

There has been a tradition of continued interest in Africa within the black community dating from the time that African captives were first brought to the shores of what is today known as the United States. While such interest has always been present, it has, however, ebbed and flowed in accordance with the changing fortunes of the black community.

One of the earliest advocates of emigration to Africa was Paul Cuffe, a black shipowner from Massachusetts who sailed for Sierra Leone in 1815 with 38 other Afro-Americans. While it is not clear what proportion of the black population supported such efforts at the time, it is clear that Cuffe was not alone in his beliefs. The names of the earliest churches, such as the African Methodist Episcopal and the Abyssinian Baptist churches, bear testimony that Africa had not been forgotten by the black community. Moreover, as a number of writers (Blassingame, 1972; Rawick, 1972; Stuckey, 1969); have shown, a great deal of African culture was retained by many of the slaves who worked on the plantations.

By the 1850s, a good number of black leaders had begun voicing their support of emigration as a solution to the injustices faced by many Afro-Americans in this country. Among the most famous advocates of this position were Martin R. Delany and Alexander Crummell. Delany was a physician who had visited Liberia and Nigeria and who was active in various colonization efforts until the outbreak of the Civil War. Bishop Crummell was probably the most important figure among black missionaries who were involved with Africa. What eventually became known as W.E.B. DuBois' theory of the "talented tenth" was actually first developed by Crummell who argued that the educated black elite in this country had a special obligation to help uplift the race.

Although interest in Africa waned somewhat following the end of the Civil War, it enjoyed a revival in the 1880s, in large part because of the activities of Bishop Henry M. Turner. It was the force of Turner's personality and his abilities as an orator that were perhaps most responsible for keeping the spirit of black nationalism alive during the late 19th and early 20th centuries. But perhaps the greatest leader in terms of forging ties between Afro-Americans and Africa was W.E.B. DuBois, who sponsored and participated in numerous conferences on Pan-Africanism (the first was held in London in 1900) and who made countless scholarly contributions toward a better understanding of Africa's past and present. Although DuBois did not advocate a return to Africa, he was committed to the belief that a powerful Africa would be of inestimable value to black people throughout the entire world.

Booker T. Washington is perhaps more often thought of as an accommodationist than as a nationalist. Yet he too played an important part in focusing the attention of the black community on Africa. In addition to sending students from Tuskegee Institute to work in various parts of Africa, Washington also tried to influence Theodore Roosevelt to improve the conditions of blacks in the Congo. At the same time, as the historian Louis Harlan (1966) has pointed out, Washington's conservatism extended to his attitudes on Africa as well and that, in principle at least, he supported colonialism there.

A list of important figures in the black community who nurtured and developed interest in Africa could easily fill several pages – names such as Carter G. Woodson, Rayford Logan, Countee Cullen, James Weldon Johnson, etc., but in terms of appeal to the black masses of America Marcus Mosiah Garvey had no equal. Through his organization, the Universal Negro Improvement Association, Garvey was able to fire the imagination of black people throughout the United States and imbue them with pride in and awareness of their historical origins. Despite Garvey's lack of success in his efforts to establish a colony in Liberia, there is little doubt concerning Garvey's contribution in drawing attention to Africa and the relationship of Afro-Americans to it.

Identification with Africa continued to be expressed by the black community in a variety of ways in the years following Garvey's demise. In 1935 the black community rallied to the support of Ethiopia during the Italian-Ethiopian War. Mass rallies were held, money was raised, and volunteers were recruited. In 1945 the Fifth Pan-African Congress was held in Manchester, England. Although DuBois was instrumental in organizing the meeting, its leadership was, for the first time primarily made up of Africans, many of whom were to see the initial realization of their goals some 12 years later when Ghana became an independent state.

*Written especially for this book.

While the 1950s were perhaps characterized, on the whole, by integrationist sentiment, the 1960s saw a considerable increase of identification with Africa on the part of many Afro-Americans. This interest manifested itself in many areas ranging from the spread of black studies programs that included courses on Africa and the formation of many organizations that focused on Africa, to the adoption of African modes of dress and the popularity of "Afro" haircuts. As the discussion until now has shown, such interest had been a recurring theme throughout the history of the black community in America although, perhaps, never before on such a wide scale.

One indication of the interest in this field has been the tremendous increase in the last decade or so of books and articles, both scholarly and popular, that deal with the relationships of Afro-Americans to the African continent. For example, from 1950 to 1960 the *New York Times* carried less than 15 articles on this topic while the period 1960-1972 saw the appearance of over 70 articles on the same subject. While most of these articles were more journalistic than scholarly, the same trend was present in academic journals where hundreds of articles in a wide range of disciplines were published. This essay will discuss some of the mory important books and articles that appeared in recent years on the subject of Afro-Americans and Africa. The period covered will be from 1960 to 1972, a period which saw millions of black people in this country actively engaged in a struggle to improve the quality of their lives in every possible way. In addition a bibliography of the relevant literature in this area, including works not touched upon in the essay, appears at the end of the chapter.

## GENERAL WORKS

*The Myth of the Negro Past* (1958) by Melville J. Herskovits is perhaps the classic work in the field of cultural relationships between Afro-Americans and Africa. Originally published in 1941 (the 1958 edition contains a new preface by the author), this book is basic reading for anyone seeking an understanding of the subject, hence its inclusion here despite its pre-1960 publication date. Generally speaking, the book is a provocative, fascinating, and wide-ranging discussion of African survivals among black people in the New World. While many of Herskovitz' assertions concerning retentions of Africanisms have been criticized as being somewhat speculative, the work succeeds admirably in refuting the then popularly held notion that African people had lost their culture upon their arrival in the New World or had never possessed a culture of their own. In a later article (1960) Herskovits replies sharply to his critics, saying that it is ridiculous to demand evidence of a perfect retention of an African behavior pattern before accepting a New World cultural practice or characteristic as being African in origin.

Another important work is *Mintu: The New African Culture* (1961) by Jahnheinz Jahn who makes a number of interesting observations on the subject, especially in his chapter on blues music. While Jahn identifies a number of similarities between the autobiographical writings of Afro-Americans and that in African music the singing accompanies the drums, whereas in Afro-American blues the opposite holds true: the singer leads and the instruments accompany (p. 221). Jahn also observes that Afro-American novels such as Ellison's *Invisible Man* (1947), Wright's *Native Son* (1940), and Baldwin's *Go Tell it on the Mountain* (1963) are not at all similar to African novels since they deal primarily with the problems of split personalities and inferiority complexes that are particularly relevant to the black experience in America. If Jahn's point was valid ten or 15 years ago, it is certainly no longer true today for we can see parallels and similarities in many areas. For example, black South African writers such as Peter Abrahams and Ezekiel Mphalele have written about the same problems of discrimination that Afro-Americans were discussing in the 1960s. Works by Africans dealing with Negritude find their equivalent in Afro-American analyses of Soul and its implications. One observer has drawn some interesting comparisons between the autobiographical writings of Afro-Americans and Africans (Bruchac, 1971), and there is an excellent book that deals exclusively with Afro-American and African writings in a broad range of areas (Cook and Henderson, 1969). On the whole, however, Jahnheinz Jahn's book is a valuable contribution toward an understanding of both African and Afro-American culture.

Roger Bastide's *African Civilizations in the New World* (1971), which originally appeared in French, is a third important work concerning African culture in the New World. In his discussion of religion, Bastide makes a number of incisive points with regard to the United States. Although many patterns of behavior are unique to black Americans, the author asserts that they are often affected by a mentality that still retains African ways of thinking – i.e., a desire for group association. While Afro-Americans have borrowed from American revivalism (which originated in Scotland) in their religious behavior, there are some important differences between the two that may be a result of the African heritage. Some examples given by Bastide are: White revivalist groups nave onlookers as well as performers, while black groups consist exclusively of performers; among whites the movements are rather disorganized and jerky as opposed to the more rhythmic and coordinated movements of the black groups. At the same time, Bastide notes that both the white revivalists and the black groups have influenced each other. The book also contains an interesting and useful discussion of African folklore and the reasons for its survival in the United States. In this discussion Bastide is careful to distinguish black folklore and that which was created by whites for the purpose of making conversion to Christianity easier (pp. 179-84). Other topics covered by the author include the varying interpretations of Negritude here and in Africa, Africanisms in the Father Divine cult, and some general problems facing Afro-Americans in their attempts to identify with Africa.

In recent years there has been a proliferation of articles describing and evaluating African survivals in the New World. Those that deal with specific forms of survival such as music or art will be covered in the section that follows. A good general introduction to the African origins of many aspects of American culture may be found in an article by Garrett (1966). Words like tote, tater, chimpanzee, etc., all stem from Africa. Dances such as the Mambo, Conga, Rhumba, and Charleston were originally African. Different tales such as Uncle Remus and other animal stories have African roots, Black-eyed peas was the food brought originally by the slaves during the Middle Passage from Africa, watermelon is still found growing wild ın

Africa, coffee comes from Kaffa, Ethiopia, and kola was originally an African drink. Although Garrett could also have made mention of Afro-American wood objects, pottery, and their African antecedents, his is a well-written and informative piece of work.

## SLAVERY

An important link in establishing the continuity of African culture in the New World has been the slave experience. Thus, a number of scholars have addressed themselves to the social and cultural structure of the African slave and the forms of African life that flourished within that community.

In his book *From Sundown to Sunup: The Making of the Black Community* (1972), George P. Rawick describes how the American slaves combined many African elements of their culture with American ones. Much of this cultural synthesis was created through the activities of the slaves at night after they had finished the long day of work in the fields. Rawick emphasizes that the reconstruction of their old world and the grafting of it to the new was essential for their survival. Relying heavily on excerpts from the slave interviews that were done in the 1930s by the Works Projects Administration, he presents a great deal of material on the social, cultural, familial, and religious lives of the slaves and demonstrates the extensive role played by the African heritage in its development. *From Sundown to Sunup* is actually the first of a 19-volume series. The other 18 volumes contain the actual slave narratives upon which much of the material is based. For those interested in gaining a full understanding of the slave experience and its connections with African life, this fascinating and authoritative book is indispensable.

Another excellent introduction to this topic is *The Slave Community: Plantation Life in the Ante-Bellum South* (1972) by John W. Blassingame, which also deals with African survivals as they appeared in slave culture. Blassingame points out (p. 2) that the slaves were able to adjust to plantation life here because many came from agrarian tribes such as the Ibo, Ewe, Wolof, Bambara, etc. Of particular interest is the author's discussion of music and dance forms that survived in various portions of the United States, especially New Orleans.

In addition to the work of Rawick and Blassingame, a number of articles dealing with this topic have appeared in earlier years. Highly recommended among these is a piece by Genovese (1960) that evaluates the slaves' ability to work on the plantation in light of their African heritage and an article by Stuckey (1969) about the African content in slave folksongs and tales.

## MUSIC AND ART

In the area of general introductions to Africanisms in Afro-American music, a good starting point is the first chapter in Harold Courlander's *Negro Folk Music, U.S.A.* (1963). Courlander stresses the importance of seeing Afro-American culture as a mixture of European and African culture and takes the position that the musical abilities of black Americans are a result of cultural rather than biological transmissions.

Perhaps the best discussions of black music in terms of African survivals appears in *Blues People* (1963) by Imamu A. Baraka and *Urban Blues* (1966) by Charles Keil. Baraka analyzes the historical development of Afro-American music in a perceptive and lucid manner. According to him, the sense of rhythm attributed to people of African descent can be traced to the fact that Africans used drums to communicate by phonetically reproducing the words, a process that required great rhythmic sensitivity. In his discussion of religion in the black community, Baraka gives a number of reasons to account for the slaves' acceptance of Christianity. Among these are the restrictions against the slaves' practicing their own religion, the fact that the African always respected the conquerors' gods, and their awareness of the practical value in adjusting to the white man's world (p. 32). Baraka also observes that Christianity, through its belief in heaven, took the slaves' minds off the idea of returning to Africa (p. 39). Keil's book is primarily about the structure, dynamics, and nature of the world of jazz. In it Keil talks about interrelationships and hybridization between European and African music: "West African folk music and European folk music are enough alike to blend easily in a seemingly infinite array of hybrids" (p. 30). Moreover, "in the blending process the African rhythmic foundation absorbs and transforms the European elements." Keil does an excellent job of portraying the subtleties and complexities of jazz and of showing how its structure is capable of absorbing within it a large variety of different types of music.

In an article dealing with similarities between West African and Afro-American music, Metcalfe (1970) finds at least two major points of comparison. The first is the social context of these songs – i.e, the popularity of work songs in both cultures – and the second is the similar tones, notes, verse forms, and call and response patterns that are found in the music of both cultures. Basically, however, this article is a review that presents very little new material and that relies heavily on quotes from other sources. While Metcalfe begins by launching a general attack on the research of white scholars in this area, saying: "No man has the right to interpret another man's past" (p. 16), he later quotes from the work of quite a few whites, among them Herskovits, Jahn, Keil, and others.

The work of Gunther Schuller is quite a bit more technical than earlier works cited and is not recommended for readers with only a casual interest in this subject. In his book *Early Jazz: Its Roots and Musical Development* (1968), Schuller explains how the African rhythms brought over by the slaves developed into early jazz. Reading this book one gets a better appreciation of the complexity of African music. In addition, the work demonstrates how Afro-Americans actually simplified their music so as to allow it to blend with European influences and styles. For those interested in obtaining hard facts concerning the African connections to Afro-American music, Schuller's book is a must. Also of value is a technical article by Lomax (1970) that attempts to evaluate and compare Afro-American and African music by using "cantometrics," a method of rating songs within the actual context of their performance in order to discover and analyze their characteristics. This approach differs from earlier ones that evaluated *printed* versions of melodies or that examined the *poetic content* of black and white spirituals (many of the earlier studies had concluded, erroneously, in Lomax' view, that the black spirituals were variants of white spirituals). Lomax' study concludes that there are indeed a great number of similarities between Afro-American and African music.

One of the best articles to appear on the subject of similarities in dance forms has been written by Cayou (1970) in which she traces the development of black dance in America and compares it to African dance forms. Cayou remarks that by trying to eliminate expressions of African culture, the plantation master may have actually aided the development of new forms of expression that were sufficiently divorced from African culture – i.e., jazz, gospel, blues, etc. Cayou also makes the important point that probably hundreds of cultural adaptations were lost through the passage of time and because they were not seen and subsequently institutionalized by the dominant white society. Articles such as the one by Cayou go a long way toward demonstrating the resilience of black culture. Inasmuch as African dance forms often expressed real-life situations, it is an indication of the black community's vitality that it was able to take these dance forms and successfully adapt them to the new lifestyles and situations of the New World.

Writing in *Blues People,* Baraka asserts that religion, music, and dance retained a great deal of their African origins as opposed to ironworking, woodcarving, and the like, which "took a new less obvious form or was wiped out altogether" (pp. 15-16). The fact that someone as knowledgeable as Baraka could make this assertion merely points up the value of Robert F. Thompson's article on African art in the United States (1969). Thompson's essay is a superb and valuable piece of work in an area that has been all but ignored. In it he presents a great deal of substantive material on the survival of many specific art forms in the United States. In his discussion of various artifacts produced in the United States by black craftsmen such as woodcarvings in New York and Georgia and stoneware in South Carolina, Thompson traces the designs and motifs back to the specific African tribes in which they originated.

## LINGUISTICS AND FOLKLORE

One of the more interesting articles to appear on the subject of linguistics has been done by David Dalby (1972). Dalby gives three reasons to explain why the contributions made by African languages to English have gone unrecognized. One reason may have been that so many languages are spoken in Africa that transferences may have occurred and gone unidentified. Second, the common belief that black people lost their languages in the United States may have contributed to this unawareness. Finally, there has been according to Dalby, a lack of proper historical documentation in this area. Dalby maintains that English contains many heretofore unnoticed words that are actually the result of English and African words converging, in addition to also having incorporated a number of expressions that were originally African. The author presents a very useful list of 80 such words, which he explains and traces back to their specific tribal origin. The importance of Dalby's article lies in the fact that it deals with far more than the usual recitation of words that were directly taken from African languages such as pinder, juju, goober, cooter, etc., and presents new material in a refreshing style. Long (1972) has also written a useful and informative article, though it is somewhat more technical than Dalby's. Long talks about the linguistic structure of African languages, particularly those spoken in West Africa, and points out that despite the existence of many different languages, the slaves were able to communicate through the use of transactional dialects that were actually a form of pidgin. Long also suggests that the linguistic peculiarities of many black southerners, such as substituting "d" and "t" in place of "th," are based on the phonetics of West African languages. We might add that while it is true that most languages lack a "th" sound, the long survival of this substitution among blacks as opposed to, say, French immigrants, is probably due to the prolonged isolation of the black community that resulted from slavery, segregation, and ghetto life.

A good introduction to the topic of Africanisms in New World folklore may be found in an article by Crowley (1962) that includes a general discussion of the area, and that takes note of some of the problems involved in locating the origins of folktales. Crowley talks about some of his own efforts to come to grips with this problem in a later piece (1970) in which he gives an account of a project he has initiated in this area. What he has done is to gather over 12,000 tales from all over the world for the purpose of analyzing their content and origin through the use of a type index and a motif index.* Vansertima (1971) has challenged Crowley's assertion that many African tales originated in Europe. Vansertima argues that such similarities as do exist may have developed out of a common, yet independent, human experience and that these similarities are coincidental rather than indicative of cultural contact. The article also touches upon the geographical origins of Afro-Americans and attributes the proliferation in this country of East African and Bantu tales to the fact that while the slaves left from West Africa many had come originally from the Lower Congo. On the whole, this is an interesting and thought-provoking article that is well worth reading.

## ATTITUDES TOWARD AFRICA

With the upsurge of interest in Africa within the Afro-American community, a number of social scientists have turned their attention to the attitudes of Afro-Americans toward the African continent. These studies have been carried out in a wide range of settings and exhibit a great deal of variation insofar as approach, methodology, findings, and quality of work are concerned. Consequently, it would be premature at this stage to make general statements and conclusions with regard to how Africa is perceived in the black community. Many of these studies do, however, provide insights and set the stage for future and more intensive investigations.

Laosebikan (1972) reports on a study on the attitudes of Afro-Americans toward Africa which employed the Social Distance Scale developed by E.S. Bogardus. Using a sample of 100 Afro-Americans, Laosebikan found that positive attitudes toward Africans ranked second out of 30 ethnic groups surveyed. This was in contrast to an earlier study (Goins and

*A type index numbers and documents tale types wherever they have appeared, and a motif index sets down incidents or characters that occur repeatedly in various contexts.

Meenes, 1960) that showed Africans in fifth place behind the French, West Indians, Northern whites in the United States, and Afro-Americans. The author suggests that this change is due to increased contact between Afro-Americans and Africans and to the development of black consciousness in recent years. On the whole, this article is somewhat superficial, especially in its failure to discuss and evaluate the positioning of the other 28 groups in the scale. Moreover, the author's conclusion that blacks are more positively oriented toward Africa in 1972 than they were ten or 15 years ago is hardly surprising.

A good study has been done by Hoadley (1972), who compared the views toward Africa of both whites and blacks in St. Louis. Based on a questionnaire distributed to both groups, Hoadley came up with a number of interesting conclusions: Among blacks and whites who evinced interest in Africa blacks had more favorable attitudes toward the Continent. Young blacks were discovered to be in favor of the United States government assuming a more active role with regard to Africa to a greater extent than older blacks. Whites were somewhat reluctant to have blacks "especially" consulted on matters pertaining to Africa and felt that both whites and blacks should be asked to contribute their views. Based on a content analysis of articles dealing with Africa, Hoadley found that more articles on Africa appeared in white St. Louis newspapers than in black ones and concluded that, in general, blacks were not more interested in Africa than were whites. The basis for this conclusion can be questioned since black newspapers generally (and certainly in St. Louis) represent primarily black middle-class interests and are not good indicators of how the young and the poor in the black community may feel. Thus, while the author's point may be valid, the evidence he presents is only applicable to the black middle-class community. Going on the assumption that white support for Africa is important in terms of general government support for the Continent, Hoadley concludes that the general lack of white enthusiasm for Africa that emerged from his study may indicate future difficulties for blacks who attempt to positively influence United States foreign policy toward Africa. While Hoadley's study would have been even more revealing had it included a comparison of different socioeconomic strata, the material presented is informative and well-handled.

In late spring of 1969, Raymond H. Giles, Jr., conducted a study of the effects of an African heritage program that was given in three Harlem elementary schools. The results (1972) raise serious questions concerning the usefulness of such programs. Giles discovered that many black Harlem schoolchildren were not positively oriented toward Africa even after an intensive, nine-month heritage program. The various classes sampled were taught by three people with different backgrounds. One was an African male, the second a white American male, and the third an Afro-American female. As a result Giles questions whether pride can be taught in the public school system as it is presently constituted. He suggests (but offers no proof) that the children's attitudes are shaped by the dominant white culture long before they enter school. One way of testing this assumption would be to interview preschool children and then interview them again after they have been in school for a few years. Giles makes a number of good suggestions for improving the awareness of children in this area, such as developing programs that concentrate on the differences as well as on the similarities between African and Afro-American culture and having teachers focus on dispelling commonly held stereotypes about Africa. This otherwise excellent investigation could have been even better had it covered the attitudes of the children *before* they began the heritage program.

A study done by Hicks and Beyer (1970) lends support to the assertion made by many in the black community that the schools have not (at least in the past) done a good job of teaching students about Africa. In an investigation of attitudes of secondary school students (seventh and twelfth graders) toward Africa south of the Sahara, it was found that while most students knew something about Africa, they had many misconceptions about the Continent, ranging from the belief that Timbuctu is most famous for its diamonds (rather than universities) to the belief that most of Africa is covered by jungles as opposed to grasslands. This despite the fact that most students have presumably learned about Africa by the time they reach the twelfth grade. In fact, a higher percentage of twelfth graders had incorrect images about Africa than did seventh graders. The authors criticize school programs for their superficiality and cite the need for improving their content. The data for this study were collected in 1967 and it is safe to assume that school programs have, generally speaking, improved quite a bit since then.

A very interesting study (Krystall *et al.,* 1970) has been made of attitudes toward integration and black consciousness in a deep South city. The data, which were gathered in 1967, concluded that a substantial number of blacks favor both integration and black consciousness and that the two positions were not mutually exclusive. A total of 506 interviews were done, 240 of which were with mothers or female guardians and 266 of which were with high school seniors. Students were more likely to be interested in visiting Africa, more likely to think of themselves as having an African heritage, and more likely to be knowledgeable about Africa although in general the level of knowledge was low compared to the intensity of positive feelings about the Continent. The study also noted that African dress or hair style is a poor indicator of separatist or integrationist views. Although many middle-class blacks were proud of their African heritage they were not as extreme in their views and were concerned as well with successfully entering the mainstream of American society. Another study of black students has been done by Wolkon (1971), who found that the Grade Point Average of students who identified with Africa was lower than that of students who did not.

Finally there are two studies of a more impressionistic nature that nevertheless offer some valuable insights into the conflicts facing black Americans in their efforts to develop a group identify. In his well-known book, *The New World of Negro Americans,* Harold R. Isaacs examined the views of 107 prominent Afro-Americans toward Africa and concluded that they had generally been ashamed of their background in the past. Considering the stereotypes of Africa that prevailed in the first half of the 20th century, this result was not very surprising. More importantly, however, Isaacs concluded that his respondents were generally uninterested in Africa and, in some cases, rather disillusioned with their ancestral homes and that there was therefore no basis for the establishment of close ties between the two groups. Although the material presented in Isaacs' book is highly interesting and stimulating, his methodological approach leaves much to be desired. The interviews he conducted were not systematic or representative of the black community as a whole. Rather they consisted of a "panel" of leaders who may well have been, because of their strategically located positions in the black community, far more cautious than the average person in expressing their true opinions to a white interviewer on a matter as sensitive as this. Another work by Inez S. Reid (1972) deals in part with the attitudes of black women toward Africa. Her interviews indicate a lack of knowledge about and interest in Africa on the part of many of her respondents. Although Reid's work contains many insights into this question, it is more descriptive than analytical and barely touches upon the issue of *why* blacks do not relate to Africa.

When one considers the rate at which interest in and awareness of Africa have grown in recent years, it becomes apparent that the studies discussed here must be viewed in terms of *when* they were carried out, for we are talking about a community that has undergone such tremendous changes in the past decade that a difference of two or three years can be very significant. We need, at this juncture, more studies of high quality to determine the future role of Africa in the Afro-American community. It is impossible to predict the future psychological importance of Africa in the black community or its cultural significance for these depend on too many factors not the least important of which is how black people come to perceive their role and their opportunities in American society. Unforseen political developments in Africa, especially South Africa, may also play a crucial role in the future involvement of Afro-Americans with the African continent. Economic opportunites or the lack of them may also exert an influence over many Afro-Americans as they attempt to carve out a satisfactory and productive environment for themselves and their families. Although the situation is sufficiently unclear at present to warrant projections into the future, it is, nonetheless, clear that Africa is continuing to play a role of great importance in the black community and that, because of its importance, this is an area that deserves even greater attention than has been the case until now.

## REFERENCES


Baldwin, James. *Go Tell it on the Mountain.* New York, Dial, 1963.

Bastide, Roger. *African Civilizations in the New World.* New York, Harper & Row, 1971.

Blassingame, John W. *The Slave Community: Plantation Life in the Ante-Bellum South.* New York, Oxford University Press, 1972.

Bruchac, Joseph. "Black Autobiography in Africa and America." *Black Academy Review,* 2, Spring 1971, 61-70.

Cayou, Dolores, K. "The Origins of Modern Jazz Dance." *Black Scholar,* 1, June 1970, 26-31.

Cook, Mercer, and Henderson, Stephen, E. *The Militant Black Writer in Africa and in the United States.* Madison, University of Wisconsin Press, 1969.

Courlander, Harold. *Negro Folk Music, U.S.A.* New York, Columbia University Press, 1963.

Crowley, Daniel J. "Negro Folklore: An Africanist's View." *Texas Quarterly,* 5, Autumn 1962, 65-71.

Crowley, Daniel J. "African Folktales in Afro-America," pp. 179-189, in John F. Szwed (Ed.), *Black America.* New York, Basic Books, 1970.

Dalby, David. "The African Element in American English," pp. 170-186, in Thomas Kochman (Ed.), *Rappin' and Stylin' Out.* Urbana, University of Illinois Press, 1972.

Ellison, Ralph. *Invisible Man.* New York, Random House, 1947.

Garrett, Romeo B. "African Survivals in American Culture." *Journal of Negro History,* 51, October 1966, 239-245.

Genovese, Eugene D. "The Negro Laborer in Africa and in the Slave South." *Phylon,* 21, Winter 1960, 343-350.

Giles, Raymond H., Jr. *Black and Ethnic Studies Programs at Public Schools: Elementary and Secondary.* Amherst, Mass., Center for International Education, School of Education, 1972, esp. pp. 29-57.

Goins, Alvin E., and Meenes, Max. "Ethnic and Class Preferences Among College Negroes." *Journal of Negro Education,* 29, Spring 1960, 128-133.

Harlan, Louis R. "Booker T. Washington and the White Man's Burden." *American Historical Review,* 71, January 1966, 441-467.

Herskovits, Melville J. *The Myth of the Negro Past.* Beacon Press, Boston, 1958.

Herskovits, Melville J. "The Ahistorical Approach to Afro-American Studies: A Critique." *American Anthropologist,* 62, August 1960, 559-568.

Hicks, E. Perry, and Beyer, Barry K. "Images of Africa." *Journal of Negro Education,* 39, Spring 1970, 158-166.

Hoadley, J. Stephen. "Black Americans and U.S. Policy Toward Africa." *Journal of Black Studies,* 2, June 1972, 489-502.

Isaacs, Harold R. *The New World of Negro Americans.* New York, John Day, 1963.

Jahn, Jahnheinz. *Muntu: The New African Culture.* New York, Grove Press, 1961.

Jones, LeRoi (Imamu Ameer Baraka). *Blues People.* New York, 1963.

Keil, Charles. *Urban Blues.* Chicago, University of Chicago Press, 1966.

Krystall, Eric R., Friedman, Neil, Howze, Glenn, and Epps, Edgar G. "Attitudes Toward Integration and Black Consciousness: Southern Negro High School Students and their Mothers." *Phylon,* 31, Summer 1970, 104-113.

Laosebikan, Supo. "Social Distance and Pan-Africanism." *Afro-American Studies,* 3 (3), 1972, 223-225.

Lomax, Alan. "The Homogeneity of African – Afro-American Musical Style," pp. 181-201, in Norman E. Whitten and John F. Szwed (Eds.), *Afro-American Anthropology: Contemporary Perspectives.* New York, Free Press, 1970.

Long, Richard A. "From Africa to the New World: The Linguistic Continuum," pp. 37-45, in W.B. Abilla (Ed.), *Source Book in Black Studies.* New York, MSS Information Corporation, 1972.

Metcalfe, Ralph., Jr. "The Western African Roots of Afro-American Music." *Black Scholar,* 8, June 1970, 16-25.

Rawick, George P. *The American Slave: A Composite Autobiography.* Volume I; *From Sundown to Sunup: The Making of the Black Community.* Westport, Conn., Greenwood Publishing Company, 1972.

Schuller, Gunther. *Early Jazz: Its Roots and Development.* New York, Oxford University Press, 1968.

Stuckey, Sterling. "Through the Prism of Folklore: The Black Ethos in Slavery" pp. 172-192, in Jules Chametzky and Sidney Kaplan (Eds.), *Black and White in American Culture: An Anthology from the Massachusetts Review.* Amherst, University of Massachusetts Press, 1969.

Thompson, Robert F. "African Influence on the Art of the United States," pp. 122-170, in Armstead L. Robinson, Craig C. Foster, and Donald H. Ogilvie (Eds.), *Black Studies in the University.* New Haven, Yale University Press, 1969.

Vansertima, Ivan. "African Linguistic and Mythological Structures in the New World," pp. 12-35, in Rhoda L. Goldstein (Ed.), *Black Life and Culture in the United States.* New York, Crowell, 1971.

Wolkon, George A. "African Identity of the Negro American and Achievement." *Journal of Social Issues,* 27 (4), 1971, 199-211.

Wright, Richard. *Native Son.* New York: Harper & Brothers, 1940.

## AFRO-AMERICANS AND AFRICA: A SELECTED BIBILIOGRAPHY

### General Works

Bastide, Roger. *African Civilizations in the New World.* New York, Harper & Row, 1971, especially pp. 162-226.

Blauner, Robert. *Racial Oppression in America.* New York: Harper & Row, 1972, especially pp. 124-161.

Garrett, Romeo B. "African Survivals in American Culture." *Journal of Negro History,* 51, October 1966, 239-245.

Herkovits, Melville J. *The Myth of the Negro Past.* Boston, Beacon Press, 1958.

Herkovits, Melville J. "The Ahistorical Approach to Afro-American Studies: A Critique." *American Anthropologist,* 62, August 1960, 559-568.

Jahn, Jahnheinz. *Muntu: The New African Culture.* New York, Grove Press, 1961.

Waterman, Richard A. "On Flogging a Dead Horse: Lessons From the Africanisms Controversy." *Ethnomusicology,* 7 (2), 1963, 83-87.

### Slavery

Blassingame, John W. *The Slave Community: Plantation Life in the Ante-Bellum South.* New York, Oxford University Press, 1972, pp. 1-40.

Genovese, Eugene D. "The Negro Laborer in Africa and in the Slave South." *Phylon,* 21, Winter 1960, 343-350.

Levine, Lawrence. "Slave Songs and Slave Consciousness: An Exploration in Neglected Sources," pp. 99-126, in T.K. Hareven (Ed.), *Anonymous Americans: Explorations in Nineteenth Century Social History.* Englewood Cliffs, N.J., Prentice-Hall, 1971.

Rawick, George P. *The American Slave: A Composite Autobiography.* Volume I; *From Sundown to Sunup: The Making of the Black Community.* Westport, Conn., Greenwood Publishing Company, 1972.

Reed, Harry A. "Slavery in Ashanti and Colonial South Carolina." *Black World,* 20, February 1971, 37.

Stuckey, Sterling. "Through the Prism of Folklore: The Black Ethos in Slavery," pp. 172-191, in Jules Chametzky and Sidney Kaplan (Eds.), *Black and White in American Culture: An Anthology from the Massachusetts Review.* Amherst, University of Massachusetts Press, 1969.

Stuckey, Sterling. "Slave Resistance as Seen Through Slave Folklore," pp. 51-60, in Inez S. Reid (Ed.), *Black Prism: Perspective on the Black Experience.* New York, Faculty Press, 1969.

### Music and Art

Bourguignon, Erika E. "Afro-American Religions: Traditions and Transformations," pp. 190-202, in John F. Szwed (Ed.), *Black America.* New York, Basic Books, 1970.

Cayou, Dolores K. "The Origins of Modern Jazz Dance." *Black Scholar,* 1, June 1970, 26-31.

Chase, Judith W. *Afro-American Art and Craft.* New York, Van Nostrand, 1971.

Courlander, Harold. *Negro Folk Music, U.S.A.* New York, Columbia University Press, 1963.

Jones, LeRoi (Imamu A. Baraka). *Blues People.* New York, 1963.

Keil, Charles. *Urban Blues.* Chicago, University of Chicago Press, 1966.

Kinney, Esi S. "Africanisms in Music and Dance of the Americas," pp. 49-63, in Rhoda L. Goldstein (Ed.), *Black Life and Culture in the United States.* New York, Crowell, 1971.

Landeck, Beatrice. *Echoes of Africa in Folk Songs of the Americas.* New York, 1961.

Levine, Lawrence. "Slave Songs and Slave Consciousness: An Exploration in Neglected Sources," pp. 99-126, in T.K. Hareven (Ed.), *Anonymous Americans: Explorations in Nineteenth Century Social History.* Englewood Cliffs, N.J., Prentice-Hall, 1971.

Lomax, Alan. *The Folk Songs of North America.* New York, Doubleday, 1960, pp. xv-xxx.

Lomax, Alan. "The Homogeneity of African – Afro-American Musical Style," pp. 181-201, in Norman E. Whitten and John F. Szwed (Eds.), *Afro-American Anthropology: Contemporary Perspectives.* New York, Free Press, 1970.

Lovell, John, Jr. *Black Song: The Forge and the Flame.* New York, Macmillan, 1972.

Merriam, Alan P. "Jazz – The Word." *Ethnomusicology,* 12, September 1968, 373-396.

Metcalfe, Ralph H., Jr. "The Western African Roots of Afro-American Music." *Black Scholar,* 8, June 1970, 16-25.

Oliver, Paul. *Savannah Syncopators: African Retentions in the Blues.* New York, Stein and Day, 1970.

Porter, James A. "The American Negro Artist Looks at Africa," pp. 293-301, in American Society of African Culture (Ed.), in *Pan-Africanism Reconsidered.* Berkeley, University of California Press, 1962.

Porter, James A. "Contemporary Black American Art," pp. 489-506, in Joseph S. Roucek and Thomas Kiernan (Eds.), *The Negro Impact on Western Civilization.* New York, Philosophical Library, 1970.

Roberts, John S. *Black Music of Two Worlds.* New York, Praeger, 1972.

Rublowsky, John. *Black Music in America.* New York, Basic Books, 1971.

Schuller, Gunther. *Early Jazz: Its Roots and Development.* New

York, Oxford University Press, 1968.

Sithole, Elkin T. "Black Folk Music," pp. 65-82, in Thomas Kochman (Ed.), *Rappin' and Stylin' Out.* Urbana: University of Illinois Press, 1972.

Southern, Eileen. *The Music of Black Americans: A History.* New York, Norton, 1971.

Szwed, John F. "Musical Adaptation Among Afro-Americans." *Journal of American Folklore,* 82 (324), 1969, 112-121.

Thompson, Robert F. "An Aesthetic of the Cool: West African Dance." *African Forum,* 2 (2), 1966, 85-102.

Thompson, Robert F. "African Influence on the Art of the United States," pp. 122-170, in Armstead L. Robinson, Craig C. Foster, Donald H. Ogilvie (Eds.), *Black Studies in the University.* New Haven: Yale University Press, 1969.

Tyler, Robert. "The Musical Culture of Afro-America." *Black Scholar,* 3 (10), 1972, 22-27.

Walton, Ortiz. *Music: Black, White, and Blue.* New York: Morrow, 1972.

**Linguistics and Folklore**

Blassingame, John W. *The Slave Community: Plantation Life in the Ante-Bellum South.* New York: Oxford University Press, 1972, pp. 1-40.

Crowley, Daniel J. "Negro Folklore: An Africanist's View." *Texas Quarterly,* 5, Autumn 1962, 65-71.

Crowley, Daniel J. "African Folktales in Afro-America," pp. 179-189, in John F. Szwed (Ed.), *Black America.* New York: Basic Books, 1970.

Dalby, David. *Black Through White: Patterns of Communication.* Bloomington, Ind.: African Studies Association, 1970.

Dalby, David. "The African Element in American English," pp. 170-186, in Thomas Kochman (Ed.), *Rappin' and Stylin' Out.* Urbana, University of Illinois Press, 1972.

Dundes, Alan. "African Tales Among the North American Indians." *Southern Folklore Quarterly,* 29, September 1965, 207-219.

Long, Richard A. "Toward a Theory of Afro-American Dialects." *Atlanta University Center for African and African American Studies Center,* Paper in Linguistics, 1, 1971.

Long, Richard A. "From Africa to the New World: The Linguistic Continuum," pp. 37-45, in W.D. Abilla (Ed.), *Source Book in Black Studies.* New York: MSS Information Corporation, 1972.

Piersen, William D. "An African Background for American Negro Folktales," *Journal of American Folklore,* 84, April-June 1971, 204-214.

Rawick, George P. *The American Slave: A Composite Autobiography.* Volume 1; *From Sundown to Sunup: The Making of the Black Community.* Westport, Conn.: Greenwood, 1972.

Stuckey, Sterling. "Through the Prism of Folklore: The Black Ethos of Slavery," pp. 172-191, in Jules Chametzky and Sidney Kaplan (Eds.), *Black and White in American Culture: An Anthology From the Massachusetts Review.* Amherst, Mass., University of Massachusetts Press, 1969.

Stuckey, Sterling. "Slave Resistance as Seen Through Slave Folklore," pp. 51-60, in Inez S. Reid (Ed.), *Black Prism: Perspectives on the Black Experience.* New York, Faculty Press, 1969.

Vansertima, Ivan. "African Linguistic and Mythological Structures in the New World," pp. 12-35, in Rhoda L. Goldstein (Ed.), *Black Life and Culture in the United States.* New York, Crowell, 1971.

Walker, Sheila. "Black English." *Black World,* 20 (8), 1971, 4-16.

Whitten, Norman E. "Contemporary Patterns of Malign Occultism Among Negroes in North Carolina." *Journal of American Folklore,* 75 (298), 1962, 311-325.

**Sociology**

Blauner, Robert. *Racial Oppression in America.* New York, Harper & Row, 1972, especially pp. 124-161.

Chick, C.A. "The American Negro's Changing Attitude Toward Africa." *Journal of Negro Education,* 31, Fall 1962, 531-535.

Friedman, Neil. "Africa and the Afro-American: The Changing Negro Identity." *Psychiatry,* 32, May 1969, 127-136.

Friedman, Neil. "Has Black Come Back to Dixie." *Society,* 9, Ma 1969, 47-53.

Giles, Raymond H., Jr. *Black and Ethnic Studies Programs at Public Schools: Elementary and Secondary.* Amherst, Mass: Center for International Education, School of Education, 1972, pp. 29-57.

Goins, Alvin E., and Meenes, Max. "Ethnic and Class Preferences Among College Negroes." *Journal of Negro Education,* 29 (2), 1960, 128-133.

Hicks, E. Perry, and Beyer, Barry K. "Images of Africa." *Journal of Negro Education,* 39, Spring 1970, 158-166.

Hoadley, J. Stephen. "Black Americans and U.S. Policy Toward Africa." *Journal of Black Studies,* 2, June 1972, 489-502.

Isaacs, Harold R. *The New World of Negro Americans.* New York, Day, 1963.

Krystall, Eric. R., Friedman, Neil, Howze, Glenn, and Epps, Edgar G. "Attitudes Toward Integration and Black Consciousness: Southern Negro High School Seniors and Their Mothers." *Phylon,* 31, Summer 1970, 104-113.

Laosebikan, Supo. "Social Distance and Pan-Africanism." *Afro-American Studies,* 3 (3), 1972, 223-225.

Pettigrew, Thomas F. *A Profile of the Negro American.* New York, Van Nostrand, 1969, especially pp. 10-12.

Reid, Inez S. *Together Black Women.* New York, Emerson-Hill, 1972, pp. 245-283.

Waiguchu, Julius M. "Black Heritage: Of Genetics, Environment, and Continuity," pp. 64-86, in Rhoda L. Goldstein (Ed.), *Black Life and Culture in the United States.* New York, Crowell, 1971.

Wolkon, George A. "African Identity of the Negro American and Achievement." *Journal of Social Issues,* 27 (4), 1971, 199-211.

# 20
# *Alternatives and Strategies in Black America: A Critique*[*]

LADUN ANISE

## INTRODUCTION

There is no dearth of literature on the culpability of white racism for the existential and psychological predicament of black people in America. In a general causal sense almost every black problem can be traced to the door of white oppression. The pathology of the ghetto, its bleakness, paralysis, and human negation; the deviancy of the atomized black individual; the tendency toward a lifestyle of reckless abandon and the resultant absence of social accountability, all have their causal explanations rooted in the very pathology of white oppression. Thus it can be argued justifiably and on teleological grounds that the visible symbols of a distorted black humanity originate from this very environment of agonizing and unrelenting oppression.

There is little or no dispute about the validity of this causal explanation. But causal explanations do not necessarily produce curative antidotes. It is necessary nonetheless to know the origin of ones troubles in order to develop effective solutions through counter action and reaction. To paraphrase an African proverb: to have an accurate knowledge of the causes of one's troubles is to have won half of the battle. Black people in America already know that white racism and white oppression through various social, economic, and political institutions are responsible for almost all of their predicaments. But this unanimity in cognition has rarely produced any unanimity either in black leadership or in the selection and articulation of black alternatives and strategies. This absence of black unity in the face of unrelenting threat to black survival attests to the tenacious viciousness of the other half of the battle.

In this essay, therefore, attention is focused not on the cognitive aspects of the black struggle, but on the analytical aspects. That is, the focus is on those aspects of black behavior and mode of analysis that constitute a dead weight on the chances for black survival. The intention in doing so is not to challenge the general validity of the prevailing style of black analysis, but to call for the abandonment of that style of analysis that is preoccupied with white-determined definitions of black alternatives and strategies.

The central thesis of this essay is simply that black people in America will survive or perish not so much by virtue of what white America does or fails to do for blacks but primarily by virtue of what black people do or fail to do for and to themselves. Black people have to do certain things *for* themselves. Black people have to do certain things *to* themselves and to many aspects of their mode of behavior. *Black analysts have to begin to focus on patterns of black behavior or social conduct that tend to destroy any advances achieved by perpetuating the dogma of white culpability without dilineating areas of black responsibility. Many black problems are caused not by white racism but by black people themselves.*

The dangers in the above orientation are obvious: Some black readers are likely to construe it as an expression of hostility by the author to the black struggle. Many white people are likely to misinterpret it as an exoneration of their culpability. The writer is acutely aware of the capacity of white America to distort any attempt at black self-criticism into an opportunity to absolve white people from their deserved burden of guilt. There is no intention here to soothe the tortured souls of white America. More importantly, no perversion by white people should be used as an excuse by black people to escape self-criticism. This black self-criticism, not competitive self-negation, is a precondition for black survival in America and elsewhere in the New World.

## BLACK ALTERNATIVES AND PREVAILING MODES OF ANALYSIS

An intentional focus on black problems offers black analysts an opportunity to probe the origin and nature of available black alternatives and the strategies of the black struggle. From the experience gained from such a frame of reference, the analyst can easily compile a litany of black problems, and with some skill and refinement such a litany can be reduced to sociopolitical, psychocultural, and economic categories. These categories can be further reduced to this general statement, variants of which the reader must have heard or read before:

*This essay is a modified and enlarged version of a lecture delivered at the Faculty Seminar, Department of Black Studies, University of Pittsburgh, March 25, 1971.

The white man is the black man's problem. Or, to put it in a non-personal form, black problems – at all levels – are said to be the white man, the white society, and all the institutional arrangements that sustain both the man and the damned society he has created. All the modes of analysis that operate at this level ignore an important variable in the general equation. *Part of black reality in America is that black people to a fantastic extent have also become a part of black people's problems.*

According to Kenneth B. Clark in *Dark Ghetto,*[1] the problem of black people in America is their objective powerlessness whose sometimes invincible and "invisible walls have been erected by the white society, by those who have power, both to confine those who have no power, and to perpetuate their powerlessness." Within this environment of powerlessness, other social, political, and economic problems have arisen. There is the objective reality of black political disenfranchisement. This has come about from socially sanctioned as well as legalized black nonparticipation in the process of authoritative allocation of values, and in the distribution of scarce resources.

*There is also the objective reality of traditional economic exploitation which has been transformed into economic ostracism for black people wherever automation and general cybernetics have rendered the exploitation of black labor virtually needless or useless.*

There is the objective reality of social alienation and social ostracism, the emasculation of black family life, and the perversion of black sexuality. There is a basic denial of black reality and objective existence in America. All these factors have produced the atomized black individual at the same time that they have nearly succeeded in creating a disordered, distorted black humanity.

According to Dr. Poussaint, the black psychiatrist, it is this environment of mangled humanity and warped values that produces the pathology of self-hate, self-negation, self-destruction, and self-emasculation among black people.[2] It also largely accounts for the self-directed nature of much of the violence in the black communities. One great loss to the black people in the evolution of this tragedy is the loss of "the power to define."[3]

It may well be that this loss of the power to define constitutes a causal explanation for the growing danger of self-defeatism in the articulation of black alternatives and in the operation of the strategies for their realization. Be that as it may, a litany of black problems can be matched by a list of articulated "black alternatives": (1) Integration, (2) Separation, (3) Revolution, and (4) Liberation. The other alternatives frequently encountered both in the literature and in social discourse (e.g., Black capitalism, Nation of Islam, Black Nationalism, the Republic of New Africa, and Back-to-Africa Movement or Neo-Garveyism) are more in the nature of strategies or variations of these four alternatives. In fact, Lerone Bennett has argued that *Black Liberation* is the one and only real alternative or objective of black people and that all the other considerations fall into the category of strategies and tactics.[4]

Perhaps the most serious indictment against the confusion that surrounds these alternatives has been articulated by Clarence Rollo Turner in the following poignant words:

> The attempts of black political activism to emend the plight of black people in this nation have failed to advance us to a self-liberation for the reason that our efforts have been, latently, the very components of a *government-controlled cycle of rebellion.* Much of the "black revolution" has been preoccupied with revisions of former strategies . . . we, in naive, efficient zeal, reinaugurate this cycle at each ominous completion. *Until we can understand that America systematically determines even the ways in which her rebels and activists can resist,* that it guides and beguiles them into continuous, blind rapport with her motive by inducing carefully manipulated rebellion against herself . . . we will be incapable of self-controlled strategies, hence of self-determination . . . Black people have not been permitted to be the free agents of their own political reactivity, for even urban revolt has been controlled by intricately devised intervention into and monitoring of black political response and communication . . . The danger of our being immobilized . . . to an irrevocable state of despair is impending at this stage.[5]

What Turner calls "the retarding politics of self-determination" and "government-controlled cycle of rebellion" constitute one level of response to those aspects of the black struggle that must be defined and controlled by black people before Liberation or Self-Determination can ever be achieved.

Another facet of the same problem that concerned Turner is to be found in the positing of black objectives, goals, alternatives, and strategies too frequently in abstract theoretical terms. This preoccupation with abstraction, and the ego-satisfying rhetorical attributes of black ivory-tower metaphysics is another source of possible spatio-temporal immobilization of black liberating energies. What, for example, is self-determination or liberation? It is said to be the control of black destiny by black people. This control of black destiny is to be achieved through the acquisition of black power over all areas of black life.

At the rhetorical, abstract level we all understand or purport to understand what all these words mean. At the concrete level we correctly argue that black power and black control of it is the ultimate avenue to self-determination or liberation. But we have really not penetrated the reality that power cannot and will never be granted for the asking; that indeed power is an abstraction; that every positive black activity constitutes a source of black power; that every negative black activity – that is, black activity directed against blacks – constitutes a dissipation of black energy, and hence, a dead weight on black survival. The determination of "negative" or "positive" black activity is considered here within a black-controlled system of adaptive response.

Nor have we penetrated the corollary reality that *power as an abstract idea cannot be taken, or seized. Only situations can be controlled; only institutions and instrumentalities of power can be taken.* And these have to be used to generate more power for black survival, and understood as black possessions and black property. For example, does the establishment of a Black Studies Department at any university and/or college campus in the nation constitute an acquisition of an amount of power by the black people in the city, the state, or the nation? *Can we argue that fragmented acquisitions of power in frag-*

*mented local situations can lead to a cumulative source of power for all black people?* If our answer to this question is positive, then we must reject the unrationalized conception of power as something we can be given or as something we can take in an abstract vacuum.

There is no doubt that the articulation of black alternatives, remaining as it does at the rhetorical level, satisfies emotional as well as ego-relevant needs. But it must be clear by now that all the mythologized, romanticized, righteous indignations of black people will not by themselves be sufficient to ensure black survival. In short, there must be a breakthrough to the level of black-controlled cycle of black resistance and black-controlled operation and definition of black alternatives and strategies.

The next facet of the problem is that all the black alternatives have either been defined and articulated for black people by the white power structure, or those alternatives articulated and defined *initially* by black leaders have, within the shortest span of time, been distorted by the white power structure via the agencies of the media. This is another way the system controls black response by manipulating the parameters of those definitions that the black people themselves ultimately accept. For example, once the black people have been manipulated to accept the definition of "integration" as the total biological as well as cultural assimilation of black reality in America into the white mold, they can only react with horror and vindictiveness toward black leaders who adhere to "integration" as a viable black alternative. The same process paves the way for the manipulation of white congenital fears by the system to keep black people from self-realization.

It is strange and depressing to observe that historically the myth of the melting pot has never been interpreted to mean integration as is now defined by the white society. *Integration within the melting pot mythology has meant only equality of opportunity, equal access to the resources of this nation, equal freedom of choice of one's subculture, place of residence, style of life, and proportionate participation in the process of authoritative allocation of values in society.*

Objectively, black analysts are aware that *the white tribes in America* engage in ruthless competition among themselves; they are aware that pluralism or polyarchy in America has done nothing to the *tribal* (ethnic) atomization, pattern of social mobility and stratification, modes of political behavior and organization in America. Black analysts know all this, but most black defenders of various black alternatives either ignore this objective reality of America or abandon it in favor of doing battle with one another over the misrepresented definitions of their assumed alternatives. Obviously, if we define integration in terms of those attributes of equality mentioned above, it would become evident that doing battle with the supporters of integration is not only a dissipation of black energy but also a dangerous pastime.

Similarly, the prevailing definitions of separation, revolution, and liberation are not subject to black-control. Those who have followed the distortion of the demands of Black Power as well as the techniques by which the Black Panthers were made to assume an irrational, self-destructive revolutionary posture, cannot fail to appreciate the manipulative capacity of the white power structure.

Why and how do black people, black leaders especially, lose control of the meaning they attribute to their objectives, goals, alternatives, and even strategies? Once they lose the control over those self-generated definitions of black reality, why do black people fall prey to the alternatives and self-defacing definitions adopted by the instrumentalities of white oppression? That is, why do black people accept the distorted definition of their own reality (sometimes already defined correctly by them) and then proceed to use the imposed definitions in doing battle against one another?

*It should be understood that the power to insist on one's definition of one's reality through a structure of self-controlled operational strategies is another precondition for the survival of black people in America.* Furthermore, this is something only the black people can do for themselves. This in no way invalidates the fact that oftentimes part of the manipulative mechanism of white society is to present black people with a meaning never articulated by them, for the sole purpose of shifting the theater of social discourse from the consideration of prevailing injustices to the defense of one's original definitions or positions. And to be put on the defensive is to lose the capacity to control the situation at hand. Thus, for example, *white society continues to refuse to define white segregation as the vicious and cruel separatism that it is, but would attack the Nation of Islam and The Republic of New Africa and other black radical movements as forms of black separatism.* What is urged here is that increasing attention be paid to this level of social manipulation; further, that a counter strategy, developed and controlled by black people, be put into operation. This would mean for a start an abandonment of glamorized black rhetoric, emotionalized black romanticism, and a cultivation of a reasoned, rationalized, calculated approach to the problems of dignified black survival in America.

## BLACK STRATEGIES AND MODES OF OPERATION

Thus far the analysis has focused on the pitfalls inherent in the definitions of black alternatives. The general conclusion to be drawn from this is that the ultimate fate of black alternatives is determined largely by white America. We know that white America will not suddenly stop the manipulation of black America but, somehow, black people must develop efficacious strategies of adaptive behavior. That there is a need for rationalized black strategies cannot be overemphasized. That the present stage of the black struggle is not characterized by this kind of rationalized strategic responses seems ominously evident.

*The issue of rationalized strategies concerns the conjunction between means and ends. A rational, efficacious strategy is that which achieves the desired goal by utilizing the most appropriate methods. Thus, a rational strategy cannot be theoretically formalized in advance of the particular configuration of the forces of oppression.* The struggle to achieve black dignity and full participation in the self-sustaining activities in this nation must, according to Malcolm X, utilize all means necessary. By *all means necessary* Malcolm meant the belief in anything that is necessary to correct injustices. He once wrote:

> I believe in anything that is necessary to correct unjust situations . . . I believe in it as long as it's intelligently

> directed and designed to get results. But I don't believe in getting involved in any kind of political action or other kind of action without sitting down and analyzing the possibilities of success or failure.[6]

The best strategy is, therefore, "that combination of energies required to determine and to translate goals into a desired social reality."[7] Thus, effective strategy involves the right combination of words and action, of pressures and self-sacrifice, and the critical evaluation of the "possibilities of success or failure."

Clark has outlined some of the strategies the black struggle has utilized thus far as follows:[8]

(1) the strategy of prayer, applied traditionally by the black church in its anticipation of earthly salvation through divine intervention; this offers escape through spiritualism;
(2) the strategy of isolation, generally utilized by secure middle-class and upper middle-class blacks whose symbols are conspicuous consumption, the Cadillac, and a visible abdication of their potential leadership roles in the black struggle;
(3) the strategy of accommodation practiced frequently by most of us depending upon our particular situations and needs;
(4) the strategy of despair or resignation practiced by several million black poor who have lost the will to hope;
(5) the strategy of alienation and separation advocated in neo-Garveyism, the Nation of Islam, and by some black nationalists;
(6) the strategy of law and maneuver practiced chiefly by the SCLC, NAACP, National Urban League, black capitalists, and other black social groups and individuals;
(7) the strategy of direct encounter practiced by CORE, SNCC, SCLC, Black Panthers, black nationalists, and black revolutionaries;
(8) the ineffective "strategy of truth," practiced by scholars who believe that an impartial analysis of the problems will bring about the desired change. This implies the assumption that the evils of racism and oppression result from ignorance which truth, discovered through reason, will automatically eliminate.

These strategies have been used singly or in various combinations by various black groups as they advance from the *"stage of passion and endurance"* to the *"stage of integration,"* characterized by "litigation, pressure-group techniques and petitions for the one-by-one admission of the oppressed into the precinct of the oppressor."[9] According to Bennett, this later stage is succeeded by the *"stage of Mass direct Action"* which in turn is transformed into the "momentous crossing of the threshold into the . . . *"stage of nationalist rebellion."*[10] The complexity of these strategies has been revealed by what Bennett also conceptualized as "the theory of seven veils . . . which suggests that the Black Rebellion is the product of the ripping away of successive veils of illusion . . . the veil of litigation, the veil of education (and) the veil of integration."[11]

The "veils of illusion" that have surrounded the choice of black strategies stem partly from the manipulative instrumentalities of white America and partly from the self-imposed stupor of black America. For a long time, black strategists have fallen victim to the paralyzing consequences of their tactics. Mao Tse-tung, for example, spoke of strategic offense within a general posture of defensive adaptation.[12] That is, given the reality of overall black "encirclement" by white oppression, black people can carve out areas of strategic offense, so that they are not continuously on the strategic defense. Lenin makes the same point this way:

> To tie our hands beforehand, openly to tell the enemy who is at present better armed than we are, whether we shall fight him, and when, is stupidity and not revolution. To accept battle at a time when it is obviously advantageous to the enemy and not to us is a crime; and the political leader of the revolutionary class who is unable to "tack, manoeuvre, and compromise," in order to avoid an obviously disadvantageous battle, is absolutely worthless.[13]

Thus, it can be argued that the veil of illusion was born out of the naivete of black credulity. Black people have historically tended to put all their eggs in one basket – the worst kind of strategy. At one time the Black Church was all pervasive; it was the answer to all black oppression. Then the veil of education came along. The belief in education was not entirely misplaced. However, three conditions associated with the strategy of education were dangerously mistaken.

First, there was the belief that black oppression would vanish if every black man received a good education. This did not take into account the possibility that black education may be anything but appropriate for black needs. Secondly, there was an incredible belief in the goodness of the white man, or, if not in his goodness, at least in his possession of a moral conscience to which appeal can be made. The latter was part of the illusion perpetrated on humanity by the European philosophy of Reason, Progress, and the infinite Perfectibility of man. Thirdly, black people underestimated the viciousness and tenacity of white racism and economic oppression. *And yet a rationalized and efficacious strategy should suggest that the black struggle will not succeed without the acquisition of adequate education, but that education alone will not solve the problem of oppression and racism.*

Furthermore there is an invidious development among young black radicals these days. They debunk education on grounds that (a) it is controlled by white America, (b) it is irrelevant to black needs. However, it is one thing to debunk white-defined education and scholarship but quite something else to debunk education per se. There is a growing tendency to glorify black mediocrity, black incompetence, and black ignorance because blacks have realized that the white criteria of excellence are not necessarily valid. It must be realized that the fact that white standards of valuation are suspect or invalid in no way invalidates the idea of excellence in itself. The belated discovery by the black people that the white criteria of education, scholarship, beauty, and excellence are invalid and racially arrogant should not send black people into the "bad trip" of rejecting these values. On the contrary, this discovery should energize black people – black educators and black scholars especially – to develop and formalize black relevant education and scholarship. Moreover, there is no reason why the criteria, so developed could not be universalized, not by violent imposition but by their inherent superiority and validity.

*Many black people have made not just tactical but more or less permanent errors by assuming that most values are white values, whereas what has happened is that white people have expropriated what ought to be understood as universal human values as white values only.* To live in decent and healthy houses and environments, to eat good food, drive good cars, wear good attire – in short, to live what classical philosophers called the good life – is not the property of white people but the natural right of all men. There is, therefore, no reason for black people either to apologize for desiring and demanding these valued objects or to renounce them on grounds that white people want and desire them. The challenge to black people everywhere is not to abandon excellence in education and other phases of life, but to cultivate it, to create it, and to make it serve human purposes. This cannot be achieved without adequate training, discipline, and a sense of personal as well as social responsibility.

## BLACK STRATEGIES, BLACK ENCAPSULATION, AND WHITE ENCIRCLEMENT

To say that the black situation in America is a complex one is to indulge in gross understatements. The black struggle in America is a life-and-death struggle. The intensity may sometimes be bewildering but so is the tenacity of racism and oppression. The black communities scattered over the dark corners of America exist in an encapsulated environment, suffocating from the political, social, economic, and psychological encirclement of white racism and oppression. Naturally, this environment generates turmoil – that is, an existential crisis that creates conflicting political strategies, varied ideological, philosophical interpretations, as well as the inevitable rituals of adaptive emotional responses. The environment creates all kinds of defense mechanisms by the necessity for human survival. It is to be expected that much of the confusion in the strategies of the black struggle would relate back to the nature of this environment. *Black people have come to live within a self-perpetuating vicious cycle.*

What we have called encapsulated black communities that exist within a perimeter of encirclement has been conceptualized by many black analysts as black colonies existing within the perimeter of Domestic Colonialism.[14] To understand the limitations as well as the dynamics of these encapsulated communities, or the defensive mechanisms they generate, it is desirable to consider a different set of black strategies. What was said earlier as a general criticism of black alternatives, their determination and articulation, is also generally true of black strategies. That is, black strategies are somewhat confused, abstract, and contradictory at many levels. This point should be borne in mind as we consider the following strategies.

### The Strategy of Permanent Confrontation

This strategy is characterized by "an ascending spiral of radicalization which has not yet reached its peak."[15] It involves not only putting maximum pressure on the sources of racism and oppression, but also sustaining such pressures overtime in order to win maximum concessions and conquer optimum positions of power. The rationale behind this is that the application of "permanent confrontation" will allow black people to extort enough resources from the white power structure to break the corroding chains of poverty and oppression. Thus, this is essentially a strategy of equal participation within America.

This strategy is frequently applied by all shades of black movements and organizations. In particular, this is the avowed strategy (now a philosophy) of black revolutionaries who, like the Panthers, have concluded that nothing but counterviolence can remedy the oppressive situation in which black people exist.* This conclusion is further reinforced by the *conception* of black communities as Domestic Colonies of America.

There are serious dangers and limitations in the "unstrategic" or "untactical" application of this strategy in accordance with the venerated remedies posited by other revolutionary theoreticians. The dangers are more real especially within those aspects of this strategy dealing with violence. First, a strategy should never be elevated to the level of philosophy or to the sanctuary of dogma. Violence has its place, perhaps more so in the American society than elsewhere. But violence can never be an end. As an end, violence is self-destructive. Bayard Rustin puts the point this way:

> . . . the tactic of violence is suicidal. White people may for a time make minor concessions to blacks who use violence – and thereby help to discredit non-violence as an effective means for achieving social change – but the point must inevitably be reached when the state will take repressive measures which will inflict untold harm upon the black community.[16]

Violence as a general philosophy of redress by blacks will reach the point of that massive white reaction known euphemistically as white *backlash* in American politics. At that point, it will immobilize the proponents by restricting their strategic options.

There are those black revolutionaries who are willing to risk the total destruction of all black people to achieve what they perceive as black people's ultimate objective. The least that can be said is to point out to them that although the price of black equality may mean the violent death of many black people who must sacrifice their lives so that other black people, the majority of black people, may live in freedom, equality, and self-determination, the aim of the black struggle is to preserve the dignified survival of black people and not to bring about their annihilation. A point is reached when any philosophy of violence as opposed to a rationalized strategic use of violence, becomes a philosophy of mass murder and nihilism.

Fanon is only situationally correct on this point when he argues in *The Wretched of the Earth* that violence (i.e., armed struggle) and violence alone is the answer to the oppression of all colonized peoples. Those who analyze the black situation in terms of Domestic Colonialism cannot afford the self-

*Stokely Carmichael's latest views are meant to resurrect this approach to solving black problems in America.

annihilating luxury of taking Fanon's situational prescriptions to its logical conclusions within the American context.[17] We must recall Lenin's haunting words already quoted, in order to learn to use violence as a strategy, whenever it is appropriate; to know when it is appropriate and when it is inappropriate. The strategy of Permanent Confrontation should mean:

> an effective, programmatic militancy ... an informed militancy, based on a clear analysis of the economic and social situation of (blacks) both in the South and in the Northern ghettos, an identification of the major institutions which can provide blacks with the maximum power and leverage in their struggle for equality, and a political strategy that can influence these institutions to serve the needs of the poor ... (For) a militancy that is based on frustration, withdrawal, and a desire to simplify or avoid reality rather than transform it will unintentionally ... destroy the possibility of solving (black) problems.[18]

Thus the aim of confrontation is to solve black problems, not to go on ego trips or distort black political reality or confuse and mislead masses of black people.

### The Strategy of Reparation, Romanticization and Self-Delusion

It became a vogue for many black groups and organizations to demand reparations from various constituent units of white America after James Forman, the director of the National Black Economic Development Conference (NBEDC) first popularized this strategy in *The Black Manifesto.* The demand for $500 million in reparations from basically religious institutions was followed by Hayward Henry's demands for $100 million from the Boston religious community.[19] This strategy developed by the NBEDC and further popularized by the Committee of Black Churchmen in Boston (CBCB) may be very effective if rationally utilized. For example, it could be effectively utilized either as a kind of *moral blackmail* to force the religious institutions to commit themselves actively and materially to the eradication of institutionalized injustices against black people or as a powerful instrument to expose the moral bankruptcy and pietistic hypocrisy of westernized, racist Christianity in America.

However, there are problems. First, it is not easy to calculate the exact amount of reparations which white America must pay to black America. For example, what is the dollar value of 400 years of oppression? What is the dollar value of mangled and distorted black humanity in America? What is the dollar value of the atomized, psychologically disinherited black individual? The dollar values for reparation are ultimately incalculable.

Secondly, these appeals, unlike the practical, political idea of "40 acres and a mule," are made mostly on ethical, not on power-political grounds. Thus the efficacy of this strategy will depend on the capacity of white America to be moved by a prick of conscience and hence the capacity to respond to valid moral arguments. It is doubtful whether white America possesses such capacity to a degree that will radically alter the oppressed situations of blacks in America.

Thirdly, there have been suggestions that the Federal Government should appropriate $10-30 billion for the total elimination of black poverty in America. The truth of the matter is that no one really knows how much money is needed to solve the problem. The danger then is that monies so allocated may not altogether meet the needs. Apart from the problems of maladministration of funds, there is the further danger that once such allocations have been made, additional black demands may be dismissed as unwarranted. Unless black leaders can demand at once all that which black people deserve, an unthinking, emotional application of the strategy of reparation can lead to black self-defeat or black self-immobilization.

The strategies of romanticization, self-indulgent delusion are sometimes appropriate and understandable defense mechanisms. That is, they are understandable as psychological adaptive responses to the threat to individual or collective black survival. But any drive to escape reality is dangerous to the prolonged survival of the human organism. Such self-indulgence is even more dangerous for the survival of black people. To survive, black people must learn to sting like the bee, while talking sweet as honey. Survival demands rational and calculated responses and a perpetual focus on, not escape from, reality.

The observable psychological need to remain at the abstract level, to substitute rhetoric for action, self-justification for discipline, pseudorevolutionary postures for genuine and constructive actions that tend toward black self-preservation, and mutual admiration for self-criticism constitutes another dead weight on black chances for survival. All these must become points of concern for black theroreticians and strategists. For unless they are reformed, no amount of concession from white America will save black people from their oppression.

Much of neo-Garveyism and perhaps the philosophy of the Republic of New Africa fall under this category. At least the Nation of Islam is taking concrete economic measures to support the religious isolation of the adherents. In fact, the latter has concretized its programs in many economic, social, and psychological ways that have revolutionized the members of the Nation. The Nation of Islam is carrying out a radical transformation of the psychology of many black people, thus inculcating a sense of discipline and social responsibility among the members. The Nation is acting out its philosophy without necessarily attacking other black movements.

By contrast, the unreality of neo-Garveyism has been aptly described by Bennett:

> ... Since no country on the face of the earth is prepared at this moment to accept 30 million Afro-American refugees and since the logistical problems of transporting 30 million Afro-Americans anywhere are staggering, and perhaps insurmountable, it seems that any viable strategy must be based on the fact that the overwhelming majority of Afro-Americans are going to win or die here.[20]

Any back-to-Africa movement is almost doomed to failure by the present African reality and by the forces of international law and national sovereignty. Moreover the idea that skilled, competent blacks could migrate permanently to Africa is dangerous, not because such migration will not help Africa, but because it will merely rob Peter to pay Paul. The migration of black talent to Africa will denude black movements of their desperately needed leadership while dooming the mass of black people in America to resignation and hopelessness. It is therefore most undesirable to advocate the kind of leadership drain implied in the permanent migration of black skills to Africa. This self-delusion persists in many quarters probably because hero worship provides psychological satisfaction to its supporters.* If Africa cannot absorb all the black people in the diaspora, she should not be encouraged to snatch the cream of black talent in the New World.

### The Strategy of Self-Negation

What is here conceptualized as the strategy of self-negation has been mentioned earlier in this essay. It is defined as negative black action precisely because such actions are directed by blacks against blacks. Such negative action takes several forms.

It is manifested in the hostility between black movements. Often, more time is consumed by the black radicals, the black revolutionaries and Black Power advocates, in publicly attacking movements like the NAACP, National Urban League, and the Civil Rights Movement, than in combating the real enemy. Such practice is destructive of black unity; it exposes black movements to further manipulation by the instrumentalities of oppression. For the white power structure, such indirect manipulation would allow black movements to destroy their own credibility and thereby delay or postpone indefinitely any consideration of black demands. The more this kind of self-immolation continues, the longer black people aid the forces of oppression and injustice in trampling black people under their feet.

Strategically, all black movements should view themselves as operating a complementary system of attack. Those who threaten the white power structure with violence may not win direct or significant concessions, but as a result of such action the white society might be willing to negotiate in earnest with the "moderates." Thus, if the Black Panthers, the revolutionaries, and the Black Power advocates can strategically force the white society to meet the demands of the Civil Rights Movement and the Urban League, black people could not be worse off for it.

Put differently, there is no reason why most of these black groups should remain at the abstract, ideological level, attacking each other's positions or ideologies while they can rationally and strategically focus on concrete and specific goals, each in its own way, until each has exhausted its area of practical productivity. This is a strategy that has seldom been tried. If the followers of the Republic of New Africa believe in physical or geographical separation, they should first concentrate on encouraging mass black migration to the five southern states they are demanding,[21] and then begin to take over the political and economic apparatus of these states instead of spending their venom on the supporters of integration and Civil Rights.

*The plans of Julian Bond and Mayor Charles Evers to concentrate in the 1970s on the massive organization of local black populations in the South to gain full political control through electioneering is a productive extension of this strategy.

It makes a substantial difference whether black movements and social groups focus on concrete action or whether they continue to emphasize the ideological differences between themselves. A quiet mobilization of black energies, black resources, and the masses of black people to help support those who can migrate to, and resettle in, those southern states which have a high percentage of black population would have far-reaching strategic consequences for the struggle against white racism and economic oppression. What effects would black control of the governorships and the houses of legislature in, say, Alabama, South Carolina, Georgia, Louisiana, or Mississippi have on the strategic configuration of political power positions in the United States? The political implications of such an eventuality would probably assume revolutionary proportions.

However, it is self-delusion to think that these states will be turned over to black people for the asking. It is also a grandiose illusion to think that the United States will ever allow these states, when controlled by blacks, to secede, or that, in case of forcible seizure of power in them, the United States Government will hesitate to put down any such attempt. Yet, many black people indulge in these grandiose illusions and seem to have substituted them for practicable actions.

It is probable that black people could take control of a number of states in this country through planned strategic migration and a voluntary resettlement aided by resources mobilized from other parts of the nation. But it should be clear from the beginning that the only alternative available to any state(s) controlled by black people is participation within the United States as (an) integral unit(s) of the federal government.

It is misleading to speak of a plebiscite supervised by the United Nations or any other international organization. It is self-delusion to contemplate a sovereign black state within the present boundaries of the United States. The American Civil War should be enough of an historical reminder to the dreamers of a sovereign black state within America. An extension of this kind of illusion is the romantic idea that 22 million strong Black Americans is potentially one of the most viable nation-states in the world – 26th largest.

This romantic chimera ignores the basic unlikelihood that all the black people scattered over America could, in the foreseeable future, migrate and resettle in a contiguous stretch of territory in America to make the attainment of such a black nation-state possible. The seers of this vision speak of the GNP of black people as if the total black economic productivity could be calculated outside the compass of the American economy. It is seldom remembered that although black people in the United States number about 11 percent of the total population, they own only 0.7 percent of the total financial assets of America, 6.5 percent of the personal income and 2 percent of assets held by households.[22] *What becomes increasingly apparent is that the language of discourse of strategies blurs the distinction between what is possible and what is not, between what can be done and what is merely emotionally pleasing and psychologically satisfying.*

Two other examples will illustrate further the utility of the strategy of concentrating on productive action while ignoring the zones of divergence between black movements. The first is the strategy of incorporating black communities into self-governing municipalities by Orzell Billingsley, the Birmingham attorney.[23] The successful incorporation of Roosevelt City in

Jefferson County, Alabama, suggests how existing patterns of segregation at least in many southern districts could be turned into oases of black political power and black pride in self-government.* Although the idea of incorporation has generated "academic" debates among whites and blacks who accuse Billingsley of separatism, this black lawyer has virtually ignored the debate precisely because it is academic, while quietly going about creating the conditions that will ensure the success of his ideas. Moreover, Billingsley undertakes all the necessary legal research and surveying largely out of his own resources without joining in a debate that could detract him from his original ideas or siphon his energies into wasteful bloodletting.

The second example is illustrated by the combination of strategies utilized by the late Whitney Young, the Director of the National Urban League. His strategy of *Quiet Diplomacy* was probably as revolutionary in its outputs as the total effect of all radical groups put together. Young's style was different to the degree that he focused always on practical goals, and to the degree that he was ready to "tack, maneuver and compromise," without betraying his people, his personal convictions, and his overall objective – which was to win participatory equality for black people in all areas of American life. He would rather go downtown and secure 2,000 jobs for black people from America's business executives than stand at the corner of a black ghetto street outshouting the radicals and the revolutionaries to prove that he was tough. By utilizing the art of strategic maneuvers, and appealing to "consciences where he found them, hard business instinct where he did not," Young's organization was able to land 40,000 jobs for black people in a single year.[24]

The effectiveness of Young's strategy is illustrated by Ernest Dunbar's appraisal of two contrasting styles at the African-American Dialogues held in Lagos, Nigeria, in March 1971. Dunbar writes:

> Towards the end of the Dialogues, Jesse Jackson indicted white America in blunt, blistering ghetto language that left electricity hanging in the air. Then Whitney spoke up, not to refute Jesse but to explain, in more refined terms, the reasons for Jesse's condemnation. White hackles rise when Jesse Jackson speaks, but though Whitney Young was saying essentially the same thing, he would leave the conference room and go swimming or drinking with the indicted.[25]

It is not the difference of style that counts so much as the complementarity of both strategies. Strategically, it takes the combination of a Jesse Jackson and a Whitney Young to move white America and get results for black people. As Dunbar put it:

> The instant anointment by the white media notwithstanding, there are real qualifications for becoming a genuine black leader, and they involve sacrifice and commitment. The ability to deliver rhetoric and bombast are simply not enough. It is not where a black leader lives that's important. Malcolm X did not live in Harlem, but in a comfortable house in New York's middle-class Queens. And it's not even his color: blue-eyed Adam Clayton Powell could have made it as a white man. It's not even whom he's married to: Jim Farmer's spouse is a white woman. The overriding considerations are: Will he be with us when we need him, and are his efforts bent on relieving our condition?[26]

No doubt, Dunbar exaggerates the aspects of the private lives of black leaders that could be safely and strategically overlooked. But he is most correct, however, in stating that the ultimate criterion of legitimate black leadership should be its concrete productive output. The strategic focus on productivity in evaluating black leaders and movements would have salutary effects on the potential complementarity of both the leadership cadres and the currently fragmented and factionalized black movements.

Unfortunately those groups and movements that gain the greatest public attention are those least inclined to adopt practical strategies in their struggle. For example, it was once announced that The Republic of New Africa (RNA) was negotiating to buy some land in Mississippi. Before the land was actually acquired, the RNA declared its intention to utilize it as the nucleus of a sovereign black state. The state officials in Mississippi reacted quickly by declaring that no such black state will ever exist in Mississippi. Whatever motivated the RNA to announce its intention, the fact remains that the public declaration was bad strategy especially when RNA's ultimate objective is taken into account.

The deeper one probes the practical consequences of black strategies currently in vogue, the more apparent it is that several of the black missionary revolutionaries are not just romantic visionaries but imposters. According to Bennett:

> the forward motion of the Rebellion has created new problems which probably cannot be resolved until the Rebellion has become more self-conscious, until it clarifies and defines its tasks and rises to a new level of awareness and organization. And since no Afro-American can fulfill himself if the Rebellion flounders and goes astray, it is incumbent upon all Afro-Americans to re-examine their strategies and commitments in the light of the needs and exigencies of the Rebellion . . . *But we have not begun to rap on the strategic problems involved in a sustained and long-range project for the radical transformation of Afro-America.*[27]

It may be argued as a rejoinder to the above that all black movements are contending for the support and mind of the same numerically few black people, and that this competition inevitably results in the overemphasis placed on ideological differences between black movements. That is, to win the minds of black people, the movements must openly debate each other and publicize their differences. It is contended here that such competition should either be in terms of practical productive outputs or it should wait altogether until each movement or group has exhausted its zones of practical productive

*The Panthers have since moved away from this posture to adopt a more pragmatic ideological position.

action. *In any case, the final test of the viability and efficacy of any black movement would not be its ability to rhetorically discredit its opponents but its capacity to prove its functional utility through concrete, practical action.*

The other ways in which blacks engage in self-negation can be found in the pathology of the ghetto itself. It was reported, for example, that the riots which took place in Washington, D.C., after the death of Dr. Martin Luther King resulted in loss of jobs for more than 4,900 people, most of whom were black.[28] Dr. Poussaint addressed the strategy of self-negation in the following eloquent words:

> We can blame many of our present conditions on whites and we would be largely right, we could say that blacks destroy other blacks because this white-regimented society is a violent one. We could say that our self-dislike is the result of racism and thus rationalize taking it out on each other. We could say that because we are powerless we are more competitive and jealous of each other's success, that's why we fight each other. We could say that the poverty and slums provide a fertile soil for the growth of the less desirable elements in human nature, and that's why we rob each other. We could speak of a white-controlled law and judiciary which discriminate against blacks and encourage black criminality, and argue that those are the reasons we kill each other. All of these indictments, in some degree, would be correct. But . . . where do we go from here? Do we wait until the sick racist whites are cured before we begin to positively mobilize ourselves and stop certain behavior? Will we say that we cannot get rid of our self-destructive drives until our "parents" change? Do we sit around and blame them while we continue to live passively in the decadence which they have created in our community – in our minds?
>
> Black people are over 21. They have had a horrible "childhood" and continue to live with oppression. Now we must combat those forces which keep us hurt and divided without diverting most of our energy into trying to cure white folks.
>
> Our black communities can no longer condone blacks hurting, killing, and exploiting other blacks. We should have no room for black heroin pushers or black gangsters who prey on the poor.[29]

Dr. Poussaint advocates community programs that begin in early childhood, both in the schools and in the homes, to instill manhood and brotherhood in black youth. The quotation from Dr. Poussaint thus illustrates the validity of the point made earlier that descriptive analysis does not necessarily produce curative antidotes. *The curative antidotes must be found largely within the inner strength of black people and not primarily from the concessions of the white power structure.*

It is equally puerile to debate whether racism or economic exploitation is the source of black problems. Both racism and the other institutionalized forms of white oppression are inextricably united in a marriage that knows no laws of divorce. It seems equally dangerous to push the strategy of Black Capitalism too far since we already know the human wreckage wrought by Corporate Capitalism in close alliance with white racism. How valuable is it to prove that a few blacks can own, operate and manage a business successfully when such proof will in fact rest on a foundation of perpetuated black exploitation?

### The Strategy of Percentages

In terms of systematic public articulation, this is perhaps the most recent of the strategic responses of black people to the problems of social and racial injustice. The strategy of percentages is concerned with the procurement of racial justice through ethnic or racial arithmetical engineering. *The ultimate and categorical demand of the strategy is the black control of at least a certain percentage of everything in America that equals the percentage of blacks in the total population.* Thus, if blacks constitute 11 percent of the total population, then they should *own* 11 percent of the gross national product, control 11 percent of all houses of legislatures, share 11 percent of all power resources, influence, and authority. In short, blacks, would control 11 percent of effective power of resource allocation and decision-making at all levels of societal governance.

It is obvious that the radical implications of a more serious effort to pursue the black struggle through the use of this strategy have not been critically examined. For example, when applied to the punitive instruments of society, this strategy would require that blacks should not constitute more than 11 percent of all the inmates of correctional institutions! Moreover, the effective application of the strategy would result in radical transformation of the social and political structure of America.

The use of such a strategy necessarily requires that black people anticipate the range of responses from white America. Given the possibility that part of the gains of some black people would also be the losses of some whites, the stage may unavoidably be set for new realignments of conflicting social groups and the intensification of other racial polarities that are currently dormant in the society.

Generally speaking, there is still wide scope for the exploitation and manipulation of this strategy for the acquisition of effective black power in the drive for proportional equality which is the hallmark of this racial arithmetic of social engineering. A more systematic exploitation of the strategy should therefore result in more flexible options for black strategic planning. Although the strategy may be attacked for institutionalizing a racial quota system of social engineering, its consistency with the objective facts of American racial history would tend to undermine that attack. In fact there is a morality of content that should allow greater gain to be made before white America could resort to their typical "white backlashes."

It appears likely that a majority of black people would welcome a successful implementation of such a strategy. However, the pursuit of this strategy would call forth a level of discipline, maturity, and mastery of skills not yet available among the present black population if the achieved powers and resources are to be managed properly, efficiently, and purposefully for effective black liberation. Paradoxically, the adoption of this strategy inevitably implies either a tacit or conscious decision to become integral, functional, and full participants in Mainstream U.S.A. To the extent that this is the case, the strategy may be nothing more than an attractive reformulation of the integrationist strategy in the form and manner consistent with the ethos of American ethnic and cultural pluralism. Therefore, this is a strategy on which more black strategists should undertake more serious and informed analysis. It is a strategy that should also command more discussion among the generality of the black public.

## MARXIST ANALYSIS AND THE BLACK STRUGGLE

A rapidly increasing number of black radicals have begun to cast their analysis of the black experience into the Marxist analytic framework. This is not radically new, as black socialists and even communists, have appeared from time to time on the sociopolitical scene since the turn of this century. Angela Davis is a most dramatic and contemporary case in point. What is important to note is the growing number of such analysis. The theoreticians of the Black Panther Party, Eldridge Cleaver, and Huey Newton, for example, view the black struggle within the context of a global rising tide of the revolutionary struggle of the oppressed, impoverished, and exploited peoples of the world against the exploitation of the propertied, oppressor, owning classes of the world.[30] For his class of black revolutionary analysts, the works of Fanon, Mao, Ho Chi Minh, Castro, and Debray have become the new scriptures. The thrust of such analysis deserves attention, for from it has arisen the conception of the black struggle as an *impending revolution.*

James Boggs, one of these revolutionary theoreticians, has described the two *necessary* conditions of this *revolution.* He writes:

> a revolution involves, first of all, an escalating struggle for power, culminating in the forced displacement of the social groups or strata who have held economic and political power, by another or other social groups who have hitherto been ruled by those in power. Secondly, a revolution involves the destruction of one form of social organization which has been developed to meet the needs of a given society but which has obviously failed to meet the needs of a significant section of that society, and its displacement by another system or form of social organization which purports to meet these needs.[31]

Boggs argues that there are only three alternatives open to America: (1) maintaining the status quo in a state of progressive deterioration, (2) the liberating of America through a successful mobilization of black revolutionary power, or (3) the mobilization of counterrevolutionary forces to thwart the objectives of black revolutionary power.[32] Although he concedes that the Black Revolution is not inevitable, Boggs believes that it is the most feasible of the three alternatives. The premises of this prediction are rather interesting.

First, the American people are said to have grown weary of the deterioration of their culture, that they have become aware that the present confusion cannot continue for long, and finally that a new system must replace the old, archaic, and chaotic system. Secondly, it is argued that the attempts of a white extremist minority to mobilize counterrevolutionary forces to destroy the emerging revolutionary forces in America would fail because their tactics would be met with revulsion and fear by the majority of the population who occupy the large space between right and left. Thirdly, it is argued that black revolutionary power would give rise to fundamental divisions, turmoil, crisis, and conflicts among the white population whose effects would be the immobilization of the large majority of people in the middle.

These arguments conceal many assumptions of the black revolutionists that should be explicitly analyzed. First, the assumption that the white population could be immobilized by desensus is utopian. Any degree of immobility among the large middle population will tend to be reflected in the same if not greater degree of desensus and immobility among black people. The enormity of black oppression has not reflected itself in greater unity or consensus among black people than we can find in the white population.

Secondly, we may grant the theoretical possibility of a successful black revolution in America. *That is, it is theoretically possible that the black people in America could overthrow the government of the United States,* in the very limited sense that revolutions are always led and carried out by a minority of a people in any country or institution. But it is utopian to think that black people could sustain such a revolution or become the ruling class in America. Different coalitions of white groups could effectuate a more or less permanent displacement of the ruling groups and cause a radical transformation of existing social structures and organizations but black people by themselves have a very slim probability of effectuating such transformations.

Thus, the call for a violent revolution requires at a minimum the coalition of many social, economic, and political groups that transcend racial boundaries. Part of the growing contradiction in the Marxist frame of analysis of the black experience results from the racial determination and motivation of the black struggle and its inability to accommodate the validity of the participation of non-blacks in such a revolution. Revolutionary Marxism assumes the coalition of the oppressed and exploited classes against the oppressor classes. Translated into the American situation, that would mean a coalition of labor, black people, student radicals, and the white poor against the existing power structure. The prospects of such a coalition are very small. Because of the exigencies of racism, black people are not psychologically inclined to favor such a coalition; for the same or similar reasons, masses of the white poor, although objectively oppressed as black people, are not likely to view the latter as equal travellers in the same social predicament. The white poor derives immense psychological satisfaction from the myth of white racial superiority. This subjective irrationality invariably supersedes the objective reality of their social and economic oppression, particularly in terms of their perception of their social-functional identification with blacks.

This last point also explodes the sterility of the revolutionary analysts' preoccupation with the purely economic aspects of black oppression. For most black Marxist analysts, white racism is only a means of rationalizing the material or economic exploitation of black people. Even if this was true at the beginning of black exploitation and oppression, it is no longer true today. White racism has become a *cause* of black exploitation and oppression. It is therefore virtually impossible to deal with racism or economic exploitation as separate phenomena. They both co-determine the objective conditions of black people in America. It is this intricate co-determination that gives the white poor their subjective feeling of superiority even over well-to-do blacks who are not subject to serious economic deprivations.

Furthermore, the assumption that white America would stop short of massive repression in the event of real threat to the survival of the present social, political, and economic structures constitutes an indulgence in fantasy. In fact it could be argued that the present level of repression reflects the capacity of the "system" to control, beguile, rechannel, and manipulate social protests by nonviolent means. Any increasing diminution in this "system's" capability will tend to reflect itself in a greater reliance on violent counterreactions to the sources of stress and threat. How this legalized control and utilization of the means of coercion can be deployed has been more than demonstrated in the treatment of the Black Panther Party. The incapacitation of the Party through massive and wanton use of legally sanctioned violence should be viewed as proof of the system's readiness to use any means necessary to protect itself against real or imagined threat. Generally speaking, as the threat of rebellion has grown in America, the system's articulation of the doctrine of "Law and Order" has also grown, thus making legally sanctioned use of violence more prevalent.

It should be realized that no matter what revolution takes place in the United States, the government and most of its institutions will continue to be dominated by white people. As a racially distinguished minority in an environment where race is a salient cognitive as well as sociopolitical factor, black people cannot become the dominant power structure of the United States. *Black people are large enough numerically and oppressed enough sociopolitically and economically to be theoretically capable of bringing about a revolution in America. But they are too few and too weak to ever be capable of maintaining and controlling a permanent revolution; they can never become the ruling class in America without at the same time establishing the most unheard-of system of minority repression in the world.*[33]

There are other questions to be answered: Can black people carry out a revolution of this type without the aid of white groups? If past and present experience is any guide, the answer is negative. First, with the possible exception of the Black Muslims, no black group, or movement – not even the Panthers or any radical black organization – has been able to do much without direct or indirect white support. Most of the money that supports and maintains the groups originates from white sources. To a degree, the source of such support tends to determine the limits of operation or antiestablishmentarian activities of such groups. This is another instrumentality of the white or government controlled cycle of black responses. Secondly, it offers very little consolation to realize that even if the black revolution were to succeed, it would result only in the establishment of another white-dominant structure of government. Thus, the initial repudiation of white participation in the revolution would imply a labor of loss.

From a strategic standpoint, every successful or unsuccessful revolution provides relatively equal opportunities for would-be revolutionairies and would-be defenders of the status quo. Every revolutionary blueprint reveals not only how a revolution can be made but also inevitably how the revolution can be defeated. The problem of world revolutions lies precisely in the fact that the sources of revolutionary strategies and ideas are available both to the believers and the infidels. *The inevitability of revolutions is precisely that the revolutionist, by declaring himself the enemy of the status quo, has put himself in a state of war against the established order. In doing so he has unwittingly sanctioned the authority of the state to declare him an enemy and to use its resources to incapacitate the revolutionist.*

When the revolutionist threatens the survival of the state, he also has granted to the state the right of self-preservation. This "double-edged" nature of revolutionary objectivity works seriously against revolutions led by minorities distinguishable especially by race. After all, there have been relatively few successful revolutions that have shaken social and political fabrics in the world: the French Revolution (1789), the Bolshevik Revolution (1917), the Chinese Revolution (1949), and the Cuban Revolution (1959). The rest are either "quiet revolutions" or pretenders to that name. Not a single one of these revolutions can be repeated, for each has limited the strategic options of future revolutionaries by instructing the defenders of the status quo how to preserve their regimes. This is the reality contained in the sentence "we shall not tolerate another Cuba in the Western hemisphere."

This does not mean that revolutions would not happen in the future; it only suggests that future revolutions must work out their unique strategies in the light of the particular manifestations and configuration of the forces of oppression; for each revolution results in reconfiguration or regrouping of the instrumentalities of oppression. Racism, like economic oppression for example, wears many faces, which parallel the many guises of imperialism in the New Nations. If a people's land is no longer colonized, their economy, culture, or mind can still be colonized to protect neo-colonialism in the guise of political independence.[34]

Finally, a fatal characteristic of black strategies is the obvious lack of "computational strategic response." This applies to all black movements including the avowed revolutionists. An elementary rule of strategic planning in warfare is the computation of one's capabilities and weaknesses and the juxtaposition of these alongside those of the enemy. The present stage of the black struggle exaggerates black strategic capabilities, while underemphasizing or altogether overlooking black weaknesses. In addition, it totally fails to analyze and compute the strategic arsenal of the white power structure. This is a particularly vexing source of black self-delusion. Much reliance is consequently placed on the moral conscience of the white power structure and little attention paid to the complex and manifold structures through which black responses can be controlled or manipulated to serve the overall objectives of the state.

These techniques of control and manipulation range from media and white "election" of black leaders, the recognition of black leaders and "revolutionary radicals," to the financial support-control mechanisms of the establishment and its affluent functionaries. They include the controlled, manipulated "funnel admission" policies of the "system" that reinforce the one-by-one admission of blacks into the very low echelons of power positions, and the carefully manipulated reward systems that silence many black articulators of black oppression. Successful black strategies would emerge only out of a computational matching of planned black strategic responses against several combinations of the strategic options open to the white power structure. Such options include the "monitoring systems" of surveillance, dossier and information-gathering – storage-and-retrieval-arms of the state.

In addition black strategic responses will inevitably have to face the agony of defining the place of the individual within the collectivity. At this present state of black consciousness, the more radical or revolutionary strategists tend to dismiss any expression of individuality. And yet the collective goal tends to be defined by a small group in the name of all. It is not always clear whether such objectives really further the self-realization of the collectivity or whether they merely lead to the self-realization of the core of elite leaders at the top.

## FRAGMENTED ACQUISITION OF POWER AND THE CRISES IN BLACK STUDIES: A CASE IN POINT

It has been argued earlier in this essay that massive power can neither be granted nor seized. Such instrumentalities of power that are either conceded to or conquered by black people will tend to be in piecemeal, fragmented forms in localized places scattered over this nation. Black Studies Departments or Programs will be established on predominantly white, individual college campuses. Model Cities Programs, Community and City Renewal Projects, Black Capitalist Ventures, Job Corps, Poverty Programs, Peace Incorporated Institutions, etc. will exist at localized districts. All these constitute fragmented sources of power for fragmented black groups and communities.

*Although most of the concessions granted by white America are probably granted in bad faith, with calculated intention of seeing the programs fail, black people must be ready to turn such concessions into black possessions and black properties.* Thus, once Departments of Black Studies and Black Studies Programs are established on university or college campuses they should be conceived from that time on as sources of black power, as part of the instrumentalities of black people, and as possessions or property of black people, to be protected, developed, and raised to the highest level of excellence. Such utilization would create other sources of reinforced black power.

In many black communities much of the inadequate grants are poorly administered if not outrightly misspent. Observations also reveal that many black people continue to regard concessions won or conquered as white possessions to be used recklessly, on the grounds that they belong to the exploiting racists. This, unfortunately, is negative black action. It is argued that because federal government appropriations are not enough, what is appropriated need not be spent judiciously. Black people have been known to "borrow" black funds, and Black Studies materials without any intention of returning them on the grounds that they belong to the white man. This pattern of black behavior constitutes a dissipation of black energy and a disservice to the black struggle as a whole.

In some black communities in Pittsburgh, Philadelphia, New York City, Syracuse, Buffalo, Columbus, Ohio, Detroit, Ann Arbor, Kalamazoo, Albion, and Grand Rapids, to name a few cities in which the author has recorded observations on black housing, many black people leave their rented houses virtually unkept generally because they do not own the property, because rents are generally outrageously exorbitant, and because it is widely believed that any attempt to maintain the property almost invariably works to the economic advantage of the money-hungry, exploiting landlords. Although many of these reasons are valid, they could and are, easily frequently used as rationalizations for general lack of regard for keeping one's environment hygienically healthy. And yet it should be realized that some black people cannot know how to keep and appreciate property unless they are encouraged to begin to care for their rented houses. This point should be taken with caution especially since there exists a vicious circle about housing that defies reason or simple prescriptions for remedy. *In any case it is the reason why black people do certain things that should be emphasized. If, in order not to help increase the profits of greedy landlords, black people allow a deterioration of their environments until they constitute serious hazards to the healthy and dignified survival of black people, then it may be in the interest of the people to maintain reasonable standards of hygiene and health for no other reason than the very survival of the black people concerned.*

The strategy of black people should therefore be directed toward the coordination of fragmented power sources so as to establish a matrix of black community energies for the elevation and self-realization of black people. Black Studies Departments and Programs especially will become supportive springs of black-relevant knowledge only if the blacks who man and operate them decide not to use them for the protection of mediocrity and incompetence. If Black Studies Departments and Programs are to succeed in spite of white America and not necessarily because of it, there will come a time when some incompetent black "scholars" will be fired, and others who have the skills needed for black survival (will be) hired to replace them. That is to suggest that black survival will require hard decisions that may go beyond protecting the source of livelihood for particular individual black persons in any part of America. Similarly, when black police officers gain effective control of the protective responsibilities of law enforcement in the black communities, they will be required by their new roles to dislodge, not protect, black criminality in all forms.

We referred earlier to the debunking of education by the rising black youth. This is happening at a time when trained and skilled black people are in decreasing supply but in increasing demand. Generally, many black students do not attend classes even when they have knowledgeable blacks as their professors. They plead all kinds of excuses, take unlimited liberties, insist on unearned good grades on grounds that some incompetent, guilt-ridden white professors are known to be destroying these black students by rewarding their irresponsibilities with unearned passing grades. When such unworthy black outputs are on record, the forces of oppression could easily turn them against black people's increasing incapacity to hold their destinies in their own hands.

The tendency toward a lifestyle of reckless abandon sucks the blood from black vitality and drains black moral energy and the power to resist.

Most of these unfortunate attributes can only be removed

by black people, not by the white society. And no amount of self-imposed delusion or rationalization will save black people from oppression; no amount of white-initiated actions or black-coerced concessions will ensure black survival until these inner and internal contradictions of black people are removed by black people themselves.

Black Studies Departments and Programs across the nation are either facing or will soon be facing a growing crisis resulting from both internal and external factors. This crisis is closely related to the conditions under which the programs were established. The white educational institutions which granted them did so under threat and pressure from the black communities and students in and around these institutions. Others were established in anticipation of black radical demands and for the overall purpose of preventive innovations. But most, if not all, such programs were granted in bad faith, in the hope that the white institutions could buy time until the "rebels" cooled off and all could return to business as usual. Some other programs were established to "buy" off some black troubleshooters whose activities were increasingly centered around protecting their "fat" salaries and "rocking the boat" as little as possible.

Like African Studies Programs, most Black Studies Departments and Programs were funded either on "soft" funds or on foundation grants that are famous for their short duration and sudden deaths. Most of these funds are beginning to dry up, if they have not done so already. When colleges and universities face increasing diminution of financial resources, these programs are usually the first to wither away because of "tight money" crises and cutbacks. Since we are concerned with strategies, it is necessary to remember that those concerned with seeing such programs survive should insist on budgets provided for within the "hard," necessary and continuous sources of funds for general college and university financing. Otherwise, whenever the foundation "start-up" funds dry up, these programs will tend to wither with them.

But the most important threat to the survival of such black institutions will probably come from within the black people themselves. Many of such programs have tended to be used as breeding grounds for adventurism and opportunism. This development represents a serious danger. Increasingly, black people view black studies as institutions where people spend money without accountability or accounting; where black "scholars" ask for salaries that defy all rationality; where prospective faculty members debunk traditional academic standards and demand positions of Assistant, Associate, of Full Professors with little to show for their academic productivity or integrity; and where those who make little or no contributions to academic excellence demand instant promotions.

These are danger signals. They represent the ambivalence of struggling black scholars, some of whom wish to disregard traditional criteria of academic disciplines only to find themselves increasingly incapable or unwilling to compete, or do the hard work by which superior scholarship is generally established. Black Studies are at a stage of development where black people must *sacrifice* and *specialize* in order to produce that alternative superior scholarship that will guarantee black survival. And yet the opposite seems to be the case; that is, many of the programs tend to be used for personal power purposes. This pattern of behavior and perception reinforces the general attitudes of black students everywhere.

The observable attitudes of many black students toward the process of learning constitutes another internal source of danger. Many of them do not seem to hold Black Studies or their faculties in high esteem. They behave as if Black Studies offer courses that demand no work, and no class attendance before the students could "earn" A's and B's. For many of these students, the fact of blackness is sufficient justification for passing any Black Studies Courses. And many of them would in fact take their professors to task should they receive F's and D's for their irresponsible academic behavior.

Everything tends to remain at the emotional, ideological, and sometimes irrational level. *Black Studies is increasingly teaching predominantly white classes. The most unfortunate part of this growing crisis is the realization that the academic satisfaction many Black Studies faculties derive from teaching comes not from their black students on the whole but from their white students.* The latter group usually completes the assignments on schedule, usually gives praiseworthy attention to the content of instruction, and undoubtedly gains more out of the courses than most black students do. Part of the problem results from lack of motivation and direction among black students. This lack is also symptomatic of the history of mis-education on the part of the average black student. But part of the problem also results from general inability on the part of the black students to separate political, student-action concerns from the demands of academic rigor. One finds that black students who fail to attend classes and who fail to do class assignments or to take scheduled examinations demand passing grades on grounds that they have been active in black students organizations! Although such experiences may be valid in themselves, they are not substitutes for required skills in say Biology, Mathematics, or African Politics.

Black studies exist for the development and dissemination of black relevant knowledge, and only the best minds with the best training and most rigorous self-discipline would be able to contribute appreciably to the development of that body of knowledge. The survival of these programs would depend largely on what the black people who manage them do or fail to do with them.

## CONCLUSION

Perhaps the reader has found this essay too critical or pessimistic; he may have found many points of disagreement. But the hope is that he could not have escaped being provoked to think in those strategic computational terms which, we suggest are a necessary condition for black survival in America. It is in this particular sense that we have advanced the thesis that the salvation of black people lies in their own hands, and that black people must do what they must to ensure a dignified survival for themselves. Half of the black struggle must be directed toward the elimination of those internal contradictions within individual blacks as well as social groups. All the concessions won from the white power structure will be of little use unless those patterns of black behavior which lead to self-negation are removed. Finally, we have suggested that whatever black alternatives are, black people are destined to participation within the United States. This realization should help many black people to avoid strategies that only lead to delusion or self-defeatism.

## NOTES

[1] Kenneth B. Clark, *Dark Ghetto,* New York, Harper & Row, 1967, p. 11

[2] Dr. Poussaint, "Why Blacks Kill Blacks," *Ebony,* Oct. 1970, pp. 149-50.

[3] Jack L. Daniel, "Black Rhetoric and the Power to Define," Faculty Seminar, Department of Black Studies, University of Pittsburgh, Feb. 1971.

[4] Lerone Bennett Jr., "Liberation," *Ebony,* August 1970, pp. 36-43.

[5] Clarence Rollo Turner, "Black Gradualism: The Retarding Politics of Self-Determination," *Black Lines: A Journal of Black Studies,* Vol. 1, No. 1, Fall 1970, p. 31 (see also pp. 31-36).

[6] Quoted by Lerone Bennett Jr., *Ebony,* August 1969, p. 34.

[7] *Dark Ghetto,* p. 199.

[8] *Ibid.,* pp. 219-222

[9] Bennett, *Ebony,* August 1969, p. 32

[10] *Ibid.,* p. 32.

[11] *Ibid.,* p. 32, italics mine.

[12] Mao Tse-tung, *On Protracted War,* Foreign Language Press, Peking, 1967, pp. 47-51.

[13] Quoted by Bennett, *Ebony* August 1969, p. 36

[14] See, for example, William K. Tabb, *The Political Economy of the Black Ghetto,* New York, Norton, 1970, Chapter 2, pp. 21-34.

[15] Bennett, *Ebony,* August 1969, p. 32.

[16] Bayard Rustin, "The Myths of the Black Revolt," *Ebony,* August 1969, p. 104.

[17] See Frantz Fanon, *The Wretched of the Earth,* New York, Grove Press, 1963, pp. 7-106.

[18] Rustin, pp. 96-97.

[19] See, for example, *Ebony,* August 1969, p. 98.

[20] Bennett, p. 38.

[21] These states are (1) Alabama, (2) South Carolina, (3) Georgia, (4) Louisiana, (5) Mississippi.

[22] See, for example, estimates by Dr. Andrew F. Brimmer in "Economic Integration and the Progress of the Negro Community," *Ebony,* August 1970, pp. 118-121.

[23] See Carlyle C. Douglass, "Incorporation: A New Tactic for Saving Black Areas," *Ibid.,* pp. 100-105.

[24] See "Whitney Young: He was a Doer," *Newsweek,* March 22, 1971, p. 29.

[25] Ernest Dunbar, "The Lost Black Leader," *Look,* April 20, 1971, p. 76.

[26] *Ibid.,* p. 76.

[27] Bennett, *op. cit.,* 1969, p. 36, Italics mine.

[28] *Ebony,* August 1969, p. 102.

[29] Dr. Poussaint, "Why Blacks Kill Blacks," *Ebony,* October 1970, pp. 149-50.

[30] See, for example, Eldridge Cleaver's *Soul on Ice.*

[31] James Boggs, "Black Revolutionary Power," *Ebony,* August 1970, p. 154.

[32] *Ibid.,* p. 155.

[33] South Africa and Rhodesia represent the only two environments where a racial minority continues to remain as the ruling class by means of coercive repression of another racial majority. The world, and black people in particular, have condemned such a system. Thus the options available to black people are limited. The logic of their predicament leads inexorably to the defense of universal human values; for they cannot seek to substitute a black system of inhumanity for a white history of inhumanity without justifying the very inhumanity they seek to destroy.

[34] For a more theoretical and detailed formulation of this view, see Regis Debray, *Revolution in the Revolution,* New York, Grove Press, 1967.

# 21
# *Radicalism and Separatism Among Four West Indians:*

## W.A. Domingo, C.L.R. James, Marcus Garvey, and Claude McKay *

DENNIS FORSYTHE

Is it possible to assess the radical status or claims of black groups and individuals in any objective way? This paper refuses to accept subjective chaos; instead we propose an objective model or *political formula,* which we will then illustrate by way of a detailed discussion of the ideologies of four West Indian radicals – W.A. Domingo, C.L.R. James, Marcus Garvey, and Claude McKay.

It is suggested here that when one discusses black radicalism one should be essentially concerned with *radicalism from the black group perspective,* on the assumption that *each group in the society faces a unique configuration of problems or sets of contradictions. A black radical or revolutionary is therefore one who attempts to change the basic contradictions of a particular society insofar as they bear down on his particular group.* The basic requisite therefore is a knowledge of the core or structural aspects of a *particular society* that significantly created and sustained the particular group problem. I believe that the best method of unravelling the various roots of the collective demise of blacks, and one that averts confusions and interpretive anarchy, is an historical analysis that specifies the key factors which historically led to the enslavement of blacks, because it may be taken that the present is the cumulative effect of slavery and its offshoots. To arrive at these factors, it is necessary that we pose two questions concerning the origin of modern Negro American slavery.

1. Why did this slavery emerge in the first place?
2. Why were blacks enslaved as opposed to any other group?

In answer to the first question, it is quite clear that it was (1) the imperatives of capitalistic competition which made slavery necessary. As for the reasons for *black enslavement,* slavery historiography suggests the operative presence of (2) *white ethnocentricism* and (3) the greater power of whites. These three factors together constituted the sufficient basis for black enslavement. Without one or the other, blacks would not have been enslaved and their descendants would not have inherited their particular status, position, and problems.

Thus conceived, a black radical should be assessed in terms of his awareness of these factors and the extent to which his ideology grapples with these three variables. If he advocates the control or countervailing of all three factors, then he can be defined as "most radical" and most realistic, for such a position offers the possibility of maximum changes from the black group perspective. Correspondingly, an individual or movement is "less radical" and more idealistic when he or it ignores or rejects the reality of these three factors, for this would mean that the degree of change that can be attained *for the group* is nil or minimal.

By means of these variables, we may therefore categorise the various modalities within black protests in terms of how they grasp the importance of these variables. Logically and substantively, we derive four types of radicals – each occupying a particular rank in the radical hierarchy.

DIAGRAM SHOWING TYPES AND DEGREES OF RADICALISM IN BLACK PROTESTS IN AMERICA

(- indicates rejection; + indicates acceptance)

| | Variables | | |
|---|---|---|---|
| Types of Radicals | Capitalism | White Ethnocentrism | White Power |
| Civil Rights (Civic radicalism) | + | + | + |
| Communism (Internationalist radicalism) | - | + | + |
| Black Capitalists (Black radicalism) | + | - | - |
| Progressive Nationalists (Progressive radicalism) | - | - | - |

### CIVIC RADICALISM

Civic radicals are essentially patriotic nationalists, with the limited goal of becoming integrated either within America or in the West Indies. They make especial point of appealing to a type of nationalistic sentiment. They tend to work in and with the system in order to effect change. This "civil rights" approach is the most reformist type of radical. In the United States they are, in essence, seeking to complete the American

*Written especially for this book.

Revolution of 1776, which was, in essence, a bourgeois revolution. They are not attempting to change the system but rather to be integrated into it, to be counted in as individuals. They do not reject capitalism or the prevalent white values in the society. Neither do they recognise and argue in terms of the uniqueness of the black experience and use this group base as a leverage. They make especial appeal to the "American Dilemma" and to the American Constitution and rely on the routine methods of the political process.

### W.A. Domingo

We will use the case of W.A. Domingo and his Jamaica Progressive League to bring out the full ramifications and weaknesses inherent in this type of West Indian radicalism. In 1918 W.A. Domingo was a young and active member of Garvey's U.N.I.A., speaking frequently on its platform and gaining notice as a good public speaker. But Domingo subsequently resigned from the U.N.I.A. because "he disagreed with the extreme form of racialism which Garvey advocated."[1] He then went into business on his own and became "a man of modest competence." In 1936 he, along with other established Jamaicans[2] in New York, "who had never forgotten their country," formed the Jamaica Progressive League of New York, under the assumption that "the awakening of consciousness of nationality is what is needed today."[3] The group stood for independence under the impetus of nationalism. In the first pamphlet put out by W.A. Roberts on behalf of the group, he stated: "I set the ideal of nationalism before all Jamaicans. There is a definite sustaining and guiding strength in national sentiment, in a national consciousness, and this can be created only along parallel lines of political action and artistic fruitfulness." Rev. Ethelred Brown, Secretary of the organisation, expressed the sentiment of the group in this Exile's Ode to Jamaica.

> Let us all our voices ring
> Let us arise and sing
> Of our dear land
> Jamaica! Here to thee
> Thy sons across the sea,
> We pledge our fealty –
> A loyal band.

Domingo lost no time in declaring that the programme of the League was "constitutional."[4] The League, he wrote, "will agitate for self-government, petition for it, make sacrifices for it, take every legal step within its power until that supreme goal has been attained."[5] Strictly working within the legalistic parameters, the Jamaica Progressive League (in alliance with the New York League) campaigned for universal suffrage, labour reforms, civil service reforms, took up the question of discrimination of steamships plying between Jamaica and America, took up with the Postmasters of Jamaica and the United States the question of the inequitable airmail postage rates between the two countries, contributed $500 for the defense of Jamaica rioters in the Frome disturbances, and presented a report on the conditions of Jamaica to the Commission appointed by England to look into the 1938 disturbances. Full support was also pledged for any political party that took up self-government as its primary concern – a promise that shortly materialised in the formation of the Peoples' National Party of Jamaica.

By "relentless pamphleteering," they agitated for reforms along legalistic lines but also resorted to appeals to consciences: "The time has arrived to ask the Mother Country to restore their ancient rights."[6] We must in the meantime, they argued, "show our aptitude for the responsibilities of liberty, or it will never be granted. . . . We must . . . begin to act as a people within the framework of the Empire, and cease speaking and thinking as apathetic subjects under a Crown Colony system."[7]

The bourgeois character of the group may be seen not only in the composition and explicit aims of the group but in its theoretical analysis. W.A. Roberts, for instance, argued that the old House of Assembly, though controlled by the planters and merchants in their own interests, was nonetheless "Jamaican," because a "nation" consisted of "any people that has seen its generations come and go on the same soil for centuries."[8] Jaime O'Meally, one of the leading theorists of the movement, urged the masses to unite with bourgeois leaders because for a long time to come, he argued, the nationalistic movement will "depend on the educated representatives of the middle class who have achieved an understanding of the historical movement."[9]

It was the fire of nationalism that burned in Domingo's soul and subordinated alternative notions of race, socialism, or radicalism. On October 18, 1938, he moved the following resolution in a meeting of the League:

> That the Board of Directors hereby condemn the raising of the Race issue as an argument for self-government, it being the settled conviction of this body that this is a nationalistic and democratic movement including all races which go to form the Jamaican people.[10]

He was equally circumspect in his radical emphasis. The P.N.P., in his defense at the time of his arrest and detainment, argued that when Domingo returned to Jamaica in 1939 to organise a branch of the League of New York "his utterances were distinguished for their moderation and good sense."[11] There should be no surprise at this because the whole philosophy of the League was opposed to "radicalism." A leading spokesman for the League once reported that they had agreed from the beginning to "make haste slowly":

> It was unanimously agreed (by the Directors of the League) that radicalism was unsuitable and not to the best interests of the Island and we would not endorse or support any radical movement whose purpose was fundamentally to change the present economic system. We agreed, however, to agitate and work for self-government and for such reforms as would benefit the majority.[12]

It is therefore understandable why the Peoples' National Party (allies of the Progressive League) expelled the four leftists (the "4-H's") from the Party and why the leader of this Party (the P.N.P.) on a subsequent tour in America assured Americans that:

> We are all resolved to oppose communism in Jamaica to the utmost and that I am confident that with active

> steps to relieve conditions and effective Trade Union activity we are well able to control and master the small group of communists actively present and working in our country.[13]

The inherent limitations of the bourgeois-nationalist ideology which they held also found expression in Domingo's conservative attitudes toward the West Indian Federation. His basic position was that "without federating with any country Jamaica single-handedly [had] secured an advanced Constitution"; that since "Jamaicans are politically more advanced and alert and aggressive and progressive than their fellow islanders," Jamaicans should go it alone, for any "inclusion of Jamaica is a great disservice to the country."[14] Being essentially a formalist, the gist of his opposition to Jamaica joining the West Indian Federation boiled down to a statistical one:

> "Big Brother" Jamaica can easily be outvoted with only 17 out of 45 seats although on the basis of population and area it is entitled to at least 22 seats in the Lower House of the Federal Parliament . . . With them it was Federation, not Jamaica first.[15]

W.A. Domingo thus resorted to the game of numbers to drive home the prudency of a "Jamaica first." Yet this same Domingo would not concede that in Jamaica, where blacks constitute 80 percent of the population, they should come "first" or at least have the power to run the society.

Despite the limitations endemic to his bourgeois-nationalistic position, Domingo continues to occupy an impressive reputation for his part in the "New Negro" movement of the 1930s and 1940s. This is, in part, due to his agitations in New York during the 1940s. After the fall of France in 1940, the United States called a conference to debate and decide upon the fate of the West Indian islands in the event that America was called upon to occupy them in self-protection. W.A. Domingo organised around this crisis, issued posters (one of which, for instance, read: "The Fate of the West Indian People Hangs in the Balance"), and called a "mass meeting" for July 15, 1940, to be held in the Renaissance Casino, New York, to hear the Declaration of Rights which was to be presented to the Havana Conference regarding the West Indian people as a result of the war. Aiding Domingo were other black notables like Attorney Hope R. Stevens (West Indies National Committee), Dr. Charles Petioni (Caribbean Union), Richard B. Moore, Dr. P. Savory, Rev. E. Elliot Durant, and Rev. Adam Clayton Powell. In a commanding tone they called upon "West Indians and Americans!" declaring that "the hour of destiny has struck for us all. . . . Every liberty loving Negro and everyone who values democratic rights will make it a point to join in this historic meeting." When the question of the establishment of Naval and Air Bases in the West Indian territories came up, there were heated discussions. The original committee formed to act at Havana was reorganised under the name of West Indies National Council, and Domingo was made its President. The Council "made strong recommendations to British and American Governments" to ensure that Jim Crowism was not introduced to the islands.

It was because of these latter activities that, on his return to Jamaica in 1941, Domingo was hauled off the ship and interned under the wartime Defense Regulations. But from the general uproar caused by his arrest, from the P.N.P.'s attestation to his "good sense," "moderation," and "strict observance of the Party's policy," to the fact that he was a specially invited guest of the Government of Jamaica at the Independence celebrations in 1962, it was shown that Domingo had not veered too far from his bourgeois-nationalist position. Toward the end of his life he became politically inactive but developed a lucrative import-export business. He finally died in 1968.

## COMMUNIST INTERNATIONAL RADICALISM

This position at least rejects capitalism and advocates the overthrow of the government through a general proletarian movement. It sees racism, however, as a part of the larger problem of class subordination. Oliver Cox, well-known Trinidadian Marxist in America, believes that "the Negro protest alone would be of virtually no effect had it not been integrated in the larger and more powerful process of democratic transformation."[16] In his reasoning, the black struggle becomes submerged to the wider proletarian mass movement: "It directs its strategy mainly to the larger problem of expediting the advent of democracy and it will employ the Negro protest and discontent as an auxiliary in seeking to expedite the democratic process."[17]

This modality suffers from too much faith in the "proletarian democratic revolution" and faith in the proletarian class itself. It starts off with a critique of capitalist society from the perspective of the working class rather than from that of the black community, despite the fact that each group is faced with a unique set of contradictions or core problems. Having been subjugated as a black category, in which the white working class played its white ethnocentric part, these radicals are attempting to overlook these differences and fight as part of a general economic category, thereby denying the universalism of ethnocentricism.

### C. L. R. James

C. L. R. James is truly the most "internationalist" of our noted black leaders. He is a citizen of the world who has lived in or had extended visits to England, the United States, France, Greece, Spain, Mexico, Ghana, Austria, and Venezuela; a man who at one moment appears as a staunch West Indian national socialist, then at the next appears in an African, English, or American guise. The tremendous range of his interests, activities, and scholarship are also living proof of the transcending universalism of James. This has been his strength and also his weakness.

In 1932 James arrived in England with many of the ideas of "19th-century intellectualism" but at that stage "knowing nothing of communism." He plunged into the radical haunts of London, read prolifically and became a member of the Independent Labour Party. By 1933, he wrote, "I was reading hard and was already a long way toward becoming a Trotskyist." James, along with Ted Grant, Henry Wicks, and others, became staunch critics of Stalinism and became the leading proponents of Trotsky's theory of "the permanent revolution."

At this stage James considered notions of "race" eerie. He

disparagingly commented that his friend Learie Constantine "had a point of view which seemed to me unduly coloured by national and racial considerations."[18] That James became committed to a working class socialist struggle, rather than to a black movement, can be explained by the fact that (as he recently admitted) "there was no black base in England."[19] He did, however, make a break with the I.L.P. in 1936 because of its reaction to the Italo-Abyssinian crisis. He and nine others formed the International Friends of Abyssinian Association, which later (1937) became known as the African Service Bureau and which was to play an important part in the initial agitation and preparation for the independence of various African nations. As late as 1959, he admitted without any reservations that though their Bureau was an African organisation, neither he nor Padmore tolerated "the slightest tinge of colour prejudice," and that "all were welcome, and various English people came there to help or to stay and fraternise."[20]

With this type of background, James went to the United States and remained there until 1953. One researcher argued that "the American period was James' most radical days, distinguished for its polemics with Max Shachtman and other Socialists as for its vehement prosecution of the 'Negro cause'."[21] James himself admitted that the trip to America "permanently altered" his attitude toward the world.[22] James became immersed in the Socialist Workers' Party and was Trotsky's adviser from 1939 onward on the "Negro question." LaGuerre commented: "James' arrival into the ranks of the S.W.P. in 1938 gave added impetus to a consideration of the 'Negro question,' not in the spirit of 'Negro chauvinism' against which Trotsky had warned Claude McKay in 1923, but in a spirit of solidarity of all exploited without consideration of colour."[23]

But how true is this? Rather, how radical was James' radicalism? If we seriously analyse James' proposals and discussions held with Leon Trotsky in Mexico, April 1939, and at the second convention of the Socialist Workers' Party, we will get a clear picture of James as the supra-colour radical.[24] Preceding the convention, James circulated his thoughts which, if followed up, would have been a remarkable and acceptable synthesis: "The Negro," he declared, "must be won for Socialism. There is no other way out for him in America or elsewhere. But he must be won on the basis of his own experience and his own activity."[25] In this same document he confessed: ". . . the Negro, fortunately for Socialism, does not want self-determination." This statement provides the key to James' thought: Socialism first, the Negro second. He discarded any idea or group that threatened socialism. Using this standard, he rejected the notion of black self-determination: "I consider the idea of separating as a step backward so far as a Socialist society is concerned . . . The danger of our advocating and injecting a policy of self-determination is that it is the surest way to divide and confuse the workers in the South." He described "self-determination" as reactionary, an opinion which even Leon Trotsky dismissed as "abstract and wrong." Garvey's racialism was successful, James said, "simply because the white workers in 1919 were not developed. There was no political organisation of any power calling upon the blacks and the whites to unite." But with the coming of the C.I.O. in 1936, the appointment of a Special Negro Department, and the New Deal gestures to Negroes, he argued that Negroes and white workers were coming together and chauvinistic movements were on the wane. Because blacks, "individually and in the mass . . . remain profoundly suspicious of whites," James proposed, as an alternative to any self-determination proposals, the formation of an all-black movement that would fight for equality in all areas but, "inevitably," the members of the Fourth International "must" exercise "a powerful influence in such an organisation." A history was also to be written to show that "the emancipation of the Negro in the United States and abroad is linked with the emancipation of the white working class," as a way to show why "in general black and white must unite." James appeared timid, especially in contrast to Trotsky, by displaying a fear of espousing any idea that smacks of racialism or black cultural nationalism. When the S.W.P. published one of its 1939 resolutions ("The S.W.P. and Negro"), in which appeared a sentence stating that the Negroes "are designated by their whole historical past to be, under adequate leadership, the very vanguard of the Proletarian revolution," James, who had been the principal architect of the resolution, shortly published a revealing alteration of the sentence: "There is," he said, "in the sentence quoted, an overstatement, in my opinion. It would be more correct to say, "in the very vanguard" and not "the very vanguard."[26] His abiding faith and hope was that "if white workers extend a hand to the Negro, he will not want self-determination." But will they? James himself at that meeting pointed out that "great numbers of these Negroes hated the Communist Party . . . up to the last convention, 79 percent of the Negro membership of the C.P. in New York State (1,579) had left the C.P. I met many of the representatives and they were now willing to form a Negro organisation but did not wish to join the Fourth International." James persistently overlooked and ignored this call for a racial colouration of socialism, because of his integrationism, albeit couched in socialist guise.

Thus, though James had changed a little (as a result of his American experience), this was not to the point of boldly embracing the uniqueness of the black experience. In 1943 he issued an internal bulletin to the Workers Party[27] in which he declared that "the building of a mass party to lead the proletariat is for us the problem." He argued that the whole history of labour in the United States indicates that the American working class needs, above all else, the theory and practice of Bolshevism, which he proposed to instill through his "marxist" paper known as *Labour Action.* In this document James clearly shows where his loyalty lay: it was with the working class: "Proletarian thought, Proletarian method," he instructed, "must be for them a challenge to the Bourgeoisie at all points . . . For them it must be a theory which marks off those who adhere to it from all others giving them pride and confidence and the consciousness of a great superiority to all, however influential or famous, who do not accept Marxism." James moved in and out of the Socialist Workers' Party several times, eventually forming his own group called the Johnson-Forest Tendency, which drew upon the original notions of the Dialectics in Hegel and Marx, and injected a populist streak in their concept of proletarian revolution. Priority in this group was given to the real proletarians who carried more prestige within the organisation. Next came housewives and individuals with semi-proletarian status. Lastly, came the intellectuals. At meetings, the proletarians had the privilege of voicing their views while the intellectuals listened. From revolutionary elitism, James ended up advocating proletarian populism.

What is revealed by this survey of James' ideological development is a man caught in the theoretical strictures of Marxism, despite the various anomalies of that perspective that were apparent to him. Though he had recognised the importance of a large number of recruits to a revolutionary party, he had confessed that the working class did not appear "ready": "In one area our comrades have taken an active and effective part in union work. They have distributed between a quarter and a half million pieces of literature among the workers. Yet the results in recruiting have been practically zero. Perhaps we now have gained 3 members, perhaps."[28] He overlooked the tremendously important role of the race factor in mobilising individuals, and continued to maintain an abiding faith in the masses – workers, farmers, and peasants. He maintained that the "African Revolution" was "contingent upon the Socialist revolution in Europe," despite the fact that, as he confessed, the Second World War brought no such revolution in Europe.[29]

This was the type of perspective which James took back with him to Trinidad in 1965. In opposition to Dr. Eric Williams, he formed the Political Action Committee which, he declared, aimed to "work for politics purged of race."[30] On August 8, 1965, he and Maharaj formed the Workers' and Farmers' Party of Trinidad and Tobago which was supposedly a national party cutting across race and aiming to give the mass "fullest participation." In the election of 1966, James and his Workers' and Farmers' Party suffered a crushing defeat, with James losing his deposit. He was, in fact, defeated by the very racial factor which he wanted, in his usual idealistic fashion, so much to ignore or transcend. In Trinidad, blacks voted for Eric Williams' P.N.M. Party, and the Indians voted for the Democratic Labour Party. James was, on the strength of his ideas, attempting to cut across this deep-seated cleavage.

One wonders why James failed or took so long to veer his ideology to acknowledge the importance of the racial factor in history. In fact he came close to it at several points. In 1943 he noted that "every great revolution is a truly national revolution, in that it represents not only the historic but the immediate interests of the nation and is recognised as such. But every party which leads such a revolution is also a national party rooted in the economic and social life, history and traditions of the nation."[31] As an instance, he pointed to the Bolshevik Party of Russia under Lenin: "This most international of all parties, learnt Marxism on a Russian basis, and could not have learnt it in any other way."[32] Why then did James not see blacks as a distinct nationality or a distinct people? Why couldn't he see an almost unbridgeable gulf between the white working class and blacks? The answer is to be sought in the cultural and ideological factors that entered into James' childhood and adult socialisation. It was only during the 1960s that James became influenced by the Black Power – Black Nationalist philosophy, and the fact that he is now a Professor of Black Studies at Federal City College, Washington, is a testimony to the thesis that James has entered the final lap of becoming a progressive black radical.

## BLACK RADICALISM

This position sees blacks as a distinct people, with a different history and a unique experience, from which flow distinct needs and interests. This modality stresses black nationalism (black ethnocentricism) and black power while at the same time advocating black capitalism or at best failing to deal adequately with the issue of socialism versus capitalism.

### Marcus Garvey

Marcus Garvey started out as a civic radical. There were many factors in his early life that predisposed him toward agitation – if only of the reformist type. He was influenced by the progressive teachings of Dr. Albert Thorne and Dr. Robert Love, who were then the acknowledged militants in Jamaica. Garvey became active in the first Political Club in Jamaica – the National Club – and learned to speak eloquently. He also acted as the leader in the Printers' Union strike in Jamaica in 1906. After this, he travelled extensively to Latin America, where he found West Indians being exploited, robbed, and brutalised. He attempted to help in various ways and was dubbed an "agitator" in Costa Rica, but he failed in the face of the entrenched nature and enormity of the evils against his people. He then travelled to London, where he was further influenced by this sojourn and specifically by the nationalistic teachings of Duse Mohammed. With this type of background and his brains "set afire," Garvey returned to Jamaica in 1914 and started the embryo of the now-famed Universal Negro Improvement Association (U.N.I.A.). Even at this stage, however, Garvey was still a reformist: he planned concerts and organised elocution contests and planned the development of a Jamaican "Tuskegee Institute." To this end, he wrote the famed Booker T. Washington, with the intention of getting organisational insights and financial backing so that he could return to Jamaica "to perfect the Jamaica organisation."

As a result of a number of factors Garvey stayed in the United States. It was this subsequent involvement in the Afro-American struggle that took him (like Dr. Robert Love before him) from his narrower embryonic phase. Dr. Love had argued in 1903 that the American struggle was of immense significance and that "blacks of the British Empire" had to pass through the same ordeal as their Afro-American brothers so as "to be made to feel the disadvantages of belonging to a race different from that of their Anglo-Saxon fellow subjects."[33] By 1921, Garvey had developed so much that he could now confidently repudiate his former ideological mentor, Booker T. Washington.

> We have been misrepresented by our leadership. We have been taught to beg rather than to make demands. Booker T. Washington was not a leader of the Negro race. We do not look to Tuskegee. The world has recognised him as a leader, but we do not.[34]

As part of the same theme he acknowledged that "if Washington had lived, he would have had to change his programme. No leader can successfully lead this race of ours without giving an interpretation of the awakened spirit of the New Negro, who does not seek industrial opportunity alone, but a political voice."[35]

Our immediate concern is not to trace the moulding or the making of Garvey, the racial radical. Rather it is to juxtapose the ideological system fashioned by Garvey beside those of the earlier (and later) radicals discussed. The diagram below gives a concise summary of Garveyism in such a way as to highlight the key variables that he stressed and to show their interconnections.

DIAGRAMMATIC SUMMARY OF GARVEYISM

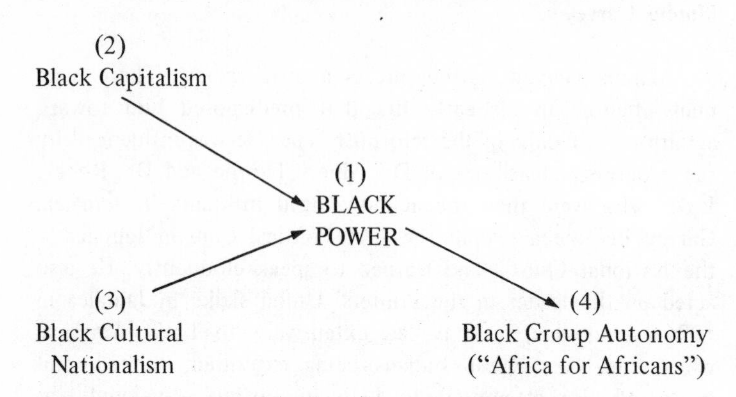


Central to Garveyism is the notion of power, around which every other aspect revolves. Garvey wrote: "If we must have justice, we must be strong; if we must be strong, we must come together; if we must come together, we can only do so through the system of organisation . . . let us not waste time in breathless appeals to the strong while we are weak."[36] Marcus Garvey realised that whites succeeded in enslaving and dominating blacks only because of "the element of forces employed." From this, he concluded, therefore, that "what-ever influence is brought to bear against the powers opposed to Negro progress must contain the element of force in order to accomplish its purpose, since it is apparent that this is the only element they recognise."[37] Garvey reasoned that the greatness of Europe, Great Britain, and the United States was not based on "prayers or petitions" but on power. He called upon blacks, therefore, "to get power of every kind. Power in education, science, industry, politics and higher government. That kind of power that will stand out signally, so that other races and nations can see, and if they will not see, will feel."[38] In like manner, Amy Garvey, the most devout Garveyite, has placed "power" at the philosophical, sociological, and political centre of the Negro problem:

> Power is the keynote of this age. When all races have acquired that, and reached a common plane of world achievements, each will grasp the other and say "Brother"; until then, the struggle continues.[39]

As a means to acquire Black Power, Marcus Garvey stressed (1) black capitalism (black economic power) and (2) black cultural nationalism. He openly embraced black capitalism. "Capitalism," he said, "is necessary to the progress of the world, and those who unreasonably and wantonly oppose or fight against it are enemies to human advancement."[40] With this perspective in mind, Garvey developed such commercial enterprises as The Black Star Steamship Company and the Negro Factory Corporation. "Why," he asked, "should not Africa give to the world its black Rockefeller, Rothschild, and Henry Ford?"[41]

Instrumental to acquiring Black Power, Garvey also stressed a staunch type of black cultural internationalism. He preached the need for a Black House as opposed to a White House, black newspapers as opposed to white newspapers, a black Congress as opposed to a white Congress, a black aristocracy as opposed to the white aristocracy, a black "God" as opposed to a white one. He called for the development of separate black institutions specific to the needs of black people. Blacks, he said, must thoroughly arm themselves with their own autonomous institutions. He therefore instituted the African Orthodox Church, the Universal African Legion, the Universal Black Cross Nurses, the Universal African Motor Corps, the Juvenile and the Black Flying Eagles – all equipped with officers and uniforms. The thorough organising of blacks around the racial theme would, according to him, effect unity. His dream was realized, if only temporarily, in the U.N.I.A. convention held in New York in 1920, which was attended by some 25,000 blacks, representatives from 25 countries, embracing all segments of the black population – black Jews, black Hindus, black Catholics, black Muslims, black Protestants of all denominations and non-sectarian black revolutionaries. Through a multitude of devices, Garvey sought to instill racial love, racial respect, and racial consciousness. In all these ways he was specifically dealing with the uniqueness of blacks at the psychological level. He noted the destructive effects of slavery upon the black psyche – an inferiority complex, a dependency complex, and self-hatred. Slavery, he said, had turned blacks "into their own worst enemies." Only with the development of the strong "African personality" will blacks be freed from the evil taints of slavery, regain their lost manhood, and feel like "somebody." Amy Garvey put this noble purpose in grandiose language:

> He [Garvey] had a message to deliver to all people everywhere – a redemptive, soul searching, yet practical, comprehensive program for his race's way of life, to prepare them really to live as real men, and be partakers in the fullness of the earth, through their own efforts and diligence.[42]

With blacks "armed" with the above economic and cultural institutions, they could consolidate this relative power in the absolute form of a nation state. The ultimate for Garvey was the establishment of black group autonomy, taking the supreme political form of a "redeemed" Africa. "Africa for the Africans, at home and abroad" was Garvey's trenchant plea. "There is," he said, "no justice but strength . . . might is right, and if you must be heard and respected you have to accumulate nationally, in Africa, those resources that will compel the unjust man to think twice before he acts."[43] He asked: "Do they lynch Englishmen, Frenchmen, German, or Japanese? No. And why? Because these people are represented by great governments, mighty nations and empires, strongly organised . . . Until the Negro reaches this point of national independence, all that he does as a race will count for naught."[44] It was this belief that prompted his crusade for the selective migration of New World blacks to Africa where they could hasten "African redemption."

One major loophole in this system of ideas was Garvey's attitude toward the issue of capitalism versus communism. Using essentially a race perspective, Garvey was primarily concerned with the conflict between blacks and whites. His overall ideological system thus dealt with the ways in which blacks, as a collectivity, could acquire and maintain their independence from whites. Garvey failed, however, to consider the problems of exploitation that could enter the black communities once they gained autonomy. Instead he seemed to assume the beneficence of capitalism, openly endorsing black carpetbaggers to go to Africa, arguing that those Negroes "who seek the White House in America could find ample play for their ambition in Africa."[45] By that period, West Indian and Afro-American migrants to Africa had already formed themselves into an elite group in West Africa, thereby adding dangerous elements of class exploitation and class snobbery into West Africa.

It is very important to understand the reasons why Garvey turned out to be an advocate of black capitalism, because in our evolutionary perspective, this was Garvey's major shortcoming. The reason is not hard to find. Garvey was by socialisation and by training, capitalistic in outlook, a man who, like most other migrants, wanted to "make good." To have changed, he would have had to be converted to an alternative mode of thinking – socialism or communism. Yet Garvey was precluded from even examining these alternatives closely by the shortcomings of the Communists. On the basis of his experiences in both Jamaica and America, Garvey reached the conclusion ("a strange paradox," as he puts it) that "the only convenient friend the Negro worker or labourer has, in America, at the present time is the white Capitalist. . . . if the Negro unionizes himself to the level of the white worker, and in affiliation with him, the choice and preference of employment is given to the white worker, without any regard or consideration for the Negro."[46] Marcus Garvey clearly perceived the reason for this, as is evident in his following reaction:

> The danger of Communism to the Negro, in countries where he forms the minority of the population, is seen in the selfish and vicious attempts of that party or group to use the Negro vote and physical numbers helping to smash and overthrow, by revolution, a system that is injurious to them as the white underdogs, the success of which would put their majority group or race still in power, not only as Communists but as white men. . .
>
> On the appeal of race-interests the Communist is as ready as ever to show his racial ascendancy or superiority to the Negro. . .
>
> Lynching mobs . . . are generally made up of 99½% of such (poor) white people. . .
>
> Potentially, every white man is a Klansman, as far as the Negro in competition with whites socially, economically and politically is concerned.[47]

It was this persistence of the racial factor even amongst the Communists that convinced Garvey that doctrinal aspirations are secondary to the reality of the racial factor. His wife stated the position categorically: "The only ground on which white people are really united is race; neither language, religion, nor political systems have as cohesive a force for all nations; and because of this knowledge many white leaders deplored the idea that Garvey, too, should organise his race."

Besides this, Garvey became peeved with the Communists who were constantly attempting to "sell" the idea of class analysis to blacks. A Communist statement of the period read:

> We desire to win over the masses, organisationally and ideologically this Association (U.N.I.A.) for the Communist program . . . We are aiming to win over these Negro masses to fight for the Negro workers on a class basis . . . under the leadership of the World Communist Party International.[48]

The tactlessness and boldness of statements like this were naturally interpreted by Garvey as part of the "master-of-all-I-survey" mentality of whites, which took concrete form in their many meddlesome pranks, as when they attempted to get the 1924 U.N.I.A. Convention and Garvey to openly declare themselves against the K.K.K., a move which would certainly have made many Negro heads roll! Garvey's puritanical zest for honesty (which had led him to declare that the K.K.K. was a better friend of the Negro because, with them the Negro knew precisely where he stood) reacted negatively at liberal efforts of deception.

For these reasons, Garvey scoffed at socialism and did not even examine the issue carefully. Otherwise he might have come up with a distinction between (1) Marxism as a doctrine or set of principles with some degree of universal applicability, and (2) Marxism as practiced by white Communists. Such a distinction would have shown the possibility of extracting the principles of socialism and applying them to the black situation. Though he did not do this, it is clear that several of his remarks showed the possibility of such a strategy:

> I should warn him [the Negro] against the *present* brand of Communism or Worker's Partizanship *as taught in America* and to be careful of the traps and pitfalls of *white* trade unionism. (My emphasis)
>
> The Negro should keep shy of Communism or the Workers' Party in America. Since they are so benevolent let them bring about their own reforms and show us how different they are to others.[49]

When one considers, in addition, that he actually proposed that the state should limit individual ownership to the maximum of one million dollars and corporations to five million,[50] one sees that Garvey was not too far away from embracing socialism.

Despite the faults of the Communists, we can see clearly that the gulf was not unbridgeable and that there were possible compromises. Both were internationalistic, of one type or other. Ideologically speaking, they were more radical than civic radicals. And when the N.A.A.C.P.ers pursued their drive to get rid of the Garvey menace, the Communists came out in his defense. The Communist Party of America signed a press release in April 1925, through its central executive committee of the Worker's Party, under the heading, "Importance of organisation of Negroes," resolving:

> The Workers [Communist] Party takes this occasion to point out to the white workers as well as Negro workers the importance of organisation of the Negro masses of this country . . . The Workers Party

> composed of Negro workers as well as white workers . . . cannot stand idly by while the Capitalist dictatorship attempts to destroy a mass organisation of the exploited Negro people .. The Workers Party calls upon the workers both Negro and white, to protest against the persecution of U.N.I.A. . . . We demand the immediate and unconditional release of Marcus Garvey . . . and that he not be deported.

The reality of a theoretical synthesis came in the 1930s with Leon Trotsky who drew upon the experiences of the Russian Revolution and the thoughts of Lenin on the "National Question." Trotsky's thoughts on the Negro question are almost identical to those of Garvey.[51]

## PROGRESSIVE NATIONALISTS

From the preceding analysis it becomes clear that there have been two paths to arriving at the progressive nationalist position: (1) some West Indians started off from a racial radicalism but progressively moved toward a more socialist position upon observing certain anomalies – Malcolm X and Stokely Carmichael; (2) other West Indian radicals started off on a socialist platform, but observing certain flaws either in the actions and attitudes of Communists or in the Marxist model itself, progressively moved towards a more black nationalist position – Claude McKay, George Padmore, Frantz Fanon and C.L.R. James.

Whatever the route, they all converge in their theoretical conceptions by commonly perceiving the importance of culture, power, and socialism. Such a perspective leads to an attempt to control and countervail the effects of capitalism, white nationalism, and white power. This modality of radicalism is also less circumscribed in its methods of protest, adopting the position of "any means necessary" – constitutional or unconstitutional.

### Claude McKay

Claude McKay may be taken as prototypical of this brand of radicalism; since his most productive years were in the 1920s and 1930s, it becomes possible to discuss him in relation to the other radicals discussed earlier. McKay migrated from his "idyllic" Jamaican background with only the political philosophy of "free thinking" and having only one desire – to be a poet. His friend, Tom Redcam, then editor of the *Jamaica Times,* warned McKay that he would be "terribly changed by America." McKay came across all the problems that typically confronted blacks in America. He also came across socialist thought in Harlem in the 1920s and later he sojourned in England where he confesses to have drunk most of the socialist ideas.

> The International Club was full of excitement with its dogmatists and doctrinaires of radical left ideas . . . For the first time, I found myself in an atmosphere of doctrinaire and dogmatic ideas in which people devoted themselves entirely to the discussion and analysis of social events from a radical or Marxist point of view. . . . The contact stimulated and broadened my social outlook and plunged me into the reading of Marx.[52]

He was invited to Russia by the Bolsheviks and worked for socialist papers both in England and America. At times he even used strict Marxist terminology, as when he wrote: ". . . it is with the Proletarian revolutionists of the world that my whole spirit revolts . . . I see no other way of upward struggle for coloured peoples, but the working class movement."[53] Despite his proclivity in this direction, McKay never joined the Communist Party, nor did he join Sylvia Pankhurst's Workers Socialist Federation in England. Part of the explanation has to do with the reservations McKay had concerning white communists (not Marxism). Though he had the time of his life in Russia with the top Communist leaders, he reflected that "the Bolshevik leaders, to satisfy the desires of the people were using me for entertainment."[54] He also noticed that in Russia the official American Communist delegates were misrepresenting and giving false impressions of America, of the Negro, and of the revolutionary potentials there.

For these reasons and others, McKay did not become a fanatical adherent of communist dogma. At the same time there were pressures and problems facing McKay as a Negro which drove him to assert his distinctiveness as a Negro and the right of blacks to their separate culture and institutions. McKay had started out for the United States armed (rather, disarmed!) with the belief that "people of all kinds are just people to me."[55] But in the United States racial discrimination propelled him toward cultural nationalism. Once, when he went as a reviewer to a theatre and was told at the door that there must have been some "mistake," he reacted bitterly:

> Suddenly the realisation came to me. I came here as a dramatic critic, a lover of theatre, and a free soul. But I was abruptly reminded – those things did not matter. The important fact, with which I was suddenly slapped in the face, was my colour. I am a Negro . . .[56]

McKay, in striking contrast to C.L.R. James, did not disregard prejudice or try to cover it up or explain it away. Instead he confronted it boldly as a black man. In response to everyday personal encounters with racial discrimination – the type many Negro Socialists rarely talk about, McKay wrote several defiant sonnets including "Baptism," "The White City," "America," "He who Gets Slapped," "The White House," and "If we must Die."[57] McKay's "Enslaved" may be cited as indicating the depth to which he felt oppressed as a black man:

> My heart grows sick with hate, becomes lead,
> For this my race that has no home on earth.
> Then from the dark depth of my soul I cried
> To the avenging angel to consume
> The white man's world of wonders utterly:
> Let it be swallowed up in earth's vast womb,
> Or upward roll as sacrificial smoke
> To liberate my people from its yoke![58]

Because of these shattering discriminatory experiences, McKay was driven back from his earlier romanticist belief to a positive affirmation of his blackness, which he accepted. He joined the staff of the *Masses* (a radical Socialist newspaper that had taken the place of *The Liberator*) and expressed his liking for it because "I felt a special interest in its sympathetic and iconoclastic items about the Negro."[59] He admitted that colour-consciousness was the fundamental cause of his restlessness, that it was "hell to belong to a suppressed minority and outcast group,"[60] and that "no White person, however sympathetic can feel fully the corroding bitterness of colour discrimination. Only the black victim can."[61] He therefore clutched onto his black group with the proverbial desperation of a drowning man. After living in several parts of the United States, McKay then went to live in Harlem, and reacted exuberantly:

> Harlem was my first positive reaction to American life . . . After two years in the blue sky desert Kansas, it was like entering a paradise of my own people . . . I give myself entirely up to getting down . . . into the rhythm [of Harlem life] which still remains one of the most pleasurable sensations of my blood.[62]

Later in his life, when he visited Marseilles and met blacks from all parts of the world, he acknowledged: "It was good to feel the strength and distinction of a group and the assurance of belonging to it." The full theoretical implications of this insight, nurtured by his life's experiences, were duly expressed in 1937 when he records in his autobiography:

> Wherever I travelled . . . I was impressed by the phenomena of the emphasis on group life. . . . But there is very little group spirit among Negroes. The American Negro group is the most advanced in the world. It possesses unique advantages for development and expansion and for assuming the world leadership of the Negro race. But it sadly lacks a group soul. And the greatest hindrance to the growth of a group soul is the wrong idea held about segregation. Negroes do not understand the difference between segregation and group aggregation. And their leaders do not enlighten them. Negro institutions and unique Negro efforts have never had a chance for full development, they are haunted by the fear of segregation. Except where they are forced against their will, Negroes in general prefer to patronise white institutions and support white causes in order to demonstrate their opposition to segregation. It is clear historical fact that different groups have won their social rights only when they developed a group spirit and strong organisation.[63]

McKay had finally arrived at a theoretical synthesis in vivid clarity. It was a position which juxtaposed him between the racial radicals like Garvey on the one hand and strict communists on the other. This may be verified by a review of McKay's dealing with Garvey. McKay contributed several articles to Garvey's *Negro World,* and in 1920 he clearly defined his ideological position and its relation to Garveyism: "Although an International Socialist, I am supporting the [Garvey] movement, for I believe that for subject peoples at least, nationalism is the open door to Communism."[64] With this attitude, in 1921 he attempted to meet with Garvey and other socialists (Cyril Briggs, Richard B. Moore, etc.) hoping to veer Garvey towards a more socialist position. But nothing came of the meeting. By 1922, McKay had dismissed Garvey as a short-sighted leader: "His spirit is revolutionary but his intellect does not understand the significance of modern revolutionary developments . . . All those who think broadly in social conditions are amazed at Garvey's ignorance and his intolerance of modern social ideas."[65]

It would seem, then, that black ideological development moves inexorably toward embracing a concept not only of Africa (as a symbol and reality of black power and black culture) but also towards the concept of socialism. Though Pan-Africanism has often been stressed (not defined) in its cultural guise (as black cultural nationalism and unity), Pan-Africanism proper – as a total black ideology – embraces both the notion of black political power and the notion of communal or socialistic values and organisations. Claude McKay thus belongs to that honourable band of evolved black ideologues whose ideological synthesis nestles comfortably under the rubric of Pan-Africanism – men like Padmore, Frantz Fanon, and Stokely Carmichael. Yet, by definition, this synthesis could not have been attained without the guidelines set and ideological groundwork laid by our precursors.

## NOTES

[1] *The Case of Domingo,* Pamphlet published by the P.N.P. Kingston, Schomburg Collection.

[2] The Board of Directors included: W.A. Roberts, Ivy Essien, R.J. Kirkpatrick, Rev. Ethelred Brown, I.A. Frazer, T.A. D'Aguilar, Dr. F. Theo Reid, C.A. Wallace, Thomas Bowen, Theodore Burrell, James O'Meally, Dorcas Thompson, R.S. Trew, and Attorney Vernal Williams.

[3] *Public Opinion,* "The Jamaica Progressive League of New York," March 20, 1937, Kingston.

[4] W.A. Domingo, "The Jamaica Progressive League," *Public Opinion,* December 17, 1937.

[5] *Onward Jamaica,* Pamphlet published by the Jamaica Progressive League of New York, 1937, Schomburg Collection.

[6] *Public Opinion, "The Jamaica Progressive League of New* York, March 20, 1937.

[7] *Ibid.*

[8] W.A. Roberts, *Jamaica: The Portrait of an Island,* New York, Coward McCann, 1955, p. 127.

[9] Jaime O'Meally, "Nationalism and the Masses," *Public Opinion,* January 22, 1938. Jaime O'Meally was a former prominent member of Garvey's U.N.I.A. and was actually Garvey's Commissioner sent along with other experts in June 1924 to start constructing camps to receive immigrants in Liberia.

[10] *The Case of Domingo.*

[11] *Ibid.*

[12] Jaime O'Meally, "Nationalism and the Masses.

[13] Norman W. Mahley, *Daily Gleaner,* March 30, 1954.

[14] W.A. Domingo, *British West Indian Federation: A Critique,* Kingston, Gleaner, 1956.

[15] *Ibid.,* p. 18.

[16] Oliver C. Cox, *Race, Caste and Class,* Garden City, N.Y., Doubleday, 1948, p. 271.

[17] *Ibid.*

[18] C.L.R. James, *Beyond the Boundary,* London, Hutchison, 1969, p. 115.

[19] James, in an interview with *Black Scholar,* September 1970, p. 36. Several other West Indians in London have expressed a similar point. Claude McKay remarked: "England is not like America, where one can take refuge from prejudice in a black belt . . . I was a very happy man when I could get out of it to go back to the Negro pale of America." Claude McKay, *A Long Way From Home,* New York, Lee Furman, 1937, p. 303.

[20] James, in *The Nation,* November 13, 1959, Port-Of-Spain.

[21] John LaGuerre, *Colonial Intellectuals in Politics,* M. Sc., Pol. Sc. Dept., U.W.I., 1968, p. 9, 41. (Master's Thesis)

[22] James, Editorial, *The Nation*, March 28, 1953.

[23] LaGuerre, *op. cit.,* p. 41.

[24] The following quotations are extracted from: Leon Trotsky *on Black Nationalism and Self-Determination,* Merit Publishers, 1967. This booklet contains the proposals and ideas of James, then using the cover name J.R. Johnson.

[25] Later published in S.W.P. *Internal Bulletin,* No. 9, June 1939.

[26] *Socialist Appeal* (S.W.P. Paper), August 22, 1939.

[27] C.L.R. James, *Education, Propaganda and Bolshevism,* 1943. Reissued in 1968 by the Facing Reality Publishing Committee.

[28] C.L.R. James, *Education, Propaganda and Bolshevism,* p. 3.

[29] C.L.R. James, *Nkrumah – Then and Now,* Mimeographed, p. 23; C.L.R. James in *The Nation,* December 4, 1959, Port-of-Spain.

[30] C.L.R. James in *We the People,* June 25, 1965, Port-of-Spain.

[31] C.L.R. James, *Education, Propaganda and Bolshevism,* p. 14.

[32] *Ibid.*

[33] Dr. Robert Love in *Jamaica Advocate,* April 18, 1903, p. 2

[34] Marcus Garvey in Baltimore's *Afro-American,* August 12, 1921.

[35] Amy Jacques Garvey, *Philosophy and Opinions of Marcus Garvey,* Vol. 1, p. 41

[36] Amy Jacques Garvey, *Philosophy and Opinions,* Vol. II, p. 12.

[37] Amy Jacques Garvey, *Philosophy and Opinions,* Vol. 1, p. 15.

[38] *Ibid.,* p. 19.

[39] Amy Jacques Garvey, *Garvey and Garveyism,* Kingston, Published by the Author, 1963.

[40] Amy Jacques Garvey, *Philosophy and Opinions,* New York, Universal Publishing House, 1923, 1925, Vo. 2, p. 72.

[41] *Ibid.,* p.68

[42] Amy Jacques Garvey, *Garvey and Garveyism,* p. 111.

[43] Amy Jacques Garvey, *Philosophy and Opinions,* Vol. 2, p. 13.

[44] *Ibid.,* Vol. 1, p. 39.

[45] *Ibid.,* Vol. 2, p. 40.

[46] *Ibid.,* pp. 70-71.

[47] *Ibid.,* pp. 70-71.

[48] *Daily Worker,* August 9, 1924.

[49] Amy Jacques Garvey, *Philosophy and Opinions,* Vol. 2, pp. 70-71.

[50] *Ibid.,* p. 72.

[51] Leon Trotsky, "The Negro Question in America" (1933). Reprinted in *Documents on the Negro Struggle,* Pioneer Publishers, 1962. For an extended discussion of Trotsky's ideas on these questions, see the author's larger study which is to be published in the future.

[52] McKay, *A Long Way from Home, op. cit.,* p. 68.

[53] McKay, "How Black Sees Green and Red," *The Liberator,* Vol. IV, June 1921, p. 20.

[54] McKay, *A Long Way from Home,* p. 173.

[55] McKay, *My Green Hills of Jamaica,* Kingston, Institute of Jamaica, Mimeographed Circa 1930, p. 57.

[56] McKay, "He Who gets Slapped," *The Liberator,* Vol, V, No. 5, May 1922.

[57] This last poem was reprinted in every leading magazine and newspaper. It was cited as evidence of Negro radicalism in the U.S. by investigating authorities. Incidentally, 20 years later, when Britain faced the threat of German invasion, Winston Churchill read "If we must Die" to the House of Commons to increase morale.

[58] McKay, "Enslaved," *The Liberator,* Vol. 15, July 1921.

[59] Quoted in Wayne Cooper, *Claude McKay,* MA Thesis, Tulane University, History Dept., 1965, p. 68.

[60] McKay, *A Long Way from Home,* p. 345.

[61] *Ibid.,* p. 135.

[62] McKay, "Review of Home to Harlem," *McClures,* Vol. LX, June 1928, p. 81.

[63] McKay, *A Long Way from Home,* pp. 349-50.

[64] McKay, "Socialism and the Negro," *Workers Dreadnought,* January 31, 1920, pp. 1-2.

[65] Quoted in Cooper, *Claude McKay,* p. 83.

# 22
# *The Internationalization of Black Power: Historical and Contemporary Perspectives**

LOCKSLEY EDMONDSON

In a civil rights march through Mississippi in June 1966, Stokely Carmichael, then Chairman of SNCC (Student Non-Violent Coordinating Committee)[2] raised the cry: "We want Black Power." This was not the first appearance of the "black power" phrase in black America. Adam Clayton Powell, Jr., then Harlem Congressman, had employed this terminology twice in speeches in May 1965 and May 1966. In 1963, an "organization for black power" was formed by Jesse Gray in New York. And, as shall be discussed in more detail, Richard Wright and Paul Robeson in the 1950s had explicitly used the phrase, though with reference to non-American situations.

If, however, Carmichael cannot be credited with coining the phrase, he is considered as the effective initiator of Black Power. This is the fact acknowledged by Martin Luther King Jr. in his discussion of the events of 16 June 1966: "The phrase had been used long before by Richard Wright and others, but never until that night had it been used as a slogan in the civil rights movement."[3]

King at the time "confidently" asserted that "the call for 'Black Power' will rapidly diminish."[4] But on the contrary the cry for "Black Power" has rapidly escalated. While it is difficult to ascertain the extent and intensity of support for the slogan it is clear that Black Power is now an entrenched phenomenon in the Black American revolution.

This article does not propose to deal with the domestic American implications of Black Power[5] – used here in capitalized form to refer to the black American formulation – except where necessary to the development of an international and comparative perspective. Instead, the writer intends to analyse Black Power against the background of its pan-Negro articulations and in terms of its internationalizing potentialities.[6] Black America, Africa, and the Caribbean constitute the main arenas of investigation and the following analysis will embody:

(1) historical and contemporary treatment of the evolution and significance of certain global black nationalist ideologies;
(2) a comparative study of their origin and diffusion;
(3) trans-national perspectives on the situations in black America, Africa and the Caribbean which may condition the future prospects of pan-Negro ideological initiation and diffusion.

A brief word may here be said about the importance of the historical dimensions in the present analysis. In a recent lecture C.L.R. James (who was closely associated with his childhood friend George Padmore in the Pan-African movement of the 1930s, after defining Black Power "not in the ordinary sense of the phrase but in terms of the emancipation of black people," observed:

> Black power is perhaps the most remarkable unplanned movement that the twentieth century has known because of consistency, steady development and constantly growing ascension and expansion. . . . Stage by stage it has mounted higher and expanded wider until it has reached the peak where it is today.[7]

In developing this contention James proceeded to trace the evolution of black emancipation strivings through the contributions of W.E.B. DuBois, Marcus Garvey, George Padmore, Martin Luther King, Frantz Fanon, Malcolm X, and Stokely Carmichael.

What is significant in James' analysis is that he has pinpointed the historically important phenomenon of the linkage of ideas and interests of black men the world over and the historical interrelationships of pan-Negro and pan-African aspirations. On these factors a British historian has commented:

> The first British Empire owed much to the triangular trade between Africa, the West Indies, and North America. The last British Empire has not been uninfluenced by another triangular trade not of pocatille, slaves, and molasses, but a commerce of ideas and politics between the descendants of the slaves in the West Indies and North America and their ancestral continent.[8]

So too the French Empire was not influenced by a trade of ideas and politics between New World Negroes and Africans:

*First published in *Mawazo*, Vol. 1, No. 4, December 1968. Reprinted with author's permission.

> What Shepperson pointed out for the British Empire was equally true for the French Third and Fourth Republics. French-speaking Africans and West Indian Negroes and Malagasies shared a common intellectual life which gave rise to the founding of the Society for African Culture in Paris, the publication of *Presence Africaine* and the death of a man like Franz [sic] Fanon from Martinique in the cause of the Algerian Liberation Movement. The concept of "Negritude" is a joint production of Senegalese poet, Leopold Senghor and Martinique poet, Aime Cesaire.[9]

Enough has been said to illustrate the significance of historical perspectives in this analysis of the internationalizing capacities of Black Power. When we turn to the contemporary setting, we are confronted with certain realities of black existence beyond the United States which have a direct bearing on the Black Power international outlook:

(1) The almost universal phenomenon of colonialism until recent times;
(2) The process of political decolonization and the facts of legal sovereignty – the formal arrival of political Black Power – in the greater part of the African and Caribbean world;
(3) The political repression of blacks by whites in certain areas in southern Africa, the world's most regressive area with regard to racism;
(4) The "Third World" revolution against poverty and the strivings for political and social integration;
(5) The economic position and relations of the white to the non-white world, and the lag between the attainment of political and economic independence;
(6) The global struggle of the black man for dignity.

So far, we have been treating Black Power as a potential pan-Negro ideology without examining the bases of such an assumption. It would therefore be appropriate to comment on the international implications of the black American revolution and, more specifically, on the evolving global interests of the Black Power movement.

What, it may be asked, is the utility of analysing Black Power, a phenomenon basically indigenous to the United States, with reference to outside contexts? Can Black Power have any bearing on the future of Africans or West Indians?

These questions may be approached initially by surveying some of the ideas in circulation within the Black Power movement. Take, for example, the following statements of prominent Black Power leaders or organizations:

> We must therefore consciously strive for an ideology which deals with racism first, and if we do that we recognize the necessity of hooking up with the nine hundred million [sic] black people in the world today. That's what we recognize. And if we recognize that, then it means that our political situation *must* become international. . . . It must be international because if we knew anything, we would recognize that the honkies don't just exploit us, they exploit the whole Third World – Asia, Africa, Latin America.[10]

> Therefore . . . we talk of international black power because of the apex of power, guided by the United States, revolves around the western, barbaric countries in relationship to the exploited peoples of the third world. . . . the Black Power we are talking about in the United States has to become an international concept.[11]
> We must learn how close America and Russia are politically . . . We must seek our poor-people movements in South America and Asia and make our alliances with them.[12]

> Black Power is coming together of black people around the world to fight, wherever they are, for their dignity, and to fight for the masses of our people who are oppressed around the world.[13] [Black Power] is more a slogan used to be a cohesive force for black people in the United States and hopefully for black people in the world.[14]

Such enunciations involve a variety of international angles: the relation of the black American struggle to "Third World" strivings; American power in the international system which in turn is symptomatic of international white power; the anatomy of super-power behaviour and the related consideration of a nonalignment response; the psychological revolution of black people in their search for dignity; the pan-Negro unifying potentialities of Black Power.

But to what extent are the expressed international interests of a few prominent Black Power proponents illustrative of a *general* international orientation within the as yet diversified Black Power movement? And to what degree do the *specific* international themes expressed by these spokesmen enjoy support at large within the movement?

The second query is less easy to resolve. However, while it may be true that some specific international formulations represent individual rather than collectively held beliefs, the foregoing illustrative statements appear to be in harmony with widely held opinions. Especially significant is the fact that the Black Power movement now does not couch its thinking in exclusively domestic American terms, a fact which is clearly evident from the tone of the Manifesto of the 1967 National Conference on Black Power (full text in Appendix).[15] What is of initial consequence is less the realisability of the hope of bringing black Americans fully within the "Third World" orbit, than that such globally oriented concerns are being articulated.

In focussing attention on Black Power conceptions of the outside world a salient background consideration involves the arrival of formal political Black Power in Africa. Not only has this development aided in boosting black American aspirations and self-conceptions, but it also has had a catalytic impact on black American nationalism and internationalism.[16] James Baldwin in 1961 succinctly pinned down this consideration: "Africa has been *black* a long time but American Negroes did not identify themselves with Africa until Africa became identified with *power.*"[17]

Black Power, as a domestic American phenomenon, cannot be isolated from race developments in the outer world. Indeed, well before its effective indigenous adoption, the idea of "Black Power" had made a limited appearance in Black American vocabulary (or ideology), but with reference to the global, or external, contexts of the race question.

Writing in 1962, a Nigerian student of the "Black Muslim" movement summed up its ideology in the following terms: "The attainment of *black power* over the whole world is relegated to the intervention of 'Almighty Allah' sometime in the future."[18] Almost a decade earlier, Richard Wright recorded his impressions of the then Gold Coast in his book *Black Power,* and in so doing counselled Prime Minister Nkrumah on ways and means of making Black Power a reality.[19] And three years after Wright's publication, Paul Robeson, in an interview with another black American, declared:

> Yes, I think a great deal of the power of black people in the world. That's why Africa means so much to me. . . . Yes, this *black power* moves me. Look at Jamaica. In a few years the white minority will be there on the suffrance of black men. If they're nice decent fellows they can stay. . . . If I could get a passport, I'd like to go to Ghana or Jamaica just to sit for a few days and observe this *black power.*[20]

Of additional relevance to the international view of, and background to, Black Power is the already evident infectiousness of the Black Power slogan beyond black America. Kwame Nkrumah recently hailed Black Power as "a vanguard movement of black people" which "opens the way for all oppressed masses" and which "heralds the long-awaited day of liberation from the shadows of obscurity."[21] There is a fairly well-developed Black Power consciousness among non-white minorities in Britain,[22] and a Black Power awareness among some Australian Aborigines,[23] black Canadians,[24] and southern African students in the United States. On the basis of interviews conducted among the latter it was speculated: "It may be that Stokely Carmichael will be as influential to this generation of African freedom fighters as Marcus Garvey was to Nkrumah's generation."[25]

The pan-Negro potentialities of Black Power can be assessed in terms of the global themes in circulation within the movement, the international racial context within which the black American assertiveness has evolved, and the initial dissemination of Black Power ideas beyond black America.[26]

George Padmore, writing in 1956, thought it significant that "the two most dynamic black nationalist ideologies. . . . had their origin in America: Garveyism and Pan-Africanism."[27] For reasons later suggested, Padmore's observation requires amplification. But for the moment we shall raise some considerations concerning the undoubtedly striking black American role in the international diffusion of race ideas.

In the first place, Negro America was one of the first black communities to gain legal political freedom and equality, but after a century the American political system has failed to convert this nominal freedom and equality into actuality. Given this discrepancy, the black American has had a long history of agitation against his actual status. In articulating his needs and strivings, he was strategically positioned to attempt to effect a linkage of ideas and aspirations with others of his race who were in large measure similarly situated in terms of white domination. Secondly, white racism has from the outset been ingrained in the American political culture,[28] thus heightening the confrontation of white racism and black nationalism over time.[29] Despite the recent retreats of overt white racism on many fronts, it remains a powerful influence in the United States.[30] A reinforcing factor lies in the demography of racial balance, for unlike their numerically dominant Caribbean and African counterparts, black Americans, who comprise less than eleven percent of the American population, have always been confronted with the elusiveness of meaningful power.

Thus in the African and Caribbean situations, black nationalism could be articulated in anti-colonial or majoritarian-democratic *political* terms to which a rigid racial emphasis was often subordinated. By contrast, in the conditions of black American existence black nationalism has inevitably involved a pervasive *racial* emphasis in its political socioeconomic, and psychological dimensions.

A related consideration – here there are many similarities with the Caribbean Negro – is the long history of direct black American exposure to the ideals and performances of Western civilization. With an intensive and extensive contact with the very civilization which enslaved him and has more often than not disregarded his worth, the black American nationalist has been well situated to mount an intensive and extensive attack on the failings of Western civilization in its treatment of black men.

Historically, the Caribbean has played a highly significant role in the initiation of global black nationalist ideas, so we are not here implying the uniqueness of the black American role in such ventures. What we have tried to do is to suggest some considerations in viewing the very prominent and consistent part played by black Americans in the dissemination of such ideas. The conclusion seems warranted that if any pan-Negro ideology was to arise in the 1960s it was most likely to originate in the United States. However, it is because of its origin and basic entrenchment in the realities of black American existence that Black Power, though conveying some ideas of relevance to the black world at large, is limited in its potential as an internationalizing force.

This contention will first be developed through a comparative exploration of the origins of the major pan-Negro ideologies of the 19th and 20th centuries. It is on this score that Padmore's comment on the "American" origin of Garveyism and Pan-Africanism requires elaboration.

Neither of these two ideologies, strictly speaking, was American in origin. It would be more correct to refer to their New World Negro origin, and even this characterisation should not lead one to ignore the contributions emanating from the African continent.

Garveyism was as much West Indian as American in origin and style. While it is true that Garveyism in *dynamic* form rose to prominence in the United States, the following facts should be borne in mind:

(1) Marcus Garvey's UNIA (Universal Negro Improvement Association) was initially established in Jamaica; its headquarters later was transferred to the United States.[31]
(2) Garvey left Jamaica for the United States at the age of 29, *after* his race emancipation programme was conceived and after his lengthy process of socialization into the West Indies race relations system. The latter influence at times led Garvey to carry over to the American race context some West Indian conceptions of colour or shade stratifi-

cation which were less relevant (though not as irrelevant as some writers suggest) to the American situation.[32]

(3) In its American origin, Garveyism was activated and initially dominated by expatriate West Indians.

Thus it is not surprising that in death Garvey has been reclaimed by Jamaica as a national hero.[33] And viewing Garveyism as a philosophy of race, rather than the specific school founded by Marcus Garvey, it may be argued that the first prominent "Garveyite" was Edward Wilmot Blyden (1832-1912), another West Indian-born pan-Negro thinker, who unlike Garvey preached his vision from an African base, having emigrated to Liberia at the age of 18.[34] Garveyism, therefore, was not exclusively a black American invention.

The same can be said of Pan-Africanism, a term used in this analysis to refer specifically to the organizational movement for continental African liberation launched in the early 20th century and later evolving into a drive for African continental political unity. This is the narrow specific definition of "Pan-Africanism." By contrast, the broader term "pan-Africanism" (with a lower case "p"), can be defined in Colin Legum's terms as "*essentially a movement of ideas and emotions;* at times it achieves a synthesis; at times it remains at the level of thesis and antithesis."[35] To illustrate this broader dimension of "pan-Africanism," Vernon McKay refers to its "complex and varied" cultural, economic, and political aspects, and adds that "It is related to the concepts of the 'brotherhood of Negro blood,' the 'African personality,' and *negritude*" and at times "has fostered ... the racist concepts of 'Black Zionism,' 'black power,' and 'blackism.' "[36] These distinctions between "Pan-Africanism" and "pan-Africanism" have been employed in part to stress the point that the former is but one (and the most important political) manifestation of the latter, and is thus interrelated in motivation to other pan-African ideas, including Garveyism. In addition such distinctions aid for precision in analysing a variety of interrelated concepts.[37]

The *effective* initiator of Pan-Africanism was a black American (W.E.B. DuBois), but the initial organizational impetus came from H. Sylvester-Williams (1868-1911), a Trinidadian barrister. It was the Pan-African Conference of 1900 convened by Williams in London which, in DuBois' words, "put the word 'Pan-African' in the dictionaries for the first time. . . ."[38] And it was here that DuBois "transformed Williams' limited conception of Pan-Africanism into a movement for self-government or independence for African people."[39] This later found more concrete and effective organizational expression in the first four Pan-African Congresses convened by DuBois between 1919 and 1927 in which the primary actors were black Americans and West Indians. It was at the Fifth Pan-African Congress of 1945 that the movement for the first time came to be predominantly African-led, but even though by this time black American participation had lagged, West Indian involvement was still significant. Indeed, during the 1930s and early '40s, it was West Indians in Britain led by Padmore who were largely responsible for keeping alive the Pan-African idea, and through their contacts with emerging African nationalists – notably Kenyatta and Nkrumah – they aided immeasurably in facilitating the transition to African leadership. It was fitting that the Trinidadian-born George Padmore (by then Nkrumah's adviser on African Affairs) was responsible for the organization of the two Pan-African Conferences which were held in Accra in 1958, and that on his death in the following year he was acknowledged as the "father of African emancipation"[40] – a designation also recently assigned to him by a biographer.[41] Thus, in origin as well as early promotion, the West Indian contribution to Pan-Africanism is at least as prominent as that of black Americans.

Dealing with cultural pan-Africanism, the major concepts of "African Personality" and "Negritude" can be treated simultaneously. As in the cases of Garveyism and Pan-Africanism, these concepts originated from a diverse international base. Blyden appears to have been the first to use the phrase "African Personality" in a lecture delivered in Sierra Leone in 1893.[42] Shortly after, John Edward Bruce (1856-1924), a black American journalist who was in regular contact with Blyden and later became an active Garveyite,[43] explicitly used the phrase and also began to express the sentiment of Negritude.[44]

The African Personality idea in the English-speaking black world was destined to become primarily an African promoted and applied concept, as witness the writings of Casely Hayford (1886-1930) of the Gold Coast,[45] and its subsequent active promotion by Nkrumah. However, neither Casely Hayford nor Nkrumah restricted his vision to black Africa. Nkrumah's pan-Negro allusions in this particular respect are perhaps less well known, but he did at least on one occasion raise this consideration. In a letter of 7 June 1962 to all the West Indian Heads of Government, pleading with them to work at maintaining the disintegrating West Indies Federation, he wrote:

> My excuse for making this appeal is the sincere conviction I hold that success in the establishment of a powerful West Indian nation would substantially assist the efforts we are making to redeem Africa's reputation in world affairs *and to re-establish the personality of the African and people of African descent everywhere.*[46]

In the meantime, the French-speaking concept of Negritude was to come to prominence in pan-Negro aspirations. The phrase first appeared in 1939, coined by Aimé Césaire of Martinique in his poem *"Cahier d'un Retour au Pays natal,"* thus paving the way for its subsequent popularisation, particularly by Senghor. Negritude's contemporary exposition is a joint African-Caribbean venture.

But prior to Negritude's explicit formulation, related ideas and influences had been in a process of pan-Negro diffusion. Mention has already been made of Blyden (the West Indian African) and Bruce (the black American). A more influential development in the parentage of Negritude was the Haitian cultural response to the American occupation of 1915. Also significant were the writings of the Afro-Cuban school which rose to prominence from 1920-1940. Marcus Garvey's role in these developments should not be overlooked: "He did not know the word Negritude but he knew the thing. With enthusiasm he would have welcomed the nomenclature, with justice claimed paternity."[47]

A closer study of black America of the early 20th century will complete the link in the triangular trade of cultural pan-African ideas. In many of DuBois' early writings this concern is prominent. Of more importance in the field of black cultural reconstruction are the contributions of Alain Locke (1886-1954) who is acknowledged as the mentor of the Harlem (or Negro) Renaissance. Black American writers (including the Jamaican-born Claude McKay) of the immediate post-World War I period had begun to give Negritude literary expression during the heyday of the Harlem Renaissance. There is now no need to speculate that "it is likely that Cesaire was aware of their work,"[48] in view of the following assertion by one of the leading members of that school:

> In France, as well as Germany, before the close of the Negro Renaissance, Harlem's poets were already being translated. Léopold Sédar Senghor of Senegal and Aimé Césaire of Martinique, the great poets of *negritude,* while still students at the Sorbonne, had read the Harlem poets and felt a bond between themselves and us. . . .
> The Harlem poets and novelists of the Twenties became an influence in faraway Africa and the West Indies – an influence till today in the literature of black men and women there. To us, *negritude* was an unknown word, but certainly pride of heritage and consciousness of race was ingrained in us.[49]

In tracing the roots and initial promotion of certain dominant pan-Negro and pan-African concepts, we have documented their transnational origins. Almost simultaneously, various ideas associated with these concepts sprang from different quarters of the black world. Their initial motivation was to serve as black internationalizing forces. Garveyism, Pan-Africanism, Negritude, and the African Personality originated as forces of African racial, rather than African continental, relevance. A variety of ideas and formulations within each school evolved into a symbiotic relationship in Negro race aspirations.

Black Power, by contrast, is more explicitly American in origin and immediate relevance. It is true that some of West Indian origin have been prominent in the promotion of Black Power,[50] but such a contribution can best be styled "indirect" from the global racial standpoint. Although their West Indian background has had an influence on their perceptions of race relations, their race thought and action essentially have been moulded by their American experience. Even if Cruse is correct in his contention that their West Indian background more often than not results in their distortions of the realities of the American race problem,[51] the fact remains that they have set out to address themselves primarily to the question of the black present and future in the United States. In any case, West Indian born activists represent but a handful of the recent crop of black American nationalists, the vast majority of whom have no direct links with the Caribbean. The same did not apply in the case of Garveyism, the most dominant prior manifestation of black American nationalism.

While dealing with the question of comparative pan-Negro ideological origins, mention can be made of the rise of other versions of "Black Power" outside the United States in recent years. For a brief time between 1961 and 1962 a new political party appeared in Jamaica under the banner of "blackmanism."[52] In 1959, Chief Remi Fani-Kayode declared in the Nigerian Parliament that "blackism is the answer to our problems,"[53] a view on which he has since elaborated:

> Blackism is a call to the states of Africa to unite. A positive, aggressive, and direct force. Naked and unashamed Blackism, a force to weld together the states of Africa into one unified entity. Not a negative force activated against anyone, but a positive force for progress, strength, and power. . . . I may as well copy the communist slogan: 'Black men of the world unite, you have nothing to lose but your shame, humiliation, suffering, and the contempt of the white man' . . .[54]

Common to the formulations of Black Power, "blackism" and "blackmanism" is that each has independently arisen as an indigenous response to situations in the United States, Africa, and the Caribbean. They have not effected a triangular linkage as did earlier forms of black political and cultural nationalism. Indeed, no active effort has been made to internationalize "blackism" and "blackmanism," nor for that matter is there any evidence of their effective slogan value in the contexts wherein they originated. Only Black Power has so far succeeded in emerging as a powerful rallying cry within its domestic sphere and only Black Power has been striving to become a major internationalizing influence within the black world. But, as we have been arguing, Black Power remains essentially rooted in the realities of black American existence. Black Power was initially articulated in terms of black American needs and only *after* it began to gain root there did talk of its internationalization emerge.

However, the questions of ideological origin and initial motivations are not sufficient tests in assessing the potentialities for transnational ideological diffusion. The fact is that there is, even today, an objective situational similarity in the black world in its relation to the white. This is the situation which James Baldwin trenchantly pinpointed in his reflections at the 1956 International Congress of Negro Writers and Artists held in Paris:

> And yet, it became clear as the debate wore on, that there *was* something which all black men held in common, something which cut across opposition points of view, and placed in the same context their widely dissimilar experience. What they held in common was their precarious, their unutterably painful relation to the white world. . . . the necessity to remake the world in their own image, to impose this image on the world, and no longer be controlled by the vision of the world, and of themselves, held by other people. What, in sum, black men held in common was their ache to come into the world as men. And this ache united people who might otherwise have been divided as to what a man should be.[55]

This underlying situational unity is manifested in the fact that in the past, as in the present, the common situation and needs of black people throughout the world have been characterised by their strivings for psychological reformation; for political independence (which is not necessarily the same thing as the acquisition of legal sovereignty), or – in the case of black minorities – political power and equality; for economic advancement and self-sufficiency and social reconstruction.

It is therefore not surprising to find some older or revised editions of pan-African and pan-Negro themes reappearing in Black Power international philosophising:[56] the Pan-African notions of African liberation,[57] and continental unity;[58] the pan-Negro premise of global racial solidarity;[59] reflections on neo-colonialism;[60] the Garveyite "Back-to-Africa" theme (here articulated in terms of political support and psychocultural linkage rather than repatriation);[61] the conceptions of the African (as of the African-American) Personality and Negritude.[62]

But it is one thing to say that black men the world over exhibit a situational unity in that they are all urgently trying to acquire *meaningful* political and economic power and are attempting to reorganize their position *vis-a-vis* the white world and redefine their self-perceptions. It is quite another thing to assume that black men will (or can) be united in formulating specific goals, in drawing up priorities, and in agreeing on tactics. The present situation in black America is evidence enough of these divergences. There the creative aspects of Black Power as a force for black unity co-exist with its uncreative potential for black disunity. Looking beyond black America it would be natural to expect that such divisions in black opinion will be accentuated. In assessing Black Power's internationalizing capacities, it is therefore necessary to examine more closely the African and Caribbean worlds of the 1960s. In this connection, *the* significant contemporary development bearing on the further prospects of pan-Negro ideological diffusion is the decolonization of most of the African and Caribbean countries.

We earlier noted the impact of the African independence movement on black American aspirations, on their growing interest in Africa's future, and on the accompanying impetus to forge at least a measure of psychological linkage with Africa. In this sense the emergence of numerous political sovereignties in Africa has broadened and strengthened black American pan-Negro feelings.

The nature of the present Caribbean link with Africa is less easy to assess. The earlier political coordination of the African and Caribbean struggles for independence, as was manifested in the Pan-African movement of the 1930s and '40s, became weaker and weaker the nearer the prospects arose of actually achieving their goals. Now in the era of actual or impending Caribbean independence two factors appear to be at work which do not always move in the same direction. On the one hand, it is certain that Caribbean knowledge of Africa has increased in scope and advanced in accuracy. It is also likely that there is a growing Caribbean interest and psychological involvement in Africa as the dominant symbol of Black Power. But another factor is that West Indians now have political communities of their own, largely black-dominant numerically and formally black-controlled politically, in which the requisites of nation building and the related establishment of national identities become immediate.

Much, of course, depends on the solution of the relationships of national identity and racial identity. On the surface, the Caribbean appears to have progressed further than most in solving the issue of multiracial existence, and considering its historical conditions the Caribbean area has managed to achieve a creditable degree of multiracial harmony. But many painful realities lie beneath the surface. The ideal of the "multiracial" (or – as some there prefer to say – "nonracial") society is frequently propagated in the Caribbean, but the multiracial composition of Caribbean societies is based on a black majority which suffers most from economic and psychological insecurities.[63] Many of the racial factors submerged could well erupt in the future unless the pressing problems of economic opportunity and maldistribution are solved.[64] But whatever adjustments are required will have to be worked out in Caribbean terms.

The strengthening of Caribbean bonds with Africa in the foreseeable future will probably be in the area of formal political contact and supports rather than in the realm of mass race unity response. Prime Minister Eric Williams was not merely officially reaffirming the ideal of multiracialism, but was addressing himself to the question of nation building as a matter of political immediacy when he stated:

> There can be no Mother India for those whose ancestors came from India. . . . There can be no Mother Africa for those of African origin, and the Trinidad and Tobago society is living a lie and heading for trouble if it seeks to create the impression or allow others to act under the delusion that Trinidad and Tobago is an African society. There can be no Mother England and no dual loyalties. . . . There can be no Mother China . . . no Mother Syria or no Mother Lebanon. A nation, like an individual, can have only one Mother. The only Mother we recognise is Mother Trinidad and Tobago, and Mother cannot discriminate between her children.[65]

What of the new Africa in its relations with its descendants in exile? With the progressive unfolding of independence, the earlier forms of racial pan-Africanism which forged a bond between New World Negroes and Africans evolved through contraction into a stress on continental Pan-Africanism.[66] But simultaneously, the imperatives of nation building have frequently led to the subordination of the Pan-African ideal. In either case, the pan-Negro dimension has declined in significance.

We have been discussing some of the operative constraints on Black Power's internationalizing mission. This is not at all meant to suggest that Black Power formulations are by definition irrelevant to many African and Caribbean conditions. As was earlier maintained, there is a large measure of situational similarity – especially in economic and psychological spheres – between black people in the contemporary global setting. And, as has been argued elsewhere, there are some Black Power programmatic and tactical formulas to which many leaders in the outer black world could well subscribe.[67]

But what is debatable is whether black Americans are in a position to set the pace and example for a fuller degree of Negro race emancipation. Unlike past times when the zeal of black Americans in the arena of race ideas was directed against institutionalized white power in most of the black world, now such global race ideas face formalized Black Power in the greater part of the black world. Some black leaders in Africa may indeed – as have some in the Caribbean – view Black Power activities as unfriendly acts. More certainly, many black

Africans and Caribbean leaders will react unfavourably to Black Power's global leadership pretensions.

This focussing of attention on leadership response ignores one important factor – namely, the potentialities of Black Power diffusion to masses rather than elites in the outer black world. Certainly the fundamental antiestablishment and anti-elitist attitudes connoted by Black Power must be taken into account in explaining – what appears surprising to many observers – why some Black Power leaders reserve some of their harshest strictures for some black elites outside the United States.[68]

Earlier pan-Negro ideologies were essentially elitist in conception and dissemination. (Garveyism differs to some extent in that it was based in origin and style on a mass appeal and response, but in his conceptions of the outer world Garvey was first and foremost concerned with the transfer of power from white to black elites.) In the present, unlike the past, the question of black elite-mass domestic relations assumes prominence. The nature and conditions of these relations vary from area to area and from country to country. The debatable thing is whether, in these variations, a race solidarity slogan can achieve a meaningful degree of transnational unity in the way that Pan-Africanism, for example, once represented a conspicuous degree of concord in the quest for the specific goal of decolonization. Add to this consideration the nature of politics in the international system which acts as a source of (and in which are reflected) the tensions arising in the relations between black-controlled sovereignties, and the conclusion is inescapable that in an era of declining colonial white power and rising postcolonial Black Power theoretical constructs of global black unity become more elusive in the undertaking.

Another limiting factor to the internationalization of Black Power derives from the pervasiveness and immediacy of the black-white American confrontation, on which we earlier commented. In view of a minority position in a predominantly white environment which has proved unresponsive and antagonistic, black American race consciousness *vis-a-vis* whites is a logical function of the conditions of black existence in America. (It is no accident that outside the United States the Black Power concept has found its greatest appeal among racial minorities in Britain, Canada, and Australia. The apparent attractiveness of the concept to southern African blacks, while in a numerical majority, constitute a political minority.) Such heightened race consciousness in the black-white context is not automatically transferable to other quarters.[69] To Ibos in Biafra, to the Afro-Shirazi in Zanzibar, to the Southern Sudanese, to the Batutsi (or, conversely, the Bahutu) in Rwanda, to some Africans in Guyana, the immediately perceived racial (or ethnic) threat in recent years has not emanated from the white world. Many black American nationalists are tempted to view the outer black world predominantly "through the thick mist of race" – to use Langston Hughes' words with reference to his first visit to Africa –[70] but such a restrictive vision can often lead to unrealism and distortion concerning the totality of African or Caribbean problems, especially in the era of their independence. Indeed, back in the 1930s the Negro internationalist George Padmore "worried about the Negro American tendency to analyse African problems in an American light."[71]

We are not here minimising the persistence of black-white adjustments as significant and explosive national and international issues. It only requires certain incidents – like those in Notting Hill (London) in 1958 or Selma (Alabama) in 1965; the Sharpeville massacre of 1960; the murder of Patrice Lumumba (at black hands but, as the feeling persists, at white instigation), and the various evidences of direct outside intervention in Congo (Kinshasa); the declaration of UDI and the hanging of black Africans by that regime; the initial invitations to South Africa to participate in the 1968 Olympics – to arouse a common pattern of strong emotional response throughout the black world. Despite this, the development and propagation of "a philosophy of "Blackness"[72] as a coordinating force and organizing principle for all black people has severe limitations in terms of the immediate realities of, and perceived needs in, the varied quarters comprising the black world.

The upshot of the foregoing arguments is that Black Power encounters many difficulties in facing the realities of the black world beyond America. Indeed, it might be argued that in spite of what some Black Power spokesmen say about its internationalizing potential, they recognise its limitations in this quest. Far from trying to organize the non-American black world, they may well be interested primarily in getting back into this world from which they have been removed physically and spiritually. The endorsement by some Black Power proponents of revolution (Fanon-style); the "nonaligned" posture openly advocated by some (see note 12); their persistent condemnation of neo-colonialism; their "Back-to-Africa" spiritual mission; the effort to effect a black American linkage with the "Third World" – all these appear to support the previous assertion. In other words, the essential function of Black Power's internationalizing mission appears to lie less in its intended external effects than in its internal consequence to the black American struggle for political, socioeconomic, and psychological emancipation.

But there are significant implications emerging from the rise of Black Power in America of the 1960s to which leaders in African and Caribbean political systems could well pay heed, for Black Power's rise brings into focus many generalized political, socioeconomic, and psychological issues bearing on the national integration question: the consequences of the arrogance and insensitivity of majority power, and of the systematic deprivation of minority groups and their relegation to a position of inferiority; the dangers of institutionalized and non-institutionalized racism (or its variations); the degree of racial and ethnic assimilation necessary and feasible; the relationships between less and more privileged economic groups; the problems arising from the psychological insecurities and low self-esteem of a sub group.

The American experience in almost two centuries of nation building has much to offer by way of instruction, both in terms of its successes and failures. The realities of multiracial and multiethnic existence in the Caribbean and Africa make it politically prudent that they study closely other experiences, if only to try to reduce the possibilities of duplicating errors which have occurred elsewhere.

This study began with a brief look at Black Power in its domestic environment and proceeded to look outward in its primary purpose of assessing the internationalizing capacities of Black Power. In conclusion, we shall return briefly from the outer to the inner context. One point will be dealt with, which is the major potential contribution that, in the author's view,

Black Power's "Third World" vision can make to Black Power in America.

In the long run, Black Power efforts to effect this "Third World" linkage may well prove the most beneficial to the internal (and external) aspects of Black Power *race* thought. For the more that "Third World" strivings are promoted, the more it will be realised that not all problems of the Negro race can be analysed at the black-white dimension. Carmichael, for example, can maintain a more harmonious dialogue with a white Fidel Castro (who has welcomed him to Cuba) than a black Eric Williams (who has banned him from entering his country of birth); with Cheddi Jagan (of East Indian origin) than with his black political opponent Forbes Burnham;[73] with Ho Chi Minh than with Hastings Banda.[74] Moreover, as Carmichael and others are aware, white masses in Latin America comprise a significant part of this "Third World" with which Black Power is striving for cooperation. Oversimplified as many of Carmichael's political and economic formulations may be in his internationalizing mission, they could aid on the other hand in expanding the Black Power vision beyond the confining world of black and white.

The greatest long-run danger facing Black Power is that it may become too dogmatically ethnocentric, which could be disastrous both in terms of its internal appeal and export value. The urgent need of Black Power is to promote race consciousness not racism; to nourish black nationalism not black chauvinism; to aid in the fight for a more meaningful degree of black self-determination without degenerating into race determinism; to work for a measure of race unity not race exclusiveness; to strive for race emanicipation while eschewing all forms of race domination. Black Power does not of necessity connote anti-white power, but it necessarily denotes anti white power. On the latter, a large measure of mutual sympathy will arise in the black world at large; on the former, black men will forever be disunited.

## APPENDIX

### Black Power Manifesto from the National Conference on Black Power

Black people who live under imperialist governments in America, Asia, Africa and Latin America stand at the crossroads of either an expanding revolution or ruthless extermination. *It is incumbent for us to get our own house in order to fully utilize the potentialities of the revolution or to resist our own execution.*

Black people have consistently expended a large part of our energy and resources reacting to white definition. It is imperative that we begin to develop the organizational and technical competence to initiate and enact our own programs.

Black people in America and in Black nationalist groups across the world have allowed ourselves to become the tool of policies of white supremacy. It is evident that it is in our own interest to develop, and propagate a philosophy of Blackness as a social psychological, political, cultural and economic directive.

The objective conditions for reversing the plight of the Black peoples reside within the Black communities of the world. It is of importance that efforts be undertaken to develop a communications system among the larger Black communities in America and the Black nations of the world.

The masses of Black people in America, after 400 years of oppression and deprivation under the white supremacist government of the United States, and the great number of Black people across the world, still remain disfranchised, colonized and enslaved.

The democratic process has failed to bring justice to Black people within the framework of the imperialist government of the United States, and within the imperialist framework of white nations throughout the world.

Control of *African* communities in America and other Black communities and nations throughout the world still remains in the hands of white supremacist oppressors.

The colonialist and neo-colonialist control of Black communities in America and many Black nations across the world by white supremacists necessarily is detrimental and destructive to the attainment of Black Power.

It is therefore resolved, *that The National Conference on Black Power sponsor the creation of an International Black Congress,* to be organized out of the soulful roots of our peoples and to reflect the new sense of power and revolution now blossoming in Black communities in America and Black nations throughout the world.

*The implementation of this Manifesto shall come through the convening of Regional Black Power Conferences* in America and in Black nations of the world.

It is recommended that these International and Regional Black Power Conferences be held before the end of this year, in the spirit of unity exhibited during this National Conference on Black Power. The Regional Conferences shall be *convened* by the *coordinated efforts of delegates to this National Conference* on Black Power *in each region, working in conjunction with the Committee on Continuation of the National Conference on Black Power.*

*These Regional Conferences shall begin to structure methods of attaining operational unity in their regions in preparation for the convening of a Second Annual International Conference on Black Power in a year's time, to be held in a Black setting.*

The International Black Congress shall act in concert with the Committee on Continuation, which shall convene the Second Annual National Conference on Black Power to establish a method of electing delegates to The National Black Congress.

The International Black Congress shall be inaugurated within the next year and a half, at which time it shall replace the Committee on Continuation in the convening of future International Black Power Conferences and in the implementation of programs for the realization of Black Power.

[The Manifesto reproduced in full above was the only *official* document approved by the Conference held in Newark, New Jersey, 20-23 July 1967. The other resolutions adopted (e.g. those at note 61 *supra*) were *advisory* to the continuing bodies set up by the Conference. L.G.E.E.]

## NOTES

[1] Some of the following arguments were first presented in my " 'Black Power,' Africa and the Caribbean"; a paper prepared for the University of East Africa Social Sciences Conference held in Dar es Salaam, 2-5-Jan. 1968 and since circulated in the Makerere Institute of Social Research *Conference Papers* (1968).

[2] SNCC, founded in 1960, recently announced that it had "terminated" its relationship with Carmichael "with regret and no pleasure" (*The New York Times,* 23 Aug. 1968.) This development should not be construed as a diminution in Black Power ardour on part of either SNCC or Carmichael, who is closely associated with the Black Panthers, a rival militant Black Power group. (See report on the deteriorating relations between SNCC and the Black Panthers in *The New York Times,* 7 Oct. 1968).

[3] Martin Luther King, Jr., *Where Do We Go From Here: Chaos or Community* (New York: Harper and Row, 1967), p. 29. Chap. 2 of King's book gives a good inside account of the immediate origins of the slogan. See also Paul Good, "The Meredith March," *New South,* XXI, No. 3 (1966), 2-16; Good, "A White Looks at Black Power," *The Nation,* 8, Aug. 1966.

[4] Martin Luther King, Jr., "Black Power," *The Progressive,* XXX (Nov. 1966), 15-17.

[5] Of the numerous relevant writings special attention should be paid to Stokely Carmichael and Charles V. Hamilton, *Black Power: The Politics of Liberation* (New York, 1967) and Nathan Wright Jr., *Black Power and Urban Unrest: Creative Possibilities* (New York, 1967). Wright organized the 1967 and 1968 National Conferences on Black Power. Carmichael has since become much more revolutionary in his formulations.

[6] Not much has been written on the international and comparative aspects of Black Power. I have attempted some such analysis in "Black Power, Africa and the Caribbean" (note 1. *supra*). See also the special issue on "Black Power and Africa," *Africa Today,* XIV, No. 6 (Dec. 1967), in which is included my "Black Power: A view from the Outside"; some relevant analyses in Floyd B. Barbour (Ed.), *The Black Power Revolt* (Boston, 1968); Inez Smith Reid, "Black Power and Uhuru," *Pan-African Journal,* I, No. 1 (1968), 23-27; The Times News Team, *The Black Man in Search of Power* (London, 1968), Chaps. 1 and 2, parts of which previously appeared in *The Times* (London), 11-16 March 1968. The major Black Power statements of international relevance will be documented below when necessary.

[7] C.L.R. James, "Black Power"; public lecture at Makerere, 21 Aug. 1968.

[8] George Shepperson, "Notes on Negro American Influences on the Emergence of African Nationalism," *Journal of African History,* I (1960), p. 229.

[9] St. Clair Drake, "Negro Americans and the Africa Interest" in John P. Davis (Ed.), *The American Negro Reference Book* (Englewood Cliffs: Prentice-Hall, 1966), p. 679, note 33.

[10] Stokely Carmichael, "A Declaration of War"; transcript of speech, 17 Feb. 1968 in Oakland, California, published in *The Running Man,* I No. 1 (May-June 1968), 17-21.

[11] James Forman: "The Concept of International Black Power," *Pan-African Journal,* II Nos. 2 and 3 (1968), p. 93.

[12] Excerpt from publication of the SNCC Chicago Office, quoted in the *International Herald Tribune* (Paris), 18 Aug. 1967.

[13] Stokely Carmichael; interview published in the *Sunday News* (Dar Es Salaam), 5 Nove. 1967. (In an earlier interview in Guinea he conceived of Black Power "in its simplest form" as "the coming together of black people throughout the world to fight for our liberation by any means necessary"; *Africa and the World,* IV, Nov. 1967, p. 19. See also interview with Carmichael published in *The Nationalist* (Dar Es Salaam), 6 Nov. 1967.

[14] *Ibid.*

[15] Held in Newark, N.J., 20-23 July 1967, this was, in the words of its Chairman Nathan Wright, "the first major national dialogue by 1,300 [a more recent figure given by another Conference Official is 1,094] Black Americans on the creative possibilities inherent in the concept of Black Power." The first such Conference, at which there were roughly 100 participants. was convened by Adam Clayton Powell in Sept. 1966 in Washington, D.C. A third Conference chaired by Wright was held in Philadelphia, Pa., 29 Aug.-1 Sept. 1968 at which there were between 3,000 and 4,000 participants (official reports unavailable at the time of writing). One *New York Times* report has it that at the 1968 Conference "it was announced that the Government of Tanzania ... had issued an invitation to the Conference to hold a meeting there."

[16] See, e.g., Rupert Emerson and Martin Kilson, "The American Dilemma in a Changing World: The Rise of Africa and the Negro American," *Daedalus,* XCIV (1965), 1055-84; Harold R. Isaacs, *The New World of Negro Americans* (New York, 1964); Thomas F. Pettigrew, *A Profile of the Negro American* (Princeton, 1964), pp. 10-12, 191-92; St. Clair Drake (note 9 *supra*).

[17] Quoted in Lewis Nkosi, *Home and Exile* (London: Longmans, 1965), p. 81, (My italics.)

[18] E.U. Essien-Udom, *Black Nationalism: A Search for an Identity in America* (New York: Dell, 1964), p. 313 (my italics); first published in Chicago in 1962.

[19] *Black Power* (London: Dennis Dobson, 1954). See especially Wright's concluding open letter to Nkrumah (pp. 342-51) excerpts from which are given a full-page reprinting by Nkrumah at the beginning of his most recent book, *Dark Days in Ghana.*

[20] Carl T. Rowan, "Has Paul Robeson Betrayed the Negro?" *Ebony* (Oct. 1957), p. 41 (my italics).

[21] Nkrumah, "The Spectre of Black Power" *Granma* (Havana), 17 Dec. 1967; also in *Africa, and the World,* IV, No. 39 (1968), 9-12.

[22] *The Observer* (London), 6 Aug. 1967; "Black Power in Britain," *Life* (16 Oct. 1967), pp. 8-17; *East African Standard* (Nairobi), 30 April 1968; The Times News Team, *The Black Man in Search of Power.*

[23] Charles Perkins, "Black Power," *The Union Recorder* (published by Sydney University Students Union), 13 June 1968, pp. 110-113. (Perkins who is part Aboriginal was until recently regarded by many as "the Australian Martin Luther King".) See also "Black Power May Emerge in Australia," *The Nationalist* (Dar Es Salaam), 23 Aug. 1968.

[24] Murray Barnard, "For Negroes in Halifax, Black Power v. ping pong," *MacLeans* (Toronto), Nov. 1967, p. 1.

[25] John Strong, "Emerging Ideological Patterns Among Southern African Students," *Africa Today,* XIV, No. 4 (1967), p. 16.

[26]SNCC (among the major black American groups) has been the spearhead of Black Power's internationalizing mission, and the two most prominent international Black Power spokesmen are James Forman (Director of International Affairs for SNCC) and Stokely Carmichael who in, 1967 visited eleven countries (Algeria, Cuba, Denmark, France, Guinea, North Vietnam, Sweden, Syria, Tanzania, the U.A.R., the U.K.). Very recently, Carmichael left the U.S. for Senegal expressly "to unite the black peoples of Africa with those of the United States." (*The Nationalist,* Dar Es Salaam, 7 Sept. 1968.)

[27]George Padmore, *Pan-Africanism or Communism?: The Coming Struggle for Africa* (London: Dennis Dobson, 1956), p. 319.

[28]This stands in inherent conflict to the egalitarian ethic also deep-rooted in the political culture but, as Seymour Martin Lipset argues, this contradiction "has, if anything, forced many Americans to think even more harshly of the Negro than they might if they lived in a more explicitly ascriptive culture. There is no justification in an egalitarian society to repress a group such as the Negroes unless they are defined as a congenitally inferior race." Lipset, *The First New Nation: The United States in Historical and Comparative Perspective* (London: Heinemann, 1964), p. 330.

[29]On the general development of black American nationalism, see Herbert Aptheker, "Consciousness of Negro Nationality: An Historical Survey," *Political Affairs* (June 1949); Essie-Udom, *Black Nationalism,* Chap. 2; C. Eric Lincoln, *The Black Muslims in America* (Boston, 1961), Chap. 2.

[30]This is given blunt official acknowledgement in the March 1968 Report of the President's National Advisory Commission on Civil Disorders.

[31]Garvey, who was in the U.S. from 1916-1927 (when he was deported), had initially planned a brief visit to launch the UNIA there and intended to return to "perfect the Jamaica organization." But because of conflicts in the Harlem UNIA branch some of its members asked him to remain on as its President. *The Philosophy and Opinions of Marcus Garvey,* compiled by Amy Jacques Garvey (2nd ed., London: Frank Cass, 1967), Part II, pp. 128-129.

[32]It has been argued that one of Garvey's major tactical errors was in transferring to the United States the white (upper class)-coloured (middle class)-black (lower class) cleavages which were West Indian, not American, phenomena. (See e.g. Edmund Cronon, *Black Moses,* Madison, 1962, pp. 9-11, 191; E. Franklin Frazier, *Black Bourgeoisie,* New York, 1962 p. 105; David Lowenthal, "Race and Color in the West Indies," *Daedalus,* XCVI (1967), pp. 613-614; Padmore, *Pan-Africanism,* p. 91.) But in the two situations there were only differences in degree. The major difference was that in terms of American (unlike West Indian) intergroup (white-black) relations, shade factors were irrelevant in the caste system. But in terms of intragroup relations, shade was not at all irrelevant in black America; the differences with the West Indies system narrowed. (See e.g. Frazier, *op. cit.,* pp. 116-117, 164-166; Frazier, *The Negro Americans,* pp. 137, 145; Gunnar Myrdal, *An American Dilemma,* New York, 1944, pp. 693-700; Malcolm X, *Autobiography,* New York, 1966, pp. 1-8, 374.)

[33]In 1956 a bronze bust of Garvey was erected in Jamaica's National Park. In 1965, three years after Jamaican independence, Garvey's remains were brought back from London (where he died in 1940) and enshrined as Jamaica's First National Hero. At that time the Jamaican Government established a £5,000 "Marcus Garvey Prize" to be awarded in 1968 to "the person who, in this generation, has contributed most significantly to the field of Human Rights."

[34]See generally Edward Blyden, *Christianity, Islam and the Negro Race* (London, 1887; Edinburgh, 1967) and Hollis R. Lynch, *Edward Wilmot Blyden: Pan-Negro Patriot,* 1832-1912 (London, OUP, 1967). Like Garvey, Blyden was a proponent of a New World Negro repatriation; his vision was one of global black race unity; and he was even more bitter than Garvey in his denunciations of mulattoes, so much so that Lynch (p. 251) speculates that Blyden probably boycotted the 1900 Pan-African Conference because of his suspicion of the mulatto leadership of DuBois and others. Lynch also states that "although so far no reference has been made to Blyden by Garvey, it seems likely that the latter . . . was well-acquainted with the writings and ideas of the former."

[35]Colin Legum, *Pan-Africanism* (New York: Praeger, 1962), p. 14. Legum, unlike the present writer uses "Pan-African" (with capitalized "P") to refer to the variety of major pan-African ideas.

[36]Vernon McKay, *Africa in World Politics* (New York: Harper and Row, 1963), p. 93. Like Legum, McKay deals with "Pan-African" political, economic, and cultural aspects. (Note that McKay's reference to "black power" is not a reference to the subject of the present analysis but to the exaltation of African and Caribbean "black power" by Wright and Robeson referred to above at notes 19-20. "Blackism" is discussed below, in Section V.)

[37]The foregoing distinctions are derived (with minor modifications) from George Shepperson, "Pan-Africanism and 'Pan-Africanism': Some Historical Notes," *Phylon,* XXIII (1962), 346-58.

[38]W.E. Burghardt DuBois, *The World and Africa* (enlarged ed., New York: International Publishers, 1965), p. 7.

[39]Rayford Logan, "The Historical Aspects of Pan-Africanism, 1900-1945," in American Society of African Culture (Ed.) *Pan-Africanism Reconsidered* (University of California Press, 1962), pp. 37-38. See also Legum, *Pan-Africanism,* pp. 24-25, and Padmore, *Pan-Africanism,* pp. 117-119.

[40]C.L.R. James, *The Black Jacobinis: Toussaint L'Ouverture and the San Domingo Revolution* (New York: Vintage Books, 2nd ed. rev., 1963), p. 399.

[41]James R. Hooker, *Black Revolutionary: George Padmore's Path from Communism to Pan-Africanism* (London: Pall Mall Press, 1967), p. 140.

[42]Lynch, *Edward Wilmot Blyden,* pp. 54-55 (note 37). See also Robert W. July, *The Origins of Modern African Thought* (New York: Praeger, 1967); Chap. 11 on "The First African Personality: Edward W. Blyden."

[43]Bruce regularly contributed a column to Garvey's *Negro World* and in 1920 was knighted by Garvey for services to the U.N.I.A.

[44]Shepperson, "Notes on Negro American Influences. . . .," pp. 309-310.

[45]See, e.g., July, *The Origins of Modern African Thought,* Chap. 21.

[46]This letter and related correspondence was published by

C.L.R. James in a pamphlet, *Kwame Knumah and the West Indies:* 1962 (San Juan, Trinidad). (My italics.)

[47] James, *Black Jacobins,* p. 397.

[48] Rupert Emerson and Martin Kilson (Eds.). *The Political Awakening of Africa* (Englewood Cliffs: Prentice-Hall, 1965), p. 21 (note 2).

[49] Langston Hughes, "The Twenties: Harlem and Its Negritude," *African Forum,* I (1966), pp. 17-18. My treatment of the origins of Negritude has benefitted from these studies: Albert H. Berrian and Richard A. Long, (Eds.), *Negritude: Essays and Studies* (Hampton, Virginia, 1967) – especially the essays on DuBois, Locke, and Price-Mars of Haiti; G.R. Coulthard, *Race and Colour In Caribbean Literature* (London, 1962); and especially Abiola Irele, "Negritude or Black Cultural Nationalism," *The Journal of Modern African Studies,* III, No. 3 (1965), 321-348.

[50] In addition to Carmichael who left Trinidad at the age of 11, there were at mid-1967 at least four other such Black Power proponents holding major offices in SNCC and CORE (Congress of Racial Equality), the two leading nationally organized Black Power organizations: Lincoln Lynch (associate director, CORE) born in Jamaica; Roy Innis (chairman, Harlem CORE) born in the Virgin Island; Ivanhoe Donaldson (director, New York office of SNCC) born in Jamaica; Cortland Cox (SNCC field secretary) lived in Trinidad. (William Brink and Louis Harris, *Black and White: A Study of U.S. Racial Attitudes Today,* New York, Simon and Schuster, 1967, p. 60.) Lynch, I understand, has since left CORE to form a new Black Power organization (official details unavailable). Innis, who apparently had succeeded Lynch as associate director, has just been elected national director of CORE (succeeding Floyd McKissick) at its reconvened 1968 national convention, at which was adopted a new constitution advocating black nationalism (*The New York Times,* 17 Sept. 1968).

[51] Harold Cruse, *The Crisis of the Negro Intellectual* (New York: William Morrow, 1967), deals extensively with historical and contemporary relations of West Indian born, and native black, Americans. See especially pp. 422-38, 550-59, where he assesses the "undercurrent of West Indian-American Negro rivalry" in present-day black American nationalism.

[52] This was the People's Progressive Party founded by a Jamaican barrister, Millard Johnson. (On its origin and philosophy see Katrin Norris, *Jamaica: The Search for an Identity,* London: Oxford University Press, 1962, pp. 57-64.) In the 1962 General Elections the party gained slightly over two percent of the total vote; it thereafter disintegrated, and Johnson left for Africa.

[53] McKay, *Africa in World Politics,* p. 127.

[54] Remi Fani-Kayode, *Blackism* (Lagos, 1965), p. 13; quoted by E.U. Essien-Udom, "Introduction" to *Philosophy and Opinions of Marcus Garvey* (2nd ed., 1967), Part I, p. xxiv.

[55] James Baldwin, *Nobody Knows My Name* (New York: Dell, 1963), p. 35.

[56] References for the following illustrative statements of Carmichael and Forman (notes 57-62 and 68) are at notes 10, 11, 13 *supra.*

[57] *Carmichael:* "... if we are going to talk about the liberation of Africa, then we prepare for a revolution." *Forman:* "... the kind of struggle for liberation which is going on in the southern half of Africa is extremely important and must be supported."
In 1967 H. Rap Brown, then Chairman of SNCC, twice sent letters to the United Nations offering black American troops to support African guerrilla movements in southern African liberation struggles (*Africa Diary,* 24-30 Sept., 1967, p. 3584; *Uganda Argus,* 7 Dec. 1967).

[58] *Carmichael*: "Many of them [i.e., African leaders] are not concerned with a united Africa. And that is absolutely absurd."

[59] *Carmichael:* "... the African world stretches wherever the African has been scattered" *Or*: "Our struggle lies in the unification of those 900,000,000 [sic] people" of African descent throughout the world. "Our base of course will be Africa – it's our Motherland." *And:* "Once the African states accept ... that this struggle is an integral part of the general Pan-African struggle, they should assist these liberation movements in the United States, in exactly the same way as they already assist the liberation movements in southern Africa .... There is absolutely no difference of principle involved. It is all one struggle for African liberation."

[60] *Carmichael:* "The [African] continent today is controlled by the white man, particularly the United States." *Forman:* "Many of us are willing to take these skills and put them in the service of the continent. ... This purpose is to free Africa to some extent from the neo-colonialism that exists." See also the "Black Power Manifesto" (text in Appendix), para. 8.

[61] *Carmichael:* "We are an African people with an African ideology, we are wandering in the United States, we are going to build a concept of peoplehood in this country or there will be no country". When asked if he favoured the return to Africa of black Americans: "No, not a complete return. At least not at this point. The best protection for Africa today is the 50,000,000 [sic] African-Americans inside the United States. ..." *Forman:* "It is paramount to get rid of the concept that we are Negroes, Afro-Americans, or even African-Americans; we are Africans living inside the United States. ..." The 1967 National Conference on Black Power adopted resolutions on the teaching of African languages and establishment of Institutes of African Studies; cementing ties with the O.A.U.; establishment of a Black Youth Exchange, Student-Teacher Exchange and International Employment Exchange Service with African countries; and promotion of African-American Home Hospitality programs for African visitors.

[62] *Carmichael:* "It seems also that the motherland has a responsibility to safeguard the humanity of Africans in countries where they live outside of Africa. They also need cultural organizations that will begin to revive and place the culture of the African back on the pedestal where it belongs." See also, "Black Power Manifesto" (paras. 3 and 9); W.A. Jeanpierre, "African Negritude – Black American Soul," *Africa Today,* XIV, No. 6 (1967), 10-11.

[63] See, e.g., David Lowenthal, "Race and Color in the West Indies," *Daedalus,* XCVI, No. 2 (1967), 580-626; Rex Nettleford, "National Identity and Attitudes to Race in Jamaica," *Race,* VII, No. 1 (1965), 59-72.

[64] This is no doubt recognised by those Caribbean Governments which have banned Carmichael's entry in person or through the printed word. I understand from a reliable source that the Governments of Trinidad and Tobago, Guyana and Jamaica have prohibited Carmichael's proposed visit, apparently

because of his remarks on the prospects of guerrilla warfare in the Caribbean. (See Carmichael interview in *The Observer*, London, 23 July, 1967.) The Jamaican Government has prohibited the importation of all publications authored or co-authored by Carmichael, Malcolm X, and Elijah Muhammad (*The Jamaican Weekly Gleaner*, 31 July, 1968. p. 34).

[65] Eric Williams, *History of the People of Trinidad and Tobago* (Port-of-Spain: PNM Publishing Co., 1962), p. 281. But the Ras Tafari cult in Jamaica thinks otherwise (Norris, *Jamaica*, Chap. 5; M.G. Smith *et al.*, *The Ras Tafari Movement in Kingston, Jamaica*, Kingston, 1960).

[66] On the evolutionary relationships of pan-Negroism and Pan-Africanism, see Legum, *Pan-Africanism*, pp. 40-44; St. Clair Drake, "Negro Americans and the Africa Interest," pp. 691-700; Ali A. Mazrui, *On Heroes and Uhuru-Worship* (London, 1967), pp. 48-49, 209-30, in which the theme of "pan-proletarianism" is also related to the former two.

[67] See my two analyses referred to in note 6 *supra.*

[68] *Carmichael:* ". . . the African continent today in general is ruled by clowns who are more concerned about big cars than the welfare of their people." *And:* ". . . the African leaders are not prepared to sacrifice. They are engaged in bourgeoisie tea party revolutions." *Forman:* ". . . within the concept of International Black Power, there is revolutionary Black Power and there is reactionary Black Power. We must not ignore the fact that some of our brothers and sisters who are leaders of certain African countries, like certain people within this country, are espousing the policy of reactionary Black Power." (It was reported that during Carmichael's 1967 visit to Tanzania, President Nyerere privately asked him "to moderate his . . . criticism of African leaders." *Uganda Argus,* 28 Nov. 1967.)

[69] President Nyerere was also reported to have privately asked Carmichael "to moderate his 'hate whites' message . . ." *Uganda Argus.*, 28 Nov. 1967. It is uncertain if Nyerere used these precise terms. Nothing that I have seen in Carmichael's 1967 speeches and interviews reported in the East Africa press can be construed as a "hate whites message." But I gathered from a reliable source that Nyerere was not fully receptive to Carmichael's uncompromising racial emphasis.

[70] Quoted in James Farmer, "An American Negro Leader's View of African Unity," *African Forum,* I No. 1 (1965), p. 70.

[71] Hooker, *Black Revolutionary* . . . p. 18. Thus when Carmichael in 1967 criticised African liberation movements on their failures, and in so doing drew on examples from black America, the African National Congress of South Africa (based in Tanzania) replied that "his attacks . . . reveal profound ignorance" and added: "The struggle in South Africa cannot be fought with bottles" against a "well armed and cruel" enemy (*Sunday Nation,* Nairobi, 12 Nov. 1967).

[72] "Black Power Manifesto," para. 3.

[73] During a recent visit to Uganda, Guyana's opposition leader Jagan said in an interview: "The majority party . . . has been completely silent on the Negro question in America. . . . My party supports the line of leaders like Stokely Carmichael. . . ." *The People,* Kampala, 30 March 1968.

[74] When visiting North Vietnam in August 1967, Carmichael said: "We are not seeking the end of the bombing or the end of the U.S. policy of aggression in Vietnam. We want to see the Vietnamese win the war, defeat the United States, and drive it out of the country" (*Keesing's Contemporary Archives,* 14-21 Oct. 1967, p. 22304). James Forman recently cited Banda as an example of "reactionary Black Power" (reference at note 11, *supra).*

# 23
# *The Dialectics of Black Separatism* *

DENNIS FORSYTHE

## A SOCIO-PSYCHOLOGICAL PERSPECTIVE

This essay is an attempt to consider the position of Blacks today from a sociopsychological perspective. This, we will argue, is the most fruitful approach, because it leads us to ask the right questions and proceeds to make sense of so many aspects of Black life which, if considered from the broader holistic perspective, would appear incomprehensible or irrational.

Among a large group of white social scientists there is today a definite bias against the sociopsychological perspective, which they dismiss as an unacceptable form of psychological reductionism. This bias is certainly unwarranted when one considers that such classic bastions of the social sciences – men like deTocqueville, Durkheim, Weber, Marx, Pareto, Michel, and Sorel – endeavoured throughout their works to show the dynamic interplay between individual personalities (egos, motivation, self-consciousness) and social structures (the social situation). In fact a whole number of sociopsychological concepts today which are basic to the social sciences, are derived from their work – concepts such as "relative deprivation," "alienation," "motivation," "consciousness," "status inconsistency," "reference group," and "marginality."

Since the 1960s, a number of white liberal sociologists have added their "liberal" orientation to their former bias against the sociopsychological approach and have questioned a large number of studies which had attempted to ascertain the effects of racism on the Black personality. Two recent articles will be taken as representative of this trend. The article by John McCarthy and William Yancey[1] is the most disturbing if only because it questions so much and offers so little. They wrote:

> In their various attempts to demonstrate the negative consequences of caste victimisation, social scientists have, in their description of the Negro American, unwittingly provided scientific credibility for many white-held stereotypes of the Negro . . . It is our contention, however, that such a view has found wide support as much because it complemented political strategy as because it was based upon solid evidence.

This is true, especially in the old debate over the so-called "docility" and "laziness" of Blacks. However, this old type of scholastic verification of white stereotypes is *very much* different in intention from those questioned by McCarthy and Yancey – studies like that of Kenneth Clark (1965), Silberman (1964), Rose (1945), and Pettigrew (1964). What these studies do in common is attempt to map out the psychological effects of racism and discrimination. Now, the only evidence that McCarthy and Yancey forward against these studies is a number of other studies that have questioned the above. (Note that these are in a substantial minority, so on the basis of the sheer Popperian majority criterion of science, we could dismiss them; but since it takes a minority to draw attention to anomalies or flaws in a scientific paradigm, we will take their remarks seriously, on their own merits.)

In their zeal to destroy stereotypes, the authors have gone to the opposite extreme by being completely unsociological because, in effect, what they do is to question the fact that slavery and racism affected the personality of Blacks at all. What of Malcolm X's claim that "the worst crime the white man has committed has been to teach us to hate ourselves"? One wonders if the authors attribute "personalities" to Blacks and, if so, what factors mold and form the contents of such personalities. Having been uniquely subjugated to so much, could Blacks have escaped particular effects on their personalities? It does not seem that the Black personality is any more resilient and any less adaptable than that of others to such external realities as oppression, conflict, and society.

It seems to me to be the height of academic hypocrisy (and ideological hypocrisy, too) to deny this. It seems ludicrous to say, as the authors do, that "Frazier's study [the *Black Bourgeoisie*] is consistent with the general tendency of this literature to characterise the Negro as pathological, no matter what his circumstances, by suggesting that the Black bourgeoisie is ambivalent about identification with the "Negro masses" and responds by a flight into a world of "make believe" based upon emulation of the "white middle class." But surely "personality" can be cramped not only by failure but also by success because this "success" may be exacted at the cost of one's racial self-respect and integrity. But this is precisely what the authors

*Written especially for this book.

cannot understand: that we are dealing with Blacks in a racist milieu. Therefore to use, as the authors do, such indicators as anomie, mental disorder, suicide, and alcoholism as rough indicators of alienation is faulty and absurd, because although it is shown that Blacks and whites do not differ significantly in these respects, it is nevertheless important to bear in mind that, regardless of the relative levels, Blacks disintegrate in these ways because of racism, whereas the reasons are different for whites. There are many sources of personal disorganisation. Blacks have uniquely suffered from racism, in addition to the other problems.

We will agree with the authors that some "formal comparison" or control group is necessary and desirable in order to find out the real effects of racism on the Black personality. In the meantime, it is better to turn to the self-analyses of Blacks themselves, to the insights of analytical and progressive Black leaders and to the works of Black psychiatrists like Frantz Fanon. In fact, *Black Skin, White Masks* is a refutation of the McCarthy and Yancey argument.

The other article to have recently appeared in the *A.J.S.* by a Japanese sociologist[2] is suggestive and more to the point. For this researcher, "the issue is whether contemporary Blacks and yellows conform to the expectation that minorities will absorb negative stereotypes regarding themselves held by the majority." The analysis suggested by the author is more structural to the extent that he sees "stereotypes as social norms" which "reflect existing social structures." Therefore, to the extent that Blacks and other minorities gain power, their self-images will change. His review of the literature for the 1930s revealed that Blacks and Japanese did in fact internalise negative traits of themselves in the 1930s. But he concluded:

> The social structure has changed. Through the civil rights movement, minority groups have gradually improved their position in society. This improvement should be reflected in their images of themselves and others. There is some evidence in the studies made around 1950 that minority absorption of images created by the dominant group considerably decreased.

Following the logic and line of reasoning of this method, we suggest that there is need to develop dichotomies of social situations facing Blacks along with their dichotomous but related psychological correlates. For example, we can visualise a continuum of racial situations ranging from a closed system (caste system) on one extreme, to an open system on the other extreme. The racial slavery system that developed in America (and the Nazi concentration camp situation described by Elkins) would approach the former extreme. These systems of coerced totalitarian subordination have peculiar traits, from which peculiar psychological consequences emanate. (Note, however, that even within the American system of slavery there were variations or departures from the ideal structure, and therefore departures from the Sambo-boy personality syndrome.) The opposite polarity is a social system that is open and noncoercive as far as Blacks are concerned. This system also generates its specific personality traits.

This simple dichotomy allows us to understand variations both in social structures and in personality types. For instance, it allows us to recognise that the "ideal system" is undermined when certain structural configurations exist such as urbanisation, large Black population, geographical and social separation and autonomy of Blacks, and Federal opposition to local discriminatory practices. Because these structural configurations are so diverse, there is no one unified Black personality, although we can see a modal type. It is therefore no wonder that McCarthy and Yancey are able to find conflicting accounts of Black psychological disposition. Each study reviewed by them is concerned with a particular group of Blacks at a particular point on the continuum, under differing structural conditions.

In 1948 Arnold Toynbee, though known as one of the most formidable racist historians, nevertheless admitted that:

> The great event of the twentieth century was the impact of the Western civilisation upon all the other living societies of the world of that day. [Historians] will say of this impact that it was so powerful and so pervasive that it turned the lives of all its victims upside down and inside out – affecting the behavior, outlook, feelings, and beliefs of individual men, women and children in an intimate way, touching chords in human souls that are not touched by mere external material forces – however ponderous and terrifying.[3]

Here we see reference being made to structural as well as to personality effects. But such overall effects (defects) have characterised all the major modes of institutionalised white-Black contact, from the 16th century to the present time.

These modes (slavery, colonisation, and migration) embrace the forms and systems of relationships that developed out of Black-white contact – all of which led to Black economic and cultural subordination, and hence to Black marginality. In simple historical chronology we may say that 25 percent of the Black population was initially enslaved and forcefully transferred as labourers or indentured servants to the New World; those who were not enslaved and transferred to this alien environment were subsequently colonised and exploited in their own native lands (50 percent); the other 25 percent was later exploited through the "voluntary" migration of native peoples into metropolitan territories in search of better economic and social opportunities which were automatically denied them in their own native territories largely as a result of the devastating and stagnating effects of slavery and colonisation upon their indigenous cultures. Whatever the form of Black-white contact, the inevitable end-product has been Black marginality.

The basic proposition of this essay, then, is that in spite of all the political and social rhetoric of white society, its essential aim vis-a-vis Blacks has been to keep Blacks in a state of marginality by means of: (1) the ideology of integration and (2) the denial of authentic Black separatism. White strategy has been to keep Blacks in a state of marginality and alienation by means of token integration, token separation, and apartheid separation.[4]

These choices have meant that Blacks could see themselves as "white," or a "no-body," or a subhuman. Either way, these available self-conceptions reflect either a condition of utter alienation, internal anguish and despair on the one hand, or a virulent type of false consciousness and delusion on the other.

The vast majority of Blacks have neither been "integrated" nor "separated," but rather in a state of limbo and "inbetweenness," suspended on the margins of both possibilities. They have been rejected by white society while at the same time they have been made powerless and dependent. Blacks have been intentionally molded into a "marginal" people, because this condition of marginality is evidently consistent with the interests of whites much more than the other two possibilities.

## THE MEANING OF BLACK MARGINALITY

What do we mean by Black marginality? Problematic, and as polemical as this concept is, we can nevertheless reduce it to its two basic components, as is reflected in the literature on marginality. Black marginality occurs in two spheres or forms – one cultural and the other social. Robert E. Park pioneered the *cultural usage* of marginality. For him, the marginal man is a cultural hybrid in that he lives in "two, not merely different but antagonistic cultures."[5] The marginal man, argues Park, is "an effect of imperialism, economic, political and cultural". . . . He is "a cultural hybrid, a man living and sharing intimately in the cultural life and traditions of two distinct peoples; never quite willing to break, even if he were permitted to do so, with its past and its traditions, and not quite accepted because of racial prejudice, in the new society in which he now sought to find a place."[6]

Stonequist followed Park in defining marginality in cultural terms. For him "culture conflict and differential are the basic factors in creating the marginal man."[7] Equally explicit, he noted that "it is the fact of cultural duality which is the determining influence in the life of the marginal man."[8] His definition of marginality often runs identical to that of Park, as when he describes the marginal man as "the individual who lives in or has ties of kinship with two or more interacting societies between which there exists sufficient incompatibility to render his own adjustment to them difficult, or impossible. He does not quite, belong or feel at home in either group."[9]

The second dimension of marginality is *social marginality* as defined in status terms. Everett Hughes sees marginality as a subjective dilemma arising from an inferior status assignment.[10] Others have come to stress this aspect of marginality. Antonovsky, for instance, includes in the definition of the marginal situation, examples "where some of the members of one group . . . come under the influence of another group . . . and where cultural and/or racial barriers serve to block full and legitimate membership within another group."[11] Continuing this emphasis, Dorothy Nelkin, in her study, argued that the relevant issue should not be the "cultural conflict" experienced by mobile individuals, rather, "the emphasis must be placed on the isolation of a group and the relatively impermeable barriers established by the dominant society. [For example] the migrant community is marginal in that it is situated on the margins of the larger society."[12] A recent advocate of this aspect of marginality is Dickie-Clark. The marginal situation applies very widely, he said, to those "hierarchical situations in which there is any inconsistency in the ranking of an individual or stratum in any of the matters falling within the scope of the hierarchy. . . . This inconsistency is taken as the essential core of sociological marginality."[13]

Blacks have long been recognised as a marginal group, living in society but not of the society, the last to be hired and the first to be fired, always living on the outside, looking in. Both aspects of marginality are important to grasp, although it seems that poor Blacks suffer more from economic marginality while middle-class Blacks suffer more from cultural marginality.

The concept of Black marginality constitutes an illuminating perspective from which to study Black institutions, Black history, and Black movements. For at this level, we can understand the forces responsible for creating this dilemma and the extent to which Black institutions or movements alleviate this problem or help to maintain it. It helps us to understand the similarities in negative attitudes found among Blacks wherever they may be, why Blacks kill Blacks, and why hypertension is the number one killer among Afro-Americans. As Kurt Lewin noted:

> It is also true that intergroup relations cannot be solved without altering certain aspects of conduct and sentiment of the minority group. Minority groups tend to accept the implicit judgement of those who have status even where the judgement is directed against themselves. There are many forces which tend to develop in the children, adolescents, and adults of minorities deep-seated antagonism to their own group. An over-degree of submissiveness, guilt, emotionality, and other causes and forms of ineffective behavior follows. Neither an individual nor a group that is at odds with itself can live normally or live happily with other groups.[14]

The concept is superior to so many others in locating Blacks and in describing their position because it involves cultural, economic, and social dimensions, and should therefore abate the misguided division of Black ideologues into cultural nationalists versus economic nationalists. While a class (economic) perspective stresses the economic deprivations encountered by Blacks, our focus on marginality points to the uniquely biorationalisation foundation of Black economic marginality, while at the same time stressing the unique cultural disorganisation resulting from white control. Thus, the Third World includes peoples who have suffered in these two respects; these are predominantly non-white peoples of the world.

## THE "IDEAL TYPE" OF BLACK OPPRESSION

The enslavement of Blacks and the institutionalisation of colonial relationships was primarily an economically motivated endeavour, whereby mediocre white Europeans collectively robbed non-whites of their labour, land, and resources as well as their self-concept. These Europeans were primarily mediocre men, marginals thrown off by the breaking up of the old feudal order and by the social and economic dislocations associated with early European capitalism such as the enclosure movements, economic depressions, famines, and the ravages of wars. This colonial process "benefited" all whites at the expense of all Blacks. On the eve of the Civil War in 1861, Jefferson Davis, the southern leader who later became the President of the Confederacy, remarked that "one of the reconciling features of the existence [of Negro slavery] is the fact that it raises white men to the same general level that it dignifies and exalts white men by the presence of a lower race."[15]

Colonialism had a specific aim and a specific method, and the scientific matching of means to aims shows up colonialism as involving a high degree of instrumental rationality. To successfully implant this colonial system, it was necessary to provide optimal conditions in which white exploitation could proceed with the minimum of disruptions in the system. Both objective and subjective conditions were thus instituted.

Subjectively, colonialism aimed at creating and differentiating two types of natives through a process involving varying mixtures of cultural manipulations and coercion. Ideally, only two types of natives were tolerated by colonialism. First there were *mechanical men,* mimic men, aides to whites, natives who were reduced to a more instrumentality or appendage of whites, and thereby exhibited little creativity and initiative. Second, there were the natives who were dehumanised to the level of *tamed animals,* and were thereby expected to be devoid of reason. Although the former (the nascent Black bourgeoisie) reaped more crumbs from colonialism, they, like the other category, were non-persons, negations of men; even where these mimic men performed their role well, they were similarly regarded with utter contempt. Following his visit to Jamaica in 1859-60, Anthony Trollope wrote of the Negro:

> He burns to be regarded as a scholar, puzzles himself with fine words, addicts himself to religion for the sake of appearance, and delights in aping the little graces of civilisation ... If you want to win his heart for an hour, call him a gentlemen; but if you want to reduce him to despairing obedience, tell him he is a filthy nigger, assure him that his father and mother had tails like monkeys, and forbid him to think that he can have a soul like a white man.[16]

Slavery crystallized the whole non-person status of Blacks. So thoroughgoing was the right of ownership of the slave's person and the consequent loss to the slave of even the right to personal security that, under Virginia law, the killing of a slave by his master was not considered a felony, for the code reasoned that "it cannot be presumed that prepensed malice should induce a man to destroy his own estate." Slaves were described in animalistic or zoological terms – "well fleshed," "strong limbed," "lusty," "healthy," "robust," and "unblemished"; later, colonialists would refer to "native quarters," the "gesticulation of natives," "swarms of natives," "the stink of natives," etc. Slaves were branded by their owners with a hot iron, with the owner's initials, and they were ranked in the same categories as horses and mules in various legislative statutes. Throughout the period, scientists and non-scientists through such concepts as "the Great Chain of Being" and Social Darwinism sought to prove that Blacks were at the bottom of the evolutionary ladder and to that extent bore remarkable resemblances to the Orangoutang or the chimpanzee. Fanon depicted this situation by pointing out that colonial settlers physically separated themselves from the "natives" by physical coercion and by also depicting them as sub-human evil things.[17] Humanity (which connoted privilege and civilisation) was restricted to whites only. Chief Justice Roger Brooke Taney concluded in his famous Dred Scott decision of 1857 that he had no ground to assert that Negroes were not "beings of an inferior order ... so far inferior that they had no rights which the white man was bound to respect."[18]

By so dehumanising and redefining Blacks, whites could thus salvage their consciences and bolster their pockets. When the sadism and barbarism of the coloniser is unleashed against the natives, the victim merely becomes a "poor brute," "poor mangled creature," or "poor devil." This explains, even to this day, the relative indifference of the white world to the suffering, murders, and catastrophies that plague underdeveloped countries. While much commotion will follow the killing of one white man by a Black, little furor will result from the mass killing of natives. This attitude, which places less value on Black lives, permeates white institutions generally insofar as they encompass Blacks. Take the legal process. Anthony Lester, a British lawyer, investigated the southern courts in 1964, and confessed that:

> Southern officials admitted to me that there are four standards of justice. First, where white is against white, there is equal protection of the law. Second, where Negro is against Negro, the common complaint is that Southern courts and police are too lenient ... Third, where a white commits a crime against a Negro, he will be punished lightly if at all, and the Negro complainant may expect reprisals.... Fourth, where a Negro commits a crime against a white, retribution is swift and severe.[19]

To create these two types of natives, Europeans methodically sought to remove and destroy the protective cultural veil which formerly protected the native personality. Culture embraces all the accepted and patterned ways of behavior of a given people – it is the sum total and the organisation of the group's ways of thinking, values, feeling and acting which becomes incorporated within the individual personality and shapes his perception of things around him. Thus defined, a cultural system is a living, vital but delicate mechanism which synchronizes a group to its environment. To make the native a tool of the new imposed economic order, it was therefore necessary to destroy the integrity, wholeness, and legitimacy of all traditional aspects of the culture which provided the natives with security, integrity, and wholesomeness – by attacking native gods and native systems of authority; by exploitation, expropriation, and spoilation; by imposing foreign languages; by outlawing certain native ways as immoral, uncivilised, and bestial; and then with the aid of superior force by imposing a compartmentalised world along caste lines. In sum, then, in the words of Fanon, "the appearance of the settler has meant in the terms of syncretism the death of the aboriginal society, cultural lethargy, and the petrification of individuals."[20] Writing of the Algerian colonial experience one author noted:

> The disintegration of the organic communities and the process of urbanisation caused by European colonialism have given birth to the man of the masses bereft of roots and traditions, of aspirations and convictions of social ties and of laws. Torn from his family surrounding and the social setting in which his entire life was spent ... placed in extremely trying material

circumstance and confronted with radically new problems the man of the masses has no choice other than indifference.[21]

Though "indifference" can certainly be one of the outcomes of colonialism, and in fact is the ideal aim of colonialism, it is important to recognise that for a number of reasons colonialists were never completely successful in nullifying the Black subjective claim to humanity. At best, colonialism was able to create only the marginal man rather than the non-person. The native was subdued but was not totally convinced of his inferiority. He retained enough integrity, feelings, and human-ness to question and to rebel; on reflection he began to question the humanity of whites themselves, like Baldwin's Leo, who asked Caleb: "Are white people – people? People like us?" *(Tell Me How Long the Train's Been Gone).* DuBois also noted that "in those sombre forests of his striving his own soul rose before him, and he saw in himself some faint revelation of his power of his mission. He began to have dim feelings that to attain his place in the world, he must be himself, and not another."[22] Though not completely successful in replicating colonialism as a subjective reality, it proved sufficiently upsetting in creating an identity problem for Blacks. Fanon, writing over a half century later, makes essentially the same point suggesting that colonialism created self-doubt in its subjects.[23] DuBois similarly reasoned that no thinking Afro-American has failed at some time or other to wonder: "What, after all, am I?"[24] We will now attempt to examine this identity problem in greater detail.

## MANIFESTATIONS OF BLACK MARGINALITY

Evidence of the "Negro-dilemma" may be found in the writings of Blacks themselves. Perceptive and introspective Black writers, irrespective of geographical origins, have constantly brought this subjective dilemma to public awareness and have thereby exposed the manner in which their cultural and economic location has affected their self-esteem, their identity, and their cognitive orientation. Most Black autobiographies, like those of Fanon and Malcolm X, along with their writings, exemplify the subjective dilemmas and conflicts of the marginal man, the constant efforts to resolve the dilemma, and the conflicts between reason and rage, revolt and reconciliation. Fanon's *Black Skin, White Masks,* for instance, provides a superb analysis of the psychological results of marginality – overemphasis on ego problems, feelings of insignificance, self-hatred, worthlessness, uneasiness, anxiety, insecurity, hypersensitivity, and a devaluation of self. There are, of course, a wide range of sociopsychological patterns related to marginality, and they vary in degree as well as in kind from group to group. For instance, in the British Caribbean, until very recent times, there was a strong white bias in the normative system, with beauty and goodness defined in white terms. But this lack of a strong racial identity was combined with a strong self-concept.

An examination of Afro-American literature will, on the other hand, reveal a particular cluster of symptoms of marginality which pervade the subjective arena of Blacks. These include feelings of being a nobody, Blackness being a burden, being walled in, and a sense of homelessness.

### "Nobodiness"

In Black literature this recurrent theme is variously expressed as that of "homelessness," "facelessness," "namelessness," or "invisibility."[25] One 30-year-old man interviewed by Kenneth B. Clark, in despair, remarked: "A lot of times, when I'm working, I become as despondent as hell and I feel like crying. I'm not a man, none of us are men. I don't own anything. I'm not a man enough to own a store; none of us are."[26] William James wrote: "No more fiendish punishment could be devised, were such a thing physically possible than that one should be turned loose in society and remain unnoticed by all the members there."[27] In his autobiographical *Black Boy,* Richard Wright stated: "I could not believe in my feelings. My personality was numb, reduced to a lumpish, loose, dissolved state. I was a non-man, something that knew vaguely that it was human but felt that it was not." In the form of a "Letter to My Nephew," James Baldwin expressed this theme:

> you were born where you were born and faced the future that you faced because you were Black and for no other reason. The limits of your ambition were, thus, expected to be set forever. You were born into a society which spelled out with brutal clarity ... that you were a worthless human being. You were not expected to aspire to excellence: you were expected to make peace with mediocrity.

It was only in Paris that James Baldwin could salvage a workable degree of identity; as long as he remained in North America, "there was not, no matter where one turned, an acceptable image of oneself, no proof of one's existence."[28] Ralph Ellison similarly exclaimed: "I am an invisible man ... simply because people refuse to see me ... that invisibility ... occurs because of a peculiar disposition of the eyes of those with whom I come into contact." When Bill Russell was kicked about by the police, he wondered, "Why did they do it? What does it make me? Am I nothing? Am I a non-person?" Malcolm X, as a result of his childhood experiences, remarks that in the eyesight of welfare workers, "We were not people ... just things." The feelings of young Black children were recently published in book form.[29] One 14-year-old child asked: "For what purpose was I born? I don't see. To speak words that no one will listen to, no matter how loud I shout."[30] For Afro-Americans, it is the very consciousness of self which is suppressed, and this basic self-doubt provides no solid anchor for great aspirations, only mediocrity.

### "Blackness as a Burden"

In Canada, Robin Winks quotes the feelings of a Black living in Halifax: "I have felt my color in my pride and I should have suffered often the pain of being skinned alive could it make me white."[31] Another researcher quoted the direct response of a Black respondent who recalled: "I got this letter from a friend of mine. He's gone to Paris and he says 'come over here. You need a rest from being a Negro.'"[32] Essayist-novelist J. Saunders Redding confessed that "one's heart is sickened at the realisation of the primal energy that goes into the sheer business of living as a Negro in the U.S.A."[33]

Another study based on the childhood experiences of 19 prominent Blacks[34] registered the point that the Black skin brought with it an exposure to "deep hurt, terror and ugly emotions." A few examples taken from these cases will serve to highlight the point. When Daisy Bates found out that her mother was raped and killed, she reacted by complete withdrawal, declaring that "if Jesus is like white people, I don't want any part of him"; as a mob approached the home of Walter F. White, he realised that "it made no difference how intelligent or talented my millions of brothers and I were, or how virtuously we lived. A curse like that of Judas was upon us, a mark of degradation fashioned with heavenly authority"; Elizabeth Adams, in desperation, wondered "how God would like it if someone called him a nigger"; Gordon Parks, after coming across racial killings, confessed that he "wondered why God had made me Black"; by the time Claude Brown was nine years old, he "had been hit by a bus, thrown in the Harlem River, hit by a car, severely beaten with chain and had set the house afire."

### "Being walled in"

Richard Wright, in *Black Boy,* says "I seemed forever condemned, ringed by walls . . . I feel trapped"; elsewhere he used the metaphor of a "steel prison" to describe his feelings. Langston Hughes in a poem, "As I Grow Older," indicated: "And the wall rose . . . /Between me and my dream . . . /Dimming/The light of my dream/Rose until it touched the sky – the wall." Will Thomas spoke, too, of walls ". . . like morning mists." W.E.B. DuBois referred constantly to "the veil" or the "colour line" or "the racial mountain" or the "caste line," which created what he called "double consciousness." In *Dusk of Dawn* he again described in vivid terms the psychological dynamics of marginality resulting from caste segregation:

> It is as though one, looking out from a dark cave in a side of an impending mountain, sees the world passing and speaks to it; speaks courteously and persuasively, showing them how these entombed souls are hindered in their natural movement, expression and development. . . . It gradually permeates the minds of the prisoners that the people passing do not hear; that some thick sheet of invisible but horribly tangible plate glass is between them and the world. . . . Some of the passing world stop in curiosity. . . . they laugh and pass on; they still either do not hear at all or hear but dimly, and even what they hear they do not understand.[35]

### "Homelessness"

Afro-Americans have been denied the advantages of a stable niche in the society, as a result, they lack that feeling of rootedness, sense of stability, and feeling of belonging. This homelessness may be seen in their folk songs and spirituals, which constantly express the longing for "Another Country" (Baldwin) or a home beyond Jordan:

(1) I'm rolling through an unfriendly worl' . . .

(2) Swing low sweet chariot
Come for to carry me home . . .

(3) Deep river, my home is over Jordan . . .

(4) I'm a poor pilgrim of sorrow . . .
I'm tryin' to make heaven my home . . .

(5) Sometimes I feel like a motherless child,
A long way from home . . .

(6) Sometimes I am tossed and driven
Sometimes I don't know where to roam,
I've heard of a city called heaven,
I've started to make it my home . . .

## THE UNIVERSALISM OF BLACK MARGINALITY

It is our contention here that for Blacks marginality is more problematic than poverty per se, for there are many social science studies which attest to the fact that the poor often work out enduring and ordered relationships in the face of poverty. Poverty becomes more problematic in a context of affluence – and when the poor are exposed to the possibility of wealth but denied the means to attain this because of so-called biological reasons. As DuBois puts the point: "To be a poor man is hard but to be a poor race in a land of dollars is the very bottom of hardships."[36] Marginality is thus viewed here as the common denominator and monstrosity against which Blacks struggle. It transcends national, economic, sex, and class frontiers. It is the basic situation faced by all Blacks whether in Africa or America, Black bourgeoisie or Black lumpen-proletariat, mulattoes as well as pure Blacks, urban as well as rural Blacks, migrant as well as native-born Blacks, French as well as British-born Blacks.

In a most telling analysis, E. Franklin Frazier argued that "the feeling of inferiority is shared by all the colored peoples of the world. This is especially true of the colored peoples who have left their country and have had contacts with the European peoples."[37] While Blacks often quibble amongst themselves and construct complicated systems of intragroup categories based on colour and class, as far as outgroup relations are concerned, "a nigger is a nigger, is a nigger." This clearly differentiates them from the poor whites who are poor but not culturally marginal, nor is their economic marginality based on their color or any other aspects of their biology. This explains why the correct Black ideology must have a nationalist content.

The case of the so-called Black bourgeoisie (nicknamed "Black Anglo-Saxons or "Black Afro-Saxons") needs to be examined in this respect since it has often been the contention of this group that their elevated class position makes them non-Negroes. Moreover, white society likes to point to the existence of the Black middle class as proof that Blacks have now entered the open society and that "being Black and qualified is the most valuable commodity in American society," or that "success is the best revenge against whites." For instance, a recent issue of the *New York Times* regarded it as a "reassuring process" that "more and more Blacks are achieving the American dream of lifting themselves into the middle class. They have become as well heeled, well housed, and well educated as their white counterparts."[38] The proof they gave was that while in 1961, 13 percent of American Blacks earned $10,000 or more a year, by 1971, 30 percent were making that amount, and 12 percent earned $15,000 or more. The article concluded: "The best guarantee of durable, amicable race relations in America is the continued growth of a strong, self-confident Black middle class."[39]

It is important to examine such claims, for what is often projected as solutions might in reality turn out to be a bogey when approached analytically. E. Franklin Frazier, C.L.R. James, Frantz Fanon, Amilcar Cabral, among others, have long decried the Black middle class for individually attempting to circumvent their marginality through assimilation. Writing in the 1950s, Frazier derided such an individual as "half a man in a white man's country," who had broken with his rural folk traditions but who had not been accepted by whites, and, as a result, "suffers from nothingness because when Negroes attain middle class status, their lives generally lose content and significance."[40] He observed and noted a cluster of psychological traits resulting from their marginality: feelings of inferiority, insecurity, guilt, frustration, racial ambivalence, immaturity, childishness, phonyness, self-hatred, and delusions. Gunnar Myrdal similarly stressed the isolation of the Black bourgeoisie when he wrote:

> This tiny upper group of the Negro community often lives in a seclusion from white society which is simply extraordinary and seldom realized by white people; there are Negro doctors, dentists, teachers, preachers, morticians and druggists in the South who might as well be living in a foreign country.[41]

Similar descriptions of the Black middle class in other parts of the world are abundant. Lord Lugard, writing on Africa, commented:

> The educated African imitates European dress and customs closely, however ill adapted to his conditions of life, and may be heard to speak of going "home" to England. He has, as a rule, little in common with the indigenous tribes of Africa, and seldom leaves his native town except to travel by sea or railway. The Europeanised African is indeed separated from the rest of the people by a gulf which no racial affinity can bridge. He must be treated – and seems to desire to be treated – as though he were of a different race. Some even appear to resent being called Negroes.[42]

Since the 1960s the Black bourgeoisie has been "nationalised" by such movements as Civil Rights and have consequently become more assertive and conscious of their Blackness. They have also become more educated, but in spite of this they remain economically marginal. The relative income gap between Blacks and whites increases with education. Siegel computed the estimated lifetime income of Blacks as a percentage of white estimated lifetime income at three educational levels, and found that the Black elementary school graduate would earn 64 percent of his white peer's lifetime income, but the Black college graduate's lifetime income would be only 50 percent of his white counterpart's lifetime earnings.[43]

Logically, it is impossible for Blacks to get absorbed into the present system *as a group* because all capitalist societies, by their very nature, need a subject group. The Civil Rights Movement, to the extent that it attained any success, allowed only for the absorption of a few token individuals into the system, but even so they are absorbed at a great cost to themselves and to the Black community. The Black middle-class person is never sure what proportion of his "success" is merited as opposed to being a token gesture. At the individual level, therefore, all forms of uncertainties and anxieties persist, but, more importantly, this option of assimilation is detrimental from the Black group perspective. Such Blacks might have full stomachs, but to them the question may still be posed: What does it profit a man to gain a little wealth but lose his group soul? As Lerone Bennett so poignantly proclaimed in the August 1973 issue of *Ebony:* "For Blacks in America, there is only one thing worse than failing in America – and that is succeeding in America." Herein lies the true dilemma of the Black man in America and of the Third World generally.

## SOCIAL SCIENCE BIAS TOWARD INTEGRATION

In spite of the failure of integrationism as is evident in the foregoing discussion of marginality, and in spite of the avowed claim to objectivity, the social sciences continue to accept integrationism as the ideal, and proceed to analyse Blacks from this perspective, which means that Blacks are seen either as cultural deviants and wayward children or as backward non-Americans gradually on their way towards being full-fledged Americans.

Most recently, Pierre Van Den Berghe noted that "the field [of race relations] has been dominated by a functionalist view of society and a definition of the race problem as one of the integration and assimilation of minorities into the mainstream of a consensus-based society."[44] A brief review of this "natural-history" perspective on race relations will serve to highlight the point. In 1926 Robert E. Park, prominent mentor of the famed Chicago School of Sociology, made this influential statement:

> In the relations of races there is a cycle which tends everywhere to repeat itself. . . . The race relations cycle which takes the form . . . of contacts, competition, accommodation and eventual assimilation, is apparently progressive and irreversible, but cannot change its direction. . . . The forces which have brought about the existing inter-penetration of peoples are so vast and irresistible that the resulting changes assume the character of a cosmic process.

W.O. Brown similarly postulated that:

> "The inevitable trend in every situation is towards equilibrium, toward status uniformity and assimilation. . . . In the long run, the only permanent solution of race conflict is the complete absorption and assimilation of the races in a common culture and social order."[45]

The famous Borgardus "Race Relations Cycles" gave the most formal expression of this view. In 1944 Gunnar Myrdal's classic statement of race relations, *An American Dilemma,* similarly expressed this assimilationist proclivity: "We assume it is to the advantage of American Negroes as individuals and as a group to become assimilated into American culture, to acquire the traits held in esteem by the dominant white Americans." In England, too, Sheila Patterson's *Dark Strangers* in 1963 applies this unilinear perspective to the study of West Indian immigrants in London. From her study, she concluded that racial conflicts and discrimination in England were merely temporary types of social maladjustments which would necessarily settle down after a period of time.

This bias toward integration has correspondingly led social scientists to ignore the important but opposite trend or dialectical inclination toward Black separatism, Black nationalism, Black ethnicity, or Black ethnocentricism. Such a trend, because of this social science bias, has been brushed aside as "extremist," "escapist," "chauvinistic," "racism-in-reverse," "Black supremacy," and as deviant and pathological. From this point on, the social sciences need to start off from real facts in order to restore objectivity, and in so doing uproot the social science foundation of the myth that assimilation and integration, rather than separation, is the only democratic way to solve racial problems.

## THE DIALECTICS OF BLACK MARGINALITY

Social scientists must therefore begin to develop dynamic models of Black development which explore the possibilities, potentials, and forms of Black separatism. It is in keeping with this need that we suggest that the concept of marginality is a useful analytical tool and organising concept. It is demonstrable that the three situations of racial contact (slave transfers, colonisation, and migration) all produce Black marginality, which in turn engender separatist impulses. Marginals are never static. As Memmi stated, "a man straddling two cultures is rarely well seated."[46] Marginality has its hidden advantages and its own dialectical tendency toward motion; it engenders insecurity, discontent, and conflict; it generates all types of reactions – ranging from drug usages, alcoholism, suicides, migrations, flights of fantasy, to reform movements and revolutionary movements. In fact, all the powerful and dynamic Black movements have been generated by such marginal Blacks rather than by those who have been satisfactorily "integrated." Models of the dialectics of Black separatism may be constructed at both the level of national states or at the level of individual psychic liberation. These levels can then be related to show their fundamental interdependence.

At the level of colonised nation-states both Fanon and Albert Memmi have shown through the logic of the dialectic method that colonialism is bound to fall because it creates an inexorable movement towards polarisation and separation in the colonies; even left-wing radicals in the colonies, according to Memmi, will sooner or later realise that they too do not belong in the world of the colonised and in their struggles. Memmi's *The Colonizer and the Colonized* is a patient explanation of the inevitability of this process:

> The colonial relationship . . . chained the coloniser and the colonised into an implacable dependence, molded their respective characters and dictated their conduct. Just as there was an obvious logic in the reciprocal behavior of the two colonial partners, another mechanism proceeding from the first, would lead inexorably to the decomposition of this dependence . . . The colonial situation, by its own internal inevitability, brings on revolt. For the colonial condition cannot be adjusted to; like an iron collar, it can only be broken.[47]

At the level of the individual, on the other hand, social psychologists in particular should develop models dealing with the processes of psychic detachment away from subjective colonialism. This psychic separation and liberation may be viewed as an "awakening" process, where the individual moves away from sleepiness as a result of some experience which qualifies as an encounter or "disturbance." Being asleep, he is not aware of his right to a separate existence, so that the contents of his thoughts are myths, illusions, and fantasies – about who he is, what he is, and about his relationship to "others." In Marxian terminology he suffers from "false-consciousness." In concrete terms this is a period of unqualified assimilation to the dominant white culture.

Usually a disturbance occurs to break the calm, sleeping repose. The disturbance might be sudden or gradual, traumatic or moderate, verbal or visual, psychological or physical. The disturbance jolts the person into at least considering a different interpretation of himself and his past. It constitutes a crisis or a turning point in the person's life. It may be the result of a single experience which climaxes a process of summation, or it may develop in a more gradual and imperceptible manner, not clearly recallable by the subject.

The important point is that such a disturbance is a necessary prerequisite. Brink and Harris discovered that the Freedom Rides "were the torch that set the smoldering civil rights battle ablaze . . . It was as if, after so many years of submission, the Negro suddenly discovered that he had a collective purpose and a collective courage."[48] Likewise, they noted a similar effect emanating from the assassination of Medgar Evers at Jackson in 1963 and the spectacle of police dogs and fire hoses turned on Negro marchers in Birmingham. As one respondent related: "You get the spirit when you see terrible things happening to others."[49] Likewise another study pointed out that the death of Martin Luther King "hurled thousands of pre-encounter Negroes into a search for a deeper understanding of the Black Power Movement. Witnessing a friend being assaulted by the police, televised reports of racial incidents or discussions with friends may 'turn a person on' to his own Blackness."[50] Not only do studies by sociologists and others reveal the vitality of such a factor, but also subjective accounts by Black respondents themselves concur to this. DuBois recalled how, as a boy at school, his card was rejected by a white girl and how this shook him up: "Then it dawned upon me with a certain suddenness that I was different from the others . . . shut out from their world by a vast veil."[51] For Malcolm X, it was his contact with the Black Muslims; for LeRoi Jones, it was the struggle for a Master's Degree in Philosophy. The disturbance shatters their complacency and prompts a reevaluation.

It is this sociopsychological perspective, by focusing on the structural effects of colonialism on the individual psyche, which explains the role of marginal middle-class Blacks in spearheading certain nationalist movements. More than any other sector of the colonised they felt the agony of "double-consciousness," not so much in their bellies as in their minds. E. Franklin Frazier in his analysis of racial and cultural contacts gave ample proof of this tendency. He remarked that "it has been the marginal man who has become the leader of the nationalist movements."[52] Frazier systematically gave proof of this in the cases of the Gold Coast, Nigeria, Indonesia, and India,[53] where the leaders of these nationalistic movements were all educated products of Western culture.

The "disturbance" may also occur through larger processes such as warfare, race riots, or through emigration to metropolitan areas, which heightens the marginality of the Black migrants. Some illustrations and discussion will serve to highlight these dialectical processes of separatism inherent to the emigration of Blacks to metropolitan areas.

Black emigration to metropolitan areas was manifestly intended to serve the labour needs of the metropolitan area, but it generated such latent consequences which operated to undermine the very metropolitan-colonial-capitalist complex which sponsored it. Fanon in *Black Skin White Masks* noted that "the Black man who has lived in France for a length of time returns radically changed," that if he goes to Europe, "he will have to reappraise his lot," and that he will learn there that "he is a Negro": "For the Negro there is a myth to be faced . . . The Negro is unaware of it as long as his existence is limited to his own environment; but the first encounter with a white man oppresses him with the whole weight of his Blackness." Claude McKay, like Fanon and so many others who migrated to metropolitan countries, left Jamaica with only the political philosophy of "free thinking" and the belief that "race" did not matter to him. But, because of the shattering discriminatory experiences abroad, he was driven back from his earlier innocence to a positive affirmation of his Blackness with the proverbial desperation of a drowning man, as is borne out by all his poems and writings. Blocked and rebuffed in their quest to identify with the dominant culture, they come to identify with their despised group, a switch similar in function to what Brinton in *The Anatomy of Revolution* calls the "transfer of allegiance of intellectuals," a process which constitutes a necessary prerequisite of revolutions. Even O. Mannoni in *Prospero and Caliban* was able to observe from his study of the Malagasian colonial situation that:

> The complexes of the "assimilated" drive them to seek the company of Europeans, but they are never received by them as equals. They are ill at ease in all societies, and the failure they embody heightens rather than diminishes consciousness of racial differences. . . . He will suffer painful psychological conflicts and will become subject to the feelings of hostility which, paradoxically but understandably enough, will be vented upon the Europeans. . . . Paradoxically, the more "civilised" the colonial inhabitants become, the greater is the awareness on both sides of irremovable racial differences. These differences acquire exactly the importance attributed to them.[54]

Mannoni went on to argue that in Madagascar "unrest occurred about the same time that a number of Europeanized Madagasies" dreaded to return to Madagascar. Those who for all intents and purposes had assimilated European lifestyles tended not to hide with their Madagascan brethren. But those who were semi-assimilated did so.[55]

Fanon is a stark verification of this thesis. After noting in *Black Skin White Masks* that he was "hated, despised and detested" resolved that "since . . . the other hesitated to recognise me there remained only one solution: to make myself known" by rebellion. In *The Wretched of the Earth* he went on to explain the functions of this severance and return to native culture not only as a way of restoring "psycho-affective equilibrium" in the native but also to rehabilitate and regenerate native states.[56]

The rediscovery of national self-hood and national culture finds expression in what amounts to be some type of cathartic jubilation, when the prodigal sons and daughters "return" to their original tribe. Aimé Césaire in his monumental poem – "Statement On My Return to my Native Country" – gave vivid expression to this phenomenon of "wisdom-through-suffering" by jubilantly exalting the Black antithesis which he had discovered: Aimé Césaire's monumental autobiographical poem – "Return to my Native Land" – was written at the age of 26, just after he had finished his studies in France and, after ten years absence, had returned to Martinique. He resolved his subjective dilemmas and his identity problem by jubilantly exalting the Black antithesis which he had rediscovered:

> Hurray for those who never invented anything
> hurray for those who never explored anything
> hurray for those who never conquered anything
> but who, in awe, give themselves up to the essence of things
> hurray for joy
> hurray for love
> hurray for the pain of incarnate tears . . .
> Give me the wild belief of the magician
> Give my hands the power to create . . .
> Turn me into a fighter against all conceit
> And yet obedient to my people's spirit . . .
> Do not turn me into a man of hate when I shall hate,
> for in order to emerge into this unique race
> You know my worldwide love . . .
> Listen to the white world
> how it resents its great efforts . . .
> Listen how their defeats sound from their victories.
> Mercy! Mercy for our omniscient, naive conquerors.[57]

## THE IDEOLOGY FOR CHANGE

While all Blacks suffer from and feel the pangs of marginality, not all understand its source nor how to go about curing themselves of those ailments. It is at this point that the issue of political movements and ideology becomes important. Without a correct ideology, which redefines and reinterprets reality, the Black potential will never be tapped, Blacks will remain a broken, disorganised, and disoriented people, and our hostilities and frustrations will be turned inward or sublimated.

Rather than dealing at this point with the whole problem of strategies and tactics for change, it is more fruitful to deal with the broader philosophy of change since the former problem can only be dealt with in a specific social context, whereas the ideology of change can be discussed so as to formulate, in a general way, the "ideal" ingredients of a Black liberation ideology, one that would obviously include ways to counteract (1) economic marginality, (2) cultural marginality, and (3) the emasculated Black self-concept.

This question of the correct Black ideology may be discussed in relationship to the role of the progressive elements of the Black intelligentsia, since it is they who must necessarily play the leading role in ideological clarification and development.

Self-reliance or a do-it-yourself determination of the people is, of course, the first and basic prerequisite. Fanon, in his battle against colonialism, became distraught with the French Communist Party, with the French proletariat, and French intellectuals (including Sartre); he renounced and denounced France, and became convinced that liberation will come only from the people. He argued that the masses must be educated to the fact that they, and only they, have the power to liberate themselves.[58]

This is not only pragmatically necessary but also psychophilosophically justified. Like the psychosomatic cripple, he must decide to get up and walk. It is only by asserting oneself that one will be recognised by "others" as a living, feeling, and thinking being. The act of rebellion makes the slave a whole being not only in terms of his own self-concept but also in terms of the accorded recognition by others:

> Man is human only to the extent to which he tries to impose his existence on another man in order to be recognised by him. As long as he has not been effectively recognised by the other, that will remain the theme of his actions. It is on that other being, on recognition by that other being that his own human worth and reality depend.[59]

In fact Fanon and other existentialist writers went to the point of asserting that it is only by practising violent activism that the long colonial psychological syndrome of dependency and inferiority can be broken so that the colonised overcomes his fears of the enemy and acquires the traits of the "new man" who could then play a meaningful role in nation building.

An emancipated slave cannot remain in the household of his former master and be anything but the slave. To consume his freedom, to realise his manhood, he has to sever ties and separate, just as a growing child must assert his independence and go out into the world in order to establish new and independent roots. The slave's rejection and rebellion against his master is an indispensable prelude for his emancipation and self-recovery. After having been rejected for so long by the master, the day must come when it is the slave who must refuse the master. Why should Blacks be any less susceptible to racial selfhood than whites?

This type of philosophical justification of separatism must, however, be buttressed by sociological analysis, and it is to this that we now turn our attention. Black marginality and its related sociopsychological syndrome expressed in feelings like "nobodiness," "Blackness as a burden," "being walled-in," and "homelessness" can be eliminated only by embracing some ideology with an important separatist orientation, as is found in such movements as Black Nationalism, Black Marxism, Pan-Africanism, Back-to-Africa, or Black Studies. In fact, in the history of the United States these movements were tremendously important in terms of their mobilizing and therapeutic effects. They deliberately aimed at combating marginality and so it is no wonder that all the positive attitudes associated today with Blackness – attitudes like Black pride, Black unity, Black is beautiful, and Black power – were nurtured in the womb of these sectarian separatist movements rather than in movements of integration. Besides, the ideology of separatism seems to unleash a creative mental energy which is not found amongst integrationists. For instance, at the beginning of the 20th century, DuBois and his followers who worked around *Crisis* magazine were more intellectually creative than Booker T. Washington and his Tuskegee group.

Separation is by far superior as a strategy to either integration or marginality. It recognises the group nature of American society (and world society in general), and attempts to mobilise Blacks on the basis of their unique experiences and their distinct interests. Any Black movement or ideology that fails to accept the dictates of this group imperative of American life is doomed to fail, for the fact of ethnic solidarity and ethnic power are firmly rooted in American society. The idea of separation is not simply or mainly spatial in connotation: it is based on shared experiences, communicative effectiveness, and interests, which together comprise the substance of their uniqueness and constitute their claim to being a "people." As Karl Deutsch stated:

> Peoples are marked off from each other by communicative barriers, by "marked gaps" in the efficiency of communication. . . . Membership in a people essentially consists in wide complementarity of social communication. It consists in the ability to communicate more effectively, and over a wider range of subjects, with members of one large group than with outsiders . . . Complementarity is greater if it permits individuals to communicate efficiently no matter how often they change their residence or their occupations . . .[60]

Separatism is therefore a necessary element for Black survival and Black advancement. The processes operating within separatist movements need some clarification, as it is important for us to understand some of the conditions under which and by which a new type of consciousness can be subjectively instated and sustained. The new reality has to be objectified essentially by processes of psychoaffective interaction and resocialisation along lines similar to the primary socialisation of children within the family, but a process which must necessarily be forceful as this is the only way to dismantle and disintegrate the previous nomic structure of subjective reality. It is indeed within Black separatist movements that one finds all the major requisites for the redefinitions of reality. In fact the only political movements to have won mass support among Blacks are those espousing some form of Black nationalism. The numerical strength of Black movements vary directly to the degree to which they cater to the identity or ego problems of Blacks as well as their solutions of bread-and-butter needs. We find historically that the most successful Black movements have been those like Garveyism and the Nation of Islam that have offered solutions to both aspects of Black marginality. These movements are all autocratic and familylike in structure and functioning with a strong father figure (Messiah) at its head, who disciplines his followers by imposing a stringent set of "do's" and "don'ts"; he protects, teaches, directs, and provides for his followers. Old loyalties and beliefs are expunged. This new form of attachment substitutes for the Black family that was disorganised by the colonisers and for the slavish attachments to the colonisers that had developed. The leader of such movements, being now role-model, provides a new self-concept and identity through discipline, through ideology, and through example. Exorcising the self of negative aspects is more like a conversion process which often takes on all the seriousness and intensity of a religious process. Recognising the negative connotations of "Negro" and the refusal of whites to substantiate their American citizenry, they offer some alternative nationality which designates their new "elect" status – "African" (Marcus Garvey), "Moor" (Noble Drew Ali), "Muslim" (Elijah Muhammad), or "Black Jews" (Rabbi Matthew). Writing of the effects of the Nation of Islam on the Black psyche Essien-Udom noted:

> Muhammad's ideological pronouncements . . . are aimed at purging lower-class Negroes of their inferiority complex. The "real" rather than the "ostensible" enemy of the Nation of Islam . . . is not the white people per se, but the Negro himself – his subculture, his image of himself and of his "place" in society, his attitude toward white people, and his idealisation of all that is white. Black nationalists, [argue that] the Negro can never be really free until he has purged from his mind all notions of white superiority and Negro inferiority and then ceases to despise himself and his group.[61]

Membership in the Nation of Islam invariably affects a personality change which is almost chemical in nature: one walks, talks, eats, dresses, works and thinks differently. The same type of analysis is applicable to other Black separatist movements like Garveyism and Noble Drew Ali. The Black Panthers were also successful up to a point, not so much in realising their famous ten demands (many of which were so unrealistic) but the very bravery and romantic boldness by which they voiced these demands enhanced the egos of not only Panther members themselves but also of Black onlookers. The Panther movement dissipated not only because of the intensity of the repression against them but because the movement was not as disciplined and as tightly organised as the Nation of Islam. Moreover, while the Panthers were primarily concerned with debunking the environing system, the energies of the Black Muslims are turned inward in an attempt to rebuild the Black personality and the Black community.

The phenomenal rise and popularity in 1973 of the so-called "Crest Theory of Color Confrontation" developed by Dr. Frances Welsing of Howard University can only be understood in terms of the ego gratification gained by those who subscribe to her ideas rather than to the scientific merits of her ideas. How uplifting it is for Blacks to be told that scientifically they are biologically superior to whites because their bodies have the power to produce melanin, an attribute which whites envy and which unleashes white frustrations and white hostilities against Blacks?! Even nonviolent movements like Martin Luther King's were successful in this limited sense since one of the latent effects was to increase the manhood of Blacks through Satyagraha or the ability to excel in soul power or moral restraint.

On the other hand, the Civil Rights Movement, which is integrationist in essence, does not cater to these unique psychological deprivations, but rather increases them because integration – both substantive and token – is one of the very sources of marginality. Historically, integration for Blacks has meant broken dreams, exploitation, frustrations, and impoverishment (psychological and economic); it is by definition a means by which false consciousness and marginality are institutionalised by failing to respect the cultural uniqueness of Blacks. Substantive separation is, on the other hand, a return to the universal of Black ethnocentricism and is the only means of reducing the costs of marginality. Historically, in order to guarantee maximum white control, whites ensured that Black separation was at its minimum. Any assertion of Black independence, any movement towards a functional Black autonomy, has been seen as a dangerous manifestation of Black rebellion and Black "uppitiness." The more Black separation there was, the less the possibility of white exploitation. For this reason, whites have always opposed separatism. For them Black separation only means insecurity, uneasiness, and powerlessness – in short, it generates or reallocates all the elements of marginality from Blacks to whites themselves. It forces them back to their original condition which was one of social marginality. Memmi depicted colonisers as very mediocre men: "Although he is everything in the colony, the colonialist knows that in his own country he would be nothing; he would go back to being a mediocre man."[62] O. Mannoni likewise agreed that "a group infected with racialism acquires a cheap superiority; the more mature personalities may scorn it, but we may be sure that the mediocre will make great play of it."[63] Mediocre whites are always the most hardened racists because racism becomes for them a compensatory bastion.

The third element of this ideal Black ideology is socialism. Here the role of the Black intelligentsia is crucial and most difficult as it involves helping the people overcome their attachment to capitalism by showing them how capitalism has created and sustained their suffering. The natural tendency is for the oppressed people to want to reap all the privileges and material affluence which have been denied them, as was so glaringly illustrated in the "Cargo cult" movements in Melanesia and Polynesia at the start of this century. Fanon observed that "What they demand is . . . the settler's place, . . . for them, there is no question of entering into competition with the settler. They want his place."[64] It is thus up to Black intellectuals to show the people the logical impossibility of this and to teach them that is absolutely necessary to *transcend* the current capitalist system. The conclusion to Fanon's *The Wretched of the Earth* dramatises the need not only to sever ties but to transcend the values and method of the capitalist European order.

> To Fanon, Europe should not serve as a role model for blacks in that her incessant search for humanity often ends in human destruction, both spiritually and physically. For example, the United States created in

> Europe's image, has in the past (and continues today) subjugated a large segment of her citizens of non-European lineage.[65]

Fanon pointed out that if we simply wanted to turn Africa into a new Europe then we might as well leave our destiny in the hands of Europeans since they are better capitalists. The last words of Fanon, penned from his deathbed, again warned the world against following the European lead, suggesting instead that for the sake of humanity, including Europe, a "new humanitarianism" must evolve.[66]

Besides this, there are other considerations which preclude capitalism as the rational choice for Blacks and Third World peoples. *Europeans have simply exhausted the capitalist technique.* Their development and progress occurred at a time when inviting, friendly, and powerless natives existed to be conquered and enslaved, when frontier regions existed in abundance, and when the resources of natives could be stolen. European wealth and affluence was based on Third World underdevelopment. No such conditions exist today – no lands that Blacks can expropriate, no people they can subjugate, and no resources they can steal. Therefore a Socialistic ideology is needed to mobilise people toward the development of their own resources, but it must be a development of the social collectivity and not one based on the exploitation of the masses by their own native bourgeoisie. These are dialectical reasons which justify Socialism for Blacks and are more appropriate than cultural claims that Africans are a noncapitalist people or that African traditional culture was based on a type of communalism revolving around the extended family. If you probe far back into the history of white societies, they too had such historical communal antecedents.

## THE CONTEXTUAL APPLICATION OF IDEOLOGY

Having sketched the ideal components of a Black ideology, it is then possible to apply and modify it to fit the constraints and nature of particular situations. For instance, separatism in the West Indies and the United States means two different things. In societies like the West Indies and Africa, where Blacks form the numerical majority, separatism refers more to psychological detachment and less to geographical separatism.

When we examine the Afro-American situation, it is in terms of a qualitative and quantitative minority having little economic and political power, suffering from a high degree of spatial and mental sprawl, living on the margins of the most powerful and highly developed capitalist system, and exhibiting a remarkable degree of adaptability to change. It would appear, therefore, that Black separation in the United States can only occur in the form of the development of a Black counterculture or subsystem. A sustained and direct military onslaught on the system with the aim of overpowering the system is overruled by tactical logics and common sense. Blacks have no choice but to develop their own counterculture.

The development of a Black subsystem adds up to Black community development, which in essence, entails three aspects:

(1) a reexamination of everything in the light of the long-run interests and needs of Blacks;
(2) the progressive detachment from white institutions and white values generally; and
(3) the creation and development of Black community institutions for Blacks and controlled by Blacks, in the spheres of politics, economics and culture.

Black community development will only come from a multidimensional attack on the basic problem of community underdevelopment, disorganisation, and powerlessness. Blacks' very survival as a distinct people depends upon this. This option is based upon the reasoning that it is easier for Afro-Americans to change and develop their own subsystem, to become a part of their own system, than it is for them to change the larger American system.

Black Americans have had a tremendous impact in advancing the tide of Black nationalism but they have had less influence in furthering the movement towards socialism in America. This is a pessimistic conclusion, especially to those myopic but well-intentioned dreamers who dream about a socialistic or a Black revolution in America. Though torn by internal contradictions, America remains the most powerful capitalist society. Black socialism will triumph first in Third World countries which form the weak links in the chain of international capitalism, and this will undoubtedly affect American society and Blacks in America. Meanwhile, all that Black Americans can do is struggle to survive as a distinct people, be less "American" in their values, and do whatever is in their power to aid Third World movements, for in the future of these movements lies the future of Black Americans.

## NOTES

[1] J. McCarthy and W. Yancey, "Uncle Tom and Mr. Charlie: Metaphysical Pathos in the Study of Racism and Personal Disorganisation," *A.J.S.*, Jan 1971.

[2] Minako Kurokawa Maykovich, "Reciprocity in Racial Stereotypes: White, Black and Yellow," *A.J.S.*, March 1972.

[3] Arnold Toynbee, *Civilisation on Trial*, New York, Oxford University Press, 1948, p. 214.

[4] "Token separation" denotes a neo-colonial situation where effective control remains in the hands of the white ruling class despite all the outward and formal appearances of independence and separation. Black Studies is a case in point; "apartheid" or caste separation occurs for example in South Africa where the people are forcefully fixated and isolated at a lower level of development and are thereby crippled and denied the normal patterns of growth and development. Blacks have experienced this in "slave quarters" on slave ships and on plantations, and later in (Black) ghettoes.

[5] Robert E. Park, *Race and Culture*, Glencoe, The Free Press, 1950, p. 373.

[6] Robert E. Park in "Introduction" to Everett V. Stonequist, "The Marginal Man," *American Journal of Sociology*, May 1928, No. 6.

[7] Stonequist, p. 215.

[8] *Ibid.*, p. 217.

[9] Stonequist, "The Marginal Character of the Jews," in I. Graeber and S. Britt (Eds.), *Jews in the Gentile World*, New

York, Macmillan, 1942, p. 297.

[10] E. Hughes, "Social Change and Status Politics: Essay on the Marginal Man," *Phylon*, X, 1, 1949.

[11] A. Antonovsky, "Toward a Refinement of the Marginal Man Concept," *Social Forces*, October 1956.

[12] Dorothy Nelkin, "A Response to Marginality: The Case of Migrant Farm Workers," *British Journal of Sociology*, XX, 4, December 1969.

[13] Dickie-Clark, *The Marginal Situation*, London, Routledge and Kegan Paul, 1966, pp. 39, 48.

[14] Kurt Lewin, *Resolving Social Conflicts*, New York, Harper and Bros., 1948, p. 213.

[15] Quoted in Michael Banton, *Race Relations*, London, Tavistock, 1967, p. 117.

[16] Anthony Trollope, *The West Indies and the Spanish Main*, 1860. Cited in Wilfred Wood and John Downing, *Vicious Circle*, SPCK, 1968, pp. 30-31.

[17] Frantz Fanon, *The Wretched of the Earth*, Penguin, 1967, pp. 31-32.

[18] Cited in Pierre Van Den Berghe, *Race and Racism*, London, Wiley & Sons, 1967, p. 78.

[19] Anthony Lester, *Justice in the American South*, London, Amnesty International, 1965, pp. 12-15.

[20] Frantz Fanon, *The Wretched of the Earth*.

[21] P. Bourdieu, *The Algerians*, Boston, Beacon Press, 1958, p. 117.

[22] W.E.B. DuBois, *The Souls of Black Folk*, Chicago, McClurg & Co., 1903, p. 81.

[23] Frantz Fanon, *The Wretched of the Earth*, New York, Grove Press, 1963, p. 250.

[24] Quoted in Essien-Udom, *Black Nationalism*, 1964 ed., p. 139.

[25] James Baldwin, *Nobody Knows My Name*, New York, Dell, 1963; Ralph Ellison, *Invisible Man*, New York, Random House, 1952; John A. Williams, *The Man Who Cried I Am*, New York, New American Library, 1968.

[26] Kenneth B. Clark, *Dark Ghetto*, New York, Harper and Row, 1965, p. 1.

[27] Quoted in Charles Silberman, *Crisis in Black and White*, New York, Random House, 1964, p. 53.

[28] *Ibid.*, p. 71.

[29] Stephen Joseph, *The Me Nobody Knows: Children Voices from the Ghetto*, New York, Avon, 1972.

[30] *Ibid.*, p. 39.

[31] Robin Winks, *Blacks in Canada*, New York, Cambridge University Press, p. 114.

[32] Bertram Karon, *The Negro Personality*, New York, Springer, 1958, p. 1.

[33] Quoted in Charles Silverman, *Crisis in Black and White*, p. 54.

[34] Jay David, *Growing Up Black*, Toronto, Simon and Schuster of Canada, 1968.

[35] W.E.B. DuBois, *Dusk of Dawn: An Essay toward an Autobiography of a Race Concept*, New York, Harcourt & Brace, 1940.

[36] W.E.B. DuBois, *The Souls of Black Folk*, p. 8.

[37] E.Franklin Frazier, *Race and Culture Contacts in the Modern World*, Boston, Beacon Press, 1957, p. 298

[38] *New York Times*, June 17, 1974, p. 17.

[39] *Ibid.*, p. 24

[40] E. Franklin Frazier, *Black Bourgeoisie*, New York, Collier Books, 1962 ed., pp. 24-25, 213.

[41] Quoted in Michael Banton, *Race Relations*, p. 338.

[42] Sir F.D. Lugard, *The Dual Mandate in British Tropical Africa*, 4th Ed. London, William Blackwood and Sons, 1929, pp. 80-81.

[43] Paul Siegel, "On the Cost of Being Negro," *Sociological Inquiry*, 35, 1965, pp. 52-55.

[44] Pierre Van Den Berghe, *Race and Racism*, p. 7.

[45] W.O. Brown, "Culture, Contact and Race Conflict," in E.B. Reuter, *Race and Culture Contacts*, New York, McGraw Hill, 1934.

[46] Albert Memmi, *The Colonizer and the Colonized*, Boston, Beacon Press, 1967.

[47] *Ibid.*, p. 128

[48] William Brink and Louis Harris, *The Negro Revolution in America*, New York, Simon & Schuster, 1969, p. 68.

[49] *Ibid.*, p. 69

[50] Dixon and Foster, *Beyond Black or White*, Boston, Little Brown, 1971, p. 101.

[51] W.E.B. DuBois, *The Souls of Black Folk*, p. 2.

[52] E. Franklin Frazier, *Race and Culture Contacts in the Modern World*.

[53] *Ibid.*

[54] O. Mannoni, *Prospero and Caliban*, New York, Praeger, 1964, pp. 75, 24, 75.

[55] *Ibid.*, p. 76.

[56] Frantz Fanon, *The Wretched of the Earth*, p. 175.

[57] See Lloyd King, "Truer than Biography: Aimé Césaire interviewed by Rene Despestre," *Savacou*. June, 1971, Kingston.

[58] Frantz Fanon, *The Wretched of the Earth*, p. 197.

[59] Frantz Fanon, *Black Skin, White Masks*, p. 216.

[60] Karl Deutsch, *Nationalism and Social Communication*, Cambridge, Mass., M.I.T. Press, 1966, p. 97.

[61] Essien-Udom, *Black Nationalism*, 1964 ed., p. 361.

[62] Albert Memmi, p. 61.

[63] O. Mannoni, p. 120.

[64] Frantz Fanon, *The Wretched of the Earth*, pp. 60-61.

[65] *Ibid.*, pp. 251 ff.

[66] *Ibid.*, p. 255.

# Part VI
# Black Separatism—Catalytic Issues or the Coin on its Edge

## INTRODUCTION

This last section is concerned with one of the perennial dilemmas of black people in America – the dilemma of powerlessness. Blacks, whether separatists or integrationists, must constantly cope with the reality that they have virtually no power to determine national policy directions. In some few instances, however, black influence may slow up or dull the policy cutting edge, but when national policy directions are charted, they reflect the will of the white majority. It is true that often some whites, too, may oppose certain policies, but seldom does an alliance between disenchanted whites and powerless blacks evolve. In any case, "majority rule" is the most powerful game in town, and blacks are usually excluded from the competition; they are seldom even accorded ringside seats, but, more often than not, they are made to observe the game indirectly or from a "safe" distance. Majority rule for blacks then becomes the "tyranny of the majority" and is thus the crux of the problem. Black separatists argue that since majority rule is the *modus operandi* of the system, and since blacks cannot become the majority, the most feasible and expedient way to solve the "majority" dilemma is to separate.

Others argue that separation is unfeasible because, among other things, whites will not allow separation. Thus, the best way to influence policy regarding black problems is to work within the system. Hence, the policy question becomes more complicated when blacks themselves are divided over certain issues. Black division may be seen in terms of socioeconomic (status) and ideological variables. However, it requires – at least for a social scientist – almost wild abandon to attribute categorically certain ideological postures to blacks "because" they occupy certain socioeconomic statuses (SES). For example, the "black masses" or "black militants" are often simply the figment of social science imagination or other arbitrary and unsubstantiated derivations. The "black masses" usually oppose "radical" ideologies, and "black militants" are usually not from the "lower class" (read: from the "black masses"). It is also often dangerous to categorize "white racists" as "southern rednecks" or "northern lower class ethnics." In short, it is risky to categorize people and predict their behavior based on arbitrary designations.

Nevertheless, however imprecise our present predictive abilities regarding human behavior, we persist in our pursuit of developing better taxonomies and the ability to predict from them. The articles in this section – though disparate and diverse – have one thing in common. They all deal with issues that may have catalytic import regarding black separation in the United States; they have potential policy implications, and there is considerable agreement between black separatists and integrationists over their importance. It should be pointed out that the authors below do not regard themselves as separatists. But they all agree that the issues they write about are policy relevant and might make important differences regarding black separatism.

Killian begins the section by indicating that the real danger to dignified black survival is the "real white backlash." He writes that meaningful change "involves radical changes in the social, economic, and political structure of American society – a peaceful revolution, if you will." It is the unwillingness of the great majority of white Americans to make these radical changes that constitutes the "real white backlash." In other words, individual and institutional racism must be simultaneously dealt with in order to promote change. But this is a tall order in a society where racism is so rampant that it becomes the "normal" mode of behavior. Consequently, attempts by blacks to alter their condition often result in "blaming the victim." A case in point is an article by a leading white social scientist who wrote that the "white backlash," which accelerated in 1967, derived in part from an upsurge in "black racism" which, in turn, seemed to fill a vacuum created by a previous decrease in "white racism." Though this individual may eschew racism across the board, he, nevertheless, in his article, leaves himself open to criticism. Lamousé-Smith's article, in fact, criticizes the "black racism" charge, indicating that white "racism in the United States has never waned, been dormant, or dead . . . and never moribund."

Among the many important policy issues affecting blacks, birth control is one of the most volatile. Some blacks charge that zero population growth (ZPG) is simply a white plot to keep blacks from reproducing in order that they remain politically powerless through numerical limitations. Willie argues that "the genocidal charge is neither 'absurd' nor 'hollow' as some whites have contended. Neither is it limited to residents of the ghetto, whether they be low-income black militants or middle-aged black moderates. Indeed, young educated blacks (also) fear black genocide." Willie further observes that many "male-dominated black militant groups call for black females to eschew the use of contraceptives because they are pushed in the black community as a 'method of exterminating black people.' " Black females often take a dim view of these exhortations because, according to Wolfman, black separatists "enjoined them to not only produce children but to raise warriors to fight battles necessary to win freedom." Moreover, the black woman's place in the revolution is often determined by "her relationship to a leading man rather than her own abilities to spellbind crowds or to formulate an ideological position." In other words, the black woman's place in the revolution is on her back conceiving "warriors" rather than on her feet using her head. Nevertheless, "black women have not responded to the woman's liberation movement because their primary identification is racial rather than sexual, and their interests are more closely aligned with those of the group as a whole rather than with women who represent the oppressors." Black women are "black first, female second," placing primary emphasis on race rather than on ideology.

Another issue on which many blacks agree is one, ironically, involving racism in education. In the first place, all agree that whites have traditionally limited or minimized black education beginning with making it an offense to teach slaves to read or write, and, after slavery, establishing separate black institutions, eventually declaring in 1896 that black and white education would be "separate but equal." Not until 1954 was this policy officially changed. Since then "integration" has been slow and painful, and presently there is a retrenchment on the policy commitment to integrate the schools. For example, the *New York Times* reported on January 26, 1975 that the New York State Board of Regents, by a vote of 9 to 4, "opted . . . to assess compliance with state integration laws in terms of schools' efforts 'to bring about equal opportunity,' but they were vague about what standards should be used to assess compliance beyond urging 'serious effort." The New York State schools, according to the *Times,* went from 72.1 percent minority children attending schools with student bodies more than half minority in 1968 to 75 percent in 1975. It may be that eventually black and white separatists will have their way!

In higher education there is also another kind of white "backlash" among some social scientists. Many now – again, to be more precise – suggest that racism, discrimination, and material and physical deprivation are not responsible for the oppressed black condition, but, rather blacks have "inferior genes." Put another way, whites are naturally smarter than blacks and intelligence is largely (some say 80 percent) hereditary. Therefore, whites "pass on" their superior intelligence to their offspring, and the environment (deprivation and oppression) accounts for only a small (20-25 percent) amount of cognitive ability.

Some blacks call the gene-I.Q. arguments another form of racism. Black academics, especially many of those in the social sciences, are alarmed over the "neo-racism" in higher education. Recently there have emerged studies by leading white scholars suggesting that: black genes are indeed inferior (Shockley); black intelligence is lower than that of whites (Jensen); slavery was not that bad and certainly not the basis for the present-day black condition in that it did not break up the black family, blacks consumed about 90 percent of what they produced, and were generally well treated (Fogel and Engerman); and that a college education is not going to make much difference in closing the economic gap between blacks and whites (Jencks). Most black academics hold opposite views on these issues. More important is the policy implication of these views, considering that most white Americans hold them in the first place. These "studies" serve to "objectify" their unarticulated assumptions.

These studies do seem to objectify their "findings" in that all of the ones mentioned above are highly mathematically and methodologically sophisticated. The layman may ask, "How could these studies involving such sophistication in methods, math, and computer techniques be erroneous or wrong?" These seemingly objective, scientifically neutral findings serve to reinforce the racial stereotypes held by those who blame blacks for their own condition and they, therefore, take solace in these "objective" data.

Black academics, of course, have another view of these "objective," "scientific," and "neutral" data. I alluded to the misuse of quantification in my introduction to Part I. Taylor calls it "quantitative racism," and defines it "as the intentional *or* unintentional misuse of statistical and quantitative methods in the behavioral sciences to show, either directly or indirectly, explicitly or implicitly, some kind or type of ethnic superiority, usually with respect to black-white differences." He further observes that "through various feats of statistical magic, black persons are made to appear 'inferior' to whites in regard to such things as 'inherited' intelligence, achievement, motivation, family structure, crime, and so forth." Taylor points out that the scientific method, "particularly in its more quantitative aspects, provides a set of criteria against which one or more studies may be judged." Hence, he examines a number of the quantitative racist studies which use "equations of oppression." In his second work, he uses a specific example of quantitative racism where the author is obviously playing the dozens (putting blacks down) with path analysis. Note that he does not reject the scientific method as do some black social scientists.

Segal, a dinner guest at a family reunion, who has listened to the frank talk and vigorous arguments, offers another perspective on black separatism, one with which black separatists (the family members) may not agree and probably prefer not to hear. But it does represent another reality of American society, a reality that separatists have constantly fought against; it is also reason devoid of paternalistic and insincere rhetoric. Walters, in the final chapter, argues that to avoid the confusion between white and black perspectives on the black experience in America, blacks should strive for a black social science – "to revive the notion of balance, what the black social scientist should seek is the balance between efficiency and humanism that puts theory and method in its proper role as servant rather than lord."

# 24
## *The Real White Backlash**

LEWIS M. KILLIAN

"White backlash" is one of those colorful, somewhat mystical terms that arises in times of social change to depict in broad strokes something that people sense is going on. The referent of such a term is never precise. It carries different connotations according to the orientations and purposes of people who use it. For example, "white backlash" is in one sense a slogan quickly picked up by members of the White resistance to convey to Black men the warning that if they don't stop being so aggressive in their demands for change, White Americans will give them their comeuppance. On the contrary, it means to many Black Americans the resistance to even the most moderate black demands which White Americans invariably mount, but afterwards conveniently forget when they have finally reluctantly made some concessions to these demands.

The term "white backlash" began to be used sometime in the period before the 1964 Presidential elections when it became evident that there was resistance to Black progress, not only in the South but in other regions of the country. Part of this resistance was symbolized by conflicts between labor unions and Black protesters when picket lines and lie-ins were staged at construction sites in northern cities. The referendum on Proposition Fourteen in California and the surprising number of votes given George Wallace in Presidential primaries outside the South also contributed to the notion that a new sort of resistance was arising. Barry Goldwater's attempt to make crime in the streets an issue in the Presidential campaign led to interpretations that he was seeking a "white backlash" vote. His failure to garner any electoral votes outside Arizona and the Deep South was widely interpreted as a sign that the "white backlash" had failed to materialize. Whether there was, indeed, such a phenomenon at all became a favorite topic of debate among social analysts. What observers seemed to be looking for under the rubric of the "white backlash" was an increase in expressions of prejudice or hostility toward Black Americans. Yet, numerous public opinion polls all along have indicated that expression of agreement with abstract notions of civil rights has been increasing in frequency in all regions of the country. Moreover, in spite of strong resistance, the Congress has since 1964 passed so many laws aimed at eliminating discrimination based on race that many White Americans ask sincerely, "What more do Black people want?"

On the other hand, Black Americans, whether classified as moderates or militants, seem to perceive a significant slowdown in the rate of progress toward the achievement of real equality. The growing verbal assent of White Americans to notions of equal rights, the glowing words of each new civil rights act, and the defeat of such candidates for public office as Mrs. Louise Day Hicks are not accompanied by reductions in the very real, material, and psychological deprivation which so many Black men experience. This failure to make substantial progress seems to point to the existence of something which is real and which may be called a "white backlash," even though it might not show up on a social distance scale.

I have suggested elsewhere that the real backlash consists of the refusal of White Americans to take "the immediate steps necessary to make possible the entrance of the Negro community into society *en masse*."[1] It is this sort of entry, not the infiltration of White society by upwardly mobile, "qualified" Negroes, that is necessary if America is to avoid Apartheid.

When non-southern Whites began to realize that the civil rights movement was demanding more than just token integration of schools and desegregation of restaurants in the South, their own latent prejudices were unmasked. These prejudices were not based on a system of symbolic segregation in which Black men were an integral and subordinate part, as in the South. They were rooted in a system of which James Baldwin wrote:

> Negroes represent nothing to [the Northerner] personally, except perhaps the dangers of carnality. He never sees Negroes, Southerners see them all the time. Northerners never think about them, whereas Southerners are never really thinking of anything else. Negroes are, therefore, ignored in the North and are under surveillance in the South, and suffer hideously in both places.[2]

After over 300 years of slavery, segregation, and discrimination, Black men find themselves an excluded and disadvantaged group in a highly structured, technological society. They are victims of handicaps and of indifference, as well as of

*Written especially for this book.

crude racism. The White man does not have to *try* to discriminate against the Black man. All he has to do is to follow his standard business practices and move in his normal social circles for the Black man to be counted out once again. Special effort is demanded to include the Black man in the society in a meaningful way. This special effort must include more than inviting selected, "qualified" Negroes to live in one's neighborhood, work in one's business, send their children to his white controlled neighborhood schools, or come across town to lend a touch of color and tone of liberalism to a party. It must involve radical changes in the social, economic, and political structure of American society – a peaceful revolution, if you will. It is the unwillingness of the great majority of White Americans to make these radical changes that constitute the real "white backlash." Tokenism has become acceptable to a large number of White Americans just at the time it has come to be recognized by Afro-Americans as a sham and an excuse for avoiding basic social reforms. What are some of these basic reforms that are needed? Or, to put it another way, what are the traditional values which, whether for the sake of poor White men or poor Black men, affluent Americans are reluctant to give up?

One is the structural pluralism which, according to Milton Gordon, causes not only Black Americans, but Jewish, Italian, and numerous other types of Americans, to live in separate social worlds despite a high degree of acculturation.[3] If this exclusiveness in communal associations and institutions extended only to intimate primary group relations and religious organizations, its preservation might be of small consequence. It extends, however, to the neighborhoods in which people must find housing and to the so-called neighborhood schools in which children are educated. Kurt and Gladys Lang analyze this type of resistance to desegregation in a study of opposition to a school pairing plan undertaken in a predominantly Jewish section of Jackson Heights. They found that many Jews who insisted that they were not prejudiced against Negroes nevertheless mounted strong resistance to this plan for desegregation of what they perceived as a neighborhood school. The Langs observed:

> For many of the Jews against the plan, the neighborhood was in certain respects an upgraded version of the familiarly comfortable but shabby, rundown ghetto from which they had escaped. Many respondents stressed the fact that they (and others) had worked hard to get here. It was a good neighborhood and they wanted nothing to spoil it.[4]

The process of invasion and succession, in which White householders defend their neighborhoods as long as they can and then exercise the option of fleeing to new lily white suburbs, is a familiar one. Open housing laws, which depend for their effectiveness on the courage and persistence of Black men in overcoming hostility and circumvention, will be no more successful in dispersing Black ghettoes than freedom of choice plans have been in eliminating segregated schools. If the ghettoes are to be dispersed, affirmative government action to relocate Black families throughout metropolitan areas is required, even if this might necessitate condemnation proceedings and the purchase or building of homes by the government for rental or sale to Black householders. This would mean the end of the free housing market as White Americans have known it. It is safe to say that there would be strong resistance to such a program by many Whites who proclaim themselves integrationists but shudder at the thought of governmental action to establish racial quotas in schools or in neighborhoods. The alternative is to accept the Black ghetto as an enduring and self-determining reality.

Another goal which seems to be highly acceptable now to many Americans is equality of job opportunities for Americans regardless of race. What is acceptable is the traditional idea that if they have equal qualifications, Black men should have the same opportunity to obtain employment and to advance as White men. What is less acceptable is the notion that in order to compensate for years of unequal treatment, Black men should receive preferential treatment in the job market when their qualifications are only equal to those of Whites. Even more serious is the problem of workers who, according to present standards, have less than equal qualifications for obtaining jobs or entering institutions of higher learning. Standards of efficiency and respectability, as measured by standardized test scores, middle-class appearance, and absence of a police record, are sacred values which are taken for granted by many White Americans. They are luxuries which many ghetto youths have not been able to afford. Color-blind application of what are actually White middle-class standards closes the door of opportunity for many people who are neither White nor middle class. Just as the myth which half a century ago held that women could not perform many of the tasks they now perform was reexamined and abandoned, our modern-day myths about job and educational qualifications must be reexamined. This has a particular bearing on the administration and implementation of federally financed self-help programs in the ghettoes. There is evidence available already that some of the most effective of such programs have been led by young Black men who seemed poorly qualified by these standards.

It is highly questionable, however, whether the normal growth of the private sector of the economy, even when accompanied by liberalization of standards of entry, will meet the problems of income. Problems of income maintenance are not limited to Black men today, although they fall disproportionately on them. It is questionable whether, with the growth of automation and the growth of the population, the economy will be able to provide jobs for all who need them. Two types of proposals are already being advanced for meeting this growing problem. One is the expansion of public services paid for by taxes, with an accompanying expansion of the number of jobs available in education, recreation, law enforcement, public health, and family services such as child care. The other is the provision of a guaranteed income through a negative income tax or family allowance. Such proposals as these would require for their implementation the sacrifice of three traditional values.

One is the idea that taxes are a necessary evil imposed by the government on the self-sufficient to take care of the undeserving poor. Taxes must come to be viewed, instead, as the price which all citizens must pay for a viable society not to be destroyed by illiteracy, crime, disease, air pollution, and alienation. The clearest manifestation of the real "white backlash" is seen in the current Congressional reluctance, sustained no doubt by millions of constituents, to increase taxes. In spite of the repeated warnings that the plight of the cities is as much a threat to the survival of American society as any external enemy, there is no groundswell of popular opinion to spend the money necessary to meet this threat.

The second value that is threatened by such proposals for income maintenance is the traditional concept of the rights or absence of rights of government employees. The right of people who are employed in the private sector of the economy to organize, negotiate, and strike is now recognized in law. That people employed in the public sector might have a similar right to influence the terms of their employment and the conditions under which they work is a new and radical idea. Comparisons of the reaction of country school boards in Florida to the walkout by public school teachers and the reaction of the city council in Memphis to the strike of garbage collectors shows that resistance to this new idea is not based simply on racial prejudice. If government employment is to become an increasingly significant type of employment, those who work for the government will not be satisfied to remain second-class citizens when compared to workers in such semiprivate industries as the steel industry, the airlines, and the railroads.

The most basic value that is challenged, however, is the ethic of work itself. In *The Secular City*, Harvey Cox makes the point that Americans are unwilling to explore other means of linking production to consumption and that this centers around the religious meanings attached to work.

> We can produce enough for everyone and we believe, or say we do, that everyone is entitled to a decent share in the productivity of the economy. But we cannot put our convictions into practice in this instance because we still feel that only by providing a market-determined job for everyone can the ludicrous imbalance between production and distribution be reconciled.[5]

He goes on to say:

> Separated from strictly market requirements, full employment immediately becomes a rational possibility [in that there is a] vast amount of work that still needs to be done in education, conservation, social work – the areas we call public sector.[6]

The most forceful way of expressing this is through the example of the mother who is an AFDC recipient. Today she is defined as an unproductive person who receives a welfare handout to keep her and her children from starving. She could be regarded as a worker who is paid for the important task of providing her children with a good home.

The catalog of traditional practices and values that might have to be given up in order to make equality of opportunity a reality instead of a paper promise for Black Americans could be lengthy. Why call the reluctance to give up these traditional values the "white backlash" if the values defended are not uniquely related to Black progress? They may be called the "white backlash" because it is this dedication to the *status quo* which makes promises of equality meaningless for Black people and because the people who have the power to change the *status quo* through normal legislative processes are, for the most part, White. But White power is aligned on the side of the *status quo*, waiting for gradual, painless changes to solve the problems of poverty and alienation without disturbing the tenor of life as it is lived on family-type TV shows. No such sense of crisis exists in the affluent, predominantly White portion of the society as prevails in the poor, disproportionately Black "other America." These affluent Americans are willing to say to the Black man, "Enter into the mainstream of American life," but they are unwilling to make the sacrifices necessary to make this mainstream something that Black men can enter. Opposition to effective gun control laws suggests that many White Americans are unwilling to give up the privilege of hunting deer in order to reduce the likelihood that some Americans can arm themselves to hunt men!

The authors of the Kerner report observe:

> Powerful forces of social and political inertia are moving the country steadily along the course of existing policies toward a divided country. This course may well involve changes in many social and economic programs – but not enough to produce fundamental alterations in the key factors of Negro concentration, racial segregation, and the lack of sufficient enrichment to arrest the decay of deprived neighborhoods.[7]

Black power is a response to the inertia of White power. To identify resistance to the achievement of pride and material security by Black people as "White racism" is to oversimplify the problem. White society must not only be opened to Black people; it must be reformed if Blacks and Whites are to live together in a united America. Black power carries a clear and urgent message for White America.

> If you will not reform the society which you control, then we will attempt to build our own separate society which we will control regardless of the cost to you. This may not appear feasible, and it may not be the kind of society which fits your model of the American way of life, but attempting to build it will be more edifying than to continue to eat the crumbs from your table. For better or worse, we will exercise power in it, and we will derive pride from knowing that it is our own creation and not a shoddy imitation of your society.

White involvement in the Black ghetto and the costs to White society of Black self-development dictate that the dominant group will not willingly aid and abet such an attempt. Furthermore, power and pride cannot be conferred or granted. To constitute the basis for full group development, they must be won in a power struggle as a consequence of which the group can envision itself as a victor, not as a beneficiary. Feelings of subordination must be eradicated. These feelings have been produced by constant demonstration of the superior power of the dominant group. They can be eliminated only by a clear demonstration that the power differential has been removed.

White Americans have not limited themselves to demonstrating the power differential through economic and political domination. One of the most important symbols of power has been the relative impunity with which White men have been able to use violence against Black men in the past. This has been demonstrated in lynchings, in the differential application of the death penalty to Black and White offenders, in assaults on nonviolent civil rights workers, and most recently in the "overkill" of Black people during ghetto insurrections. Tragically, therefore, the stage has been set for the manifestation of Black power not only through economic and political means, but through violence. Jean Paul Sartre has said, "the rebel's weapon is the proof of his humanity."[8] It may be predicted many Black men will feel that the proof of their humanity and the reality of their power is the ability to use violence as freely as the White man has. Such violence would be retaliatory, but not in the sense of retaliation by a specific act. It would be retaliation for years of living in fear of the brutal policeman, the Ku Klux Klan, or simply the White man who feels confident that "I don't have to take nothing from no uppity niggers." This violence will not be safe for those who commit it, and there will not be assurance that it will lead to any sort of victory. But, as Sartre suggests, it is not simply overcoming the dominant group, but the mere act of attacking it which produces a new spirit and a new unity in the minority.

Black power seems to constitute a revolutionary rejection of traditional American values. Yet, there remains a strong cultural tie between Black men in revolution and the culture which they have shared as part of American society. One strand of this culture has been the American tradition of violence. It should not be surprising, therefore, that the use of violence should become a symbol of Black pride and Black power. Nor should it be surprising that there should arise what seems to be a *new* "white backlash" in the form of demands for violent repression of Black insurrection. Yet this new backlash may be viewed as only the ultimate manifestation of the real "white backlash," the unwillingness of White Americans to accept the drastic reforms required to make possible a meaningful place in the social system for Black men. As Black men have shown that they are willing to demand these reforms by whatever means are necessary, a large and influential segment of White America has displayed its determination to defend the *status quo* by the ultimate but traditional method of violence.

## NOTES

[1] Lewis M. Killian, *The Impossible Revolution?* New York; Random House, 1968, p. 133.

[2] *Nobody Knows My Name,* New York; Dell Co., 1961, p. 70.

[3] *Assimilation in American Life*, New York; Oxford University Press, 1964.

[4] "Resistance to School Desegregation: A Case Study of Backlash Among Jews," *Sociological Inquiry,* 35, Winter 1965, p. 103.

[5] New York, Macmillan, 1965, p. 183.

[6] *Ibid.*, p. 187.

[7] *Report of the National Advisory Commission on Civil Disorders,* New York; Bantam Books, 1968), p. 396.

[8] Frantz Fanon, *The Wretched of the Earth*, Constance Farrington, trans., New York; Grove Press, 1963, p. 18.

# 25

# *The Myth of Black Neo-Racism in the United States* *

W. BEDIAKO LAMOUSÉ-SMITH

*Intolerance tends to cease with conversion or recantation, while race prejudice abhors the very idea of conversion.*

Oliver C. Cox

In *Transition 41* Pierre van den Berghe presented an analysis of recent Black militant protests in the United States under the title of "neo-racism in the U.S.A." According to van den Berghe neo-racism is a brand of racism fostered by Afro-Americans against Whites. The goals of this paper are: to refute that argument; to raise questions which van den Berghe avoided; to provide as much information as possible within the limited space in order to correct the erroneous picture which the nonobserver of the American race scène was offered; and to provide some of the existing plausible explanations for the upsurge of racial and ethnic consciousness in the United States. It is important to bear in mind that the complexity and dynamism of American society permits the modest types of explanation at the level of plausibility more than of probability.

## INTO PERSPECTIVE

The world of academia (but not necessarily the academies) has always harbored scholars of all shades of skin color, ideological views, theoretical orientations, religious beliefs, and political inclinations. Many scholars reach fame by universal acclaim of their contribution to the advancement of science. Others snatch fame by successfully pouring old wines into new bottles. Some reach respectability via promotion matched only by Madison Avenue advertisers. "Scratch my back and I scratch your back" is not a maxim limited to the untamed or domesticated ape. A vociferous few receive audience by their exceptional ability to think aloud and verbalize whatever fury their imagination gives vent to. Flowery language replaces painstaking observation and founded evidence. These few are frequently celebrated in some quarters for possessing "fertile minds" and "versatile imagination." The charlatan beats the confidence man at his game. Some scholars proclaim themselves the experts and theoreticians in "difficult" areas of virtual virginity where competition from their colleagues (especially of other schools of thought) is nearly or wholly nonexistent – reminiscent of the "old school" ethnographer who describes the colors of a Kalahari Desert butterfly observed by him incidentally while he was watching an initiation ceremony of the Bushmen. Nobody dares question what he saw and his description of it.

With the diversity of shades, views, orientations, beliefs, and inclinations in the field, any assertion that smacks of dogmatic finality is at best suspect unless data are produced to substantiate the pronouncements. The suspicion is especially heightened when a claim has been made for a "dispassionate analysis." It is, of course, an elementary sociological observation of Mannheim that we are affected by our sociocultural origins in our perceptions of reality. Again, the stochastic epistemological problem raised by Popper with the concomitant quest for intersubjectivity is to caution overzealous claim of the immunity called "dispassionate analysis." Dispassionate from whose view? And why should any scientist prejudice an analysis which can stand on its own factual merits and interpretive truth by a plea to the emotion? Indeed these questions cannot be avoided when the topic of the "dispassionate analysis" is race.

W.E.B. Dubois' prophetic statement of 1903 that "the problem of the Twentieth Century is the problem of the colour-line" can be extended to the 21st century.[2] The extension is warranted by historical facts as well as by the present situation of race problems in the United States. The problem of the 20th has not been solved and is nowhere near solution. Our ability to solve technological problems has not been matched by our skill in eliminating undesirable social and human conditions. B.F. Skinner's *Beyond Freedom and Dignity* does not only propose alternative methods for human problem-solution effort, but also underlines the profound complexity of the human mind in making choices for human dignity.[3] The problem of color line is one of human dignity and society's readiness or unreadiness to solve it. I submit that the centuries-old race problem of the United States cannot be eliminated as long as there are "experts" who portray only those aspects of the color-line problem that they see as advantageous or suitable for their self-satisfying political inclinations or ideological views. And, unfortunately, social scientists who have paid any serious attention to problems of race relations have addressed them-

*By permission of the author.

selves in the light of their ideologies, ranging from "moral responsibilities" through "pariah systems"; "Marxian socialism" to "Herrenvolk democracy."

"Herrenvolk," meaning master race, a key concept in van den Berghe's widely acknowledged analysis of race conflict, happens to have been as central to the race theory of Adolf Hitler and Nationalism Socialism as the idea of competition for spatial expansionism. By the propagation of the Herrenvolk doctrine, with the intellectual backing of various scholars, naturally, Hitler succeeded in capturing Germans to sustain the holocaust. I do not imagine that the choice of "Herrenvolk" for a concept by any social scientist after the Nazi era would be accidental or excusable on the grounds of inexpediency. Those persons fleetingly acquainted with *Mein Kampf* would recall Hitler's designation of the negroid races in connection with his ridicule of the British for trying to civilize the "barbarous" peoples of its colonies and thinking of allowing the colonies to govern themselves. ". . . it is an act of criminal insanity to train a being who is only an anthropoid by birth until the pretense can be made that he has been turned into a lawyer."[4] Since "Herrenvolk democracy" and "competition" are basic concepts to van den Berghe's race theory, and the "competition" argument is reiterated in his article under consideration, the reader has to be made aware of where van den Berghe "is coming from."

## NEO-RACISM

Racism in the United States has never been dormant or dead. Race and racism are ingrained throughout the various institutions of the American society and are recognized as such by astute observers of the society as given.[5] Van den Berghe's assertion that there is a "revival of racism in the last few years" and that there had been prior to that period a "general trend away from this pernicious brand of nonsense" indicates that he is either not well informed of the subject he chose to write about and is, therefore, not familiar with the generalities of the contemporary American scene or that he is consciously hoodwinking a reading audience that is likely to be largely non-American. A senior editor of *Newsweek* reported on February 19, 1973:

> . . . now the great surge that carried racial justice briefly to the top of the nation's domestic agenda in the 1960s has been stalemated by war, economics, the flame-out of the old civil rights coalition and the rise to power of a new American Majority. Blacks and their special problems have gone out of fashion in government, in politics and in civic concern.[6]

The "surge" of activities initiated and the programs drawn up by government and private organizations in the 1960s to combat the acts of racism perpetrated against Afro-Americans indicate at least one fact – namely, racism in the United States was never moribund.

What van den Berghe did not understand was that the 1960s and "the last few years" have witnessed methods and strategies which Afro-Americans have always used in this country in their quest for that which is basic to common human dignity and decency. The accentuation of their efforts *to be free* constitutes for van den Berghe "a pernicious brand of nonsense." This so-called "neo-racism," the call for Black Nationalism and/or separation has always been part of the American sociopolitical scene. Black nationalists who have stood up over the years fighting against "Herrenvolk" supremacist racism in the United States have included Paul Cuffe, Nat Turner, Martin Delany, Bishop Turner, Marcus Garvey, Frederick Douglass, Booker T. Washington, Sutton E. Griggs, Elijah Muhammad, Malcolm X, *et al.*

"In the last few years of American history" when "white racism waned [and] black racism waxed" according to van den Berghe, The Report of the Presidential Commission on Civil Disorders was stating that from 1957 to 1967 white racism showed no signs of abating.[7] No empirical evidence available throughout the United States would support the contention that "white racism waned." Careful studies on those concrete realities, which substantiate or deny the existence and operation of racism – e.g., residential preferences, education, medical services, employment, income distribution, etc. – show that white racism did not decline at any time. The studies on urban housing distribution by Taueber and Taueber[8] and the analysis by Rashi Fein of the social and economic lags forced upon Afro-Americans are only a few of the available facts which reject van den Berghe's notion of white racism waning,[9] not to mention the proposed $34 million annual budget for policing and enforcing federal laws of anti-discrimination.[10] Rashi Fein's study of 1964 is reechoed in 1973 by Theodore Cross, editor of *Business and Society Review* and a public governor of the American Stock Exchange.

> . . .in the United States, conditions of poverty, hunger, substandard medical care, dilapidated housing, and inferior education among blacks run twice the rate of the same circumstances among whites.
>
> These conditions of group inequality are reflected in the widening gap between the income of whites and blacks. Current Census Bureau figures show that the difference between the income of the median white family in the United States and the median black family was $2,602 in 1960. The gap increased to $4,232 in 1971. So black people actually lost ground during the very period when we as a nation claimed the greatest expansion of rights and opportunities for minorities in our entire history.[11]

Black people lose ground because white racism did not wane. They could not close the gaps because white racism waxed. They could not exercise the rights and opportunities claimed to have been expanded during the 1960s because the '60s were not any different from the centuries of white racist practices and oppression.

The "two worlds of race" as the noted Black historian John Hope Franklin described American society, is a present reality as it has always been.[12] The dreamers of integration and assimilation have not realized their fantasies because, in their naivety or excessive idealism, they have not consciously recognized the forces which determine and construct their dreams – namely, white racism. As Peter Goldman noted in his article of February 19, 1973, aptly entitled "Black America Now,"

> Integration ... has been all but abandoned as an affirmative goal of national policy. Spending on the poor – who remain disproportionately black – has flattened out. And civil-rights enforcement, the U.S. Civil Rights Commission charged last week, 'is not adequate or even close to it.' So depressed is the situation that the administration resists attention for what it has actually done. Said one Justice Department official: 'We'll do whatever we can for the blacks that won't piss other people off.'[13]

Those persons who will be "pissed off" should anything be done toward ameliorating the lot of Blacks are clearly not Black.

## RACISM

No extraordinary imagination is required to perceive that an oppressor cannot sense oppression. Racism is not a mere "set of beliefs" that peoples' behavior and abilities are determined by their physical appearance, as van den Berghe would want us to believe. Neither is it the quip he makes of an American secretary transcribing a taped dictation correctly, nor the one he makes of "zionist conspiracy." I do not see the meaning of the latter quip except as a category worthy of interpretation in the A-F scale of the Authoritarian Personality by Adorno *et al.*[14] The overrepresentation of scholars of Jewish descent in the intellectual centers of the world is a well-known fact. The history of this fact is equally established and undeniable. Given the intellectual skills and supremacy which Jews hold in virtually all academic disciplines, plus the sociopolitical realities of American ethnicity, it is intriguing that van den Berghe should choose for a stepping stone toward the definition of racism "the over-representation of Jews among psychoanalysts and college professors." For me, the definition of racism is no farfetched exercise. It means a willfully premeditated action or behavior by one person against another on the grounds of the latter's visible racial characteristics. Racism is concrete. It is not "a set of beliefs" lurking idly in the crevices of people's minds.

To suggest that racism in the United States is an "insidious nonsense" is not only a reflection of a total misapprehension of race problems in the United States but also a negation of the benefits bestowed on many by the existence of the "invisible wall."[15] Those Afro-Americans who are confined to the vermin-infested ghetto slums of the inner cities and who are the victims of racist manipulations do not consider racism nonsense. Those careful and serious *white* scholars like Pettigrew and Lee Rainwater of Harvard University, who have devoted a lifetime of attention to studying the dynamics and consequences of American racism do not write it off as nonsense or see it ever buried in the graveyard of Western intellectualism.[16] The concreteness of racism never permitted itself to be buried in illusive intellectualism nor did it erupt out of the blue "around 1967" when the Presidential Commission on Civil Disorders was ending its investigations in racism.

If white racism had waned, as van den Berghe asserts, why was there a need for the Civil Rights movement during the 1960s to fight for the concrete exercise of common basic rights which Blacks had and still have under the United States Constitution? A waning of white racism should have facilitated the unfettered exercise of the rights categorically stated in the Constitution for Blacks and should have made the rise and marches of the Civil Rights movements utterly unnecessary. The Civil Rights movements' tactics appear to have been those that appeal to van den Berghe. They were "profoundly humanistic and liberating." Evidently, the strategies of the militant Blacks fell out of the parameters of some social system thinkers and hence could not and cannot be appreciated. Those persons whose knowledge of Blacks in the United States is woefully shallow found themselves at a loss when they heard the age-old "Dark Ghetto" phrases of "black power," "black pride," and "black identity." The speeches of Marcus Garvey, the works of Langston Hughes and other Black writers and artists during the Harlem Renaissance of the 1920s were full of these phrases.[17]

There was never "a qualitative shift among militant blacks ... around 1967." Rather there was a quantitative shift in the numbers loudly demanding jobs, equal pay for equal work, schools, health care, habitable housing, fair justice in the courts, equal chance to participate and share in the prosperity and achievements of the country which was built on their blood, sweat, and suffering.[18] There was also a shift in the number of leaders who were willing to stand up and make extreme demands, often non-negotiable, since they had witnessed the deceits and failures in compromises. Neither the leadership nor the following masses shifted in the age-old pent-up feelings which needed no trained eyes to see in Harlem, Watts, Newark, or Hough. To misinterpret the events of the latter 1960s as new and unexpected is to obfuscate constructive analysis for an understanding of the "Negro Problem." But, of course, I am willing to concede that those who are not well read in the history of Afro-Americans and always thought of Blacks as docile and imbecile saw events "around 1967" as a "qualitative shift." A cursory perusal of *Black Nationalism in America* by Bracey, Meier, and Rudwick would have shown that nothing new was happening.[19]

## BLACK: GROUND AGAINST THE INDIVIDUAL?

*The Black Metropolis* of St. Clair Drake and Horace Cayton has a lot to say about the concept of "Race Man."[20] This study, like many others before and after it, denies all conjectures by van den Berghe that "the new black 'radicals' accepted as their first postulate the validity, indeed the legitimacy, of racial categorization." No Black person has need to accept a categorization to which and in which he belongs by birth. All he needs is the color of his skin. The "race man" concept underlined the premium which Blacks have always put on their concern for group advancement. As Kenneth B. Clark reports in *Dark Ghetto*, "Loren Miller, a Los Angeles attorney and a vice president of the NAACP, points out that because the liberal's historic concern has been with individual rights, he sees progress in the admission of a few Negro children to a hitherto white school; while the Negro, who also wants individual rights, nevertheless regards the raising of status of the group 'to which he has been consigned' as his own immediate problem and spurns the evidence of individual progress as mere tokenism."[21]

The experiences of Black Africans in the United States show

that "racial categorization" is not the choice of the person being categorized. The autobiographies of Kwame Nkrumah and Nnamdi Azikiwe; the recent experiences of Pepper Clark's in *America, Their America*; the incident which brought the Ghanaian Minister of Finance, Komla Gbedemah, to breakfast in the White House, were all categorizations which did not wait upon "the new black 'radicals.' "[22]

No "basic change ... from a perspective advocating equal incorporation of individuals to one putting the main stress on group equality" occurred all of a sudden "around 1967." The Black sociologist Oliver C. Cox made far-reaching observations about Black individual vs. group obligations and equality with Whites in that excellent analysis of *Caste, Class and Race:*

> Two principal ideas of racial policy seem to divide the allegiance of Negroes, the one that 'Negroes should stick together' and the other that 'Negroes should shift themselves individually, since the individual can advance more easily than the group as a whole.' In reality, however, these two plans of action are correlated. The first is a necessity, the second an aspiration. Negroes 'stick together' when, in attempting to act as individuals, they are rebuffed or disadvantaged. Nevertheless, there is a continuing ideal that they should be free to act on their individual merits. As social pressure about them is relieved, they automatically become individualists.[23]

The recognition of a group strategy was not invented by the "radicals," neither has there been a negation of the individual person's desires and accomplishments. The "radicals" did not need to reassert the obligations of a "race man" to remind Black people that they were not White and that the color of their skin and racial features were the criteria for their categorized status in the United States.

## SUPERIORITY MYTHOLOGIES

The Black Muslims have always preached Black racial superiority over Whites.[24] In fact, their methods of propagation have been parallel to those used by Whites to assure Blacks of how God ordained their inferiority through the fall of Ham. Up until today many Blacks have been vocal about their rejection of the racial inferiority attributed to them by Whites, including the latter day scholars of the Jensen-Jenck-Schockley School. Black Muslims apart, it is not true that the militants have made mythological substitutions their primary occupation. The initial concern of reclaiming pride and identity presupposes a rejection of the White superiority mythology. It behooves Blacks to have a new view of themselves. Hence, the fervor for a discovery of their African ancestry to locate those cultural distinctions which can enable them to look into the face of any other American who has Italy, Belgium, Poland, Ireland, or Germany to romanticize about. In the words of the psychologist Erik H. Erikson:

> ... identity also contains a complementarity of past and future both in the individual and in society: it links the actuality of a living past with that of a promising future.[25]

America is a land of ethnics. The Federal appropriation of millions of dollars to universities for the purpose of developing ethnic heritage studies underlies the national recognition of that fact in American society, as does the validity of celebrating Italian Day by Italians, St. Patrick's Day by the Irish, Copernicus' Birthday by the Polish, Shevchenko's Day by Ukrainians, etc. The city of Syracuse, which is statistically representative of America in many respects, boasts of its clearly distinguishable ethnic groups. The Director of the Syracuse Cultural Resources Council is pointing to the obvious when he asks the rhetorical question, "... what could be more uniquely American or more distinctively Syracuse than a composite identity? ... We're an international city already, with lots of strong ethnic groups. Let's develop that identity by encouraging the ethnic neighborhoods circling the downtown."

An officer of the Syracuse Metropolitan Development Association put it more colorfully, looking down at the city from a towering skyscraper,

> There's that solid, old German section, I often eat over there. And there's the Italian North Side, with its fine restaurants and churches. [He pointed west.] There's Tipperary Hill. What an important Irish section. And the Ukrainian area over near the Polish West End."[26]

The latter day Black militants were not the creators of the "ethnic pride" which "holds promise for [the] city" or the breakers of the "Melting Pot." In fact, Moynihan's "Melting Pot" of ethnic groups coagulated back into indestructible lumps after the pot had cooled. Afro-Americans falling back on Africa for romanticism know jolly well that their struggle and survival lie in the United States, not in Africa, despite Stokely Carmichael.

To suggest that militant Blacks of post 1967 "invented a 'black culture" in America" is as disturbing as Moynihan's dictum that Afro-Americans never made any contribution to the culture of the American society because they had none. "The Negro is only an American, and nothing else. He has no values and culture to guard and protect."[27] The entertainment of such a view on Black culture in the United States is not only a flagrant distortion of history and facts but also a dubious reflection on the reliability of the scholarship behind it. "Value-free" claims are often posited by scholars like van den Berghe who cloak their personal prejudices and stereotypes in innocent phraseology while claiming the immunity of "dispassionate analysis" to pontificate over the plight of Afro-Americans in the United States. Camps in the social sciences have always sheltered those disciples of the "right view" who can above all have the courage to declare that their work is an exercise in value-free science.

Soul is no elusive quality. Few white social scientists have studied Afro-Americans more than Lee Rainwater of Harvard University, the editor of a book entitled *Black Experience: Soul.*[28] Among others, the contributors to that book show unequivocally that Soul is not a recent creation of the imagination of the militant Black. The meaning of Soul in the Afro-American culture, its operational definitions, and its empirical referents in the daily lives of the Afro-Americans are elucidated clearly in that volume. A casual reading of W.E.B. DuBois' *The Souls of Black Folk*, along with the collection of essays in

Rainwater's compilation would have restrained the derogation of Soul by van den Berge.[29]

Soul was no new concept to the racially oppressed. Neither were Black nationalism and separatism, whose mention immediately evokes familiar names like Richard Allen, Absolom Jones, Marcus Garvey, and Elijah Muhammad. All of these leaders appeared before Frantz Fanon but the similarities between what they fought against and what Fanon described cannot be overlooked. The economics of the Black ghetto present a striking structural similarity with the imperial economic operations of the colonial powers in their overseas colonies. The political economy of the ghetto as analyzed by William Tabb offers a picture which cannot deny the coincidence in the similarity.[30] The militants did not wait for Fanon to appreciate the likeness between the conditions here in the United States and conditions elsewhere. They always made use of comparative ideas which enabled them to understand the forces within their own country – the forces of human and economic exploitation over which they have no control. It, therefore, constituted a serious error in judgment to equate the popularity of Fanon's writings with the adoption of strategies that have had a long history in the United States. If anybody was ever aware that the pigmentation of his skin and its bearing on the labor market were epiphenomenon, it was the Afro-American.

## AMERICANS: APATHETIC?

It is certainly misleading to suggest that a majority of the American people were too apathetic to be bothered by the "rhetoric and ideology of black nationalism." If this were true, one may ask van den Berghe, what was the purpose of the Kerner Commission.[31] Why was it that the entire FBI pursued the militants, especially Black Panthers, as the number one threat to the stability of the country? Why is it that whenever Stokely Carmichael returns to the United States from Guinea he makes headlines in the national newspapers and is especially mentioned in the FBI's annual report? If the "silent majority" of Spiro Agnew did not care, what explains the incarceration, exile, and cold-blooded murders of leaders of most of the Black militant organizations of the late '60s? The diligence with which law enforcement officers pursued the militants was equaled by the concern expressed by a majority of both Black and White Americans over the murderous activities of some Black militants against those men they perceive as representatives of the forces of brutality and racial oppression. The recent study of Robert Daley, *Target Blue*, shows that no apathy exists over the behavior of the Black Liberation Army and other militants. Truth is that opinions and loyalties are divided, even among Blacks.[32]

The question of whether "Black 'militancy' is a great step backward in the position of Blacks" is an open one which is best judged by looking back at history. Those who are astute observers of the American scene see that some gains, however slight, have been made as a result of the militancy. The many Black-oriented programs instituted locally and federally have been in direct response to the militancy.

## SOUTHERN SANITY

Perhaps nowhere does van den Berghe's efforts to conceal his true views about Afro-Americans fail more than in his assertion that only the South remained sane while militants were allowed to "rant" elsewhere. Whenever the concept of caste has been used to describe the status of Afro-Americans in the United States, social arrangements between the races in the South have been the frame of reference. In a caste society, of course, all should be quiet, lest the ever present but latent repressive sanctions are given manifest exercise. The South of Ku Klux Klan lynchings, where White racism maintains itself through a traditional acknowledgement of delineated lines, is the region which presents sanity and humanism for van den Berghe. It becomes exceedingly clear that van den Berghe cannot come to terms with the fact that Afro-Americans would reject their disadvantaged, inferior status in America by using the "any means necessary" of Malcolm X. He presents the militants as blind, violent characters who do not know their own country and therefore cannot be expected to understand it. Incidentally, violence as a method for achieving goals is not foreign to the American society as Hugh D. Graham and Ted R. Gurr have unequivocally reported in *The History of Violence in America.*[33] When violence emanates from southern Whites, it is "sane" and laudable; when Blacks move to reject oppression, it is dismissed by van den Berghe as "nonsense" and damnable. This naked partisan expression is not tribute to "dispassionate analysis." Why has the sanity of the South not stopped the continuing emigration of Afro-Americans to the West and the North of the United States?

The use of the concept of pariah for any part of the United States is not only a denial of the kind of society Americans stand for and strive for – namely, an open democratic society – but is also indicative of the author's inner wish as to how Afro-Americans should be treated and looked upon. Afro-Americans

> have been subject to 'victimization' in the sense that a system of social relations operates in such a way as to deprive them of a chance to share in the more desirable material and nonmaterial products of a society which is dependent, in part, upon their labor and loyalty. They are victimized, 'also because they do not have the same degree of access which others have to the attributes needed for rising in the general class system – money, education, 'contact,' and 'know-how.'[34]

This quotation from St. Clair Drake is precise in its description of the disadvantaged status of Afro-Americans. They are, certainly, deprived and rendered powerless through the machinations of others; but they are *not* and cannot be relegated to the social status of untouchables. In fact, were they a pariah, Afro-Americans would not dare rebel. Some of the psychological reactions to the ever-present victimization of Afro-Americans have been skillfully studied by Thomas Pettigrew in *A Profile of the Negro American*, by Kenneth Clark in *Dark Ghetto*, by Grier and Cobbs in *Black Rage*, and by Alvin Poussaint *Why Blacks Kill Blacks*, etc.[35]

These and similar studies have demonstrated the psychology of why Afro-Americans engage in aggressive protests. No serious scholar would call their reactions "nonsense."

## INTEGRATION OR SEPARATION?

Whether or not the Afro-American in America would survive through integration or separation is a moot question. However, it is apparent that van den Berghe does not comprehend the strategies used by Afro-Americans to ameliorate their victimization. For many Afro-Americans, integration or separation is neither an immediate day-to-day concern nor a vital issue worth daydreaming about. They are first and foremost concerned with solving the concrete problems of basic biological survival – food to eat, shelter for cover, clothes to wear, money to visit a doctor, peace from police assaults and brutality, etc. The strategic use of integration tactics by the NAACP or separation tactics by the Black Muslims do initially achieve one goal – public attention, which in turn sometimes produces token redress. The dilemma of the American Black is that when he wants to integrate into a wholesome society with the Whites, he is rejected; and when he wants to separate to build up his own self-contained subsociety, he is forbidden.

This dilemma cannot be belittled by whatever van den Berghe's views are. The absence of factual figures on how many Afro-Americans gave support of any kind to the separatists and nationalists does not permit a judgment of "few" or "many." If the numbers of Black communities across the country which were involved in the riots of the late 1960s are any indicator of those who "bought separatism, nationalism and racial politics," I would not call the number few.

To blame "White liberals and radicals" and "especially those associated with the colleges and universities" for the birth of Black nationalism is to belie the common fact that the Black Panthers, the Black Muslims, and the Black Liberation Army were not, and are not, campus-originated. Those Whites on the campuses who faced the vent of Black frustration and anger did not act because they were liberals or radicals. They acted for the simple reason that they could no longer avoid the issue. It was ordinary decency and conscience in the face of "law-and-order" hawks, not liberalism or radicalism. These "White intellectuals" did not consider it a "damage" as van den Berghe thinks, to build bridges for purposeful living and studying together on the campus. Indeed, theirs was a demonstration of sensitivity to the injustices in the society and an ordinary human response to the frustrations of many.

It is significant that van den Berghe pitches "angry white young women and their "pussy power" against "angry Black young men." One would leave the sexist implications of this juxtaposition to the Women's Libbers. Did anyone ever think of calling "ruling-class organizations" such as the Ku Klux Klan or the Weathermen "pussy power"?

For a serious "dispassionate analysis," a heuristic balance to any of these White nationalist groups would have been more helpful. "Pussy power" is surely not what an oppressed people fight for in an open society. The "pussy power" of white women is already earning them a definite insertion of a clause into the United States Constitution. Thirty states have ratified the Equal Rights Amendment for safeguarding the rights of women.

## BLACK STUDENTS AND WHITE CAMPUSES

The protests of Black students in the 1960s did not begin "the ghettoization of the campus." Most "White universities" have had an unenviable history of forcing residential segregation on Black students. As John W. Blassingame of Yale University has pointed out,

> The demands of black students for separate, autonomous black studies departments, separate social centers, and dormitories have been a godsend to white racists . . . Ivy League Ku Klux Klansmen applaud and vigorously support such demands. The immediate capitulation of white colleges to such demands is understandable: They support their traditional beliefs and practices.[36]

Harvard University was notorious for its "necessity of excluding Negroes" from White dormitories and its unanimous vote of 1923 that "men of the white and Negro races shall not be compelled to live together." The Greek fraternities and sororities of White students, even in their decadence and weak patronages of today, are living symbols of campus restrictive practices which reflect what exists in the general society. In fact, to suggest that the campus has accepted separation while the rest of the society has rejected it is to confuse facts with imagination. Studies of White campuses since 1968 show that there has been more integration in university life than in the general society.[37] Perhaps a single visit to a Black Cultural Center would have made van den Berghe a witness to a spectacle he could hardly imagine possible in the United States. The music and language heard in these cultural centers and the menus served could convince anyone that Afro-Americans have a body of culture which is theirs and theirs alone. The cultural centers enable them to give expression to that which the southern sanity had brutally suppressed during the last four centuries. And, incidentally, one might unexpectedly meet a White mayor and his family eating at one of these centers, as well as White students who prefer life at the Black Cultural Center to the Greek fraternity ballroom.

Contrary to van den Berghe, a more mature understanding of the demands of Black students for their own dormitories, dining halls, cultural centers, etc., is expressed by Steven V. Roberts of the *New York Times.* This demand "runs against the integrationist ethic and undoubtedly has some unhealthy ramifications; it is strange to see blacks doing to themselves what the segregationists did to them for so long. But it is probably useful and necessary. Blacks feel they have to get themselves together before they can deal with the White world on an equal basis, and that seems fair enough. Do the same people who object to a Black social center or dormitory object to a Newman Club or the desire of Jewish students to live together?"[38] On every White campus there is a Newman Center for Catholics and a Hillel House for Jewish students.

In 1969 *Newsweek* research into "Black Mood on Campus" investigated Black students' demands for separate amenities.

> Social integration – so often the bugaboo of white parents – is for all purposes moribund on most U.S. college campuses; many black students don't want it

> . . . [At Wayne State University] Twenty years ago the blacks were ostracized by white students. Today, the tables are turned. 'We're not anti-white,' says a black freshman, 'but we just don't make them a social habit!' Her words sum up the basis for a new attitude among blacks: We can make it on our own. Nearly every black student interviewed . . . regardless of his degree of militancy, expressed an attitude of self-reliance.[39]

This and other studies dealing with the "new" Black students on White campuses and analyses by nationally respected writers in higher education were available for van den Berghe to have read before he let his pen loose. It has been necessary to quote extensively from studies made by diligent and knowledgeable investigators so that no doubt is left on the complexity of the "Negro Problem" in the United States, in which Black students, radicals and nationalists form only a small part of the story. The condemnation and slighting offered by van den Berghe reflects more his sense of balance than the "rantings of Black racists."

Van den Berghe misses the point completely when he condemns "academic white liberals" for admitting "less qualified minority students" and giving them "preferential treatment." What he cannot deny is the fact that Harvard University is accustomed to accepting students from the underdeveloped nations of Europe and the Third World "on a kind of 'implicit quota' system." As Harvard' Professor Henry Rosovsky argued prior to the establishment of Afro-American Studies at Harvard.

> . . . if the foreign students had been selected simply on the basis of formal academic qualifications far fewer individuals from underdeveloped countries would have gained admission; . . . we somehow recognized our obligations toward the less developed world and set aside certain places for these students . . . If we had social obligations to foreigners, clearly we had at least equally urgent obligations to American Negroes . . . We believed that there existed in this country qualified Negro applicants; and that while some of them might require special help – the way a good many foreign students did – by the time these black students received advanced degrees they would be able to compete on equal terms with everybody else.[40]

Quotas made available for Afro-Americans' university education in their own country should be the last thing expected to be attacked by a nouveau arrive as "insidious nonsense."

The difficulties were real ones which college administrators were confronted with when the Black assertion for entry into predominantly White universities began.

> Even the best-meaning college administrators [are] grossly unprepared for the impact of these young blacks on the campuses. Many of these students come straight from urban ghettos, [possessing] their own special attitudes and more few white academicians can understand. . . . It does no one . . . any good to ignore the fact that many of the new black students are unprepared academically, socially and culturally for the environment of a big college campus. Many whites are not much better prepared, even a well-adjusted kid from Scarsdale. Imagine what it must be like for a kid from Harlem![41]

This quotation from Steven V. Roberts is not meant to plead excuses for any Black student. The purpose is solely to help van den Berghe grasp what he sees but cannot, or refuses, to understand, although no terribly exacting training is required of a sociologist to perceive the meaning in this situation. Roberts' observations have been corroborated by many independent studies of what went on and is going on on the campuses.

From van den Berghe's own "rantings," it is obvious that he is so steeped in the traditional thought patterns about university education oriented to corporate employment that he is unable to accept the fact that persons would attend a university with any view other than graduating to enter the "middle-class sambo." Three years ago a well-known Black political scientist, Professor Charles V. Hamilton, was asked of the goals of Black students.

> Today they're understanding that they are black, and that as they go into these colleges . . . they are going to be black and skilled at the same time. Somehow or other, whatever skills they acquire, they are going to make sure that these skills can be applied to the development of Black America. The big test, of course, is what they do with their skills after they leave college. When they go to IBM with their skills, are they going to make sure that they develop a legitimate hiring policy?[42]

A year after Hamilton's statement, Roberts was making a similar observation:

> As much as anything else, the students were rebelling against the fact that the university seemed to be training them for jobs in the great corporate establishment. . . . What they want are courses that will really analyze the society, that will show them how and why decisions are made, that will give them the understanding, and the skills, to try to alter those decisions. . . . This is the full meaning of the revolt against affluence. We now have a student generation that can afford to worry about things other than money.[43]

Without appreciating the Black students and understanding "where they're coming from," lame critics dismiss the demand for "relevant education" and "black pride" as infantile fulminations and hide their dismal ignorance of Black problems in confident arrogance.

In a critical assessment of Black students' demands, the Chancellor of Morgan State College, Dr. King V. Cheek, said among other things:

> Although in many instances the tactics of black students were misguided, they helped to give us hope and progress toward emancipation. . . . They helped to place in bold relief the mockery of law and order slogans [revealing] a little more the reality of America

> and deepened our conviction that so long as any of our brothers and sisters are enslaved, likewise the rest of us are dehumanized by the conditions which permit their bondage.... In short the wave of concern they created in turn generated action and many responsible changes.[44]

These responsible changes were on the campuses, in ghettos, and in the country at large. Some were shortlived, others are still working.

Van den Berghe's apparent incompetence in the subject he chose to write about should be evident by now. I have taken the trouble to let the reader be supplied with facts and responsible interpretations. This trouble is warranted by the experience that it is far easier to talk in unfounded and glib generalities than to substantiate pronouncements with evidence.

The impression given by van den Berghe that special academic programs for Black children in ghetto schools to correct their disabilities have been a total waste of funds is simplistic. The implication of this impression for higher education is that money spent on compensatory programs for Afro-American students would go down the drain. This implication is as deplorable as it is objectionable. The social psychologist, Kenneth B. Clark, has a lengthy report on how successful and effective remedial programs instituted to improve the learning capacities of ghetto schoolchildren were.[45] But, more important, he also describes those racist forces behind the schools and how they determine the fate of the programs.

> A pre-primary program ... has begun. But in other ways, business as usual is underway despite the public support ... It is almost as though a pilot demonstration was meant to serve as a diversionary method and was never intended as a test whose results would lead to action ... it is especially cruel to the neglected child to offer him hope by showing that he can succeed if someone believes in him and then to withdraw that hope.[46]

Similar techniques have been employed in many universities across the country to kill the Black Studies programs they founded when the protests were loud.

For the relationship between race and class, Oliver C. Cox' *Caste, Class and Race* is still very instructive and recommends itself highly to all who think that to attack racism against Blacks in the United States is to "tackle a very superficial aspect of the phenomenon."

A discussion of Black Studies, affirmative action, and the position of the Black middle class on Black nationalism and student protests, for the purpose of refuting van den Berghe's misinterpretation of them would require another article. Suffice it to say that Black Studies have come to be recognized as a viable disciplinary area second to none in academic content and quality. Harvard and Yale universities are leaders in establishing the scholarly credentials of Black Studies. The organizational, recruitment, and curricular problems faced by the Black Studies programs are enormous and quite often serious.

Affirmative action programs on university campuses, just as in government and private sectors of the economy, have the sole aim of assuring fair employment practices toward minority groups (Afro-Americans, American Indians, Puerto Ricans, Mexicans, Women, etc.) to balance the monopoly of White Males. Since the operation of these programs, White women *seem* to have been employed more than the victimized racial and ethnic groups. The *quantitative* minority of Afro-Americans, American Indians, Puerto Ricans, etc., is deliberately mixed up with the *qualitative* minority (power) of the White woman. The winner has not been the Afro-American. In the employment statistics both he and the White woman appear under minority group. "Male chauvinist pigs" are notorious for their esoteric conjectures against the employment of women and other ethnic minorities as defined by law.

If ever there was a time in the history of Afro-Americans that the Black middle class and wealthy became mindful of their common destiny with those in the ghetto, and ostensibly came out to fulfill the role of "the race man," it was the period covered by the discussion in this paper. Most of the leaders of the hot summers of the 1960s and a majority of the Black students who organized against racism on white university campuses for positive attitudinal changes, originated from middle-class families.[47] In these roles, the Black middle class indeed fulfilled the Robert Michels axiom of the leadership of the aggressor class. "Every great class movement in history has arisen upon the instigation, with the cooperation, and under the leadership of men sprung from the very class against which the movement was directed."[48] The riots of the 1960s were also against the American middle class, the class of ultimate power in the United States.

In 1964 Kenneth Clark made one of the most perceptive observations about those Whites who could not tolerate the changes in techniques of Blacks to demand changes in their status:

> At times of overt social unrest, many white persons who claim to be in favor of civil rights and assert that they are "friends" of the Negro ... demonstrate mistaken assumptions concerning the nature and dynamics of Negro protest. It is argued, for example, that Negroes should "choose" only those techniques, tactics, and demonstrations which do not inconvenience the dominant white society; the oppressed are urged to be concerned about the comfort and sensitivities of those they regard as their oppressors. The implication is that if they do not, middle-class whites will use their own power to retaliate against all Negroes. Negroes are increasingly reminded of the sting of the "white backlash".... The "white backlash" is a new name for an old phenomenon, white resistance to the acceptance of the Negro as a human being.

In their effort to melt away white racism in order to make a constructive social change possible,

> The Negro cannot any longer feel, if he ever did, that he should have to prove himself "worthy" in order to gain his full freedom – the rights guaranteed to all other American citizens, including those most recently naturalized. The Negro cannot be asked to prove that he "deserves" the rights and responsibilities of democracy, nor can he be told that others must first be

> persuaded "in heart and mind" to accept him. Such tests and trials by fire are not applied to others. To impose them on the Negro is racist condescension. . . . To demand that he demonstrates virtues not ordinarily found in more privileged people, before he may enjoy the benefits of democracy, is not only irrational and inconsistent but gratuitously cruel.[49]

## NOTES

[1] Oliver C. Cox, *Caste, Class and Race,* New York, Modern Reader Paperbacks, 1970, p. 481.

[2] W.E.B. DuBois, *The Souls of Black Folk,* London, Longmans, Green, 1965, p. vi.

[3] B.F. Skinner, *Beyond Freedom and Dignity,* New York, Knopf, 1971.

[4] Adolf Hitler, *Mein Kampf,* authorized translation, Hurst and Blackett, London, 1939, p. 359.; Pierre L. van den Berghe, *Race and Racism, A Comparative Perspective,* New York, Wiley, 1967.

[5] See, for example, Gunnar Myrdal, *An American Dilemma,* Vols. I and II, New York, Harper Torchbooks, 1969; Talcott Parsons and Kenneth B. Clark (Eds.), *The Negro American,* Boston, Beacon Press, 1967.

[6] Peter Goldman, "Black America Now" in *Newsweek,* February 19, 1973, p. 29.

[7] Otto Kerner, *U.S. National Advisory Commission on Civil Disorders,* New York, Bantam Books, 1968.

[8] Karl E. Taueber and Alma F. Taueber, *Negroes in Cities, Residential Segregation and Neighbourhood Change,* New York, Atheneum, 1969.

[9] Rashi Fein, "An Economic and Social Profile of the Negro American," in Parsons and Clark, pp. 102-133.

[10] Theodore Cross, "How About Job-Equality Role for the Exchanges?" in *The New York Times,* Business and Finance, February 25, 1973, p. 17.

[11] *Ibid.*

[12] John Hope Franklin, "The Two Worlds of Race – An Historical View," in Parsons and Clark, pp. 47-68.

[13] Peter Goldman, p. 29.

[14] Theodor W. Adorno *et al., The Authoritarian Personality,* New York, Harper, 1950, is still useful for determining anti-Semitism and, by extension, negrophobic tendencies.

[15] Kenneth B. Clark, *Dark Ghetto – Dilemmas of Social Power,* New York & Evanston, Harper Torchbooks, 1967, pp. 11-62.

[16] See, for example, Thom. F. Pettigrew, *A Profile of the Negro American,* Princeton, N.J., Van Nostrand, 1964. Also by the same author, "Complexity and Change in American Racial Patterns: A Social Psychological View," in Parsons & Clark, pp. 325-359; Lee Rainwater, *Behind Ghetto Walls – Black Family Life in a Federal Slum,* Chicago, Aldine, 1970.

[17] See E. David Cronon, *Black Moses – The Story of Marcus Garvey,* Madison, The University of Wisconsin Press, 1969; Langston Hughes, "The Negro Artist and the Racial Mountain," in *Nation Magazine,* June 1926; Nathan I. Huggins, *Harlem Renaissance,* New York, Oxford University Press, 1971.

[18] An easy to read, factual survey of their suffering is available in John Hope Franklin, *From Slavery to Freedom,* New York, Vintage Books, 1969.

[19] John H. Bracey, August Meier, and Elliot Rudwick (Eds.), *Black Nationalism in America,* Indianapolis and New York, Bobbs-Merrill, 1970.

[20] St. Clair Drake and Horace R. Cayton, *Black Metropolis,* New York and Evanston, Harper Torchbooks, 1962, especially Volume II.

[21] Kenneth B. Clark, *Dark Ghetto,* p. 231.

[22] Kwame Nkrumah, *Ghana – The Autobiography of Kwame Nkrumah,* Edinburgh, Thomas Nelson & Sons, 1959; Nnamdi Azikiwe, *My Odyssey: An Autobiography,* London, C. Hurst, 1970; J.P. Clark, *America Their America,* London, Heinemann Educational Books, 1970.

[23] Oliver C. Cox, *Caste, Class and Race,* p. 571.

[24] For exact Black Muslim mythology see Hon. Elijah Muhammed, *The Supreme Wisdom,* 2 volumes, University of Islam (no date); further see C. Eric Lincoln, *The Black Muslims in America,* Boston, Beacon Press, 1969; E.U. Essien-Udom, *Black Nationalism – A Search for an Identity in America,* Chicago & London, The University of Chicago Press, 1969.

[25] Erik H. Erikson, "The Concept of Identity in Race Relations – Notes and Queries" in Parsons and Clark, p. 243.

[26] Robert W. Andrews and James Woolsey, "Ethnic Pride Holds Promise for City," *Syracuse Post-Standard,* April 25, 1973, p. 18.

[27] Nathan Glazer and Daniel P. Moynihan, *Beyond the Melting Pot,* Cambridge, The M.I.T. Press & The Harvard University Press, 1963, p. 51.

[28] Lee Rainwater (Ed.), *Black Experience – Soul,* New Brunswick, New Jersey, Transaction, 1970.

[29] W.E.B. DuBois, *The Souls of Black Folk.*

[30] William K. Tabb, *The Political Economy of the Ghetto,* New York, Norton, 1970.

[31] Otto Kerner, *Commission on Civil Disorders.*

[32] Robert Daley, *Target Blue,* New York, The Delacorte Press, 1973. Excerpts in *New York,* February 12, 1973, pp. 34-46.

[33] Hugh D. Graham and Ted Robert Gurr, *The History of Violence in America,* New York, Bantam Books, 1969.

[34] St. Clair Drake, "The Social and Economic Status of the Negro in the United States," in Parsons & Clark, p. 4.

[35] William H. Grier and Price M. Cobbs, *Black Rage,* New York, Bantam Books, 1968; Alvin F. Poussaint, *Why Blacks Kill Blacks,* New York, Emerson Hall, 1972.

[36] John W. Blassingame, "Black Studies: An Intellectual Crisis," *The American Scholar,* Vol. 38, August 1969, p. 555.

[37] Charles Willie and Alline Sakuma McCord, *Black Student at White Colleges,* New York, Praeger, 1972.

[38] Steven V. Roberts, "Black Studies," More Than 'Soul Courses,' " *Commonweal,* Vol. 91, January 1970, pp. 478-479.

[39] O. Elliot, "Black Mood on Campus," *Newsweek,* February 10, 1969, p. 54.

[40] Henry Rosovsky; "Black Studies at Harvard – Personal Reflections Concerning Recent Events," *The American Scholar,* Vol. 38, August 1969, p. 563.

[41] Steven V. Roberts, "Black Studies," p. 478.

[42] O. Elliot, "Black Mood," p. 53-4.

[43] Steven V. Roberts, "Black Studies," p. 479.

[44] King V. Cheek, Jr., "Reflections in Retrospect on the Legacy of Black Student Protest," Address delivered at Annual Banquet of the Association for the Study of Negro Life and History, *Journal of Negro History.* Vol. 57, 1972, p. 76.

[45] Kenneth B. Clark, *Dark Ghetto,* pp. 139-148.
[46] Kenneth B. Clark, *Dark Ghetto,* p. 151.
[47] John H. Bracey *et al., Black Nationalism in America,* p. LIX.
[48] Robert Michels, *Political Parties,* trans. by Eden and Cedar Paul, New York, Dover, 1959, pp. 238-239.
[49] Kenneth Clark, *Dark Ghetto,* pp. 16-19.

# 26
# *Planned Parenthood or Black Genocide* *

CHARLES V. WILLIE

My intention is to present a perspective on national population policy from the point of view of a social scientist who is black, has lived in both northern and southern regions of the United States, and has experienced poverty and a measure of affluence.

First, I must state categorically that many people in the black community are deeply suspicious of any family planning program initiated by whites. You probably have heard about, but not taken seriously, the call by some male-dominated black militant groups for black females to eschew the use of contraceptives because they are pushed in the black community as "a method of exterminating black people." While black females often take a different view about contraceptives than their male militant companions, they too are concerned about the possibility of black genocide in America.

The genocidal charge is neither "absurd" nor "hollow" as some whites have contended. Neither is it limited to residents of the ghetto, whether they be low-income black militants or middle-aged black moderates. Indeed my studies of black students at white colleges indicate that young, educated blacks fear black genocide.

This statement from a black female student in the spring of 1970 is representative of the thinking of so many other blacks. She said: "The institutions in society are so strong. The CIA is everywhere. I believe that America desires to perpetuate concentration camps for political opponents of the system of this country. People who speak out against the system are being systematically cut down – Eldridge Cleaver, the Chicago Seven, the Black Panthers." She concluded her recitation of despair with this depressing thought: "I wouldn't say that this society is against all-out genocide for black people." While there is uncertainty in her accusation, there is no mood of hope.

I designate the death of Martin Luther King, Jr., as the beginning of serious concern among blacks about the possibility of genocide in America. There were lynchings, murders and manslaughters in the past. But the assassination of Dr. King was too much. In Dr. King, many blacks believed they had presented their best. He was scorned, spat upon, and slain. If America could not accept Dr. King, then many felt that no black person in America was safe. For no other could match the magnificent qualities of this great man. Yet they were not enough; and so he was cut down by the bullet of a white assassin in a crime that remains mysterious, considering the help that the assassin received in escaping to a foreign land.

I dwell upon this event of our modern history because the Commission on Population Growth and the American Future must consider the present as well as the recent past, which is the context within which it must plan. This context cannot be ignored. Unless the American society can assure black people that it is committed to their survival with dignity and equality, they will refuse to cooperate with any national population plan. The Commission must demonstrate that participation in any national plan will serve the self-interests of blacks as well as the nation.

This Commission on Population Growth is carrying excess baggage which it did not pack and does not need. To some blacks, any call today by a federal commission for a national population policy, especially if it focuses on family planning, sounds similar to a call yesterday by a federal official for a national program to stabilize the black family. That call was set forth in *The Negro Family, A Case for National Action,* which was prepared by the U.S. Labor Department and published in 1965. Its chief author was Daniel Patrick Moynihan. I need not remind you of the negative reaction of blacks to the Moynihan report. Many blacks got the idea that the national policy Dr. Moynihan was pushing was designed to make over blacks in the image of whites. They got this idea from his allegation that a matriarchal family structure exists among blacks and this has seriously retarded their progress, "*because it is so out of line with the rest of the American society.*"[1] In an article published later in *Daedalus,* Dr. Moynihan described the black family as being in a state of "unmistakable crisis." He concluded that the crisis was acute because of "the extraordinary rise in Negro population."[2]

While Dr. Moynihan may not have intended to give this impression, his two statements seem to me to call for a national policy to obliterate any family form among blacks which might be different from the family forms found among whites. Moreover, he suggested that the nation should act fast to make over blacks in the image of whites because blacks were gaining on whites in numbers. These statements came from one who has been an intimate consultant to two presidents, including Presi-

*Written especially for this book.

dent Richard Nixon. Blacks were suspicious of Dr. Moynihan's call for national policy which focused upon the black family. The Moynihan report on the Negro family therefore is excess baggage which this Commission does not need and from which it should separate itself. *The Commission should make it clear to the public that the national population policy which it is attempting to formulate is not merely an extension and a refinement of the Moynihan call for a national program to stabilize the black family.*

If the Commission on Population Growth and the American Future is to promulgate a national population policy, it must gather up the goals and aspirations which blacks themselves have identified as important. A national population policy must demonstrate that it is more concerned about the *health* and *wealth* of black people than it is about the number of children they have. I am talking about a *positive population policy,* which is the preferred way to deal with a negative effect.

Social scientists know that people tend to act in accordance with their beliefs. If blacks *believe* that family planning programs are insidiously designed by whites to exterminate blacks, then blacks will not cooperate with any national population policy which focuses only upon family planning.

Let me explain why blacks believe any national program for family stability which focuses only upon family planning is a desperation move on the part of whites to remain in control. Whites were not concerned about the family structure of blacks a century and a half ago. Then blacks were nearly one-fifth (18.4 percent) of the total population. This, of course, was during the age of slavery, during the 1820s. Then, blacks were not free. They were no challenge to whites. Although they represented one out of every five persons in the United States, and although the family assumed even more functions for the growth, development, and well-being of individuals then than it probably does today, American whites were not concerned about the fertility or stability of the black family. Indeed, there were attempts to breed healthy male black slaves with healthy female black slaves, disregarding any family connections and even prohibiting marriage. In his famous book, *An American Dilemma*, Gunnar Myrdal wrote, "most slave owners . . . did not care about the marital state of their slaves. . . ."[3] Neither the size of the black population nor their circumstances of family life worried white Americans before black people were free.

But, in the mid-1960s and 1970s, when the throttle to the Freedom Movement was open and demonstrations for self-determination were going full blast, white Americans became concerned about the size and the stability of the black family. Daniel Patrick Moynihan tipped off blacks about what was in the minds of whites when he described the situation as "acute" because of the *extraordinary* rise in Negro population." The size and stability of the black family was of no concern to white Americans when black people were enslaved. The size and stability of the black family is a cause for alarm among white Americans, requiring a national program of family control, now that black people are beginning to achieve freedom and equality.

Blacks, of course, would not claim that there has been an extraordinary rise in the Negro population. The black population in America has increased from 9.9 percent in 1920 to approximately 11.4 percent today – no cause for alarm. But then maybe an increase of between one and two percentage points of the total population is an extraordinary rise if one believes that it is. Social scientists know that if people believe a situation is real, it tends to be real in its consequences. Sociologist Robert Merton of Columbia University has written that "self-hypnosis through one's own propaganda is not an infrequent phase of the self-fulfilling prophecy."[4]

Moreover, a population increase of one to two percentage points of the total creates an acute situation and is cause for alarm if the ultimate national goal is to eliminate black people; for such an increase, although small, indicates that they will not go away.

The genocidal charge of black people is anchored in good data. Blacks point out that a leading government spokesman has declared that an increase in black people of one to two percentage points of the total population is "extraordinary." Blacks also point out that whites were not concerned about their family form and size during the age of slavery. Even after the days of slavery, blacks point out that over the years the greatest contributor to family instability among the members of their race has been the death of the male spouse rather than divorce or desertion. Moreover, blacks point out that the major control upon the black fertility rate in the past has been deaths of very young children.

Back in 1910, 27 percent of black females were members of broken families because their husbands were dead. During that same year, only six percent of the black families were broken because of divorce or desertion of the male spouse. Thus, death was four times more frequently a contributor to family disruption than other social causes. I should add that death of the husband was the chief cause for marital breakup for black families compared with desertion or divorce up through 1963. Thus, divorce and desertion, which was highlighted by Dr. Moynihan as reasons why a national program to stabilize the black family was needed, are newcomers as chief causes of family breakup for black people. The information on trends in marital status comparing the relative contributions was obtained from an article written by Dr. Reynolds Farley of the University of Michigan and may be found in a recent book which I edited on the *Family Life of Black People.*

It would seem that whites were not concerned about the stability of the black family when it was broken largely because black men were dying prematurely. It would seem that whites are concerned about the size and stability of the black family now only because the number of *black men who are dying prematurely is decreasing and the number of black children born who survive is increasing.* If you can understand the basis of the alarm among white liberals about this situation, then you can understand the basis for the charge of genocide which is made by black militants.

Essentially, I am saying what several distinguished demographers already have said. Irene Taeuber of the Office of Population Research at Princeton University, for example, has said that "the test of future population policies, planned and unplanned, will be in the speed and the completeness of the obliteration of those demographies that can be categorized by the color of the skin or the subcultures of origin."[5] In other words, Dr. Taeuber was saying that "the demography of black Americans is a product of, and component in, the demography of all Americans."[6] This must be a guiding principle for the Commission on Population Growth. Professor Kingsley Davis of the University of California at Berkeley has pointed out often in his writings and lectures that a Population Commission should avoid the pitfall of the Moynihan report. It should promulgate a national population policy for all people in the United States but recognize that such a policy should have different emphases for different groups. Such a policy must consider the variations in historical and contemporary experiences of black, brown, and white people.

All that has been said thus far should clearly indicate that a national population policy cannot succeed if it focuses only on reproduction; family size or family planning, particularly with reference to size, is often a function of other socioeconomic opportunities. Clyde Kiser, an outstanding demographer with the Milbank Memorial Fund, and Myrna Frank have discovered *that black women over 25 years of age who have a college education or who are married to professional men tend to have a fertility rate that is much lower than that for whites of similar circumstances.*[7]

Dr. Taeuber also refers to the socioeconomic facts of life. She states that "trends in the fertility of the blacks in future years will be influenced both by rapidity of the upward economic and social movements and by that complex of factors that influences national fertility, white or black . . ."[8]

It can be stated in general that an inverse relationship exists between fertility and socioeconomic status factors. People of higher income, occupation, and education tend to have fewer children.

However, the association between fertility and socioeconomic factors is a bit more complex when one is dealing with blacks. Reynolds Farley of the University of Michigan tells us that among urban blacks, "after 1940, fertility rate . . . increased rapidly . . ." and that in 1960 "urban fertility rates (for blacks) were higher than those in rural areas."[9] He further points out that a general increase in fertility has occurred among blacks, which has involved all social classes; he concludes that this is probably due to improved health conditions resulting in decreased death rates, particularly infant and maternal mortality.[10]

The Commission should understand that blacks have begun to make only modest gains in fertility only because of increased health care. Historical adversities and recent opportunities for blacks must be taken into consideration when formulating a national population policy and enlisting their cooperation.

Because so little trust exists between the races in the United States, when whites speak of limiting fertility or controlling the family in any way, many blacks believe that whites are planning to return to a modified Malthusian plan which has controlled black family life in the past. Blacks know that their families have been disrupted and limited in the past because of deaths. They therefore are suspicious of any plan that does not assure them that death again, individually or collectively, will not be the chief controlling variable.

In a jocular vein, Dr. Moynihan, writing for *America* magazine, the national Catholic weekly review, said "while the rich of America do whatever it is they do, the poor are begetting children."[11]

I should point out in a not so jocular vein that many of the children begotten by the black poor in the past died before reaching manhood or womanhood and that these children are beginning to live today, so that the proportion of black people in the total population is increased by one to two percentage points of the total. The increase in fertility due to these achievements in health care therefore is no cause for alarm. Indeed, the Commission on Population Growth should urge and encourage a fertility that is not impeded by disease and death.

If the poor beget children and if the number they beget is counterproductive for the future welfare of the total nation, and if there is an inverse association between fertility and socioeconomic status, then it would seem that a national population policy should have as a major plank a program to guarantee equality in economic and educational opportunities for all people in this nation. This means that a national population policy must come out strong against racial and ethnic discrimination. Herman Miller of the U.S. Census Bureau tells us that "the average Negro earns less than the average white, even when he has the same years of schooling and does the same kind of work." This conclusion comes from the analysis of income figures which, according to Dr. Miller, "provide the unarguable evidence on which public policy should rest."[12]

It is for this reason that I conclude that a national population policy which would serve the best interests of blacks as well as the other citizens of this nation should focus not only on family planning, family size, or family stability, but also on enhancing the *health* and *wealth* of every household in America.

## NOTES

[1] U.S. Department of Labor, *The Negro Family,* Washington, D.C., Government Printing Office, 1965, p. 29.

[2] Daniel P. Moynihan, "The Ordeal of the Negro Family," in Charles V. Willie (Ed.), *The Family Life of Black People,* Columbus, Merrill, 1970, p. 175.

[3] Gunnar, Myrdal, *An American Dilemma,* New York, Harper & Row, 1944, p. 185.

[4] Robert K. Merton, *Social Theory and Social Structure,* Glencoe, The Free Press, 1949, p. 185.

[5] Irene B. Taeuber, Discussion at Milbank Round Table on Demographic Aspects of the Black Community, *The Milbank Memorial Fund Quarterly XLVIII,* Part 2, April 1970, p. 37.

[6] *Ibid.*

[7] Clyde V. Kiser and Myrna E. Franks, "Factors Associated with Low Fertility of Nonwhite Women of College Attainment," in Charles V. Willie (Ed.), *The Family Life of Black People,* pp. 42-43.

[8] Irene B. Taeuber, p. 39.

[9] Reynolds, Farley, "Fertility Among Urban Blacks," *Milbank Memorial Fund Quarterly XLVIII,* Part 2, April 1970, p. 189.

[10] *Ibid.*, pp. 194-195.

[11] Daniel P. Moynihan, "A Family Policy for the Nation," in Lee Rainwater and William L. Yancey (Eds.), *The Moynihan Report and the Politics of Controversy,* Cambridge, the MIT Press, 1967, p. 392.

[12] Herman P. Miller, *Rich Man, Poor Man,* New York, Crowell, 1964, p. xxi.

# 27
# *Black First, Female Second* *

BRUNETTA R. WOLFMAN

"A man who suffers much,
knows much;
Everyday brings him
new wisdom."
Ewe Proverb

This bit of West American folk wisdom might be paraphrased to rather accurately describe the condition of Black women in American life, and it might provide some clues to explain the relationship of Black women to the women's liberation movement and the separatist Black movements. It is often noted with surprise that the number of Black women active in the activist women's groups is very small; periodic attempts to involve them generally meet with little success. The reasons for this lack of participation may be attributed to the traditionally independent position of Black women, their supportive role within the Black community, and their responsibility in actualizing the aspirations of the racial group.

The tradition of passive participant and ornament of a male benefactor which is associated with the role of women in many cultures was not present in the West African societies from which Black Americans are descended. Women in West Africa then and now are important to the economy, in trading and farming; they could and do exist as independent economic entities and they amass wealth in their own right (Herskovits, 1958, pp. 58-62). This legacy embedded in racial memory may have contributed to the survival of Black women and helped the adaptation to American society. It perhaps contributed to their usefulness in a slave society where females were a vital part of the workforce.

The Black woman in the slave society worked in the fields along with the men, did the domestic chores for the master's family, provided new slaves, and served as a sexual outlet in a society which feared sexuality and dichotomized women according to race. White women were placed on an idealized pedestal and given the illusion that they were ethereal, sacred, and not to be concerned with the base aspects of life, such as sex or sensual feelings. Black women then became the opposite – earthy, physical, passionate, and profane; they were used as sexual objects, to release tensions, and for learning about sex. Thus the women of both races became enslaved by stereotypes, mores, and modes of behavior that are still functional and affect the ways in which they perceive one another. Black and white women are separated from one another and kept from working together by these images of purity and debasement which can be traced to the period of slavery.

With the end of bondage, there was a great statutory change but a rather insignificant change in the economic status of Blacks; they were used as a source of cheap labor in the South and North since it was a period when physical strength was desirable and machines had not been devised to perform many simple tasks. Since Blacks as a group were at the lowest levels of the socioeconomic scale, it was of the utmost necessity that women work. The small wages which the women earned were needed to eke out a meager subsistence; there was little possibility that Black women could choose to work or not because of the economic position of the group. Most of the jobs available to them were in private households as domestic servants working for Caucasian women: this helped perpetuate the mistress-servant relationship of slavery, though changing it to accommodate a money exchange and extending it into the North as well as in the South.

Even the Black women who were educated beyond the elementary level or who received college training for such sub-professions as teaching or nursing did not anticipate short-term careers with retirement at marriage as did their Caucasian counterparts; it was taken for granted that childbirth or geographic relocations would only mean interruptions in the work pattern. The income, though greater than that earned by domestics, was less than that of white teachers and nurses but was necessary for the maintenance of Black families. Frequently these women were married to men who had lower status jobs than they; this became a fairly common pattern for educated Black women, or they remained single because there were no eligible mates. Thus they, unlike their Caucasian counterparts, could not achieve upward mobility through marriage but had to find sources of satisfaction other than through status marriages (Bernard, 1966, p. 90).

Unionization and fair employment practices legislation have helped raise the economic position of Blacks so that the 1970 Census notes a more equal distribution of Blacks in the major occupational groups, a marked contrast to earlier periods when

*Written especially for this book.

they were concentrated in service, unskilled laborer, and private household categories (U.S. Bureau of Census, 1972, pp. 65-68). However, in spite of improvements in the economic position, more Black women are in the labor force than are white women because of the still depressed economic status of Blacks and the need for the income earned by women.

Since the Black woman has traditionally had an independent economic role, she has assumed more independence in relationships with males than has the white woman. Relationships with men have been based on romantic affection (Bernard; 1966, p. 138), and the women have used their sense of independence to end relationships which proved to be unsuccessful for any reason. This may be partially attributed to the position of Black women within the community – that of a pillar of society.

Though Black women have been held in low esteem by the majority society, they have assumed important positions within the organizational structure of the Black community; however Black women have not been the public spokesmen or leaders of these voluntary associations. They have served as the main support and provided the impetus for the Black church, fraternal lodges, uplift and social groups, and civil rights organizations. It has been this organizational affiliation which has provided psychic fulfillment to assuage the hurts of prejudice and discrimination and which has provided a spiritual center for the lives of Black women. These groups have helped Black women carry out their obligations to their families in the time available after work; the socializing role of the mother has been supplemented by the churches, lodges, social uplift clubs, and civil rights organizations.

The Black church has been the source of the greatest commitment of time and loyalty and the source of the greatest solace for Black women through the centuries in America. Just as women in many European cultures provide the largest constituency of active churchgoers and supporters, so Black women have provided the stability to sustain the largest social organization within the Black society. The women of the usher boards, guilds, missionary associations, and Sunday school groups have raised the money through the years to provide the physical facilities and financial support for ministers. The church has served as a social center for Black rural and urban populations, providing a direct contrast to the other social outlets available, such as saloons, pool halls, or sporting houses. Church activities scheduled for every night of the week and all day Sunday were a means by which Black mothers could fill their lives and those of their family; social contacts made within the church were dignified and free of the oppressive attitudes of the work-a-day world of the larger society. A scrub woman or maid could aspire to be the head of the usher board and a valuable, respected member of the congregation; this was as true for the storefront as for the conventional church structure built or bought by the members. The occupational status of the members did not automatically determine the status or prestige accorded a church member by fellow parishoners, since roles and deeds within the church were used as the basis for according prestige and position. Though Black women have been integral parts of the Black church, they have seldom assumed public leadership roles; they have been instrumental in the ministerial selection process and their support vital for continuance in office, but the instances of women heading large congregations have been extremely rare. Black women by and large have been content to take supportive and secondary roles in the church, finding satisfactions, meaning, and shelter from a prejudiced society in the maintenance of a nurturing institution.

The ceremony and regalia of the fraternal lodges have provided an additional source of associational activity and secondary relationships. Women have created counterparts of all the male groups with parallel structures so that couples may participate in the programs, attending meetings and conventions and socializing within the same social circle. This aspect of the Black associational life is very important for upwardly mobile lower and working class people who desire respectability; membership is restricted to persons who can find sponsors who will attest to their good character and to the fact that they are gainfully employed. Women's membership is usually dependent upon a marriage or family relationship with a male member of a lodge, and the women's groups must have the support and actual participation of male "patrons" in order to exist or continue functioning.

In the churches and lodges, Black women have not had the leading roles nor have they been the charismatic leaders, except in those aspects that are devoted exclusively to women or children. This has also been the case with the civil rights organizations, even in crisis situations precipitated by a woman, as in Birmingham by Rosa Parks. The Niagara Movement, forerunner of the NAACP, the Urban League, and the Southern Christian Leadership Conference have all been responses to crises; the purpose of these groups has been to extend the rights of Black people through legislation, appeals to the conscience of the majority, protests, and economic boycotts. The founders and titular leaders have consistently been males, Black and white, but there has been token female representation on the boards of directors. Often white women have been given a more visible role in the leadership structure than have Black women, but this may be partially attributed to the need to have the financial support and prestige of wealthy whites in order to gain acceptance and credibility in the majority society. The volunteer and paid leadership of the civil rights organizations has usually come from ministers, businessmen, professionals, or civil rights organizers; Mrs. Coretta King is an exception in that she has become a public spokeswoman, but it is because of her role as the widow of a civil rights martyr rather than her own leadership abilities.

Since the civil rights organizations have used forms and techniques which parallel those of the Black churches, Black women have formed a natural group of workers who could be called upon to attend meetings, take care of the organizational details, and raise funds through social events. Local and regional units of the NAACP and Urban League have had occasional women leaders, but the usual pattern is one of women assuming the secondary roles in deference to male leadership. There has been little concern or agitation on the part of Black women to assume greater roles or to create new civil rights organizations since they have been content to follow the traditional patterns. Few Black women have used their participation in civil rights activities as a springboard for political involvement, though they have worked for Black candidates for political office. The few Black women in political life are admired but not used as role models because their primary activities are outside the Black community, which continues to be the focus of life for most

Black women.

The churches and civil rights organizations have not provided the only social outlet available to Black women because some women have devised secular ways of expressing their hopes and aspirations through voluntary associations concerned with self-education, racial progress, and the improvement of conditions for Black children and adults. Many of these uplift groups had their beginnings in the period before the turn of the century and often were related to fund-raising efforts for Black schools or charities (Lerner, 1973, pp. 435-437). This avenue also provided an opportunity for socially mobile women to distinguish themselves from lower class or working class women because they could form relationships with other Black women with similar class aspirations and values. Philanthropic activities with a heavy overlay of social activities have made these groups important determinants of status in Black communities and have provided many women with an opportunity to express their aspirations in concrete ways. The programs of these groups have been so encompassing and absorbing for their members that there has been little desire to go outside the Black community for social or charitable activities; however, a few Black women have participated in social service agencies such as the YWCA. However, this has been considered to be community service necessary for an enhanced image of the race in the perceptions of the majority community.

While the Black churches and civil rights organizations expect women to fulfill traditional roles and tasks, the separatist movements have lifted Black women onto pedestals to be admired, glorified, and propagandized at the same time that they are subservient to the wishes and desires of males. These groups have taken a persistent theme in Black American life – that of the sacred "Mother" – and made it a keystone of race propaganda exhortation. The pervading image of the Black mother is that of a woman who offers ever-welcome arms and comforting bosom, who suffers the hurts inflicted on her children, who sacrifices her potential pleasures to protect her children or to have them realize her aspirations. Mother love is the cushion which protects the Black child throughout his life from the arbitrary pain of being Black in a white world, and one of the most vile insults in the Black community is one which heaps abuse on another's mother. This romantic sense of nobility, purity, and race pride personified in the Black woman is exemplified in Marcus Garvey's "The Black Woman".

> Black queen of beauty, thou hast given color to the world!
> Among other women thou art royal and the fairest!
> Like the brightest jewels in the regal diadem,
> Shin'st thou, Goddess of Africa, Nature's purest emblem!
>
> Black men worship at thy virginal shrine of purest love,
> Because in thine eyes are virtue's steady and holy mark,
> As we see no other, clothed in silk or fine linen,
> From ancient, Venus, the Goddess, to mythical Helen.

The glorification of Black women is an important part of nationalist ideology and a necessary theme used in developing positive racial identification or one of racial and moral superiority. The women are extolled not only as the mothers of the race or potential mothers but are used to counter racist propaganda which equates feminine physical beauty and purity with white women. Racial pride must be founded on an appreciation of the external and internal attributes of the group, and the woman becomes a proper focus for creating a positive self-image. Abstract adulation of Black women also allows the nationalists to expunge their guilt and make amends for their helplessness and inability to protect their women from the physical and economic exploitation of whites; much of the self-hypnotic propaganda focuses on the ways in which Black men will protect and free their communities from the oppressive bonds of discrimination. Thus, nationalist mythology does not deviate from traditional modes and reinforces the traditional male role of protecting women so that she can fulfill her divine mission of procreation.

The Garvey movement took on the trappings of the lodges, the zeal of a revivalist movement, and captured the imaginations of Black masses building on their frustrations and loss of faith in the America of the post-World War I era. The Universal Negro Improvement Association organized its members with great flair and style according to their anticipated and traditional sex roles; the men were alluded to be the potential warriors and were in the African Legion or the Universal Motor Corps, while the women were enlisted into the Black Cross Nurses. They had no medical or first-aid training but wore uniforms, marched in parades, attended mass rallies, and generated enthusiasm for the tenets of the movement (Cronin, 1966, pp. 63-64). There are unresolved contradictions in a movement which promoted black dolls for little girls and a Black Madonna and child but does not encourage women to emulate the women on the continent to which they were planning to emigrate. Women were not given leadership roles in the general movement, only in the section catering to their own sex, but they evidently gained satisfaction and fulfillment redemption in a return to Africa.

Perhaps the Black Muslims provide a link between the Garveyite's tacit acceptance of a passive role for women in a separatist movement and the bombastic discussions of women's place in the nationalists worldview of the 1960s. Elijah Muhammad and his followers have very explicit views and teachings about the duties of girls and women. They are expected to be subservient to the head of the family, accepting the decisions made by him, and remaining within the confines of the home (Essien-Udom, 1965, pp. 136-139). The movement proscribes the activities of girls and women so that the focus is on those traditional housewifely chores of cleaning, cooking, sewing, and caring for the family. The dietary restrictions and the emphasis on Muslim nutrition takes much of their time as do the welfare tasks associated with the mosques; their dress and demeanor are also subject to the controls of the group and are learned along with the religious principles in classes conducted by the Moslem Girls' Training and General Civilization Class. The Muslims have taken the idealized Euro-American image of the middle-class wife and mother and made it the norm for the sect so that the women members must reject the traditional independence of Black women, adopting another style in the name of a separatist religious ideology. In return, Muslim men must respect and protect their women, a necessary complement to demands placed on the females. Moral restraints and sanctions imposed by guilt and group membership give emphasis to the Muslim actions that is missing in secular movements without the force of religion behind their teachings.

The secular nationalists of the post-Civil Rights era found

inspiration not in the writings of American religious leaders but in the poets and analysts of Africa – Aime Cesaire, Leopold Senghor, Frantz Fanon. The latter was able to take his psychoanalytic observations of the effects of colonialism and revolution on the Black psyche and develop a case for "consciousness of self" which had universal meaning for Blacks (Fanon, 1967, pp. 216-222). This was often translated into the American vernacular in the form of adaptations of African dress, hair styles, and a renewed discussion of the meaning of Blackness. Black women were urged to adopt standards of beauty not derived from white society but based on the realities of Black physical attributes – dark skin, kinky hair, full lips, broad noses, round buttocks, and a sense of coordinated movement. As is usual in American life, this opened up new areas of commercial exploitation designed to meet the consumer demands of an aroused Black nationalism; new products, long needed, were marketed to enhance the natural qualities and beauties of Black women. The promulgation of the slogan "Black is Beautiful" along with the idealization of the beautiful Black woman helped create a more positive self-image and lessen what Grier and Cobbs (1968, pp. 24-40) call the "surrender of femininity." Many of their women patients appeared to be prematurely aged because they had given up trying to be attractive since they associated feminine beauty with the white ideal.

At the same time that Black women were being glorified, the separatists had little for them to do other than be the movement followers and produce the children of the future Black nation. Black women were told that they must not be in the forefront because they had been the pawns of the white oppressors and helped emasculate Black men, that they had functioned with a matriarchy and robbed Black men of their rightful role in running the Black community.

E. Franklin Frazier's concept of the matriarchy (1966, pp. 102-113) has been a popular one used to describe the Black family, though Frazier did note that middle class Black families were similar to those of Caucasians. The analogy of a matriarchy and a disorganized family structure applies only in part to the lower class Blacks who have adapted to the pressures of discrimination by having a loose network of relationships; there is no wealth to be handed on to daughters or granddaughters and decisions about the family are usually made by governmental agents and statutes rather than by the socalled matriarchs. Much of the rationale behind such a formulation obscures the causes of the behavior and tends to place the blame on the oppressed group rather than the oppressor; this was the purpose of the Moynihan report and the cause of the subsequent furor about it. Such a discussion tends to distort the reality that well over two-thirds of all Black families are intact and headed by a male, but the main implication of attacks on female-headed families is that they are distortions and deviations from the norm and inherently destructive. There is a need for more objective non-sexist studies of the strengths of different forms of family life.

The militant separatists of the '60s idealized the stereotyped characteristics of the lower class Black and elevated them into attributes that were to be emulated and desired. Women in the movement were to be promiscuous and given to pleasure in service to the "people"; an occasional woman was given a public role to play in the movement, but often this was again a reflection of her relationship to a leading man rather than to her own abilities to spellbind crowds or to formulate an ideological position.

Black women were enjoined to not only produce children but to raise warriors to fight the battles necessary to win freedom; they were told that there was no choice but to have children as a counterattack on the racist plan for genocide in the form of birth control programs. Contrary to the demand of the white women's movement for control of their bodies, Black women were told that their main function in life was to have babies. This was not contrary to a general value of lower class Blacks who have tended to associate adulthood with having children, so a young girl achieves womanhood when she has a child and a young man attains manhood when he fathers a child. An informant of Robert Coles expressed this value: ". . . To me, having a baby inside me is the only time I'm really alive. I know I can make something, do something, no matter what color my skin is, and what names people call me. When the baby gets born I see him, and he's full of life, or she is; and I think to myself that it doesn't make any difference what happens later, at least now we've got a chance, or the baby does . . ." (Coles; 1964, pp. 368-369).

Through the years, the Black separatist groups have approached their goals from different perspectives and have had different expectations of member behaviors, but there has been a common expectation of a subordinate position for women. Generally, women have been ignored and expected to stay in the background performing those tasks that were necessary to keep the movement going and operating within the tenets of the movements. They were not the public voices nor did they provide the ideological or tactical leadership for the movements. They have often been given the responsibility of discussing the problem of fraternization with the "enemy" whites and hours of their time have been spent clarifying the reasons for not fraternizing with whites and castigating Black men who became involved with white women. There has been concern about the disproportionate ratio of men to women and the need to keep Black men from establishing alliances with white women, thus further distorting the ratios.

Women in the movements of the '60s were given the responsibility for keeping Black men from becoming involved with white women; this was done through harangues and a modification of the old Communist "criticism and self-criticism." Much of the rationale was based on themes of race and ideological purity along with the necessity of providing social companionship for the Black women in the movement. This duty is in keeping with a traditional feminine role, that of modifying or being responsible for the behavior of the group in general and the males in particular.

Black women were never participants in any noticeable numbers in left wing political organizations; the few who were involved did so as a result of trade union activity or a local issue. Defense organizations set up to work on behalf of a political or racial "cause celebre" have often captured the interests of Black women as spectators at rallies and meetings for brief periods of times. The Angela Davis case, a Black woman Communist professor charged with murder and participation in a prison break, was one of the most unusual cases of this type because a Black woman was the center of the controversy and directed the legal and public efforts to obtain her freedom. Usually left wing cases have not been overtly ideological or political but have been based on criminal convictions or arrests of Blacks who have been "framed" by the authorities, and generally the defense has been headed by men.

One might conclude that the "mainstream aspirations" of Black women are such that they have not been attracted to the separatist movements outside the Black community and only to those within the Black community that are traditional in nature or in form. The Garvey movement, the only successful nationalist group, attracted the fervor and devotion of thousands of Black lower and working class women, but the organizational form and tasks were quite similar to that of the lodges. The movement also required zeal and offered salvation from the burden of being Black in the United States and the hope of redemption in the bosom of Mother Africa.

The women's liberation movement has inherited the mantle of early 20th-century feminism but is of far different character since it is a melange of concerns and lifestyles reflecting the radically new perspectives of the latter 20th century. It is a creature of educated middle-class women, which encompasses unmarried, married, heterosexual, homosexual, celibate, employed, and unemployed. Its most radical demands and tactics have made the movement an easy target for satire in the mass media. However, its extreme demands have affected the thinking and programs of women and women's organizations. Opinion polls indicate that the majority of the American public favors equal pay for equal rights and is less hostile to the reality of women working; of course, the latter is affected by the presence of thousands of women in the labor force.

The demands of the women's liberation movement for freedom to control their bodies, to determine such matters as birth control and abortion, for child-care centers, an end to sexual stereotypes, freedom from the traditional marriage bonds, an end to laws that regard women as the chattel of their husbands are demands that well might help the social and economic position of Black women. However, the movement has been led by and closely identified with college-educated Caucasian women who have many more privileges than poor or working class women but little in common with the masses of Black women. The demands made by the leaders of the movement have been seen as frivolous and class oriented; Black women have been the domestic workers for this class of women and find little identification with them. Since Blacks must confront the issues of economic survival and political development, there is not much interest in becoming involved with a group which is seen as radical and ephemeral; the class orientation and origins of the leaders of the women's liberation movement make them appear to be antagonistic to the interests of Black women.

As Shulamith Firestone (1971, p. 435) notes, the movement was inspired by and borrowed from the civil rights movement; the language and tactics were adapted from that used by the civil rights activists who were attempting to gain greater freedom for Blacks. Picketing, sit-ins, strikes, marches, petitions, rallies, newsletters, legislative lobbying were some of the methods which were taken from the Black movement and have been a source of resentment among Black women. Since some of the tactics had been taken from the labor movement and have no copyrights, they were not the exclusive property of the Black movement either. However the resentment has been voiced more by Black men who find that many of the gains of the civil rights bills of the Equal Rights Act of 1968 have been made by women, particularly white women. This may be partially attributed to the pool of white women who were professionally trained and skilled but had not been in the labor force or were underemployed; this was true to a lesser extent for Blacks.

Black women have not responded to the women's liberation movement because their primary identification is racial rather than sexual and their interests are more closely aligned with those of the group as a whole rather than with women who represent the oppressors. Their future is seen being more directly linked to legislation or gains won for all Blacks.

There is also a strong conservative element within the Black community with a faith in the "American Dream" which is an obstacle to becoming a part of a radical group outside the mainstream of America or the Black community. If the women's movement had achieved more respectability or status in the perceptions of the majority community, it is likely that a few Black women would be involved on the same basis as some are members of groups like the YWCA. They would consider it a duty to have token participation because it would be seen as benefiting the race. However, they will not become a part of a movement that is seen as frivolous and set on gaining additional luxuries for women who already have a higher status than that of Black women. The more the movement is ridiculed by the mass media, the fewer Black women will participate because it is counter to the quest for respectability, and it is likely that more politically conscious Black women will set up a parallel organization to concentrate on realizing greater freedom for Black women.

Many Black women have achieved a strong sense of self and the sense of independence which is a goal of many of the participants in the women's lib movement. They are not concerned about sex dependency and clarifying sex roles in the same way that white women seeking independent identities are, because Black women are identified by American society as Black first and female second. It is in this way that Black women identify themselves, recognizing that the majority in the society considers them to be the polar opposite of the feminine ideal.

Black women want to achieve equal rights and opportunities for the group and consider that goal paramount over any interests they may have in sexual discrimination. They function as the conservators of tradition in Black communities, maintaining those institutions and associations which supplement the role of the family; their primary role of socializing the young exerts great force in keeping the community within traditional limits. Black women not only maintain the cultural interests of the racial group but are a cohesive force in the community, helping it adjust to changing conditions and keeping it from being enveloped by a hostile society.

As a conservative force within the Black community, Black women have avoided and will continue to avoid involvement with groups that are outside the mainstream of the Black community. Their eyes are on the stars while their hands are on the plow, and they will continue to play the traditional helping role of women while asserting the strong sense of self necessary for survival.

## REFERENCES


Bernard, Jessie. *Marriage and Family Among Negroes.* Englewood Cliffs: Prentice-Hall, 1966.

Coles, Robert. *Children of Crisis.* Boston: Little, Brown, 1964.

Cronon, Edmund D. *Black Moses: The Story of Marcus Garvey and the Universal Negro Improvement Association.* Madison: The University of Wisconsin Press, 1966.

Essien-Udom, E.U. *Black Nationalism: A Search for Identity in America.* New York: Dell, 1965.

Fanon, Frantz. *Black Skin, White Masks* New York: Grove Press, 1967.

Firestone, Shulamith. "The Women's Rights Movement in the U.S.: A New View," in *Voices From Women's Liberation,* edited by Leslie B. Tanner. New York: The New American Library, 1971.

Frazier, E. Franklin. *The Negro Family in the United States.* Chicago: University of Chicago Press, 1966.

Grier, William H., and Cobbs, Price M. *Black Rage.* New York: Bantam Books, 1968.

Herskovits, Melville J. *The Myth of the Negro Past.* Boston: Beacon Press, 1958.

Lerner, Gerda (Ed.). *Black Women in White America: A Documentary History.* New York: Vintage Books, 1973.

United States Department of Commerce, Bureau of the Census. *The Social and Economic Status of the Black Population in the United States, 1971,* Washington, D.C.: U.S. Government Printing Office, 1972.

# 28
# *The Equations of Oppression* *

HOWARD F. TAYLOR

This essay is about the statistical equations that ultimately result in the increased oppression of black people. They are the equations of oppression. They reflect what I call "quantitative racism," a variety of racism that results in oppression in the same manner as any other form or type of racism. I define *quantitative racism* as the intentional *or* unintentional misuse of statistical and quantitative methods in the behavioral sciences to show, either directly or indirectly, explicitly or implicitly, some kind or type of ethnic superiority, usually with respect to black-white differences. Through various feats of statistical magic, black persons are made to appear "inferior" to whites in regard to such things as "inherited" intelligence, achievement, motivation, family structure, crime, and so forth. It is possible to clearly locate statistical and methodological fallacies and errors in certain studies precisely because the scientific method, particularly in its more quantitative aspects, provides a set of criteria against which one or more studies may be judged. To the degree that a particular study or inquiry draws conclusions that blacks are in some way inferior to whites, and to the degree that it also violates clearly identifiable principles of quantitative research in doing so, then to that degree the study or inquiry in question is racist.

The purpose of this essay is to identify some fallacious applications of statistical methods which are common to a number of recent studies in the professional behavioral science literature, especially studies concerning black and white intelligence. Although I cite various treatises below, I will focus on the following four: (a) Jensen's (1969) well-known, well-publicized article on the racial "heritability" of I.Q.; (b) a recent book by H.J. Eysenck (1971), which is little more than a sloppy, ill-written popularization of Jensen, and which has received wide and favorable promotion in such "respectable" media as *The New York Times Book Review;* (c) a popular *Atlantic* magazine article on the history of I.Q. testing by R. Herrnstein (1971), later written up, virtually unchanged, as a book (Herrnstein, 1973); and (d) an article by S. Scarr-Salapatek (1971a; cf. 1971b), published in *Science,* which, though methodologically more sound than the other works, nevertheless reveals certain errors. Eysenck's book and Herrnstein's article were written primarily for popular consumption, whereas the works of Jensen and Scarr-Salapatek are intended primarily for professional behavioral scientists.

Although Jensen's paper has already been heavily criticized,[1] it is being considered here for two reasons: First, some criticisms given below have not yet appeared in the professional literature; and second, there are methodological-statistical errors which are common to the work of the four scientists, errors which can be best understood by examining them as a group. In brief, this essay is a short lesson on "how to lie with statistics in the study of black-white differences in intelligence."

## RACE, HERITABILITY, AND I.Q.: COMMON FALLACIES AND ERRORS

The core thesis of Jensen and Eysenck, and to a great extent Herrnstein, is precisely as follows: (a) Blacks and whites differ significantly and markedly in average I.Q. Overall, the mean I.Q. of blacks is approximately 15 points below that of whites. (b) Differences in (the "variance" in) I.Q. are largely explainable by hereditary (genetic) factors; the "heritability" of I.Q. (for white populations) is approximately .80, or 80 percent, which means, statistically speaking, that 80 percent of the total variance in human I.Q. is attributable to genetic endowment, and the remainder (20 percent) to environmental variables and/or to the statistical interaction of heredity and environment. (c) Blacks constitute a "breeding population" in the sense that child-producing unions are more likely to occur among blacks than between whites and blacks. (d) There are many genetic differences between races which are clearly measurable (certain anatomical differences; sickle-cell anemia, etc.). (e) Therefore, all things considered, black people *genetically inherit* less intelligence than white people.

This line of reasoning is not new, of course. It goes even farther back in antiquity than Hitler or even Galton himself, the alleged originator of the "theory" of genetic racial inferiority. What *is* new is the recent marshalling of massive bodies of quantitative, statistical "evidence" and modern research methodology to support the claim. But the evidence and pro-

*Revision, prepared for this volume, of an earlier article by the author (Taylor, 1972).

cedures are faulty. The work of these scientists reads like a textbook on what *not* to do in quantitative research. Let us turn to a close look at the kinds of errors that are made.

*1. The fallacies of reification and unidimensionality.* "Intelligence" is an abstract concept, like the abstract concepts of "social class," or even "race" itself, and is only imperfectly measurable. Nonetheless, current research procedure in the behavioral sciences demands that concepts be at least somehow measurable by means of operational definitions or "indicators"; otherwise, empirical research would be impossible. Social class is commonly measured by such indicators as occupation, education, or income; race, by such observable indicators as skin color, hair texture, and so on; and intelligence, by where a person puts a pencil mark on an "intelligence test."

To presume that intelligence is *that which* is measured by current intelligence tests is to make concept and indicator one and the same – to "reify" the concept. To reify is fallacious because literally any concept used in research is subject to a great range of possible sources of measurement error, many of which are neither recognizable nor controllable. Perhaps I.Q. tests do not tap recently recognized or "newer" dimensions of intelligence, such as creativity (measurement error due to inadequate "sampling of indicators"); or, as in the case of black populations, perhaps I.Q. tests do not tap relevant aspects of black language or culture (measurement error due to culture bias); or, perhaps black children do not like to take tests from white teachers (measurement error due to factors in the "test situation"); and so on through other possible sources of measurement error, which are numerous.

The fallacy of reification is so old and well recognized in the behavioral sciences that any Ph.D. candidate, black or white, is expected to be thoroughly familiar with its intricacies and pitfalls. This is why it is perplexing that certain behavioral scientists such as Jensen, Eysenck, and Herrnstein, state quite clearly that for their purposes, there is really not much more of importance to the concept of "general intelligence" than what has been measured by popular I.Q. tests such as the Binet, Wechsler, or Thorndike-Lorge. These scientists base their argument primarily upon two beliefs: First, that I.Q. revealed in early childhood is linearly correlated with later performance in school, college, and jobs; namely, that a person's I.Q. has a certain "predictive validity." But this conclusion is based on research done almost exclusively on white populations, and even among whites the prediction is subject to considerable qualification. Among blacks, the prediction is even more tenuous. The second belief involves the supposed "unidimensionality" of human intelligence.

The so-called finding that intelligence is unidimensional is a fallacy closely allied to the reification fallacy, and it is somewhat easier to document. In brief, if most of the indicators of a concept (the actual questions or items on an I.Q. test) intercorrelate highly with each other across a large sample of people, then the concept is usually regarded as "unidimensional." If two or more sets or "clusters" of intercorrelations appear, then the usual inference is that the concept could well be "multidimensional."

The dimensionality of the concept of intelligence is generally examined through the technique of factor analysis.[2] Eysenck, Herrnstein, Scarr-Salapatek, and especially Jensen, all argue that factor analyses of white samples consistently reveal a single factor or dimension underlying I.Q. tests; this "general factor" has been labeled "*g*," or "general intelligence." But there is a consistent error involved here: Literally all of the factor analysis studies cited by Jensen, and most of those cited by the other authors, use what is called the *principal component* factor extraction, a procedure which mathematically solves for a first factor from the correlation matrix by maximizing the correlation between itself and each item on the I.Q. test, and which thus permits any remaining factors to correlate relatively less with the test items. What this all means is that principal component technique is *designed* to explain the maximum possible variance among the test items, thus running the risk of allowing one to conclude, as do Jensen and the others, that intelligence is "unidimensional." But arriving at a single factor or "dimension" is more a *property of the technique* used, not a property of the test items. Can one justifiably conclude that intelligence is "unidimensional" if one bases that conclusion on a statistical technique which in effect makes it unidimensional? I don't think so. There are, of course, factor analysis procedures other than the principal component option which are available; studies using these other techniques are rarely cited by Jensen and the others.

Another problem is that inferences about the dimensionality of intelligence are based almost exclusively on white samples.[3] It could be that intelligence is unidimensional for white populations, but multidimensional for black populations. The fact is, no one really knows. To infer from data gathered *on whites* that the dimensionality of black people's intelligence is the same (or nearly so) as that of whites, is clearly nonsensical. Nevertheless, many behavioral scientists such as those cited will insist on making the inference anyway.

*2. Erroneous calculations of "heritability."* The principle of heritability, borrowed from genetics by Jensen and the three others (all psychologists), is theoretically defined as the percent of the total variance in any observable or "phenotypic" variable (as tested I.Q.) that is attributable to genotypic (genetic or hereditary) variables. This works out to be the square of the correlation between any genetic variable and any phenotypic variable. An analysis of variance statistical model (discussed again below) is employed by Jensen and the others in estimating heritability. But since the genes "for" intelligence cannot be assessed as directly as for other phenotypic traits – say, eye color, or height; Jensen and the others openly acknowledge this – the estimate of I.Q. heritability is made by what is euphemistically called "indirect" methods. The indirect method usually employed is to correlate the I.Q.s of monozygotic (identical) twins who were raised in (presumably) different environments, since monozygotic twins are known to have exactly the same genes. If their environments are in fact uncorrelated with each other, then the correlation between their I.Q.s (or so the argument goes) could be attributable to genes only. Based on Jensen, Eysenck, and Herrnstein, this (squared) correlation comes out to be about .80; or, the "heritability" of I.Q. is approximately 80 percent, which means that only 20 percent is attributable to environment or to genetic-environment interaction.

While this procedure may sound interesting and even make sense to some, it is faulty. Here is why:

a. Monozygotic twins probably also have similar, or even identical, *prenatal environments.* The prenatal environment, including such things as nutrition, blood supply, and a host of other things, is an environmental set of variables, not a genetic set, and these prenatal environmental variables can in turn be heavily affected by one's social environment – what one eats, medical care, and so on. Thus similarity in prenatal environment is confounded within the above twin-correlation of .80; and thus, the effects of genes cannot be separated from the effects of similar prenatal environmental variables. Hence, the monozygotic twin correlation is not a true estimate of heritability, but an overestimate of it. Because of this, a true heritability coefficient, using the data Jensen himself cites, would necessarily have to be less than .80.

b. There is considerable evidence, uncovered since the original Jensen (1969) article, that the twin pairs cited by Jensen, Herrnstein, and Eysenck – twins who were presumably raised in uncorrelated environments – were nevertheless raised in highly similar (thus correlated) environments (Kamin, 1974). In fact, many of the supposed "separated" twins were raised in different branches of the *same* family, in the same neighborhoods, attended the same schools, and often even played together. Furthermore, a fair number of twins were not separated in any way whatever until relatively late in life – that is, after the effect of considerable environmental similarity. Thus, a fair amount, indeed a great amount, of the correlation between their I.Q.s is explainable by environment. The correlation (the estimate of "heritability") is thus artificially inflated.

c. Statistical estimates of heritability, *even in a theoretical sense,* are highly unstable (unreliable) if any analysis of variance model is used because of what is called "multicollinearity" (or "covariance") between the genetic and environmental sets of variables. Any estimate of genotype-phenotype correlation is highly unreliable, and interpretations of explained variance are difficult if not impossible. Furthermore, if multicollinearity (covariance) exists, then a certain amount of the variation in I.Q. will be explainable by it, and thus, the percent explained by 'genes" will be relatively less. By not considering this, Jensen and the others once again artificially inflate the "heritability" estimate.

d. Eysenck and Herrnstein base their heritability estimate on Jensen, who in turn based his estimates on studies using relatively small sample sizes. A small sample size increases the unreliability of *any* statistic gotten on the particular sample.

e. Eysenck (on p. 112) states that the 80 percent figure is a "fact" and "... not really in dispute." This is a gross lie. It is in great dispute; the professional literature has been filled with criticism of it, most of which was published *before* Eysenck's book was written.[4] Similarly, Herrnstein does not appear to be aware of the fact that the .80 percent figure has come under great dispute.

f. Jensen and Eysenck both attempt to generalize the .80 heritability estimate, gotten on white samples, to black samples. This is simply not possible to do, as any elementary statistics textbook will clearly indicate. Eysenck (on p. 67) even goes so far as to state that heritability estimates for blacks "... would not differ very greatly from the 80 percent or so quoted for white populations." Herrnstein makes the same mistake (on p. 55 of his article). This conclusion is utterly absurd; even Scarr-Salapatek (1971a) in studying black monozygotic twins, has found the black twin-correlation to be considerably *less* than the supposed 80 percent figure for white twins (i.e., about 40 percent).

g. It must be pointed out that *even if* one were to obtain reliable heritability estimates separately for *both* black and white twins, one could still not infer, even statistically, that blacks "inherit" less I.Q. Essentially, this is because such an inference would be about a *between-race* comparison but based on *within-race* data. Yet, investigators like Jensen, Eysenck, and Herrnstein will insist that such a totally fallacious inference is valid.

*3. The syllogistic fallacy.* Herrnstein (1971 and 1973) advances an argument in the form of a logical syllogism that is frequently heard, an argument which forms the central thesis of his entire article and book. Its logic might sound compelling to some at first glance:

a. (First premise) if differences in mental abilities are largely inherited, and
b. (Second premise) if success, earnings, and prestige in society require those abilities,
c. (Conclusion) *then* success, earnings, and prestige will depend upon inherited differences among people.

Thus, Herrnstein concludes that people tend to genetically inherit success in society, and, by thinly veiled implication, since black people are obviously less "successful" than whites, the inferior genes possessed by blacks are primarily responsible. Herrnstein bases the first premise on the syllogism on the exceedingly questionable .80 heritability estimate discussed above. Let us assume, *just for the sake of argument,* that this is a correct figure. *Even* if it is correct, it can be shown that the conclusion to the syllogism does not necessarily follow.

Herrnstein's syllogism may be restated in correlational terms, with no loss of meaning, and without misstating Herrnstein:

1. The greater a person's genetic endowment (abbreviated "G"), the greater his measured I.Q. score. Namely, the correlation between G and I.Q., abbreviated $r_{G,\ IQ}$, is high and positive (assume that this squared correlation is approximately .80).
2. The greater a person's I.Q. score, the greater his success, earnings, and prestige (abbreviated "S") in society. Namely, the correlation $r_{IQ,\ S}$ is positive (rather than negative).
3. Therefore, the greater a person's genetic endowment (G), the greater his success, earnings, and prestige (S). Namely, the correlaton $r_{G,\ S}$ will be positive, not negative.

What is being said here in effect is that if one variable (G) is positively correlated with a second variable (IQ), and if this second variable is positively correlated with a third (S), then the first (G) will be positively correlated with the third (S). While this may sound quite logical, even to those with some elementary training in statistics and correlation procedure, it is not necessarily so. Here is why: The first two positive correlations, $r_{G,\ IQ}$ and $r_{IQ,\ S}$, must be of a certain magnitude or greater in order to even predict whether or not the third correlation, that between G and S, will be positive or negative. Dealing *only* with these three variables (i.e., without introducing any other "control" variables or comparisons), it is statistically possible for the correlations $r_{G,\ IQ}$ and $r_{IQ,\ S}$ to be positive, but the $r_{G,\ S}$ correlation to be *negative* or even zero (nonexistent).

**TABLE 1**

A Simple Illustration of Inability to Predict the Sign of $r_{13}$ from Knowing the Signs of $r_{12}$ and $r_{23}$

| | Variable 1 | Variable 2 | Variable 3 |
|---|---|---|---|
| Person 1 | 1 | 1 | 3 |
| Person 2 | 3 | 4 | 3 |
| Person 3 | 5 | 2 | 1 |

$$r_{12} = +.33$$
$$r_{23} = +.19$$
$$r_{13} = -.88$$

A simple example will prove convincing; consult Table 1. Here, a small sample of three (hypothetical) people have scores on three variables. The correlation between variable 1 and variable 2 is positive (+.33); the correlation between variable 2 and variable 3 is also positive (+.19). But – contrary to what we might expect "logically" – variable 1 is *negatively* (not positively) correlated with variable 3 (and the correlation is quite high, at -.88). The reader is invited to check the calculations for himself. Thus, one cannot necessarily predict the direction of sign (+,-) of a third correlation from knowing the signs of the other two correlations. This is what Herrnstein's "syllogism" attempts to do.

In general, it can be shown that given *any* three variables, the sign of the third linear correlation can be predicted *if* (without further assumptions) the following condition holds for the first two correlations (cf. Costner and Leik, 1964; Yule and Kendall, 1950, pp. 301-302):

$$r^2_{12} + r^2_{23} \geqslant 1.00.$$

Thus, only if the square of the first two correlations sum to 1.00 or greater can one predict the sign of the third correlation (i.e., $r_{13}$). Using the Jensen-Herrnstein estimate of heritability (that $r^2_{G,IQ}$=.80), then

$$\begin{aligned} \text{let } r^2_{G,IQ} + r^2_{IQ,S} &= 1.00 \\ \text{thus } .80 + r^2_{IQ,S} &= 1.00 \\ \text{or } 80 + (.45)^2 &= 1.00 \\ \text{or } 80 + .20 &= 1.00, \end{aligned}$$

which means that the (unsquared) correlation between I.Q. and success *must be .45 or greater* in order for the conclusion to the syllogism to hold necessarily. The figure .45 is moderately high; neither Jensen nor Herrnstein present any evidence whatsoever regarding the I.Q. – success correlation or anything approximating it.

Recall that the heritability estimate of .80 is itself most tenuous and subject to great error. Other researchers have found heritability estimates as low as .40 (Scarr-Salapatek, 1971a), and others, as low as *zero* (Kamin, 1974). But even using the figure of .40 for $r^2_{G,IQ}$, then:

$$\begin{aligned} .40 + .60 &= 1.00 \\ \text{or } .40 + (.78)^2 &= 1.00, \end{aligned}$$

which means that the unsquared correlation between I.Q. and success would have to be quite high at approximately .78 or greater in order for the syllogism to hold. There is no evidence for this whatsoever. In sum, the syllogistic reasoning employed by Herrnstein, which was in turn based primarily upon Jensen's heritability estimate, simply does not hold up under close statistical scrutiny.

*4. The fallacy of equating socioeconomic status with "environment."* Consult Table 2, taken from Jensen's article. Note that the percent of children with I.Q.s below 75 (i.e., those who are presumably "retarded") increases as socioeconomic status (SES) decreases, both for whites and blacks separately, and that at each SES level, the percent of below-75 I.Q.s is always higher for blacks. Jensen (1969, p. 83) argues that the table shows "the environment" has little effect upon I.Q., since large differences between blacks and whites exist at all SES levels, even at the upper levels.

**TABLE 2**

Percent of Children With I.Q.s Below 75, by Socioeconomic Status (SES) and Race[a]

| SES | White | Black | Difference[b] |
|---|---|---|---|
| High 1 | 0.5 | 3.1 | 2.6 |
| 2 | 0.8 | 14.5 | 13.7 |
| 3 | 2.1 | 22.8 | 20.7 |
| 4 | 3.1 | 37.8 | 34.7 |
| Low 5 | 7.8 | 42.9 | 35.1 |

[a]Source: Jensen (1969, p. 83).
[b]These differences do not appear in Jensen's article.

Jensen (and Eysenck) manages to make *three* errors in this interpretation, all based on his failure to realize that "SES" and "environment" are not the same variable – a simple point, but somehow missed by him. Clearly, SES is only one extremely small part of one's environment, especially where black-white differences are concerned. (a) Thus, one may not conclude, as he does, that the table negates an "environmentalist" argument. (b) One may not assume, as he does, that blacks are comparable to whites even at a *given* SES level. Thus, the class 1 percent for whites (.5 percent) is not comparable to the class 1 percent for blacks (3.1 percent), and similarly for the other classes; there are a lot more differences in this society between "being black" and "being white" even if SES is similar, and these differences could well account for the findings. In short, additional environmental variables (as controls) would have to be introduced into such a table. Furthermore, the measure used for SES in the original study cited by Jensen appears to have been inadequate, even as a measure of SES alone. (c) Note the percentage differences in the last column of Table 2. These differences (or any other appropriate comparison, such as ratios) are not given in Jensen's article. What they show is that as SES increases, or becomes more "favorable," the differences in black versus white I.Q. *decrease* in a smooth fashion, and the differences at the highest SES level are quite small relative to the other differences. This would seem to support an "environmentalist" hypothesis rather than a "genetic" one, contrary to what Jensen says; or, at the very least, an hypothesis that SES and race *interact* statistically in a very marked way. Furthermore, it suggests that gene-environment interaction may not be zero, as Jensen consistently assumes.

The mistake of equating SES with environment is made in many places by Eysenck (1971). For example, on p. 103, he states that "... when educational and socio-economic differences between samples of blacks and whites compared for I.Q. are reduced or eliminated, marked score differences still remain ..." and thus, "these facts do not accord well with the environmentalist hypothesis." He even goes so far as to make a logically related kind of error – that of equating "black" with "nonwhite" (on p. 91), a fallacy so obvious and well-known that it needs no further comment ("black" and "nonwhite" are not equivalent categories).

5. *Misreading (their own) tables and figures.* An instance of Jensen's misreading his own tables and data was cited above. There are other instances in Jensen which could be discussed. A clear occurrence of misinterpretation occurs in Scarr-Salapatek's article; consult Table 3, taken directly from her article.

**TABLE 3**

Intercorrelations of Test Scores by Race and Social Class [a,b]

A. Black

| Test | Aptitude | | | Achievement | | | |
|---|---|---|---|---|---|---|---|
| | Verbal | Non Verbal | Total | Vocabulary | Reading | Language | Arithmetic |
| | | | Below median group (N=351)[c] | | | | |
| NV | .57 | | | | | | |
| T | .84 | .87 | | | | | |
| Vo | .56 | .44 | .54 | | | | |
| R | .56 | .47 | .59 | .64 | | | |
| L | .59 | .54 | .64 | .67 | .67 | | |
| A | .53 | .58 | .62 | .57 | .66 | .67 | |
| C | .64 | .57 | .67 | .82 | .84 | .86 | .83 |
| | | | Middle group (N=125) | | | | |
| NV | .71 | | | | | | |
| T | .90 | .89 | | | | | |
| Vo | .54 | .47 | .56 | | | | |
| R | .64 | .56 | .66 | .66 | | | |
| L | .67 | .54 | .65 | .66 | .75 | | |
| A | .60 | .53 | .60 | .64 | .72 | .73 | |
| C | .70 | .59 | .70 | .83 | .89 | .90 | .85 |
| | | | Above-median group (N=51) | | | | |
| NV | .53 | | | | | | |
| T | .82 | .86 | | | | | |
| Vo | .60 | .35 | .53 | | | | |
| R | .62 | .56 | .68 | .71 | | | |
| L | .68 | .55 | .71 | .74 | .87 | | |
| A | .55 | .65 | .68 | .61 | .81 | .77 | |
| C | .67 | .57 | .71 | .83 | .94 | .93 | .87 |

a. *From Scarr-Salapatek (1971a, p. 1289)*
b. *Abbreviations are: Nonverbal (NV), Total (T), Vocabulary (Vo), Reading (R), Language (L), Arithmetic (A), Composite (C).*
c *"Below median" means roughly "low SES," "middle group" means "middle SES," and "above-median" means "high SES."*

Table 3 (cont.) B. White

| Test | Aptitude | | | Achievement | | | |
|---|---|---|---|---|---|---|---|
| | Verbal | Non Verbal | Total | Vocabulary | Reading | Language | Arithmetic |
| | | | | Below-n | | | |
| NV | .44 | | | | | | |
| T | .81 | .83 | | | | | |
| Vo | .53 | -.04 | .31 | | | | |
| R | .62 | .30 | .51 | .61 | | | |
| L | .76 | .28 | .61 | .69 | .79 | | |
| A | .67 | .37 | .59 | .58 | .77 | .79 | |
| C | .75 | .26 | .58 | .81 | .87 | .92 | .89 |
| | | | | Middle group (N=43) | | | |
| NV | .57 | | | | | | |
| T | .88 | .85 | | | | | |
| Vo | .81 | .49 | .71 | | | | |
| R | .84 | .59 | .79 | .88 | | | |
| L | .71 | .51 | .69 | .75 | .85 | | |
| A | .60 | .52 | .63 | .64 | .71 | .77 | |
| C | .78 | .61 | .77 | .86 | .93 | .94 | .85 |
| | | | | Above-median group (N=147) | | | |
| NV | .66 | | | | | | |
| T | .81 | .88 | | | | | |
| Vo | .71 | .49 | .59 | | | | |
| R | .68 | .53 | .60 | .78 | | | |
| L | .69 | .61 | .66 | .73 | .74 | | |
| A | .70 | .70 | .74 | .66 | .71 | .78 | |
| C | .77 | .64 | .72 | .87 | .90 | .88 | .87 |

The table presents intercorrelations among various aspects (dimensions) of I.Q., especially with regard to how the so-called "aptitude" dimensions – (verbal (V), nonverbal (NV), and total (T) – correlate with the "achievement" dimensions – vocabulary (Vo), reading (R), language (L), arithmetic (A), and composite achievement score (C). In support of a currently held view among many educational psychologists, the author concludes that aptitude scores predict achievement scores equally well for blacks as for whites. She asserts: "As [the] table shows, the patterns of correlation among aptitude and achievement scores were quite similar in all groups, *regardless* of race or social class" (p. 1291, italics added).

But the table itself (Table 3) shows something strikingly different. Each entry represents a test intercorrelation for six separate race/class groups. Intercorrelations between aptitude and achievement dimensions are indicated by the enclosed box for each subtable. Thus, in Table 3A, the first entry, the figure .56, that for the "verbal" column and the "Vo" row, indicates that the correlation between verbal score (an aptitude dimension) and the vocabularly score (an achievement dimension) is .56.

Compare this figure in Table 3A (for low-SES blacks) to the one for low-SES whites (it is slightly less, at .53). Thus, for this given comparison, aptitude score is a slightly better predictor of achievement score for blacks than for whites. Noting that there are 15 such comparisons between low-SES blacks (Table 3A) and low-SES whites (Table 3B), the black correlation is higher than the white correlation in 11 of these 15 comparisons. Thus, aptitude-to-achievement predictions are somewhat more accurate for lower class blacks than for lower class whites.

But the correlations for the middle and high-SES groups show the direct *opposite:* In 12 (of 15 possible) comparisons for middle-SES blacks versus middle-SES whites, the *white* aptitude-to-achievement correlation is *higher* than for blacks. Similarly, for the high-SES groups, the white correlation is higher than the black one in 13 out of 15 comparisons (almost all of them).

What this means is that as SES increases, aptitude scores predict achievement scores better for whites than for blacks. *This is a clear general pattern revealed in Table 3.* This is discrepant with Scarr-Salapatek's interpretation of these very same data. It is most surprising that she does, in fact, conclude equal aptitude-achievement predictability for "all groups, regardless of race or social class."

Similar kinds of misinterpretation of tables can be seen in Eysenck.[5] For each of these instances of misinterpretation occurring in Jensen, Eysenck, and Scarr-Salapatek, the misinterpretations are almost always in the direction of supporting their own pet hypotheses.

*6. The culture-bias fallacy and a suggestion.* A well-known criticism of I.Q. testing, the idea that the tests have a built-in white and/or middle-class bias, deserves some comment. Jensen, Eysenck, Herrnstein, and Scarr-Salapatek all argue that certain "culture-free" types of tests (such as the Raven Progressive Matrices test) yield the same, or even larger black-white I.Q. differences, holding class constant, as do many of the culture-loaded tests such as the Binet, Weschler, or Thorndike-Lorge. Eysenck spends considerable time in his book stating that this is even further evidence that blacks "inherit" less intelligence than whites, since the "culture-free" tests can reveal larger differences.

There are two obvious faults in this reasoning. First, it is probably impossible to construct a truly "culture-free" or "culture-fair" test (even Jensen briefly alludes to this), since *any* test of any sort is bound to have certain cultural biases built into it. Simply learning the English language is itself a "culture bias." Second, these researchers ignore the *logical* possibility that a test be neither white-biased nor culture-free, but explicitly and intentionally black-biased. While this idea has certainly occurred to black psychologists (e.g., Williams, 1975), what has not yet been accomplished is the administration of a black-biased test to a large, cross-national sample of both blacks and whites (and possibly other groups also).

If such a test were developed, validated, and standardized on a relatively large scale, and if blacks averaged higher than whites on the test (they should, since this would in intself be part of the definition of a "black-biased" test), it is intriguing to note that if heritability coefficients were calculated using Jensen's (and the others') *own* procedures (i.e., monozygotic twin correlations), then one would conclude that blacks *inherit more* intelligence than whites! Naturally, however, such a conclusion would be subject to some of the very same criticisms discussed throughout this paper. The point is that *if* the very same methodological and statistical procedures employed by the others were used, and if a statistically significant I.Q. difference between black and white samples appeared, then this is precisely what one would *necessarily* have to conclude. Such a conclusion would then have the exact same validity in the scientific community as the conclusions of the scientists that I have cited. Clearly, the idea is worth some very serious investigation.

## OTHER FALLACIES AND ERRORS INVOLVING I.Q.

There are additional fallacies and errors cited which should be briefly mentioned. These involve: attempts to "snow" the reader with statistical manipulations which are unnecessary for the author's own purpose; the mathematical indeterminacy of heritability; fallacious inferences about causation; a disagreement between Eysenck and Herrnstein concerning heritability and its effect upon the "regression toward the mean" phenomenon; and the use of rats to study humans.

*7. Statistical "snow jobs."* Jensen is fond of presenting to the reader formulas and equations which, though correct in themselves, have no immediate bearing on his argument, and thus appear to be attempts to "snow" the reader. A case in point is his relatively famous and quite lengthy variance formula (Jensen, 1969, p. 34):

$$V_P \quad \frac{(V_G + V_{AM}) + V_D + V_I}{V_H} + \frac{V_E + 2Cov_{HE} + V_I}{V_E} + V_e$$

The components of this equation are: $V_P$= the total variance in the dependent phenotype variable (namely, I.Q.); $V_G$= variance attributable to the additive effect of genes; $V_{AM}$= variance attributable to "assortative" (selective) mating; $V_D$= variance attributable to genetic dominance-recessiveness; $V_i$=variance attributable to interaction among genes themselves. All these components refer to heredity ($V_H$) as a source of variance in I.Q. The environmental sources of variance are: $V_E$= variance due to all environmental variables; $2Cov_{HE}$= covariance (multicollinearity) between genetic and environmental variables; $V_I$= variance due to statistical interaction of heredity and environment; and $V_e$= variance due to measurement error (test unreliability).

This formula might seem most impressive to the casual reader. But it reduces to a simpler formula. Briefly,

a. Due to (yet another) misprint in the original article, the denominators $V_H$ and $V_E$ are not actually part of the formula, but were clearly intended by means of brackets and not division lines, as *labels* for the "heredity" (H) and environmental (E) components of the formula.[6] Hence, the two denominators drop out of the formula.

b. Although he briefly defines $V_{AM}$, $V_D$, and $V_i$, Jensen does not employ them in his later analysis. Thus, they could be usefully subsumed under the symbol, $V_H$ since mathematically $V_H$=$V_G$+$V_{AM}$+$V_D$+$V_i$.[7]

c. If one assumes an analysis of variance model with equal subclass samples (a model Jensen implicitly employs), then the correlation (covariance; multicollinearity) between H and E will be zero, and $2Cov_{HE}$=0, hence out of the formula.

Hence, we are left with a much simpler formula:

$$V_P = V_H + V_E + V_I + V_e,$$

which means: "The total variance in I.Q. is equal to the arithmetic sum of the variance explained by all heredity variables ($V_H$), the variance explained by all environmental variables ($V_E$), the variance explained by statistical interaction of heredity and environment ($V_I$), plus error ($V_e$)." This latter equation is simpler to comprehend, more to the point, more in line with the entirety of Jensen's article, and runs less of a risk of snowing the reader with unneccessary statistical magic.

d. Another error in the formula deserves mention. The "error term," $V_e$, contains far more than only "measurement error," contrary to Jensen. It would also contain variance due to nonlinearity, and variance due to other unspecified sources. By inadvertently leaving this out of $V_e$, Jensen (again) artificially inflates the heritability component ($V_H$).

e. Finally, we must note that even this latter formula (as the former one) is largely theoretical and relatively useless as it stands in actual data analysis. In order to apply it directly, one would require direct measurement of the "genes for" intelligence, and direct measurement of a very large range of environmental variables, both of which are utterly impossible.

*8. The indeterminacy of heritability.* Another attempt to "snow" the reader is somewhat more subtle. Jensen gives one the idea that heritability defined theoretically (i.e., as $V_H$) is somehow an empirically estimable quantity which one can actually obtain "by subtraction" if one can estimate the other components of the equation. But this is not the case. It can be shown (Taylor, 1973; 1974) that *even if* such things as $V_{AM}$ and $V_D$ are zero, there are still, at the minimum, *seven* unknown components of the total variance in IQ (i.e., $V_P$). Without going into detail, the true equation is:

$$\begin{aligned} V_P &= V_H + V_E + V_I \\ &+ 2Cov_{HE} + 2Cov_{HI} + 2Cov_{EI} \\ &+ V_e. \end{aligned}$$

This equation contains terms for the "multicollinearity" (covariance) between H and I ($2Cov_{HI}$) and between E and I ($2Cov_{EI}$). In other words, what is being considered here is the effect of heredity (H) *upon* interaction (I), and the effect of environment (E) *upon* interaction also. (Thus, interaction is being treated as a separate variable.) So, in sum, Jensen actually underestimates his task: There are an even greater number of unknowns in the situation than Jensen suspected. Not even *one* of these seven unknowns is empirically estimable (Layzer, 1974; Lewontin, 1974). Hence, the "heritability" of I.Q. is, mathematically speaking, indeterminate.

*9. Fallacious causal inferences.* In attempting the inference from the twin data that the heritability of I.Q. is approximately .80 (which is identical to saying that the $V_H$ component of the above formula is .80), Jensen and Eysenck also infer that there is a *causal* relation between genes and I.Q.; namely, that certain genes "cause" higher or lesser I.Q. scores.

Causal inferences[8] of this nature are not possible, primarily for three reasons: (a) In order to infer even tentatively that a set of heredity variables (H) are causally related to I.Q., a large range of environmental (E) variables would have to be held constant statistically. This, in fact, is what the above variance formula demands, according to recognized, standard statistical procedures. Most studies simply do not control for very many environmental variables; most studies in actuality control only for SES and then, as discussed above, commit the fallacy of equating SES with "environment." (b) Jensen and Eysenck do not treat E-variables as a set of causal variables in their own right. That is to say, they tend to ignore the possible ways in which E-variables can influence I.Q., and more importantly, the ways in which they directly influence *heredity* variables as well. It is known, for example, that environment *can* affect genes, as in the case of height in the U.S. and in Japan, which has increased markedly over the years due to medical advances – an environmental variable (Crow, 1969). Thus, even if H-variables determine I.Q., these H-variables can conceivably themselves become altered over a few generations due to environmental improvements. In contrast to what some might think, even a nearly perfect heritability coefficient (as in the case of height, which has heritability of nearly 1.00) does *not* mean "no environmental influences." (c) Finally, it should be noted that if in fact variance in H causes variance in E, which in turn causes variance in I.Q., with no direct causal connection between H and I.Q., then "equalizing" the environment among persons (as, by making education more equal) will *reduce* the heritability of I.Q. (Taylor, 1975), not increase it, as Herrnstein (1973) and some others (especially Jencks, 1972) have recently maintained.

*10. Heritability and "regression toward the mean."* A phenomenon long noted by geneticists is that a phenotypic trait of a child, such as his or her I.Q., is not the exact average of the I.Q.s of the parents, but tends to be closer to the population mean (an I.Q. of 100) rather than halfway between the I.Q.s of the parents. Thus, two parents with exceptionally high I.Q.s will have children whose I.Q.s are somewhat less than the average of their own (and thus closer to the mean of 100), and two parents with exceptionally low I.Q.s will have children whose I.Q.s are somewhat greater than theirs (thus closer to the mean). The child's I.Q. tends to be "pulled" or "regressed" in the direction of the mean, being pulled "up" in the case of parents who are below the population mean, and being pulled "down" in the case of parents who are above the mean.

Herrnstein (1971, p. 58) clearly states that the greater the heritability of a phenotypic trait, the *less* will be its tendency to regress toward the mean. But Eysenck (1971, p. 64) implies the direct opposite: The greater the heritability, the *more* the regression effect. Clearly, either Herrnstein is wrong and Eysenck is right, or vice versa. This is a clear out-and-out contradiction between two so-called "experts" on a simple statistical matter. One necessarily invalidates the other.

*11. Using rats to study humans.* Both Jensen and Eysenck insist on citing studies of rats and other animals to somehow support the contention that intelligence in humans is basically inherited. Despite the hesitancy of other psychologists to generalize findings on rats to humans, both of them do it anyway. They conclude, for example, that "maze bright" rats can be selectively mated, and over a few generations be clearly distinguished from "maze dull" rats, thus presumably showing that "intelligence" in rats is primarily inherited.

I am not going to argue the point of whether or not intelligence in rats, whatever that means, is primarily hereditary or primarily environmental. But to report rat data in an article or book about racial differences in human intelligence is stretching a point, to say the least. Neither author qualifies his conclusions about rats very much; each simply presents findings, and allows the reader to draw his own conclusions. Fortunately, most readers, even the most bigoted, are likely to conclude that rat studies (even those involving white rats versus black rats!) have very little to do with human racial differences.

## ERRORS IN OTHER AREAS OF BEHAVIORAL RESEARCH

The bulk of this essay was devoted to errors in present-day quantitative research which involve the question of black-white I.Q. differences. But errors of a methodological nature are not confined to the I.Q. issue. For example, we see major errors involving black versus white family structure in the notorious Moynihan report;[9] we see incorrect inferences concerning motivation and achievement differences among black and white schoolchildren in the Coleman report.[10] Still other kinds of errors are present, and difficult to document, simply because they appear in so many studies in sociology, psychology, and other behavioral sciences. Three examples are:

a. What is known in modern sociology as the dangers of *ecological correlation* – assuming that correlations among aggregate variables permit conclusions about people. For example, one often hears that "the higher the percent of blacks in a neighborhood, the higher the crime rate." To infer from this that blacks commit more crime than whites is erroneous, since there are a number of plausible explanations for this finding (it could be that the higher the percent of blacks in an area, causes the *whites* in those areas to commit crimes).[11] It must be mentioned that Scarr-Salapatek's article, discussed above, attempts to measure the social class of the *individual*, both black and white, by measuring the socioeconomic characteristics of the individual's *neighborhood – a crystal-clear instance of the ecological fallacy.*

b. *Extreme unreliability of measurement* for such "social disorganization" indicators as crime data, suicide data, and so on. As is well-known, crime data tend to be grossly unreliable for studying black-white differences, since a black committing a given crime is far more likely to be booked and included in the Uniform Crime Reports (a basic source of crime data for sociologists) than is a white who commits the exact same crime. Similarly, suicide data, used widely by some sociologists, is notoriously unreliable since suicides get recorded in vital statistics departments as nonsuicides in higher proportion for white and/or middle-class persons, thus artificially inflating the suicide rate for black and/or lower class persons. Despite the fact that certain sociologists recognize such errors in crime and suicide data, they nevertheless write lengthy articles about black-white differences in crime and suicide – and then conclude that blacks are "more unstable" or "more alientated" than whites, or some such nonsense.

c. *Errors in the U.S. Census.* A major source of data for the study of black-white differences, the U.S. Census, itself is subject to sources of measurement error. The inaccuracies growing out of blacks' answers to questions asked at the door by white Census interviewers are no doubt numerous and, more importantly, relatively uncodified and unknown. Furthermore, sampling error in Census data could well be great. And a whole range of other kinds of errors probably exist with Census data. Yet, hundreds of articles on black-white differences based upon Census data appear in the professional sociology and psychology journals every day.

## CONCLUDING REMARKS

This essay advances the view that while certain uses and applications of the scientific method are racist, the scientific method itself is relatively free from institutional racism. In fact, the canons of "good" research themselves become the criteria for critically evaluating the Jensens, Eysencks, and Herrnsteins; they can be shown to be wrong mainly through comparing them against certain identifiable methodological principles as done above. In this way, the scientific method is in effect used "against itself."

Black scholars might also address themselves to a second, related issue: Given that certain applications of scientific principles are racist, is it because the scientific method is itself racist? (This distinction very roughly parallels an analogous controversy among black psychologists and psychiatrists concerning whether, for example, the "basic" psychological make-up of whites and blacks is similar, and differs only in consequence and adaptive ability – a view advanced by Grier and Cobbs (1968) among others – or whether observable differences in black and white culture and personality are due to fundamental psychodynamic differences – a view held by White and Poussaint, among others.)[12]

Regardless of which view one holds, it is nevertheless clear that black scientists and scholars must begin to criticize, *in detail,* the work of racist researchers to a greater degree than they have in the past. To simply state angrily, as do many black scholars and scientists, that "Jensen is just wrong, and that is that," is perhaps necessary, but it is definitely not sufficient. What is needed is critical attention to detail, close scrutiny of figures and methods, and extensive codification of fallacies. We are reminded of the nuclear scientists' vain cry that they "never intended" their findings to be used for the massive destruction of the people of a single race by means of an inconceivably powerful bomb. It therefore sounds familiarly unconvincing when Jensen and Eysenck state, as they have, that they "never intended" their conclusions to be used for the suppression or destruction of a race. This "warning" is particularly hollow when we see that on February 24, 1972, Arthur R. Jensen presented his findings before the U.S. Senate Select Committee on Education.[13] Science is indeed the racist's most potent weapon. The dismantling of this weapon must come not only from white academicians of liberal disposition, as in the past, but in addition, from black scientists and scholars themselves.

## NOTES

[1] See, for example, *Harvard Educational Review* (1969a, 1969b). Since this early criticism, Jensen and the others have been extensively criticized in the scientific literature.

[2] For detailed descriptions of the factor analysis technique, see Harman (1960) and Rummel (1970). For a complete discussion of related techniques involving cluster analysis and hierarchical multidimensional arrangement of indicators, see Sokal and Sneath (1963).

[3] One exception is Scarr-Salapatek (1971a). Although her own data (p. 1289) show different dimensions for black as opposed to white samples, she does not point this out in her article. More on this later.

[4] No less than 12 articles criticizing the original Jensen article and its heritability estimates appeared in immediately following issues of the *Harvard Educational Review,* all well

before Eysenck's book (1971) was written. For reprints of the 12 papers, see *Harvard Educational Review* 1969a, 1969b). See also Scarr-Salapatek (1971) for different heritability estimates based on twins.

[5] As one example, Eysenck (1971, p. 53) clearly misinterprets his own table which relates "evoked potentials" (brain waves), a presumed indicator of intelligence, to I.Q. scores. While he says that the table shows "wave lengths are shortest for the brightest, longest for the dullest subjects," one table on the very same page shows the opposite. In addition, he assumes that "evoked potentials" have some bearing on intelligence, an hypothesis for which there is very little, if any, evidence to date.

[6] The formula is stated as given above in Jensen's original article. However, in a subsequent article, the formula is given without denominators, which is in fact correct, since the formula is a standard equation for the sum of components of variance (variation). In this subsequent article, the formula is given as follows (see Jensen, 1970, p. 80):

$$V_P = (V_G + V_{AM}) + V_D + V_i + V_E + 2Cov_{HE} + V_I + V_e$$

where $V_H = (V_G + V_{AM}) + V_D + V_i$

and $V_E = V_E + 2Cov_{HE} + V_I$

[7] It is worth noting yet another possible error in the formula. Variance due to assortative mating, $V_{AM}$, should appear under the environmental ($V_E$) component, and not under the heredity ($V_H$) component. Any variance due to assortative or "selective" mating is a social, or environmental phenomenon, not a genetic one. Hence, $V_{AM}$ is mis-classified, and causes false inflation of the $V_H$ component, and thus false inflation of the theoretical estimate of heritability. Hence, we see yet another source of false inflation of the heritability estimate.

[8] My criticisms (Taylor, 1975) in regard to causation are based primarily upon work in sociology on the logic of causal inference. For example, see Blalock (1961, 1971), Duncan (1966), and Heise (1969), among others.

[9] See, for example, Staples (1970).

[10] See, for example, Grant (1972).

[11] It can be shown that with a *given* body of data, the correlation between X and Y can be in one direction (positive, negative) using collectives (neighborhoods) as the unit of analysis (hence, giving an "ecological correlation"), and in the other direction using the very same data but treating the person as the unit of analysis. See Robinson (1950). In certain instances one can, however, infer individual correlations from ecological correlations. See Cartwright (1969), and Shiveley (1969).

[12] See the March 1970 issue of *The Black Scholar,* devoted to black psychology.

[13] Arthur R. Jensen, Statement Before the Senate Select Committee on Education, February, 1972, manuscript. In this statement, Jensen reiterates his original position: "It is a reasonable hypothesis that genetic factors are involved in the average black-white I.Q. difference . . ." and that "The fact that the high heritability of I.Q., therefore, makes it a very reasonable and likely hypothesis that genetic factors are involved in the black-white I.Q. difference."

## REFERENCES


Blalock, Hubert M. *Causal Inferences in Nonexperimental Research,* Chapel Hill: University of North Carolina Press, 1961.

Blalock, Hubert M. *Causal Models in the Social Sciences,* Chicago: Aldine-Atherton, 1971.

Cartwright, Desmond S. "Ecological Variables," in Edgar F. Borgatta (Ed.)., *Sociological Methodology1969,* San Francisco: Jossey-Bass, 1969.

Costner, Herbert L., and Leik, Robert K. "Deductions from Axiomatic Theory." *American Sociological Review*, 29, December 1969, pp. 819-835.

Crow, James F. "Genetic Theories and Influences: Comments on the Value of Diversity." *Harvard Educational Review,* 39, Spring 1969.

Duncan, O. Dudley. "Path Analysis: Sociological Examples." *American Journal of Sociology,* 72, July 1966, pp. 1-16.

Eysenck, H.J. *The I.Q. Argument.* New York: Library Press, 1971.

Grant, Gerald. "Review Essay." *Harvard Educational Review,* 42 February 1972, pp. 109-125.

Grier, William H. and Cobbs, Price M. *Black Rage.* New York: Bantam, 1968.

Harman, Harry H. *Modern Factor Analysis.* Chicago: University of Chicago Press, 1960.

*Harvard Educational Review. Environment, Heredity, and Intelligence.* Reprint Series No. 2, Cambridge, Mass., 1969a.

*Harvard Educational Review. Science, Heritability, and I.Q.,* Reprint Series No. 4, Cambridge, Mass., 1969b.

Heise, David R. "Problems in Path Analysis and Causal Inference," in Edgar F. Borgatta, (Ed.), *Sociological Methodology.* San Francisco: Jossey-Bass, 1969.

Herrnstein, Richard J. "I.Q." *The Atlantic,* 228, September 1971, pp. 43-64.

Herrnstein, Richard J. *I.Q. in the Meritocracy.* Boston: Atlantic-Little, Brown, 1973.

Jencks, Christopher, *et al. Inequality: A Reassessment of the Effects of Family and Schooling in America.* New York: Basic Books, 1972.

Jensen, Arthur R. "How Much Can We Boost I.Q. and Scholastic Achievement?", *Harvard Educational Review,* 39 (Winter, 1969, Cambridge, Mass.), pp. 1-123.

Jensen, Arthur R. "Another Look at Culture-Fair Testing," *in Jerome Hellmuth,* (Ed.), *Disadvantaged Child,* Vol. 3, New York, Brunner-Mazel, 1970.

Jensen, Arthur R. *Statement Before the Senate Select Committee on Education* February 24, 1972, manuscript.

Kamin, Leon J. *The Science and Politics of I.Q.* New York: Wiley, 1974.

Layzer, David. "Heritability Analyses of I.Q. Scores: Science or Numerology?" *Science,* 183, March 29, 1974, pp. 1259-1266.

Lewontin, Richard C. "The Analysis of Variance and The Analysis of Causes," *American Journal of Human Genetics,* 26, 1974, pp. 400-411.

Robinson, W.S. "Ecological Correlations and the Behavior of Individuals," *American Sociological Review,* 15, June 1950, pp. 351-357.

Rummel, R.J. *Applied Factor Analysis,* Evanston: Northwestern University Press, 1970.

Scarr-Salapatek, Sandra "Race, Social Class and I.Q." *Science,* 174, December, 1971a, pp. 1285-1295.

Scarr-Salapatek, Sandra "Unknown in the I.Q. Equation," *Science,* 172, December, 1971b, pp. 1223-1228.

Shively, W. Phillips. "Ecological Inference," *American Political Science Review,* December, 1969, pp. 1183-1196.

Sokal, R.R., and Sneath, P.H.A. *Principles of Numerical Taxonomy.* San Francisco: Freeman, 1963.

Staples, Robert. "The Myth of Black Matriarchy," *The Black Scholar,* February, 1970.

Taylor, Howard F. "Quantitative Racism: A Partial Documentation." *Journal of Afro-American Issues,* 1, Summer, 1972, pp. 1-20.

Taylor, Howard F. "Playing the Dozens with Path Analysis: Methodological Pitfalls in Jencks *et al., Inequality,*" *Sociology of Education,* 46, Fall, 1973, pp. 433-450.

Taylor, Howard F. "Review Essay." *Journal of the American Statistical Association,* 69, December, 1974, pp. 1043-1044.

Taylor, Howard F. "A Causal Analysis of 'Meritocracy' Arguments," manuscript, Cornell Conference on Genetics and Social Policy, Ithaca, N.Y., 1975.

Williams, Robert L. "The BITCH-100: A Culture-Specific Test." *Journal of Afro-American Issues,* 3, Winter, 1975, pp. 103-116.

Yule, G. Udny, and Kendall, M.G. *An Introduction to the Theory of Statistics,* New York: Hafner, 1950

# 29
## *Playing the Dozens with Path Analysis* *†

HOWARD F. TAYLOR

As some may already know, black people of all ages frequently play an interpersonal one-upsmanship game called "the Dozens." The basic idea of the game is to cleverly insult someone by insulting members of one's family, usually by making derisive comments, preferably of a sexual nature, about one's mother. One ordinarily learns the game during the elementary school years, and often continues to play it on into adulthood. To be good at it, one must possess considerable wit and "street" verbal facility – also an ability to take it as well as dish it out. The game can involve varying degrees of sophistication, such that one who insults the other by indirect, roundabout references to the other's mother is more likely to "win" (that is, receive approval of the audience) than someone who merely makes more obvious, direct unimaginative verbal attacks. The level of sophistication of the game increases as the ridicule of the mother and/or family becomes more indirect and oblique.[1]

Certainly a high level of sophistication in Dozens-playing has now been achieved by Christopher Jencks and his associates at Harvard in their recently published and much publicized study, *Inequality* (Jencks *et al.*, 1972). While Jencks himself may not know it, his analysis represents the Dozens at its best. Employing the sophisticated techniques of multiple linear regression and path analysis, and using data previously gathered in the Coleman *et al.* (1966) report and in other studies such as Project Talent and the Blau-Duncan (1967) study of American occupations, the Jencks' study finds, among other things, that: (a) the number of years a person spends in school has little effect upon later occupational and income attainment, and therefore (b) the main determinants of occupational and income success in society lie not with the amount of education that a person gets, but with what he brings to school with him, such as his genes, his "inherited" intelligence, his family background, and of course, his "luck" or lack of it, a set of variables which appear in the analysis as – quite appropriately – unexplained variance." In fact, that which Jencks and Co. do not explain greatly exceeds that which they do manage to explain, and we have a 400-page document about how not to find anything in social research.

The clear policy implication, as discussed by Jencks, is that modifying the education institution will do very little in the way of eliminating occupational and income inequality, and thus, the income distribution in society should be *made* to be more equal by a program of income insurance. A further policy implication, though denied by Jencks after publication of the report (Jencks, 1972), is that federal and state funding to education should be reduced, and money used in the past to attempt to educate the poor (and largely black) population would better be spent on something else.

Moynihan has tried the Dozens before, arguing that the so-called "inadequate matriarchal" structure of the black family prevents the success of blacks in society, but a lack of statistical sophistication in the Moynihan report made it suspect. The Coleman (1966) report similarly concluded, among other things, that the ills of blacks were, so to speak, "all in the family." But Coleman did so by being one-up on Moynihan through the use of the elaborate sophistications of multiple regression. Finally, we now have even more statistical sophistication in the "Jencks' report," as it will no doubt come to be called, which, using the quantitative magic of path analysis, reaches new heights in playing the Dozens.

### THE PITFALLS OF PATH ANALYSIS

The virtual entirety of the Jencks' study is based upon one technique, path analysis, where the path coefficients, as measures of the effects of variables, are derived from zero-order correlations obtained in past studies. The zero-order correlations, rather than actual data matrices, serve as the input for the path analyses. Two kinds of analyses are performed: those analyzing occupational and income inequality as the dependent variables (in Appendix B and chapters two, and five through seven); and those assessing the "heritability" of IQ scores (in Appendix A and chapter three). The majority of the text discussion is based upon the two appendices.

A good part (certainly not all) of Jencks' conclusions about inequality in America is based on one path model, presented here as Fig. 1, where the path coefficients (accompanying the single-headed arrows) and correlations (accompanying the

*I would like to thank the following people for helpful comments on an earlier draft of this review: Al Mazur, Dave Edelstein, Lou Kriesberg, Robert Althauser, Kent Smith, and Barbara Gunn.

†From *Sociology of Education,* Vol. 46, No. 4, Fall 1973, 433-450, by permission.

double-headed arrows) are given in the conventional manner. The square of any given path coefficient, $p_{ij}^2$, represents the proportion of variance in variable *i* that is explained by variable *j*, with other assumed causally prior variables stated in the model held constant. Thus it is seen, for example, that $(.883)^2$ or 78 percent of the variance in income is left unexplained by all variables in the model; that education has little effect upon income; and that IQ heritability ($h^2$) is assumed here to be $(.707)^2$ or about 50 percent, meaning that approximately 50 percent of the variance in IQ is explained by genes. (They use a different estimate of heritability in other places in the report; more on this later.) The investigators term this single path model their "best effort at describing the determinants of adult success in America . . ." (p. 346).

**Fig. 1 A Path Model of Effects Upon Income and Occupation, for Native White Nonfarm Males***

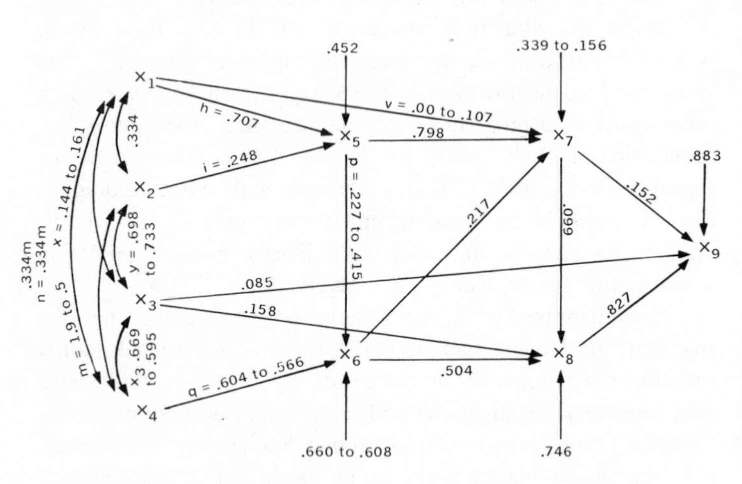


$X_1$ = respondent's genotype
$X_2$ = family background, IQ
$X_3$ = father's occupation
$X_4$ = family background, education
$X_5$ = respondent's child IQ score, measured at grade six
$X_6$ = respondent's education
$X_7$ = respondent's adult IQ, measured on a military classification test
$X_8$ = respondent's occupation
$X_9$ = respondent's income

Note: $X_1$, $X_2$, and $X_4$ are unmeasured constructs; all remaining variables are measured variables.

*Adapted from Jencks *et al.* (1972), p. 346.

It is unfortunate that Jencks and associates chose to rely so heavily upon path analysis, with all of its severe limitations, to draw conclusions so important in their policy implications. These difficulties which involve not only Fig. 1 but all path analyses in the report, difficulties which are well recognized in the methodological literature in the behavioral sciences but barely alluded to by the investigators are:

1. *Their use of path analysis did not permit the systematic elimination of alternative causal models.* Path analysis is designed to yield estimates of the partial effect of one variable on another *if* one assumes *a priori* the correctness of the causal model being used. By this procedure (employed by Jencks), the input zero-order correlation matrix is used to calculate path coefficients, since according to the "path theorem," any given correlation coefficient can be expressed mathematically as a function of one or more path coefficients and one or more correlations.[2] But in order to decide what path coefficients to include in the resulting "path estimation equations," one must first posit or suggest a given causal model. In this respect, the variety of path analysis used by Jencks does not "test for" or eliminate causal models that could be implausible or false.

While Jencks alludes to this pitfall in the briefest possible way, he makes no real attempts to suggest and test for alternative models anywhere in the study. He does not even cite literature which discusses explicit procedures for eliminating alternative models. For instance, Blalock's extensive work (for example, 1962, 1964, 1968, and 1971) on the elimination of implausible causal models is well-known in the social sciences; yet, none of Blalock's work is given mention, nor is the related work of Simon (1957) or other pertinent literature. Heise (1969) has discussed a technique[3] for systematically eliminating causal models which integrates Blalock's insights with the use of path estimation equations, but such techniques are untreated by Jencks. Hence, Jencks' estimates of effects upon occupation and income could be off base, both in Fig. 1 and in other models used. How far off is anyone's guess, and Jencks' own guesses would undoubtedly have been better if he proceeded systematically to eliminate false causal models, which he evidently did not.

2. *Their use of path analysis assumes recursiveness.* "Recursiveness" means that if any variable $X_i$ is assumed to be either a direct or an indirect (through one or more other variables) cause of another variable, $X_j$, then the possibility of $X_j$ causing $X_i$ either directly or indirectly, must be ruled out in order to solve the path estimation equations. This rules out any consideration of "two-way" or "feedback" causation. Examination of Fig. 1 appears at first glance to lend itself easily to the recursiveness restriction: certain sets of variables have a "natural" hierarchical ordering (for example, IQ score in school ($X_5$) can affect later occupation ($X_8$), but the latter cannot possibly affect the former). In many ways, it seems that this is precisely why Jencks chose the variables that he did for analysis, and why he chose to rely so heavily on path analysis as the technique for analyzing them. It becomes evident, then, that a number of conceivably important variables were never included in the analysis – variables that did not lend themselves easily to a nice hierarchical ordering. There is no way to tell how many variables were eliminated because of this. Even considering the variables that Jencks *did* include, both Fig. 1 and other path models employed suggest that nonrecursiveness was given very little thought in the broader scope of the study, even though path analysis can be accomplished without the recursiveness restriction (Goldberger, 1964; Henry and Hummon, 1971).

3. *Their use of path analysis assumes interval measurement.* In order to perform their analysis, Jencks and associates had to use only variables which they assumed represented interval scales. This no doubt produced the elimination of many variables conceivably related to occupational and income success. Furthermore, sticking with the (few) independent

variables that they did use, they had to assume interval measurement even where this assumption itself is questionable (are occupational prestige rank and IQ scores interval scales?).

What might have been statistically wiser would have been to consider modifications of path analysis which do not require interval measurement of variables. Boyles' (1970) technique, for example, involves coding procedures and assumptions for path analysis on nominal and ordinal data. Boyle's technique is based on binary or "dummy" coding, a procedure which has in turn grown out of work on the General Linear Model (Cohen, 1968; Fennessey, 1968; Suits, 1957; Ward *et al.*, 1970), work which is not mentioned by Jencks.

4. *Their use of path analysis assumes linearity.* This means that any and all relationships between variables that were to varying degrees nonlinear had to be ignored. Jencks does indicate (p. 336) that there seemed to be little departure from linearity in a few, select relationships that he took time to look at, but what he says is unconvincing. Elimination of nonlinearity has one important implication: Any multiple correlation, $R^2_{1.2,3,...,k}$ assuming linearity is *necessarily* always less than or equal to a comparable multiple $R'^2_{1.2,3,...,k}$ using a technique not requiring linearity (such as binary coding.)[4] This means that *if* Jencks originally set out to show that education and other things have very little effect upon income and occupation, and if "explained variance" is the criterion for assessing the magnitude of such effects (as it was), then Jencks is "stacking the deck" in his favor: he has chosen a technique which will necessarily give relatively lower estimates of explained variance. That is simply not playing the science game fairly (but it is a good move in playing the Dozens).

5. *Their use of path analysis assumes additivity.* Stacking the deck in favor of lower estimates of explained variance occurs in a second respect – via the restriction of additivity in path analysis. The fact is, path analysis *can* be performed without restricting oneself to additivity, though it is problematic (cf. Althauser, 1971). Again, Jencks briefly refers to a test or two for interaction (p. 337), but no results are given, the tests employed did not appear to have been done on the data he used in the study, and what he says is therefore decidedly unconvincing. He even goes so far as to admit that different measures of "family background" could have strong interaction effects, but he performs no analyses of these suspected effects. What he might have done would be to define "interaction variables" by combining two or more independent variables with each other (as, by multiplying their values, or some other procedure), and then treat the resultant interaction variables as independent variable in their own right. While it is true that the original data would have to be obtained in order to accomplish this (recall that Jencks used only zero-order correlations as his basic input), it would not have been at all difficult to obtain the original data. The result would *necessarily* have been higher estimates of explained variance. Just how much higher is of course open to question, and could be settled only upon reanalysis.

6. *They used wild guesses for certain exogenous correlations and certain path coefficients.* As will be noted from Fig. 1, and from other models appearing throughout the report, estimates of correlations among variables must be made in order to solve for the path coefficients. In the Jencks' analysis, certain of these variables are actually unmeasured constructs (for example, child's genotype, family IQ, and family education, all represented in Fig. 1), whereas other variables are measured in some way, with some degree of error, in the original data source (for example, father's occupation is one such measured variable). It therefore became necessary for the investigators to simply guess at what the correlations among some unmeasured constructs would be. This resulted in some pretty wild guessing, to say the least. A good example is correlation "*m*" in Fig. 1, that between family IQ ($X_2$) and family education ($X_4$); it is "estimated" (and I use the term very loosely) to be anywhere from .5 to perfect, or 1.00. Furthermore, the "heritability" estimate ($h$) of .707, a path coefficient, is itself the resultant of some pretty wild guessing for correlations used in an analysis made prior to that displayed in Fig. 1.

There are some other places where such guessing takes place, and the result – not surprisingly – is wild fluctuation in the values of the resulting path coefficients. In general, the greater the amount of such guessing for the values of correlations, the more the values of the path coefficients will vary. It is understandable that Jencks and associates *had* to make out-and-out guesses for some correlations. They simply had no choice. But coupled with the other weaknesses discussed throughout this paper, the careful reader is nevertheless left with the feeling that the report is simply not to be trusted, and that its exceptionally strong policy implications simply do not follow at all from its methodology.

7. *Explained variance is dependent upon variable ordering.* It is well understood that if one relates any $X_1$ to Y with $X_2$ constant, and then relates $X_1$ to Y with both $X_2$ and $X_3$ constant, and then with $X_2$, $X_3$, and $X_4$ constant, and so on, then usually (though not necessarily), the proportion of the total variance in Y that will be explained by $X_1$ will become progressively less and less. At each stage, less residual variance in Y is left over *to be* explained. Now let us assume, as we have already, that Jencks set out to *show* that his independent variables do not explain much of the variance in income and occupation. If this is so, then he has (again) stacked the deck in his favor. From Fig. 1, the effect of schooling ($X_6$) on income ($X_9$) is substantially reduced simply because adult IQ, child IQ, respondent's occupation, and father's occupation are all held constant simultaneously. (This is particularly true if, in the "true" causal model, there is no direct causal arrow from eduction to income, as hypothesized in Fig. 1.) This criticism gains importance when one considers the above-mentioned "deck-stacking" shortcomings of the report: Jencks has structured his analysis to virtually assure that certain variables, like education, have very little effect on income and occupation.

8. *Every path analysis in the entire study leaves out blacks altogether.* In the text portion of the report, Jencks himself takes considerable liberties in discussing the effects of integration, segregation, race, etc., upon occupational and income inequality. He clearly infers that education is not related to success for black people; that if blacks want more money, then more education will not get it. But this inference is based upon path analyses done only on native white nonfarm males who took an armed forces IQ test! Who can say that causal models and estimates based on native white nonfarm males are applicable to blacks? Not one single path analysis in the entire report is performed on even one black sample. The error in

simple logic here is embarrassingly evident. Even more embarrassing is the realization that this kind of error, studying whites and then generalizing to blacks without studying blacks directly, is *consistently* made in "important" social science research documents, and many social scientists are tiring very rapidly of this fallacy. Moynihan (1965) in effect did it; Jensen (1969) did it, and so have others. Although Jencks indeed uses sources other than his own path analyses to draw conclusions about blacks, he nevertheless falls victim to the fallacy; he clearly intends his path analysis results to apply not only to blacks, but also to women, farmers, nonnative persons, and to persons who did not take an armed services IQ test, as well.

9. All things considered, we are left with the following: (a) The path analysis restrictions of interval measurement, linearity, additivity, and variable ordering, all point to the conclusion that the effects of various things upon occupational and income inequality in American society, particularly the effects of education, are actually *underestimated* in the report. Higher estimates would necessarily result from techniques employing noninterval measurement, nonlinearity, nonadditivity (interaction), and experimentation with different variable orderings. How much higher the estimates of effects would go is, of course, open to question. The investigators go so far as to say that their models are "as [accurate] as any alternative model now available" (p. 337). This simply does not appear to be true. (b) The inability to eliminate alternative causal models, the recursiveness assumption, and the haphazard guessing for certain unknown correlations and certain path coefficients, all affect the question of whether plausible causal models were used, and even given these questionable models, whether the path coefficients obtained using them are worth any attention at all by social scientists and policymakers.

Further, there is the question of whether the investigators even included "important" independent variables in their models. Some serious omissions come to mind: There is no systematic attempt to assess the effects of school quality, school "prestige," grades, peer-group pressures, how much a person actually learned while in school, participation in extracurricular activities, and a host of other potentially important variables. Jencks did not even control for the respondent's *age* in any of his path analyses. (Is the relationship between education and income the same for all age groups?) Additionally, one may criticize the report for assuming that income and occupation are the only valid measures of "success" in society. A still further criticism is the investigators' failure to consider dynamic or longitudinal processes, involving measurements of a given variable at two or more points in time, a procedure readily adaptable to path analysis (Heise, 1970).[5] Finally, the attempt to generalize empirical findings obtained only on native nonfarm white males to other populations, such as blacks, is a very substantial mistake.

## IQ HERITABILITY, STATISTICAL INTERACTION, AND RACE

*Estimating heritability.* While Appendix B and accompanying text are devoted to the analysis of inequality, Appendix A and chapter three are devoted to the matter of empirically estimating, via path analysis, the "heritability" of IQ scores, where measured IQ becomes the dependent variable, and the constructs "genotype" (G) and "environment" (E) become the unmeasured independent variables. Theoretically, the heritability ($h^2$) of any observed or "phenotypic" variable, such as measured IQ, is the proportion of the total variance in it which is explained statistically by any genotypic variable, with environmental variables held constant (see Fig. 2A). Since environmental variables can never really be held constant experimentally *or* by conventional statistical procedures, heritability must be assessed by "indirect" methods. Trying to measure IQ heritability has recently concerned many behavioral scientists, most notably Jensen (1969, 1970), Herrnstein (1971), Shockley (in numerous articles, essays, memos, and proposals), Eysenck (1971), and Scarr-Salapatek (1971), who study the matter with greatly varying degrees of quantitative sophistication, cleverness, trickery, and Dozens-playing, and whose merits and demerits I discuss in the previous chapter and elsewhere (Taylor, 1972 and 1973a). In the Jencks' treatment, suffice it to say that we have what Stinchcombe (1972, p. 603) has recently called "the best in the literature."

The Jencks treatment of IQ heritability is indeed "the best in the literature," but the literature leaves quite a bit to be desired. It is perplexing that Jencks and his associates choose to enter the controversial world of heritability estimation, for concern with it is really not central to the basic purposes of their analysis. Perhaps one encouraging thing to be said is that Jencks concludes that IQ heritability is considerably less than it was thought to be by researchers such as Jensen, and Jencks introduces many admirable statistical corrections that Jensen never dreamed of. While Jensen figured $h^2$ at approximately 80 percent, Jencks concludes that approximately 45 percent of the variance in measured IQ is explained by genes (this is $h^2$), approximately 35 percent is explained by environment (called $e^2$), and the remainder (20 percent) is explained by the correlation (covariance or multicollinearity) between genes and environment. They state quite clearly that these figures are tentative, and estimate that $h^2$ could be as low as 25 percent, or as high as 65 percent. This departs most markedly from the notorious 80 percent figure used religiously by Jensen, Herrnstein, Eysenck, Shockley, and others.

**Fig. 2** Some Alternative Path Models of the Effects of Environment and Genotype Upon IQ

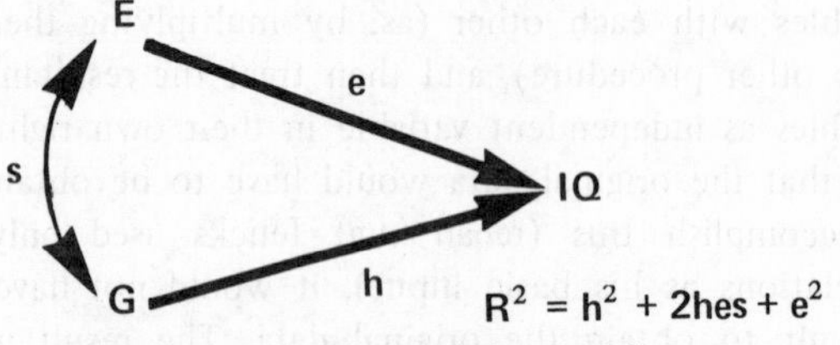


Fig. 2A Jencks' Additive Model

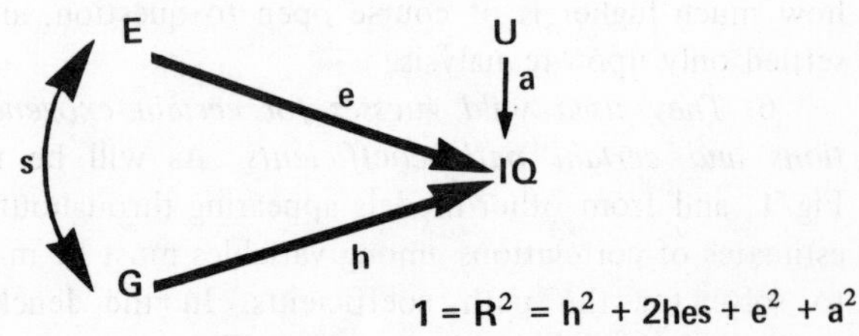


Fig. 2B An Alternative Additive Model

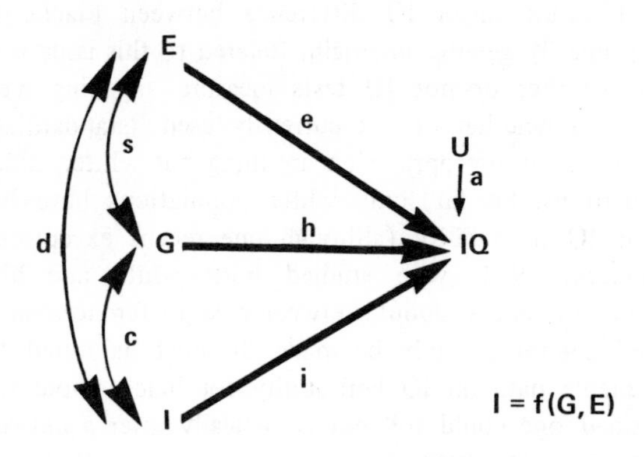


$$1 = R^2 = h^2 + e^2 + i^2 + 2hes + 2hic + 2die + a^2$$

**Fig. 2C** A Nonadditive Model

Partitioning out the variance in IQ that is attributable to gene-environment correlation is a major methodological advance in the study of heritability, and Jencks and associates deserve credit for it. Their basic strategy was this: First, they directly estimate certain correlations and certain path coefficients by means of available data. Path coefficient $h$ in Fig. 2A is estimated in this way, for example. Second, they use either evidence from past studies, or "educated guesses," for certain other correlation and path coefficients appearing in the path models (not shown in Fig. 2). (As noted earlier, this procedure caused some wide fluctuation in the values of path coefficients. In one place, estimates of $h^2$ to go from .29 to as high as .76.) Third, the estimates obtained in the first two steps are inserted into path estimation equations, and the remaining coefficients, treated as unknowns, are then solved empirically.

This procedure is certainly methodologically "cute," even ingenious, and while it gets around some of the difficulties of past literature, it still leaves many important problems unsolved. One past problem which they evidently get around is this: Jensen (1969, 1970) and others have used the correlation between the IQs of monozygotic (identical) twins raised apart as a direct measure of $h^2$. The logic of Jensen's procedure was that since monozygotic twins are known to have the same genes, if they are raised apart, their environments may be assumed to be uncorrelated. Hence, any correlation between their IQs should be due to genes only, and hence it is an estimate of the heritability of IQ. This procedure has (understandably) been soundly criticized, and Jencks manages to get around it by making cross-comparisons between and among monozygotic (identical) twins raised together, monozygotic twins raised apart, dyzygotic (fraternal) together, dyzgotic apart, siblings raised together and apart, and unrelated persons together and apart.

Here are some examples of problems and issues that Jencks does not appear to have solved:

a. Only four studies of monozygotic twins raised apart have been conducted, and these four studies – the same ones used by Jensen (1969, 1970) – use small samples (one study uses an $N$ of only 12 twin-pairs), and the data from all four studies are pooled.

b. Jencks (p. 273) assumes that "assortative mating" (non-random or "selective" mating of males and females) is based upon IQ alone, and then proceeds to calculate path coefficients on the basis of this assumption. This assumption is vastly unrealistic. People very definitely choose each other as mates on bases other than IQ alone.

c. In order to determine whether twins are in fact monozygotic or dyzgotic, some reliable measure of zygosity must be employed. On p. 284, they indicate that only one study they used had "adequate" tests for zygosity, and on p. 317, in a footnote, that "We have not attempted to correct any of the . . . correlations for errors in diagnosis of zygosity." Thus, one has no way of knowing exactly how many dyzygotic twins used were actually monozygotic, or vice versa.

d. Dyzgotic twins who were of opposite sex were eliminated from the Jencks analysis altogether, due to lack of available data. Only dyzygotic twins of the same sex were studied.

e. A troublesome issue in past literature has been the question of whether monozygotic twins have the same prenatal (Intrauterine) environemnts, or whether the prenatal environments of monozygotic twins are different in important respects. In contrast to what one might ordinarily suspect, there is some evidence that monozygotic twins may well differ in certain biochemical respects in their intrauterine environments (Darlington, 1954). Yet Jencks, for purposes of his path analyses, assumes that the intrauterine environments of monozygotic twins are identical (p. 312).

f. The path models used in the appendix by Jencks to estimate IQ heritability all assume additivity. That is, Jencks' models assume that the effects of genotype (G) upon IQ are the same for different environments (E); or, equivalently, that the effects of different environments are the same for different genotypes. This is somewhat perplexing, since certain portions of the nontechnical text clearly imply interaction. While I cannot detail this issue as much as I would like, a brief look at some alternative models and equations will be instructive.

Consider first Fig. 2A, the additive Jencks model, where $h$ and $e$ are path coefficients, and $s$ is the correlation between variables G and E. From the path theorem, the correlations $r_{IQ,G}$ and $r_{IQ,E}$ can be expressed as:

$$r_{IQ,G} = h + e(s)$$
$$r_{IQ,E} = e + h(s).$$

Assuming additivity (and linearity), the multiple correlation $R^2_{IQ,G,E}$ can be expressed as follows (Jencks *et al.*, 1972, pp.269 *et passim*):

$$R^2_{IQ,E} = h(r_{IQ,G}) + e(r_{IQ,E}).$$

Substituting,

$$R^2_{IQ,G,E} = h(h + es) + e(e + hs).$$

Or, more simply,

$$R^2_{IQ,G,E} = h^2 + 2hes + e^2, \qquad \text{(Eq. 1)}$$

which means that the variance in IQ that is explained by the model can be partitioned into that explained by genes ($h^2$), that explained by environment ($e^2$), and that explained by the correlation or covariance between genes and environment (*2hes*). This equation (Eq. 1) is basic to the Jencks analysis.

Jencks assumes that $R^2_{IQ,G,E}$ in Eq. 1 is unity (1.00), which means, theoretically, that *all* the variance in IQ is due to genes, environment, and covariance. But what is not being considered here is IQ variance that may be due to nonlinearity, and/or to interaction, and/or to other covariances. Of particular importance is interaction, which can be thought of as a separate variable. Presumably, these sources of variance in IQ are subsumed under a residual or error term, *which, however, is unstated in their model* (Fig. 2A).[6]

This can be shown by Fig. 2B, which explicitly shows a residual variable (U), and its path coefficient, *a*. Here, using Jencks' own logic,

$$1 = R^2_{IQ,G,E} = h(h + es) + e(e + hs) + a^2,$$
$$= h^2 + 2hes + e^2 + a^2 \qquad \text{(Eq. 2)}$$

which states formally that all variance in IQ can be partitioned into variance due to genes, environment, covariance, plus error ($a^2$). Hence, only if $a = 0$, will $h^2 + 2hes + e^2 = 1.00$; otherwise, this component will be less than 1.00.

Consider finally an interaction model (Fig. 2C), where an interaction variable (I) is defined by G and E, as by multiplying the values of G and E for each case, a standard procedure (cf. Taylor, 1973b). Model 2C in effect removes interaction variance from the error term of model 2B. The path coefficient, *i*, is in effect of interaction upon IQ with G and E constant; *d* represents the correlation between environment and interaction; and *c* represents the correlation between genes and interaction. Thus,

$$r_{IQ,G} = h + es + ic;$$
$$r_{IQ,E} = e + hs + id;$$
$$r_{IQ,I} = i + ed + hc.$$

Thus,

$$1 = R^2_{IQ,G,E,I} = h\,(r_{IQ,E}) + i\,(r_{IQ,I}) + a^2.$$

Or, finally.

$$1 = R^2_{IQ,G,E,I} = h^2 + e^2 + i^2 + 2hes + 2hic + 2die + a^2, \qquad \text{(Eq. 3)}$$

which means that the total variance in IQ is due to variance explained by genes ($h^2$), environment ($e^2$) gene-environment interaction ($i^2$), gene-environment correlation (*2hes*), gene-interaction correlation (*2hic*), environment-interaction correlation (*2die*), and finally, by error ($a^2$) due to any remaining interaction not captured by a multiplicative procedure.

The point of all this is to show that Jencks actually assumed *a priori* that four separate possible effects are all zero, whereas they may not be: the direct effect of interaction (*i*), the effect due to the two correlations *c* and *d*, and remaining error, *a*. Thus, it would appear that Jencks and associates are in error with their assumption that $h^2 + 2hes + e^2 = 1.00$, the basic equation which guided their entire analysis.[7]

*A note on IQ heritability and race.* Considerable controversy has recently arisen around not only the estimation of IQ heritability in general, but around whether or not the observed 15-point mean IQ difference between blacks and whites is primarily genetic in origin. Related to this issue is the matter of whether or not IQ tests measure anything worth measuring, and whether or not currently used "standardized" IQ tests are at all appropriate on anything but white, middle-class populations. So far, only white populations have been studied for IQ heritability (although one recent exception is Scarr-Salapatek, 1971, who studied both white and black twins), and inferences about between-race differences in IQ "genotype" cannot possibly be made. It must be noted that *even* if reliable data on IQ heritability for black populations were obtained one could still not statistically infer a between-race difference in genotypes.

Jencks and his associates evidently do not wish to enter this controversy, but they do inadvertently slide into it nevertheless. While all path analyses are performed only on whites, they frequently slip and generalize both *to* blacks *and to* between-race differences. For example, on p. 83, they briefly allude to the possibility that the black-white IQ difference is genetic, stating that "given the wide range of other physical differences between ethnic groups, such a difference in IQ genotypes is certainly conceivable."

While I cannot go into detail here, the crucial point missed by Jencks is that it can be shown statistically that even given high heritability for *both* groups, *and* given that the white mean IQ is higher than the black mean IQ, it is still equally *probable* and *plausible* that the black mean genotype is equal to the white mean genotype. Namely, the groups can differ on phenotype (measured IQ) without differing on genotype, even if heritability is exceptionally high at nearly 1.00 – which is itself, of course, very doubtful. Furthermore, a third distinct statistical possibility is for the black mean *phenotype* to be less than the white, but for the black mean *genotype* to be *greater* – still assuming high heritability.

Consequently, Jencks' assertion that a genetic racial difference "is certainly conceivable" is misleading, vague, and technically incorrect, since it is equally "conceivable" that mean genotypes do not differ; or, further, that the black mean genotype is higher. All three alternatives assume high heritability, and all three alternatives are equally likely, statistically speaking. Given this, it is unfortunate that Jencks seems to favor the alternative that he does, and his statement in this regard is actually quite careless.

## OTHER PITFALLS

Beyond the issues discussed above, there are other methodological shortcomings in Jencks which should be given mention: (a) Jencks states (p. 73 *et passim*) that "one inevitable result of elimination of environmental inequality would be to increase the correlation between IQ genotype and IQ scores," and thus increase $h^2$ in the general population. This argument has been made before (as, by Herrnstein, 1971), and it is fallacious. The opposite would happen *if* one assumes no direct causal link between genotype and IQ, but only, say, causal links from genotype to environment of IQ, in which case $h^2$ would theoretically fall to zero (Blalock, 1962, 1964, 1971). (b) In the text portion of the report, Jencks generalizes about the effects of "school quality" upon success; yet, "school quality" does not appear in any of the path analyses. In addition, the investigators ignore important literature on the "structural effects" of school context (e.g., Davis, 1966; Nelson, 1972). (c) Since much of Jencks' analysis is based upon the Coleman *et al.* (1966) data, criticisms previously leveled at the Coleman report, such as sampling error resulting from 30 percent nonresponse of schools originally selected (Sewell, 1967), can also be leveled at Jencks. (d) Jencks (pp. 57-58) admits that currently used IQ tests carry a heavy culture bias, but he nonetheless uses these tests in his own analysis without employing results from newer tests, such as tests involving the measurement of "creative" abilities, or even tests designed explicitly for minority persons. He states that "There is no evidence . . . to support the theory that black children are more disadvantaged on verbal tests than on other standardized tests" (p. 82). This is simply not true (see Jones, 1972; Hall *et al.*, 1972).

## CONCLUDING REMARKS

All things considered, the Jencks volume really cannot be taken seriously. Unfortunately, it already has been, if its wide promotion via the mass media is any indication. While this study in many respects is innovative, its numerous methodological shortcomings simply do not lend support to the exceptionally strong policy recommendations made or implied in it – policies of income insurance (quite literally taking from the rich and giving to the poor), and decreasing federal and local funding of education. In fact, the book's elaborate methodology is *unnecessary* for its policy recommendations. One is thus forced to conclude that sophisticated analyses are given merely to impress senators and other policymakers. The book is fine as an exercise in Dozens-playing and "cute" methodology, and it is excellent as after-dinner conversation for Ph.D. students in the behavioral sciences. But its methodology bears no recognizable connection to its conclusions and recommendations.

The study's shortcomings encourage some rather precise recommendations: First, a complete reanalysis of Jencks' original data sources, using path models which permit nonrecursiveness, noninterval measurement, nonlinearity, nonadditivity, alternate variable orderings, the elimination of implausible causal models, considerably less wild guessing for the values of unknown path coefficients and correlations, and considerably less "deck-stacking." Second, instead of studying white people to draw conclusions about black people, why not study black people? Third, introduce some *new* variables into the analysis. Fourth, perform some "structural effects" analysis, taking attained occupation and income as the dependent variables, and examine the effects of different "group units" such as the family, the school, the peer group.

Finally, in reference to perhaps the greatest omission of all in the Jencks report, consider the effects of institutional racism (and sexism, etc.) upon why some people are "successful" in society and why some are not. In discussing the various determinants of success among blacks, for some unfathomable reason, Jencks utterly omits the painfully obvious one of racism. Since Jencks takes considerable liberty in inserting "unmeasured" constructs into his path models, why not insert the "unmeasured construct" of institutional racism? Doesn't that seem fair enough? Jencks' omission of any analysis or discussion whatever of racism, in a book presumably analyzing "inequality" in society, is an omission almost beyond conception.

## NOTES

[1] A related game, called "signifyin'," is in some ways related to playing the Dozens. In general, while "signifyin' " involves derision and clever comment about the other as a person as well as about one's family, playing the Dozens is usually thought of as involving comments *only* about one's family, especially one's mother. Thus, "playing the Dozens" might be thought of as a subset of "signifyin'."

[2] Clear introductory discussions of the path theorem, the construction of path estimation equations, and the original work of Sewall Wright in path analysis, can be found in Duncan (1966), Land (1969), and Heise (1969). The basic idea is to express any correlation, $r_{li}$, as a function of other correlations and path coefficients appearing in the postulated model. Thus:

$$r_{li} = p_{li} + \sum_{\substack{j=2 \\ j \neq i}}^{n} p_{lj},$$

which is the "path theorem," where $p$ is any path coefficient. Path coefficients can be obtained either from the data matrix or from the correlation matrix.

[3] The technique involves first postulating some "parsimonious" model (where one or more path coefficients are set at zero), and then calculating *expected* correlations on the basis of that model, and then working in this way toward "fuller" or more complete models. At each stage, the expected correlations are compared to the observed correlations of the original correlation matrix. Each time some non-zero path coefficient is included in the appropriate path estimation equation, the value of the expected correlation approaches the value of the observed correlation, until with a full model, the observed correlations are reproduced exactly. If, at some point, the expected correlations are "close" to the observed correlations, then that particular parsimonious model is not rejected (it becomes plausible).

[4] On p. 336, Jencks makes brief reference to "multiple classification analysis," a binary technique which permits nonlinearity. However, he cites only one past study which uses it, and does not appear to have used it in his own analysis.

[5] Unfortunately, in the original Coleman study, identification of the subjects is impossible, as individuals were not "tagged" (Sewell, 1967). This means that repeated measures on given variables on the same individuals cannot be accomplished. Yet, Jencks uses data other than Coleman's. Also, there is no detailed discussion, with or without data, of longitudinal processes anywhere in Jencks' book, so the criticism still holds.

[6] In fact, they admit (p. 266) that their procedures often resulted in an $R^2$ of *greater* than 1.00, thus allowing no real basis at all to assume that $R^2$ is unity.

[7] In order to empirically form an interaction variable (I), actual values (scores) for variables G and E across cases would have to be obtained. This is impossible, since G and E are unmeasured constructs. However, through simulation, it would seem to be possible to generate alternative distributions for G and E, and then form an interaction term, although problems of collinearity and the resulting interpretability of the coefficient of interaction would arise (Althauser, 1971). Nonetheless, simulation seems especially feasible since considerable liberty is taken away by Jencks to estimate certain construct-correlations, and simulation would give some guidelines concerning the *maximum* possible effects of gene-environment interaction upon IQ. Furthermore, Fig. 2C and accompanying equations, taken only as theoretical, nevertheless show that Jencks implicitly assumed correlations *c* and *d*, and path coefficients *i* and *a*, to be zero.

## REFERENCES


Althauser, R.P. "Multicollinearity and Nonadditive Regression Models," in H.M. Blalock, Jr. (Ed.), *Causal Models in the Social Sciences.* Chicago: Aldine-Atherton, 1971.

Blalock, H.M., Jr. "Four-Variable Causal Models and Partial Correlations." *American Journal of Sociology,* 68, September, 1962, 182-194.

Blalock, H.M., Jr. *Causal Inferences in Nonexperimental Research.* Chapel Hill: University of North Carolina Press, 1964.

Blalock, H.M., Jr. "Theory Building and Causal Inferences" in H.M. Blalock, Jr., and A.B. Blalock, (Eds.), *Methodology in Social Research.* New York: McGraw-Hill, 1968.

Blalock, H.M., Jr. *Causal Models in the Social Sciences.* Chicago, Aldine-Atherton, 1971.

Blau, P., and Duncan, O.D. *The American Occupational Structure.* New York: Wiley, 1967.

Boyle, R.P. "Path Analysis and Ordinal Data." *American Journal of Sociology,* 75, January 1970, 461-480.

Cohen, J. "Multiple Regression as a General Data-Analytic System." *Psychological Bulletin,* 70 (6) 1968, 426-443.

Coleman, J.S., Campbell, E.Q., McPartland, J., Mood, A.M., Wenfeld, F.D. and York, R.L. *Equality of Educational Opportunity.* Washington, D.C.: U.S. Government Printing Office, 1966.

Darlington, D.C. "Heredity and Environment." Proceedings IX International Congress of Genetics, Caryologia, 190 1959, 370-381.

Davis, J.A. "The Campus as a Frog Pond: An Application of the Theory of Relative Deprivation to Career Decisions of College Men." *American Journal of Sociology,* 72, July 1966, 17-31.

Duncan, O.D. "Path Analysis: Sociological Examples." *American Journal of Sociology,* 72, July 1966. 17-31.

Eysenck, H.J. *The IQ Argument.* New York: Library Press, 1971. 1971.

Fenessey, J. "The General Linear Model: A New Perspective on Some Familiar Topics." *American Journal of Sociology.* 74, July 1968, 1-27.

Goldberger, A.S. *Econometric Theory.* New York: Wiley, 1964.

Hall, W.S., Cross, Jr., W.E., and Freedle, R. "Stages in the Development of Black Awareness: An Exploratory Investigation," in R.L. Jones (Ed.), *Black Psychology.* New York: Harper and Row, 1972.

Heise, D.R. "Problems in Path Analysis and Causal Inference," in E.F. Borgatta, (Ed.), *Sociological Methodology 1969.* San Francisco: Jossey-Bass, 1969.

Heise, D.R. "Causal Inference From Panel Data," in E.F. Borgatta and G.W. Bohrnstedt (Eds.), *Sociological Methodology 1970.* San Francisco: Jossey-Bass., 1970.

Henry, N.W., and Hummon, N.P. "An Example of Estimation Procedures in a Nonrecursive System." *American Sociological Review.* 36, December 1971, 1099-1102.

Herrnstein, R. "IQ." *The Atlantic,* 228, September 1971, 43-64.

Jencks, C. *Statement in the Boston Globe,* evening edition, December 8, 1972.

Jencks, C., Smith, M., Acland, H., Bane, M.J., Cohen, D., Gintis, H., Heyns, B., and Michelson, S. *Inequality: A Reassessment of the Effects of Family and Schooling in America.* New York: Basic Books, 1972.

Jensen, A.R. "How Much Can We Boost IQ and Scholastic Achievement?" *Harvard Educational Review.* 39, Winter 1969, 1-123.

Jensen, A.R. "IQs of Identical Twins Reared Apart." *Behavior Genetics,* 1(2) 1970, 133-146.

Jones, R.L. *Black Psychology.* New York: Harper and Row, 1972.

Land, K.C. "Principles of Path Analysis," in E.F. Borgatta (Ed.), *Sociological Methodology 1969.* San Francisco: Jossey-Bass, 1969.

Moynihan, D.P., and Barton, P. *The Negro Family: The Case for National Action.* U.S. Department of Labor, Office of Policy Planning and Research, 1965.

Nelson, J.I. "High School Context and College Plans: The Impact of Social Structure on Aspirations." *American Sociological Review,* 37, April 1972, 143-148.

Scarr-Salapatek, S. "Race, Social Class, and IQ." *Science,* 174, December 1971, 1285-1295.

Sewell, W.H. *Review Symposium. American Sociological Review,* 32, June 1967, 475-479.

Simon, H.A. "Spurious Correlation: A Causal Interpretation," in H.A. Simon, *Models of Man.* New York: Wiley, 1957.

Stinchcombe, A. "The Social Determinants of Success." *Science,* 178, November 10, 1972, 603-604.

Suits, D.B. "Use of Dummy Variables in Regression Equations." *Journal of the American Statistical Association.* 25, December 1957, 548-551.

Taylor, H.F. "Quantitative Racism: A Partial Documentation." *The Journal of Afro-American Issues,* I, Summer 1972, 1-20.

Taylor, H.F. "Jensen on Heredity, Race, and IQ," in A. McCord, (Ed.), *Educational Opportunity and the Ghetto Child.* Manuscript, forthcoming, 1973a.

Taylor, H.F. "Linear Models of Consistency: Some Extensions of Blalock's Strategy." *American Journal of Sociology,* 78, March 1973b, 1192-1215.

Ward, J.H., Jennings, E., and Bottenberg, R. "A New Vector Approach to Regression Analysis and Computers in Research." Manuscript. Washington, D.C.: Control Data Corporation, 1970.

# 30
# *Black Separatism and American Quicksand: Planting One Foot in the Land of the Dream**

BERNARD E. SEGAL

## BY WAY OF INTRODUCTION

Most writers probably have a prospective audience in mind when they first sit down at their typewriters. Mine is made up of most of the other people who have written the selections in this book. I am going to take on a different task from theirs, trying to introduce some different perspectives. I am self-conscious about my task, for I am one of few white writers in a book that has been largely written by black people. Moreover, I sat down to compose my essay after having the chance to read what the others had already put down on paper. I feel like a man who came to dinner at a family reunion, one who has listened to the frank talk and heard the vigorous arguments of family members who share a certain solidarity in which he is not included. The family squabbles. Somewhere between dessert and cigars someone turns to the guest to seek his opinions. The guest wishes to be polite. He wants to be honest and helpful, but tactful and courteous as well, particularly because he has not learned intimate family details and because of his impression that a few of the family members are wondering just who he is, how the devil he got there, and what he can possibly say that might interest them. The guest finds it best to begin by explaining who he is and where his vantage point lies. He thinks he can then go on to show how the momentarily heated emotions of some family members may have kept them from hearing all that some other relatives have had to say.

It should be obvious that I would find it pleasant to be able to think that I was objective in what follows. Not very many other people are likely to think that I have managed to do so. Readers may actually be better than I at judging how much my presentation depends on my own proclivities rather than on the true character of the subjects I treat. In order to judge, however, they need to know something about what those proclivities are. The guest therefore begs his host's indulgence, requesting a few pages to identify himself a bit more. He hopes he may be pardoned for being so personal, especially because it would have been less satisfying, though not difficult, to have eliminated his egos in favor of some more vague set of alters. Maybe you think his satisfaction should not be at issue here. Perhaps you'll change your mind after recalling that a family reunion is, after all, a kind of party; and that an ego trip is one of the worst kinds to have to take alone.

My family history and black history intersected directly for the first time about 15 years ago, shortly before black people began to live in a house I used to live in. The house is on what is and was a nicer and quieter street than most of the others in its neighborhood on the Roxbury-Dorchester border. Most of the families who used to live there were working and lower middle-class Jewish people. My street was only about two blocks away from the school that Jonathan Kozol wrote about in *Death at an Early Age.* My sister attended it for a couple of years, before any black children did, until she left for Girls' Latin. It wasn't so long ago. Maybe some of the teachers who treated my sister reasonably well were some of the same ones Kozol criticized so bitterly for their stupidly unthinking treatment of black children.

I was in graduate school by the time my immediate family left the neighborhood. They would have gone long before, but didn't want to leave behind my widowed grandmother. She would have been alone in her downstairs flat, and she didn't want to move away. However, my parents' 20-year dream of wanting to live in a handsome suburb finally won out. Most of their friends already lived in Newton or Brookline. The beginning of the arrival of black people in the old neighborhood was the final push. My grandmother stayed, no longer a landlady, but a tenant of a black family. About two years later, my grandmother moved to another apartment, once again on the margin of the black ghetto but in a piece of what was still left of the Jewish second settlement area in Mattapan. After five or six years there, she moved again. The ghetto had spread; drunks and junkies were turning up in the entryways of most of the apartment buildings in the area. Besides, when my mother and her sister drove in from the suburbs to visit, they were reluctant to leave their Cadillacs untended on the street. My grandmother lived in Brookline, in a new apartment building full of Jewish old people, until she died a little over a year ago.

Multiply my family by tens of thousands in Boston, or by millions nationally. The product is an enormous social force impinging on the people left in old ghettoes or forming new ones. My family's leaving made a little room, but also took away some of Boston's tax base. My family illustrates that white people tend to have more options than black ones, and

*Written especially for this book.

that one of those options is the chance of moving away, even if people don't like to think that they have been pushed to exercise it. Residental segregation is white separatism.

My mother is now old and far away. Probably she will never again find herself in anything remotely approaching residential integration. In that respect, my sister and I are slightly different. She lives in Lexington among Harvard and M.I.T. intellectuals and technocrats. I live in New Hampshire in a college town where liberalism is so much the dominant mode that we are intolerant of departures from its moderate and gentle middle way. In both places, the last five years have seen integration begin on a small and carefully controlled scale. The screen of social class stands tall, making certain that the only people who can live among us are those who have acquired enough money and enough of the proper sort of credentials – usually educational. Other people, too bulky to climb over the screen or too gross to filter through it, stay out. I'll use the title of one of James Herndon's books to say that in a country which combines strong traditions of classbound neighborhoods and local autonomy, it often seems *That's the Way It S'pose To Be.* Many of my neighbors and I happen not to approve of that norm. So what? We aren't moving, and so we're taking advantage of it and passing the advantage on to our children.

Among white people, ethnic assimilation has been part of a more general pattern in which upward mobility has been both solvent and source of the perpetuation of status advantage between generations. The same pattern occurs among black people and other minorities considered racial. It is still too early to tell how widespread it will become, or how many of them will either be able or will go on choosing to play the game.

## A DEFINITION AND SOME POSSIBLE CONCLUSIONS

My definition of black separatism is black people choosing to stay out of the larger society. The choice may be based on the calculation that integration has not worked and cannot, or it may be based on the fear of being rebuffed again. It may be a choice saying wait-and-see, that doors may open later to items worth stretching to gather, or it may be a choice trying to formulate ways of inventing and creating rewards of a new and different kind. It may aim to be permanent, total, and categorical, involving all efforts of the whole black population in building a new nation, or it may set its horizons lower, more as a tactic than as a strategy, aiming, say, for local control of schools and some jobs but not the whole labor market, using leverage and pressure where they can be used effectively so that other techniques, including those based on integration, can be brought to bear in other spheres or at other times.

What black people do, white people tend to stereotype. I think most of the white population is not aware that separatism has so many themes, that there are so many variations on them, and that black people argue heatedly even over how to strike a given chord. I also think that most white people are hostile to separatism, not just in principle and not just in those cases where it seems that a separatist proposal may take something from them that they do not wish to relinquish. Many white people find separatism insulting, because it says straightforwardly that hallowed American values have been and will go on being fraudulently applied. Hardly anyone doubts past fraud, but why insist that it will go on? Have there not been great changes in American race relations for about the last 20 years, or ever since Brown vs. Board of Education?

Criticism of separatism in principle is not too hard to make, or to take. Any black person who wishes to support separatism can merely cite other principles in its defense. After all, in principle (such a splendid all-purpose phrase!) autonomy and self-determination and pluralism are pretty good things. Almost everybody likes 'em. Far more serious is that white criticism on the level of principle is almost certainly just the visible ideational tip of a firmly established reluctance to provide black areas with the kinds and quantities of resources that would make it possible for those areas to be or shortly become self-sustaining at a decent standard. The criticism and the reluctance are intertwined. Anyone not wanting a separatist proposal to work and yet afraid that it might, would hardly rush to do what could facilitate its becoming viable.

As I read other contributions to this volume, they suggest to me that it is possible to set black responses to this set of circumstances at two poles. At one is found the call for power through solidarity and threat; enough power to wrest away the resources, including the territory, that would allow black people to live alone and determine their own destiny, relying on white America for nothing more than what is implied in the interdependence of conventional international relations. (Underdeveloped countries that are already politically independent also complain that rich countries limit their autonomy and keep them subordinate, but that's another story.) The other pole appears to rest on the twin beliefs that black people are edging into and making their way in the larger society, and that they have no alternative to doing so. The reason there is no alternative is not that the larger society is so splendidly rewarding; it is, rather, that the white majority which sees separatism as insulting also sees it as a way of getting off the hook.

There is not much doubt that white folks do sympathize with one another. First they had to be dragged kicking and screaming to let some black folks in, and just when they were getting around to doing it, some other black folks began to shout that the first one shouldn't go. Well then, if that's how it is, a common white view holds, if black people want to go it alone, why not let them? Time enough, the argument sometimes goes on, to let them try for our acceptance once again after they've prospered and become respectable. Still, that's a matter we won't have to face for a long time, because they probably can't do it. Besides, there are always the cops and the Guard to make sure they won't get away with anything too radical.

No wonder that black people also have sympathy for one another. Not only are they damned if they do and damned if they don't by many white people, but by many of their own intellectuals as well. Public opinion polls show that what most black people most want are decent steady jobs, adequate living conditions, and solid educations for their children. These people seem little concerned about ideology. There is not much doubt that the separatist thrust would disappear if they could meet their desires through integrationist means.

Yet many people assert that anyone still holding out hope for the possibility of being incorporated into the larger society suffers from a severe limitation of consciousness. People left out or kept out of the system for so long, they point out, ought to be able to see its contradictions and strains, and look ahead to its destruction or radical change. Let's draw a distinction. There is separatism that withdraws, and radical separatism that attacks; or, more precisely, separatism that concentrates on creating change in a given community that is within though not fully a part of the general society, and separatism that levels real or ideological guns against that society and its agents of control.

Forms of separatism that in effect accommodate themselves to being inexorably surrounded by the larger society may be more or less tolerated. I have in mind the Nation of Islam. Wishing to be left alone to develop its own program and carry out its own activities, it does not attack the larger society, the vehemence of its own mostly internally directed rhetoric notwithstanding. True, the Nation has been ridiculed and questioned because its membership is black and because its religious basis is foreign to the Judeo-Christian tradition. And, although there is some reluctance to grant full legitimacy to its religious standing, the span of tolerance for its activities is wider on account of that religious base. Moreover, the Nation is reformist and rehabilitative, and the ascetic character of its behavioral code sometimes makes it seem not more Catholic than the Pope but more Calvinistic than Calvin. In general, therefore, the Muslims are ignored except when they draw attention to themselves, on the relatively rare occasions when the group or a prominent member is involved in a political issue. Examples are Muhammad Ali's fight against the draft, or prison authorities blaming Muslims and Muslim influence for prison rebellions.

A black organization with an avowedly radical position soon finds itself in a different set of circumstances. The Black Panthers, for example, held that revolution alone could bring black and other poor people what was their due. Moreover, society's debt to such people was more than economic, and Panther anger and bitterness were not the whole of their message. Like many other contemporary young Marxists, they also emphasized their socialist humanism, their vision of a more decent society where all once-poor people would be free not merely from their poverty but from degradation and from the limitations that had been placed on their capacity to develop their own faculties. The Panther message was important, but the group was isolated. Its ties were not with the white working and lower classes, but with higher ranking people – a few of the rich, and students at the more intellectually inclined universities. When the Panthers' revolutionary pitch brought the authorities down hard on them, the isolation meant that there was no way for the group to generalize its struggle against authority and official perfidy. Moreover, the organization suffered internally from arguments over doctrine, over how to adapt doctrine to different local or regional circumstances, and over how much its local leaders were to be subordinate to the national leadership.

The central Panther dilemma, however, concerned its ideology and isolation. It serves as a particularly dramatic example of a more general black dilemma. When black people attempt to make clear that their situation and prospects are the product of systematic arrangements biased in favor of the great corporate and individual holders of wealth and productive property, and that these arrangements strike immense numbers of white people almost as hard as black ones, the second part of the message is not listened to. Instead, racist ticket-thinking goes to work, and the radicalism is heard as a black shout rather than a human plea. Very large numbers of white people know, but don't want to hear black people say (even larger numbers may not know and do not wish to hear anyone say) that a great proportion of this society, white and black, suffers from over control, from unreasonable income distribution, from stultifying work, from leaders who accommodate, and from a consequent lack of honest and effective lower and working class inventiveness, creativity, and leadership.

Politics, it has been often said, is the art of the possible. From backroom deals to street demonstrations, the statement applies to black politics too, with the additional specification that black politics particularly aims at lengthening the span of the possible. Yet at any given time, the possible is almost never what anyone might wish it to be; it is limited, sometimes by severely restraining conditions. One of these conditions in American society is that one of the likeliest ways of having important but unpopular ideas dismissed rather than attended to is to have them be thought the property or the product of black people. The circumstances that make struggle necessary also serve to make it more difficult.

For documentation, consider these three items: (1) recent census figures show that the percentage gap between the median incomes of black and white families has increased slightly in the past two years after having narrowed through the 1960s. (2) After comparing black and white attitudes on a number of important issues, the *Harris Survey* for November 23, 1972, concluded, "Now there is a distinct sense of being relegated back across the tracks, left without a great deal of concern by a dominant white society. At least as far as blacks are concerned, the charge of 'two Americas – one black and one white,' made in a Presidential commission report in 1968, never seemed more accurate than in late 1972." (3) A Quayle survey carried out in the key bellwether state of Illinois, published in the May 1973 *Harper's,* found that 60 percent of the white voters thought that the country had already gone far enough (41 percent) or too far (19 percent) in helping blacks achieve equality. *Harper's* led into it dramatically: ". . . the easiest way for a liberal Democrat to lose in 1976 would be to advocate justice – racial justice." Nevertheless, it appears in sum that white Illinois voters approve of measures which, under white control, would help upgrade black populations while keeping them at a distance. I wonder if it is inaccurate or uncharitable to summarize white opinion from this survey in a different and blunter way, stating that it says, in essence, "Keep 'em away and buy 'em off." Select the summary you prefer. Either one makes clear that white attitudes allow nothing but compromise for black desires, whether these be integrationist or separatist.

Now a fourth and last item, this one stimulated by, but not fully treated in, *The Times'* account of a statement to the National Education Association by Albert Shanker, head of New York's United Federation of Teachers. Mr. Shanker, responding to criticism, insisted that his union had not been racist in the New York school strikes and community control controversy of 1968. He went on to point out that his union was now the spokesman and bargaining agent for thousands of black and Puerto Rican paraprofessionals.

Readers may recall how, at the height of the crisis, advocates for community control made great claims for the educational benefits that would follow from having minority teaching staffs and greater neighborhood involvement in local schools. Subsequent studies show the claims to have been greatly exaggerated, although I suppose one could always argue that not enough minority teachers were hired, or that they did not have the proper mentality, or that the experiment was never allowed to mature, or that the communities were not fully enough involved, etc. I do not know if the claims made for better education were intended to be genuine educational predictions. I do know that they constituted a strong rallying point for trying to build solidarity in districts that until that time had shown remarkably little. Moreover, as David Cohen subsequently pointed out in his article "The Price of Community Control," education in the sense of readin', writin', and figurin' was in a very important way no more than a surface issue. Below it, moving it, were the issues of education as value training and of legitimacy. Cohen suggests that what really mattered was what minority children were going to be taught to believe, who was going to have access to jobs to teach it to them, what the appropriate techniques were for finding or creating and filling job openings, and to whom people in school positions would be responsible. In sum, educational concerns, as customarily conceived, were the cover for a political and cultural contest being carried out between a new group of aspiring black professionals who needed places to go but saw their way blocked, and a largely Jewish lower middle-class group that was trying to hang on. It is hardly surprising that in these circumstances, as in other similar ones, the best available educational research data – the Coleman Report, for example – were used selectively and in such fashion that ambiguous results were almost invariably interpreted so as to correspond with the interests of particular groups. *Sic transit gloria datorum.*

Neither side got all it wanted. Neither side lost everything. The union is probably stronger than ever; certainly with the new paraprofessional members it is in a better position to argue for its fairness if similar issues arise again. On the other hand, there are the minority paraprofessionals who are now represented by a strong union even if they don't control it; minority influence over minority schools is not complete, but there is more of it; and more minority people are staffing these schools.

When the heat got turned up in New York, integrationists got closer to separatists. Community control offered a way for both to try to apply policy without departing from principles; besides, both had common foes in the union and in the overwhelming majority of the white parents of New York's schoolchildren. But consider the following questions. Would even the compromise outcomes have taken place without an issue as general as community control? Would community control have counted for so much if it had not been fueled by a flow of separatist militance and rhetoric? Would the issue ever have arisen had New York ceased to be a *de facto* segregated city? Would New York's race relations problems have been so massively severe if the city had not in some ways (as tough a place as it may be) been a better place to live than the rural South or the San Juan slums? Was one measure of that difference the very presence of young black professionals, many of them not yet as well off as whites but already far more comfortable than their own parents? The questions are all rhetorical. That the answer to all is "no" does not mean there are no further questions to ask. It does suggest, however, and quite strongly at that, that in a city which is neither closed nor open, the slogans which move people do not necessarily explain them.

## LOYALTY AND FAITH, MEANS AND ENDS

The use of the term legitimacy in the last section may have suggested to some readers that conflicts between separatist and integrationist viewpoints (as well as between both and that segment of white opinion wanting to defer changes based on either for as long as possible) are not merely conflicts over how to choose the most efficient means for reaching given ends. In particular, when separatists use the term integrationist in disparaging reference to other people, black or white, they are making what is at least an implicit statement about the hopelessness of trying to deal with the white majority on its own terms. However, when the term is used to disparage black people, it has another facet as well, for it then becomes an indirect call for black loyalty. Separatists tend to call for exclusive loyalty. Exclusive loyalty is close to utter conviction. To grant it means to allow oneself no room for being seduced or sidetracked, tempted or co-opted. Exclusive loyalty is hard to find, and harder to keep. Perhaps that is one reason why leaders don't just ask for it but tend to demand it, insist on it, try to invent disciplines and organizations to maintain it. Frequently, when we call a leader charismatic we mean no more than that he can inspire that sort of loyalty. I like to call that sort of leader a prophet.

Loyalty is important for any change-oriented movement under attack or preparing to do battle, whether or not it has a prophet, whether or not it departs drastically from current majority expectations and standards. Loyalty is bedrock. Without loyalty there is no solidarity, and without solidarity – particularly among those short of other resources like money and technical skills – no movement can be sustained. However, in diverse societies that do allow some room for upward mobility, many minority people, like others, are often loyal to more than one group and to more than one set of standards. They are often people trying on new roles and trying out new lives. Consequently, in a society made complex by cross-cutting racial, ethnic, and class differences, if one is seeking understanding rather than adherents, it is more useful to think in relative terms than categorical ones. Then the question is not whether or not A or B or C is a loyal individual, but how loyal he is, and to what.

Loyalty is so affective and traditional, so often an end in itself, that it is easy to feel offended upon seeing it used in a deliberately calculating way. When someone plays on others' deep emotions without being convinced that he is also trying to serve them, it is a serious violation of trust (except in the love and war that make anything fair). It is common, therefore, for one group to cry hypocrisy in an attempt to demean another's prophet. Sometimes the cry is also a denial of another aim, for a conflict of loyalty can surely reflect a deeper conflict of interest. But a group will desert its own prophet too, if it decides that he has feigned his conviction or if it traps him in what it considers to be moral inconsistencies. Indeed, since a prophet is often a symbol of the group and the vessel of its belief and hope, it is probably more important that he appear convinced and dedicated than that he always make accurate judgments.

A prophet is always dangerous for an established order, for fear or desperation at men's backs merely drive them forward. Loyalty in their breasts can pull them ahead, can sustain their conviction that there is something better that will soon be their own. On the other hand, prophets do not often achieve great success, even though men are frequently desperate, and desperate men need loyalty and faith. The desperate may be ready to clutch at straws, but they are also skeptics. Having often failed, they have become tired of having each new failure add to the sting of the last. No wonder that most prophets never attain all their goals. They face an often intractable world, and, in addition, run the double risk of being snuffed out by the enmity of their antagonists or of being forgotten or overwhelmed by the disenchantment of their erstwhile supporters and followers. Leading the better-off is far easier. They have had the training and have the time to reflect on what they have earned or won and do not wish to lose. The better-off, however, have less need than the desperate of faith and loyalty, leadership and trust. Here, then, as with wealth, distributive justice is an ideal to be sought, not the customary condition to be expected.

Loyalties and faith also concern morality more than fact, feelings more than intellect. We do not use words like accurate and inaccurate, correct or mistaken, efficient or inefficient to describe loyalties and commitment. Moreover, if loyalty were not a basic existential issue it would not lie at the heart of what current fashion calls identity crises. Yet the question, "Who am I?" is frequently no more than a shopworn label hastily pasted over more troublesome questions such as, "To whom do I belong? For whom am I responsible? In what can I believe? To what should I devote myself?"

There are three reasons why it is difficult to resolve problems of loyalty, and why many people need group support to do so. The first is that many people belong to many different kinds of individuals. Consequently, they need to weigh what it might mean to themselves and others to follow one group's standards rather than another's. Such weighing by itself introduces a note of pragmatism into what might otherwise seem immediate and elemental, devoid of calculation. A second reason introduces practical considerations more directly. When a diverse variety of groups exists, with each having a program for achieving at least some of the common goals sought by all or most of the smaller groups in a larger congeries, the effectiveness of the program rather than the identification of a given group with a given goal may become the basis of loyal attachment. A person who selects this option lays himself open to charges of hypocrisy and compromises. Indeed, since he cannot base a claim of legitimate action on his unswerving whatever-the-cost devotion to some group or leader, he may be driven to still further compromise in order to make his program more effective. Finally, many people who possess common status characteristics or otherwise find themselves in circumstances where it is at least possible for them to be members of more than one group that questions the program or the sincerity of others, feel their tensions heightened by such questioning. Split or divided loyalties are hard to tolerate, so that it is frequently easier to line up on one side or another than to go on alone, trying to steer an independent course by borrowing a keel from here, a rudder from there, a mast from someplace else. A patched-up craft may be satisfactory enough in fair weather, but tends to founder quite easily in an approaching storm.

Many movements based upon group loyalty therefore try to create or capitalize on the impression or fact that other groups are enemies. They may do so in many different ways. These include expressing aggression directly on a random or systematic basis; or controlling the amount and modes in which aggression may be expressed while reserving and rechanneling some of it into other efforts; or transforming it into its opposite, as in doctrines emphasizing that enemies will be defeated not by hate and scorn, but by love and pity, that they will not so much be beaten as won over. Choosing among these modes, one man may select as his dream what is another's nightmare.

I can identify five sources of serious discrepancy between observers of a movement and its participants, or between participants in different branches of a similar movement. The five are as follows: (a) disagreement over goals, ends, or values; (b) disagreement over norms of appropriateness or legality governing the choice of methods used to reach goals; (c) disagreement over the calculation of the most effective means for maximizing the probability of attaining given goals; (d) disagreement over choosing more appropriate methods rather than more effective ones; and (e) disagreement over whether a given activity is only a means or method for reaching a more distant goal or is a primary end in its own right.

The fans of effectiveness maximization, of whom I am one, like to strike balances between pragmatic and affective criteria and motivations. They like to point out that antagonists' responses must not be neglected, so that what is merely convention for the conformist must be part of the conscious changer's formula for estimating prospective outcomes. They like to see means and ends laid out one after another, like the links of extended chains. In contrast, the fans of goal or value or end maximization have often had quite enough of chains of any kind, including metaphorical ones. The single giant stride they urge may seem more like a blind leap of faith to others, for they are more inclined to call for the long bomb than to slog ahead with three yards in a cloud of dust. Ball control is safer but duller. It also depends on team discipline and internal cooperation, but can't work for a light and weak squad no matter how great its team spirit. How much more grace and daring in a sudden strike to a streaking, darting flanker! Alas, how much likelier that he will fumble when hit, or perhaps never even get his hands on the ball.

Until we arrived at the stadium, it may have seemed that the issues I have raised in this section were abstract, merely academic. They are not. Contributors to this volume have turned to them again and again, wrestling with them themsleves or reporting on how others have wrestled with them. In doing so, they have raised many other similar questions. Where does loyalty lie? What is the best way of expressing it? Is it necessary to tolerate ambivalence? When is compromise legitimate? When and how can personal goals be consonant with group goals? If there is conflict between them, which should be preeminent?

Furthermore, it is not just the other writers who have raised such queries. I know they speak for others, for I have seen and heard black students grapple less systematically with problems of the same kind.

Many of the black students I know have had to try, all at once, to carry the obligation of performing well for themselves and for others who have been watching them, depending on them, sacrificing for them; of overcoming educational handicaps that place them at a disadvantage against well-trained white students; and of trying to decide what they wish to do with their education, not for their own sake alone but with and for other black people as well. It is a great deal to ask of young people, and I have seen a few who, although they were quite competent, turned out to be academic casualties, hobbled by social and emotional problems that kept them from studying at all well. True, I have seen white students in the same position, but not in the same proportion. I have also heard the folly of white students wishing they were black, to have something to believe, to overcome their loneliness or harness their anger. It is a folly, for they have not had to understand that having something to believe is not the same as being able to grasp it, and that there are so many ways of believing that it is often difficult to choose just one and then resist the pressures that come from having chosen it. Perhaps there are black students elsewhere, away from countryside Dartmouth, or the rest of the Ivy League, who find themselves more easily. From those who are here, however, I have first-hand evidence of how dear the price of change can be. I have yet to meet a black student who did not know, however, that high as that cost is, it is cheaper than the blood and grimy sweat that went to make the down-payment.

Is it improper for me, a white man, to have made note of these tender undersides of black pride? I do not think so, not when so many other white people still see only militance, hear only rhetoric, go on fearing bravado. I know, after all, that many black students doubt that they belong here and are yet reluctant to leave. Though the choice should and must be theirs to make, I do not share their doubt. I get paid here; they pay tuition or get scholarship aid. In that, we are equally insiders.

## A SKEPTICAL VIEW OF SUBJECTIVISM, DETERMINISM, AND TIME

Many Marxists in and out of academia in countries poor and rich have made honest attempts to answer some of the same questions I am about to raise. Whether or not they intended to, they have also helped to perform an important service for Western social science in general, forcing many of us to shake loose the cobwebs of an established way of thinking that we had begun to treat almost as if it had been revealed wisdom. (If it needs a name, call it "early '60s liberal behaviorism.") That totem has fallen, chopped down not just by its critics, but by Cuba, China, and Vietnam, by Watts, Detroit, and Harlem. And just in case these axe blows hadn't been enough, along came Watergate to finish off the job.

What will the new symbol be? What kind of social science perspective can lay legitimate claim to the right to stand tall among us now? I recommend something well balanced and not easily toppled: social phenomena are too complex and too quickly shifting to be grasped adequately by onesided or prejudged points of view.

There are two major reasons why I think a Weberian perspective is wider and better balanced than a Marxist one. As hooks to hang these reasons on, I'll say in an overly simple way that they concern subjectivity and certainty. A third item, about which I find myself somewhere midway between Weber's and Marx's positions, concerns the place of ideas as forces of stability and change.

Weber tried to make clear, especially in the essays included in *The Methodology of the Social Sciences,* that a difference had to be maintained between the forms of analysis and presentation that were respectively appropriate for desk and lectern on the one hand, altar and stump on the other. Thus, while Marx held, as in the *Theses on Feuerbach,* that the task of philosophy until his time had been to interpret the world and that the hour had arrived for philosophy now to change it as well, Weber would have held that the philosopher's (for which read social scientist's or even scholar's) task had not changed so drastically. The chance and obligation to change the world lay not with the man of learning or knowledge, but with the man of action. The two roles, Weber held, were to be kept distinct, even in the case of the individual person who occupied both, one at one time and place, the other at another. The man of action was limited by the world he encountered; the man of knowledge, in a different way. His was the limitation of reporting no more than, but also no less than, all that he came to know through his studies. Note that the word is know, not believe or hope, even though what we call knowledge is necessarily tentative and subject to change. One gets to know only through applying such an explicit method of reviewing, reporting, and interpreting data that anyone coming later could also apply it, and, by so doing, arrive at the same conclusion. In addition to his care with method, however, the man of knowledge may not accept the presuppositions or fixed assumptions of others who have come before him, nor can he let their conceptions of the proper and the desirable fix his horizons and define his rules for making interpretations and drawing conclusions. To do so would be to engage in moral axiology rather than social science. By the same token, he may not predict or forecast just on the basis of his own hope or desire or belief. That is faith, not social science. Nor is he to urge his beliefs on others, except for the belief in knowledge for its own sake and in the rules for acquiring it, and then only to those who have also elected to be men of knowledge. To do otherwise is to engage in proselytizing, not demonstration.

Let us make no mistake. Weber was no scientificist. He insisted on the greatest possible detachment, to be sure, but about what? About analysis that concerned what was important to people in their own time or ours – analyses, he held, could not pretend to adequacy unless they showed how what mattered to men affected what they believed and how they acted. There is no ground for asserting that Weber misunderstood or underestimated the importance and force of commitment to emotion or ideals, or that he believed it was actually possible for him or any other social scientist to be as objective as the ideal for which he strove in the one limited sphere of social science. One limited sphere – the term is worth repeating. A field of study coterminous with life, or servant to the circles and agencies that regulate life, or bound by the preconceptions normally assumed and accepted in the very social contexts from which social scientists come – such a field of study is not and cannot be social science. A social science slave to life could not only not make contributions that were sensible and useful for correcting error, but would make it more difficult for us all to avoid having our lives increasingly subject to rational calculation, with only constantly diminishing spheres open for the play of emotion, the support of attachment, the bursts of spirit. Objectivity and dispassionate analysis, as Weber would have us use them, are therefore not the same as lack of involvement in our subjects; instead, he leads us to be as wary of the clean cut of an uncaring scalpel as we are of the brute force of an angry bludgeon.

A great many people have eagerly used some of these ideas in a one-sided way, using them to attack intellectual or social antagonists. At times their eagerness to dismiss others has been equal only to their reluctance to apply these considerations to their own thoughts and programs. "You and not I," they seem to be saying, "have to be more objective. I am convinced that what I say is so; an objective doctrine shows it so. I shall also demonstrate it to be so, quite conclusively, as soon as a sufficient number of others also accept it, acting upon it as if it were." What a big contingency is there implied! Instead of stopping to consider what people do and accept, it simply makes the doctrine its own touchstone. The concern for evidence is secondary. Under the circumstances, it is hardly surprising that many of the people who espouse such a view feel some need to make it more secure. What better way than to endow it with inevitability? The "if" of collective belief and of its force thereby disappears, lost in a framework asserting that proper belief as accurate fact is tomorrow's basis of social organization. The Marxist method, applied not to what has already happened but to what might occur, is often an attempt at a self-fulfilling prophecy, propelled by moral fervor and conviction, backed up by a mass of apparent evidence that in the recent past poor people in many different parts of the world have changed their destiny consciously setting out to make their history.

A quick look at recent history suggests that Marx was right. However, a more detailed examination gives us some ground for hesitating before accepting all the implications of the argument. There is enormous variation from one so-called Marxist-Leninist nation to another. Some quite old-fashioned problems of international trade, of comparative advantage, and of national sovereignty have far from disappeared in states considering themselves already to have passed into at least the first stage of socialism. Continuing the examination, we cannot avoid seeing a new capitalist titan of a nation in Japan; and the awakening sleepy giant of Brazil, whether we like it or not an unsteady Cyclops with one eye focused on growth rather than general welfare. The examination also shows that even among the more egalitarian countries, there is no universally necessary connection among the following four items commonly found as foundationstones of revolutionist platforms: increased political autonomy, greater equality of living standards, more prosperity resting on a self-sustaining economic base, and a spread of individual and minority group liberties.

Still, the major thrust of the Marxist argument is more nearly correct than not. In general, there has been a movement toward greater control by, and greater sharing of available wealth among, the world's poorer people within their own countries. In many cases, the changes have occurred with a rapidity no less astonishing than the long length of time that had to pass before the changes began. Nevertheless, it would be useful if available predictions were more specific. What changes does political change bring in its wake? How do stratification systems shift? How can economies be made simultaneously less dependent and more productive? How is it possible to combine past tradition with modern arrangement in order that initial enthusiasm continue and not turn to dullness or resentment? Are answers appropriate for places where the deprived have been overwhelming majorities also appropriate for where they have been minorities?

Examination over. What, then, the prognosis? That a random patient will surely die one day, probably of cancer or heart disease, but perhaps of an accident or influenza? Predictions much more accurate than that are not available, whether from econo-determinist schools of thought or from others that are currently fashionable. Men have made and will go on making their own history. Yet until now they have certainly not done so in any consistent way, even when ostensibly relying upon an essentially similar doctrine. On the contrary, the doctrines themselves have been shaped to circumstances, showing a certain ironic similarity to what Marx said was true of the so-called laws of classical economics. They, he said, were not universals at all, only descriptions of how economics worked in given times and places.

Despite my tentativeness, there are people who feel certain. Perhaps they agree with a proposition embodied in a quotation from Victor Hugo that appears on a poster I have on my office wall. It reads, "Nothing can withstand the force of an idea whose time has come." We know that Marx, fighting against the ghost of Hegel (or is it Geist?) as well as against some of the other currents of the thought of his time, held that ideas were merely emanations from more basic and fundamentally economic conditions. When he did attribute causative force to systems of ideas, he tended to dismiss those that were not in accord with his own as mere ideology, as the conscious or unconscious defense of class interests, or as ignorance, as in the case of the peasantry that was responsible for what he and Engels called the idiocy of rural life. Marx would have liked those words of Hugo's in reference to an idea linked to the force and drive of an ascendant proletariat. Neither he nor Hugo himself, for that matter, would have wanted to apply them to the ideas that helped put Louis Napoleon at the head of France.

Both Weber and Marx would have thought, I think, that Hugo's statement was not intended to be a tautology, but a declaration of hope, an implicit assertion that newer and better values would triumph over old ones. But consider. How do we know when an idea's time has come? It is not sufficient to decide at some time after the idea has triumphed. That is merely to let time make all things right or, as some of my colleagues would put it, to indulge in a *post hoc, ergo propter hoc* kind of analysis. Moreover, many ideas must have come and gone without finding their time, precisely because there was a good deal that could withstand them. If an idea misses even though its time was almost right, as the times seem to have been almost right for Garvey's ideas, will it ever find its time again? Maybe . . . maybe not. The Russian Empire suffered

1905 before the Soviet Union had its 1917, but Paris has had so many unsuccessful rebellions since 1789 that only experts are likely to remember them all.

## RAILING AGAINST ONE-TRACK DIALECTICS

The force of an idea is not autonomous and self-propelling. Instead, it can neither be harnessed nor set free apart from appropriate cultural, political, and economic circumstances. Take the case of the two twinkled-toed modern sisters – science and technology. They refuse to perform without the right sorts of stages. Or think how hard it is to find judge, cop, or convict endorsing the poet's view that stone walls and iron bars do not prisons or cages make. Yet there is a difficulty here that my feeble attempts at cute phrasing cannot resolve, for the range of covariation among different sorts of idea systems and social institutions is very wide. By way of example, consider that science may be as well developed in a totalitarian state as in a nominally democratic one, or that there may be more purely political equality in a highly stratified nation than in another appearing to be more nearly leveled out. Attempting to summarize, I suppose that if, like Hugo, we find ourselves wanting to say that the time is right for an idea, we are actually letting the term "time" stand for a particular set of social arrangements, recognizing at the same time that it is not necessarily just those arrangements, but conceivably others as well, which could be equally or nearly equally correct for that idea.

I think my formulation amends a more orthodox Marxist position. Many Marxists assert that belief, knowledge, and material conditions ought to pull together like a cooperative troika, and that when they do not it is because the belief is wrong, the knowledge inaccurate, and the consciousness false. Because they work with a vision of a road that *will* be followed and that when followed will lead to a better future, they dismiss detours as aberrations. They further assert that the aberrations are not random, but are directly determined products of an order different from and antagonistic to the one they envision. A common argument of this sort holds that a working class which does not have consciousness in and for itself has been duped into accepting part of an ideological superstructure that actually belongs to and serves the ruling class.

It takes only a small step to get from that argument to the proposition that the only way for a class to free itself (these days the same point is made about other categories like racial, religious, or sexual ones) is either to do away with the social order that has been dominating it, or, in a separatist variant, to get out from under by moving away and constructing anew. The proposition is quite persuasive when two other conditions hold: (a) it is possible to prove that the class or other social category in question has actually been deprived or abused; (b) it is also possible to show that the deprivation or abuse has been continuous even where it differs in form in accordance with changes in the larger social order that have not been so great as to have changed its fundamental character. Then it is easy to say, "We must prevent them from doing what they do, or we must avoid it, for no matter what their actions, we are the ones who are used and who get the short end."

I have tried to do justice to the argument by presenting it consistently. Nevertheless, I think it is open to three possibly serious sources of error. First, discriminatory ideas or systems of thought are not necessarily direct emanations from economic orders. Second, calling a social or economic order by the same name despite recognizable changes in it over time leads to oversimplifications that make it harder to plan conscious additional change. Third, the residue of past relations between a superordinate and a subordinate group which differ in terms of a visible or otherwise well-established membership criterion (such as religion or language) is likely to include an ideology that is affected by the groups' present relative class positions and interests but is not identical with them; that ideology has, as a consequence, demonstrable effects across class lines within each group, particularly vis-a-vis members' orientations toward nonmembers.

People have devoted entire careers to considering these three points. I do not have the space to treat them with all the attention they deserve, and so I must try to handle them briefly. I treat the first two in this section and give the third a place of its own in the section that follows, concentrating on conditions helping to account for contemporary black consciousness rather than on the majority's continuing racism.

I begin with an example of a discriminatory belief system that may have begun with, and certainly became beyond any doubt, a direct emanation from an economic order. I think that in the entire Western Hemisphere, particularly in its northern half, racial prejudice had its greatest significance as a justification for economic exploitation in what was a massive complex of slavery and plantation agriculture. In the United States, the very formation of the national state had to do obeisance to the economic interests of the southern planters. The conflict over slavery later nearly broke the Union, but the paper principles of three postbellum amendments intended to undo slavery's effects were largely symbolic, not even serving to decorate the reality that slavery had merely been replaced by a kind of serfdom called sharecropping.

Nevertheless, not all forms of prejudice and discrimination have such obvious economic roots, even though they almost always have important economic implications. The Spanish Inquisition is a good example. Religion was the central issue, despite both the Church's and Crown's playing for significant political and economic stakes. Surely the Jews who were put to the fire could not have been thinking that they were protecting their class status or possessions through their martyrdom, not when many could and did go free by converting. However, because their case is closer to representing the force of group membership, my third point, I shall go no further here except to say that factors other than class also lead men to perform well or badly, or to define their interests in ways which may seem strange at first glance.

Returning to the main theme, I'll take a moment to recapitulate. Although racism may not have been invented by capitalists, it certainly came to serve the needs of one form of American capitalism and was then nourished and sustained by other and later forms of it, not only for an elite but among ordinary groups living in a competitive order that led them to push and tug at one another. Black people in general have never drawn any but a short lot in this society, and the society has always been capitalist in one way or another. Black people here have served as the society's consensual bottom ever since their arrival, working as slaves, as serfs, or for low wages, in all three cases bolstering the self-esteem of others who had no better way for feeling themselves at all well off.

However, it is mere rhetoric to equate today's conditions with those of one of the harshest forms of slavery the world has known by calling them both by the same name – white capitalism. It is closer to reality, but still rhetorical, to equate the kinds of legal and political control over black people in a contemporary northern ghetto with the terror of lynching or the threat of starvation that controlled black people in 1920 southern villages and towns, and then to call both kinds of control repression by the white capitalist power structure. I am impatient with such misguided or frankly propagandistic pitches which boil down to saying simply that the country was and is racist and evil because it was and is white and capitalist. It is now 1975, and enough has changed so that all of us ought to be able to see oversimplifications and part-truths for what they are, even if we sympathize with the aims or understand the motivations of the people who make them.

Not all has changed, and the change has not been sufficient. Nevertheless, now in 1975 black people, some of them at "servant-of-the-power-structure" universities and some of them in this book, are together writing more articles and books about American race relations in a year than many of us could read in five. This is a time when it is easy to assert, but hard to prove, that racism in New York or Chicago or Los Angeles serves economic interests more than it dents and bends them. Arguing that all that is necessary is for racism to serve some whites' interests even if it damages an economy in general, since white solidarity demands and enjoys racism's being tolerated, is shifting the ground. It is to say, that is, that racism has its own force apart from class. I think it does have its own force, in line with my third point above. For now, the more limited point is that if racism is not necessarily good for capitalism, or if major capitalists are indifferent to it in some important respects, it is probably incorrect to go on holding that as long as American capitalism exists, then American racism must exist too.

Instead, and very much like 19th- and 20th-century European anti-Semitism, American racism is a splendid example of how idea systems, or sets of beliefs that originated in one epoch or set of circumstances for which they were "appropriate" (in the limited sense of fitting well with dominant institutions), go on exercising great influence under new circumstances to which they are linked but for which they are neither appropriate nor ineluctable. Consider that now, in 1975, blacks are still last hired and first fired at Ford and GM, still have less seniority than whites in the UAW. But skin color makes far less difference to those organizations as prospective employers or bargaining agents than it does to Poles in Hamtramck as prospective neighbors concerned about prestige, property values (yes, yes, of course I know that's economic), and maintaining their own community. In this instance, racism is stronger at the bottom, where it's based on convention and sentiment as much or more than on calculation, than at the top, where power really lies, and where racism could really pay off if the controllers wanted to try to use it that way. Some readers may wish to counter my argument, holding they couldn't use it that way, couldn't get away with it, not with so many black people already in the union, not with so many prospective black voters. They would be making my point for me. There have been some important changes in this American capitalist society; its politics do reflect, but are not merely a reflection of, the corporate interests that are now the major factor in the American economic system. I simply think that it is always a good idea for those who are involved in and planning change to see that institutions do vary over time, that the relations among those institutions also change, and that different people are linked to those institutions in many, many different ways. To forget these sources of variation in an attempt to make a neater and cleaner theoretical argument or a more powerful rhetorical appeal is to lose sight of some very good openings for wedging in levers of change.

## CLOSING THE RING TO OPEN THE DOOR

Race and class are still inextricably linked in American society, still mutually reinforcing, but they are not the same things, and neither is coterminous with the American political system, though both exercise enormous effects upon it. Put somewhat less succinctly but more precisely, racial distinctions go on adding to and perpetuating class distinctions; class inferiority sustains racial distinctions and rationalizes what turns out to be differential treatment even under ostensibly universalistic or meritocratic circumstances such as are assumed in usual civil service requirements; and the political system has turned from having been just a perpetrator of class and racial differences to something more responsive, sometimes perpetuating and sometimes changing them, in some limited circumstances even insisting that racial criteria be made to counterbalance the class-associated residue of three centuries of enforced low status. After 50 or 60 years in which the black population has been moving rather rapidly from traditional, more personal, rural settings to modern, more anonymous, urban industrial ones, it is not surprising that the effects of class differences should count for more and be felt more bitterly than before, even while older caste distinctions diminish in prevalence and intensity.

Class factors help to explain the thrust of today's black liberation movements, but it is obvious that the movements are not based on class alone. On the contrary, every day they come to depend more upon black internal organization and black political activity. These operate across class lines within black areas, black districts, black ghettoes, trying to make communities of them, not just neutral descriptions based on location or demographic concentration. Furthermore, although white Americans have traditionally responded to black ones primarily in terms of racial difference, that is not the whole explanation of why black Americans now more and more wish to respond to one another primarily in terms of their own race.

A more complete explanation has to consider some ways that class and racial factors have interacted in the recent past. Keep in mind that race has become a preeminent basis for *positive* and widespread minority identification only after caste lines were weakened. No longer is there little or no upward mobility among the minority; no longer is it nearly categorically correct to say that minority members rank lower than majority members in general class terms. On the contrary, *relative* deprivation has been a more important mobilizing factor as absolute deprivation has lessened, but with no certainty that remaining inequities would disappear or sharply diminish over a brief period of time.

The following are some other conditions that need to be kept in mind for a satisfactory explanation of emergent black consciousness and the separatist thrust. Some of them stem directly from class and material considerations; others, while obviously related to them, do not.

1. *Broad contextual circumstances*

Black people live under conditions practically identical with the classically hypothecated ones for mobilizing political protest: residential concentration in massive urban agglomerations, increases in education without correlative boosts in income, rapid means of mass communication, threats of employment layoffs, and easy identification of real or assumed oppressors.

2. *The neglect of the ghettoes*

Most of today's major protest and consciousness-building activity is occurring in the urban ghettoes. Ghettoes have higher proportions than other areas of people who are ill-informed, unskilled, unlettered; of people who bear other burdens or carry other stigmata; delinquents and criminals, prostitutes and pimps, alcoholics and addicts. The ghetto is the refuse heap where the society stacks the lives and bodies of the unwanted, leaving them to pile up and to prey and be preyed upon by one another. Add the old and the sick, for these normally debilitating problems occur among black people, too, and they are more difficult when people are poor.

Neither movements nor riots are generally built from such people. The Kerner Commission Report showed, for example, that riot participants were badly educated and likelier than others to have been recently unemployed, but they were young, healthy, and strong, nearly representative of the people of their age living in the riot areas, themselves poorer than other ghetto districts. Movements are not often built from the expendables and the leftovers, not from the lumpen. But they may be built *for* them, partly on their behalf, partly using them as symbols of a country's reluctance to keep its promises. Forty acres and a mule? More like it was 40 years of chopping someone else's cotton than a bone-shaking run up the Illinois Central from the Delta to the South Side.

Who could possibly care for these people, reshape or retrain them, give them a reason for change or the strength to carry on? Who was there to tell them that a bent back was reason enough to hold head high? White people wouldn't do it; white people didn't want these blacks whose records made them unreliable, unacceptable.

An important part of black pride and the separatist thrust grew from a confusing complex concatenation of events and conditions: the failure of integration to work, as white individuals withdrew themselves and their money from central cities; the terrible, crying, shameful need in the black ghettoes with no one but blacks to meet it; the successful example of some black efforts at self-help and self-organization; black individual and social successes against great odds; whites throwing in the towel and giving blacks some resources to try to clean up the mess themselves; the fear of ghetto revolt; Vietnam as documentation – if more were needed – of national perfidy; the assassination of two white brothers who had befriended black men, and of two black men who may have been the greatest leaders their people have ever had in this country. Civil rights coalitions were dead or dying and it was clear that riots could not make a revolution. By 1968, blacks' pride and their autonomous drive were the residue, a new hope born of broken promises and deadened dreams. The present already calls for new tasks and higher levels of expertise, less assumption of instant liberation and more measured judgments. In the meantime, it is clear that black people will never willingly go back to thinking and acting as they did as short a time as five or ten years ago, in the days when self-hatred was more apparent than pride, or even in those days when an ethic of universal brotherliness tried to tame anger by urging Christian love and forbearance in the face of brutality.

3. *The rise of the new middle class*

Another catalyst deserves special mention, for it concerns a group that is critical far beyond its numbers. That group is the young, disaffected black middle class. The black middle class as a whole counters a common white stereotype that ghettoes are merely jungles and a less common black stereotype holding that American racial minorities are condemned to ranks no higher than that of the working class while whites all rise to the middle and beyond. More directly important is that the younger portion of the black middle class is today a major source of black intellectual and organizational leadership.

Such people do not have the fear of their elders. That fear, we must remember, is by no means unjustified. When what Frazier called the black bourgeoise played its own status games in deadly earnest, living in what he called their world of make believe, they had little assurance of being able to maintain a precarious respectability or to lay a solid foundation for their children to build upon. Many young black readers of Frazier seem to concentrate only upon his criticisms, forgetting that he tried also to explain what he described. Is it reasonable, after all, to expect sainthood from people whose lives carried so large a chunk of sociohistorical determination?

Today's younger and well-educated blacks do have less to fear, for there is more they can win and hold securely. But they are also realists who know that what they have won they have gained more as prizes of battle than as gifts from a contritely generous larger society. It was they who, after the fires last time, posted their edicts and took the Luther-like stands that swung open the gates of the nation's most important universities. It was they who, commuting in and out of the imitations of universities called community colleges, carried and spread that gospel of the contemporary poor intellectual, the Marxist-Leninist text. It was they who, for a short time, became the darlings of the liberal young whites on campus and the central actors in dramas performed on radical chic stages, bringing the rich a taste of a world thought "real" because its lives, like those of many white grandfathers, were nasty, brutish, and short. It was they who, having done and won all these things, heard the galling whispers that their accomplishments weren't real, weren't achieved by talent, but came through political pressure. It is now they who are coming to know that in working to win they sacrificed, for already there are younger and better trained brothers who are following paths they blazed and who, before long, will pass them. Tomorrow it will be they who will know that though their reward may be less than full, they will have done what they said could not be done before them, and that is for black men in America to have earned their manhood.

Unblemished heroes? Of course not, and not supermen either. Smaller proportions of black people than whites attend the top quality universities; and in strong universities or weak ones, fewer black than white students concentrate on the more stringent but ultimately more useful disciplines. Engineering, economics, and pre-med courses are tougher and drier than education, sociology, and history. Moreover, the prestige and deference rewards for black universitarians in black communities, as well as calls for leadership from them, tend to make them ready to claim elite prerogatives that often run beyond their talents and experience. They sometimes remind me of their counterparts in Latin America who also espouse more rapid and radical change than they can bring about by themselves. Another parallel may be less flattering still, for both Latin American and black American universitarians commonly have far more eagerness to urge and to work for egalitarian change than they do to give up very much of what they have earned for themselves. Color aside, many young people start out by criticizing others for weaseling away from complete and ultimate conviction, and then end up doing pretty much the same thing themselves once they've gotten to have about as much as the others, and to think, as the others do, that they have earned it. It isn't just power that corrupts; prosperity seduces, and mobility co-opts.

I need to strike two balances. One is that I have written as if all the people in this new kind of black generation are the same. Of course they are not; all of us know many different kinds of them. The second balance is that each is a separate person. Separate people combine motivations and performances that are sometimes good, sometimes bad, sometimes ephemeral, sometimes lasting. However, if someone were to ask me for my personal opinion about this generational group as a whole, I'd sum up by saying that it has met its obligations not perfectly but well. Other than to ask that it go on doing so, it is hard to expect much more.

4. *White response and separatist momentum*

A substantial number of white people still assume that almost any black person is essentially or ultimately inferior or undesirable, whether on his own account or because his presence is taken as a harbinger of the coming of his less well-off or less well-trained brothers. Furthermore, the majority still puts prejudice into practice by indirect ways of leaving the minority segregated in inferior facilities, even after direct ways for putting and keeping it there have come to have less scope and less widespread approval. Common examples are withdrawal to newer and better facilities, or reluctance to impose taxes high enough to pay for bringing minority facilities closer to the level of their own. It is not even necessary that such discriminatory outcomes be consciously linked to prejudice or stem from a clear intent to maintain relative superiority and inferiority. Effects may be similar where majority performances are predicated on nothing more than the willingness to tolerate others' preferences, so as to avoid upsetting friends or relatives, neighbors or business associates. Outside of the South, in fact, white prejudice and discrimination have usually depended more on such informal means of social control than on formal ones, calling out the cops or calling in the Guard only as a last resort. Class-based differences in power and control have done the rest of what needed to be done.

Many minority efforts have been directed toward securing state-enforced means for making it impossible for white people to go on exercising such informal but powerful practices. Such efforts were often easily understood and thought to be more or less legitimate, even by white people, when they were directed toward letting black people in, as in limiting employment discrimination or eliminating restrictive housing covenants. White resistance has been far stronger, however, to rules or programs that, although essentially integrationist, have sought to limit white options or move white people into black areas. Suburban whites wish neither to pay for nor be included in plans to educate central city children, nor do they tolerate the idea of their children being transported to schools in predominantly black districts.

Most white people have been equally hostile toward black attempts to exert direct control over school systems or police forces. Let us not make the mistake of assuming that these agencies are just like any others. On the contrary, to question them or their operation is to question how the general society socializes its young and insures final control. Many white preferences and options, such as moving away from ghetto border areas, do affect black communities significantly, but at one step removed. Not so police forces and school systems, although whites are no more accustomed to thinking of these two agencies in racial terms than they do of the electric or the water company. Yet, when almost all the other whites have gone, except for the shopkeepers, police and schools are still there in the ghettoes, serving as representatives of the larger – that is, non black – society. Their impact is direct; their symbolism, obvious. They are agencies of the state.

What the community organizers have told us is, "Work with the grievances a community already has. Ideology is less important than helping to show people how they can make a difference right where they live." A large part of what is called separatism is no more than black people trying to follow that advice, counseled by other black people rather than by outside experts or volunteers. A large part of what is called separatism is merely a collective effort to try to influence agencies that regulate as much as serve black people, agencies like police and schools, welfare and housing authorities.

When a problem is at home and an enemy can be identified, a movement can take on new strength, building on itself for as long as its victories are neither pyrrhic nor merely symbolic. In the long run, however, it is important to identify enemies correctly. If not, neutrality or even the possible support of outsiders may be needlessly sacrificed. A concrete example is at hand. It was a mistake to let anti-Semitism slip into the New York City school controversy in 1968. It was a mistake despite the fact that some Jews were and are racists, and despite the contention that the teachers' union took only a small bit of black anti-Semitism and blew it out of all proportion for its own propaganda purposes. Precisely. The union could not have done so if others hadn't carelessly given it the chance.

In any case, once the separatist and community control movements of the 1960s picked up steam, they created their own momentum. The direction of black effort changed, placing more emphasis on reconstruction from within and on antagonism toward outsiders rather than hopeful cooperation with them. The majority also pulled back, recoiling from the less and less veiled hostility that was being directed against it, more conscious of protecting its own interests. It has become more difficult to build class-based coalitions across racial lines. Today the majority may also sense that minorities are displaying less power than they did three and four and five years ago when tangible threats backed up innumerable postings of non-negotiable demands.

Add unfortunate internal divisions in the black communities, for there are presently many places where black people are sapping their own strength in bitter controversies over the one best way to win change. There is no one best way, only many good ways. They range from breakfast programs to selective boycotts, on through joint interracial union lobbying where it's possible, all the way to voting together with whites for a liberal candidate thought unsatisfactory but still preferable to his Neanderthal opponent.

Internally divided movements that find it hard to coalesce with others sharing some similar class interests are not new in American history. Group ties resting on the primarily affective bases of faith or ethnicity have long kept class cleavage from being felt as strongly here as in many sister states in Western Europe. It seems to take quite a long time, moreover, before groups which have often been betrayed get to feel secure enough to let themselves trust the principle that alliances need not be more than temporary in order to work.

## CONCLUSION

I have spent a large part of this paper questioning some of the assumptions of the black left. Here I merely point out that it is just at the point of asking Lenin's question, "What Is To Be Done?" that much of the black left suddenly swerves away from dialectical materialism to bump an ideational curb. It is, after all, a pretty thoroughly idealist position which holds that black liberation will assuredly follow from black consciousness, black desire, black pride, and black solidarity. Yet the argument is important. Only in the realm of ideas can people perform the acrobatically impossible task of lifting themselves by their own bootstraps. The idea takes strap from boot and gives people something higher to hang it on. Yet belief must do more than create elan. If not, elan turns out to be just more pie in the sky, and in America, as Mr. Brown pointed out, pie is often blood-red like cherry, served a la mode on a plate of violence. Nobody, or almost nobody, really likes that dish, but it's more easily digested by those with the bigger guns.

That is why black pressure must be unrelenting and flexible, but applied against obstacles that can be pushed, and that, when pushed, will give. There is no need to make the majority's anger an end in itself and a measure of success. Nevertheless, there is also no way to avoid that anger. The better established majority could not abide the Irish use of politics; they called it dirty, graft-ridden, and nepotistic – and they were not always wrong. The better established could not abide the Jewish and, later, the Japanese-American reliance on education; they called it a grinding, obsessive, overanxious approach to learning – and they were not always wrong. These are techniques that appear to be becoming more available and better used by blacks. In the meantime, the better established can't abide black emphasis on common concern and closed organizational techniques; they call it separatist, short-sighted, and selfish. It frightens and offends them – and they are not always wrong. But what will mean more to black people – benign neglect or concessions won from an antagonist who may be angry but still has to recognize that pushes come from power?

Calling another brother and meaning it, reaching out to hold his hand – these are not material actions, but they are more than mere metaphors. They are not yet power, but they are an inspiration that can be converted to power. I do not underestimate inspiration. (I'd like to borrow the phrase "the lift of a driving dream," but, since I know its source, it's probably better to leave it out.) Inspiration is not all, of course, Muhammad and Moses were deeply inspired men, and yet their God did not move mountains for them. One walked; the other climbed.

Perhaps a case can be made that at least one of the two men makes a fine study in economic determinism as well as in inspiration. Moses, after all, is reputed to have been leading the first generation of ex-slaves and their children. Yet, surely, now that the age of miracles is long gone, we cannot say that very many of the economic and political implications of the belief he so strengthened were either foreseen or intended by him or by any of his contemporaries. It should be obvious by this time that I have a certain fondness for Moses. Maybe that's why I think it no more reasonable to make him responsible for my family's moving from Roxbury to Newton than to blame him for the "final solution." I'll share Moses with others, or let them pick their own favorite prophets. I ask only that we not ask too much of them or attribute too much to them; that we not underestimate belief but frame and limit our estimates of its effects by considering its surrounding circumstances; and that we not confuse a true believer's glimmer of hope with a beam that must illuminate the paths to be taken.

# 31
# *Toward A Black Social Science**

RONALD WALTERS

Whether or not one believes in the possibility that there exists a body of knowledge about black life which can be disciplined and made useful in the survival and development of black people depends upon many factors. Among them are (1) a determination that such knowledge can be disciplined and (2) a determination that in such a disciplined state, the knowledge when applied to actual problems the community faces will be useful in the solution.

For years both black and white scholars denied that the "stuff" of black life constituted a respectable enough body of knowledge to even bother about recording for posterity. Recently, however, there has been a recognition of this gross oversight and a grudging admission that perhaps there is such a thing as black history (after all, a people have only to have existed to have a history). This was an important admission because (in addition to the protest by black students) it was this small bit of intellectual awareness that was a major factor that led university faculties to vote in favor of adopting Black Studies in the last few years. Once having established such programs, it was easy to see, from a perusal of some sample curricula that the humanities were legitimate because blacks have produced some of the most original art forms the country has had and in some areas constitute the most dominant and dynamic forces existent today. But there is definitely no black science and no black social science.

Secondly, another question arises when those involved in black education assume that the application of the knowledge of African history and culture is essential to black progress. Most whites and blacks still do not believe this! Standing in the residue of program after program fashioned by so-called "experts" to reconstruct the black community, using white social science, these doubters know that something is wrong but refuse to believe that there is some efficacy in their own black being, some black power which, when added to other relevant factors, constitute the necessary ingredient for the solution. It is all the more confusing when solutions are not found because white social science has acquired a reputation for its "social change" orientation and the development of "intervention" strategies.

One source of this reputation has been the operation of white social science in the Third World. After World War II, when many countries in Africa and Asia were becoming independent, there were many social scientists studying the problem of the transition of "old societies" into "new states"[1] (a process commonly called modernization) and the factors which impeded such a transition. Some of the lessons of this experience were that significant change depended either upon (1) the operation of powerful incentives or (2) the application of selective force. In any case, white social science may have discovered these laws but it still has not been able to control the factors that lead to development or modernization in spite of the fact that many such "new states" have Western social scientists and technicians in every ministry of their governments.

The reputation has done little to bring about results in the domestic scene in the United States as well. Part of this failure is political in the sense that no matter how relevant the information gathered, priorities of the politician are usually different because the modernization process in this country is taking place with a black minority. None other than Daniel Moynihan, after chronicling the failure of the political management and the functions of social scientists in the construction of the OEO Program, exhibits his own ambivalence about the role of social science.

> But is there something called social science, a body of knowledge, a methodology that men of quite disparate politics and temperaments will nonetheless agree upon, that can contribute to the formulation of policy? I will propose that the answer is a limited but emphatic yes.[2]

Then he poses a somewhat analogous question further on, and he suggests an answer.

> What institutional role may the social sciences expect to play in public affairs? The answer seems clear enough. *The role of social science lies not in the formulation of social policy, but in the measurement of results.*[3]

What seems here to be not only ambivalence but downright contradiction belies the proof of a powerful missing ingredient

*Reprinted by permission of the author.

in the study of black life which would be useful in both the formulation and evaluation of policy within this specific range of problems. Besides the ambivalence manifested by such social scientist, other causes of the dysfunction of white social science may be accounted for by three prime factors: (1) an ideological bias, (2) a structural bias, and (3) a methodological bias.

The ideology of social science planning for social change is rooted in the diverse theories and assumptions of the nature of the problems they address. Because they have no familiarity with the real culture from which these problems arise, they have created something synthetic – a "culture of poverty"[4] thesis to explain the reality of why black and a significant number of white people are poor in this country, as if by this single factor analysis they could also satisfactorily analyze all the roots of black oppression. One element of this ideology is that the poor are poor because they are bad managers of resources, and they, therefore, should have resources managed for them and "services" provided. The theory goes on, if an individual is adept at providing his own services, he will learn how to accumulate and utilize resources and will get on in this society. Under this ideology, black people are seen as children for whom the system (upon which they must depend) has to provide. This view, it should be noted, is not far from the "childlike" thesis of the nature of black people provided us by social scientists like Stanley Elkins who studied black slavery.[5] Never once have the theorists who have followed this line of reasoning stopped to consider how it was that in the Depression, for example, during the darkest period this nation faced since slavery, black people were able to manage resources. How was it that a people who lived on the very margin of existence were able to survive by hustling, by adapting their diet so as to make a delicacy out of the leftover waste of a pig, and how they shared even that with others. Considering the nature of the opposition black people have faced historically, someone must have been managing some resources somewhere.

There is also an administrative or structural bias concerning the way in which ideology is translated into strategy.[6] "Services" are structured to be available in ways that are suitable to those dispensing them. They are available at certain hours (which may or may not be the hours of highest need in the community) and at certain places (which may be inaccessible to those needing the services); and they are dispensed in certain ways (which are dehumanizing to the recipient). But even these problems would seem minor if a person were able to leave a service center having been truly aided in some way. In fact, there are scores of cases in evidence which detail the breakdown of such systems of services and their failure to deliver the services originally provided for.

There have been some recent administrative experiments designed to make the delivery systems more efficient, such as Program Planning Budgeting Systems,[7] but this method seems more applicable to institutions dealing in "hardware" and physical resources than it does in planning for delivery of human resources of the "software" variety. It has been and always will be difficult to quantify need beyond the most elementary material levels.

The problem of administrative methodology can be traced to social science research methodology in part. The sum of it can be found in the doctrine of "scientism"[8] – that the sum of what we believe must be right and, therefore, factual. These "facts" then become the basis upon which theories of black life are shaped into ideologies, which are shaped into strategies, which are shaped into programs. Rather than examining the substance of the consensus they reached as representative of a narrow area of truth which has limitations for them qualified by their collective backgrounds and experiences as white people, they have gone a step further and made their theories take on the quality of universal norms. That the sum of white experiences (and therefore theorizing) does not add up to black "fact" or reality can be seen in the following (and I hesitate to call it this) "analysis" by an American sociologist.

> [The Negroes] were without ancestral pride or family tradition. They had no distinctive language or religion. These, like their folkways and moral customs were but recently acquired from the whites and furnished no nucleus for a racial unity. The group was without even a tradition of historic unity or of racial achievement. There were no historic names, no great achievements, no body of literature, no artistic productions. The whole record of the race was one of servile or barbarian status apparently without a point about which a sentimental complex could be formed.[9]

This study, published originally in 1927 (and reissued recently in the wake of the panic publishing on blacks) gives the impression of some authority, as the author cites 33 separate pieces of "consensus" for the "facts" in the chapter from which this quote was taken. Some of the pieces of evidence he generally cites are from white and black authors and, no doubt, today one could take the same sources and manage a "modern" interpretation of the nature of black life. This suggests, at least to this writer, that the business of utilizing methods in arriving at the truth which appears to be objective (for Reuter had one of the best reputations of his day for objectivity) often does little more than yield to "voguism" in the social sciences.

One author has located what he thinks to be the reason for this problem in the fact that research has been oriented toward the prejudices of the discipline without the researcher understanding or purposefully hiding the fact that his finds are oriented toward his personal prejudices as well. The person is important because he has tended to hide behind the shield of "ethical neutrality," and this has enabled him to obviate the moral implications of his works. In fact, other prejudices derived from the institution he serves and the profession (discipline) of which he is a part assist the researcher in developing the shield between himself and the subject.[10]

The university or research institute has become a convenient place from which to sally forth occasionally to gather data, then to return to its sterile atmosphere to cogitate fantasies about their validity based on one's own narrow experiences using methodology that has its own inaccuracies and eccentricities. One also uses the resources of the university to produce results – the computer, the time off, the research grants, and the research assistants are all valuable supportive aids in this work. The other important thing about the university is (besides the fact that such researchers are not accountable to the people they research) that researchers are supported and reinforced in the disciplinary characteristics of their work by it. The department or other administrative unit has come to know and anticipate what the needs of various social science divisions will be in terms of resources and is adept at searching through the various foundations and government agencies for sources of support; at the same time, the black social scientist in the same unit has to fend for himself. There is also remarkably little internal ferment in these disciplinary units on the question of the nature of the discipline (the methodological argument aside), little cross fertilization with others, and a certain smugness about the legitimacy of these disciplines outside of the occasional salvoes from the "radical" professor on the left. Such attitudes make the research and the discipline mutually adaptive, reinforcing systems.

The results of the default of researchers, hiding behind the ethical neutrality we spoke of, together with the individual who has purpose in his distortion of the truths of black life, is that white social science has been ineffective with respect to the solution of black problems, it has become a weapon in defense of white interests, and an instrument of black social control.

> Information gathering systems or research methods always promise the existence and use of some system of social control. It is not only that the information they yield may be used by systems of social control, *but that they themselves are systems of social control.*[11] [Emphasis mine]

The evidence for this continues to mount but includes such items as the widespread use of drug therapy on so-called "hypersensitive children."[12] It is within the realm of this writer's own personal experience to have witnessed (and reported to the black community) the existence of white psychiatrists pronouncing black children "mentally retarded" or "mentally disturbed," which classified these children for special classes and special programs where they became guinea pigs for researchers who experiment with amphetamine injections, supposedly to make them "manageable."

The psychologists and psychiatrists are currently pushing the concept of "mental health" in the black community despite the fact that concepts they are peddling come out of white psychological experiences.[13] Many of these concepts are "individual-oriented," which is a strategy counter to the historic lessons of black survival (and future survival) which was and still is in terms of group dependence. The American "rugged individualist" ideology places a great deal of emphasis on individual effort, but what would have happened if the black man had tried to stand alone to endure or to escape from slavery; and what will happen if the black man tries to stand alone today and be defined as a human being outside of his blackness in this country? That is right, he would really be crazy! Finally, if one reads the military Riot Manual which is published by the Department of Defense and pays particular attention to the sections dealing with individual and group behavior, it is clear that these control agents are paying a great deal of attention to the social scientists and to the research that has been done on black behavior.[14] In fact, agencies like the Department of Defense spend millions of dollars annually on such research, and the so-called leading social scientists in universities all over the nation participate, as a recent governmental report will indicate.[15]

These facts are crucial when one considers that the balance of such activity and information is in the hands of the decision makers and, hence, the decision enforcers. Very recently the State of Massachusetts wanted some expertise on the performance of the State's Racial Imbalance Law as it was coming up for a review. The Education Commissioner turned to the Harvard School of Education and contracted for a study which will no doubt give the decision makers (not the black community) a basis on which to decide the matter compatible with the interest of the State. Parenthetically, one of the reasons the political system in the black community is so weak is that the monopoly of information about the way the system works, and not incidentally about the black community, is in the hands of white decision makers. What we need, therefore, is a black-controlled and black-informed social science that will yield the desired strategies for social change commensurate with the texture and aspirations of life of black people.

## BLACK SOCIAL SCIENCE

Those concepts that discipline (or bring order to) the study of the history and culture of black people constitute a working definition of the term.[16] Writing at the beginning of the development of black social science, one can only say what it might become. One hint in the area of sociology is in the writings of Robert Staples, Nathan Hare, Andrew Billingsley, and Joyce Ladner; in political sociology – the work of Gerald McWorter and James Turner; in history – the work of Harold Cruse, Lerone Bennet, Jr., John Clarke, and Vincent Harding; in political economy – Robert Browne, Earl Ofari, and James Boggs; in politics – Charles Hamilton. This list is not meant to be exhaustive and is a subjective selection of the work of black social scientists who have had the courage to try to criticize wrong-headed approaches whether from whites or blacks and the originality to try and create a black framework for their analyses.

One should not rejoice prematurely, however, by this meager listing because the white scholar is still winning the race to the documents and to the publishing houses and, thereby, still is in a position to exercise a great deal of influence over what the younger brothers and sisters read and think. New works by Tauber and Tauber, Theodore Draper, Philip Foner, Joanne Grant, Melvin Brimmer, Tabb, Meier, Rudwick, Pettigrew, Factor, Marx, Fox, and many others still come out weekly. Despite the beginning effort there is very little internal intellectual black ferment. For example, in black history there is very little consensus but no significant debate over periodization or the significance of various social, political, and cultural movements; in sociology no consensus and no black debate over the structure and function of the black social system; in economics there is a waning argument over the efficacy of "black capitalism" but there should be a great debate over the "isms" black people have historically been sold, in order to clarify our choices. Very generally, the dominant features of black intellectual energy at the present time seems to be concerned with a consideration of Pan-Africanism (which is absolutely necessary) and still, to a considerable extent, we are in the finishing stages of having to react to the challenge to the legitimacy of black social science by white and black skeptics.

We are also in the midst of developing embryonic organizations and settling their ideology and operations, hoping they will be the base of activities that will consistently feed attempts of black social scientists to relate their craft to the struggles of black people. In any case, the lack of volume in our activity may be attributed to many causes, but perhaps it may be as a student of mine said recently (sister Joyce Martin) that in this period we are like the old mule who lashed out with his heels to kick the wagon and start it rolling and who is simply rearing back to strike again.

What is clearest at this point is that in the works that have been produced, the ideology is profoundly different from that of white social science. Perhaps it would suffice to take a few samples from the work of the authors listed above as evidence for this assertion. In discussing Black Nationalism, James Turner states that biased sociological studies have accepted the census model,

> But while consensus models accept the core values of the dominant group as functional for society, some of these values may in fact be inimical to particular groups, who are thus increasingly led to question the legitimacy of the social system. Proper study of Black Nationalism employs a conflict perspective[17]

and he continues to define the concept.

Harold Cruse performs a valuable service, writing in the same issue of *Black World,* by pushing black scholars toward social criticism:

> I reiterate this critical assault on black social, political, and cultural thought was premeditated [speaking of his book *Crisis of the Negro Intellectual*]. It was my conviction that black social thought of all varieties was in dire need of some ultra-radical overhauling if it was to meet the comprehensive test imposed by the sixties. Now that the sixties are history, I am still convinced – even more so – that black social thought is in need of ultra-radical overhauling. In fact, the arrival of the seventies revealed to me that I had underestimated the critical reassessing black social thought really needed.[18]

And he goes on to imply that our political theory needs to be seriously grounded in local conditions and perspectives, using the experiences of other political events in other countries selectively. In his subsequent article (Part II) in *Black World,*[19] he chides the black scholar for not having dealt critically with the revered black historians of the past, and he is oh so right.

John Henrike Clarke has a partial answer to the role of the contemporary black scholar in the struggle for black liberation when he says that he must be a "scholar-activist" and adds (speaking of the formation of the African Heritage Studies Association),

> We interpret African History from a Pan-Africanist perspective that defines all black people as African People.... Our program has as its objective the restoration of the cultural, economic, and political life of African people everywhere.[20]

In the realm of sociology, Andrew Billingsley points to the fact that "white social science" excludes consideration of the complexity and strength of the black family as factors of prime importance mainly because

> To understand family functioning in the black community, the chief fault is the attribution of an inverse cause and effect relationship between family and society [ignoring] the forces of institutionalized racism. Analyses such as these stem almost unchecked from the white Anglo-conformity perspective which judges black people outside the context of their unique anchor in history, their treatment in this country, and their contemporary social conditions. More important, such analyses ignore the existence of a black subculture, and the strength of the black community and the black family which enabled black people to survive in a hostile environment for over 300 years.[21]

Methodologically, he feels that social science disciplines are "already too old and rigid to give us the knowledge of black families we need without a major renewal of those disciplines themselves."[22] This point is expressed here but illustrated in his book, *Black Families in White America,* as he gives to this work not only a sociological but a strongly historical frame of reference.

The ideas of Earl Ofari and James Boggs in Political Economy make a powerful argument as they analyze the reasons for the failure of black economic life. In looking at the failure of black business, Earl Ofari finds that the sum of traditional literature suggests the following:

> Examples abound throughout the voluminous reports and studies the mythmakers of black business have conducted. The blame for black business failure for a long time was laid on black people themselves. The main argument [citing E. Franklin Frazier's study, *The Negro in the United States,* p. 410] can be easily summarized: black proprietors are inefficient, lazy, lack education, have little business experience, are slow and discourteous. Black businesses fail because the very economic system in which they are trying to succeed is stacked against them.[23]

If this is true, then brother's Boggs' statement seems to point up the solution as he says,

> Any program for the development of the black community must be based on large-scale social ownership rather than on private individual enterprise. In this period of large-scale production and distribution, private individual enterprise [or small business] can only remain marginal and dependent, adding to the sense of hopelessness and powerlessness inside the black community.[24]

Central to this particular problem seems to be the discussion of whether or not racism in America is endemic to capitalism. This point was settled long ago by one of our most brilliant and neglected black scholars, Oliver Cox, who listed racism as one of the features of capitalism.[25] But the debate over the form and substance of the system which will guarantee equality to blacks proceeds from the perceived need to have radical change in the distribution of wealth. Thus far the center of this debate has been over the value of "black capitalism," but as it begins to appear in social science literature there is a recognition of the need for new concepts. As S.E. Anderson says,

> Paradoxically, black business education and most of the relatively few black economists have made the tragic mistake of embracing, unequivocally the principles and practices of American Capitalism; the same system that white people manipulate and scheme to deny black people significant participation.[26]

He goes on to say, in a fashion not dissimilar to Boggs, that if black people are to be liberated under capitalism they must have the power and control to affect significant changes in their current status. The answers to black economic development have not been found within the concepts of white social science because it assumes the ideology of the capitalist system.

This discussion has been based on the knowledge that there are questions inherent in the black experience which have been approached incorrectly by the utilization of both the ideology and the methodology of white social science. But the black truth does not necessarily proceed in dialectical fashion because of the intimate juxtaposition of black people to whites in the history and culture of America.

> The black scholar must develop new and appropriate norms and values, new institutional structures, and in order to be effective in this regard, he must also develop and be guided by a new ideology. Out of this new ideology will evolve new methodology. Though in some regards it will subsume and overlap existing norms of scholarly endeavor.[27]

Nevertheless, black life has been distinctive enough and separate enough to constitute its own uniqueness, and it is on the basis of that uniqueness that the ideology and the methodology of black social science rests.

## IDEOLOGY

In the works cited above it is possible to identify certain elements that contribute as an ideology for black social science, and they refer to radicalism and conflict theory as well as an infusion of the substances of blackness – Africanism, nationalism, history, cultural style, self-determination, and consciousness of racism. Elsewhere I have dealt with this problem of using Brother Basil Matthews' term the "Unity and Order of Blackness."[28] I believe this term (which he is in the process of applying to research as the "Black knowledge process") to be comprehensive enough to include all aspects of a black social science ideology. Also, concepts of "unity" and "order" may be looked upon as operations which when performed upon the data help to discipline them. Here, however, I would turn to the seminal works of Gerald McWorter and Preston Wilcox in order to give to the discussion of ideology a more specific quality. In his article, "The Ideology of Black Social Science" Brother McWorter says,

> Social Science has constructed a set of terms to explain black people and their experiences and, for the most part, these terms have suffered from being based on sterile analytical theory that attempts to *classify* social reality and not *explain* its essential nature. [His emphasis.][29]

He then goes on to classify and explain the terms of black social science by contrasting them with the terms of white social science.[30]

| *White Social Science* | *Black Social Science* |
|---|---|
| Negro | African (black) |
| Segregation | Colonization |
| Tokenism | Neo-Colonialism |
| Integration | Liberation |
| Equality | Freedom |
| Assimilation | Africanization |

Preston Wilcox also performs a transforming function on terms which to him are examples of the "rhetoric of oppression," by his use of a black educational ideology and a taxonomy resulting from the comparison of scientific colonialism and scientific humanism.[31]

| | | |
|---|---|---|
| Urban Renewal | really means | Negro Removal |
| Model Cities | " | Model Colonies |
| Human Relations | " | Colonial Relations |
| Culturally Deprived | " | Illegally Deprived |
| Public Welfare | " | Public Starvation |
| Code Enforcement | " | Tenant Exploitation |
| School Decentralization | " | School Recentralization |

In each case the writer "translated" from the white into the black terminology using his sense of black consciousness as the cutting edge to redefine reality so that the black terms that resulted are congruent with the objective black situation.

Terms alone, however, do not make an ideology. If, therefore, we can distill the essential experience which the collectivity of these terms represent, perhaps we may present the ideology that results below as a model of relations.

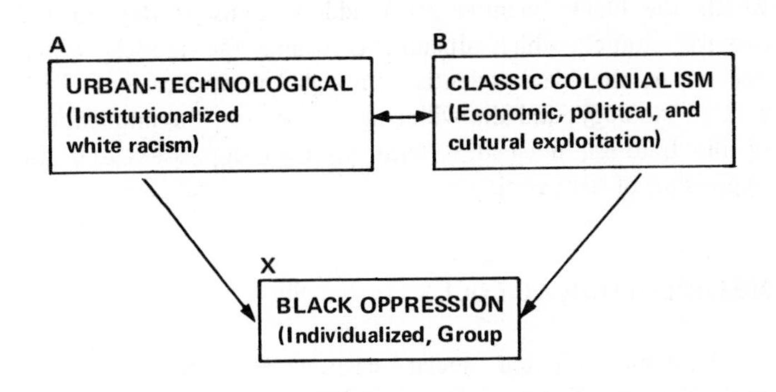

Without going into the details of either A – X or B – X relationship (which would be beyond the scope of this paper and volumes, perhaps a comment on each would suffice to relate what the reader must most assuredly know to be some of the facts to the subject at hand.

*Variable A.* Many of the analyses, particularly in the historical cultural, and political realm, do not yet take into account the pervasiveness of technology as a weapon against us and an impediment to the full expression of our blackness, the ways in which technology can be utilized in order to enhance those elements of our culture we should like to emphasize, and how we can control such technology to make this possible. The result of the functioning of such technology in an urban environment we know has increased the effectiveness of institutionalized racism by expelling more black people from institutions which would theoretically make them productive, and by using such institutions to objectively control our lives – one has only to mention the press in this regard, among other institutions. The distorted picture of black life presented in the national media will only be informed by the participation of black people in significant ways, and until that happens, it will continue to constitute an item of oppression upon black communities. Increasing levels of unemployment, and the disparity between white and black income and economic opportunities makes this relationship of oppression starkly evident.

*Variable B.* The explosive work *Black Power* contains within it the colonial paradigm[32] which explains the relationship between the white and black communities with respect to power relationships, and, thus, to all the attendant relationships which logically follow as a result. Sociologist Robert Blauner, notes this model and applies it to an analysis of the black community in Los Angeles as a rationale for the rebellion of 1965.[33] The use of this model is no accident, the objective conditions of power prevailing between the groups, plus the fact of an easily identifiable black group as the target, together with the geographical unity of most black communities, give every evidence of the colonial characteristic. That such relationships deal in exploitation is a necessary corollary to the existence of the colonial condition, as is the fact that such exploitation is traditionally interpreted by the exploited as base oppression.

Both variables A and B interact with each other in the American context to produce circumstances of unique and unequaled social quality. Together they constitute a powerful source of black oppression – that is, the consistent reality to which the black scientist must address himself. Beyond the massive studies which document it and the models which explain it, the black scientist, through the application of his skill to ideology, and the willingness to act out the implications of his findings, must deal with his own oppression and the oppression of his people.

## METHODOLOGICAL FOCUS

Liberation-oriented social science must have a rather explicit focus. The suggestion by Billingsley that perhaps the existing disciplines need to be revitalized could begin with the construction of black social science. For example, there is nothing new about the field of political sociology as one can readily see by reference to the studies compiled by brother McWorter,[34] but in the dichotomy between it and mere sociology is the realization that there is often the necessity for the inclusion of an operative ideology, and, at the least, the recognition that it may be impossible to draw a hard and fast boundary between the fields. Perhaps a sociology rooted in black social science on balance would emphasize the "end-use" as well as an analysis of the structure and function of black social institutions. The result is that political sociology would be emphasized more than the implicitly neutral sociology.

The same argument, of course, could be made for economics. Black social scientists should not only be concerned with the analysis of the economic system or the state of black economy, but should seek to develop and utilize theories that lead to the production of economic resources. In this case, we could take a page from Chapter Seven of *Dusk of Dawn* by W.E.B. DuBois, where, as he often did, he made an analysis of the state of black society, concluded that capitalism was antithetical to black accumulation of wealth, and put forth a plan of action to radically change the situation. In both the discipline of sociology and economics discussed above briefly, the focus should be the acquisition of influence (or control or power) over choices in each sector of society; to the extent, we should recognize the inherent political activity involved in the development and espousal of such concepts and in their employment in real situations. Certainly, in the other disciplines of social science the same suggestion about focus could be made, which does not in each case involve the use of the term political, but which understands clearly what is involved in emphasizing the "end-use" dimension of their discipline.

## TECHNIQUE

Many of the existing methodologies are valid for the analysis of black life but I would argue here as elsewhere that it is the black researcher's "field experience" in being black that gives to him a better potential understanding of the techniques of analysis that are more relevant in a given situation. In a way, such a position mirrors the older conflict between traditionalist researchers who have the knowledge of substance, be it geographical or historical, and the technician who is skilled in the technique of his particular discipline at the expense of substance. My position is that a proper marriage – that is, the balance between substance and technique – is preferable and that the deficiencies in white social science are revealed, when in dealing with black life the analyst comes prepared only with methodology. Studies that are produced in this way are seriously in need of reinterpretation by black scholars with a liberation orientation. The question of achieving a proper balance, though important, is most often possible to assess only after the results of the research are in, and therefore at the outset caution is a greater requirement. Nevertheless, it is possible to suggest that either extreme, using the traditional interpretation or the overly quantitative approaches, are unsatisfactory for most questions that deal with any human life. Since the current quantitative fad is in full swing in academic life, perhaps a word should be said about it here.

Of course the assumption upon which quantification is

based is that there are units of analysis which stand for a given amount of social value, which, when manipulated mathematically, reveal aspects of social reality either real or theoretical. The wish of the user is to come as close to the real situation as possible and even perhaps be able to anticipate and plan for human responses to given situations or events. It strikes this writer as highly plausible that one of the fruits of a highly technological society such as this one is the notion of 'precise value" – that is, there are so many things produced and developed in a manner which makes them amenable to the quantitative approach; this is true from material goods to social services. Indeed many problems in the field of administrating social services revolve around the necessity to monitor value precisely in quantitative terms, not necessarily for the sake of the user but for the sake of the decision maker who allocates resources. The writer is not at all sure – in fact, is skeptical – that either African or Afro-American culture is thus amenable to the quantitative approach. This is the subject of another discourse but the problem suggests itself here; phrased in these terms – to what extent is the exercise of "blackness" compatible with the vagaries of a Western technological situation. We should be aware that the material aspects of such a civilization have a powerful influence on the way in which we are able to perceive and to express our culture. One of the wonders of black culture is the way in which it has survived and still flourishes, buffeted by strong historical events, both quantitative and qualitative. But the question of compatibility is important on another level due to the increased desire for analysts to learn and utilize the tools of systems analysis in the disposition of black problems. The cost-benefit type of analysis has been adapted to "software" output only with questionable results,[35] thus, if there are problems at that level of analysis, the utilization of such techniques of analysis on black problems would be even less effective. One then has to cope with the effectiveness of the instrument itself, as well as the fact that even now some of the most elementary facts about black people, such as an accurate population count, are still in a questionable state of existence, and such data are the life of the quantitative approach.

This discussion leads directly to challenge the assumption upon which some developing graduate programs in Black Studies are founded. One basic assumption is that one should get a degree in an established discipline, while the subject of the research for the dissertation may be in the area of black life. Graduate students also need the substantive as well as the methodological training if such work is to be accurate as well as profitable. *Treating the substance of black life as something second-hand which can be "picked up" at will, or as something "we already know," that does not need systematic and constant elucidation, clarification, and development is an insult to the quality and complexity of the black experience and perpetuates the racists' attitude which graduate schools have of the value of the study of black life in general.*

The caution urged here, then, is in the use of extremes of theory and methodology and in substantive areas also. To revive the notion of balance, what the black social scientist should seek is the balance between efficiency and humanism that puts technique in its proper role as servant rather than lord.

## NOTES

[1] There are many such studies in the literature. But see, as a representative sample, Vera Micheles Dean, *The Nature of the Non-Western World,* Mentor, 1957; also Lucy Mair, *New Nations,* University of Chicago, 1963, particularly Chapter Seven.

[2] Daniel Moynihan, *Maximum Feasible Misunderstanding,* Free Press, 1969. Here one should read his entire chapter on Social Science and Social Policy, but see particularly p. 191.

[3] *Ibid.* p. 193.

[4] A representative grouping of essays on this topic in this vein may be found in *Poverty American Style,* Herman P. Miller (Ed.), Wadsworth, 1968. See especially Section Three and an essay by anthropologist Oscar Lewis, pp. 51-54.

[5] I refer here to the "Sambo" thesis in Stanley Elkins, *Slavery,* University of Chicago Press, 1968.

[6] This suggestion is from "The Sociology of Knowledge and the Problems of the Inner Cities," by Prof. Roland Warren, Florence Heller Graduate School for Advanced Studies in Social Welfare, Brandeis University, 1970, unpublished.

[7] The philosophy of "systems" theory as applied to the social sciences was developed by Ludwig Von Bartalanfy, now President of the Society for General Systems Research, but the technique was adapted with some success to problems of management in the Department of Defense by Secretary McNamara.

[8] See an important new work in sociology, Alvin Gouldner, *The Coming Crisis in Western Sociology,* Basic Books, 1970, p. 53.

[9] Edward B. Reuter, *The American Race Problem,* Crowell, 1970, p. 365.

[10] See "Interviewer-Respondent Interaction," *Sociometry,* Vol. 27, September 1964, pp. 338-352 and "Interviewer Role Performance," *Public Opinion Quarterly,* Vol. 32, Summer 1968, pp. 287-294, both by J. Allen Williams Jr. These articles show that bias will occur in the research when there is social and (cultural) distance between the subject and the researcher. Also, mention is made of this fact by A.R. Radcliffe-Brown, in *The Andaman Islanders,* who says, "Indeed it may be urged . . . that attempts to interpret . . . beliefs . . . without any first-hand knowledge of the people whose beliefs are in question are at the best unsatisfactory and open to many possibilities of error," in *Field Work: An Introduction to the Social Sciences,* Buford H. Junker, University of Chicago Press, 1960, p. 20. The reason such studies will result in inaccuracies is due to the complexities of any culture: "The major consideration that makes the evaluation of reports of subjective data difficult is the fact that they are *too highly situational."* (Emphasis mine.) *Elite and Specialized Interviewing,* Lewis Anthony Dexter, Northwestern University Press, 1970, p. 122.

[11] Gouldner, p. 50.

[12] Recent press reports indicate that a subcommittee of the House Education and Labor Committee in the U.S. Congress has begun an investigation into what is reputed to be a widespread national phenomenon, but the case which provoked the inquiries was discovered in Minneapolis, Minnesota.

[13] Recently I had the opportunity of speaking before a

group involved in mental health community work and discovered that their concepts and practices were taken verbatim from the work of a white psychiatrist unchanged to fit the nuances these workers would encounter in the culture of black people.

[14]This writer has read a copy of this manual but I understand that it is not now publicly available.

[15]"Behavioral sciences and the National Security," Report No. 4, Subcommittee on International Organizations and Movements, Committee on Foreign Affairs, House of Representatives, December 6, 1965.

[16]It has been a traditional practice to define items not only by genus but also by function and application as the term "Black" fixed to the phenomenon "Social Science" implies. To wit, one would catch hell if he used a left-handed monkey wrench to turn a right-handed bolt, which would suggest the necessity to obtain the right tool in the first place!

[17]"Black Nationalism the Inevitable Response," *Black World,* January 1971, p. 9.

[18]"Black and White: Outlines of the Next Stage," *Black World,* January 1971, p. 9.

[19]"Black and White: Outlines of the Next Stage," Part II, *Black World,* March 1971, pp. 9-14.

[20]"The Meaning of Black History," *Black World,* February 1971.

[21]Andrew Billingsley, "Black Families and White Social Science," *Journal of Social Issues,* Vol. 26, No. 3, 1970, p. 131.

[22]*Ibid.,* p. 135

[23]Earl Ofari, *The Myth of Black Capitalism,* Monthly Review Press, 1970, p. 77.

[24]James Boggs, *Racism and the Class Struggle,* Monthly Review Press, 1970, p. 141.

[25]Oliver Cox, *Capitalism as a System,* Monthly Review Press, 1964, pp. 32, 65-66.

[26]*The Black Scholar,* Vol. 2, No. 2, October 1970, p. 11.

[27]Nathan Hare, "The Challenge of a Black Scholar," *The Black Scholar,* Vol. 1, No. 2, December, 1969, p. 62.

[28]Ronald W. Walters, "The Discipline of Black Studies," *The Negro Education Review,* Vol. 21, No. 4, October 1970, pp. 138-144.

[29]*The Black Scholar,* December 1969, p. 31.

[30]*Ibid.*

[31]*Negro Digest,* Part III, March 1970, p. 83.

[32]Stokely Carmichael and Charles Hamilton, *Black Power: The Politics of Liberation in America,* Chapter 1, "White Power: The Colonial Situation," Random House, 1967.

[33]Robert Blauner, "Internal Colonialism and Ghetto Revolt," *Social Problems,* Vol. 16, No. 4, Spring 1969.

[34]Gerald A. McWorter, *The Political Sociology of the Negro,* Anti-Defamation League of B'nai B'rith, p. 31. Pamphlet.

[35]President Johnson directed the Bureau of the Budget to install PPBS analysis through the government in 1966. In 1968 this writer was conducting interviews in the Department of State pursuant to a Doctoral Dissertation and he discovered that many Bureaus had written negative appraisals of the extent to which the new system had been successful. Some had, in fact, recommended that it not be further used, which points to the vulnerability of this method of analysis when used on products such as foreign policy, which are difficult to quantify. See also "The Politics of the Budgetary Process," James Oliver, Ph.D. Dissertation, American University, 1970, unpublished, for some of the difficulties involved.

# Name Index

# Subject Index